MATTHEW

Matthew

A Life Application Commentary

David John Costa

XULON PRESS

Xulon Press
2301 Lucien Way #415
Maitland, FL 32751
407.339.4217
www.xulonpress.com

Printed in the United States of America.

ISBN-13: 9781545606360

Author's preface

This Bible Commentary was specifically designed with the aim of providing help to teachers and ordinary laypersons who in his or her busy life seldom have enough time to prepare adequately for Bible study.

Because most Bible Commentaries out there are either unhelpfully brief, unduly long, or overly technical to be used in a real bible study setting. It was the author's goal to produce a Commentary that would be practical to both individual and group bible classes, providing the teacher and layperson with the hands-on tools necessary for holding and developing their own Bible study.

In order to achieve this goal, it was necessary to have a Commentary that was both exegetical in nature, as well as concise in its interpretation, and practical in its application.

To fulfill all these requirements this Commentary was formatted in a way that deals first with the **"Exegesis of the verse"** [shaded in gray]. Which includes defining and expounding on the various words, phrases, and Greek terms, also drawing on other bible translations (e.g. K.J.V., A.V., N.E.B., R.S.V., L.B.V. etc.). As well as the Vines Expository dictionary of Greek words (keyed to the Strong's reference numbers).

This is then followed by a **"Concise interpretation of the verse"**, drawing on the scholarly consensus, as well as personal insights, giving the student the overall explanation and gist of what is being taught.

And finally the **"Message & Application"**, which includes various ways in which the teaching can be applied to the believer's daily life.

The applications provided by the author are not exhaustive in themselves, but rather are only meant to get the bible study group moving in the right direction. The author is confident that under the guidance of the Holy Spirit the group will be able to apply even greater applications and insights to the teachings.

Also included in this Commentary are valuable outlines of chapters and passages, as well as cross-references.

The book is also linked to the website "www.matthewlifeapplication.com" where teachers & students can find additional notes, maps, pictures, and visual aids from the author, as well as post their own notes & applications.

David J. Costa

Special thanks goes to the Holy Spirit and to those Pastors, Ministers, and Teachers who went before me, who without they're work this commentary would have been impossible.

This book is dedicated to the edification of believers everywhere who love God's word.

Hermeneutics
Principles of Interpretation

Historical/Cultural Analysis:

The field of study that determines the meaning of a passage by identifying the historical and cultural context. Identify the passage within the political, economic and social situation. Determine the religious and cultural customs, as well as the geographical setting.

Contextual Analysis:

The field of study that determines the meaning of a passage by identifying the context. Determine how the passage under study relates to the blocks of material immediately preceding and following it. Know that no individual word, sentence, or paragraph stands alone. The meaning the author intended is always found in its context, thus bound to what precedes and follows in a discourse or narrative. A verse of scripture must always be understood in light of the verses which precede and follow it. (A text without a context often becomes a pretext, which can be interpreted to mean whatever a person wants). The context can usually be found in the part of a text or statement that surrounds a particular word or passage. Clues to finding the context are performed by observing explicit statements, repeated words or phrases. As well as observing any issues that are focused on with exhorting remarks.

Lexical /Syntactical Analysis:

The field of study that determines the meaning of a passage by identifying the various word, phrases, and clauses in a verse. Recognize when an author intends his words to be taken literally, figuratively, symbolically, typologically or hyperbole. Determine the meaning of words by identifying the literary form the author is using, are they "Prose" (ordinary vocabulary) "Poetry" (proverbial) "Apocalyptic" (symbolic) or "Parabolic" (Simile, metaphor, allegorical).
Determine the various possible meanings of ancient words by identifying their Greek and Hebrew definitions and grammar.

"Syntax" (grammar) is the field of study that determines the different ways in which words are combined to form phrases, clauses, and sentences. Syntax deals with the way thoughts are expressed through Hebrew or Greek grammar, thus the various forms that words can take in the function of tense, mood, phrase, and clause.

Theological /Doctrine Analysis:

The field of study that determines the meaning of a passage by identifying how it fits in with the total pattern of God's revelation. Determine how the passage fits with God's character and nature (theological). Determine how the passage fits within the doctrines of grace, law, faith, redemption, and justification (doctrinal). Identify and define the theological implications of certain words and phrases (e.g. "Kingdom of heaven", "Son of man", etc.) Identify the spiritual nature of the passage.

Application Analysis:

The field of study that determines how the teaching of the passage is applied to the believer's daily life. Determine whether the passage should be applied for the purpose of exhorting, reproving, correcting, or instructing.

Identify which principles in the passage are meant to be applied spiritually, morally, or theologically. Determine the various ways in which the principles of the discourse, narrative, or story has relevance for the contemporary believer.

Determine the Application of the passage in the immediate context of its original hearers, then its wider relevance for the believer. A good practice in the Application is to first meditate on the passage, asking the Holy Spirit to reveal how to apply it. A good tool to use when applying scriptures is always to ask the questions "What is God trying to tell me" or "What does this mean for my life"?

General Areas of Application:

- A Sin I need to forsake.
- A Victory I can claim.
- A Promise I can claim.
- A Command for me to obey.
- A Blessing I can enjoy.
- A Failure I can learn from.
- A Truth about God, Jesus, the Holy Spirit, Satan, man, etc.
- A Doctrinal adjustment for me to make.
- A Truth about myself.

Abbreviations

A.D.	after Christ's birth
App.	application
B. C.	before Christ's birth
cf.	compare
Chp.	chapter
e.g.	for example
etc.	so on/so forth
Grk.	Greek
Heb.	Hebrew
i.e.	that is
Lit.	literally
LXX.	Septuagint (Greek Translation O.T.)
Lat.	Latin
MSS.	manuscripts
Metph.	metaphor
N.T.	New Testament
O.T.	Old Testament
Pg.	page
Ref.	references
Syn.	synonyms
V./Vs.	verse/verses
Viz.	that is to say, namely.
506	Strong's reference numbers
◙	visual aids/pictures on website
💻=🌎	more notes & applications on website

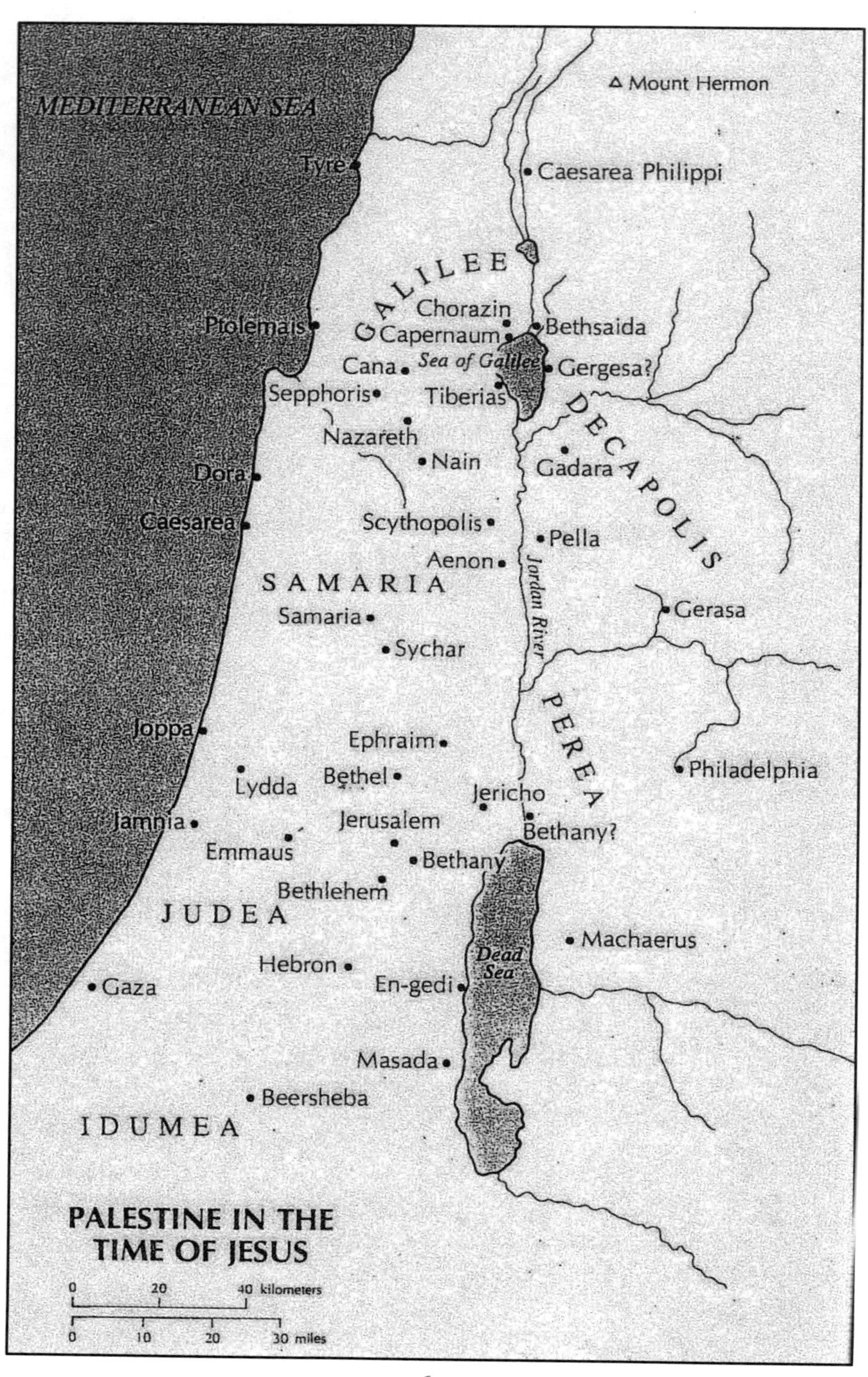
MEDITERRANEAN SEA
Mount Hermon
Tyre
Caesarea Philippi
GALILEE
Chorazin
Bethsaida
Ptolemais
Capernaum
Cana
Sea of Galilee
Gergesa?
Sepphoris
Tiberias
DECAPOLIS
Nazareth
Nain
Gadara
Dora
Caesarea
Scythopolis
Pella
Aenon
SAMARIA
Jordan River
Samaria
Gerasa
Sychar
PEREA
Joppa
Ephraim
Philadelphia
Lydda
Bethel
Jericho
Jamnia
Jerusalem
Bethany?
Emmaus
Bethany
Bethlehem
JUDEA
Machaerus
Dead Sea
Hebron
Gaza
En-gedi
Masada
Beersheba
IDUMEA
PALESTINE IN THE TIME OF JESUS
0 20 40 kilometers
0 10 20 30 miles

Author:

Name: Matthew (meaning "Gift of God", "Levi",-(Mark 2:14-15)
Occupation: Tax Collector, disciple of Jesus-(9: 9-10)
Age: Uncertain (Between 20 & 40 years of age)
Father: Alphaeus-(Mark 2:14)
Nationality: Jewish
Birth place: Palestine
Residence: In the vicinity of lake Galilee-(Mark 2:13-15)

Date, Place & Sources of writing:

1) The earliest proposed date is A.D. 50 (Some argue 70 or later).
2) The Jewish nature of Gospel places it in Palestine.
3) The modern consensus of the day is that Matthew used Mark' gospel as his main source (already in circulation) In addition to other outside sources as well called Q.

Recipients/Readers:

Based upon the text they were Jewish Christians evident from:

- Matthew's many references to O.T. text.
- His tracing of Jesus' descent from Abraham-(1:1-17).
- Lack of explanation of Jewish customs & culture.
- Use of Jewish terminology (e.g. Son of David)

Structure:

The Scholarly consensus is that Matthew had formatted his gospel around 5 major discourses. This division suggests that he had molded his book on the structure of the "Pentateuch" (First five books of O.T.) Possibly with the intention of presenting his Gospel as a new "Torah" (Law) and Jesus as a new and greater Moses. Following 5 divisions:

1).......5:1-7:28 (Sermon on the Mount/teachings on discipleship)
2)......10:1-42 (Jesus' teachings on Missionary work)
3) ....13:1-53 (Jesus' teachings in Parables)
4) ....18:1-35 (Jesus' teachings on relationships among believers)
5) ...... 24-25 (Jesus' Olivet discourse on Tribulation & Return)

Purpose: Historical & Theological

A) To have a historical record of Jesus' life & ministry.
B) To convert that Jesus is the Savior of the World.
C) To instruct and teach.
D) To prove that Jesus fulfilled many of the O.T. prophecies.

Pharisees:

Their origins have been traced all the way back to Ezra's time, eventually coming to prominence as a religious sect after the Maccabean revolt under the Hasmonean dynasty 2nd B.C.
The name means "Separate ones" from the fact that they intentionally kept themselves separate from that which they considered unclean. Along with the Torah, they accepted with equal authority their "Oral Traditions". A rabbinical interpretation of the law believed to have been passed down orally from Moses to Rabbis, who intern, eventually put it in written form in a book called the "Mishnah" (found in the first part of the "Talmud" compiled in 200 A.D.) They were a legalistic & separatist group who emphasized ritual purity, tithing, and fasting. They were legalistic when it came to the Law of Moses and the unwritten "Tradition of the Elders". They were often at odds with Jesus over matters of the law, (i.e. Sabbath violations, fasting).

Doctrines

- They believed in the resurrection of the dead.
- They believed in the immortality of the soul and rewards or punishment after death.
- They believed in angels & an organized spirit world.
- They believed Salvation was based on good works.

Sadducees:

Their origins have been traced back to "Zodak", first high priest, only coming into prominence as a political party during the Maccabee & Hasmonean dynasty (166-63 B.C.). They and their descendants would eventually assume the Temple leadership for many centuries. The Sadducee party would eventually become the priestly aristocratic heads of state, also making up part of the Sanhedrin. Many of their beliefs and doctrines were at odds with that of the Pharisees, their religious counterparts. Their demise occurred in 70 A.D. with the fall of the Temple and Jerusalem.

Doctrines

- They denied the "Oral traditions" of the Pharisees.
- They were very scrupulous when it came to Levitical purity.
- They denied the resurrection of the dead.
- They believed the soul died with the body.
- They viewed only the 5 books of Moses as authoritative.
- They denied the existence of angels & other spirits.

Scribes:

Their Jewish origins have been traced back to the time of Moses, only coming to prominence during the post-Babylonian exile and return (70 years later) to Jerusalem under Ezra (5th century B.C.). They were well versed in dictation, copy, study and the interpreting and teaching of the Torah (first five books of Moses). In the modern sense, they were the religious scholars and theologians of their day.

They were often associated with the Pharisees, some even belonging to their sect. They were sometimes called "Lawyers" which implied that they were experts in the "Law of Moses" thus "Lawyer" would become a synonym for "Scribe". They were well known for their ability to give judicial advice based on scriptural exegesis.

They held important positions within the Sanhedrin. They were often at odds with Jesus over His observances of the Law of Moses.

Chief Priests:

Their origins have been traced back to the Levitical priesthood, only coming into prominence in postexilic times. A title that designated the heads of priestly families.

They were a body of clerics who had oversight of the cultus, control of the Temple, administration of the Temple treasury-(Matt 27:6) and the supervision of priestly duties and disciplines.

We're also members of the Sanhedrin. They were often at odds with Jesus and were instrumental in arresting, condemning and sentencing Jesus to death. Their demise occurred in 70 A.D. with the fall of the Temple & Jerusalem.

Elders:

Their origins have been traced back to the Patriarchs.

They were ruling heads over family or clans, and leaders of aristocratic Jewish families. They served both administrative and judicial functions in local Jewish communities as well as in foreign affairs.

They were also community leaders who presided over civic and Synagogue affairs. Their title was generally used to describe all the lay leaders that constituted the 3rd and least influential group within the Sanhedrin.

High Priest:

Their origins have been traced back to the Aaron priesthood, only coming to prominence in exilic and postexilic times under the leadership of Ezra and Nehemiah.
During the Maccabean period, the kingship and the High priest were often combined. They were given even greater power by Roman procurators, the most actively known in the New Testament were Annas, Caiaphas-(who ruled at the time of Jesus' trial & crucifixion) and Ananias.
Their duties included officiating in regular priestly tasks, overseeing special religious days such as the "Day of Atonement", in which only the high priest could enter the Holy of Holies once a year.
They presided as head council over the Sanhedrin.
Their office usually was conferred for life.
Their demise came to an end with the destruction of the Temple by Titus in 70 A.D. The last high priest to serve was "Phannias".

Sanhedrin:

Its origins have been traced back to Moses-(Numb. 11:16) and Joshua-(Numb. 27:22-23) It wasn't until the Maccabean and Hasmonean dynasties that the Sanhedrin became prominent. The name "Sanhedrin" comes from the Greek meaning "Counsel or Assembly".
The court itself was made up of 71 judges (members comprising of Pharisees, Sadducees, Elders, and Chief priests, with the High Priest presiding as head judge). The council met in the chamber known as the "Hall of Hewn Stone" located in the Temple complex. It functioned as Israel's Supreme court making rulings on lower civil court decisions as well as decisions in criminal cases involving; rebellion, Sabbath violations, and common laws. Though they had authority to render verdicts they had no power to carry out capital punishments, a right which was retained by the Roman authorities.
They were instrumental in making the final decision to put Jesus to death. Their demise occurred in 70 A.D. with the fall of Jerusalem and destruction of the Temple by Rome.

Biography of the Twelve Disciples

1) **Peter:** (Heb. "Cephus" meaning: "Rock"-(Matt 16:17-18) Greek "Simon")
Home: "Bathsaida" of Galilee-(Jn. 1:44)
Occupation: Originally a Fisherman-(Mark 1:16)
Father: John (Jonah)-(Jn. 1:42, Matt 16:17)
Brother: Andrew-(Jn. 1:40, Mark 1:16)
Wife: Wife unknown -(Mark 1: 30, 1-Corn. 9:5)
Character traits: Impulsive, later bold.
Died: Church tradition was crucified upside down on a cross-(Jn 21:18-19).
Best known for:
- Was one of three disciples in Jesus' inner circle-(Mark 5:37, 9:2, 13:3)
- Being the spokesman for the twelve.
- His great confession-(Matt 16:16)
- His foundational role in the Church-(Matt 16:18)
- His denial of Christ and later reinstatement-(Matt 26, Jn. 21:15- 17)
- First preaching on the day of Pentecost-(Acts 2:14-40)
- Authored the Pastoral letters of 1 & 2 Peter.

2) **Andrew:** (Greek meaning "Manly")
Brother: Peter.
Father: John-(John. 1: 40-42)
Occupation: Originally a Fisherman-(Mark 1: 16)
Character traits: Eager to bring others to Christ.
Died: Church tradition was crucified on an X-shaped cross by Rome.
Best known for:
- Was one of Jesus' first followers-(John 1:35-40)
- Pointed out Jesus to Peter as the Messiah-(John 1:40)
- Calling out attention to the boy with the loaves and fishes-(John 6:8-9)

3) **James:** (brother to John) Surname "Boanerges" Grk-"Sons of Thunder"
Occupation: Originally Fishermen with Peter & Andrew-(Luke 5:10)
Father: Zebedee-(Matt 4: 21)
Mother: Salome-(Mark 15:40)
Character traits: Ambitious, short-tempered, judgmental, committed.
Died: By beheading-(Acts 12:2)
Best known for:
- Was one of three disciples in Jesus' inner circle-(Mark 5:37, 9:2, 13:3)
- Fiery temperament-(Mark 9:38-41, Luke 9:51-54)
- Requested to sit on Jesus left and right in His Kingdom-(Matt 20:20-21)
- Witnessed Jesus' transfiguration-(Matt. 17: 1-2

4) **John:** (brother to James) Surname "Boanerges" Grk-"Sons of Thunder"
Occupation: Originally Fishermen with Peter & Andrew-(Luke 5:10)
Father: Zebedee-(Matt 4: 21)
Mother: Salome-(Mark 15:40)
Character traits: Ambitious, judgmental, and later very loving.
Died: Exiled to Patmos-(Rev. 1:9) Church tradition died in Ephesus.
Best known for:

- Was one of three disciples in Jesus' inner circle-(Mark 5:37, 9:2, 13:3)
- Witnessed Jesus' transfiguration-(Matt. 17: 1-2)
- Requested to sit on Jesus left and right in His Kingdom-(Matt 20:20-21)
- Known for the one whom Jesus loved-(John. 13: 23, 19:26)
- Only one to witness the crucifixion-(John. 19:25-26)
- Given responsibility in caring for Jesus' mother Mary-(John. 19: 26-27)
- Authored the Gospel of "John" and 3 Epistles-(1-3 John) "Revelation".

5) **Philip:** Greek meaning "lover of horses"
Home: "Bethsaida" by the sea of Galilee-(John. 1:44)
Character traits: Questioning.
Died: Church tradition was crucified on a cross at Hierapolis (Turkey).
Best known for:

- The third disciple to be called by Jesus-(John 1:43)
- Pointing Jesus out to Nathanael as the One Moses wrote about-(Jn. 1: 45)
- Requested of Jesus to see the Father-(John. 14:8)

6) **Bartholomew:** Surname "Nathaniel" Greek "God's gift"-(John 1:45)
Home: "Canna" in Galilee-(John. 21:2)
Character traits: Honest, straightforward.
Died: Church tradition holds that he was flayed alive in Armenia.
Best known for:

- Announced by Jesus as a true Israelite-(John. 1:47)
- Declared Jesus to be the Messiah King of Israel-(John. 1:49)
- Church tradition holds that he ministered in Asia minor and India and was the founder of the Armenian Church.

7) **Thomas:** Greek "Didymus" meaning "Twin"- (John 11: 16)
Occupation: Church tradition holds that he was a carpenter.
Character traits: Pessimistic, doubting, and courageous.
Died: Church tradition was killed by a spear for his faith, buried in India.
Best Known For:

- His pessimism and loyalty to die with Jesus-(John 11: 16)
- Demanded evidence of Jesus' resurrection-(John. 20: 24-25)
- Gave the highest declaration of faith-(John. 20: 28)
- The "Apocryphal" Gospel of Thomas is attributed to him.
- Church tradition holds that he founded a Church in India.

8) **Matthew:** Greek meaning "Gift of God" Hebrew "Levi"-(Luke 5: 27)
Occupation: Originally a Tax collector-(Matt. 9: 9)
Home: "Capernaum" near the Sea of Galilee-(Matt 9:1,10)
Father: Alphaeus-(Mark 2:14)
Character traits: Despised outcast.
Died: Church tradition was martyred by being stoned then beheaded.
Best known for:

- Following Jesus immediately when called-(Matt. 9:9)
- The dinner he held in his home in honor of Jesus-(Matt 9:10)
- Writing the Gospel of "Matthew".
- Church tradition, went on to minister the Gospel in Persia, Macedonia, Syria, Parthia, Media, and Ethiopia.

9) **James:** Also known as "James the Younger"-(Mark 15:40).
Father: Alphaeus- (Matt 10:3) (possibly the brother of Matthew)
Mother: Mary-(Mark 15: 40)
Brother: Joses-(Mark 15: 40)
Occupation: Church tradition, revolutionist, associated with the Zealots.
Character traits: Unknown.
Died: Church tradition was thrown off the Temple and beaten to death.
Best known for:

- Mothers attendance at crucifixion, discovery of empty tomb-(Mark 15:40)

10) **Thaddaeus:** Also known as "Judas son of James". (Name was probably changed to distinguish him from Judas Iscariot. John 14: 22)
Father: James-(Luke 6:16)
Occupation: Church tradition, that he belonged to the Zealots.
Character traits: Unknown.
Died: Church tradition, that he was shot to death with arrows.
Best known for:

- Questioning Jesus concerning reappearance to the disciples (Jn. 14: 22)
- Church tradition, that he authored the book of Jude. (Others that it was Judas the brother of Jesus).

11) **Simon:** Greek "Simeon" the "Cananaean"-(Mark 3:18 R.S.V.)
The "Zealot" (do to his revolutionary & patriotic zeal)-(Matt 10:4)
Occupation: Member of a revolutionary political party the "Zealots".
Character traits: Fierce patriotism.
Best known for:

- Church tradition was the bridegroom at the wedding in Cana.
- Church tradition was a missionary in Persia.

12) **Judas Iscariot:** Heb. meaning either "Man of Kerioth" or "Daggerman".
Home: Village of "Kerioth".
Father: Simon-(John. 6:11)
Character traits: Treacherous, greedy.
Died: Committed suicide by hanging himself-(Matt 27:3-10)
Best known for:

- His charge of the money bag and being a thief-(John 12: 6)
- Betrayed Jesus for money-(Matt 26: 14-16)
- Criticized the use of expensive perfume to anoint Jesus-(John 12:4-8)
- Betrays Jesus with a kiss-(Matt. 26:47-49)
- Feeling remorse returned blood money committed suicide-(Matt. 27:3-5)
- Being replaced by "Matthias"-(Acts 1:26)

CONTENTS

Jesus' Ancestral Line

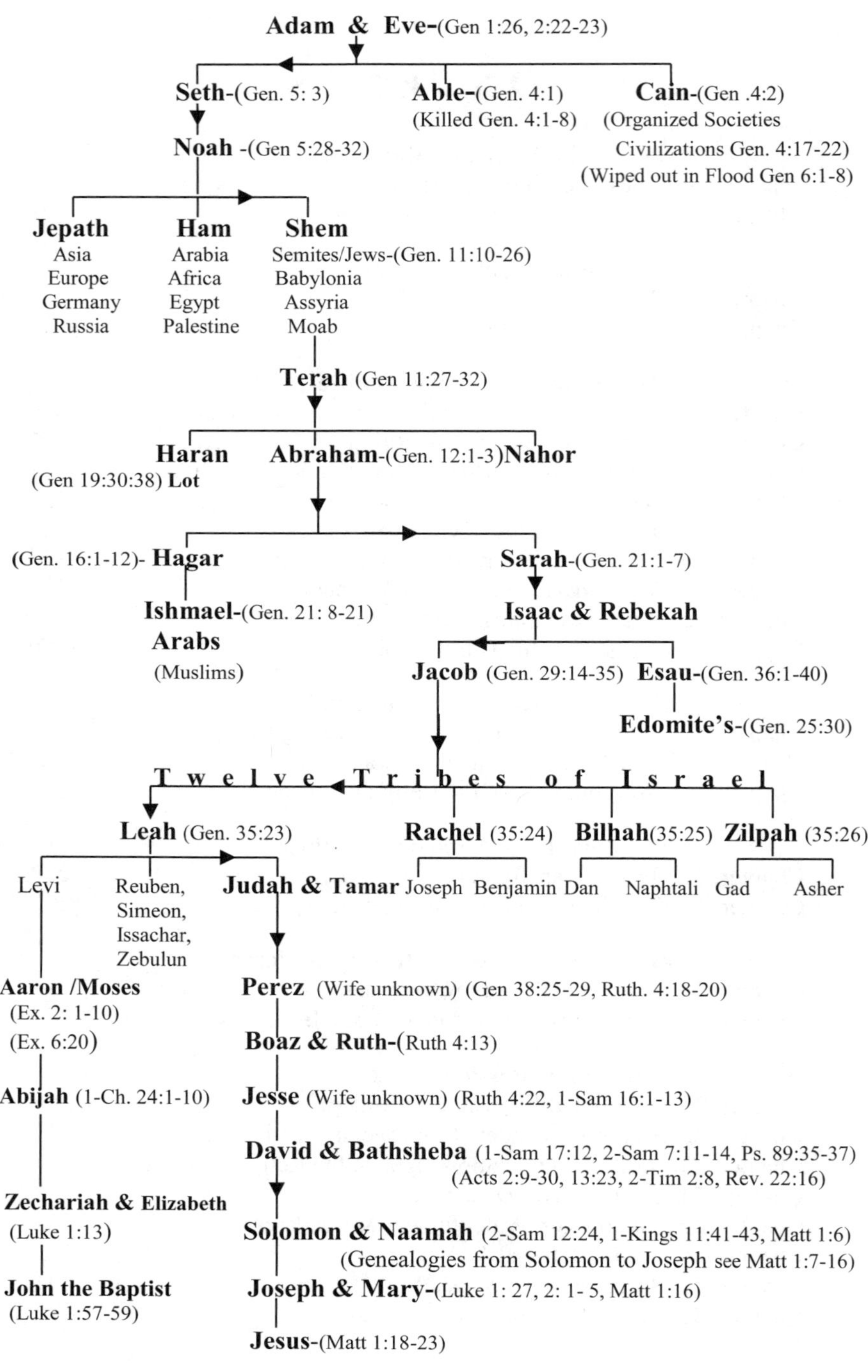

Chapter One

Jesus' Genealogy & Miraculous Conception

- **The Genealogy of Jesus-** Matthew traces Jesus' ancestry showing how He fulfilled the Messianic promises made to Abraham & David-(Vs. 1-17)
- **The Birth of Jesus Christ-**Matthew records the events surrounding the Messiah's /Christ's miraculous conception-(Vs. 18-25)

The Genealogy of Jesus-(N.I.V.)

1:1 A record (Syn.-account, archive, document, book-K.J.V., table-N.E.B.) **of the genealogy** (generation-K.J.V.-1078-*Denotes "an origin, lineage or birth"*. Syn.-family tree/line, roots, ancestors-L.B.V.) **of Jesus** (2424-*Heb-Joshua, meaning "Jehovah is Salvation".)* **Christ** (5547-*Grk.-Christos, "Anointed one", "Messiah".)* **the son** (Syn.-descendant) **of David,** (Expresses Jesus' Messianic royal descent from king David.-{Mark 12:35, Luke 20:41}) **the son** (Syn.-descendant) **of Abraham:** (Suggests: The reversal of the order of the chronology was meant to connect Jesus first with His royal heritage, and then to His fulfillment of the Messianic covenant promises made to Abraham.)

Matthew traces Jesus' ancestral line in Salvation history through the Messianic prophecies & promises made to Abraham & David.

<u>Message & Application</u> 💻=(🌎)

- Shows believers how Jesus is the culmination & fulfillment of all of God's promises. (Know the promises of God are always yes in Christ).
- Assures believers how God is always faithful in keeping His word and promises, that He makes good on every word He has spoken!
- Teaches though God's mercies be delayed, they do not weaken His promises.(Though God's promise are postpone they will not fall short)
- Emphasizes God's work in bringing about our healing & redemption. (Know God's love for you, having sent His Son to die for your sins).
- Teaches how Jesus was also human, flesh & blood just like us. (Trust that Jesus is able to sympathize with your failures & shortcomings).

-***David***-By tracing Jesus' ancestry back to David shows how it fulfilled God's promise that the Messiah would be of the royal line of king David, and would sit on his throne forever. (See 2-Sam 7:13-16, Ps. 89:35, Is 9:6-7, Jer. 23:5, 33:15-17, Luke 1:12, Acts 2:29)

–***Abraham***-By tracing Jesus' ancestry back to Abraham shows how it fulfilled God's covenant promise. That it would be through Abraham's offspring that all peoples (Nations) on earth would be blessed (Saved). (See Gen. 12:3, 22:18, 26:2-4, 28:14, Acts 13:23)

1:2 Abraham was the father (begot-K.J.V.) **of Isaac, Isaac the father of Jacob,** (Israel-{Gen. 32:27-28}) **Jacob the father of Judah and his brothers,** (i.e. Twelve tribes of Israel: Ruben, Simeon, Issachar, Zebulun, Joseph, Benjamin, Dan, Naphtali, Gad, Asher, Levi.-{Gen. 38:1} Suggests: The brothers are included because all the patriarchs were considered heirs of the Messianic promises.)

Matthew follows Jesus' ancestral line in Salvation history through the patriarchs.

Message & Application 💻=🌎

☞ Both Genealogies are the same from Abraham & David. But from David on they differ, most common explanations for this was either:

A) Matthew only uses the legal heirs to the throne. While Luke traces the complete line to David. Thus Matthew provides the Royal and Luke the Natural. (See dig. below)

B) Matthew traces the genealogy on Joseph's side only, while Luke traces the genealogy on the mother's side, Mary. Thus Mary's line of descent came through Nathan- (Luke 3:31) (not prophet) another son of both David & Bathsheba. (See 2-Sam 5:13-14, 1-Chron. 3:5)

➢ Differences between Matthew & Luke's genealogies is as follows:

- Matthew begins with Abraham and moves forward.
- Luke begins with Jesus and moves backwards to Adam. (Suggesting Jesus' ties to the whole human race)

Matthew & Luke's Genealogies

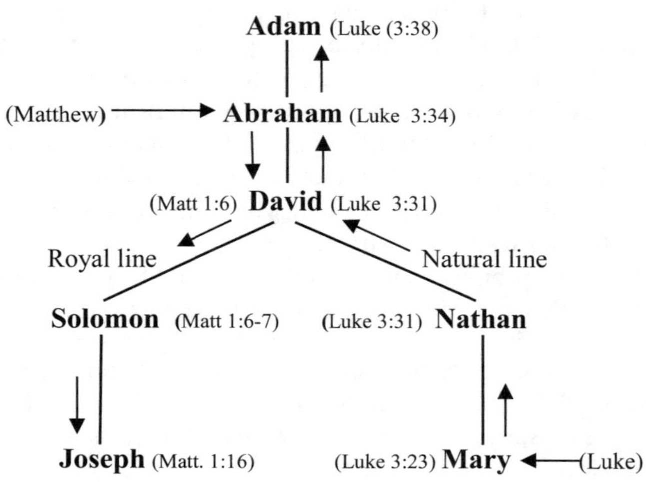

1:3 Judah the father of Perez and Zerah, (i.e. Twins-{Gen. 38:27-30}) **whose mother was Tamar** (i.e. Daughter-in-law of Judah-{See Gen. 38:1-26, Ruth 4:12}) **Perez the father of Hezron, Hezron the father of Ram,**-{Ruth 4:18-19}
4 Ram the father of Amminadab, {Ruth 4:19 b} **Amminadab the father of Nahshon,** {Numb. 1:7, Ruth 4:20 a} **Nahshon the father of Salmon,**{Ruth 4:20 b}
5 Salmon the father of Boaz, {Ruth 4:21} **whose mother was Rahab** (Jericho prostitute-{Josh. 2:1, 6:22-23}) **Boaz the father of Obed,** {Ruth 4:21} **whose mother was Ruth** (Suggests: Moabite and gentile nationality.-{Ruth 1:4}) **Obed the father of Jesse,** {Ruth 4:22 a}
6 and Jesse the father of King David. {Ruth 4:22 b} **David was the father of Solomon, whose mother had been Uriah's wife,** (i.e. Bathsheba.-{2-Sam. 1-27}

Matthew follows Jesus' ancestral line in Salvation history through some reputable & unsavory characters.

Message & Application 💻=🌍

- ❖ Shows believers how God's grace & mercy extends to all people regardless of race, culture, flaws, or character.
- ❖ Calls for not allowing our sinful past or checkered history to keep us from coming to Christ. (Know that God's grace is for everyone!).
- ❖ Displays the grace of God, that no matter how ruined our lives are, God can take flawed sinners like us and use them for His glory.
- ❖ Encourages believers of God's love & mercy regardless of our past sins. (Don't allow past failures, shame, or guilt keep you from Christ).

☞ What's noticeably different here from Judah to David are the women that are included which have been variously interpreted to show either:

A) God's plan of bringing Salvation to all people, not just the Jews.
-Rahab- Being a Canaanite.-(Josh. 2:1-24)
-Ruth- Being a Moabite.-(Ruth 1:4)

B) God's mercy & grace, for each had questionable character:
-Tamar- Had seduced her father-in-law (Judah) in making her pregnant.-(Gen 38:1-26)
-Rahab- Had been a prostitute of Jericho.- (Jos. 2:1-22)
-Ruth- Had been a "Polytheistic" worshiper of many god's.- (Ruth 1:4,15)
-Bathsheba- Had committed adultery.- (2-Sam 11:1-4)

C) God's favor towards these women for their righteous character.
-Tamar- For carrying on Judah's line.-(Gen 38:26)
–Rahab- For hiding the Spies.- (Jos. 6:25)
-Ruth- For giving up her Pagan god's.-(Ruth 1:16-17)
-Bathsheba- For submitting to David's oath.-(1-King 1-28-31)

1:7 Solomon the father of Rehoboam, (wicked king.-{1-King. 12:1-24}) **Rehoboam the father of Abijah,** (wicked king.-{1-King 15:1-8}) **Abijah the father of Asa,** (good king.-{1-King. 15:9-24})
8 Asa the father of Jehoshaphat, (good king.-{1-King 22:41-50}) **Jehoshaphat the father of Jehoram,** (wicked king-{2-King. 8:16-24}) **Jehoram the father** (i.e. Great Grandfather) **of Uzziah,** (good king.-{2-Kings 15:34})
9 Uzziah {Azariah-2-King. 15:1-7, 2-Chron. 26:1-23}) **the father of Jotham,** (good king.-{2-King. 15:30-38}) **Jotham the father of Ahaz,** (wicked king-{2-King. 16:1-20} **Ahaz the father of Hezekiah,** (Very good king.-{2-King. 18:1-16})
10 Hezekiah the father of Manasseh, (wicked king.-{2-King 21:18}) **Manasseh the father of Amon,** (Very wicked king.-{2-King. 21:19-26}) **Amon the father of Josiah,** (Very good king.-{2-King 22:1-20, 23:1-30})
11 and Josiah the father of Jeconiah (wicked king, Jehoiakim.-{2-King. 23:36-37, 24:1-6}) **and his brothers at the time** (i.e. 586 B.C.) **of the exile to Babylon** (i.e. Israel taken into Captivity to Babylon [modern day Iraq] which lasted 70 years.-{See 2-Kings 24:10-16, 2-Corn. 36:15-21})

Matthew follows Jesus' ancestral line in Salvation history through the Kingly & Royal line of Judah.

<u>Message & Application</u> 💻=🌍

- Shows believers God's goodness & mercy in using not just the best or the brightest, but also the weak things and those who are not perfect.
- Teaches just as God's grace does not run in the blood, neither does reigning sin. (Trust God's power to break the cycle of sin in your life).
- Teaches that if God can bring triumph and success through the failures of others, just think what He can do in your own life!
- Warns how those who continue in their sins and reject God's ways will only lead to bondage and destruction. (V. 11)

☞ This list of genealogies follows 1-Chron. 3:10-17 and speaks of the royal line through the kings of Judah after the kingdom was divided. (1-Kings 12:1-24)

☞ When comparing the two lists what is noticeably missing are the three kings Ahaziah, Joash, Amaziah that come between Jehoram & Uzziah. Reasons for their not being omitted is variously attributed to either:

- They may have been dropped because of their connection with "Ahab" and his wife "Jezebel" who were considered evil. (cf.2-Kings 8:25-27, See also chart on page 23)
- They may have been dropped for systematic purposes, thus to keep to the 3-fourteen generation structure. (Matt 1:17)

1:12 After the exile to Babylon: (i.e. After Israel came out of captivity.) **Jeconiah was the father of Shealtiel, Shealtiel the father of Zerubbabel,**
13 Zerubbabel the father of Abiud, Abiud the father of Eliakim, Eliakim the father of Azor, (Note: No O.T. historical records of these men. {See note below})
14 Azor the father of Zadok, Zadok the father of Akim, Akim the father of Eliud, (Suggests: Again, no O.T. historical record of these men.)
15 Eliud the father of Eleazar, Eleazar the father of Matthan, Matthan the father of Jacob, (Suggests: Again no historical record of these men.)

Matthew follows Jesus' ancestral line in Salvation history through the princes & priests of Judah.

Message & Application 💻=🌎

- ❖ Shows believers that no matter how far our sins take us, we will never cease to be objects of God's mercy and grace.
- ❖ Assures believers that God will never allow us to be lost completely in the captivity of our sins.
- ❖ Teaches believers no matter how far our sins take's us, God still has a specific purpose and plan for our lives as we faithfully serve Him.
- ☞ This list of names from "Zerubbabel" on are not found in the O.T. They may have been taken from public or family registries, of which Matthew being both a Jew & tax collector would have had access too.

1:16 and Jacob the father of Joseph, the husband of Mary, of whom was born Jesus, (2424-*Joshua, meaning "Jehovah is Salvation".)* **who is called Christ** (5547-*Grk-"Christos" meaning; Anointed One/Messiah.)*

Matthew completes Jesus' ancestral line in Salvation history through Joseph, the legal heir to the throne of David.

Message & Application 💻=🌎

- ❖ Shows how God can do extraordinary things through ordinary people.
- ❖ Assures believers of Jesus' divine appointment and qualification to be our Redeemer and Savior.
- ❖ Encourages believers how God can take our weaknesses and imperfections and use them for His glory.
- ❖ Teaches though our role may not seem very important compared to others, but God still has a specific purpose and plan in our redemption.
- ☞ After Jacob, the regular formula of father is dropped and Matthew simply lists Joseph as Mary's husband, signifying both Jesus' virgin conception, as well as Joseph being only the legal, not the natural father of Jesus.

1:17 Thus, there were fourteen generations (1074-*Origin, lineage, birth, genesis.* i.e. Either descent of a family from the birth of a father to the death of a son, or a group of people.) **in all from Abraham to David, fourteen from David to the exile to Babylon, and fourteen from the exile to the Christ.**

Matthew concludes Jesus' ancestral line in Salvation history as the culmination of God's sovereign work and plan.

Message & Application 

-Fourteen generations-The numerical significance of using 3 sets of fourteen generations has been variously interpreted as either:

- As an easy way to help remember such a long list to memory.
- They equal the total value for each of the Hebrew vowels in David's name (D=4, V=6, D=4 totals 14) (cf. Rev. 13:17-18)
- They represent each of the 3 covenant periods:
  1) Abrahamic 2) Davidic 3) Grace
- They represent turning points in Israel's history.
  1) The establishment of David's throne.
  2) The removal of it. (i.e. Babylon captivity)
  3) The final reestablishment of it by Christ

Purpose of Jesus' Genealogies:

- To show how Jesus fulfilled the Messianic prophecies made to Abraham & David. (See Gen. 12:3, 22:18, 26:2-4, 2-Sam 7:12-16)
- To show Jesus' legitimacy to the throne of king David (See Is. 9:7, Luke 1:32, Rom. 1:3)
- To explain Jesus' virgin birth by Mary, and her role in line with the Messianic promises. (See Gen. 3:15, Luke's 3:23)
- To show Jesus' identity with both Gentile's and sinners. (Explains the anomaly for including several women in the geology- (See Vs. 3-5)
- To show Jesus' relationship to the whole human race, rather than just to Judaism. (See Luke 3:38)
- To show how Jesus could be both the son of David and Son of God. (See Luke 3:38)

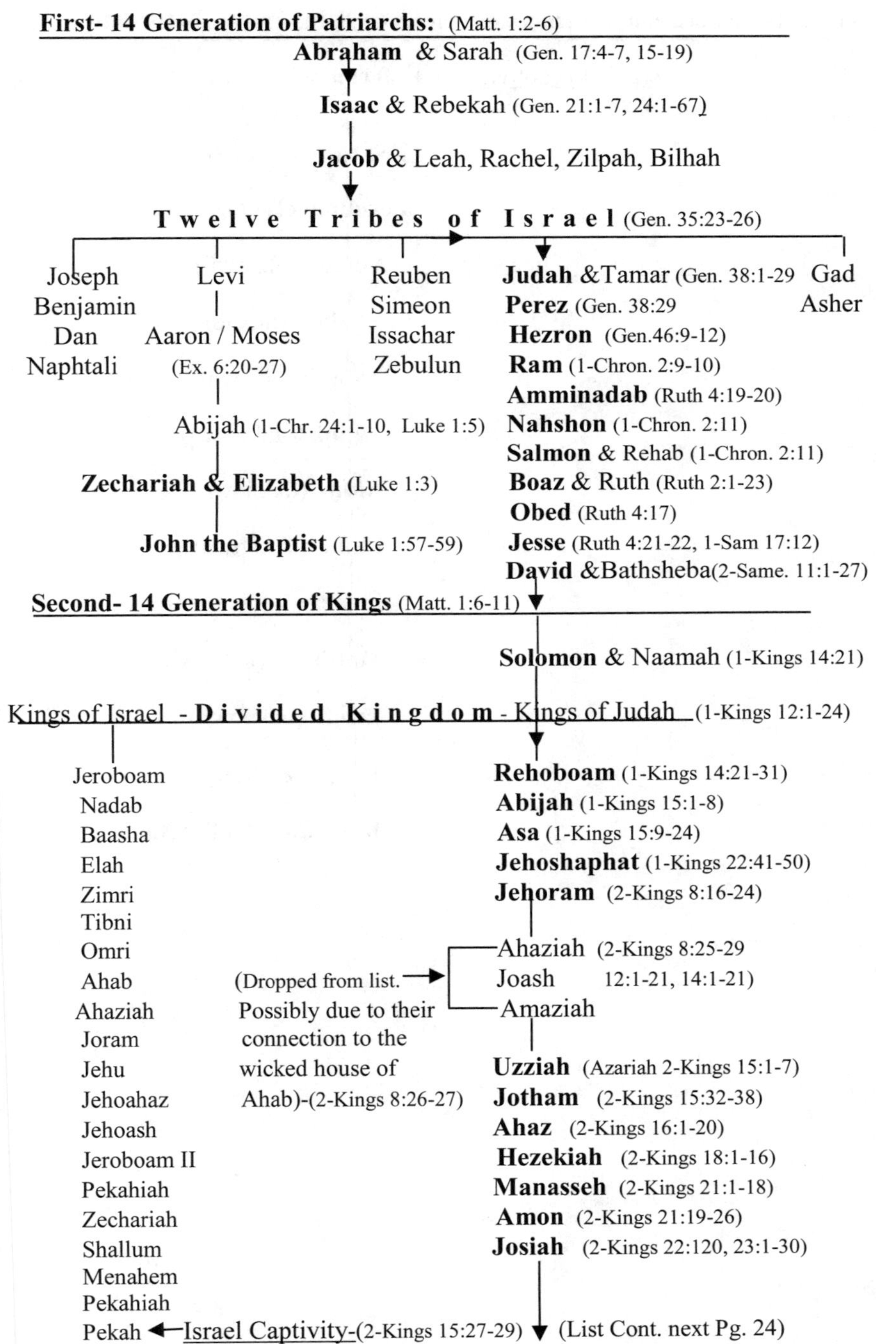

First- 14 Generation of Patriarchs: (Matt. 1:2-6)
Abraham & Sarah (Gen. 17:4-7, 15-19)
Isaac & Rebekah (Gen. 21:1-7, 24:1-67)
Jacob & Leah, Rachel, Zilpah, Bilhah
Twelve Tribes of Israel (Gen. 35:23-26)
Joseph
Benjamin
Dan
Naphtali
Levi
Aaron / Moses
(Ex. 6:20-27)
Abijah (1-Chr. 24:1-10, Luke 1:5)
Zechariah & Elizabeth (Luke 1:3)
John the Baptist (Luke 1:57-59)
Reuben
Simeon
Issachar
Zebulun
Judah &Tamar (Gen. 38:1-29
Perez (Gen. 38:29
Hezron (Gen.46:9-12)
Ram (1-Chron. 2:9-10)
Amminadab (Ruth 4:19-20)
Nahshon (1-Chron. 2:11)
Salmon & Rehab (1-Chron. 2:11)
Boaz & Ruth (Ruth 2:1-23)
Obed (Ruth 4:17)
Jesse (Ruth 4:21-22, 1-Sam 17:12)
David &Bathsheba(2-Same. 11:1-27)
Gad
Asher
Second- 14 Generation of Kings (Matt. 1:6-11)
Solomon & Naamah (1-Kings 14:21)
Kings of Israel - Divided Kingdom - Kings of Judah (1-Kings 12:1-24)
Jeroboam
Nadab
Baasha
Elah
Zimri
Tibni
Omri
Ahab
Ahaziah
Joram
Jehu
Jehoahaz
Jehoash
Jeroboam II
Pekahiah
Zechariah
Shallum
Menahem
Pekahiah
Pekah
Israel Captivity-(2-Kings 15:27-29)
(Dropped from list.
Possibly due to their
connection to the
wicked house of
Ahab)-(2-Kings 8:26-27)
Rehoboam (1-Kings 14:21-31)
Abijah (1-Kings 15:1-8)
Asa (1-Kings 15:9-24)
Jehoshaphat (1-Kings 22:41-50)
Jehoram (2-Kings 8:16-24)
Ahaziah (2-Kings 8:25-29
Joash 12:1-21, 14:1-21)
Amaziah
Uzziah (Azariah 2-Kings 15:1-7)
Jotham (2-Kings 15:32-38)
Ahaz (2-Kings 16:1-20)
Hezekiah (2-Kings 18:1-16)
Manasseh (2-Kings 21:1-18)
Amon (2-Kings 21:19-26)
Josiah (2-Kings 22:120, 23:1-30)
(List Cont. next Pg. 24)

Third-14 Generation of Princes & Priests (Matt. 1:12-15, 2-Kings 25:27, Ezra 2:1-70)

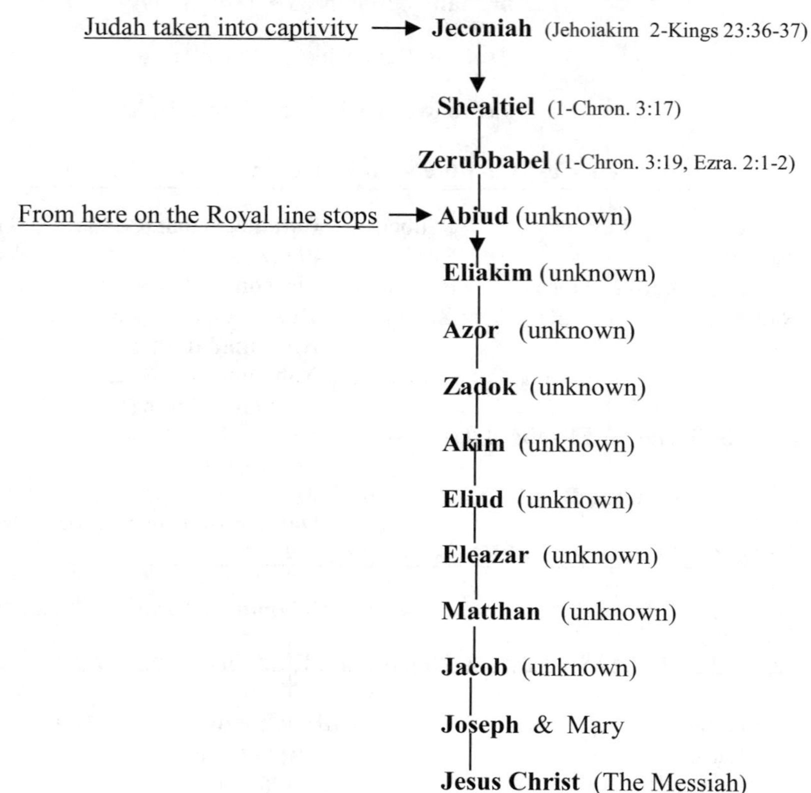

The Birth of Jesus Christ-(N.I.V.)

1:18 This is how the birth of Jesus Christ came about: His mother Mary was pledged to be married (betrothed-K.J.V. Syn.-Engaged.) **to Joseph, but before they came together,** (i.e. Before they were officially married, or consummated the marriage.) **she was found** (i.e. By Joseph.) **to be with child** (Suggests: Either confessed openly by Mary. Or Mary's pregnancy began to show itself through her baby bump/bulging belly.) **through** (i.e. By way/agency of.) **the Holy Spirit.**

Mary is found to be with child through the miraculous conception of the Holy Spirit.

Message & Application 💻=🌎

- ❖ Shows the supernatural power of God in taking ordinary people and turning them into willing vessels for His honor & glory. (Luke 1:30-38)
- ❖ Displays how the power and promises of God often show up in the most unusual and unexpected ways.
- ❖ Reminds believers how sometimes the future we're preparing for is not always what God has in store for us.
- 🗝 Even today, believers must be prepared for the unusual circumstances and supernatural ways the Holy Spirit may be working in our lives!

Marriage Customs & Practices:

- No Biblical restrictions stated for the proper age of marriage. More than likely girls were married at an early age, while still in their youth (after puberty). (Prov. 2:17, 5:18) According to the "Talmud" rabbis set the minimum age for marriage at 12 years for girls and 13 years for boys. (From this some conclude Mary was anywhere between 14 & 16 years of age when she was engaged-[Infancy Gospel of Thomas-8:3-8, 12:7-9]
- Marriages were pre-arranged based on family and tribal loyalty. Parents often arranged marriages for their children, usually with the father securing wives for their sons.(Gen. 24:3)
- Marriage contracts were made between the two families and sealed by a payment to the parents of the bride in the form of a "Dowry", either of gifts, money or other compensation.
- The engagement period lasted a year in which abstinence was to be maintained until the marriage was consummated.
- The wedding ceremony usually lasted a week with the bridegroom's father preparing the wedding banquet at his house with the wedding feast being celebrated at night-(Matt. 25:1)

1:19 Because Joseph her husband was a righteous man (just-K.J.V.-1342–*without prejudice or partiality.* Syn.-fair, merciful, gracious, compassionate. Not that Joseph was without sin, but only that he was characterized as being virtues & compassionate at heart.) **and did not want to expose her to public disgrace** (3856-*Expose to infamy, put to open shame.* i.e. Scandal, humiliation, adultery, stoning-{Duet. 22:21-24}) **he had in mind to divorce her quietly.** (i.e. To give a bill of divorce before two witnesses without going to court.{Deut. 24:1}

Because Joseph was a compassionate man, he did not want to expose Mary as an adulterous.

Message & Application =

- ❖ Shows how believers are to always be inclined towards others with godly compassion & love. (Always put the dignity of others first!).
- ❖ Calls believers away from a victim mentality in making it all about us and our rights, to putting the needs and welfare of others first.
- ❖ Calls for being merciful & fair in our deliberations and judgments.
- ⊶ Even today we're to see that our deliberations are guided by God, and not ruled by our feelings or emotions. (How would you respond if cheated on, will it be with godly love or with anger & bitterness?)

1:20 But after he had considered this, an angel of the Lord (Gabriel-{Luke 1:26-27}) **appeared to him in a dream and said, "Joseph, son of David,** (Expresses Joseph's legal descent from the royal line of King David.-{Luke 2:4}) **do not be afraid** (Syn.-Troubled, misgivings, don't hesitate-L.B.V.) **to take Mary home as your wife, because what is conceived in her is from the Holy Spirit.** (Holy Ghost-K.J.V. Suggests: Mary's birth was Divinely conceived.)

Joseph is assured of Mary's fidelity because her conception was divinely conceived.

Message & Application =

- ❖ Shows how God eases the fears & anxieties of the faithful, that when we're at a loss and our wit's end God always shows up with an answer!
- ❖ Displays how at times we think we only have two options when often God will provide a third way that we never even thought of before!
- ❖ Calls for the willingness to stay true to what God wants no matter the social stigma, public gossip, or low approval it may bring from others.
- ⊶ Even today we're not to allow the fear of losing friends, business, public opinion, or reputation to keep us from pressing forward in the work and mission that God has called us to. (In what ways has God called you to do something that was challenging to your faith?)

1:21 She will give birth to a son, and you are to give him the name Jesus,- (2424-*"Yehoshua" Grk. "Joshua" meaning-"Jehovah Saves".)* **because he will save** (4982-*To deliver, heal, rescue, set free.* Syn.-cleanse, atone, redeem, reconcile) **his people from** (out of) **their sins."** (266-*Missing the mark, falling short of the divine standard, estrangement from God.* Expresses Jesus' work in Saving & rescuing people from the penalty, power, and consequence of their sins.-{Rom. 5:9-10, Eph.-5:25-27, Col. 1:13-14, 1-John 2:2})

Shows Jesus' very purpose of coming into the world to Save and deliver people from their sins.

Message & Application 💻=🌎

- ❖ Shows believers how Jesus came not only to Save us from the penalty of sin, but also from the power and bondage of sin as well. (1-Pet. 2:24)
- ❖ Displays how Jesus didn't come to cheer us up or make us feel better about ourselves, but to rescue us from the sewer of sin that we're in!
- ❖ Teaches how we should be crying out to Jesus to Save us from our sin, and not about granting us a successful career, marriage, or business.
- 🗝 Even today if our greatest need was info, God would have sent us an educator, or if it was pleasure, God would have sent us an entertainer, or if it was money, God would have sent us an economist.
But our greatest need was forgiveness, so God sent us a SAVIOR!

1:22 All this took place to fulfill what the Lord had said through the prophet: 23 The virgin (3933-*Woman who has never had sexual intercourse. Young maiden.*) **will be with child and will give birth to a son, and they will call him Immanuel which means "God with us."** (Not meant to be a proper name, but only a declaration of Jesus' divine presence, nature, work in Salvation. {Is. 7:14})

Mary's miraculous conception fulfilled Isaiah's prophecy that a virgin would give birth to a son who would be God incarnate.

Message & Application

- ❖ Shows how we have in Jesus a God who loves us, cares for us, and who's on our side, always forgiving, supporting, and fighting for us!
- ❖ Comforts believers in knowing that no matter how far we fall into sin, despair, or hopelessness, God's presence is with us! (cf. Matt. 28:20)
- ❖ Encourages believers in knowing that we have a God who will be with us through the struggles, trials, and difficulties of life.
- 🗝 Even today the next time you're going through a hard time or facing a health crises, financial burden, or a messy divorce. You never have to feel alone or abandoned, knowing God is there to walk you through it!

1:24 When Joseph woke up, he did what the angel of the Lord had commanded him and took Mary home (To Nazareth.-{Luke 2:4-5}) **as his wife. 25 But he had no union with her** (knew her not-K.J.V., no intercourse-N.E.B. remained a virgin-L.B.V. i.e. Joseph had no sexual relations with Mary.) **until she gave birth to a son.** (Firstborn son-K.J.V.-Some draw from this as implying that Joseph would later have other children by Mary, which he eventually did. {cf. Matt. 12:46, 13:55-56}) **And he gave him the name Jesus.** (Suggests: In obedience to the divine appointment.-{1:21} That it was given to Jesus eight days later at His circumcision.-{cf. Luke 2:21})

Joseph in faithful obedience to God's will takes Mary home as his wife and names the baby Jesus.

Message & Application

- ❖ Shows believers how true faith will obey & follow through in what God commands, even if we don't fully understand it at the moment.
- ❖ Displays how true faith will do what God asks despite the uncertainties, reservations, or misgivings we may have.
- ❖ Teaches though we may not always know why God has called us to do something, but we can know He will use our faithfulness for His glory.
- ❖ Calls for a faith that will follow through with what God wants, even if it wasn't part of our plan, or what we would have chosen.
- ❖ Calls for making our relationships a sacred and holy thing, always putting Christ's honor & glory above our own natural desires. (V. 25)
- ❖ Calls for believing and trusting in God despite all the evidence to the contrary. (Will you accept yourself a sinner, even if all feels well?)
- ⊶ Even today, believers are to trust in the plans & purposes of God. Knowing that God can take a bad marriage, relationship, job, investment, and anything else and see that good comes out of it!

Reasons for the Virgin Birth:

- In order that Jesus would not inherit man's fallen sinful nature passed down from Adam. (Rom. 5:12-19, Heb. 4:15, 1-John 3:5)
- In order that Jesus could be both human & divine. (John 1:18, 14:9, Philip. 2:6-8, Col. 1:15-19).
- In order that Jesus could offer His body as a perfect sacrifice in the Salvation of man. (Gen 3:15, Gal 3:16, Col. 1:20-22, Heb. 10:1-10).
- In order that Jesus could enter our struggles and share in our humanity. (Heb. 2:14-18)

Chapter Two

Jesus' Birth & Escape to Egypt

- **Visit of the Magi**-Teaches the proper response to Jesus is one of worships & praise-(Vs. 1-12)
- **Jesus' escape to Egypt**-God takes divine protection & care of all who follow Him.-(Vs. 13-18)
- **Jesus' return to Nazareth**-God takes divine providence in the return of His Son to Israel-(Vs. 19-23)

The Visit of the Magi-(N.I.V.)

2:1 After Jesus was born in Bethlehem in Judea, during the time (i.e. Reign) **of King Herod** ("Herod the Great", 6-4 B.C. First of three Herod's to be mentioned in the N.T.) **Magi-◙** (3097-*"Magos", magician, sorcerer, astrologers, priest.* Wise men-K.J.V., Kings.-[Church tradition]-{Is. 60:1-7}) **from the east** (i.e. Persia or Babylon-[today Iraq]. A 900 mile and 3-month journey.) **came to Jerusalem.**

Astrologers from the East set off from Persia to see the new King.

Message & Application 💻=🌎

❖ Shows how believers are to spare no expense or cost in pursuing a relationship with Jesus. (The wise still seek Him!).

❖ Teaches those who are truly seeking after Jesus will go to any length despite the obstacles, hardship, and difficulties. (cf. Jer. 29:12-14)

❖ Displays how God's Saving grace is open to all people regardless of race, culture, religion, status, history, or background. (cf. Eph. 3:1-12)

-***Magi***-Scholarly consensus is that they were a priestly caste in ancient Persia or Babylon who belonged to a monotheistic religion known as "Zoroastrianism" who worshiped one God. That they were skilled in astrology, divination, magic, and dreams. They were also familiar with the Jewish religion, having access to such scriptures like Danial and Numbers, dating back centuries earlier during Israel's captivity and release from Babylon-(Dan. 2:2, 2:48, Numb. 24:15) According to Church legend gives their names as "Gaspar", "Balthasear", and "Melchior".

⊶ Even today, believers must be willing to make every effort to follow after Jesus regardless of the journey, risks, or costs. How far would you go to make it to Church or bible study? Would you be willing to get up early, drive a great distance, miss a ball game? Or even risk being bored, uncomfortable, scrutinized, judged, or looked at.

☞ The number of those who came to King Herod is uncertain, Church tradition places the number at 3, a calculation based upon the 3 gifts.

"King Herod's" Family Line

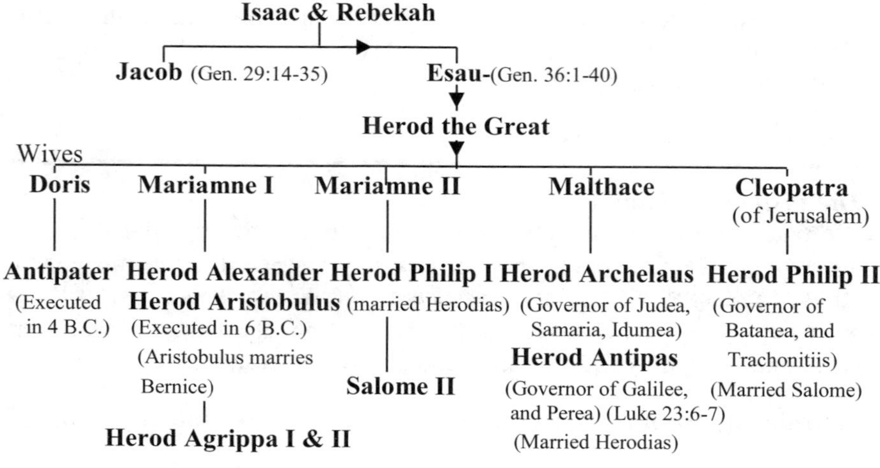

King Herod's Background

King Herod's birth and reign 73-4 B.C. Made king of Judea by the Roman senate in 40 B.C.
Herod was an "Idumean" (a descendant of Esau) his father's name was Antipater. Wife's name's were; Doris, Mariamme I & II, Malthace, and Cleopatra. (See above)
Herod ruled his subjects with an iron fist.
Was universally unpopular with the Jews because of his foreign origin and favoritism with Rome.
Was well known for his temper & paranoia, indiscriminately putting down any sign of revolt or conspiracy, even having his wife, brother-in-law, and two son's executed.
Was renowned for his building projects such as the rebuilding of the Jewish Temple, the building of his own palace, the construction of a large amphitheater in Caesarea, and the rebuilding of many fortresses.
The successor to his rule was passed on to his son "Herod Antipas". His last will also conferred a dividing up of his kingdom between his other three sons, Archelaus-governor of Judea, Samaria, and Idumea. Antipas was given Galilee & Perea. And Philip was given Batanea & Trachonitiis.

2:2 and asked, "Where is the one who has been born king of the Jews? (Suggests: They were already familiar with Balaam's prophecy concerning a coming Messiah.-{Numb.24:15-17}) **We saw his star in the east** (i.e. While in Persia) **and have come to worship him.**(4352-*Pay homage, bow to the ground.*)

The Magi take the appearance of the star as fulfillment of Balaam's prophecy and come pay homage to a new King.

Message & Application =

❖ Shows believers how the proper response to God's Saving mercy & grace is one of worship, praise, and devotion! (cf. Rom. 1:19-23)

❖ Teaches the importance of consulting God's word and seeking His help when we get lost, off course, and headed in the wrong direction.

⊶ Even today God may use different signs to lead a person to faith in Jesus. Whether its a sermon, book, friend, bible tract, television program, song, etc. Or even a life-altering crises, tragedy, or event.

-Star- Has been variously interpreted as either:

- Planetary conjunction of Saturn & Jupiter in 7 B.C.
- A Comet, possibly Haley's which appeared in 12 or 11 B.C.
- A supernova, meteor, or asteroid.
- The Shekinah glory of the Lord/God.

2:3 When King Herod heard this he was disturbed, (Syn.-agitated, deeply troubled, in turmoil, etc. Suggests: His Fear of being overthrown by a rival King.) **and all Jerusalem with him**. (Suggests: The people fearing King Herod's temper, rage, and cruelty he would go to in maintaining his throne and power.)

Herod being a Roman appointee to the throne feared a legitimate King would arise and overthrow him.

Message & Application =

❖ Shows how many are uneasy in coming to Jesus, fearing the changes He would bring. (Many see Jesus as a threat to their way of life).

❖ Calls for staying open & public with our praise and devotion of Jesus, even if it makes those around us feel uneasy and uncomfortable.

❖ Displays how many would rather stay in their comfort zones, fearing the struggles and Christ's claims on their lives would be too great.

❖ Displays how many are hesitant in coming to Jesus, fearing He will upset the status-quo, or interfere with their personal goals and plans.

⊶ Even today those who don't want to give up their sins, or who fear having their livelihoods, businesses, and social life's turned upside down will see Jesus as a threat.

2:4 When he (i.e. Herod) **had called together all the people's chief priests and teachers of the law,** (Scribes-K.J.V. Taken together the Jewish religious authorities and bible scholars of the day.) **he asked them where the Christ** (5547-*Grk-Christos, Anointed One, Messiah.*) **was to be born.** (Suggests: Since Herod refers to this King as "Christ" demonstrates that he understood the Messianic implications of the Magi's announcement.)
5 "In Bethlehem in Judea," they replied, "for this is what the prophet has written: (i.e. Foretold by the prophet Micah 700 years earlier.-{Micah 5:2 LXX})
6 "'But you, Bethlehem, in the land of Judah, are by no means least among the rulers of Judah; (Though it be insignificant city, It would be highly honored & celebrated as the birthplace of the Messiah.) **for out of you will come a ruler who will be the shepherd** (Metph-Lord, Savior, deliverer) **of my people Israel."**

By quoting Mica 5:2 the religious leaders identify Bethlehem as the Messiah/kings birthplace.

Message & Application 💻=🌎

- ❖ Shows how it's not about knowing all the facts about Jesus that Saves you, but whether or not you truly repented & trusted in Him!
- ❖ Teaches how God's word is the sole authority for all truth, wisdom, and direction in life. (cf. 2-Tim. 3:14-17)
- ❖ Teaches how the bible is there to help us know, obey, and follow God, and not just a set of historical facts or interesting stories.
- ❖ Displays how many can know a lot about bible history, prophecies, and facts, and yet still miss the truth and be far from Jesus. (2-Tim. 3:7)
- ❖ Displays how many only approach God's word on an intellectual level and never on a spiritual level in allowing it to talk to their hearts. (Religious academics is no substitute for a Saving faith in Jesus!)
- ❖ Teaches how men can be well instructed in the bible, but indifferent to its truths. (Many can have head knowledge, but not heart knowledge!).
- 🗝 Even today just because you're knowledgeable of the bible, know a lot of bible trivia, and able to quote bible verses from memory doesn't mean a thing if you're not applying its truths to your lives in being changed and transformed by it! (cf. John 5:39-40, James 1:22-24)
- ☞ Note how the religious leaders knew what the prophecies said about Christ but didn't do anything with it themselves. That they never rejoiced or even made an effort to join the Magi on their short five-mile hike to Bethlehem!
- ☞ In context, the quoted passage of Micah is in reference to the future invasion of Jerusalem by Nebuchadnezzar king of Babylon. But as a word of encouragement the Prophet predicts that in the distant future a Messiah-Ruler will be born in Bethlehem. (See Mic. 5:1-5)

2:7 Then Herod called the Magi secretly (Suggests: In order to keep his fears, jealousy, or murderous plot hidden from the Jews.) **and found out from them the exact time the star had appeared.** (i.e. Two years earlier.-{2:16} Suggests: That by doing a little math Herod could ascertain the child's age, and then have all the male babies killed who were born around that time.)
8 He sent them to Bethlehem and said, "Go and make a careful search for the child. (Search diligently-K.J.V., A.V.-199-*Accurately, exactly.* Leave no stone unturned-M.B.V. Suggests Herod's desire to locate the right child.) **As soon as you find him, report to me, so that I too may go and worship him".** (4352-*Pay homage, bow down.* Suggests: A false pretense of paying homage in order to convince the Magi in revealing the location of the child once they found Him.)

Under a false pretense of worship, Herod attempts to trick the Magi into revealing the location of the Messiah.

Message & Application 💻=🌎

- ❖ Shows how believers are to see that we're showing up to worship with earnest & sincere hearts, and not just putting on a religious show.
- ❖ Warns the folly of thinking we can frustrate the purposes and plans of God by our own manipulation, schemes, and designs. (V. 7)
- ❖ Warns how passion & fear can have mastery over reason and conscience, plunging us into even greater evil and cruelty. (V. 7)
- ❖ Warns believers against laziness in expecting our pastors to spoon feed us when we should be in God's word for ourselves. (V. 7)
- ❖ Displays how fraud and wickedness often conceals itself under a mask of religious piety and show.
- ❖ Calls believers in being aware of those who make loud professions of faith, least we unknowingly aid them in their evil design.
- ❖ Displays how many only become religious when it suits their political needs in getting votes, making sales, or for business opportunities.

⊶ Even today believers need to see that were coming to worship to draw near to the Lord, and not for the purpose of being entertained, meeting friends, catching up on the latest gossip, or how prosperous we can become.

☞ What's strange here is that none of the religious leaders, nor Herod himself went with them. Possible explanations for this is that the religious leaders did not want to go, fearing Herod would suspect they were going to revolt against him. And that Herod did not want to go, out of fear of either causing the parents to hide the child or that the Jewish leaders would suspect he wanted to kill the child.

2:9 After they had heard the king, they went on their way, and the star they had seen in the east went ahead of them (went before-K.J.V. Appeared again-L. B. V.) **until it stopped over the place** (i.e. Bethlehem) **where the child was. 10 When they saw the star, they were overjoyed.** (i.e. For the second time. Expresses a joy filled with laughing, shouting, crying, and jumping up & down!)

God guides the Magi to His Son the Christ.

Message & Application =

- ❖ Shows believers who are truly responding & seeking after Christ will find divine guidance and direction in steering them in the right way.
- ❖ Calls for not allowing the indifference and unconcern of others to deter us from seeking after Christ, even if we have to go it alone.
- ❖ Displays how God deals rightly with those who seek answers & truth, that if we follow the light He gives, He will give us even more light!
- ❖ Displays how those who encounter Jesus will never end up empty, dissatisfied, or unfulfilled! (V. 10 cf. John 4:14, Rom. 15:13, Philp. 4:11-12)
- ⊶ Even today those who will take the next step in their walk with Jesus will find a joy & peace that they've never imagined or known before!

2:11 On coming to the house, (Not finding Jesus in a manger/stable as the shepherds did.–{Luke 2:7} That Jesus was probably 2 years old at this time.) **they saw the child with his mother Mary, and they bowed down and worshipped him.**(4352-*To pay honor, homage, reverence, by kneeling down on the ground*) **Then they opened their treasures-◙** 2344-*Treasure-chest, strongbox.*) **and presented him with gifts of gold-◙ and of incense-◙** (Frankincense-K.J.V.) **and of myrrh.-◙** (Suggests: Taken together gum resins obtained from trees used in perfumes and as medicinal ointments.)

The Magi as an act of worship present their gifts to Christ.

Message & Application =

- ❖ Shows believers how true worship of Jesus will honor Him with everything we have and all that is dear and valuable to us.
- ❖ Teaches how true worship of Jesus will do all we can in giving Him the best we have to offer. (Come not with lips, but all the rest!).
- ⊶ Even today those who know Jesus for who He is and all that He has done will bow down and give all worship, praise, and devotion to Him!
- ➢ Symbolic values in the three gifts signifying:

Gold –Jesus' royalty & Kingship. (Ps. 72:15)
Incense –Jesus' divinity & priestly office. (Lev. 2:2, Is 60:6)
Myrrh –Jesus' anointing, suffering, death. (John 19:38-40)

2:12 And having been warned in a dream (3560-*To put in the mind, divinely admonished.* i.e. Indirectly by God-K.J.V.) **not to go back to Herod,** (i.e. Not To report their discovery to king Herod.) **they** (i.e. Magi) **returned** (departed-K.J.V.-402-*Give place, withdraw, retired.*) **to their country** (i.e. Persia or Babylon.) **by another route.** (Suggests: They took a different direction home, bypassing Jerusalem and king Herod altogether.)

Having been warned by God of Herod's murderous plot, the Magi bypass Jerusalem altogether, escaping Herod's reach.

Message & Application =

- ❖ Shows believers how coming to Christ requires taking our lives in a different direction, one that is responsive & obedient to God's leading.
- ❖ Displays how those who encounter Jesus will have their lives forever altered & changed. (Those who come to Christ never leave the same!).
- ❖ Calls for expecting detours and U-turns in our walk of faith. (Though God leads us home, it may not be the journey we expected!).
- ❖ Calls for staying true to the path God has called us to, even if it means detours in life, or going into unfamiliar territories we're not used too.
- ❖ Warns how others will use our generous hearts and good nature for their own abuse. (Know that not all will have Christlike intentions).
- ❖ Promises believers in having God's guidance and protection from whatever dangers we encounter as we honor and follow Jesus.

⊶ Even today we need to take our lives in a new direction, never to return to our old patterns and ways of living. (In what ways has Christ affected the direction of your life, and what steps have you taken?).

–***Another route***-Unclear as to which way the Magi used to return home. Some have concluded that they must have gone east of Jerusalem, then traveling north along the upper part of the Dead Sea.
Taking roads that were not usually traveled on or well protected. (Demonstrates the lengths they were willing to endure to avoid Herod, even if it meant exposing themselves to hostile & dangerous territory).

Three Ways People Respond to Christ:

- **Magi-**joyful, faithful, diligent, worshipping, devoted, humble, reverent, zealous.
- **Chief Priests-**indifferent, skeptical, oblivious, disobedient, apathetic, uncaring.
- **Herod-**hostile, defiant, conniving, scheming, manipulative, self-centered.

From this verse here* (V. 13) *to verse* (V. 18) *God takes divine providence in the protection of His Son from Herod.

***The Escape to Egypt*-(N.I.V.)**

2:13 When they had gone, (i.e. Magi's departure back to their own country. That Joseph's escape and the Magi's departure occurred on the same night.) **an angel of the Lord appeared to Joseph in a dream. "Get up,"** (Syn.-awake, make haste.) **he said, "take the child** (i.e. Jesus) **and his mother** (i.e. Mary. The Child is put first due to the special providence and protection.) **and escape** (Syn.-flee, run) **to Egypt.** (Suggests a 200-mile journey that would put them safely outside of Herod's jurisdiction.) **Stay there until I tell you,** (i.e. Until God says it's safe to return.) **for Herod is going to search for the child to kill him."**

God takes sovereign providence in preserving His Son Jesus from Herod's murderous plot.

Message & Application 💻=🌎

❖ Shows believers when God commands us to do something know that it's for our own good and wellbeing, no matter where it takes us.
❖ Displays how throughout our lives the Lord will show up, warning and protecting us from going down the wrong path/road.
❖ Assures believers that when we find ourselves facing a difficult issue or an insurmountable problem the Lord will always provide a way out!
❖ Teaches no matter the hassles we face in life, God is working to help see us through it. (When life is threatening, God is protecting!).
❖ Teaches how God can make the worst of places the best of havens. (What may seem at first places of hardship; prisons, drug programs, homeless shelters, etc. can be places of refuge, recovery, and safety!

🗝 Even today though God may not speak to us directly through angels or dreams. Yet He does speak to us through His written word, giving us guidance and direction that we may avoid the things of drugs, alcoholism, pride, greed, selfishness, gossip, etc.(2-Tim. 3:16, Heb. 1:1-4)

***-Egypt*–**Chosen either because:

- It was the closest Roman province of Judea and yet outside of Herod's jurisdiction.
- It was a place of refuge for Israel during times of political turmoil. (1-Kings 11:40, 46, 2-Kings 25:26)
- It had a large Jewish population.

☞ Some have suggested that they went to Alexandria due to the large Jewish population already there. And that they may likely have used the Magi's gifts to pay for their traveling and living expenses.

2:14 So he got up, (Expresses Joseph's prompt obedience to the divine command.-{V. 13}) **took the child and his mother** (Suggests: The child is put first as primary importance and Mary's honor of caring for the child, or that Joseph was not the biological father.) **during the night** (Suggests: In order to avoid detection by Herod or by witnesses.) **and left for Egypt-◙** (i.e. A ten day journey spanning 200 Miles.)
15 where he stayed until the death of Herod (i.e. In 4 B.C.) **And so was fulfilled what the Lord had said through the prophet:** (i.e. Hosea 1:11, 700 years earlier) **"Out of Egypt I called my son."** (Portrays Israel's historical escape from their slavery & bondage in Egypt. But in a wider context, typologically fulfilled in Jesus' Saving work, calling us out of a life of sin, bondage, and idolatry.)

Joseph by taking Jesus to Egypt fulfilled Hosea's prophecy of God Saving His people from their sins.

Message & Application 💻=🌎

❖ Shows how true faith responds immediately & obediently without question or delay. (Don't argue or rationalize, just trust and obey!).
❖ Teaches though God gives guidance and direction in getting us out of our dilemmas, it's still our responsibility to obey and follow through!
❖ Teaches even when God's plans & ways don't make sense, or fit with what we would have chosen, don't question or hesitate just obey!
❖ Calls for following & trusting in God even if we don't understand it all. (If God brought you to it, He'll bring you through it!) (Prov. 3:5-6)
❖ Teaches no matter how great our bondage and afflictions are, God loves us too much to leave us in a bad situation.
❖ Promises that no matter how much we've wandered, strayed, and backslidden God will never abandon or forsake us. (Though divine deliverance be delayed it will not last forever or fall short!) (V. 15)
❖ Displays no matter how enslaved we are to sin, there's nothing too hard or too difficult that God can't break and deliver us from. (V. 15)

🗝 Even today, believers can take comfort & encouragement that even when we find ourselves falling into a life of sin, or trapped in a life of drugs, gangs, prisons, and homelessness, know that God is working out our Salvation, healing, and deliverance!

☞ In context, the quoted passage is in reference to Hosea's recounting Israel's history and birth. From God bringing the Israelites out of their bondage in Egypt to their rebellion in turning from God to idols. (Hos. 11:1-11, Ex. Chps. 4, 5, 6, 7,8, 9, 10) In a wider context, the prophecy is now more fully fulfilled by God in a greater Exodus in delivering sinners from the bondage & slavery to sin through the Saving and redeeming work of His Son Christ Jesus!

2:16 When Herod realized that he had been outwitted (mocked-K.J.V. Syn.-duped, conned, hoodwinked, played the fool.) **by the Magi, he was furious,** (Syn.-boiling, livid, went ballistic/ape, blew his lid, saw-red.) **and he gave orders** (i.e. To Roman soldiers) **to kill all the boys in Bethlehem and its vicinity who were two years old and under, in accordance with the time he had learned from the Magi.** (Due to the total population of Bethlehem, being around 1000 at this time. Estimates have set the number of infants at about a hundred, with the number of boys 2 years old and under at no more than a few dozen.)

Herod realizing the Magi were wise to his plot, in a mad rage, he orders the massacre of boys two years old and under.

Message & Application 💻=🌎

❖ Shows believers rather than trying to hold onto control & power, we need to let go and put Jesus on the throne of our lives.
❖ Warns how uncontrolled anger and passions can get the better of us. (We often fight against the very things God is trying to help us with).
❖ Warns believers when we fail to bend our knees to the Lordship of Christ, we only end up hurting our self's and those around us.
❖ Prepares believers to expect persecution for no other reason than our proximity and closeness to Christ. (cf. John 15:20-21, 16:33, 2-Tim. 3:12)
❖ Warns of what can happen when we let our fears & insecurities get the better of us, hanging onto power at all costs no matter who we hurt.
⊶ Even today many are more interested in saving their way of life than Saving their souls. Thinking that Jesus only wants to take things away, not realizing that Jesus only wants to give us real peace and joy. (Will you trust that Jesus only wants to change your life for the better).
☞ Many accept this event do to the fact that such atrocities were not out of character for Herod who even had his wife & sons killed suspecting they were trying to depose him. Thus it's not improbable that his fear of a potential king would stop him from killing a few babies.
☞ Many overcome the atrocity of such an evil act as a grim reminder of the consequences of Adam & Eve's fall in the garden of Eden, having used their freewill to bring sin & rebellion against God into the world.
➢ Lack of corroborating accounts to such an atrocity is due to either:
- Historians would not have been aware of such an act, due to the obscurity of a small town like Bethlehem.
- Historians would not think it worthwhile recording such an event, due to the other atrocities committed by Herod.
- Historians would not have wanted to record anything that would appear to confirm Christianity.

2:17 Then what was said through the prophet Jeremiah was fulfilled:
18 "A voice is heard in Ramah, (i.e. An O.T. village near the tribal area of Benjamin. Was the staging point for Judah's march into exile to Babylon.) **weeping and great mourning,** (Expresses: Great grief & sorrow by crying and lamenting.) **Rachel** (i.e. Jacob's favorite wife.) **weeping for her children** (i.e. Not her literal children, but symbolically of her descendants the nation of Israel.) **and refusing to be comforted, because they are no more."**(In the historical context the Israelites who were killed or taken into captivity to Babylon. But in a wider context fulfilled of the babies killed by Herod.) {Jer. 31:15}

Herod's slaughter of the innocents in Bethlehem fulfilled Jeremiah's prediction of Rachel mourning over the massacre.

Message & Application 💻=🌍

- ❖ Shows how believers are not to allow the tragedies & difficulties of life to hinder our relationship and walk with God.
- ❖ Warns against allowing life's grief's to have the last word or to take our faith & hope away from God. (We may mourn, but not murmur!).
- ❖ Calls for not allowing the pain and sorrows of life to cause us to lose sight of God's love and compassion. (cf. John 14:1-6)
- ❖ Teaches that no matter how evil or bad things become, know it can never thwart or frustrate the plans and purposes of God. (cf. Rom. 8:28)
- ❖ Warns against allowing tragedies to steal our faith or harden our hearts. (No greater challenge to our faith than when we lose a loved one!).
- ❖ Warns how being wrapped up in our own grief & self-pity can become obstacles to God's promises. (Focus on what's left, not what's lost!).
- ❖ Warns believers against allowing the tragedies and setbacks of life to become roots of anger, bitterness, and discontentment with God.

⊶ Even today, believers are not to allow the loss of a child, death of a loved one, or a broken marriage to become bitter roots of anger towards God. That somehow it's God's fault, that He let us down, not realizing that God is with us in it and working all things out for His glory and our good!

☞ In context, the passage is in reference to Jeremiah recalling how, because of Israel's idolatry and unfaithfulness to God, God allowed His people to be exiled to Babylon by Nebuchadnezzar-(586 B.C.). But in a wider context, the passage also includes the future hope of God's comfort and grace: *"Restrain your voice from weeping and your eyes from tears, declares the Lord. They will return from the land of the enemy. So there is hope for the future." "Your children will return to their own land"*. (cf. Jer. 31:16-17)

From this verse here (V. 19) to the end of the chapter, God takes providence in His Son's return to Israel.

The Return to Nazareth-(N.I.V.)

2:19 After Herod died, (Historical records report Herod's death at Jericho in March or April 4 B.C. at the age of 70. According to the historian Josephus, Herod died from Dysentery, a disease of the lower intestines. {Jos. Antiq. 17-5}) **an angel of the Lord appeared in a dream to Joseph in Egypt**
20 and said, "Get up, take the child and his mother and go to the land of Israel, for those (i.e. King Herod and his henchmen/soldiers.) **who were trying to take the child's life are dead."**
21 So he got up, took the child and his mother and went to the land of Israel.
22 But when he heard that Archelaus was reigning in Judea in place of his father Herod, he was afraid to go there. (Suggests: That Archelaus possessed the same cruel and brutal disposition as that of his father king Herod. Even having 3000 people put to death during one Passover.-{cf. Joseph. Book 17, 9:3}) **Having been warned in a dream, he withdrew to the district of Galilee,-◙** (Suggests: Governed by Herod's son Antipas, who having a milder disposition.)

God takes providence in the safety & return of His Son to Israel by assuring Joseph of Herod's death.

Message & Application 💻=🌎

- ❖ Shows how we can count on God's daily care & provisions in easing any fears, worries, and doubts we may have while following Him.
- ❖ Teaches how it's better to wait for God's guidance and direction rather than thinking we have to take matters into our own hands.
- ❖ Displays the watchful providence of God, that in all of life's journey's, sorrows, and setbacks, God is always looking out for us!
- ❖ Gives encouragement that no matter how terrifying our adversities and troubles may seem, there only temporary and will not last forever.
- ❖ Calls believers in trusting that God is still working in our situation, even if all the details aren't exactly perfect as we expected. (V. 22)
- ❖ Reminds believers even when we're obeying God's will expect evil to be lurking around every corner, trying to take us down. (V. 22)
- ❖ Calls for prudence & common sense when taking on the tasks that God has called us too. (Common sense tells us to be careful, faith tells us to wait on God's timing).

🗝 Even today when your in the middle of God's will and the path He's called you too, and things don't work out as expected. Do you try to push through anyway, or wait for God's guidance and timing?

2:23 and he went and lived in a town called Nazareth.-■ (3478-*Grk.-"As in a watchtower or guard place" Heb.-"Shoot or Sprout".* Syn.-Bean-town, Hick-town. i.e. A small village in Galilee, total population being between 500-1500.) **So was fulfilled what was said through the prophets: He will be called a Nazarene.**(3480-*Inhabitant of Nazareth, a title of reproach, contempt, and rejection, as being insignificant and despised.* Syn.-hillbilly, redneck, hick. Many assume because the words and title are not found in any of the O.T. Books. That it's in reference to the overall prophetic theme concerning the Messiah's character as being humble, lowly, and despised.)

Jesus by moving to Nazareth fulfilled the prophetic theme that the Messiah would be despised & rejected.

Message & Application 💻=🌎

- ❖ Shows believers Jesus' willingness in being despised & rejected on our behalf that we may be Saved and delivered. (Is. 53:3-5, Philp. 2:6-8)
- ❖ Portrays the extent of Jesus' love, that He was willing to endure rejection and disgrace that we may find purpose and significance.
- ❖ Gives comfort that Jesus knows the pain of what it means to be rejected, shunned, and marginalized, having experienced it Himself.
- ❖ Calls believers in not allowing our upbringing or poor reputations define who we are in God, or what He can do through us.
- ❖ Comforts believers that no matter how poor and insignificant we feel we are, God has a great plan and purpose for our lives!
- ❖ Prepares believers how being a Christian may mean being unpopular.
- 🗝 Even today we need to stay true to God's calling on our lives no matter how much we're ridiculed and labeled by family and friends as being weird, weak, foolish, gullible, fanatic, radical, Jesus freaks, etc.

-Called a Nazarene–Variously interpreted as either:

- Was a prophetic theme signifying that the Messiah would come from humble beginnings and be despised and rejected. (cf. John 1:46, 7:52, Ps. 22:6-8, 69:9-10, Is. 53:1-3)
- Was a play on the word *"Neser"* which in Hebrew means shoot or branch, thereby signifying the Messiah would be a descendant of king David. (cf. Is. 11:1, Jer. 23:5)
- Was a title given to Jesus, having resided and grown up in Nazareth. (cf. Matt 26:71, John 18:5, 7, Acts 2:22)
- Was in fulfillment of the "Nazarite vow", Jesus having been consecrated and separated to God's service.-(cf. Numb. 6:1-5) (Most reject this explanation due to the fact that Jesus drank wine and would often go near dead bodies.-cf. Matt. 11:19, Luke 7:11-14)

Chapter Three

John the Baptist Prepares the way

- **John prepares the way**-John shows what true repentance is and what it should look like.-(Vs. 1-12)
- **The Baptism of Jesus**-Jesus identifies Himself with sinners and those He came to Save.-(Vs. 13-17)

John the Baptist Prepares The Way-(N.I.V.)

3:1 In those days (i.e. 30 years later.) **John the Baptist came, preaching in the Desert** (Metph.-Spiritual renewal, restoration, new beginnings.) **of Judea-◙**
2 and saying, "Repent, (3340-*To change one's heart, mind, and thinking, A turning from sin to God.* Expresses a reorientation of life that is making a complete U-turn and going in the opposite direction, from living for sin to living for God.) **for the kingdom of heaven is near."**(at hand-K.J.V.-932-*God's power, rule, reign.* Expresses the Saving reign and work of Jesus in redemption.)

John the Baptist is calling people to turn from their sinful lives in preparation for the Messiah's arrival.

Message & Application 💻=🌎

- ❖ Shows believers the need for acknowledging we're sinners who need to repent and turn back to God. (cf. Rom. 3:23, 1-John. 1:9)
- ❖ Calls for a change of heart & mind about sin, that it is displeasing and offensive in God's eyes and has no place in our lives. (cf. Gen. 39:9)
- ❖ Calls for a heart that is willing to agree with God's view of sin, that it is wrong and out of character with who He's called us to be.
- ❖ Teaches how repentance is a gift that allows us to move forward in God's love & mercy, no longer tied to the guilt and shame of the past.

⊶ Even today many will admit their not perfect but stop short in actually acknowledging their sinners who are heading for hell. Or they'll see their lives as a big improvement from who they used to be in the past, not realizing just how worthless, wretched, and lost they really are.

☞ Repentance is not feeling sorry or regretful because you got caught in a particular sin or grieved over the consequences of sin.-(2-Corn. 7:10) But rather it's about having a change of heart & mind that is turning from sin to turning to God and righteousness.

Proper Responses in Repentance:

- Willingness in having a change of heart, mind, and thinking that results in a change of life and living.
- Willingness in taking our lives in a different direction, one that is turning from sin to turning to God.
- Willingness to confess and die daily to sin.

3:3 This is he who was spoken of through the prophet Isaiah: "A voice of one calling in the desert Prepare the way (Hearts) **for the Lord make straight paths for him.** (i.e. By repenting of sin, unbelief, self-righteousness, etc. {Is. 40:3 LXX})

John the Baptist is calling for repentance & moral reform in preparation for the Messiah's arrival.

Message & Application 💻=🌎

❖ Shows how we're to come with open & prepared hearts in seeing ourselves as sinners who need God's forgiveness! (cf. 1-John 1:7-10)

❖ Calls for turning from any sin, habit, attitude, thinking, or behavior that's keeping the Lord from moving and operating in our lives.

❖ Calls for seeing that we're not allowing the obstacles of sin, doubt, anger, greed, bitterness, or pride to keep us from receiving Jesus.

–***Make straight paths***-The Roman practice of preparing highways by fixing, smoothing, and removing obstacles off the road in preparation for a king's arrival. But in a wider context portrays a heart that's willing to admit that they're a sinner who needs God's forgiveness.

🗝 Even today "Obstacles" that can block God can be anything from an Ego barrier that keeps one from seeing they're a sinner. Or emotional barrier, having been hurt & abused by others in the past. Or a spiritual barrier that doubts God's love & goodness due to the evil in the world.

☞ According to Luke's Gospel the call to "Prepare straight paths" is extended to include: *"Valley shall be filled in"*-Symbolic of filling up with what is lacking, such as faith & good works. *"Mountains and hills made low"*-Symbolic of removing the barriers of pride & self-righteousness. *"Crooked roads shall become straight"*-Symbolic of no longer living wickedly & sinfully, but holy & righteously. (cf. Luke 3:5)

3:4 John's clothes were made of camel's hair-◙ (rough, coarse) **and he had a leather belt around his waist. His food was locusts and wild honey.**

John the Baptists lifestyle & ministry was consistent with the role of a true Prophet.

Message & Application 💻=🌎

❖ Shows how believers are to see that we're looking the part, that our lifestyle is consistent with being a Christian and follower of God.

❖ Teaches those who received God's Saving grace won't care if they don't fit in, or about how other people will perceive us.

❖ Calls for a life of humility and simplicity, that we're finding our purpose and fulfillment in Christ alone and not in material things.

3:5 People went out to him from Jerusalem and all Judea and the whole region of the Jordan. (i.e. Gentiles. Not literally every person, but is indicating a large number of people. That John's preaching was reaching all classes of society and culture, from the rich & poor, good & bad, heathen & religious.)
6 Confessing their sins (1843-*"To acknowledge or agree fully with God"*. Syn.- coming clean, owning up, admitting guilt, accountability, wrongdoing.) **they were baptized-◙** (907-*Dying of a garment, to immerse, plunge, dip.*) **by him in the Jordan River.-◙** (Suggests: An ideal place where water was abundantly available. At Aenon.-{cf. John 3:23})

Those who received John's message proved their repentance by acknowledging their sins openly and honestly before God.

Message & Application

- ❖ Shows believers instead of covering up & minimizing our sin, we need to come clean and confess it openly and honestly to God.
- ❖ Calls for realizing that no matter how good we are, we've all sinned and fallen short of the glory of God. (cf. Rom. 3:23, 5:12-21)
- ❖ Calls for the humility in recognizing that we're no better than anybody else, that we stand just as guilty and sinful as the next guy.
- ❖ Teaches how those who are serious about getting right with God will display it in real visible and public ways.
- ❖ Teaches rather than denying and excusing, we need to take personal accountability for our sins!
- 🗝 Even today rather than excusing & minimizing our sins by calling it another name as a "Mistake", "Error of judgment", "Indiscretion", "Moment of weakness", "Poor decision", "Alternate lifestyle", etc. we need to confess it for what it really is, a "Sin" against God!
- ☞ Baptism for believers is an outward sign/symbol of our public confession of faith in Jesus. That we're saying to the world we're leaving our old life of sin behind and embracing our new life in Christ Jesus. (cf. Luke 3:10-14, 1-Tim. 6:12, 1-Pet. 3:21)

The Meaning & Purpose of Baptism:

- Displays the believer's public declaration of their faith, commitment, and conversion to Christ. (Acts 2:38-41)
- Displays the believer's participation in Jesus' death, burial, and resurrection, dying to sin & rising to new life. (Rom. 6:3-4)
- Displays the believer's act of obedience in recognition of all ordinances ordained and exemplified by Christ. (28:18-20)

3:7 But when he saw many of the Pharisees (5330-*Heb.Origin-Separate One's*) **and Sadducees** (4523-*Heb.-The righteous.*) **coming to where he was baptizing,** (Suggests: Not for repentance, but rather for interrogation.-{cf. John 1:19-24}) **he said to them "You brood** (3555-*"Nest"*. Syn.-family, offspring, generation-K.J.V. sons-L.B.V.) **of vipers!-◙** (2191-*Any species of small poisonous snakes. We're usually known for eating their way out of their mother's womb, killing her in the process.* Expresses a term of reproach as the "Offspring of Satan". Being that they were poisonous, cunning, deceitful, wicked, and corrupt. Modern cliché "Snakes in the grass".) **Who warned you** (Expresses: Doubt, insincerity.) **to flee from the coming wrath?** (Lit. Snakes slithering out of their nests to escape a wildfire. Metph.-The inevitable day of God's judgment against sin.-{Rev.20:11-15} Was a rhetorical question challenging the sincerity of their repentance due to their hypocritical and self-righteous views of themselves.)

Due to the religious leaders hypocritical & self-righteous views of themselves, John doubted the genuineness of their repentance.

Message & Application 💻=🌎

- ❖ Shows how believers are to see that we're coming to baptism for the right reasons, and not out of pretense or for appearance sake.
- ❖ Warns believers against a repentance that is hollow, shallow, and superficial. (God wants true repentance, not lip service!).
- ❖ Calls for seeing that we're not just following the crowd or going through the motions of what's popular, but are truly repenting.
- ❖ Displays how some can have the right intentions, but the wrong motives in seeking baptism as a token of respect or a badge of honor.
- ❖ Warns how pride can harden our hearts, giving us a false sense of security and self-righteous opinion of ourselves that we're so good.
- ❖ Calls for confronting the sin and hypocrisies of others for their own spiritual welfare, no matter the costs involved.

⊶ Even today, believers need to see that we're submitting to baptism for the right reasons, not just because it's popular or as some sort of insurance policy, safeguard, or appeasement. The latter in only satisfying pastors, parents, and spouses.

☞ According to the Gospel of John, the religious leaders had only come with the intent of interrogating and subduing John the Baptist, fearing he was undermining their authority and influence with the people. (cf. John 1:19-22)

Pharisees

- Held the entire old testament and their oral traditions as authoritative and binding.
- Accepted the resurrection of the dead and the hierarchy of angels & spirits.
- We're careful to avoid and separate themselves from anything that was unclean.
- We're religiously scrupulous in matters of ritual purity, tithing, fasting, and Sabbath observances.
- Were legalistic, ritualists, ultra-orthodox, formalists, externalists, religiously devoted.
- We're corrupt, proud, haughty, sectarian, hypocritical, and self-righteous.
- Were ostentatious in worship, putting on a show of piety in order to impress others.

Sadducees

- Held only the Pentateuch (first five books of Moses) as authoritative and binding.
- They denied the resurrection, angels, and ministering spirits.
- Were aristocrats, more concerned with politics than religion.
- We're skeptics, rationalists, sensual.
- We're scrupulous in areas of Levitical purity.
- Were carnal, secular, worldly, and materialistic.
- Were modernist, liberal, compromising, free-thinkers, political opportunists.
- We're interested in power, money, and status.

3:8 Produce (Syn.-exhibit, manifest) **fruit** (Metph-Godly character, conduct, behavior, good deeds.) **in keeping with** (Syn.-consistent, agreeable, befitting) **repentance.** (3341-*Change of mind, a turning from sin to turning to God.*)

John calls on the religious leaders to prove their repentance by living changed lives.

Message & Application 💻=🌎

❖ Shows how true repentance will prove itself by a change of life and conduct. (Can others see the transformation and changes in you?)
❖ Warns believers against saying to God that you're sorry for your sins, and please forgive me, and then go right back to sinning again.
❖ Calls for a repentance that is consistent with a change of lifestyle and behavior, that we're no longer living the way we used to. (Eph. 4:22-26)
🗝 Even today does your actions & words show that you really repented and changed, or are you still lying, cheating, and hurting other people?
☞ This is not saying that we're expected to live perfect life's in never sinning. But rather it's about one who knows what needs to be done and turns back to the Lord. (cf. 1-Corn. 7:10-12, 2-Corn. 12:21, 2-Sam. 12:13)

3:9 And do not think (Syn.-presume, take for granted.) **you can say to yourselves, 'We have Abraham as our father."** (Suggests: They thought because they were descendants of Abraham they had an in-road to Salvation.) **I tell you that out of these stones-◙** (Lit. Stones lying in the Jordon river. Metph-Gentiles, heathens, sinners.) **God can raise up** (Syn.-produce.) **children for Abraham.** (Expresses spiritual offspring of the faith of Abraham.-{cf. Rom.4:1-18})

John warns the religious leaders against trusting in their Jewish ancestry from Abraham to Save them.

Message & Application 💻=🌎

❖ Shows how believers are to see that we've truly repented and put our faith in Jesus, that we're not just Christians in status and name only.
❖ Warns against trusting in our religious degrees, credentials, and positions to Save us. (God wants a Saving relationship, not pedigree!).
❖ Warns believers against thinking that God will simply give us a free pass because we grew up in the Church and were baptized as infants.
❖ Displays the Saving power of God's mercy & grace, that God can take the most hardened sinners and use them for His purpose and glory!
🗝 Even today many believers can still make the wrong assumptions, thinking they're Saved because they were raised in a Christian home, born of believing parents, or were lifelong members of a Church.

3:10 The ax-◙ (Metph-God's judgment, Christ's arrival.) **is already at the root of the trees,** (Metph-Jewish nation, unrepentant sinner. Expresses impending Judgment and doom. The image may have been taken from a lumberjack who has laid his ax down to take his coat off, that he might wield his blows more powerfully.) **and every tree** (person) **that does not produce good fruit** (Metph-genuine repentance, conversion, holy living.) **will be cut down and thrown into the fire.** (Expresses to suffer eternity in Hell in the Lake of fire.-{cf. Rev. 20:14-15})

John warns of impending judgment in Hell for those who bear no evidence of genuine repentance and holy living.

Message & Application 💻=🌎

- ❖ Shows how God expects believers to be living fruitful & productive life's for Him. (God has no use for those who live unchanged lives!).
- ❖ Warns of the danger in thinking we have all the time in the world to deal with our sins and clean up our lives. (Luke 13:6-9, Rom. 2:4)
- ❖ Warns that when it comes to sin in our lives there can be no gray areas, no drawing the line, downplaying it, or thinking we're good enough.
- ❖ Warns against superficial repentance, or putting Christ off for another day. (Know that there is no room for fakers or idle pretenses!).
- ❖ Warns believers of the dangers of simply going through the motions, that our lives must match our Christian profession.

🗝 Even today if not careful we can slowly start to gloss over our sins as minor and insignificant as compared to axe-murderers and rapists. Or that God will simply accept us the way we are, thinking that *"We're not so bad"* or that *"Nobody's perfect"*. (cf. 1-Cor. 6:9, Eph. 5:3-5)

☞ According to Luke's Gospel, the people respond by asking *"What should we then do?"*. To which John replies how the fruits of true repentance will display itself in everyday living & work through acts of love, charity, kindness, compassion, and honesty. (cf. Luke 3:12-14)

Types of Fruits Expected of Believers:

- Fruits of holiness, humility, submission, obedience, confession, brokenness, sorrow, gratefulness, etc.
- Fruits of love, joy, peace, patience, kindness, goodness, faithfulness, gentleness, and self-control.-(Gal. 5:22-23)
- Fruits of integrity, charity, honesty, and compassion. (Luke 3:10-14)
- Fruits of praise, devotion, witness, testimony, soul-winning.-(Matt. 5:13-16, 10:32)

3:11 "I baptize you with water for repentance. (As an external rite & pledge of a repentant life.) **But after me will come one** (i.e. Jesus) **who is more powerful than I, whose sandals I am not fit to carry.** (Expresses the duty of a slave in taking their Masters sandals off as he entered the home. Expresses profound humility.) **He will baptize** (Syn.-immerse, fill, indwell, infuse.) **you with** (by) **the Holy Spirit and with fire.** (4442-*Means of divine judgment, testing, purification.* Syn.-refine, cleanse, purge, purify. Expresses the indwelling work of the Holy Spirit in cleansing and purging away the dross of the old sin nature.)

Where John the Baptist only brought people to repentance, Jesus will permanently fill & cleanse believers with the Holy Spirit.

Message & Application

- Shows the transforming work of the Holy Spirit in changing us from the inside out, turning us from the love of sin to the love of God.
- Emphasizes the "Regenerating work" of the Holy Spirit, transforming believers into living holy and sanctified lives. (cf. John 16:8, 13)
- Portrays the "Consuming work" of the Holy Spirit, igniting believers in living Spirit-filled lives that are on fire for the Lord. (cf. Luke 24:32)
- Displays the "Indwelling work" of the Holy Spirit, empowering believers for service, witness, and ministry.(Acts 1:4-8, 4:31, 1-Thess. 5:19)

-With fire-Variously interpreted as either:

- As a means of the Holy Spirits work in purifying/cleansing believers. (Supported by most) (cf. 1-Pet 1:6-7, Zech. 13:9, Mal. 3:1-3, 1-Corn. 3:13)
- As an act of final judgment upon the unrepentant and unbeliever. (Supported by some due to the judgmental fire of verses-10 & 12)

Even today, believers who have been baptized in the fire of the Holy Spirit will be fully consumed with the things of God, Church, bible study, witness, and prayer!

☞ Most view this baptism of the Holy Spirit here as a one-time event at conversion. (1-Corn. 12:13) Others view a second outpouring of the Holy Spirit after Salvation, which a believer receives greater anointing, power, and gifts for service. (John 20:22, Acts 1:2-5, 2:1-4, 8:13-17, 19:2-6)

Other Ministries of the Holy Spirit:

- Converting, Reproving, and Convicting. (John 16:7-15, Rom. 8:16, 1-John 5:6-8)
- Filling & Empowering for service.- (Gal. 5:16)
- Sealing & Assuring Salvation. (John Eph. 1:13-14)
- Illumination & Discernment. (John 16:13, 1-Corn. 2:12, 1-John 2:27)

3:12 His (i.e. Messiah/Jesus) **winnowing fork-◙** (fan-K.J.V. Lit.-pitchfork, rake. Metph-Gospel, judgment.) **is in his hand,** (Expresses an image evoking power, judgment, authority, or nearness, close proximity.) **and he will clear his threshing floor,-◙** (Lit.-A hard flat circular area used for treading grain by Oxen. Metph-Israel, world, Church, hearts.) **gathering his wheat-◙** (Lit.-cereal grasses. Metph-Righteous, useful, godly, regenerated) **into the barn** (Metph-heaven, paradise, God's kingdom.) **and burning up the chaff** (Lit.-husks, stalks, and straw which were burned as fuel in clay ovens. Metph-Christ's spiritual work in burning off the carnal cravings, sinful habits, and fleshy-appetites of an individual, be it sin, vice, pride, vanity, ego, worldliness, self-righteousness.) **with unquenchable fire.** (Expresses eternal suffering in Hell.-{cf. Rev. 20:14-15})

On the day of judgment, Jesus will separate Spirit-filled believers from unbelievers.

Message & Application

- ❖ Shows how believers are to see that we're allowing Jesus to burn all the sin and junk out of our lives that's not of Him. (cf. Heb. 12:14)
- ❖ Reminds believers if we're going to become valuable tools in the Lord's hands, all the useless chaff and rubbish in our lives has to go!
- ❖ Teaches how we can either resist Jesus and suffer the consequences, or allow Him to bring us under His rule and operation.
- ❖ Calls for allowing God to sweep away all the undesirable components from our lives, no matter how difficult or painful the process may be.
- ❖ Teaches how sometimes God has to chasten us from time to time, that we may see our sin/rebelliousness and turn back to Him. (Heb. 12:5-11)

-***Winnowing***-The agricultural practice that after the threshing of grain by Oxen in separating it from its stalk. A farmer would then proceed to use a shovel type tool in separating the wheat kernels from the straw by tossing it up in the air and allowing the wind to blow the light chaff away, while the heavier kernels fall to the ground.

⊶ Even today no matter how uncomfortable or painful the process, we need to let the Lord determine what needs to stay and what needs to go from our lives. Whether it's a sin or attitude we're still hanging onto or an area of pride, greed, and selfishness we need to let go of.

☞ Today God's winnowing process in getting us back on track can be performed in a variety of ways. That God may speak to us through the voice of our conscience or the bible. Or through times of trials and testing that we may turn back to Him. (cf. Rom. 5:1-5, 1-Pet. 1:6-7)

☞ Most view the separating of the "Wheat & Chaff" here as the dividing off of the good & bad aspects of a person. Others view it only as God separating true believers from unbelievers on the "Day of judgment".

***The Baptism of Jesus-(*N.I.V.)

3:13 Then Jesus came from Galilee (i.e. Nazareth of Galilee, a 60-mile journey by foot. Jesus was about 30 years old at this time.) **to the Jordan-◙** (i.e. Jordan river. Bethany.-{John 1:28}) **to be baptized** (907-*immersed, submerged)* **by John.**
14 But John tried to deter him, (forbad-K.J.V.-2697-*A persistence effort to prevent, discourage, dissuade.* Syn.-protest, dissuade, talk out of. Expresses: No casual hesitation, but a strenuous & earnest protest.) **saying, "I need to be baptized by you' and do you come to me?"**(Expresses John's reluctance, being aware of his own sinfulness in light of Jesus' righteousness and divine nature.)

John sensing his own sinfulness feels his need to be cleansed by Jesus with the Holy Spirit.

Message & Application 💻=🌎

❖ Shows the importance in recognizing our lost & sinful condition and our desperate need for God's forgiveness. (Rom. 3:9, 3:23, 1-John 1:8-10)
❖ Teaches how baptism is a personal journey and a conscious decision of one's own accord, and not something that you feel pressured to do.
❖ Calls for obeying God's will and call on our lives no matter the pain, journey, or adversities. (Are you willing to go as far as it takes?) (V 13)
❖ Calls for the humility in admitting that no matter how perfect we think we are, there's always room for improvement! (Matt. 6:12, Philp. 3:12-14)
❖ Calls for realizing that Jesus is the only hope we have, that we can't make it into heaven on our own efforts and good works.
❖ Calls for recognizing how helpless and inadequate we are, that without Jesus we stand condemned before a holy and righteous God!
❖ Displays how even in light of all our sins, failures, and mistakes, we can still become vessels for God's use and service!
❖ Teaches even when God's ways may seem strange to us, trust that His plans will work. (Don't try to understand, just comply!).
🗝 Even today, believers need to acknowledge that outside of Christ's Saving work, we have no hope of standing righteous before a holy God.
☞ Jesus coming to be baptized was not because He had sin to repent of, for He was already sinless!-(2-Corn. 5:21, 1-Pet. 2:2, Heb. 7:26) But rather undertook it in obedience to all that God commands & requires. (V.15)
☞ Though the exact location of Jesus' baptism is uncertain, Church tradition places it at the ford just before the Jordan river flows into the Dead Sea, known today as "Yardenit" ("Little Jordan"). According to the Gospel of John, it was on the banks of the Jordan river just across from Bethany, home of Mary, Martha & Lazarus. (cf. John 1:28-29)

3:15 Jesus replied, "Let it be so now; it is proper (Syn.-appropriate, correct, agreeable, God ordained.) **for us to do this** (i.e. Baptism) **to fulfill** (4137-*Make full, satisfy, bring to completion.*) **all righteousness.**(1343-*To conform to the will, plan, and ordinances of all that God commands & ordains.* Expresses Jesus' obedience in identifying with sinners by fulfilling God's plan of Salvation & redemption.) **Then John consented.** (i.e. Yielded, administered the baptism.)

Jesus submits to John's baptism out of obedience to the Father's will that He identify Himself with sinners.

<u>Message & Application</u> 💻=🌎

- ❖ Shows Jesus' readiness in carrying out God's will & plan of Salvation by standing in the place of sinners.(cf. Is. 53:11-12, 2-Corn. 5:21, Philp. 2:6-8)
- ❖ Displays Jesus' willingness in identifying with us in our plights, that He understands our pain and what we're going through. (Heb. 4:14-16)
- ❖ Displays how obeying and submitting to God's will in all things is the first step on the path to righteous and holy living.
- ❖ Teaches how it's every believer's duty to honor & observe all that God ordains, even if we feel exempt. (cf. Matt.17:24-27, Philp. 2:6-8)
- ❖ Displays how true righteousness will do all that God instructs and requires, even if it's things that we're not bound to or obligated by.
- ❖ Teaches how Jesus will never command us to do anything that He Himself is unwilling to do!

–***Fulfill all righteousness***-Variously interpreted as either:

- Out of obedience to God's will, though sinless Jesus identifies Himself with sinners. (Is. 53:10-12, Heb.5:8)
- Out of obedience in observing all religious duties & ordinances ordained by God, including John the Baptist. (Luke 2:21-24)
- Served as an example for believers to follow. (Rom. 6:3-11,1-John 2:6)

🗝 Even today, believers must be willing to surrender & submit ourselves in all that God asks of us no matter where it may take us, or how costly, challenging, or uncomfortable it may be.

<u>The purpose of Jesus' Baptism:</u>

- Jesus' obedience to God's will in identifying Himself with sinners.
- Jesus' obedience in allowing John the Baptist reveal Him to the people as the Messiah.
- Jesus' obedience in submitting to all divinely appointed ordinances and institutions.

3:16 As soon as Jesus was baptized, he went up out of the water. (Confirms baptism by submersion.) **At that moment heaven was opened, and he** (i.e. Jesus or John as well.-{John 1:32}) **saw the Spirit of God** (Holy Spirit) **descending like a dove and lighting on him** (i.e. Either the form or movement of a dove as it slowly descends and lands on Jesus. Expresses divine confirmation of Jesus' innocence, purity, and meekness. As well as Jesus' anointing for ministry work.) **17 And a voice from heaven said, "This is my son, whom I love;** (Expresses: Only Son, begotten by the Father, object of love from eternity past.) **with him I am well pleased.**"(Expresses God's approval in Jesus' sinless character and obedience in suffering for sin while undertaking the work of man's Salvation.)

As the Holy Spirit anoints Jesus for ministry, God gives His approval of Jesus' obedience in bearing the sins of the world.

Message & Application =

- ❖ Shows believers Jesus' divine approval & qualifications in carrying out our Salvation and redemption. (cf. Eph. 3:11-12)
- ❖ Assures believers in being fully equipped, having God's anointing and seal of approval as we step forth in ministry and service.
- ❖ Comforts believers in knowing that no matter who we are or what we've done, we're still a child of God and dearly loved by Him!
- ❖ Calls for caring less of what others think about us, that it's God's approval that counts. (Know that you're never a loser in God's eyes!)
- ❖ Teaches how we can be open and honest with God about our sins, that God will never disinherit, disown, or write us out of His will and love!
- ❖ Displays God's unconditional love, that God doesn't hold us to some level of performance or perfection, but loves us just the way we are! (Know you're always operating out of God's grace, not for His grace!).

-***Spirit descending like a dove on him***-Not that Jesus received the Holy Spirit at this time.-(Matt.1:18, 20) But rather is interpreted either as a symbol of Jesus' meekness, purity, and perfection. Or as a special anointing upon Jesus, empowering Him in carrying out His work.

⊶ Even today with all our sin, failures, and mistakes we can stand secure knowing that we're a child of God, dearly loved & forgiven by Him!

➢ Following Revelations signifying:
- **Heavens opened**-Signifying Jesus' intervention in opening the way up to God's forgiveness.
- **Spirit of God descending**-Signifying Jesus' public anointing as Messiah and empowering for ministry work.
- **This is my Son, whom I love and well pleased**-Signifying Jesus' sinlessness & divine qualifications as our substitute in suffering and dying for the sins of the world.

Chapter Four

Jesus' Temptation

- **Jesus' temptation-**Satan tries to tempt Jesus away from God's will in suffering for sin.-(Vs. 1-11)
- **Jesus begins to preach-**Jesus begins preaching ministry in Galilee.-(Vs. 12-17)
- **Jesus calls first disciples-**Jesus calls His first disciples in the work of ministry.-(Vs. 18-22)
- **Jesus' heals the sick-**Jesus begins a threefold ministry of preaching, teaching, and healing.-(Vs. 23-25)

The Temptation of Jesus-(N.I.V.)

4:1 Then (Following Jesus' baptism) **Jesus was led by the Spirit** (Yielded to the Holy Spirit, full of the Holy Spirit.{Luke 4:1}) **into the desert** (wilderness-K.J.V. Expresses: How even when alone, drifting, and wandering doesn't mean God is not with us.) **to be tempted** (3985-*Test or solicit to sin, make a trial of*) **by the devil.** (Satan's attempt to deter Jesus away from God's will in suffering for sin.)

Jesus' obedience in obeying God's will in suffering for sin is put to the test by Satan.

Message & Application 💻=🌎

❖ Shows Jesus' qualification & fitness in helping us overcome our own struggles with sin, having been tempted like us. (cf. Heb. 2:18, 4:14-16)

❖ Teaches how temptations usually occur when we are coming out of a great spiritual victory, or when we think our faith is the strongest.

❖ Teaches how victory over sin and temptation comes not by our own willpower and might, but by the Holy Spirit's power & strength.

🗝 Even today, believers can expect Satan to use our spiritual highs, victories, and breakthroughs to attack us. (cf. 1-Corn. 10:12)

☞ Emphasizes a common experience many face having given our lives to Jesus, Satan now attacks us, trying to draw us back to himself.

☞ Believers need to remember that temptation itself is not a sin, but only an opportunity to sin. Or becomes a sin when we entertain it and yield to it. That God may be using our trials & temptations to grow our faith.

Purposes of Jesus' Temptations:

- **To overcome what Adam & Eve couldn't in the Garden.** Since Adam & Eve faced the same temptations in the garden of Eden. (Lust of the flesh, lust of the eyes, pride of life). (Gen 3:1-7)
- **To overcome what Israel couldn't in the Wilderness.** Since both faced the same temptations in the desert, Israel for 40 years, Jesus for 40 days. (Grumbled for bread & water, tested God's presence, worshiped a Golden calf). (Deut. 6:13, 6:16, 8:1-3)

4:2 After fasting (3521-*Abstinence from food*) **for forty days and forty nights, he was hungry.** (Expresses Jesus' human nature & vulnerability to temptation.)

Jesus prepares Himself spiritually for the extreme trials & temptations that lie ahead.

Message & Application

- ❖ Shows how believers can better prepare ourselves spiritually for trials and temptations by seeking God's strength through prayer and fasting.
- ❖ Displays how Satan's temptations usually come when we're at our weakest & lowest point, losing a job, family problems, breakups, etc.
- ⊶ Even today Satan will use whatever struggles we have in the areas of pride, doubt, lust, anger, greed, addiction, etc. to launch his attack.

4:3 The tempter (Expresses Satan's work in soliciting men to sin.) **came to him and said, "If** (Viz.-Since, seeing that.) **you are the Son of God,** (Suggests: Proclamation made at Jesus' baptism.) **tell these stones to become bread"**

Satan is tempting Jesus away from God's will in suffering for sin to using His Divine powers for His own ends.

Message & Application

- ❖ Shows how Satan often tempts us to act independently of God, getting us to put our own needs & wants above what God wants.
- ❖ Warns against thinking that God is not providing in the way He should, that we start looking to other things to get our needs met.
- ❖ Warns how Satan often tempts us to take matters into our own hands, that we deserve better after all we've suffered and been through.
- ⊶ Even today, believers can be tempted in meeting a legitimate need in an illegitimate way. Whether it's cheating on an exam in order to graduate, fudging on our taxes to pay the mortgage, stripping at night to pay the bills, or gambling on-line to pay the rent.

Satan's Three Areas of Temptations:

Stones to bread-"Lust of the flesh"-Satan's efforts to get us to gratify the sinful cravings & desires of the flesh outside the will of God. (Rom. 13:14, Gal. 5:19-21)

Throw yourself down-"The Pride of Life"-Satan's effort to get us to seek a life of status, recognition, self-reliance, and self-dependence apart from God. (Gen. 3:6)

Kingdoms of the world-"Lust of the eyes"-Satan's efforts to draw us away from God for a life of money, wealth, fame, and materialism. (1-John 2:15-16)

4:4 Jesus answered, 'It is written: 'Man does not live by bread alone, (Food, shelter) **but on every word that comes from the mouth of God'.** {Duet. 8:2-3}

Jesus overcomes Satan's first temptation by putting God's word & will above His own wants and needs.

Message & Application 

- ❖ Shows how believers can have victory over sin & temptation by standing on the truth of God's word & promises.(2-Corn.10:5, 1-Pet.1:22)
- ❖ Calls for always keeping God in the equation of our daily actions and decision. (Never live a day without considering God into your plans!).
- ❖ Teaches how we're not just flesh & blood, that there's also a spiritual side of us that needs to be nourished & refreshed daily by God's word.
- ❖ Teaches how defeating temptation is not a matter of willpower, argument, or debate, but about simply yielding to the word of God.
- ⊷ Even today, believers can have victory over sin & temptation by knowing when something is contrary to God's word & truth. (Eph. 6:17)

4:5 Then (Expresses the tenacity of Satan, that He doesn't give up easily.) **the devil took him to the holy city-◙** (i.e. Jerusalem) **and had him stand on the highest point of the temple-◙** (i.e. Temple wall 450 ft. above the Kidron valley.) **6 If you are the Son of God, he said, throw yourself down. For it is written "'He will command his angels concerning you, and they will lift you up in their hands so that you will not strike your foot against a stone.**{Ps.91:11-12,Mal. 3:1}

Satan is tempting Jesus to test God's faithfulness or to win public approval through a spectacular miracle.

Message & Application 

- ❖ Shows how Satan often tempts us to question our standing with God or to question the character of God's love, power, and goodness.
- ❖ Warns how Satan often tempts us to doubt God's care when going through difficult times, or God's forgiveness when we fall into sin.
- ⊷ Even today we can be tempted to presume upon God saying; *"Lord if you get me out of this mess, I'll know your real"*. Or will manipulate God into giving us what we want saying; *"Lord if you'll do this for me, then I'll know that you love me"*. Or will presume upon God's grace thinking: *"God won't send me to Hell for this one little sin"*. Or will even twist scripture around in order to justify some wrong action.
- ☞ Satan by cleverly omitting the rest of the verse *"in all your ways"* takes the Psalm out of context. Which was really showing how one is only protected when their walking in the path and will of God.

4:7 Jesus answered him, "It is also written: 'Do not put the Lord your God to the test. (tempt-K.J.V.-3985-*To try, test, prove.* Syn.-Put to trial/proof. Expresses to make a trial of God's power, faithfulness, goodness.) {cf. Duet. 6:16}

Jesus overcomes Satan's second temptation by showing how men are not to make a trial of God's faithfulness & goodness.

Message & Application 💻=🌎

- ❖ Shows how believers are not to test whether or not God is as good as His word. (Trust what God promises He will do!). (cf. 2-Corn. 5:7)
- ❖ Warns believers against carelessness, expecting God to always be there to rescue and bail us out of our reckless and foolish behavior!
- 🗝 Even today we can think because we're Christians were strong enough to go to wild parties/concerts and God will be there to bail us out.

4:8 Again, (Expresses how Satan seldom gives up with just one try.) **the devil took him to a very high mountain and showed him** (In an instant.-{Luke 4:5}-Suggests: A visionary experience) **all the kingdoms** (i.e. Empires/Nations) **of the world and their splendor.**(Glory-K.J.V. Syn.-power, wealth, riches, pomp, etc.) **9 "All this I will give you," he said,** (Not that Satan owns the world, but rather has free reign as a result of man's fallen humanity.-{2-Corn. 4:4}) **if you will bow down and worship me.**(i.e. To bow down to the forces & sway of sinful desires.)

Satan is tempting Jesus with a shortcut to world dominion without having to suffer on the Cross.

Message & Application 💻=🌎

- ❖ Shows how Satan often tempts us away from God to craving the pleasures and things that this world has to offer. (cf. Matt. 16:26)
- ❖ Warns against thinking that money, wealth, and material things can bring us happiness or a better way of life than what God can give us.
- ❖ Warns how Satan often shows us all the pleasures of sin, while hiding the consequences in all the bondage, misery, and ruin it brings!
- ❖ Warns how Satan will make it seem that God's a killjoy, and will take away all the fun and joy in life.
- ❖ Displays how Satan often tries to get us off track by tempting us to take shortcuts or the easy way out, rather than doing the right thing.
- 🗝 Even today we can be tempted to seek short-term gratification now in what feels good, thinking; *"Why wait for marriage, when I can find intimacy now"*, or *"Why allow the anxiety & troubles of life to worry us, when we can find escape through drugs & alcohol"*, or *"Why wait to be successful, when I can achieve it through dishonest means"*.

4:10 Jesus said to him, "Away from me, Satan! (Syn.-beat it, get packing. Expresses a form of rebuke, rejection, indignation.) **For it is written: 'Worship** (Syn.-love, honor, obey) **the Lord your God, and serve him only'."**(Suggests: To worship Satan would have been an act of idolatry.) {Deut. 6:13}

Jesus overcomes Satan's third temptation by showing how obeying & serving God takes priority over all other things.

Message & Application 💻=🌎

- ❖ Shows how believers can have victory over Satan by always putting what God wants first above what we want or what the world dictates.
- ❖ Warns how there can be no room for compromise in our Christian walk, that everything must be done on God's terms, not ours!
- ❖ Calls for doing things God's way, even if it feels like we're missing out on certain things, or we're getting the short end of the stick.
- 🗝 Today we can have victory over temptation, knowing that there's not enough that Satan or the world can offer us to get us to turn from God.

4:11 Then the devil left him, (until an opportune time.-{Luke 4:13}-Suggests Jesus was never free from temptations, nor will we be!) **and angels came and attended him.** (ministered-K.J.V. i.e. Food, spiritual comfort of the soul, etc.)

Having successfully defeated Satan's temptations, God sends angels to comfort and encourage Jesus.

Message & Application 💻=🌎

- ❖ Shows believers how when we abide in God's word & will, Satan will flee from us. (cf. James 4:7, Eph. 6:10-13)
- ❖ Having defeated Satan, Jesus is better able to sympathize with our weaknesses, helping us in our times of temptations. (cf. Heb. 4:15)
- ❖ Teaches how God will not leave us to fight our battles alone but will bring spiritual strength to overcome them. (cf. 1-Corn. 10:13, Heb. 13:5)
- ☞ Satan flees not just because Jesus quoted scripture, but because Jesus placed Himself under the authority of God's Word & Will!

Lessons learned from Jesus' Victory over Temptation:

- Stay spiritually prepared by praying, fasting, and being filled with the Holy Spirit. (4:1-2)
- Stay alert for Satan's areas of attack, know your weaknesses. (4:2)
- Stay anchored in the word of God, know what scripture says. (4:4)
- Stay worshipping, serving, and putting God first. (4:8-10)

From this verse here (V. 12) to verse (V. 17) Jesus' begins preaching ministry in Galilee.

Jesus Begins to Preach-(N.I.V.)

4:12 When Jesus heard that John (i.e. The Baptist) **had been put in prison,** (By Herod Antipas for reproving his adulterous affair.-{Matt. 14:1-12}) **he returned** (departed-K.J.V.-402-*Give place, turn aside, withdraw)* **to Galilee.** (i.e. His hometown of Nazareth, eventually moving His ministry to Capernaum.-{V. 13})

Hearing of John the Baptist's imprisonment by Herod, Jesus for His own safety moves His ministry to Galilee.

Message & Application 💻=🌎

- ❖ Shows how believers are not to allow life's setbacks to delay us from doing God's will. (When the going gets tough, the tough get going!).
- ❖ Comforts believers in knowing that Jesus hears our cries and is well aware of the burdens, trials, and persecutions we suffer.
- ❖ Teaches rather than get frustrated & discouraged by opposition, see it as an opportunity towards a new phase of ministry and outreach.
- ❖ Teaches when God closes one door, He always opens another! (Expect God to provide the provisions in ministry wherever you go!).
- ⊶ Even today it shouldn't come as a shock/surprise that when we speak words of hope, truth and accountability people will persecute us for it.
- ☞ According to the synoptic Gospels attribute John's imprisonment as a result of having reproved King Herod for his adulterous marriage to Herodias his brother Philips' wife. (cf. Matt. 14:3-5). According to the Jewish historian Josephus, identifies the prison as the fortified castle of "Macherus" located on a mountain top 4 miles east of the Dead Sea.

-***Returned to Galilee***-Jesus' withdraw is variously attributed to:

- Not in fear of Herod, since Galilee was under Herod's jurisdiction. But of prudence in not provoking the envy and malice of the religious leaders in Jerusalem. (cf. John 4:1-3)
- Was staying to God's divine timetable, that His appointed time had not yet come to suffer on the Cross.
- Was building upon the movement of John's earlier ministry.

☞ John's Gospel records a time lapse of about a year, in which several events took place prior to Jesus' move to Galilee:
Jesus' attends wedding at Canaan, turning water to wine-(Jn 2:10)
Jesus' clearing of the temple in Jerusalem during Passover-(Jn 2:12-25)
Jesus' meeting with Nicodemus & Samaritan woman-(Jn 3:1-21, 4:1-26)

4:13 Leaving Nazareth, (i.e. Having been ousted & rejected by His own people.-{cf. Luke 4:14-30}) **he went and lived in Capernaum,-◙** (i.e. A city that Jesus adopted as headquarters for His ministry.) **which was by the lake-◙** (i.e. On the N-W shore of the Sea of Galilee.) **in the area of Zebulun and Naphtali-** (Suggests: O.T. lands allotted to two of the Twelve Tribes of Israel, after Joshua's conquest of Canaan. That Capernaum lay within these O.T. Borders.)
14 to fulfill what was said through the prophet Isaiah: {cf. Isaiah 9:1-2}
15 "Land of Zebulun and land of Naphtali, the way to the sea, (Suggests: O.T. tribal areas that skirted the Sea of Galilee.) **along the Jordan-◙** (beyond the Jordan-K.J.V. Either "Perea" or the "Decapolis"-[Grk.-"Ten-cities"] which lay just southeast of the Jordan river.) **Galilee of the Gentiles—**(i.e. Non-Jews living in the northern part of Galilee, chiefly the cities of Tyre and Sidon.)
16 the people living (Syn.-walking, residing, bound.) **in darkness** (Metph.-Spiritual blindness, error, sin, hopelessness, ignorance, rebellion, etc.) **have seen a great light;** (Metph-Jesus, hope, rescue, Salvation, Gospel.) **on those living in the land of the shadow of death** (Metph-Eternal death, bondage, misery, damnation, condemnation, etc.) **a light has dawned."** (Suggests: The Messiah's arrival, beginning of Christ's ministry of teaching and healing.)

By moving to Capernaum Jesus fulfilled Isaiah's prophecy of the Messiah bringing hope and Salvation to the Gentiles.

Message & Application 💻=🌎

❖ Shows the Saving grace of Jesus in coming into the world, lifting us out of the darkness of our sins, hopelessness, and despair!
❖ Displays Jesus' ability to call us out of our life of sin and brokenness, to one of hope, peace, and new life! (cf. John 12:46)
❖ Teaches regardless of how bleak and hopeless things look, know that with Jesus there's always a light at the end of the tunnel!
❖ Teaches the transforming power of Christ, calling us out of our sinful ways of living to His truth, light, and right way of living.
❖ Teaches that no matter how grim and hopeless our problems with addiction and depression may look, Jesus can pull us out of it!
⊶ Even today, believers can take comfort that no matter how gloomy things look in our marriages, finances, business, sobriety, health, etc. Jesus will be there helping to guide us through it.
☞ In context, the quoted passage of Isaiah is in reference to how even though God had used Assyria's invasion of the northern kingdom of Israel to humble & turn her from her idolatrous ways. But God would not allow the calamity of their captivity to overtake them, promising their future deliverance by king Hezekiah, now more fully fulfilled through the work & ministry of Christ. (2-Kings Chaps.17, 18, 19, Is. 8:3-8)

4:17 From that time on (i.e. From Jesus' arrival in Capernaum, or after John's imprisonment.-{Mark 1:14} May also express the beginning of Jesus' public ministry.) **Jesus began to preach,** (2784-*To proclaim, exhort, and declare as a herald.)* **"Repent,** (3340-*Afterthought, "To have a change of mind involving both a turning from sin and a turning to God".* Expresses: More than just being sorry for your sins, but having a change of heart, mind, and direction, making a complete U-turn from living life our way to living it God's way.) **for the kingdom of heaven is near."** (at hand-K.J.V. Suggests: The arrival of the Messiah through the person and work of Jesus' ministry. But in a wider context expresses the sovereign rule & reign of Christ over the hearts and lives of believers. {cf. Mark 1:15, Luke 17:20-21} Note: Matthew may have substituted the word "God" for "heaven" out of reverence for the holy name of God.)

Jesus begins preaching ministry by calling people to turn from their sins and receive Him as their rightful Lord over their lives.

Message & Application

- Shows how believers are to give up control of being in charge of our lives to surrendering it over to Christ's direction and control.
- Calls believers in turning from a life of self-centeredness and sin-centeredness to Christ-centeredness!
- Calls believers in taking our lives in a new direction, no longer cooperating with sin to cooperating with God.
- Calls for taking "Self" off the throne to making Christ the rightful Ruler & King over our lives. (Will you allow Jesus to call the shots?).
- Calls for turning from anything that is keeping us from fully surrendering ourselves over to the rule and Lordship of Christ.
- Calls for putting our lives under the "New management" of Christ, that Jesus can do so much better with our lives than we can!

Even today repentance is more than just about "Altar Calls" or saying the "Sinners Prayer". But rather it's about putting every aspect of our lives under the rule and direction of Christ. (cf. 1-John 1:9-10)

Proper Responses in Repentance:

- Stop living for self and start living for God.
- Stop seeking other things & start seeking God's Kingdom.
- Continually forsake and renounce daily sins to God.
- Bear the fruits of a changed & reformed life.
- Turn from the service of sin to the service of God.
- Turn from self-centeredness to God-centeredness.

From this verse here (V. 18) to verse (V. 22) Jesus calls His first four disciples in being preachers & soul winners for the Gospel.

The Calling of the First Disciples-(N.I.V.)

4:18 As Jesus was walking beside the Sea of Galilee,-◙ he saw two brothers,
Simon called Peter (4074-*Grk.-Petro's or Cephas, meaning "Rock or a Stone".)*
and his brother Andrew. They were casting a net into the lake,-◙ (i.e. Standing
on the shoreline or boat while tossing a circular weighted net into the sea.) **for**
they were fishermen. (Expresses their occupation, trade, business.)
19 "Come, follow me, (190-*Union, to be in the same way with. To join as or*
become a disciple. Expresses a call to discipleship, service, commitment, and
obedience.) **Jesus said," and I will make you fishers of men.** (Metph-Ministers,
Gospel preachers, souls winners for Christ, etc.)

Peter & Andrew are called in becoming disciples and soul winners for Christ.

Message & Application 💻=🌎

❖ Shows how believers are to lay aside our own personal goals & pursuits in favor of Christ's higher calling on our lives.
❖ Calls for being sold out for Jesus, knowing He has a better purpose and calling on our lives than what we can see now.
❖ Assures believers that whatever Christ has called us to do He will see that we're able and fit to do it! (cf. Philp. 4:13, Eph. 6:10, Luke 22:35)
❖ Reminds believers no matter how poor, uneducated, or unqualified we feel we are, God can still use us and make something out of our lives!

🗝 Even today whatever calling God has put on our lives must come first, even if it means leaving family & friends to serve Him overseas, or changing jobs, careers, and vocations in midlife. Or simply being bold in witnessing the Gospel as we go about the daily routines of life.

Qualifying Fishing Traits for Witness:

- **Courage & Patience**–Like fishing, Gospel witness will be hard work, requiring persistence and perseverance.
- **Alertness & Discernment**-Like fishing, Gospel witness will require strategy, knowing the right time, being ready at a moments notice, and being vigilant.
- **Cooperation & Ingenuity**-Like fishing, Gospel witness will require teamwork, adaptability, flexibility, and finesse.

4:20 At once (immediately-K.J.V. Expresses: Without hesitation or delay.) **they left their net** (i.e. Occupations, employments, trade, business.) **and followed him.** (Suggests: Took Jesus up on His call to become His disciples.)

In response to Jesus' call, Peter & Andrew immediately leave their fishing business and become His disciples.

Message & Application

- ❖ Shows believers how following Jesus requires an immediate response, one without excuses, reservation, or regrets.
- ❖ Calls believers in the willingness in forsaking all in following Jesus.
- ❖ Teaches how there can be no half-measures or holding back when following Jesus, either you're all in or you're not!
- ☞ This is not saying that all believers must leave their jobs, careers, and livelihoods, or drop out of school and college. But rather only if those things are interfering with Christ's greater call on our lives.

-At once followed Him-Variously attributed to either:

- Were already familiar with Jesus as the Messiah, having been introduced to Jesus as the "lamb of God" by John the Baptist months earlier. (cf. John 1:35-42).
- Were already familiar with Jesus as the Messiah, having witnessed earlier that morning the miraculous catch of fish that Jesus performed in Peter's boat. (cf. Luke 5:1-11)
- Were convinced Jesus was the Messiah by the powerful impression that He made upon their hearts & souls. (cf. Luke 24:32)

4:21 Going on from there, he saw two other brothers, James son of Zebedee and his brother John. They were in a boat with their father Zebedee, preparing their nets. Jesus called them, (Expresses to become disciples.)

James & John are called in becoming disciples and soul winners for Christ.

Message & Application

- ❖ Shows the brotherly love that should be found among ministers. (No better companion to share our work with than a fellow believer!).
- ❖ Teaches the importance of industry and diligence in our Christian vocations and callings. (It is commendable to make what we have go as far, and last as long as possible).
- ❖ Teaches how it's good when Christ returns, that we're not idle but employed and busy in our calling. (It's good to be found doing and obeying when Jesus returns).

4:22 and immediately they left the boat and their father (i.e. occupations, business, trade. Some contend they did not leave their father in dire circumstances, due to the fact that hired help was present.-{cf. Mark 1:20}) **and followed him.** (Suggests: Took up Jesus' call to become His disciples.)

In response to Jesus' call, James & John immediately leave their occupations and become His disciples.

Message & Application =

- ❖ Shows how following Jesus takes priority over all other commitments, including occupations and family. (Don't be restrained by ties of family, career, or profession).
- ❖ Teaches how discipleship requires an immediate response in obedience and faith. (Follow Jesus no matter the cost or where it leads you!).
- ⊶ Even today for believers there should be nothing so precious or dear to us that we are unwilling to part with in following Jesus. (Will you let go of whatever is holding you back or keeping you from giving yourself fully to Jesus?).

-Immediately followed Him-As with Peter & Andrew it is attributed to:

- Were already familiar with Jesus as the Messiah, having previously been introduced to Jesus as the "Lamb of God" by John the Baptist months earlier. (John 1:35-40)
- Were already familiar with Jesus as the Messiah, having both been present when Jesus performed the miraculous catch of fish in Peter's boat earlier that morning.(Luke 5:1-10a) (Suggests the reason why they were mending their nets -Matt. 4:21)
- Were convinced Jesus was the Messiah by the powerful impression that He made upon their hearts & souls. (Luke 24:32)

How to be Fishers of Men:

- **Fish**-around for those who are open and receptive to the word.
- **Anchor-**the Gospel upon their hearts & souls.
- **Bait-**them with bible tracts and literature.
- **Lure-**them to your Church/Christian website.
- **Cast-**your testimony & witness before them.
- **Lead**-them by example of your own Christian life and walk.
- **Hook & reel**-them by convicting them of being sinners in need of God's forgiveness.

From this verse here (V. 23) to end of the chapter, Jesus begins three-fold ministry of teaching, preaching, and healing.

Jesus Heals the Sick-(N.I.V.)

4:23 Jesus went throughout Galilee, (Suggests: A circuit covering 70 miles & 200 cities & villages.) **teaching in their synagogues,-◙** (4864-*Greek-Assembly, places of worship.*) **preaching the good news of the kingdom** (Metph.-Gospel, God's Saving grace, His arrival as Messiah.-{Luke 4:18-19}) **and healing every disease** (i.e. Chronic illness, epilepsy, blindness, tumors, etc.) **and sickness** (i.e. Emotional & mental disorders, demon possession, etc.) **among the people.**

Jesus begins a tour of Galilee, confirming the Gospel with a threefold ministry of teaching, preaching, and healing.

Message & Application 💻=🌎

- ❖ Shows believers Jesus' compassion & commitment in bringing healing and wholeness to every area of our lives, both body and soul!
- ❖ Teaches how Jesus will go to any distance and to any extreme to bring healing into our lives and all that He has called us to be!
- ❖ Calls for following the same example in reaching out to the lost and hurting with acts of love, kindness, and compassion.
- 🗝 Even today the Church needs to follow the same pattern in confirming the Gospel message through acts of compassion, charity, and love.

4:24 News about him (i.e. His popularity, celebrity, fame-K.J.V.) **spread all over Syria-◙** (i.e. Provinces north of Galilee, present day Lebanon.) **and people brought to him all who were ill with various diseases, those suffering severe pain, the demon-possessed, those having seizures,** (lunatic-K.J.V., epilepsy) **and the paralysed,** (cripple, lame, disabled) **and he healed them.** (Suggests: By word or touch. Expresses sufficiency of Christ' compassion and divine power.)

As the reports of Jesus' miracles spread, people as far as the Roman province of Syria came to be healed by Him.

Message & Application 💻=🌎

- ❖ Shows how believers can bring those who are sick & paralyzed by sin to Jesus that they may be healed and set free.
- ❖ Teaches how there is no sin or burden too great or too small for Jesus to handle. (No one is ever too bad or too far gone for Jesus to heal!).
- 🗝 Even today, believers are to reach out and share Jesus with those who are hurting, broken, and lost, that they can be healed and Saved as well.

4:25 Large crowds from Galilee, (i.e. Northern Palestine west of the Sea of Galilee.) **the Decapolis-◙** (1179-*Grk.-Deca="Ten", polis="cities". i.e. "Ten cities".* i.e. A district located south of the Sea of Galilee and just east of the Jordan river. So named for the confederation of ten cities that resided there, consisting chiefly of foreign Gentiles [Greeks].) **Jerusalem, Judea-◙** (i.e. Southern Palestine situated on the west side of the Dead Sea.) **and the region across** (beyond-K.J.V., A.V.) **the Jordan** (i.e. "Perea" a region of land south of Decapolis and east of the Jordan river.{See Map. Pg. 6}) **followed him** (Expresses a mixed multitude of people, nationalities, and backgrounds. That they were only following Jesus for healing and not for who He was.)

The popularity of Jesus' ministry was attracting a wide range of diverse peoples and nationalities.

Message & Application 💻=🌎

- ❖ Shows believers who have been touched & impacted by Jesus will extend the time, energy, and effort to follow after Him!
- ❖ Calls believers in seeing that we're making following Jesus our priority, passion, and walk in life.
- ❖ Teaches how investing and spending time with Jesus is the best way to make the most out of our lives.
- ❖ Teaches how being a follower of Christ is not a spectator sport of just sitting on the sideline, but about being actively involved.
- ❖ Calls believers in counting the costs, that following Jesus is the best thing in life, no matter the obstacles, hardships, or inconveniences. (Know that you have come too far to turn back now!).
- ❖ Calls for seeing that we're not just following Jesus for healings or what we can get, but for who He is and all that He has already done.
- ❖ Calls believers in seeing that we're patterning our lives off of Jesus' message & teachings, and not just looking for the here and now!

-Decapolis-An area of land that sat on the east side of the sea of Galilee-(Mark 7:31) and stretching south along the Jordan river. It finds it's name due to the fact that it consisted chiefly of ten major cities.
In the Old Testament, it was the track of land allotted to the Tribe of "Manasseh". According to the historian "Pliny the younger" (62-113 A.D.) these cities were: Damascus, Opoton, Philadelphia, Raphana, Scythopolis, Gadara, Hippondion, Pella, Galasa, and Canatha.

🗝 Even today true followers of Jesus will extend the time, effort, and energy in making it to church, bible study, and prayer, no matter how difficult or inconvenient it may be. (Don't let anything or anyone keep you from your blessing!)

Chapter Five

Sermon on the Mount

- **Beatitudes-**Teaches on the qualities, virtues, and traits believers are to possess.-(5:3-12)
- **Salt & Light-**Teaches on character & influence.-(5:13-16)
- **Fulfillment of the Law-**Teaches on an inner righteousness that comes from the heart-(5:17-48)
- **Proper religious observances-** Teaches against putting on a religious/spiritual show-(6:1-18)
- **Treasures in Heaven-**Teaches on correct perspective and value towards money/wealth-(6:19-24)
- **Do not worry-**Teaches against worry & anxiety-(6:25-34)
- **Judging Others-**Warns against judgmental and condemning attitudes towards others-(7:1-6)
- **Ask, Seek, Knock-**Teaches on being persistent in prayer-(7:7-12)
- **The narrow and Wide Gates-** Teaches how Jesus is the only way to Heaven and eternal life-(7:13-14)
- **Tree and its Fruit-**Warns against false teachers & doctrines-(Vs. 15-23)
- **Wise & Foolish Builders-**Teaches on the importance of putting Jesus' teachings into practice-(7:24-27)

5:1 Now when he saw the crowds, (i.e. Those that had followed Him.-4:25) **he went up on a mountainside** (Suggests: As a convenient place to be heard. Was probably a hillside in the vicinity of Capernaum near the sea of Galilee. Church tradition locates the site as the "Horns of Hattin".-◙ Expresses possibly Matthew's way of presenting Jesus as a new and greater Moses!) **and sat down.** (Expresses: A customary posture of Rabbis who were about to teach & instruct.) **His disciples** (3101-*pupil, student.* The Twelve.) **came to him,**
2 and he began to teach them (i.e. The Twelve disciples, as the crowds listened on.–{7:28}) **saying:** (Syn.-preaching, discoursing, exhorting, opened his mouth-K.J.V.-Expresses to speak solemnly, earnestly, and loudly.)

Jesus presents Himself as a new and greater Moses as He begins His Sermon on the mount.

Message & Application 💻=🌎

- ❖ Shows how Christ will always direct us towards the essential qualities of character and virtues expected of those who follow Him.
- ❖ Calls believers in making the most of every opportunity to learn from Jesus of the type of character that honors and pleases God the Father.
- ⊶ Even today those who desire to be taught by Jesus must be willing to draw close to Him.(Better to sit at Christ' feet than stand at a distance)
- ☞ This verse here marks the first five-set division of discourses.(See Intro.)

Sermon on the Mount's Message:

- A description of the character, qualities, and virtues to be manifested by authentic Christians.
- A call in going beyond outward actions to the inner motives and attitude of the heart.
- A higher standard of righteousness that is meant to drive men to seek God's grace.
- A means of moving believers to strive for perfection without becoming complacent or self-righteous.
- A description of God's kingdom to be established at Christ's millennial reign and second coming. (Dispensationalists view)

Following Beatitudes

Believer's Relationship to God

Blessed are the Poor in spirit-(V.3)
One who knows their bankruptcy before God.
Blessed are those who mourn-(V. 4)
One who is remorseful & regretful over sin.
Blessed are those who are meek-(V.5)
One who humbly surrenders control to God.
Those who Hunger for righteousness-(V.6)
One who longs for a life that is right with God.

Believer's Relationship to Others

Blessed are those who are merciful-(V.
One who is loving & forgiving of others.
Blessed are the pure in heart-(V.8)
One who is honest & genuine with others.
Blessed are the peacemakers-(V. 9)
One who lives in harmony with others.
Those persecuted for righteousness-(V.10)
One who suffers for doing what is right.

Beatitudes-(N.I.V.)

5:3 "Blessed (3106-*Pronounce happy, favored, approved by God.* Lat.-beatitude. Syn.-congratulated, privileged, approved/favored by God, Be-Attitude.) **are the poor in spirit,** (4434-*To crouch & cower as helpless, to be reduced to beggary.* Syn.-spiritual poverty/bankruptcy, empty, broken, contrite, wretched, inadequate, end of oneself, end of your rope-M.B.V.) **for theirs is the kingdom of heaven.** (Expresses: Either the Gospel of grace is composed just for such as these. Or such qualities and traits will facilitate entrance into heaven.)

Approved are believers who acknowledge their spiritual poverty and bankruptcy before God.

Message & Application 💻=🌍

- ❖ Shows a person who recognizes they're a lost & hopeless sinner who is in desperate need of God's forgiveness & Saving grace. (Rom. 3:23)
- ❖ Calls for coming to the table with open hands, that we have nothing to offer or commend ourselves before God. (Only to the Cross I cling!)
- ❖ Calls for coming to an end in ourselves, that we're powerless in managing and changing our lives on our own without God's help!
- ❖ Calls for recognizing our destitute condition before God, that we have no way of making it to heaven on our own efforts or good works.

-Poor in spirit-Meaning not one who takes a vow of material poverty or lives like a monk. Nor is it one who is always down on themselves, that they have no value and can't do anything right. Or who withdraws from the world and lives in poverty. But rather it is one who humbly knows they are completely dependent on God's care and support. One who knows that even at their best, with all their success and accomplishments they will always fall short. One who knows they deserve nothing but the judgment and grace of God.

How to Grow Poor in Spirit:

- Be mindful that everything is by God's grace, and not by your own merit or efforts.
- Be willing to stop doing things by your own strength to depending more on God's strength.
- Be open to putting every detail of your life into God's hands, that He knows what's best.
- Be ready to lay down your pride, that you're utterly hopeless without Jesus in your life.

5:4 Blessed {see V.3} **are those who mourn,** (3996-*Lament, sorrow over sin.* Syn.-remorseful, contrite, penitent, grief-stricken, deep anguish, godly sorrow.) **for they will be comforted.** (Expresses to be consoled here and now by the promises of God's love, grace, and forgiveness as held out in the Gospel. Or the peace of having the comforting presence of the Holy Spirit in removing the guilt over it as soon as we repent and own up to it. {John 14:15-17, 26-27, 1-John 1:8-9}

Approved are believers who are remorseful & repentant over sin.

Message & Application =

- Shows a believer who is grieved & remorseful over personal sins. (Be sensitive to what offends God, look at sins the way God does!).
- Calls believers in coming to hate & loathe sin that we truly want it out of our lives. (See your sins as abhorrent & detestable in God's sight).
- Calls for a heart that is grieved over the costly effect of our sins, and how much suffering and pain it cost Jesus in being nailed to the Cross.
- Teaches that before the Lord can help heal us we need to recognize that we have a sin/addiction problem that needs fixing. (cf. James 4:8-10)
- Portrays one who is broken over the sin that is going on in their lives and the world around them, and who want to do something about it.

-***Mourn***-Meaning not self-pity or one who mopes around looking sad, miserable, and down in the dumps. Or that one can never laugh, smile, or enjoy life. Nor is it just about grieving over the loss of a loved one, disappointments of life, or the brokenness of the world, though it may include this. But rather, it's one who stops rationalizing & minimizing their sins as insignificant to calling it for what it really is. One who can agree with God that sin is sin no matter how small or trivial it may be. Whether it was a hurtful word to our wives, impatient remark to our children, unkind act to a neighbor, or judgmental attitude to a stranger.

How to Grow Mournful Over Sin:

- Be sure to acknowledge areas where you've failed God and your need to repent & change.
- Be sorrowful over the painful effects of sin, and how it has hurt & broke God's heart.
- Be sincere in turning from a sinful behavior or habit, that it doesn't happen again.
- Be honest enough to stop excusing/defending to taking personal responsibility for the sin.

5:5 Blessed are the meek, (4239-*One who is mild and humble, power under control, a wild horse that's been broken.* Syn.-humble, gentle, patient, submissive, flexible, yielded, content, God-controlled.) **for they will inherit the earth.** (Does not mean believers will own the world, but rather of ruling & reigning with Christ when He establishes a New heaven & New earth.-{cf. Rev. 21:7}. Or expresses those who can find satisfaction & contentment in whatever situation they're in, knowing they're going to have it all one day anyway!)

Approved are believers who humbly submit their life's over to God's authority & control.

Message & Application

- ❖ Shows a believer who can humbly surrender & submit to God's control, guidance, and direction in life.
- ❖ Displays a believer who can humbly accept God's dealings with them as just and fair, without ever arguing or disputing.
- ❖ Displays one who can humbly accept correction from God and others when they're wrong, without getting angry or defensive. (James 1:19-20)
- ❖ Portrays one who doesn't need to display or prove their strength to everyone, but instead, allows their character to speak for itself.
- ❖ Emphasizes a believer who exhibits gentleness & self-control in the face of insults and criticism. (cf. Matt. 5:39, 1-Corn. 4:12-13, Gal. 5:22-23)

-***Meek***-Meaning, not one who is shy, timid or weak. Or allows themselves to be doormats and walked on by others. Nor is it one who is passive & easy going. But rather it's one who is teachable and open to correction without being offended. One who does not boast about their own abilities and accomplishments, but gives all the glory to God. One who knows they're no better in God's eyes than anyone else.

How to Grow in Meekness:

- Be mindful about how much God has forgiven you, and the grace He has shown you.
- Be conscious of your daily dependence on God's guidance and direction in all things.
- Be accepting of God's dealings as just & fair without getting angry or bitter.
- Be willing to endure injuries patiently, trusting God to vindicate and defend you in the end.
- Be humble & open to follow where God leads and to bloom where God plants you.

5:6 "Blessed-{V. 3} **are those who hunger and thirst** (Metph.-earnest desire, deepest cravings, driving need, all-consuming passion. Present tense suggests a continual action.) **for righteousness,** (1343-*A right relationship and standing with God. The character of behaving & living right.* Syn.-holiness, integrity, godliness. Expresses a spiritual hunger for godly living and Christ-likeness.) **for they will be filled.** (Suggests: God will provide the grace for all who have put their faith in a Saving relationship with Jesus.-{cf. Rom. 3:21-26} Or God will supply the grace and strength in living holy and Spirit-filled lives we long for.)

Approved are believers who earnestly long to live a life that is right with God.

Message & Application

- ❖ Shows a believer who is hungering to have God's rule & ways perfected in our lives, becoming more and more like Christ.
- ❖ Displays a believer who longs to be free and done with sin, always loving what God loves and hating what God hates.
- ❖ Warns if there's no hunger in your life to know God, then its a pretty good indicator that something is wrong with your spiritual life!
- ❖ Displays a believer who no longer finds satisfaction in worldly things and pleasures, but now longs after Christ and Godly things.
- ❖ Portrays a believer who starts to sound and look different from the world around them to preferring more and more the things of God.

-Thirst for Righteousness-Is not just about seeing injustices righted and wrongs corrected. Nor is it about an imputed righteousness, already won by Christ. Or about attaining a perfect life in never doing wrong. But rather it is one who keeps turning from sin back to God, even when they've messed up and blown it. One who continually seeks God's help over the pollution and power of sin. One who does not let a day go by that their not praying, fellowshipping, and in God's word!

How to Grow in Righteousness:

- Be invested in reading & studying the bible, applying its truths to your daily life.
- Be connected with a Church, see that your fellowshipping with Spirit-filled believers.
- Be passionate about the things of God, always seeking to grow in a deeper relationship.
- Be filled with a life that is faithfully following, serving, and believing on Jesus.

5:7 Blessed {V. 3} **are the merciful,** (3628-*One who is moved with compassion & action towards the plight/suffering of others.* Syn.-forgiving, forbearing, goodwill.) **for they will be shown mercy.** (Suggests: Not in the sense as *"What comes around goes around"*, that if we're merciful, the world will be merciful to us. Or that by acts of mercy we can force God's arm to bless us. But rather our mercy towards others determines if our hearts ever received God's mercy.)

Approved are believers who bear the same mercy & compassion towards others that God has shown them.

Message & Application 💻=🌎

❖ Shows a believer who has received God's grace & mercy will extend that same grace and mercy towards others. (cf. Eph. 4:31-32)
❖ Teaches how there should be no limit to our mercy, that there should be no sin too great to forgive, and no debt too large to pardon.
❖ Calls for dealing mercifully with others since we too are sinners, having shared the same temptations, struggles, and shortcomings.
❖ Calls for a heart that is less critical & judgmental, to one that is patient, loving, and forgiving, that we all stumble now and again.

-Merciful-Meaning is not just about giving handouts to the homeless, or saying "I feel your pain". But rather its one who's willing to stand with others in their struggles and addictions. Or one who's mercy shows up even in the little everyday acts as giving up a seat on the bus, or being patient with someone in the check-out line, or allowing a car to cut in front of us, or overlooking the insensitive comment of a co-worker.

☞ Such mercies extend to both the physical & spiritual. Meeting their material needs, such as shelter, food, clothing, etc. And their spiritual needs, such as love, comfort, forgiveness, counsel, encouragement, etc.

How to Grow in Mercy:

- Be lovingly inclined & concerned for those who are lost and heading for Hell.
- Be charitable & openhanded towards the hurting and suffering around you.
- Be open minded and understanding of where others are coming from.
- Be sympathetic to the difficulties and struggles that others are going through.

5:8 Blessed {See V. 3} **are the pure in heart** (1506-*Unmixed, unalloyed, refined.* Syn.-undivided-affections, single-mindedness, fully-devoted, sincere, genuine, authentic, transparent, without guile.) **for they will see God.** (Expresses to spend eternity with God in heaven. Or to have a greater perception of knowing the power, love, and presence of God moving and working in our lives.)

Approved are believers who desire to live a life that is holy & pleasing to God.

Message & Application

- Shows a believer who is sincerely striving to live a clean & holy life that's pleasing to God. (cf. Rom. 12:1-2, 1-Thess. 4:1-12, 1-John 3:3)
- Calls for a heart that's always seeking God's help in overcoming the sinful habits, issues, and weaknesses we're struggling with. (Rom. 7:18)
- Teaches how it's not enough just to clean up the outside, we need to allow God to change us on the inside as well. (cf. 1-Sam. 16:7, Ps. 51:10)
- Teaches how God wants more than just a reformed life that's free of bad habits, to one that is pure in motives and intentions as well.
- Calls for a life of openness and transparency, that we're not whitewashing, downplaying, or concealing anything from God.
- Teaches how God doesn't expect a perfect life, but rather a heart that is genuinely striving to follow after Him.

–***Pure in heart***-Meaning not sinless perfection, or one who never lies. But rather one who is constantly confessing their sins & weaknesses openly to God. Or one who's language is the same around friends as it is in Church. Or who's humor is the same around co-workers as around church members. Or one who's interests and entertainment is the same around the home as around their Church family.

How to Grow Pure in Heart:

- Be ready to acknowledge & confess a specific sin or habit that needs to be gone from your life.
- Be eager to spend daily time in God's word, learning how to grow in its principals and truths.
- Be single-mindedly focused on always living for God's will and glory.
- Be determined to stay in the battle and press forward, even if you stumble and fall.
- Be gentle, loving, and forgiving, not allowing anger, hate, or bitterness to take root.

5:9 Blessed{V.3} **are the peacemakers,** (1515-*One who seeks to bring harmony, unity, and reconciliation between men.* Syn.-bridge-builders, fence-menders) **for they will be called** (Syn.-counted, characterized.) **sons of God.** (Expresses one who reflects the character of God, always loving and forgiving. Or one who carries out the Gospel message of peace and reconciliation to a lost world.)

Approved are believers who promote the Gospel and live in harmony with others.

Message & Application 💻=🌎

- Shows how believers are to be agents of hope & peace in reconciling people back to God by sharing the Gospel message. (cf. 2-Corn 5:19-21)
- Calls for laying down any grievances and pettiness that's keeping us from praying for others. (Be peacemakers, not trouble makers!)
- Displays one who is willing to compromise on personal demands for the sake of unity & peace. (Put relationships above personal rights!).
- Teaches how it's better to cooperate and compromise than to cause conflict, quarrels, and fights. (Be part of the solution, not the problem)
- Calls believers in taking the high road in never becoming abrasive or confrontational when Christian values and principals are not at risk.

-***Peacemaker***-Meaning, not one who remains passive and appeasing for the sake of conflicts. Or one who compromises their convictions in order to avoid fights. Or who seeks peace at any price even at the cost of their integrity. But rather it's one who's always bearing the love and forgiveness of God into every problem and negative situation. One who for the sake of peace will be the first to apologize and admit their wrong, even if they feel their right. One who does not argue over the non-essentials of the faith, that most things are trivial, petty, and not worth bickering and fighting about.

How to Grow as a Peacemaker:

- Be agreeable to living in harmony with others.
- Be available instruments & channels of God's love and mercy to a lost and troubled world.
- Be quick to make amends by apologizing and asking for forgiveness, even if your right.
- Be passionate in standing up against injustice & abuse by coming to the defensive of others.

5:10 Blessed {V. 3} **are those who are persecuted** (1377-*To put to flight, pursue, drive away.* Syn.-harassed, rejected, hated, ridiculed, ostracized.) **because of righteousness** (i.e. godly living, Christian values, principles, morals, etc.) **for theirs is the kingdom of heaven.** (Expresses how the persecution we suffer can't compare to the eternal glory that awaits us in heaven! {2-Corn.4:17})

Approved are believers who suffer for doing what is right.

Message & Application 💻=🌎

- ❖ Shows how a believer can expect to be harassed & mistreated by the world as we stay standing and living for Christ. (cf. 1-Pet. 4:1-4, 4:12-16)
- ❖ Calls for staying true to our Christian values without compromising what we know is right just in order to fit in or go along with the crowd.
- ❖ Calls for staying true to Jesus without giving into the ways of the world, or bending to the latest trends, popular culture, or status quo.
- ❖ Calls believers in standing with Christ even if it means being un-hip, unpopular, marginalized, and out-casted. (cf. Luke 6:22-23)

-Persecuted for Righteousness-Meaning, not one who goes's looking for ways to be persecuted. Or that persecution qualifies one for Salvation or special reward with God. Nor is it one who suffers persecution at their own hands for being rude, obnoxious, and an inconsiderate jerk! Or one who suffers termination or disciplinary action for performing poorly at their job. But rather its about one who suffers persecution for staying true to their Christian values. One who would rather lose a job or a promotion than engage in unethical and immoral practices.
Or one who would rather face ostracism from friends and co-workers than participate in their dirty jokes, crude behavior, and hateful gossip. Or one who would rather lose a boyfriend or girlfriend than be rushed into having sex, or pressured into drinking, smoking, and cursing.

Virtues in Suffering Persecution:

- Allows one to overcome evil by doing good.
- Allows one to better witness the way of Christ's love and forgiveness to others.
- Allows one to forge greater Christlike character & virtue to those around them.
- Allows one to better stay true to self without compromising their values and principals.

5:11"Blessed are you when (Expresses how it's not a matter of "If" but "when", that persecution is inevitable.) **people insult you,** (revile-K.J.V. Syn.-criticize, discredit, scorn, ridicule, belittle, butt-of-jokes.) **persecute you** (Syn.-harassed, abused, ill-treated.) **and falsely say all kinds of evil against you** (Syn.-vilify, belittle, slander.) **because of me.** (i.e. Devotion and commitment to Christ.)
12 Rejoice (Syn.-welcome.) **and be glad,** (Syn.-celebrate, jump for joy, exult.-{Acts 5:40-42}) **because great is your reward in heaven,** (Eternal life with God.) **for in the same way they persecuted the prophets** (O.T. Prophets) **who were before you.** (Expresses how believers can take comfort in knowing we stand in good company in a long line of holy men and woman who stood up for God.)

Approved are believers who endure persecution in their loyalty and faithfulness to Jesus.

Message & Application 💻=🌎

- ❖ Shows how believers can take comfort & joy that no matter how much we're mistreated, we belong to God and have Heaven waiting for us.
- ❖ Calls believers in not allowing insults or personal attacks to take away our peace and joy in the work we're doing for the Lord.
- ❖ Reminds believers if were not experiencing persecution in one form or the other, then we need to question what kind of faith we really have.
- ❖ Calls for staying sold out for Jesus and His truth, knowing that we're going down a proper path that's going to lead us in the right way.
- ❖ Calls for seeing persecution as a sign that we're no longer living under the principles & patterns of this world but the right way as God wants.
- 🗝 Even today as we live out the other eight beatitudes we can expect to be treated differently by the world around us. Who will criticize us as being weak & simple, that we have to use God as a crutch. Or they'll ridicule us as being a "Bible-thumper" or "Jesus Freak" because we talk about Christ at school or at work. Or they'll accuse us of being bigoted & narrow-minded because we hold that Jesus is the only way to heaven. Or they'll ostracize us for being odd & weird because we would rather go to church or to bible study than to go out and party.

How to respond to Persecution:

- See persecution as God's way of perfecting stronger faith, character, and growth.
- See persecutions as insignificant compared to our eternal glory that awaits us in heaven.
- See persecutions as evidence that we're in a right relationship with Christ.

Beatitude Values	Vs.	Worldly Values
Poor in Spirit-(V. 3)		Self-sufficient Self-reliant Self-confident
Mourn-(V. 4)		Self-gratification Pursuit of happiness You only live once
Meek-(V. 5)		Be aggressive/assertive Fiercely Competitive Stand up for yourself Might makes right Nice guys finish last
Hunger for righteousness-(V. 6)		Compromise Worldly-minded Materialistic If it feels good do it
Merciful-(V. 7)		Don't get mad, get even No place for losers Cut-throat/Dog eat dog Survival of the fittest
Pure in heart-(V. 8)		Open minded Crafty/Manipulative Self-serving
Peacemakers-(V. 9)		Don't rock the boat Go along with the crowd Fence riders
Persecuted for Righteousness-(V. 10)		Tolerant/broadminded Adaptable Stay the Status quo Crowd-pleasers Live & let Live Join the club Go with the flow

From this verse here (V. 13) to verse (V.16) Jesus teaches on Christian character & influence.

Salt and Light-(N.I.V.)

5:13 "You are the salt of the earth.(Metph-Ones moral & purifying influence, admiral qualities, authenticity.) **But if the salt** (Metph.-Christian character, qualities.) **loses its saltiness,** (Lit.-The chemical leaching reaction that takes place when impure salt comes into contact with other earthly substances. Metph.-Loss of moral character, effectiveness, witness, testimony.) **how can it be made salty again? It is no longer good for anything,** (neither for soil or the manure pile.-{Luke 14:35}-Suggests: It could not even be used as fertilizer.) **except to be thrown out** (Metph.-rejected) **and trampled by men** (Lit-Used to harden paths, keep walkways free of vegetation. Expresses how a hypocritical lifestyle will be rejected and treated with disdain, contempt, and ridicule.)

Believers are to have a moral and purifying influence on society and the world around them.

Message & Application 💻=🌎

- Shows believers how our godly lives are to have a positive influence and impact on the lives of those around us.
- Teaches believers only by living out Christ's love, kindness, and compassion, can we hope to influence, change, and affect others.
- Calls for seeing that our Christian walk is authentic. (Inconsistent lifestyle is the chief cause in repelling others from Jesus).
- Calls for living such victorious & godly life's that it makes others thirsty for Christ. (Move people to want the peace & Savior you have).

-*Salt*-Meaning: Without refrigeration, salt was used as a preservative in keeping fish & meat from spoiling, was also used as seasoning and disinfectant. Other characteristics of "Salt"- it flavors, penetrates, preserves, purifies, pervades, transforms, savors, and parches.

🗝 Even today, believers can lose our influence and witness when we compromise our Christian principles for worldly values, e.g. immodest dress, unsavory talk, materialism, mingling with the wrong crowd, etc.

Ways Believers can impact the World:

- Put into practice Jesus' teachings and example.
- Donate time to Christian charities and outreaches.
- Participate in social reforms, vote for Christians.
- Use social media to share your faith with others.

5:14 "You are the light of the world (Metph-witness, testimony) **A city on a hill cannot be hidden.** (Lit.-Because it reflects the sun, glows at night. Expresses public example and witness. Christian character will be under scrutiny by all.)
15 Neither do people light a lamp-◙ (Lit.-clay lamp. Metph-Christian character, Gospel witness.) **and put it under a bowl.** (Bed-{Luke 8:16}, Metph.-hide, conceal, veil, neglect, hold back.) **Instead, they put it on its stand, and it gives light to everyone in the house.** (Metph.-Enlightens, directs, benefits, exposes.)
16 In the same way, let your light (Metph.-good deeds, godly lives, virtuous character, Gospel witness. Other qualities of "light", it reveals, exposes, diffuses, enlightens, directs.) **shine** (Syn.-excel, stand out, be evident) **before men,** (Syn.-work, home, society) **that they may see your good deeds** (works-K.J.V. Metph.-faithfulness, integrity, transformation, Christian character.) **and praise** (glorify-K.J.V. Syn.-worship, hope in) **your Father in heaven.** (Suggests: Having seen God's transforming power in your own life, thereby giving their lives over to Christ. That witness is driven not by recognition, but God's glory.)

Believers godly lives are to be a witness and testimony in leading others to Jesus.

Message & Application 

❖ Shows believers how our Christian lives are to be a witness and Saving influence on others around us in bringing them to Christ.
❖ Warns against an inconsistent witness and unholy living. (Always live a clean life that brings honor, glory, and praise to God).(Vs. 15-16)
❖ Calls for becoming a beacon of comfort, hope, and Salvation by sharing the Gospel and God's love with others, either by word or deed.
❖ Calls believers in sharing the liberating power of the Gospel to those who are lost in sin, darkness, and bondage.
🗝 Even today we're to live in a way that's having a Saving influence on others in winning them over to the Lord. Whether it's a kindly gesture to a stranger or a kind act of love to a neighbor or co-worker.
☞ Jesus is not saying that we have to witness to everyone we meet. But rather we allow Christ and the changes He's made in our own lives speak to what He can do for others.

Ways Believers can be a Light of the World:

- Stand for Christian principals without compromise.
- Keep your faith and devotion when no one else does.
- Love and care for people that nobody else will.
- Persevere in doing good in spite of all the immorality.

From this verse here (V. 17) to verse (V. 20) Jesus teaches on the spirit & inner intent of the Law.

***The fulfillment of the Law*-(N.I.V.)**

5:17 Do not think (conclude, assume) **that I have come to abolish** (destroy-K.J.V.-2647-*To overthrow, tear down.* Syn.-Scrap, replace, throw-out, do away with.) **the Law or the Prophets;** (Expresses the entire O.T. Suggests: That Jesus was dispelling any notion that He was setting aside God's commands by His reinterpretation of the Law as spelled out in the following Sermon on the Mount.) **I have not come to abolish them but to fulfill them.** (4137-*To make complete, or to supply what is lacking.* Syn.-internalize, transcend, deepen, perfect, exemplify, embody, draw out, etc. Expresses Jesus' transcending the law by teaching it's deeper spiritual principals and inner intent.)

Jesus came to fulfill the true spiritual meaning and inner intent of the Law.

Message & Application

- Shows believers how Jesus came to give us a fuller understanding of God's word and what true righteousness should look like.
- Assures believers how Jesus will see to it that we're following God's word the right way, the way it was intended and meant to be!
- Teaches how we no longer have to try to win God' favor or acceptance by what we do, but by trusting in what Christ has already done for us.

–***Fulfill the law***-Meaning: Jesus fulfills the law by meeting its spiritual design and inner intent by His teachings and way of life. But in a wider context, Jesus also meets the righteous requirements of the Law, as well as all the sacrificial types, ceremonies, and prophecies that were pointing to His suffering and death. (cf. Heb. 4:15, 10:1-22)

Even today all believers have to do is look to Jesus to understand the type of heart, character, and righteousness that God expects as we live our lives out for Him.

LAW	SPIRIT
Murder	No Anger
Adultery	No Lust
Divorce	Commitment
Oath-taking	Speak the truth
Retaliation	Forgiveness
Hate your enemy	Love your enemy

5:18 I tell you the truth, until heaven and earth disappear, (Expresses how God's word will be more enduring than creation itself.) **not the smallest letter,** (jot-K.J.V.) **not the least stroke** (tittle-K.J.V.) **of a pen-◙** (i.e. The smallest dot or dash used in Hebrew letters. Similar to a dot on an "i" or a cross on a "t". Metph.-Smallest of details.) **will by any means disappear from the Law until everything is accomplished.** (i.e. God's work in the redemption of mankind.)

God's moral law down to its smallest details will always be a guiding principle in the believer's life.

Message & Application 💻=🌎

- ❖ Shows believers the enduring & trustworthiness of God's word. (Know that God's word will always have relevance for your life).
- ❖ Warns against thinking God's word is irrelevant or out of date.
- ☞ Though we are free from the ceremonial law (now fulfilled by Christ) we are not free from the spiritual principles of the moral Law.
- ➢ Reasons for the Law's perpetual presence:
  - The law defines & convicts of sin. (Rom. 5:20, 7:7)
  - The law leads a person to Christ. (Gal. 3:24)
  - The law teaches godly morals & standards. (2-Tim. 3:16-17)

5:19 Anyone who breaks (Syn.-minimizes, downplays, trivializes-M.B.V.) **one of the least** (Syn.-insignificant) **of these commandments** (i.e. Moral precepts of the Law.) **and teach others** (i.e. Either by doctrine or example.) **to do the same will be called least** (i.e. Held in low esteem, bottom of the totem pole.) **in the kingdom of heaven, but whoever practices** (Syn.-obeys, follows, upholds, takes seriously-M.B.V.) **and teaches these commands will be called great** (i.e. Highly exalted, or held in high regard by God.) **in the kingdom of heaven.**

Warns believers against neglecting & diminishing God's commandments or loosening its moral obligations.

Message & Application 💻=🌎

- ❖ Shows how believers are to treat all of God's word as important. (You can't pick and choose which parts of the bible you like and don't like!).
- ❖ Warns believers against playing it fast & loose with the word of God. (Don't try to lower the bar or create loopholes so you can live it up!).
- ❖ Teaches how true believers will always seek to follow God as closely as possible, and not try to get away with as much as possible.
- 🗝 Even today we need to be careful that we're not watering down or sugar coating God's word to suit our lifestyle, or to make sin appear less sinful!

5:20 For I tell you that unless your righteousness (1343-*Right relationship and standing with God.* Syn.-godly character, right living.) **surpasses** (Syn.-transcends, outstrips. Suggests: Not in quantity or degree, but quality & kind.) **that of the Pharisees and the teachers of the law,** (Suggests: That they were legalistic and self-righteous.) **you will certainly not enter the kingdom of heaven.** (Expresses having all the precepts that are in-line with the character, norms, and standards of heaven.)

Calls believers for a righteousness that goes beyond outward behavior to obeying God from the heart.

Message & Application 💻=🌎

❖ Shows believers how God wants more than outward performance of just looking and sounding holy to actually living and being holy!
❖ Reminds believers how it's not just about reforming bad habits and acting nice, but about being truly changed from the inside out.
❖ Teaches how God is more concerned with genuine inner change than outward appearances. (God wants Christians who are the real deal!).
❖ Teaches how our focus should be more than just about "right conduct" & "rule keeping" to becoming the new person God created us to be!
🗝 Even today a believer's life should be more than just about religious performance of simply showing up to Church, fasting, tithing, singing in the choir, to actually growing in a personal relationship with God.
☞ Jesus is not saying that believers must try harder, that unless we're living up to God's perfect standards of holiness will never make it into heaven. But rather is calling for a heart-righteousness that is keeping it real with God in our private lives as we are in our public lives. (Will you get real with God with that part of your life which nobody sees?)
☞ Jesus' statement must have shocked the disciples, that if the Pharisees, by their scrupulous observance of the Law were thought to be the most righteous people around, then what hope was there for them!

Examples of a Righteousness that Surpasses:

- Do you put into practice what you profess and preach?
- Do you practice your faith only to be seen, praised, and admired by others?
- Do you come by your own self-centered righteousness and goodness, rather than trusting in God's mercy & grace?
- Do you base your relationship with God on performance?
- Do you put religious rules above mercy and compassion?

From this verse here (V. 21) to verse (V. 26) Jesus warns against a brooding anger of the heart.

Murder-(N.I.V.)

5:21 "You have heard that it was said to the people long ago, (i.e. By God through Moses.) **'Do not murder,** (i.e. 6th commandment) **and anyone who murders will be subject to judgment.'** (i.e. Capital punishment.{cf. Deut. 21:22})
22 But I tell you that anyone who is angry (i.e. A simmering, stewing, brooding anger.) **with his brother will be subject to judgment. Again, anyone who says to his brother Raca,** (4469-*Empty head, stupid.* Syn.-idiot, moron, blockhead) **is answerable to the Sanhedrin.** (Taken to court for defamation.) **But anyone who says, You fool!** (3474-*To damn one's heart & character.* Syn.-loser, low-life, worthless, good-for-nothing.) **will be in danger of the fire of hell.**

Anger & hate are just as guilty as murder because it shows the true desires and intent of the heart.

Message & Application

- ❖ Shows how believers are not only to avoid the outward act of murder but also the anger and hate that gives rise to it.
- ❖ Teaches how God wants us to take all sin seriously, not just in our actions, but also in our thoughts, attitudes, and motives as well.
- ❖ Teaches how hateful and vengeful attitudes, as well as insults and name calling reveals a heart that is far from God. (cf. 1-John 3:15)
- ⊶ Even today we often downplay and excuse our anger by calling it by other names; *"I just have a short temper/fuse"*, or *"That's just the way I am"*, or *"I just fly off the handle"*. Or we will try to justify our anger by blaming other people saying; *"They kept pushing my buttons"*!
- ☞ Jesus is not just talking about a self-righteous anger as when God's honor is at stake or when someone is wronged. But about a brooding & festering anger that lingers day after day into bitterness and contempt.

Other ways we can Murder People:

- By giving up on them, writing them off as dead to us and a total waste of time.
- By character assassination in damaging their reputation through our gossip and slander.
- By destroying them emotionally & spiritually through our careless and hurtful words.

5:23 Therefore, if you are offering your gift (Metph.-Religious service, tithe.) **at the altar-◙** (1041-*Table/platform.* i.e. Time of Worship.) **and there remember that your brother has something against you,** (i.e. A quarrel, fault, or grudge.) **24 leave your gift there in front of the altar. First, go and be reconciled** (i.e. Apologize, make amends.) **to your brother; then come and offer your gift.**

Believers are to initiate the process of reconciliation, even above that of worship and the religious stuff.

Message & Application 💻=🌎

❖ Shows how God would rather we make peace with others than come to worship with a heart that is angry, bitter, and far from Him.
❖ Warns believers of the hypocrisy in seeking God's forgiveness while harboring an unforgiving heart/spirit towards others around us.
❖ Teaches how we're responsible for taking the initiative to correct the wrong and cut off the chain of anger and bitterness before it escalates.
❖ Warns how unresolved anger can poison one's spiritual life, that religion must examine itself, that it's living up to what it's proclaiming.
🗝 Even today we're to see that our Christian faith/devotion is not coming off as hypocritical, but is matched by a life of love and forgiveness.

5:25 "Settle matters (i.e. End the riff, make it right.) **quickly with your adversary** (Metph.-anger, hate, guilt, sin, etc.) **who is taking you to court. Do it while you are still with him on the way,** (Lit.-Before the trial, present life.) **or he may hand you over to the judge,** (Christ) **and the judge may hand you over to the officer,** (God) **and you may be thrown into prison.** (Metph.-Hell)
26 I tell you the truth, you will not get out until you have paid the last penny. (Expresses inevitable penalty, the full measure of guilt and accountability.)

Believers are to reconcile any unresolved anger and sin issues before the day of God's judgment.

Message & Application 💻=🌎

❖ Shows how believers are to get any unresolved anger & sin issues right before we have to stand before God. (cf. Rom. 14:10)
❖ Teaches the importance of repenting and coming clean in confessing sin or it will catch up with us, eventually finding us out.
❖ Warns of the danger in leaving anger & sin unresolved. (The longer we wait, greater the bondage, guilt, and bitterness becomes).
🗝 Even today, believers need to deal with anger & sin before it becomes a bigger issue in poisoning our walk and relationship with God, or before it starts to damage our influence and witness with others.

From this verse here (V. 27) to verse (V. 30) Jesus warns against the sinful desires & lusts of the heart.

Adultery-(N.I.V.)

5:27 "You have heard that it was said, {V. 21} **'Do not commit adultery.'** (Syn.-infidelity, cheating, messing around, etc. The 7th commandment.-{Ex. 20:14})
28 But I tell you that anyone who looks at (Syn.-gawks, leers, ogles, check-outs.) **a woman lustfully** (Syn.-sexually, luridly, lasciviously, flirtatiously.) **has already committed adultery with her in his heart.** (2588-*Ones mental activity, willful desire.* Expresses one's true desires, main ambition, greatest wish.)

Lust and sexual longing are just as guilty as adultery because it shows the true desires and intent of the heart.

<u>**Message & Application**</u> 💻=🌎

- ❖ Shows how believers are not only to avoid the act of adultery, but also the lustful thoughts and desires that give rise to it.
- ❖ Teaches how God is not only concerned with our outward actions, but also with the inner thoughts, lusts, and desires of the heart as well.
- ❖ Warns against the imaginations of the heart that would entertain immoral acts if there were no consequences and no one ever found out.
- ❖ Calls for keeping lustful thoughts in check. (Passing glances may be unavoidable, but it's that second and third look that is to be averted!).
- 🗝 Even today, believers need to be careful of the kind of movies, T.V. shows, and websites we're viewing, and ask ourselves are we watching it for its entertainment value or its sexual appeal? Do you watch "Dancing with the Stars" or "Baywatch" for the celebrities or for the scanty outfits? Or when dining out, are you going to "Hooters" or "Twin Peaks" for the fine food, or to check out the waitresses? Or when channel surfing, what do you find yourself pausing on?
- ☞ Jesus is not just talking about passing glances, as when a beautiful girl crosses your path. Or God-given attractions towards the opposite sex or the sexual pleasure enjoyed in marriage. But rather He's talking about one who deliberately fills their minds with erotic fantasies that would be immoral if acted out. Or one who misuses & mishandles God-given desires that are outside the boundaries and standards He has set.
- ☞ Though the teaching here is directed primarily towards men, it is also a plea for women to do their part as well in helping men by not dressing so provocatively.

5:29 If your right eye (Expresses: The inward lusts & desires of the heart.) **causes you to sin,** (offend thee-K.J.V. Syn.-lead astray) **gouge it out** (separate, get rid, *"Nip it in the bud"*.) **and throw it away. It is better for you to lose one part of your body than for your whole body** (Person) **to be thrown into hell.**
30 And if your right hand (What is acted upon through the agency of the flesh in one's work/living.) **causes you to sin, cut it off and throw it away. It is better for you to lose one part of your body than for your whole body to go into hell.** (Expresses: Better to deal with the sin now, than risk spending eternity in hell!)

Believers must be willing to deal with lust and temptation radically and severely.

Message & Application 💻=🌎

- ❖ Shows how believers are to take drastic measures in dealing with sin and temptation. (Rather than cater to sin, make no provision for it!).
- ❖ Calls believers for a decisive decision in breaking away from any sinful habit, practice, and activity before it starts to take root.
- ❖ Demonstrates how when believers take drastic and radical measures against lust, it shows that we have it in our hearts to be done with sin.
- 🗝 Even today, believers need to take radicle measures in cutting off sin. Whether it's moving to another town, taking another job, getting new friends, etc. Or it may take throwing out your computer, smartphone, and tablet if your struggle is with things like gambling or pornography.
- ☞ Jesus is not here teaching self-mutilation, but rather the importance of taking decisive action in dealing with any sinful activity that can jeopardize our spiritual life and walk with God no matter the cost!
- ☞ Jesus is not saying that sin originates in the organs of the body, for even a blind man can lust. But rather is calling for heart surgery.

How to Deal with Sin & Temptation:

- **Avoid the avenues that encourage you to sin.** (Get rid of any videos, books, magazines, friends, internet)
- **Know your vulnerabilities & weakness.** (Know when your upset, tired, lonely, bored, stressed out)
- **Know the consequences that sin can cause**. (See beyond the temporary pleasures of sin to the evil, guilt, regret, and ruin it can bring in your walk with God)
- **Stay studying & meditating on God's word.** (Be willing to recognize and confess sin for what it is)
- **Pray for God's help & strength.** (Wait patiently that God to help you overcome the sin)

From this verse here (V. 31) to verse (V. 32) Jesus teaches on fidelity & commitment in marriage.

Divorce-(N.I.V.)

5:31 "It has been said, Anyone who divorces his wife must give her a certificate of divorce.' (i.e. Divorce papers, bill of divorcement.-{Deut. 24:1-4})
32 But I tell you that anyone who divorces his wife, except for marital Unfaithfulness (fornication-K.J.V.-4202-*Illicit sexual intercourse, adultery, homosexuality, bestiality.* Syn.-adultery, infidelity, cheating, extramarital affair) **causes** (Syn.-stigmatizes, labels, forces) **her to become an adulteress and anyone who marries the divorced woman commits adultery.** (Suggests: Because in God's eyes she was not legally divorced from her first husband.)

Marriage between a husband and wife is a permanent union except where infidelity & adultery is committed.

Message & Application =

- ❖ Shows how believers are to stay true to our covenant promises in marriage as a lifelong commitment rather than trying to find a way out.
- ❖ Teaches how marriage should never be trivialized or taken lightly, but entered into as a sacred bond between two people.
- ❖ Warns against the lusts of the heart in allowing the issues of money, beauty, sex, or any other superficial reasons to seek a divorce.
- ❖ Teaches rather than looking at divorce as an option and easy way out, have the heart that is willing to stick together and work it out.
- ❖ Teaches rather than seeking a divorce we should be praying for God's grace in bearing patiently and quietly with a spouse's imperfections.

–***Marital unfaithfulness***-Variously interpreted as either:

- A single act of adultery (Widely accepted by most)
- Premarital promiscuity (cf. Matt. 1:19, Deut. 22:20-21)
- A sexual immoral lifestyle not formally confessed.

⊶ Even today no matter how much you try to whitewash divorce by claiming; *"Irreconcilable differences"*, *"We've grown apart"*, *"We're not in love anymore"*, etc. does not hold water in God's eyes.

☞ Divorce should be avoided at all costs due to the brokenness it creates in family's, and the loss of character and witness it produces.

☞ By prohibiting the option of divorce spouses are more readily to forgive, reconcile, and work through their differences.

☞ By entering into marriage as a lifelong commitment provides couples with security, stability, and strength in difficult times.

Sins that result in Divorce:

- The believing spouse violates a covenant that in God's eyes was intended to be permanent.
- The believing spouse fails to display Christian love by forgiving transgressions and seeking reconciliation.
- The believing spouse falls into spiritual pride in thinking his wife is not good enough, or that he could do better.
- The believing spouse abandons his obligation to care and forgive his wife when she falls into grievous sickness or sinful error.
- The believing spouse neglects and disregards the welfare of his children.

Only Scriptural Grounds for Divorce:

1) The death of a spouse.-(Rom. 7:1-3)
2) The act of sexual infidelity.-(Matt. 5:32)
3) The desertion of an unbelieving spouse. (1-Corn. 7:10-15)

Principles for a Successful Marriage:

- Be willing to understand & accept each other's personal differences (Have open communication).
- Be open to seeking pastoral advice and Christian counseling when difficult conflicts arise. (Always seek God's help).
- Be willing to devote yourselves in prayer, bible study, and worship. (Prioritize God's glory first).
- Be willing to maintain a submissive spirit, be humble, loving, forgiving, and patient.
- Be willing to make sacrifices. (Put the spiritual condition and welfare of the other spouse first).

From this verse here (V. 33) to verse (V. 37) Jesus teaches on the need for truthfulness & integrity in speech.

Oaths-(N.I.V.)
5:33 "Again, you have heard that it was said to the people long ago, 'Do not break your oath, (forswear-K.J.V.-1964-*To commit perjury.* Expresses: To break one's word, promise, or pledge.) **but keep the oaths you have made to the Lord.** (Suggests: Not a direct quote, but a summary of vows.-{cf. Deut. 23:21-23})
34 But I tell you, {See V.22} **Do not swear at all** (3660-*A solemn appeal to a person, thing, or God as a witness.* e.g. *"I swear to God"* or *"Let God strike me dead if I'm lying"*.) **either by heaven, for it is God's throne;** (Metph.-Dwelling)
35 or by the earth, for it is his footstool; (Metph.-Ownership) **or by Jerusalem for it is the city of the Great King.** (i.e. God. Taken together that whatever one swears by is ultimately related to God in one way or another.)
36 And do not swear by your head, (i.e. On one's self/life, e.g. *"I swear on my life"*.) **for you cannot make even one hair white** (i.e. Gray) **or black.** (Expresses how even one's life is under God's creation, domain, and ownership.)

Believers are to be people of honesty & integrity, always speaking the truth without the need for oaths.

Message & Application 💻=🌎

- ❖ Shows believers rather than looking for clever & sophisticated ways of getting out of our promises, we are to be people of our word.
- ❖ Calls believers in being accountable for the words we speak, that were going to stay true to our promises and commitments no matter what!
- ❖ Teaches how believers should not have to legitimize the truthfulness of our words or promises by swearing in order to be believed.
- ❖ Warns no matter how much we try to manipulate the situation, God is watching & will hold us accountable whether we use His name or not!
- ⊶ Even today we often do the same things by crossing our fingers behind our back in order to get out of our promises. Or we reinforce our word saying: *"Cross my heart and hope to die, stick a needle in my eye"*.
- ☞ Those who need oaths or who are swearing up & down shows their word is unreliable, that they're prone to lying and can't be trusted!
- ☞ Jesus is not prohibited believers from taking an oath as in a court of law or as in wedding vows. But rather, what He is condemning is the practice of making empty promises which we never intended to keep in the first place. Or always looking for fanciful ways of escaping our promises without involving God's name.

5:37 Simply let your 'Yes' be 'Yes', and your 'No', 'No'; (Expresses: Believers word should be good enough, no additional safeguards needed.) **anything beyond this comes from the evil one.** (i.e. Satan. That when one swears it can usually be traced back to false motives, wicked intentions, and deceitfulness.)

Believers are to be people of their word.

Message & Application 💻=🌎

❖ Shows believers how our word should be good enough without adding anything else to it. (Let your character and actions speak for itself!).
❖ Calls for living a life of integrity and transparency. (Admit when you're wrong, own your mistakes, don't cover up or make excuses).
❖ Calls for being such faithful and trustworthy people that we can be counted on to follow through with what we say 100% of the time!
❖ Warns how failure to keep our word can destroy our trust, bringing our Christian character into question. (If we lie about little things, who's going to believe us when it comes to the Gospel and spiritual things!).
❖ Warns how Satan desires to ensnare us by binding us to oaths we can't keep that he may ruin our testimony and witness with others.

🗝 Even today we're to be people of our word, that if we say "Yes" we're going to be some place or we're going to tutor someone we do it! Or if we say "Yes" we're going to be to work on time we do it! Or if we say "Yes" we're going to help someone move or fix their car we do it!

☞ Jesus is not saying that we can never change our answers. But rather a single word is sufficient enough without adding anything else to it!

Common Oaths to avoid:

- I swear on my mother's grave.
- I swear on my life.
- I swear on a stack of Bibles.

Common Curses to avoid:

- Well, I'll be damned.
- Cross my heart and hope to die.
- May God strike me dead if I'm lying.

Common Euphemism to avoid:

- Geez or Gee-whiz. (Slang for Jesus)
- Gosh, golly, gad. (Slang for God)
- Gaddang, doggone. (Slang for GD)
- OMG (Slang for Oh my God!)

From this verse here (V. 38) to verse (V. 42) Jesus teaches against retaliation & revenge to one of love and forgiveness.

An Eye for an Eye-(N.I.V.)

5:38 "You have heard that it was said, 'Eye for eye, and tooth for tooth.' (Expresses O.T. Law prohibiting excessive revenge.-{Ex. 21:23-25, Lev. 24:19-20})
39 But I tell you, Do not resist (Syn.-contest, quarrel, retaliate-against) **an evil person.** (i.e. Don't take matters into your own hands, don't repay evil for evil.) **If someone strikes you on the right cheek** (Not a vicious blow, but a backhanded slap as the greatest form of insult.) **turn to him the other also.** (Don't retaliate.)
40 And if someone wants to sue you and take your tunic,-◙ (Undergarment) **let him have your cloak-◙** (coat) **as well.** (Expresses to make the extra effort, amend, appease. Modern cliché *"Give the shirt off his back"*.)
41 If someone forces you to go one mile, (29-*Roman custom of pressing citizens into military service.*) **go with him two miles.** (Expresses to go above and beyond the call of duty. Modern cliché *"Go the extra mile"*.)
42 Give to the one who asks you, and do not turn away from the one who wants to borrow from you. (Expresses: To always be charitable and generous.)

Rather than retaliate over trivial matters believers are to seek peace.

Message & Application 💻=🌎

- ❖ Shows how believers are to put the law of love & relationships above personal rights. (Put people above possessions and personal rights).
- ❖ Calls for being gracious and tolerant of others no matter what it might cost us personally. (Put redemptive love above personal rights).
- ❖ Calls believers away from assuming an attitude of vindictiveness, revenge, and getting even, to one of love, patience, and forgiveness.
- ⊶ Even today because most things are trivial and not worth contending about, better to suffer loss then to lose a brother or one's witness.
- ☞ Jesus is not here teaching pacifism or allowing oneself to be treated as doormats. But rather that we take the high road in not becoming confrontational over trivial matters for the sake of peace and witness.

Reasons against Retaliating:

- It only escalates matters, making things worse.
- We lose our witness & testimony.
- Displays a lack of faith & trust in God.
- Teaches vindictiveness and not forgiveness.

From this verse here (V. 43) to verse (V. 48) Jesus teaches on loving & praying for enemies.

5:43 You have heard that it was said, 'Love your neighbor and hate your enemy'. (Former based on Lev. 19:18.Latter conclusion formed by the Pharisees)
44 But I tell you: Love (25-*Agapao, to exhibit/esteem goodwill*) **your enemies and pray** (i.e. For their Salvation, that God may change their hearts) **for those who persecute you** (Bless them that curse you, do good to them that hate you, pray for them that despitefully use you-K.J.V.-Not found in oldest Grk. MSS.)
45 that you may be sons of your Father in heaven. (Expresses to be followers and imitators of God) **He causes his sun to rise on the evil and the good, and sends rain on the righteous and the unrighteous.** (Expresses just as God is impartial and unbiased in His goodness to a fallen world, so too believers.)

Believers are to follow God's example in displaying undiscriminating love to all people, even our enemies.

<u>Message & Application</u> 💻=🌎

- ❖ Shows believers rather than seek retribution & revenge for the wrong done to us, we're to love, forgive, and leave them in God's hands.
- ❖ Calls believers for a redemptive love that always sees others in the light that God sees them. (Be channels of God's love to others).
- ❖ Teaches rather than allow others to bring out the worst in us, bring out the best, that we're not returning insults with hate but with love!
- ❖ Teaches how loving and praying for our enemies can free us from the feelings of anger, hatred, resentment, and bitterness.
- 🗝 Even today we're not to allow the mean & hateful things people have done to us to keep us from praying for them and seeing them Saved, that God may touch their hearts and change them. (cf. Luke 23:34)
- ☞ The love & forgiveness that Jesus is calling for is never within our own strength but must be relied upon daily by God and the Holy Spirit.

<u>How to keep Love for Enemies:</u>

- Know that he or she may be going through difficult times and personal crises.
- Know that he or she may have misinterpreted your actions or words.
- Know that he or she is acting out of anger/hurt.
- Know that he or she is prone to mistakes.
- Know that he or she is loved by God.

5:46 If you love {V. 44} **those who love you, what reward** (Syn.-praise, recommendation, benefit, credit) **will you get? Are not even the tax collectors** (publicans-K.J.V. scoundrels-L.B.V. Metph.-Sinners, wicked) **doing that?**
47 And if you greet (salute-K.J.V. Syn.-welcome, inclined, disposed of, kind-N.L.T., friendly-L.B.V.) **only your brothers** (i.e. Fellow believers/Christians) **what are you doing more than others?** (Expresses no different from anyone else.) **Do not even pagans** (i.e. Unbelievers, heathens, non-religious) **do that?**

Believers love and friendship must be shown as distinctly different from the world around them.

Message & Application 💻=🌎

❖ Shows believers that if we don't broaden our application of love to include all people we are no better than the world around us.
❖ Warns that if a believer's standard of love is no higher than the world around us, we have little hope of making an impact on others.
❖ Calls for going outside our own circles/natural affections. (Be willing to associate with those you wouldn't normally get along with).
❖ Teaches how we must never stop loving a person just because there's something annoying about them, or something we dislike about them!
🗝 Even today, believers need to reach out to the unlovable, to those we wouldn't normally associate with by inviting them into our inner circle.

5:48 Be perfect, (5046-*Complete, mature, full grown.* Syn.-all-inclusive, fully-equipped, consistent, ready & able, etc.) **therefore,** (Suggests: Conclusion drawn from the call for a higher morality of love.-{Vs. 43-47}) **as your heavenly Father** (i.e. God) **is perfect.** (Syn.-all loving, all goodness-N.E.B.)

Believers love must be universal and all-inclusive just as God's love is universal and all inclusive.

Message & Application 💻=🌎

❖ Shows how believers are to have the same gracious & compassionate nature of God. (As God is merciful so to believers must be merciful!).
❖ Calls for extending unconditional love, mercy, and forgiveness towards all people. (Always see the worth, value, and good in others!).
❖ Calls for a love that looks beyond people's character defects. (Will you accept people no matter how undesirable they might seem to be?)
🗝 Even today, believers are to have a love that reaches out to all types of people, be it criminals, drunkards, homosexuals, the self-righteous, etc.
☞ Jesus is not calling for moral & sinless perfection, but rather about having a "Love" that is all inclusive, never failing to include all people.

Chapter Six

From this verse here (V. 1) to verse (V. 18) Jesus teaches on the proper motivations behind good deeds.

6:1 "Be careful (take heed-K.J.V. Syn.-mindful, think twice, take care-L.B.V.) **not to do** (Syn.-flaunt, parade, showboat) **your 'acts of righteousness'** (alms-K.J.V.-1654-*Any acts of kindness & mercy freely done for the relief of the poor.* Suggests: In context any good deed or religious observance including Charity-{Vs. 2-4}, Prayer-{Vs. 5-8}, Fasting-{Vs. 16-18}. Not limited to, but also including worship, serving, missionary work, etc.) **before men,** (Syn.-ostentatiously, recognition, publicly) **to be seen** (Syn.-observed, applauded, praised, honored, admired-L.B.V.) **by them. If you do, you will have no reward** (Syn.-praise, blessings, good-conscience, peace.) **from your Father in heaven.** (Suggests: Because the believers giving was done not to glorify God but only self.)

Warns believers against making a show of our religious virtues simply to win the approval and praise of others.

Message & Application 💻=🌎

- ❖ Shows how believers are not to make a performance out of our good deeds simply to win the approval and admiration of others.
- ❖ Calls for always finding our self-worth & value in God and not in the approval of others. (Always seek God's approval, not man's).
- ❖ Demonstrates how many can do the right things for the wrong reasons. (One can appear their serving God when they're really serving self!).
- ❖ Calls for seeing that we're doing things to meet a pressing need in sharing God's love & concern, and not to draw attention to ourselves.
- ❖ Teaches how good deeds should always be about bringing praise and glory to the Lord, and not to boost our stock or to gain favor with God.
- ❖ Teaches how the motives behind acts of kindness and charity should always be done out of our love for Jesus and not for our own praise.
- ❖ Teaches the importance of always communicating and serving God in a way that keeps the focus on Him and not on ourselves!
- ⊶ Even today, believers need to be careful to remember that the purpose behind any good deed and spiritual discipline is to bring glory to God, or it can become an act of self-glorification.
- ☞ Jesus is not here contradicting what He taught earlier about "*Letting your light shine before men that they may see your good deeds*".(5:16) Because there the motive is directed towards God's glory and not self.
- ☞ A good gauge for believers in checking our motives is to always ask ourselves; "If nobody was watching, would I still act this way"?

From this verse here (V. 2) to verse (V. 4) Jesus warns against putting on a religious show of charity.

Giving to the Needy-(N.I.V.)

6:2 So when you give(alms-K.J.V. Syn.-charity, donation, handout) **to the needy** (i.e. Poor, homeless, panhandler.) **do not announce it with trumpets,** (Metph.-parade, fanfare, toot-ones-horn.) **as the hypocrites** (Syn.-Play actor, holy-roller) **do in the synagogues** (Viz. Church fundraisers, prayer meetings-M.B.V.) **and on the streets,** (Metph.-publicly, openly.) **to be honoured** (Syn.-praised, admired, approved, applauded.) **by men. I tell you the truth, they have received their reward in full.** (i.e. Human praise, slap on the back, nothing more from God.)

Warns believers against making a show of their charity in order to impress others of their piety.

Message & Application =

- ❖ Shows how believers are not to brag about our charity or the good deeds we have done. (Deeds should have its own reward in eternity!).
- ❖ Teaches how true righteousness does not seek praise for what it does.
- ❖ Calls believers in being careful that when we're trying to do good we don't make a show or performance out of it.
- ⊶ Today acts of charity must be done out of compassion, not reward.

6:3 But when you give (Suggests: Is to be a regular part of the believer's life.) **to the needy** (i.e. Poor, homeless, panhandler) **do not let your left hand know what your right hand is doing,** (Expresses: Privately, anonymously, low profile.)
4 so that your giving may be in secret. (Syn.-private, nameless) **Then your Father,** (God) **who sees what is done in secret, will reward you** (openly-K.J.V. i.e. In the form of eternal rewards or increase of blessings for giving even more.)

Believers charity should always be done secretly, quietly, and anonymously.

Message & Application

- ❖ Shows how believers are not to gloat or admire our own generosity.
- ❖ Teaches how we're to give freely, liberally, and all without calculation, that it's always done for God's sake.
- ❖ Teaches how charity should find its reward in eternity & good feelings.
- ⊶ Even today, believers are not to calculate our giving based on appreciation, thankfulness, or one-upmanship.
- ☞ Jesus is not here condoning poor record keeping or shoddy business practices, nor is He against taking bills or cost of living into account.

From this verse here (V. 5) to verse (V. 15) Jesus warns against putting on a religious show of praying.

Prayer-(N.I.V.)

6:5 "And when you pray, do not be like the hypocrites, for they love to pray standing (Metph.-observable, ostentatiously) **in the synagogues-◙ and on the street corners** (Lit.-Town squares. Metph.-publicly) **to be seen** (Syn.-praised, admired) **by men. I tell you the truth, they have received their reward in full.** (Expresses: Human recognition, admiration, nothing more from God.)

Warns believers against praying simply in order to impress others of how religiously devout we are.

Message & Application 💻=🌎

- ❖ Shows believers how prayer should always be about growing closer to God, and not for those listening!
- ❖ Teaches prayer should be about developing an intimate relationship with God, not about gaining a reputation or admiration of others.
- ☞ Jesus is not prohibiting prayer meetings or prayer groups. But only the ostentatious display of prayer for the purpose of impressing others.

6:6 But when you pray, go into your room, (closet-K.J.V. Lit.-storeroom in a Jewish home.-◙ Metph.-privately, inner heart) **close the door and pray to your Father, who is unseen.** (i.e. Spirit) **Then your Father, who sees what is done in secret,** (i.e. Sincerely, true motives. Expresses God's omnipotence.) **will reward you.** (Suggests: Answer to prayer or a deeper relationship with God.)

God wants prayers that are genuine, sincere, and heartfelt.

Message & Application 💻=🌎

- ❖ Shows how believers are to direct our prayers to God in a genuine & sincere manner. (Know that honest prayers get answered by God!).
- ❖ By praying privately allows us to be ourselves in pouring out our true feelings to God without being embarrassed, distracted, or interrupted.
- ❖ Teaches how praying privately allows us to shut out worldly distraction, that we may better hear the still and small voice of God.
- ⊶ Even today praying privately allows us to bear our hearts & souls openly before God, sharing our deepest hurts, pains, and struggles.
- ☞ Today a "Prayer closet" can be anything from a commute to work, a walk in a park, a chair on the porch, a dorm room, a kitchen table, etc.

6:7 And when you pray, {V. 5} **do not keep on babbling** (vain repetitions-K.J.V.-945-*The meaningless and mechanical repeating of phrases.* Syn.-yammering, rambling, rattling, blah-blah-blah, heap up empty phrases-R.S.V., recite the same prayer over and over-L.B.V.) **like pagans,** (i.e. unbelievers, non-Christians) **for they think they will be heard because of their many words.** (Much speaking-K.J.V., repeating-L.B.V. Syn.-chants, religious phraseology, vocabulary)
8 Do not be like them, for your Father (i.e. God) **knows** (exactly-L.B.V.) **what you need before you ask him.** (Suggests: Prayers to God must be given in faith. Or prayers must be given by trusting that God knows what's best for us.)

Warns believers against reciting prayers that are empty of thought and feeling.

Message & Application 💻=🌎

❖ Shows how God wants the kind of prayer that comes from the heart, not just the mouth. (God hears the heart more than the tongue!).
❖ Warns how prayers that are repetitive in nature often lack thought and sincere feelings. (Be personal in your prayers to God!).
❖ Warns believers against mindlessly memorizing or reciting prayers. (Prayer should always come from one's heart and true feelings).
❖ Calls for keeping our prayers short, simple, and to the point. (God doesn't need a lot of religious jargon to understand your needs!).
❖ Teaches how prayer is not about magic formulas or fancy speech, but simply about pouring out our hearts and being genuine with God.

–***Babbling-***Meaning: A Greek term describing a man who hung about the streets and market places, picking up scraps of words or teachings secondhand. Then repeated them without any real understanding of their true meaning. In a religious sense, it is ritual jargon in which words are often recited without thought and meaning.

–***Vain repetitions-***K.J.V.-Meaning: Repeating of words that are empty of thought. Some view the Catholic "Rosary" (5 to 15 Hail Mary's) as falling closely along these lines of thoughtless repetition. Even the "Lords Prayer" is sometimes often recited without much thought behind the words. (Be conscious of what the words mean!).

☞ The reason why "Repetition Prayer" is bad is because it suggests that by repeating things over & over again God is unable to understand our needs, that God has to be motivated and bullied to do His duty. Or that God is reluctant and needs to be persuaded in giving us what we want.

☞ Jesus is not condemning long prayers or the repetition of the same prayer. But rather only of prayers that are empty of thought & feelings. (cf. Luke 6:12, 11;5-9, 18:1-8, Matt. 7:7, 26:42-44)

The Lords [Disciples] Prayer-(Authors Insert)

6:9 "This, then, is how (Syn.-manner, pattern, model) **you should pray: "'Our Father in heaven, hallowed be your name** (Reverence of God' character/name)
10 your kingdom come (i.e. Gospel success, conversion of sinners, end to evil) **your will be done on earth as it is in heaven.** (Expresses obedience to God's will and purposes, that we confidently and cheerfully accept God's decisions.)
11 Give us today our daily bread (Expresses day to day dependence on God.)
12 Forgive us our debts, (Metph.-sins, offenses, shortcomings, failures, moral lapses, etc.) **as we also have forgiven our debtors.** (Suggests: Receiving God's daily mercies is dependent on having a forgiving spirit towards others.)
13 And lead us not into temptation, (Expresses a call that seeks God's help against daily struggles with sin, temptations, lusts, and wrong behavior.) **but deliver us from the evil one.** (Expresses a prayer for help against the snares, traps, deceits of Satan. For thine is the kingdom, and the power, and the glory forever. Amen.-K.J.V.-[Not found in earliest Greek MSS] Expresses confidence in God's sovereign reign, dominion, and power to accomplish what we seek.)

Believers are to pattern their prayers by giving praise & glory to God first before seeking their own needs & wants.

Message & Application =

–***Our father in heaven***-Meaning: Prayer that addresses God on a intimate and personal level, knowing God as one who loves and cares for our welfare. (Takes into account our redemptive relationship with God).

-***Hallowed be your name***-Meaning: Prayer that praises & thanks God for who He is and all He has done, that everything we have belongs to Him. (Also promises to live in ways that bring praise/honor to God).

-***Your kingdom come***-Meaning: Prayer that yields to God's supreme sovereignty and authority over everything. Affirms and welcomes God's rule, reign, and values in our own lives and the world to come.

-***Your will be done***-Meaning: Prayer that seeks to live out God's will in our lives, humbly submitting to His purposes and plans. One who recognizes and trusts that God knows what is good and best for us.

–***Daily bread***-Meaning: Prayer that looks to God who is able to meet our physical & spiritual needs, i.e. food, clothing, work, health, peace, joy, comfort, etc. (Also signifies one's day to day dependence on God).

–***Forgive us our debts***-Meaning: Prayer that asks for God's help and daily cleansing of our offenses, shortcomings, and moral lapses. (Does not mean the forgiveness of sins already paid in full by Christ).

–***Lead us not into temptation***-Meaning: Prayer that acknowledges our weakness & need of God's strength in not yielding to sin & temptation. (Not that God entices us to do evil or He not test our faith.)-(James 1:12)

Proper Practices in Praying:

- Keep prayers genuine, sincere, and heartfelt. (Be open and honest in your conversations with God as if you were talking to a friend!).
- Keep prayers short, simple, and to the point (Be specific of your needs).
- Keep prayer as a natural part of your daily life. (Offer prayers during normal everyday tasks of walking, driving, shopping, working, etc.)
- Keep confident & faithful in prayer. (Trust that God hears and will answer your prayers).
- Keep persevering in prayer (set a time and place aside, bedtime, morning, grace before meals, etc.).
- Keep praying with other believers. (Have a prayer partner).

Areas for Prayer:

- Pray for forgiveness of sins. (Both sins of omission and commission).
- Pray for the healing and Salvation of others.
- Pray for God's help, guidance, and assistance.
- Pray for insight, understanding of God's will.
- Pray on behalf of others. (Intercessory prayer)

Hindrances to Prayer:

- I don't know what to say.
- I run out of things to pray about.
- I feel that God doesn't hear me, that my prayers just bounce off the ceiling.
- I feel that my prayers come across as artificial and insincere.
- I feel there's not enough time in the day.
- I feel my prayers amount to little more than a laundry list, I recite.
- I feel that God is too busy for my petty requests.
- I feel since God already knows my needs, why should I have to tell Him?

6:14 For if you forgive men when they sin against you (Expresses any personal injury, hurt, or wrong.) **your heavenly Father will also forgive you.** (Suggests: In context, answer to prayer and daily blessings sought from God.) **15 But if you do not forgive men their sins, your Father will not forgive your sins.** (trespasses-K.J.V. Expresses daily misdeeds, shortcomings, failures, etc.)

Believers willingness to forgive others determines God's daily mercies to them.

Message & Application 💻=🌎

- ❖ Shows how believers cannot expect God's blessing & daily mercies while holding an unforgiving and grudging heart towards others.
- ❖ Teaches how forgiving others demonstrates an awareness of our own weaknesses, shortcomings, and need of God's daily cleansing.
- ❖ Warns that when we refuse to forgive others, we put ourselves above God as judge. (Remember it is God's place to judge, not yours!).
- ❖ Those who have experienced God's grace will be gracious to others. (If God forgave us when we didn't deserve it, can't we do the same).
- ❖ Warns believers how holding onto anger and bitterness can poison our spiritual life and hinder our relationship with God and other people.
- ☞ The forgiveness Jesus is calling for here is not about letting them off, trusting them again, liking them again, or minimizing the offense. But it's about releasing our right to stay angry & bitter with them, knowing how much God has forgiven our sins. That we're putting it all in God's hands, trusting Him to give us the strength to let it go and move past it.
- ☞Jesus is not saying God will stay angry with us if we remain angry with others. Or that God will take away our Salvation if we're not forgiving everyone we meet. But rather is warning how an unforgiving spirit can affect our daily fellowship and walk with God, hindering both our prayer life and the flow of God's love, joy, peace, and blessings.

Purposes in being Forgiving:

- Believers by forgiving others gets rid of growing anger, bitterness, and resentment towards them.
- Believers by forgiving others are better able to reflect God's love and mercy.
- Believers by forgiving others frees our guilt, brings peace of mind, keeps Satan from gaining a foothold.
- Believers resentment & unforgiveness can leave a bad witness of our faith to the rest of the world.

From this verse here (V. 16) to verse (V. 18) Jesus warns against putting on a religious show of fasting.

Fasting-(N.I.V.)

6:16 "When you fast (3522-*To abstain from food & drink for spiritual purposes.*) **do not look somber** (Depressed, dreary, sullen, dismal, gloomy) **as the hypocrites do,** (In context the Scribes and Pharisees.) **for they disfigure their faces** (i.e. Leaving the face unwashed, unshaven, hair uncombed. Was meant to convey a mournful gesture, and to draw attention to their great grief, plight, and affliction.) **to show** (display, flaunt) **men they are fasting.** (Suggests: Purpose being to impress others of their spirituality/devoutness.) **I tell you the truth,** (Expresses a strong confirmation & reliability.) **they have received their reward in full.** (Suggests: Admiration, sympathy from men, no closer to God.)

Warns believers against making a show of their fasting simply to impress others of their piety.

Message & Application 💻=🌎

- ❖ Shows how believers are not to use fasting as a way to gain the recognition and the admiration of others of how spiritual we are.
- ❖ Teaches how fasting is to be practiced for the right motives & reasons, in hungering to draw closer to God, and not in order to impress others.
- ❖ Warns against using fasting as some sort of hunger strike in twisting God's arm to bless us and answer our prayers.
- ❖ Warns against using fasting as a way to convince others of our spirituality or how devoted we are to God.
- ❖ Warns against using fasting as some sort of self-punishment or as a way of gaining favor with God.(Give God confession & repentance).

-Disfigure their faces-Meaning: The practice of smearing ashes on one's head and face. Or not washing or combing ones hair in order to display their religious piety before men. (Some view the Roman Catholics observance of "Ash Wednesday" as falling closely along these lines).

–Fasting-Meaning: The voluntary abstinence from food for the sake of some spiritual purpose or religious devotion. (See notes on Vs. 17-18). The Bible doesn't mandate time limits for fasting. A majority of Church's observe it anywhere between 24 hours to several days.

➢ Other areas of fasting may also include:
  - Media fasts-(T.V., movies, newspaper, internet, etc.)
  - Activity fasts-(Shopping, sports, hobbies, etc.)
  - People fasts-(Social gatherings, sexual intimacy, etc.)

6:17 But when you fast, (Suggests: Expects fasting to be a regular part of the believer's life.) **put oil on your head** (anoint thine head-K.J.V. e.g. moose, gel, balm, ointment, Shampoo-M.B.V., comb your hair-N.L.T.) **and wash your face,** (Expresses: Collectively to appear as usual, follow your normal daily routine.)
18 so that it will not be obvious (Syn.-noticeable) **to men** (i.e. People) **that you are fasting,** (Syn.-depriving yourself) **but only to your Father,** (i.e. God) **who is unseen;** (i.e. Spirit) **and your Father, who sees** (i.e. God's Omniscient.) **what is done in secret,** (i.e. What is done sincerely with the right attitude & motive) **will reward you.** (Openly-K.J.V.-(Not found in the earliest or must authentic Greek MSS. Suggests: Having more of God's presence, guidance, and direction in life.)

Rather than draw attention to ourselves while fasting, believers are to maintain a regular appearance.

Message & Application

❖ Shows believers how fasting is to be a private matter between you and God, and not in order to impress others of how spiritual we are.
❖ Teaches how "Fasting" should always be motivated as a means for seeking God's guidance and direction and not for appearance sake.
❖ Reminds believers how all spiritual disciplines, including fasting, should be pursued for the right reasons in building inner character.
❖ Teaches how fasting should be practiced in a pleasing and joyful way, and not to impress others of how much we sacrificed for the Lord.
⊶ Today fasting is to be practiced for the right reasons in growing closer to God. And not as some tool to increase our chances of getting our prayers answered, or as some sort of fast-track for losing weight.

Proper Areas for Fasting:

- As an act of humility and for drawing closer to God.
- As a sign of deep sorrow & remorse over sin.
- As a spiritual discipline in bringing the physical appetites under God and the Holy Spirit's control.
- As an appeal in seeking God's deliverance in times of burdens, crises, and trials.
- As an appeal to God in seeking wisdom & direction when making important decisions.
- As an appeal in seeking God's help in the deliverance from the struggles & temptations of sin.
- As an appeal to God when beginning a new spiritual movement or special ministry.

From this verse here (V. 19) to verse (V. 24) Jesus teaches on the proper values towards money & wealth.

Treasures in Heaven-(N.I.V.)

6:19 "Do not store up (covet, hoard) **for yourselves treasures on earth,** (i.e.-money, wealth, status, career, possessions, appearances, etc.) **where moth and rust destroys,** (Work of moths eating holes in clothes,-▣ rust eroding coins.) **and where thieves break in and steal.** (break through-K.J.V. Suggests: Houses that were made of mud/clay made it easy for a burglar to dig through the wall.)
20 But store up (Metph.-invest, devote) **for yourselves treasures in heaven,** (Metph.-godly-character, charity, missionary work, good deeds, soul-winning, etc.) **where moth and rust do not destroy, and where thieves do not break in and steal.** (Suggests: Being that they are imperishable, spiritual, and eternal.)
21 For where your treasure is, (Syn.-values, interests, love, profits.) **there your heart** (Syn.-loyalty, goals, devotion, interests, personal worth) **will be also.** (Expresses what we value and hold dear will begin to orient our hearts & lives.)

Teaches believers rather than invest ourselves in material things, invest it in a life that is serving & glorifying God.

Message & Application 💻=🌎

❖ Shows how believers are to be investing ourselves for eternity in things that are serving God and helping others. (cf. 1-Tim. 6:9-10, 17-19)
❖ Calls for seeing that we're using our time, energy, and finances for God's glory, and not for our own satisfactions and pleasures.
❖ Calls for finding our value, worth, and security in God and not in the fleeting and temporary things of life. (cf. Luke 12:16-21)
❖ Warns against getting caught up in the material things of life, always wanting the bigger house, better car, coolest clothes, faster computer.
⊶ Today all one has to do is look at our credit cards, bank accounts, and checkbooks to see where our hearts are at and where we are spiritually.
☞ Jesus is not saying you can't save for a rainy day or invest for the future. But is warning against the relentless pursuit of materialism.

Ways to lay up Treasures in Heaven:

- Be sure your born-again and believing on Christ.
- Be charitable, generous, and giving of others.
- Be loving, kind, and forgiving of others.
- Be soul-winners for Christ and the Gospel.
- Be invested in reading & growing in God's word.

6:22 The eye (Metph.-spiritual vision, heart) **is the lamp** (guide, director) **of the body.** (i.e. life, conduct) **If your eyes are good,** (single-K.J.V. Metph.-Single-minded devotion to God. Or generous & liberal.) **your whole body will be full of light.**(i.e. One who's life is devoted towards charity, generosity, godly things.) **23 But if your eyes are bad,** (evil-K.J.V. Metph-stingy, greedy, covetous.) **your whole body will be full of darkness. If then the light within you is darkness how great is that darkness.** (A heart that is cold, empty, and far from God.)

Teaches believers the need to keep our spiritual eyes focused on God if we're going to see wealth rightly.

Message & Application 💻=🌍

❖ Shows if we're going to navigate successfully through life and make healthy/moral choices along the way we need to stay focused on God.
❖ Displays how a heart that loves God will be less concerned about money, and more concerned about blessing and helping others.
🗝 Even today those who's hearts are following God will see the beauty of charity & generosity more important than money & material things.

6:24 "No-one can serve two masters. (God & wealth) **Either he will hate the one and love the other, or he will be devoted to the one and despise the other. You cannot serve both God and Money.** (mammon-K.J.V. Syn.-wealth.)

Because of their opposing values, one cannot serve both God and wealth simultaneously.

Message & Application 💻=🌍

❖ Shows believers if not careful material things can start to become an idol, slowly enslaving and pulling our hearts away from God.
❖ Warns against thinking we can have it both ways, that we can be consumed with the things of this world while still living for God.
🗝 Even today if not careful money can start to be the primary decision maker in our lives rather than God. That we start turning to money to find security, satisfaction, and pleasure rather than to God.

Signs that you may be Serving Money:

- Is money your primary filter for decision making, do you put off Church to make more money?
- Is money the thing you worry & fret about the most.
- Do you find it hard to be generous in the Lord's work?
- Are you preoccupied with your net-worth, always checking your bank account, credit cards, and stocks.

From this verse here (V. 25) to verse (V.34) Jesus teaches against the worry & anxiety of life.

Do Not Worry-(N.I.V.)

6:25 "Therefore (Conclusion drawn from those who have decided to serve God and not wealth.–{V.24}) **I tell you, do not worry** (3309-*To be choked or strangled with the cares of life, be pulled or torn apart.* Syn.-fretting, obsessing, stressing, worry-warts.) **about your life what you will eat or drink; or about your body, what you will wear.** (i.e. Daily necessities of life. Not limited to, but also including jobs, finances, retirement, healthcare, tuitions.) **Is not life** (Syn.-person, soul) **more important than food, and the body more important than clothes?** (Jesus argues from the greater to the lesser. That if God has given the greatest gift of life, surely we can trust Him to maintain and care for it as well.)

Believers are not to worry about daily necessities because God places great value on our life's.

Message & Application 💻=🌎

❖ Shows believers since God created us and gave us life, surely we can trust Him to provide what we need for our survival. (cf. Philp. 4:6-7)
❖ Warns against the type of worrying that acts as if God doesn't exist, or if He does He can't be counted on to supply our needs.
❖ Warns against proclaiming our love for God and all that He has done for us, and then live as if there is no God.
❖ Warns how worry/anxiety is a great sin because it distrusts in the love & power of God. (Worry can lead others in thinking God is unreliable).
🗝 Even today many Christians can believe that God can Save them from their sins, give them eternal life, and bring them to heaven, yet still distrust Him to get them through the next couple of days.
☞ Jesus is not prohibiting believers from making adequate provisions for the future or look to our financial security. But is warning against compulsively worrying about all the "What if's" that can go wrong.

Reasons against Worrying:

- Worrying invites a lack of faith & trust in God's love, care, and providence.
- Worrying can paralyze our faith, cripple our walk, and distract us from God's work.
- Worrying can hinder our witness & testimony.
- Worrying can sap & drain our spiritual lives.

6:26 Look at (behold-K.J.V. Syn.-consider, contemplate, reflect upon) **the birds of the air,-◙** (i.e. Any species of fowls.) **they do not sow-◙** (Plant) **or reap-◙** (i.e. Harvest, glean) **or store away in barns-◙** (Viz.-Storehouses, refrigerators, freezers, pantries, etc.) **and yet your heavenly Father feeds them. Are you not much more valuable** (Syn.-nobler, excellent, superior.) **than they?**

If God sees to it that inferior creatures are fed how much more will He care for believers who are created in His image.

Message & Application 💻=🌎

- ❖ Shows if God takes care of the insignificant & lesser things of life, surely He will provide and care for us who are even more valuable.
- ❖ Teaches as we go about living responsible and hardworking lives we can trust God to care for us and look after us!
- ❖ Emphasizes how even nature bears witness to God's faithfulness and goodness. (Know you can count on God to supply your daily needs!).
- ❖ Encourages believers in the bounty of God's resources & provisions. (Trust that God has a variety of methods and ways to meet your needs).
- ☞ Jesus is not saying here that believers can just sit back and take it easy, for even birds must hunt and search for food. (2-Thess. 3:10) But rather is simply teaching us to trust God to provide the talents, abilities, and resources in finding work so that we can feed and support ourselves.

6:27 Who of you by worrying (taking thought-K.J.V. Syn.-stressing, fretting.) **can add a single hour** (cubit-K.J.V.-4083-*Forearm, "The length of distance from the elbow to the tip of the middle finger", about 18 inches.*) **to his life** (unto his statute-K.J.V.-2244-*(a)-Height, looks, (b)-Age, length, or span of life.* Expresses how no one can worry themselves to long life. Or, since one's life is in God's hands, He determines when it's our time to go. {cf. Heb. 9:27, Is. 38:5})

Worrying is foolish because it accomplishes nothing.

Message & Application 💻=🌎

- ❖ Shows believers how worrying is pointless because it changes nothing.
- ❖ Teaches believers since most things are outside our ability to control, all the more reason to leave such matters in God's hands.
- ❖ Teaches rather than try to worry our self's to good health, trust that in the end it's really God who numbers our days and orders our steps.
- ⊶ Even today worrying can have the opposite effects, it can actually shorten one's life, causing ulcers, high blood pressure, depression, suicide, etc. Not to mention addiction to drugs & alcohol in trying to suppress those worries.

6:28 "And why do you worry (Syn.-fret, stress, fuss) **about clothes?** (i.e. Latest fashions/outfits) **See** (Expresses: Spiritual reflection.) **how the lilies-◙ of the field grow.** (i.e. Any wild species of trumpet-shaped lilies.) **They do not labor or spin.-◙** (Lit.-Women's work in spinning wool, silk, and cotton into clothing.)
29 Yet I tell you that not even Solomon (i.e. King Solomon) **in all his splendor-◙** (glory-K.J.V. Expresses the royal robes worn by kings . Metph.-wealth, riches, pomp, opulence.) **was dressed like one of these.**

If God sees to it that flowers are properly adorn how much more will He see to it that believers are properly cared for.

Message & Application

- ❖ Shows believers if God gives such beauty & grace to the little things of life, how much more will He care and provide for us. (cf. 1-Pet. 5:7)
- ❖ Rather than be concerned about self-image or finding acceptance with others, know that you're already beautiful and precious in God's sight!
- ❖ Teaches how it's better to look to God's provisions since they far exceed anything we could ever accomplish or acquire on our own.
- ⊶ Even today, believers can trust that God knows better than we do in what will bless, enrich, and beautify our lives.

6:30 If that is how God clothes the grass of the field, which is here today and tomorrow thrown into the fire,-◙ (oven-K.J.V. Suggests: Wild grasses that were cut down and used as fuel in clay cooking ovens.) **will he not much more clothe you, O** (Expresses: Wonder, reproach.) **you of little faith** (Expresses a tender rebuke for distrusting/doubting God's providence, sovereignty, and care.)

If divine providence provides for that which is temporary how much more will God provide believers for eternity.

Message & Application

- ❖ Shows believers that if God gives such attention & detail to things that are temporary and of little worth, how much more will God care for us.
- ❖ Emphasizes the great amount of love, care, and devotion that God places on each of us, that we're never forgotten or undervalued.
- ❖ Teaches if God gives so much time and effort to things that are of little value, surely God will take pride in us, and do what's best for us!
- ❖ Reminds believers if God created the universe & world, surely He can provide for us in putting food on our tables and clothes on our backs.
- ⊶ Even today, believers can proclaim their faith in God, but then distrust Him for the tiny details of our lives when it comes to our car payment, mortgage, rent, utility bills, grocery bills, etc. (cf. Jer. 29:11)

6:31 So do not worry, (Syn.-renounce, bar, banish, forbid, stop) **saying,** (Syn.-cultivating, magnifying) **'What shall we eat?' or 'What shall we drink?' or 'What shall we wear?** (Expresses: Worries over the general necessities of life.) **32 For the pagans** (gentiles-K.J.V.-Non-Jews, non-believers) **run after** (Syn.-madly pursue, chief concern, #1 priority) **all these things,** (i.e. Daily needs) **and your heavenly Father knows that you need them.** (Expresses how God is already familiar and acquainted with the welfare and needs of His children.)

Believers are not to live like the rest of the world in making daily necessities a priority because God already knows all our needs.

Message & Application 💻=🌎

- ❖ Shows how believers don't have to worry like the rest of the world because God is already acquainted with all our needs. (cf. Philp. 4:6-7)
- ❖ Teaches how we're not to make the world's priorities our priorities.
- ❖ Warns how worrying about daily needs is to live like people who don't have hope, and who don't know God as their personal Father.
- ⊶ Even today believers can live differently from the people around us, knowing that God as our Father is already familiar with our needs and acquainted with our expenses, bills, income, finances, and budgets.

6:33 But seek first (Expresses to actively pursue, strive, first importance, top priority, sold-out, etc.) **his kingdom** (Metph.-God's will, rule, cause, glory, interests.) **and his righteousness,** (1343-*Justice, uprightness.* Expresses: The need in letting God's word & will to set the standard for our life. To make heaven our end and holiness our way.) **and all these things** (Not life' luxuries, but the daily necessities of clothing, food, shelter. Not limited too, but also including peace, joy, wholeness, stability, etc.) **will be given to you as well.**

As believers live for God & His word, He will see to it that our daily needs are met.

Message & Application 💻=🌎

- ❖ Shows believers as we live our lives out for the Lord's work and business with it will come God's daily blessings and provision.
- ❖ Assures believers as we do our part in serving, praising, and lifting God up, He'll do His part and all the rest! (cf. Philp. 1:6, 4:19, James 4:8)
- ❖ Teaches believers as we put God first everything will start to fall into place and work itself out, if not, then things will start to fall apart!
- ⊶ Even today those who are putting God first will begin to live happier and healthier lives, even our marriages, finances, and sobriety will start to improve and get better.

6:34 Therefore (Suggests: A conclusion drawn from having chosen to give God first place and top priority in life.-{V. 33}) **do not worry** (Syn.-fretting, stressing.) **about tomorrow,** (Is not forbidding foresight & planning. But of perplexing over future calamities and catastrophes.) **for tomorrow will worry about itself.** (Expresses God's presence in helping us to deal with whatever tomorrow brings.) **Each day has enough trouble of its own.** (sufficient unto the day is evil-K.J.V. Expresses everyday has enough hardships, burdens, and temptations to deal with. That we're not to add tomorrows worries with today's concerns.)

Since each day has its own challenges, believers are to focus on the present and leave tomorrow in God's hands.

Message & Application

- ❖ Shows how believers are to live for today and leave tomorrow's worries & burdens in God's hands. (Though you may not know what tomorrow holds, but know who holds tomorrow!).
- ❖ Calls for focusing on present duties, trusting that God will provide the fresh grace and strength to see us through another day.
- ❖ Warns how worrying about tomorrow's burdens can rob us of our capacity in dealing with today's trials and struggles.
- ❖ Warns of the unreasonableness of worrying about things beyond our immediate needs and control. (Let God determine what's important!)
- ❖ Teaches instead of worrying about tomorrow, we can better use that energy in dealing with daily struggles and temptations.
- ❖ Teaches instead of focusing on how big our problems, focus on how big our God is. (You do the serving and let God do the worrying!).
- 🗝 Even today, believers can live with the peace & joy of knowing that if God was there for us yesterday, God will be there to help us today, tomorrow, and the day after that! (cf. Mal. 3:6, Heb. 13:8, James 1:17)
- ☞ Jesus is not saying here that we can't set goals for ourselves or make plans and provisions for the future. But rather we're not to let worries about tomorrow affect our relationship and walk with God today!
- ☞ Since each day has its own challenges and problems it is folly to add more to it by worrying about what may or may not happen tomorrow. (Know that 95% of what you worry about never happens!)

Four Reasons not to Worry:

- Know your under God's sovereign rule & providence.
- Know that worrying doesn't change anything.
- Know you're a child of God and dearly loved by Him.
- Know that God will always be there for you tomorrow.

Chapter Seven

From this verse here (V. 1) to verse (V.6) Jesus warns against critical & judgmental attitudes.

Judging Others-(N.I.V.)

7:1 "Do not judge, (Syn.-critical, judgmental, faultfinding, pass-sentence, cynical, nit-pick, tear-down. Expresses how believers are not to assume the right to condemn others.) **or you too will be judged.** (Suggests: The same critical standard of judgments we hold of others God will apply to us!)
2 For in the same way (Syn.-manner, treatment, dealings) **as you judge** (treat-L.B.V.) **others, you will be judged,** (treated-L.B.V.) **and with the measure** (Syn.-standards, principles, rules) **you use,** (mete out-K.J.V.-Syn.-apply, impose, exact, dish-out, deal out-N.E.B.) **it will be measured to you.** (Suggests: Not that God will remove a believers Salvation. But rather will use the same critical examinations when evaluating their walk and service to Him.)

Believers are not to manifest a condemning or judgmental attitude towards others.

Message & Application 💻=🌎

- ❖ Shows how believers are not to possess a critical or faultfinding heart towards others. (Don't go digging or suspecting the worst in others).
- ❖ Warns against assuming that we know the motives of another's heart. (Don't lump all people together into the same category).
- ❖ Warns how no believer has the right to set themselves up or usurp God's place as judge. (Judging others is God's role, not yours!).
- ❖ Warns believers against the kind of judgmental attitude of tearing others down in order to build ourselves up.
- ❖ Warns against the type of critical spirit that is always nitpicking and jumping on others for their failures and criticizing their faults.
- ❖ Teaches how critical judgments of others can have a boomerang effect, people will either shrink from us or hold us to the same standards.
- ☞ Jesus' command here is not a blanket statement in overlooking all wrong behavior, but rather is calling for being discerning rather than always negative.
- ☞ What's condemned here is the hypocritical judgment in holding others to a higher standard that we ourselves are not willing to live by.
- ☞ This verse here is one of the most misquoted passages in the Bible that people frequently recite in shaming Christian against making any moral judgments on others, that we must be more accepting and tolerant of another's lifestyle.

Areas of Judging:

Believers are "Not" to judge:

- A persons faith (Rom. 14:1)
- Believers motives (1-Corn. 4:5)
- Outward appearances (John 7:24, Gal. 2:6)
- Believers service (Rom. 14:4)
- Eternal destiny (1-Corn. 7:16)

Believers are to judge:

- Disputes (1-Corn. 6:1-8)
- Sinful behavior/conduct (1-Corn. 5:9-23)
- False teachings/doctrines (1-Corn. 14:29)
- Unbelievers (2-Corn. 6:14)
- Qualifications (1-Tim. 3:1-13)

Reasons against Judging others:

- Can cause others to become discouraged.
- Can cause divisions and estrangements.
- Can cause one to become hypocritical.
- Can produce a spirit of pride/self-righteousness.
- Can invite severe judgment of others.
- Can foster a spirit of rejection and hate.
- Can demonstrate a lack of mercy & forgiveness.
- Can invite harsh judgments and rash decisions.

7:3 "Why do you look at the speck of sawdust (mote-K.J.V.) **in your brother's eye** (Metph-Small faults, minute sins, shortcomings.) **and pay no attention to the plank in your own eye?** (Metph-major faults, sins, vices, etc.)
4 How can you say to your brother, 'Let me take the speck out of your eye,' when all the time there is a plank in your own eye? (Metph.-life, character)
5 You hypocrite, first take the plank out of your own eye, and then you will see clearly to remove (reprove/correct) **the speck from your brother's eye.**

Warns believers against hypocritically judging the small faults of others while having major faults of their own.

Message & Application 💻=🌎

- ❖ Shows how believers are to make an honest self-appraisal of our own house/life first before we go around correcting others for their faults.
- ❖ Teaches only by getting right with God first with our own faults and shortcomings, our evaluations of others will come from a better place.
- ❖ Believers by taking into account our own faults are better able to help others with theirs. (Efforts won't seem hypocritical, but genuine).
- ❖ Demonstrates how the true desire to help others is seen in the honest and moral reformation that we make in our own lives first.
- 🗝 Even today when we learn to take into account our own failings we won't be so quick to criticize the failings and shortcomings of others.

7:6 "Do not give dogs (Metph.-arrogant, quarrelsome, scoffers, mockers, hard-heart.) **what is sacred;** (Metph.-Gospel teachings.) **do not throw your pearls** (Metph-Holy advice, Gospel/spiritual truths.) **to pigs** (Metph-depraved, corrupt.) **If you do, they may trample them under their feet,** (Metph.-spurn, scorn, reject.) **and then turn and tear you to pieces.** (Expresses to continually reprove leads only to anger & resentment, not all are grateful for correction!)

Though believers are not to be judgmental they are not to throw away all discernment.

Message & Application 💻=🌎

- ❖ Shows believers how being a nonjudgmental person does not mean being undiscerning. (Be not judges, but not simpletons or fools either).
- ❖ Teaches how being nonjudgmental does not mean we ignore another's sin or look the other way. (Never throw a cloak over a brother's faults).
- 🗝 Even today though believers are not to be overly critical, we must at the same time not be overly accepting or tolerant either!
- ☞ Can also be a warning against forcing spiritual truths on those who willfully reject the Gospel and scorn our witness and testimony.

From this verse here (V. 7) to verse (V. 12) Jesus teaches on the need for persistence in prayer.

Ask, Seek, Knock-(N.I.V.)

7:7 "Ask (Pray) **and it will be given to you;** (i.e. According to God's will) **seek**
(Metph.-strive, diligent.) **and you will find; knock** (Metph.-earnest, persistent)
and the door will be opened to you. (Calls for continual action & persistence.)
8 For everyone who asks receives; he who seeks finds; and to him who
knocks, the door will be opened. (Expresses: Earnest prayers get answered.)

Believers who are earnest & persistent in prayer are assured of being heard and answered by God.

Message & Application 💻=🌎

- ❖ Shows how believers can go to God in prayer for those areas in which we need to grow, becoming more of the person He expects us to be.
- ❖ Teaches how we can go to the Lord for help in freeing us from any wrong attitudes, thinking, and behaviors that are not of Him.
- ⊶ Even today we can go to God in prayer for help in growing us more in the areas of prudence, sensitivity, tolerance, non-judgementalism, etc.
- ☞ Jesus is not here giving us a blank check, that if we pray hard God will give us what we want, but only of virtues that are earnestly sought.

7:9 "Which of you, if his son asks for bread, will give him a stone? (Similarities
being both were flat, round, and smooth. Expresses: Paternal love, provision.)
10 Or if he asks for a fish will give him a snake (i.e. eel mistaken for a snake.)
11 If you, then, though you are evil, know how to give good gifts to your
children, how much more will your Father in heaven give good gifts (i.e. Daily
empowerment, graces, etc. Holy Spirit.-{Luke 11:13}) **to those who ask him!**

If sinful humanity can be kind to their own children, how much more will an all loving God answer believer's prayers.

Message & Application

- ❖ Shows believers the assurance we can have in prayer, knowing God's readiness and willingness to bless and provide us in all we ask!
- ❖ Teaches how God bestows His blessings based on what He thinks is best, and not what we want. (See prayer withheld as prayer answered!)
- ❖ Reminds believers how God is not a reluctant bystander who needs to be coerced, cajoled, or bullied in order to answer our prayers.
- ⊶ Even today God knows if something is going to do more harm than good, whether it's going to grow us spiritually or only hinder us.

The Golden Rule-(Authors insert)

7:12 So (Suggests: A conclusion drawn from the overall summary of the Sermon on the mount against murder & adultery-{5:21-28}, retaliation & revenge-{5:38-42}, condemning & judging.-{7:1-6}) **in everything,** (i.e. In word, deed, prayer.) **do to others what you would have them do to you, for this sums up** (Syn.-fulfills, summarizes, encapsulates.) **the Law and the Prophets.** (Expresses the entire O. T. The "Law" by its moral principles. The "Prophets" by their call for maintaining love, justice, and mercy.{Is. 1:17, Jer. 7:5, Ezek. 18:7})

Believers are to treat others with the same mercy and compassion as they would like to be treated.

Message & Application 💻=🌍

❖ Shows how believers are always to be proactive in seeking out the higher good in others. (Be lovingly inclined towards all people!).
❖ Calls for a kindness and compassion that takes into consideration that we're all prone to shortcomings, defects, and mistakes.
❖ Calls for always taking the initiative in putting the interests, needs, and burdens of others first before they have to ask us.
❖ Moves believers, rather than hating, condemning, or writing others off, we should be holding out a loving and patient spirit for them.
🗝 Even today believers must be able to relate with others, understanding their mood, nature, temperament, and struggles before judging them.
☞ Jesus is not the first to invent the "Golden rule" it was already around and used by other religions. But Jesus is the first to take it from its negative form *"Refrain from doing to others what you would not want done to yourself "* to making it a positive volition for action and love.

"**Golden Rule's" Spiritual Values:**

- Allows one to see value and worth in others.
- Allows one to rise above retaliation, cruelty, harshness, criticism, bigotry, and hate.
- Allows one to live in an atmosphere of equality, justice, and love.
- Allows one to help promote the welfare and interests of others.
- Allows one to foster generosity and goodwill.
- Allows one to treat others with kindness, compassion, courtesy, and respect.
- Allows one to sympathize with the needs and burdens of others first.

From this verse here (V. 13) to verse (V. 14) Jesus teaches on the true way to heaven & eternal life.

The Narrow and Wide Gates-(N.I.V.)

7:13"Enter through the narrow gate-◙ (Lit. Ancient walled cities with small gates to enter through at night. Metph-Faith in Christ, self-denial, Sermon on the Mtn. ethics.) **For wide is the gate and broad is the road** (Metph.-accepting, tolerant, accommodating, broad minded, anything goes.) **that leads to destruction,** (Metph.-Hell, eternal death) **and many enter through it.** (i.e. The religious who have walked by their own goodness & self-righteous ways. Or those who have rejected Christ and followed their sinful passions & pleasures.)
14 But small is the gate and narrow the road that leads to life, (Metph.-Salvation, eternal life, abundant life, etc.) **and only a few find it.**

Believers must choose to follow Jesus and His truth as the only way to heaven & eternal life.

Message & Application 💻=🌎

- ❖ Shows how believers must be willing to leave both the crowd and former sin baggage behind. (Are you willing to put sin & self behind!)
- ❖ Calls for leaving everything that stands between us and God, be it cherished sins, worldliness, self-righteousness, self-dependence, etc.
- ❖ Calls believers in seeing that our lives are going to be defined by God's word and truth, and not by what everybody else is doing.
- ❖ Prepares believers how doing the right thing may be hard, with no quick payoffs, but in the end, its going to take us in the right direction!
- ❖ Calls for staying the course, that we're not going to start cutting corners or compromising for what is easier & popular. (Know that what is cozy, safe, and convenient is not always what's best!).

–*Narrow gate*-Variously interpreted as involving either:

- Salvation in Christ only. (John 10:9, 14:6, Acts 4:12, 1-Tim. 2:5-6)
- Righteous character, strict morals, no sin baggage. (Eph. 4:22-24)
- The way of faith, grace, repentance, and self-denial. (Eph. 2:8)

🗝 Even today, believers need to stay true to our walk with Christ no matter how unpopular, uncomfortable, or challenging it may be. That we're not going to allow culture or friends to pressure us into acting and behaving a certain way just to fit in and feel accepted.

☞ Jesus is not making it hard to become Christians but is warning against going with the flow of popular opinion. That just because the majority adhere to some philosophy or belief doesn't mean it's always correct!

From this verse here (V. 15) to verse (V.23) Jesus warns about false teachers & false prophets in the Church.

A Tree and Its Fruit-(N.I.V.)

7:15 "Watch out for false prophets. (Metph.-false teachers. Suggests: In context a call for diligence and spiritual alertness for those who will try to lead us down the wide path-{V.13}.) **They come to you in sheep's clothing,** (Metph-harmless, authentic, sincere. Suggests: A pretense of appearing genuine, godly, holy, and theologically-correct.) **but inwardly they are ferocious wolves.** (ravening-K.J.V.-727-*greedy, preying, covetous, exploiting, a robber.* Metph.-Predatory, extorting, self-seeking, self-promoting, rip you off-M.B.V. Suggests: Their intentions will be malicious at heart, motivated only by greed, prestige, power, and fame. Exploiting those who are naive, immature, and gullible.)

A warning to believers to beware of false teachers who will distort the Gospel message.

Message & Application 💻=🌎

❖ Shows believers the need to be alert for false teachers who are preaching a message that is different to the Gospel message. (Gal. 1:6-9)
❖ Warns against being misled by those who will twist/distort the Gospel, preaching a different Jesus than the one you came to know.
❖ Teaches the importance of seeing that the teachings and doctrines of preachers are lining up with the word of God.
❖ Prepares believers how not all people are really out to serve Christ but themselves and what they can get out of it. (cf. Philp. 1:15-18)
🗝 Even today, believers need to be alert for those who will try to water down the Gospel, always preaching on health, wealth, and everything else, and never on sin, death, judgment, and repentance.
☞ In context, Jesus is warning against those who will offer an alternative way of Salvation and lifestyle contrary to His narrow way. (Vs. 13-14)

How to Recognize False Teachers:

- Their prophecies don't come to pass.
- Their profession does not match their walk.
- Their motivated by greed, prestige, power.
- Their teachings and doctrines are unbiblical.

7:16 By their fruit (Metph-doctrine, teaching, message, conduct, etc.) **you will recognize them. Do people pick grapes from thornbushes,-◙ or figs-◙ from thistles?-◙** (Suggests: Character will be easily distinguishable and obvious.)
17 Likewise, every good tree (Metph.-Genuine believer, regenerate heart.) **bears good fruit,** (Metph-sound doctrines/teachings, good conduct, righteous character.) **but a bad tree** (corrupt-K.J.V. Metph.-wicked, self-seeking) **bears bad fruit.** (Metph-False doctrines/teachings, conduct, behavior, etc.)
18 A good tree cannot bear bad fruit and a bad tree cannot bear good fruit.

Believers can discern false teachers by their message and character.

Message & Application 💻=🌎

- ❖ Shows how believers can detect false teachers by seeing if their teachings and lives are lining up with the word of God. (cf.1-John 4:1-6)
- ❖ Teaches how though men can lie, their character and conduct cannot. (Know that sooner or later their true colors will reveal itself!).
- ❖ Calls for looking beyond a person's charisma, doctorates, and charm, to what kind of message and Gospel they're preaching.
- ⊶ Even today false teachers/prophets are often betrayed by their greediness, lavish lifestyles, and immoral living.
- ☞ Today we can determine false teachers by seeing if the fruits of the Holy Spirit, fruits of love, joy, peace, patience is operating in their life.

7:19 Every tree (Metph.-teacher, preacher, pastor, minister, believer) **that does not bear good fruit** (Metph-Gospel teachings, truthfulness, genuineness, humility, etc.) **is cut down and thrown into the fire.** (Metph-hell) **Thus, by their fruit** (Metph.-teachings, doctrines, character.) **you will recognize them.**

A warning of impending judgment for false teachers who do not properly promote and teach the Gospel.

Message & Application 💻=🌎

- ❖ Shows believers the need to see that Christian profession & character is being lived out in agreement with God's word and truth.
- ❖ Calls for an honest evaluation, that we're not just talking a good game, but that we're truly living and embracing God's word in our own lives.
- ☞ Jesus is not here saying that He expects believers to be living perfect lives, but that we're living lives that are honest & authentic with God.
- ☞ Jesus is not here calling for witch-hunts or throwing out pastors who are less than perfect. But rather it's about evaluating their overall character and teachings with the Word of God.

7:21 "Not everyone who says to me, 'Lord, Lord,' (Expresses a profession of religious zeal, with no real commitment or devotion.) **will enter the kingdom of heaven,** (Metph.-eternal life, glory) **but only he who does the will of my Father who is in heaven.** (i.e. Foremost to repent and believe on Jesus-{cf. John 6:40}, followed by a life of submission and obedient living.-{cf. 1-John. 2:3-6})

Warns that without genuine faith & godly living, Christian profession and religious service will not Save a person.

Message & Application 💻=🌎

- ❖ Shows believers how simply paying lip-service to Jesus without a life of holy and obedient living won't cut it. (cf. James 2:17-26)
- ❖ Teaches how God is more concerned about our walk than our talk, that He sees doing right as more important than just saying the right things.
- ❖ Warns how believers can't claim to be followers of Christ and then live as we want and do as we want.
- 🗝 Even today many can profess Jesus as Lord, know all the right words, and do all the religious things, yet will give Him no say when it comes to how they should live, or how they should run their life's.

7:22 Many will say to me on that day, (i.e. Day of Judgment.) **'Lord, Lord, did we not prophesy** (Teach, preach) **in your name,** (i.e. To your credit, glory, praise.) **and in your name drive out demons and perform many miracles?'**
23 Then I will tell them plainly, (Syn.-openly, frankly) **'I never knew you** (Expresses: Never had a personal relationship with Jesus, never truly Saved.) **Away from me you evildoers!'** (work iniquity-K.J.V. Expresses their lives were sinful, extremely immoral, works were deceitful, self-promoting, self-indulging.)

Jesus will not acknowledge anyone who sounds religious but does not have a personal relationship with Him.

Message & Application 💻=🌎

- ❖ Shows believers how Christ wants not religious works, but lives that are truly surrendered and submitted to Him.
- ❖ Warns that without a Saving relationship with Jesus no amount of religious works and good deeds will make you right with God.
- 🗝 Even today it's not about how much we went to Church, or how much we've witnessed for the Lord, or how many we brought to Christ. But rather about whether we were ever in a Saving relationship with Jesus!
- ☞ Jesus is not saying here that He expects us to live perfect life's in never sinning or doing wrong, or that we must work harder. But rather He's looking for those who are allowing Him to move & work in their lives.

From this verse here (V.24) to the end of the chapter, Jesus teaches the importance of putting His teachings into practice.

The Wise and Foolish Builders-(N.I.V.)

7:24 Therefore everyone who hears these words of mine (Sermon on the
Mtn.) **and puts them into practice is like a wise man** (Metph.-sensible,
prudent, diligent) **who built his house** (i.e. life/Character) **on the rock.** (Christ)
25 The rain came down, the streams rose, and the winds blew (Metph.-life's
trials, struggles.) **and beat against that house;** (Metph-life, character.) **yet it
did not fall,** (apostatize, backslide) **because it had its foundation on the rock.**
**26 But everyone who hears these words of mine and does not put them into
practice is like a foolish man** (Metph.-carless, reckless) **who built his house on
sand.** (Metph-Worldly philosophies, human reasoning, natural strengths, etc.)
**27 The rain came down, the streams rose, and the winds blew and beat
against that house, and it fell with a great crash."** (Expresses an image
conveying utter ruin, doomed to destruction, or final judgment/punishment.)

Believers who apply & practice Jesus' teachings will be able to withstand the trials and adversities of life.

Message & Application 

❖ Shows believers who are building their lives on Christ are better able to weather the storms and challenges of life.
❖ Reminds believers how staying in the word will keep us safe from things that will try to wreck our lives and shake our faith in Jesus.
❖ Teaches how staying rooted in the word will give us the strength to overcome the unexpected bumps in the road that life may throw at us.
❖ Teaches believers who are investing time in God's word will find peace, security, and stability in difficult times.

⊶ Even today the storms of sickness, job loss, divorce, betrayal, relapse, etc. are bound to come. But it's how we stay grounded in God's word will we find strength and stability to get through it!

☞ Jesus is not saying that by following His teachings will keep us from all the troubles & trials of life, though we will certainly avoid most of them. But that we will not fall under the gravity and weight of them!

–***Rain came down***- An image that conveys the calamities of life:
e.g. sickness, financial crises, legal bills, laid off, etc.

–***Streams rose***- An image that conveys fleshy & worldly passions:
e.g. temptations, lust, sinful vices, etc.

–***Winds blew***- An image that conveys evil and destructive forces:
e.g. false teachings, persecutions, evil plots.

7:28 When Jesus had finished saying these things, (i.e. Jesus' Sermon on the Mount discourse.-{Chps. 5-7} Expresses a structural formula woven within Matthews Gospel that marks the end of the "first" five-set division discourse that began in 5:1. Suggesting a shift from teaching on discipleship-(Chps. 5-7) to the next phase of Jesus' ministry of miracles and instructions on Missionary work.-(Chaps. 8-10)) **the crowds were amazed** (astonished-K.J.V.-1605-*To stand outside oneself, to be exceedingly struck in mind.* Syn.-awestruck, speechless, blown away, spellbound) **at his teaching,** (doctrine-K.J.V. i.e. His wisdom, knowledge, insight, simplicity. Suggests: Jesus' teachings were hitting people's hearts and conscience's to what true righteousness should look like.)
29 because he taught as one who had authority, (1849-*The privilege to control and demand, the power & liberty to do as one pleases.* Syn.-divine authority, approval) **and not as their teachers of the law.** (scribes-K.J.V. Suggests: The scribes had only quoted and recited the teachings of others Rabbis. That they always spoke by the authority of others never by their own opinion.)

Jesus spoke by the authority of His own teachings rather than reciting or quoting other Rabbis.

Message & Application

- ❖ Shows how believers are to give Jesus the ultimate authority & final say over our lives. (Will you see Jesus' words as the words of God?).
- ❖ Calls believers in having the same type of open and receptive heart that what we're reading and hearing is the Word of God Himself!
- ❖ Calls believers in seeing Jesus as the genuine dispenser of all truth and wisdom, that He is the true source of which all life proceeds. (Col. 1:16)
- ❖ Assures of having in God's word everything necessary in making us the people He called us to be.(Will you allow the word to change you).
- ❖ Teaches the impossibility for people to admire good preaching and not be affected and impacted by it in some way!
- ❖ Teaches how we lead and serve should always emanate from our character and not from our degrees, titles, or accomplishments.
- ❖ Calls for accepting everything that Jesus says about us is true, and the changes we need to make.
- ❖ Calls for the willingness of allowing Jesus' teachings to hit home, even if its not what we want to hear. (Are you willing to accept the truth about yourself?)
- ⊶ Even today we need to be open & honest enough in acknowledging that everything Jesus is talking about is exactly how we're living or not living, that there's a huge gulf between His teachings and our walk and the changes we need to make.

Chapter Eight

Jesus' Miracles

- **"Man with Leprosy"** Miracle affirming Jesus' power to cleanse men of sin.-(8:1-4)
- **"Roman Centurion's Servant"** Miracle affirming the power of faith.-(8:5-13)
- **"Peter's Mother-in-law** Miracle affirming Jesus' authority over sickness.-(8:14-17)
- **"Calming of the storm"** Miracle affirming Jesus' power over the storms of life.-(8:23-34)
- **"Two demon-possessed men"** Miracle affirming Jesus' power over the demonic.- (8:28-34)
- **"Paralyzed Man"**-Miracle affirming Jesus' power and authority over the paralyzing effects of sin.-(9:1-8)
- **"Jairus' Daughter/Hemorrhaging woman"**-Miracles affirming Jesus' power & authority over disease and death.-(9:18-26)
- **"Two blind/demon possessed men"**-Miracles affirming Jesus' power over spiritual blindness & unbelief.-(9:27-34)
- **"The workers are few"**-Jesus calls for Ministers in sharing the Gospel with the lost- (9:35-38)

The Man With Leprosy-(N.I.V.)

8:1 When he came down from the mountainside, (i.e. Having just delivered His Sermon on the Mount.-{Chaps. 5-7}) **large crowds followed him.**
2 A man with leprosy-◙ (3015-*A disease that causes discoloration & scaly patches of skin.* In severe cases disfigurement & deformity. Was thought to be a curse from God due to sin.) **came and knelt before him** (Expresses: Humility) **and said, "Lord, if you are willing,** (Expresses his faith in Jesus' power & ability to heal him, but was uncertain Jesus would touch him and risk infection. Or felt he was undeserving because of his sin.) **you can make me clean."**

A man with leprosy humbly places his faith in Jesus' power & compassion to heal him.

Message & Application 💻=🌍

- ❖ Shows the need for recognizing our lost & broken condition, that we're sinners who need to be cleansed & Saved by Jesus. (1-Tim.1:15)
- ❖ Teaches how some can be confident in the power of God but not in the love of God. (No matter how unlovable, God wants to heal you!)
- ❖ Calls for humbly accepting the Lord's choices and decisions as to what's best for us, whether He grants our healing now or in eternity!
- ❖ Displays how many have no problem believing God for the impossible, but sometimes doubt whether this is something God can fix or forgive.

🗝 Even today no matter how unworthy or undeserving you feel you are, know that Jesus loves you and wants to help Save you out of a life of sin and addiction your in! (cf. John 9:25, 1-John 1:9)

8:3 Jesus reached out his hand and touched the man. (Expresses a gesture of love, compassion, acceptance, reassurance.) **"I am willing"** (Expresses Jesus' willingness to suspend Levitical regulations against ceremonial defilement.-{Lev. 13:44-46}. Or Jesus' infinite mercy & grace.) **he said. "Be clean! Immediately he was cured of his leprosy.** (Expresses the supernatural nature of the miracle, that it was instant & complete, much the way Christ cleanses away all our sins!) **4 Then Jesus said to him,** (straitly charged-K.J.V.-1690-*To warn with earnest admonition, stern tone.)* **"See that you don't tell anyone.** (Suggests: Jesus did not want the popularity of only being known as a miracle worker and faith healer. Or wanted people to come to Him by faith and not miracles.) **But go, show yourself to the priest and offer the gift Moses commanded, as a testimony to them."** (Suggests: A sacrificial offering as evidence to confirm to the priests that the cleansing was of Levitical standards. That he then be allowed back into society and mingle with the people.-{Lev. 14:1-8}) Or Jesus observed the ceremonies prescribed by Law till the time He would fulfill them.)

Displays Jesus' compassion & willingness to heal the man's affliction with leprosy.

Message and Application 💻=🌎

- ❖ Shows believers Jesus' compassion & willingness in reaching out and cleansing us of our sins. (cf. Eph. 2:4-5, 1-John 1:7-10)
- ❖ Displays how we have a Savior who still has compassion even for the misguided decisions and sinful choices we make in life.
- ❖ Teaches no one ever has to feel ashamed or embarrassed, that there's no sin so ugly or repulsive that Jesus isn't willing to forgive & forget!
- ❖ Displays how we don't have to clean up our act or get our lives together first, that Jesus will meet us right in the mire and sin we're in!
- ❖ Teaches how Jesus knows the areas where we need healing the most, whether it's a touch of love, compassion, understanding, or acceptance.
- ❖ Teaches how only through Christ's merciful touch can we be restored back into a right relationship with God, family, and society. (V. 4)
- ❖ Teaches how the best medicine against relapse is to offer our healed lives to the praise, glory, and service of God. (V. 4)
- ❖ Assures how believers can go out in the name of the Lord completely healed, delivered, and set free! (V. 4)
- ❖ Displays how there's nothing that speaks more effectively of God's healing power than the testimony of a life changed by Jesus! (V. 4)

⊷ Even today, we need the same love & compassion in reaching out to drug addicts, alcoholics, and social outcasts, letting them know that they're loved by Jesus!(Will you reach out and touch the untouchable?)

Purpose of Jesus' Miracles:

- Established Jesus' claims to deity, Messiahship, and were evidence He was sent by God. (John 3:2, 6:14,10:38, 14:11)
- Authenticated Jesus teachings & message, gave proof of His power & authority to forgive sin. (Matt 8:27, 9:5-6, 10:7-8, John 2:8)
- Demonstrates God's love, compassion, and mercy for the needy. (Matt. 9:22, 29, 20:30-34)
- Were instruments used to lead people to Saving faith & repentance. (Matt. 9:22, 29, 15:28, 11:20-21, John 4:48, 7:31)
- Displays how God's reign/Kingdom had arrived. (Matt. 4:23, 9:35, 10:7-8)
- Fulfilled Messianic prophecy. (Matt. 1:22-23, 8:17, 11:5, Is. 29:18, 35:5-6, 53:4)
- Were metaphorical and parabolic illustrations. (Matt. 14:15-20, 21:18-19)

Following Category of Miracles:

- Jesus' power over diseases-(8:1-4)
- Jesus' power over disabilities-(8:5-17)
- Jesus' power over Nature-(8:23-26)
- Jesus' power over demons-(8:28-32)
- Jesus' power over sins-(9:1-13)
- Jesus' power over death-(9:18-25)

Proper Responses in Miracles:

- Worship, praise, glory- (8:1-3, 27, 9:18, 33)
- Faith, humility-(8:5-13, 9:20-22, 9:28-29)
- Hospitality, service- (8:14-15, 8:34)
- Discipleship-(8:18-22, 9:36-38)

From this verse here (V. 5) to verse (V. 13) Teaches on the power of faith when rightly placed in Jesus.

8:5 When Jesus had entered Capernaum a centurion-◙ (1543-*Roman soldier in charge of a hundred men.* Syn.-Sergeant.) **came to him, asking for help.**
6 "Lord," he said, my servant lies at home paralyzed and in terrible suffering.
7 Jesus said to him, "I will go and heal him." (Expresses Jesus' compassion.)
8 The centurion replied, Lord, I do not deserve to have you come under my roof. (Suggests: He didn't want Jesus to defile Himself in a Gentiles home or saw himself as a sinner.) **But just say the word, and my servant will be healed.**

A Roman officer humbly places his faith in Jesus' divine power and authority to heal his servant.

Message & Application 💻=🌎

- ❖ Shows how believers are not to allow pride, power, or position to keep us from humbly reaching out to Jesus and asking for help.
- ❖ Teaches how great faith knows "Who" to turn to for help in times of suffering and despair. (Is Jesus your first choice or your last resort?)
- ❖ Calls for a compassionate heart that is acting on behalf of family and friends who are paralyzed by sin and who need Jesus' help. (V. 6)
- ❖ Calls for coming empty-handed, that we have no merits or goodness to offer God, but are solely dependent on His grace. (V. 8a)
- ⊶ Even today, believers are to come in the same spirit of humility, owning ourselves as unworthy and undeserving of any special favors from God, that we're always dependent on His mercy and grace.

8:9 For I myself am a man under authority (i.e. Subject to Caesar) **with soldiers under me. I tell this one, 'Go** (i.e. In exercises, marches, battles, death) **and he goes; and that one, 'Come,'** (i.e. Call to duty/arms) **and he comes. I say to my servant, Do this, and he does it.** (i.e. Orders are obediently followed & obeyed)

As a superior officer's orders are followed & obeyed, how much more will sin and sickness obey Christ's authority!

Message & Application

- ❖ Shows believers how Jesus' power & authority outranks and exceeds any sin, sickness, and problem we may be facing! (cf. Eph. 3:20)
- ❖ Encourages believers in knowing that with Jesus our healing and deliverance comes from the highest authority, God Himself!
- ⊶ Even today, believers can walk away with the confidence of knowing that whatever we're going through Jesus has charge & authority over it.

8:10 When Jesus heard this, he was astonished and said to those following him, "I tell you the truth, I have not found anyone in Israel with such great faith. (Syn.-humble, persevering, rare, unwavering, unconditional.)
11 I say to you that many (i.e. Gentiles) **will come from the east and the west** (Viz. All over the world.) **and will take their places at the feast with Abraham, Isaac, and Jacob in the Kingdom of heaven.** (Expresses: Future Messianic banquet. Patriarchs participation, having lived by faith under the old convent.)
12 But the subjects of the kingdom (i.e. Jews) **will be thrown outside into the darkness,** (Metph-Hell) **where there will be weeping and gnashing** (i.e. Grinding) **of teeth.** (Expresses sorrow and remorse, mixed with great suffering, torment, and pain in hell for having rejected Christ.)

Many from all around the world who put their faith in Jesus will be Saved, whereas Israel who rejected Christ will be lost.

<u>Message & Application</u> 💻=🌎

- ❖ Shows believers how Christ honors the type of faith that doesn't set limits on what He can do and accomplish in our lives. (cf. Heb. 11:1-13)
- ❖ Calls for a faith that doesn't need signs, wonders, or facts to prove to us that Jesus is real and working in our lives! (cf. Matt. 28:20)
- ❖ Calls for the kind of faith that will keep praising God despite the challenges, trials, and setbacks of life! (cf. 2-Corn. 12:7-10)
- ❖ Calls for a faith that believes God can break us out of the cycle of sin and any other problem were struggling with regardless of the situation.
- 🔑 Even today, believers need the same type of faith, that despite our battles with drugs, depression, alcohol, pornography, etc. we're still trusting Jesus to heal us and give us the breakthrough were looking for.

8:13 Then Jesus said to the centurion, It will be done just as you believed it would. And his servant was healed at that very hour. (Instantly/immediately)

As a result of the Centurions faith in Jesus' power and authority, his servant is immediately healed.

<u>Message & Application</u> 💻=🌎

- ❖ Shows believers how Christ always meets us in our crises, seeing that we get the healing and relief we so desperately need.
- ❖ Teaches how faith opens the door to seeing God's amazing grace and power moving in our lives. (cf. James 1:6-8)
- ❖ Teaches how faith brings God's power to bear upon any circumstance!
- 🔑 Even today for believers the quality of our trust & faith in Christ plays a major role in what Jesus can accomplish and do in our lives.

From this verse here (V. 14) to verse (V. 15) Jesus displays His healing power over sickness and illness.

Jesus Heals Many-(N.I.V.)

8:14 When Jesus came into Peter's house,-◙ (After that days healing miracles Jesus continued to Peter's home for rest and refreshments.) **he saw Peter's mother-in-law** (Suggests: Peter was married and caring for his wife's widowed mother.) **lying in bed with a fever.** (i.e. The fever was keeping her bedridden. High fever-{Luke 4:38}-That the illness was gravely serious, even life threatening)
15 He touched her hand (Expresses a gesture of tenderness and compassion. Or the means in which the miracle was produced.) **and the fever left her, and she got up and began to wait on him.** (Ministering-K.J.V..-1247-*"To be an attendant", "To serve and wait upon"*. Prepared a meal.-L.B.V. Suggests: The healing was instantaneous, that she recovered in both health and strength. That serving dinner was a gesture of her gratitude for Jesus having healed her.)

Displays Jesus' power & authority to heal & restore those who are suffering.

Message & Application 💻=🌎

- ❖ Shows believers as we invite Jesus into our lives He'll start to lift our burdens, fix our issues, and get us back on our feet again!
- ❖ Teaches how the Lord cares for His own, often giving us strength for the hour and day even before we ask!
- ❖ Displays how a grateful and thankful heart in all that Jesus has done for us will look for ways to use our healing for His service.
- ❖ Calls for reaching out in using our recovery to encourage others in theirs. (Will you get up and help drug addicts in their sobriety!)
- ❖ Teaches how Jesus brings not only healing & health but also restores purpose & meaning to our lives. (Know you were "Saved to Serve"!)
- ❖ Teaches that when the Lord gives us faith & hope, or when He brings us through something it's for a reason, to better praise and serve Him!
- ⊶ Even today in what ways have you used the Lord's help in getting you out of that addiction and difficult mess you were in to better serve and minister for Him? (cf. 2-Corn. 5:14-15, Eph. 2:1-5)
- ☞ Many use this verse to refute the Roman Catholic Church's position on celibacy for Priest's, seeing that Peter (first Pope) was himself married.
- ➢ Miracles metaphorical implications suggests:
    - Christ's love & concern for believers in their service to Him.
    - Christ's acceptance of women into ministry.

From this verse here (V. 16) to verse (V. 17) Jesus displays His power & authority over demonic forces.

8:16 When evening came (Suggests: Due to the prohibition against working on the Sabbath, they waited until it was over.-{Ex.20:8-10}) **many who were demon-possessed** (1139-*To be possessed or vexed by a demonic spirit*) **were brought to him,** (i.e. While at Peter's house.) **and he drove out** (i.e. Exorcized) **the spirits with a word** (Suggests: Unlike other exorcists who used rites and incantations, Jesus used His own power and authority.) **and healed all the sick.**

Jesus displays His power & authority over evil spirits and demonic forces.

Message & Application 💻=🌍

- ❖ Shows believers Jesus' power & authority to heal whatever sin and sickness that's been tormenting and afflicting our lives.
- ❖ Displays Jesus' boundless love and compassion for the suffering, that no one is ever an inconvenience, nuisance, or low priority to Him!
- ❖ Calls for a compassionate heart in bringing those who have been robbed of their sobriety, morals, and sanity to Jesus that they be healed.
- ❖ Displays how Jesus heals all people irrespective of their sin, history, status, background, or age, turning none away who come to Him.
- ❖ Teaches how when Jesus is shared whole communities can be healed, changed, and transformed!
- ❖ Calls for trusting that God has an answer, even if it goes against what professional counseling, therapy, and medical wisdom may say.
- ❖ Teaches how there is no sin, perversion, or deviant behavior in existence that Christ Jesus can't defeat, subdue, and overcome!
- 🗝 Even today, believers can count on Jesus' help in setting us free from the demonic voices behind anger, frustration, unfairness, depression, addiction, pornography, homosexuality, and anything else we face!

Disorders that Jesus can Heal

- Personality/Mental disorders
- Eating disorders
- Obsessive-compulsive disorders
- Anxiety/Panic disorders
- Substance/Addiction disorders
- Posttraumatic stress disorders

8:17 This (i.e. Jesus' divine healing power over demons and sickness.-{V.16}) **was to fulfill what was spoken** (700 years earlier) **through the prophet Isaiah:** {Is. 53:4 LXX} **"He took up** (353-*To seize, remove.* Syn.-addressed, tackled, dealt with, unburden.) **our infirmities** (769-*Lack of strength, feebleness of health or sickness, of trials & troubles.* Syn.-miseries, struggles, weaknesses, baggage, etc.) **and carried our diseases.**(sicknesses-K.J.V. Sorrows.-{Is. 53:4} Syn.-anguish, afflictions, griefs, pains, wounds, brokenness. Expresses: Taken together Christ's work in alleviating the spiritual maladies and evil effects of the fall.)

Jesus' power over demonic forces fulfilled Isaiah's prophecy of the Messiah bringing deliverance over the sickness of sin.

Message & Application 💻=🌎

- ❖ Shows how Jesus came not only to Save us from the penalty of sin, but also from the curse and sickness of sin as well. (cf. 1-Pet. 2:24-25)
- ❖ Teaches how Jesus wants to bring complete healing and wholeness to every part of our lives, both body, soul, and spirit!
- ❖ Displays the ultimate healing work of Christ in taking away the deeper spiritual issues and underlining causes of our sins. (cf. Jer. 17:9)
- ❖ Teaches how believers no longer have to bear the wounds of sin, guilt, and shame alone, knowing that Jesus carried them away on the Cross.
- ❖ Comforts believers in having Jesus' presence standing beside us through the daily hurt, pains, and burdens of life.
- ❖ Teaches how the Lord identifies with us, that He knows & understands the inner pain of rejection, betrayal, loneliness, and loss.
- ❖ Invites believers in surrendering our emotional wounds/baggage over to Jesus' healing touch, that we can leave the torture of the past behind.

-Took up our infirmities & diseases-Meaning: The work of Christ in reversing the effects of the curse of living in a fallen world. That in the Atonement Jesus provided not only physical healing (to be more fully realized at the resurrection). But also spiritual healing in carrying away all the guilt, shame, bondage, and sickness that sin produces as well.

🗝 Even today, believers can bring the emotional wounds of abuse, anger, fear, guilt, grief, bitterness, resentment, frustration, despair, hopelessness, etc. to Jesus for healing and strength to move past it.

☞ This verse here is not teaching that believers will have perfect health and never get sick or struggle, for even the Apostles suffered from illnesses.-(2-Corn. 12:7-10, Rom. 7:15-25) But rather assures Christ's work in bringing healing and wholeness over the emotional pains & hurts that's been plaguing our lives.

From this verse here (V. 18) to verse (V. 22) Jesus teaches on counting the cost in discipleship.

The Cost of Following Jesus-(N.I.V.)

8:18 When Jesus saw (1492-*Primarily denoting to perceive, notice, discern.* Syn.-appraised, evaluated, gauged, ascertained.) **the crowd around him,** (i.e. Not the sick, but rather those who were only interested in Jesus' miracles than any real desire in having their hearts and life's changed by Him.) **he gave orders to cross to the other side of the lake.** (i.e. Leaving Capernaum sailing east across the sea of Galilee to a Gentile area known as the Decapolis.-{V. 28} Metph.-The willingness in leaving the kingdom of sin/darkness for the kingdom of light, or the willingness in leaving all for a greater commitment to Christ.)

Because the crowds were only curious of His popularity, Jesus separates the earnest from the superficial.

Message & Application 

- ❖ Shows believers how Christ wants full commitment, not casual loyalty. (When it comes to Jesus are you a spectator, a follower, or just a fan?).
- ❖ Warns against superficial and half-hearted commitment, that Jesus wants authentic converts, not part-time followers and hanger-on's .
- ❖ Calls for reevaluating our commitment to Jesus, is it exclusive, total, and wholehearted, or just casual? (Is your faith serious or superficial)
- ❖ Teaches how we're either fully committed or we're not, that we can't have one foot in the boat and one foot in the world.
- ❖ Teaches if we're going to get on board with Jesus we need to get out of our comfort zones in all that is safe, comfortable, and convenient.
- ❖ Displays how many only want the benefits and blessings of Jesus, without any of the demands and requirements that go with it.
- 🗝 Even today we need to go beyond just showing up to church and warming the pews, to growing and maturing in a relationship with Jesus, becoming the type of person He has called us to be.

Signs of being a Nominal Christian

- You only show up to church to catch up with friends and the latest gossip, and not what's behind the message.
- You prioritize sports, movies, and going out with friends above bible study, prayer, witness, and outreach.
- You shy away from confrontations of faith & practice or passively sit by while others are on the road to hell.

8:19 Then a teacher of the law (certain scribe-K.J.V. Jewish religious teacher) **came to him and said, "Teacher, I will follow you wherever you go."** (Expresses his eagerness and enthusiasm in becoming a permanent disciple.)
20 Jesus replied, "Foxes have holes-◙ (i.e. Homes) **and birds of the air have nests,** (i.e. Homes) **but the Son of Man** (Expresses a Messianic title signifying the Messiah's human origins and headship over mankind.-{Dan 7:13-14}) **has nowhere to lay his head."** (Expresses Jesus' willingness in suffering rejection from His own people. Or Jesus' humility in emptying Himself of His glory in heaven to suffer for sin. Taken together is calling for believers to count the costs of hardships, trials, and sacrifices as we follow Jesus.)

Believers must be willing to count the cost of hardships, poverty, and even homelessness as they follow Jesus.

Message & Application 💻=🌍

- ❖ Shows how believers must be willing to sacrifice the luxuries and comforts of life in our commitment and walk with Jesus.
- ❖ Teaches those who count the cost with a clear & objective mind won't be tempted to turn back when hardships, difficulties, and trials come.
- ❖ Warns against rash commitments, that being a disciple of Christ is not an emotional spur of the moment decision but a lifelong call.
- ❖ Displays how some can respond with enthusiasm at the outset but are unprepared for the hardships and daily struggles that lie ahead.
- ❖ Calls for laying down anything in our devotion and service to Christ, knowing how much the Lord has suffered and sacrificed for us.
- ❖ Warns against following Christ for selfish reasons. (Don't be wooed to Jesus with promises of prosperity, wealth, or a carefree life).

🗝 Even today, believers can make a spur of the moment decision for Christ with no real follow-through of what it might cost them personally in the way of giving up certain lifestyles, luxuries, jobs, promotions, status, popularity, and friendships along the way.

☞ Jesus is not saying that we must sell all our possessions, become homeless, and live on beans & burritos the rest of our lives. But rather we must be willing to give up any comforts and pursuits that might become potential obstacles in our walk and relationship with Christ.

☞ Jesus is not being overly demanding, but rather is either challenging the man's commitment in his willingness in giving up all the luxuries, honor, and prestige that came with being a Scribe. Or was confronting the man with the truth, that his real motive was only for temporal advantages of prosperity, fame, and glory by cashing in on Christ's popularity.

8:21 Another disciple (i.e. Not of the twelve, but the multitudes. That after great contemplation and effort he made a decision for Christ.) **said to him, Lord** (2962-*Sir, master.)* **first** (Expresses a first conditional clause.) **let me go and bury my father.** (Expresses: Not of burial preparations, but in caring for his aged father until he collects his inheritance. Suggests: Unlike the scribe who was "Overeager and Unprepared", this man was "Under-eager and Reluctant".) **22 But Jesus told him, "Follow me, and let the dead** (i.e. Unsaved/non-disciple. Expresses Spiritually dead or dead in sin.) **bury their own dead."** (i.e. Let those who have not responded to the Gospel or to Christ see to mundane things.)

Commitment to Jesus takes precedence over all other obligations and loyalties including family.

Message & Application 💻=🌎

- ❖ Shows how believers are to prioritize following Jesus first and foremost over all other duties and relationships.
- ❖ Warns against waiting for a convenient time to serve the Lord. (Uncommitted mind will find some excuse or other pressing need!).
- ❖ Teaches how it's not Jesus who must adjust Himself around our lives and our schedules, but it's we who must adjust our lives around Jesus!
- ❖ Reminds believers no matter the good intentions and noble causes we embark on, nothing trumps Jesus' call on our lives. (cf. Matt. 10:37)
- 🗝 Even today many often plead the requirements of work, careers, and family obligations to duck and dodge Jesus' greater call on their lives. Or they will try to justify their postponement in coming to Jesus on the grounds that they're still in school, or they haven't found the right Church, or they just need more time to straighten their lives out first.
- ☞ Most soften the harshness of Jesus' reply by suggesting the father was not actually dead. If he was the man would have been home mourning and following the Jewish custom of burying the dead within the first 24-hours and not talking with Jesus. But rather, he was only asking that he be allowed to take care of his aged father until he died.
- ☞ Jesus is not calling for abandoning one's responsibility to family, but rather is saying when choices have to be made, duty goes to Him first'

Similar Excuses used Today:

- Let me wait until I finish school or get my degree.
- Let me wait until I get married or divorced.
- Let me wait until I get rid of my vices & bad habits.
- Let me wait until I find a good Church.

From this verse here (V. 23) to verse (V. 27) Teaches on Jesus' ability to rescue us from the daily storms & trials of life.

Jesus Calms the Storm-(N.I.V.)

8:23 Then he (i.e. Jesus) **got into the boat-◙ and his disciples followed him.**
24 Without warning, a furious storm (great tempest-K.J.V.-4578-*A great shaking, seismic, quake.* Syn.-typhoon, hurricane, gale-force winds, furious squall.-{Mark 4:37} Metph.-Life's unexpected storms & trials.) **came up on the lake,-◙** (Sea of Galilee) **so that the waves swept over the boat.** (Suggests: The boat was taking on water & being flooded. Metph.-overwhelmed, sinking, overwrought.) **But Jesus was sleeping.** (On a cushion in the stern of the boat.-{Mark 4:38}. Expresses: The humanity side of Jesus, being exhausted from that day's ministry. Or Jesus' confidence/trust in the Father's care and protection.)
25 The disciples went and woke him, saying, "Lord, save us! (Syn.-rescue, protect.) **We're going to drown!".** (Suggests: This was no ordinary storm, for even the disciples, who were seasoned fishermen/sailors were all frightened.)

Shows believers no matter the storms & trials of life, we can have faith that Jesus will see us through it.

Message & Application 💻=🌍

- ❖ Shows believers how in the storms & trials of life we can always cry out to Jesus for help. (Know you can run to Jesus in times of trouble!)
- ❖ Teaches how God doesn't guarantee He's going to keep us from the storms of life, but that He's going to be there for us when they come!
- ❖ Teaches even when doing good & following the Lord trials are bound to come, but it's how we stay trusting in Jesus that gets us through it! (Know storms are temporary and will soon pass, so don't bail!)
- ❖ Teaches how God never promised us a life of smooth sailing, but of safe passage. (If God brings you to it, He will bring you through it!).
- ❖ Reminds believers just because bad things happen does not mean God doesn't love us or care for us, or that we've done something wrong.
- ❖ Prepares believers how it's not if storms come, but when they come, and how we can trust in Jesus to get us through it!
- ❖ Reminds believers when the storms of life hit, rather than wait to the last minute or try to handle them ourselves we need to cry out to Jesus!

⊶ Even today when were going through the storms of a divorce, financial crises, health issue, job loss, etc. It can feel that Jesus just doesn't care, or that He's checked out on us. Not realizing the whole time Jesus was right there in the boat with us, not allowing anything to sink or defeat us! (Trust Jesus to give you the strength to carry you through it!)

8:26 He replied, You of little faith, (Syn.-weak, doubtful, distrustful. Expresses: Not that they had no faith, but that they lost sight of Who was with them, God Himself, creator of the Universe) **why are you so afraid?** (fearful, anxious) **Then he got up and rebuked the winds and the waves, and it was completely calm. 27 The men were amazed** (Syn.-awestruck, terrified-{Mark 4:41}) **and asked, "What kind of man** (mortal) **is this?** (Expresses a rhetorical question, denoting beyond mortal man, having divine power as well, that He must be God Himself!) **Even the winds and the waves obey him!"** (Expresses Jesus' divine authority not only over spiritual forces but over the material world as well.)

Displays Jesus' divine power & authority in calming the trials and storms of life.

Message & Application =

- ❖ Shows how believers never have to fear, that Jesus will be there to help us weather any trial or storm that comes our way.
- ❖ Calls for trusting that if God is leading us to do something, He will also be there to provide our safety and security in it!
- ❖ Warns how its a great dishonor to the Lord when we take our sight off of His love and power and start to allow our fears to control us instead.
- ❖ Teaches how we can all fall short, having seen the Lord work great miracles in the past, but still distrust Him for the presence.
- ❖ Teaches how worry has no place in the Christian life when Jesus is with us. (Know that with Jesus in your boat you'll never go under!).
- ❖ Displays how there are no storms beyond Christ's ability to quell and control. (Know there's no problem Jesus can't see you through!).
- ❖ Displays the calming effect that Jesus can have on our hearts, giving us the peace to cope with any crises and turmoil that comes our way!
- ❖ Reminds believers of the kind of mighty Savior/God we serve, that there's nothing in life that He can't stop, fix, or put down. (V. 27)

–***You of little faith***-Meaning: Rebuke is variously attributed to either:

- Failing to trust in Jesus' divine power, having already witnessed that day's miracle healings.
- Failing to trust in Jesus' divine presence in protecting and securing their safety, having commanded the trip across the sea.

⊶ Even today, believers never have to worry or fear, knowing that Jesus will give us the peace & strength to deal with any tragedy, calamity, cr difficulty that comes our way. Or at worst we die and go to be with the Lord in heaven anyway! (cf. John 14:1-3, 16:33, Rom. 8:17- 18, 35-39, Philp. 1:21- 23, 2-Tim. 1:7, Ps. 107:23-31)

Types of Storms Believers may face

- **Economic-**Unemployment, recessions.
- **Spiritual-**Temptations, addictions.
- **Health-**Sickness, illnesses, death.
- **Domestic**-Homelessness, poverty.
- **Relationships**-Divorces, abuse.
- **Natural disasters**- Accidents, violence.

Why God Allows the Storms of life

- **In order to test & strengthen our faith.** (Producing patience, steadfastness, perseverance, hope, and trust).
- **In order to grow & perfect us in holiness**. (Producing character, obedience, strength, Christ-likeness).
- **In order to edify & encourage others.** (Produces compassion, empathy, caring, mercy, personal-testimony, witness).
- **In order to bring us back to God.** (Produces remorse, guilt, despair, repentance, self-surrender, Salvation).
- **In order to correct & discipline.** (Keeping us from pride, arrogance, self-righteousness, judgmental attitudes).

How to Overcome life's Storms

- Keep trusting in God's love, grace, peace, and strength.
- Keep trusting that God is in full control of the situation.
- Keep trusting that God has a purpose for it, and is working all things for our good.
- Keep focused on God's word, promises, and plans for your life.
- Know that storms are temporary and will not last forever, but will soon pass.
- See storms as opportunities to grow and witness to others of our faith in Christ.

From this verse here (V. 28) to the end of the chapter, Jesus displays His power & authority over the demonic forces of evil.

The Two Demon-possessed Men-(N.I.V.)

8:28 When he arrived at the other side in the region of the Gadarenes,-◙ (i.e. A Gentile area on the east side of the sea of Galilee, not far from the town of "Gadara" one of ten cities of the Decapolis) **two demon-possessed men coming from the tombs-◙** (Caves which served as their homes.) **met him. They were so violent** (Syn.-difficult, dangerous, hard to deal with.) **that no-one could pass that way.** (i.e. They harassed & terrorized those who walked by. No one could bind him, not even with a chain.-{cf. Mark 5:3} Jesus asked him, "What is your name", "Legion" [4-6 thousand soldiers] he replied for we are many.-{Mark 5:9})
29 "What do you want with us, (Expresses resentment at Jesus' intruding into their realm.) **Son of God? they shouted. "Have you come here to torture us before the appointed time?** (Expresses their fear of eternal torment on the Day of Judgment in the lake of fire.-{Rev. 20:14} Or being cast out from the men.)

Aware of Jesus' divine power & authority the demons fear being condemned to hell.

Message & Application 💻=🌎

- ❖ Shows the powerful arrival of Jesus into our lives, setting us free from the sin and demonic influences that are controlling and tormenting us.
- ❖ Displays the rescuing work of Jesus in crossing all boundaries in order to disrupt the sin that's been controlling our lives.
- ❖ Encourages believers though our demons can keep us away from everything else, they cannot keep us away from Jesus.
- ❖ Warns of the self-destructive power of sin, making our lives unmanageable and ungovernable. (cf. Mark 5:5, John 10:10)
- ❖ Warns of what sin can do in cutting us off from home, family, and community, condemning us to a life of loneliness and isolation.
- 🗝 Even today we become our own worst enemies when we open our self's up to the wrong things of drugs, alcohol, and pornography. Causing us to eventually lose everything, our freedom, marriages, relationships, house, car, kids, job, etc. Not to mention our dignity and self-respect as well.-(cf. Luke 8:27) Or even worse, ending up in the gutter or jail and wondering how we got there?
- ➢ Illustrates several things about demons:
  - They shun being in a disembodied state.
  - They know of the general judgment.
  - They cannot act without divine permission.

The Origins and Existence of Demons:

- Appears most likely to be that of the fallen angels who rebelled with Satan against God, and were cast out of heaven down to earth.-(Rev. 12:4-9, Jude 1:6, Is. 14:12-15, Ezek. 28:12-17)
- Some teach that demons are the result of the union of fallen angels with the daughters of men.-(Gen. 6:1-4) (Not widely accepted by most)
- Others hold to what's called the "Gap theory" that demons are a pre-Adamic race who lived in the first earth age before God created Adam & Eve. (Most reject this having no biblical basis)

Purposes in Demonic Possession:

- To destroy and torment human beings. (cf. 1-Sam. 6:14-15, Mark 9:17-21, Luke 13:16)
- To seduce people to sin and do evil. (cf. Gen. 3:2-5, 1-Sam. 18:10, Luke 22:3, 2-Pet. 2:14)
- To frustrate God's purposes and plans. (cf. Matt. 16:23, John 10:10, Eph. 6:12, Rev. 17:13-14)
- To propagate idolatry and false doctrines. (cf. Deut. 32:17, 1-Corn. 10:20-21, 1-Tim. 4:1)
- To oppose the spread of the Gospel. (cf. 1-Tim. 4:1-3, 1-John 4:1-6, 2-Corn. 11:13-16)

Areas of Demonic Afflictions:

Mental Disorders

- Insanity (Paranoia)-(Mark. 9:22)
- Manic depression (Suicidal)-(Mark 9:22)
- Masochism (Self-mutilation) (Mark 5:5)
- Hysteria (Madness) (Luke 9:39)

Spiritual Disorders

- Temptations (Sinful compulsions)
- Immorality (Sexual perversions)
- Vises (Addictions, drugs, alcohol)
- Occultism (fortune-telling, Satanism)

8:30 Some distance from them a large herd of pigs was feeding.
31 The demons begged Jesus If you drive us out, send us into the herd of pigs. (Suggests: Their plea is attributed to either as a last ditch effort in avoiding being tortured in hell, or a result of their hatred for all of God's creatures, or a ploy to stir up hatred for the Jews. [The latter favored by most due to the people's hostility towards Jesus for ruining their livelihoods].-{cf. V. 34})
32 He said to them, "Go!" So they came out and went into the pigs, and the whole herd (2000-{Mark 5:13}) **rushed down** (i.e. Stampeded, mad-dash, panic-stricken.) **the steep bank into the lake and died** (i.e. Drowned.) **in the water.**

Jesus' divine power & authority extends even over that of evil and demonic forces.

Message & Application 💻=🌎

- ❖ Shows believers Jesus' power over the sin & evil that's in our lives, going no further than He permits, doing no more than He allows.
- ❖ Displays the uncalculated value Christ places on every tortured soul in seeing to our healing and deliverance.
- ❖ Warns of the dangerous consequences of living in sin, rushing us ultimately over the edge to our own ruin and doom.
- ❖ Warns how Satan's only goal is to hurry us towards sin, ruin, and self-destruction. (So stay spiritually vigilant and prepared!). (cf. John 10:10)
- 🗝 Even today some will try to bargain & negotiate terms of Salvation & repentance. That Jesus can be Lord in one area of our lives but not in other areas where we want to maintain authority and control
- ➢ Jesus' permitting them to go into the swine is attributed to either:
  - Jesus as Master over nature has the right to do as He pleases.
  - They're being a fitting host, unclean spirits for unclean animals.
  - To prevent them from becoming a menace to other people.
  - As punishment on the Jewish owners for keeping unclean animals.

Traits of Demon Possession:

- They are often violent, hateful, abusive, combative, disobedient, rebellious, self-destructive, and antisocial.
- They have an aversion towards religious objects or are resistant towards the things of God, church, the bible.
- They have an unhealthy interest in immoral and demonic activities. (i.e. occultism, pornography, etc.)
- They have a fixation & preoccupation with death and the dead or the torturing and tormenting of animals.

8:33 Those tending the pigs ran off, went into the town and reported all this, (Pigs drowning) **including what had happened to the demon-possessed men. 34 Then the whole town went out to meet Jesus.** (i.e. Probably with the attention to arrest Jesus for ruining their livelihoods.) **And when they saw him,** (Either Jesus or the man previously possessed by the legion of demons.) **they pleaded with him to leave their region** (i.e. Gadarenes. Suggests: That they were more concerned with the economic loss than the healing of the man.)

The owners fearing for their livelihoods asked Jesus to leave their region.

Message & Application

- ❖ Shows believers the danger of misplaced values, putting more importance on revenue & possessions above a relationship with Jesus.
- ❖ Teaches those who have witnessed and experienced Christ's healing power will want to share it with family, friends, and neighbors. (V. 33)
- ❖ Warns the foolishness of having Jesus leave us without finishing His work in us, fearing the demands and sacrifices are too great.
- ❖ Teaches how no upheavals, inconvenience, or personal costs should be too much to endure in light of all that Christ brings to the table.

–***Leave their region***-Meaning: Variously attributed to either:

- Out of concern for their livelihood, fearing the loss of any more pigs could have a serious financial impact on their income.
- As a result of their own sinfulness.
- Saw the drowning of the pigs as a judgment from God for keeping unclean animals, therefore feared further punishment. (Luke 8:37)

- ❖ Prepares believers for the changes and disruptions Jesus will bring into our lives. That Jesus' values will often clash with our values.

⊶ Even today many are hesitant in receiving Jesus, fearing that it will come at the cost of changing their lifestyle or having to deal with some things that are not right in their lives. Or they will simply shut Jesus out because He upsets the balance of their lives when it comes to their personal comforts, pleasures, and future plans.

Ways People shun Jesus today:

- Fear of losing their way of life, freedom, lifestyle.
- Fear of losing family and friends.
- Fear of losing jobs, positions, and promotions.
- Fear of losing reputation, standing, and influence.
- Fear of losing securities, comforts, and pleasures.

Chapter Nine

From this verse here (V. 1) to verse (V. 8) Jesus displays His power & authority over the paralyzing effects of sin and guilt.

Jesus Heals a Paralytic-(N.I.V.)

9:1 Jesus stepped into a boat, crossed over and came to his own town. (i.e.
Capernaum, a city adopted by Jesus. Teaching at Peter's house.-{Luke 5:17})
2 Some men brought to him a paralytic, lying on a mat. (i.e. A makeshift
stretcher. Finding no room in the house because of the crowd, they lowered
him through the roof.-{Luke 5:18-19}) **When Jesus saw their faith** (Expresses
both the paralytic in consenting, and the effort/determination of the men
bringing him to Jesus.) **he said to the paralytic, "Take heart,** (i.e. Cheer up, perk
up, don't despair.) **son; your sins are forgiven".** (Expresses: Was meant to ease
the man's fear, thinking he was too great a sinner to be healed by God. Or that
his paralyses was a result of his own sinful/reckless behavior. {cf. James 1:14-15})

Jesus responds to the man's more urgent need of spiritual healing and announces his sins forgiven.

Message & Application 💻=🌎

- ❖ Shows believers how our greatest urgency is not our physical needs, but our spiritual needs in having our sins forgiven and our guilt lifted.
- ❖ Calls for caring enough in having the same determination in getting our family & friends to Jesus that they may be healed & Saved!
- ❖ Teaches those who are sorry for what they've done can take heart that God no longer condemns them or holds their sins against them. (Stand on the assurance of God's forgiveness, not the sins of the past).
- ❖ Calls for allowing Jesus to get to the real issues, that He's not just here to treat the symptoms but also the root cause!
- ❖ Teaches how Jesus heals us where we need it the most, not necessarily what we want the most. (Trust Christ to minister to your real need!).
- ⊶ Even today our greatest need is not about having our social, financial, or health problems resolved. But about allowing Jesus to get to the issues behind our drinking, gambling, and self-destructive behavior.

The Healing Power of Forgiveness:

- Brings freedom & hope in the midst of guilt, shame, grief, rejection, and despair.
- Brings a sense of meaning, purpose, value, self-worth/importance, self-esteem, usefulness.
- Brings renewed relationship, fellowship, love, companionship, the connection of belonging.

9:3 At this (i.e. Jesus' declaration having forgiven the paralytic's sins.-{V.2}) **some of the teachers of the law said to themselves "This fellow** (3353-*A plague, pest, a pestilent.*) **is blaspheming!"** (987-*To speak slanderously of God, or to take prerogatives belonging to God.* Punishable by stoning).-{cf. Lev. 24:16}

The religious leaders accuse Jesus of blasphemy for proclaiming rights that belong only to God.

Message & Application 💻=🌎

- ❖ Shows how a heart that is skeptical & critical can block Jesus from doing a divine work and healing in our lives.
- ❖ Teaches those who are legalistic and uncharitable at heart will always become critical when someone gets healed and Saved by grace.
- ❖ Warns against allowing doubt and discouragement to set in that we start questioning who Jesus is, or whether our healing is real or not.
- ⊶ Even today, believers can give into doubt and frustration after falling into some sin. That we know what God has said and what He's spoken in our situation. Yet we begin to question our Salvation & forgiveness, that maybe we didn't believe right, or we didn't pray the right prayer.

9:4 Knowing their thoughts, (Expresses Jesus' divine Omniscient.) **Jesus said, "Why do you entertain** (Syn.-foster, harbor) **evil thoughts in your hearts?** (Expresses their hardhearted skepticism and unbelief in Jesus' claims.-{V. 3})
5 Which is easier: to say, 'Your sins (266-*missing the mark, falling short of the glory of God*) **are forgiven' or to say, 'Get up and walk'** (Expresses a rhetorical question, implying that neither would have been too difficult for Jesus.)

Jesus would not have pronounced the man's sins forgiven if He wasn't God!

Message & Application

- ❖ Shows how failure to see Jesus' ability to heal & Save us is not an intellectual problem, but a matter of the heart that is disbelieving.
- ❖ Displays how it's not that Jesus hasn't revealed enough, the problem is that there is something in our hearts that keeps us from receiving Him.
- ❖ Teaches how the problem is not a lack of physical evidence or proof, but a spiritual paralysis of the heart that is limiting God.
- ❖ Warns how even the sins of the heart are open, that nothing is hidden from God's sight. (Guard your heart against doubt and skepticism!).
- ⊶ Even today, believers can struggle in the same way, that it's easy for us to believe that God can Save us from our sins. But that it's more difficult for God to forgive us, heal us, or meet our financial burdens.

9:6 But so that you may know that the Son of Man (i.e. Jesus. Expresses a Messianic title signifying the Messiah's human origins and divine headship over humanity.) **has authority on earth to forgive sins.** (863-*To send forth, send away, remit.* Syn.-pardon, atone) **"Then he said to the paralytic, "Get up, take your mat and go home."** (Suggests: The man went home healed in both body & soul, no longer bound by sin or guilt. That he was to be a living witness to his family or to repay them for the care & support they had given him for so long.) **7 And the man got up and went home.** (Praising & glorifying God.-{Luke 5:25})

Jesus proves His divine power & authority to forgive sins by healing the paralytic.

Message & Application =

- ❖ Shows believers the transforming power of Jesus' word in giving us the strength to walk away from the sin that's been paralyzing our lives.
- ❖ Teaches how Jesus will never call us to do something without giving us the strength to do it! (True faith will take Christ at His word!).
- ❖ Teaches as soon as we start to obey and act on what Christ commands will we begin to move forward in new life, healing, and wholeness!
- ❖ Teaches if Jesus' healing is going to take effect, we need to do our part in rolling up our bed of excuses, crutches, and blame games.
- ❖ Calls for acting on Jesus' word, that our sobriety and recovery is real, that we're not the same person as before!
- ⊶ Even today believers need to arm ourselves with the same attitude. That from here on out things are going to be different. That we're no longer tied to some sin, scandal, grudge, or failure of the past. That we can be set free from it, no longer having to drag it around with us.

9:8 When the crowd saw this, they were filled with awe; (marveled-K.J.V., A.V. Expresses a mixture of wonder, gratitude, and reverential fear.) **and they praised God, who had given such authority** (Syn.-power) **to men.** (Suggests: They were never moved to faith in Jesus' divine power, but only to admiration.)

The crowds were only filled with admiration over Jesus' healing work and never moved to faith.

Message & Application =

- ❖ Shows how believers can miss Jesus' divine presence when we only own Him as a mere man and not as God Himself!
- ⊶ Even today some can be honest enough to admit what they have seen and heard, but miss the fuller truths that Jesus is God in the flesh who can Save them from they're sins.

From this verse here (V. 9) to verse (V. 13) Jesus displays His love for outcasts & sinners, bringing them back to God.

The Calling of Matthew-(N.I.V.)

9:9 As Jesus went on from there, (i.e. From healing the Paralytic.) **he saw a man named Matthew sitting at the tax collector's booth.-◙** (Suggests: A makeshift hut or table set-up along trade routes.) **"Follow me,"** (190-*A call to discipleship.)* **he told him, and Matthew got up and followed him.** (Suggests: He immediately left his employment, wealth, became a permanent disciple.)

Jesus calls Matthew to Salvation and discipleship.

Message & Application 💻=🌎

- ❖ Shows Jesus' love & acceptance in reaching out to outcasts and sinners and bringing them back to God. (cf. 2-Corn. 5:18-19, Col. 1:13-22)
- ❖ Displays how Jesus actively seeks out and pursues lost and broken sinners, giving them a fresh start and a whole new lease on life!
- ❖ Teaches no matter how sinful, corrupt, or despicable a person may be, they're never beyond the reach of God's mercy and grace!
- ❖ Displays how Jesus doesn't ask for certain qualifications or approval first, that sinners can follow Him just the way they are!
- ❖ Teaches how Jesus' call to Salvation requires an immediate response, one without hesitation or reservation. (cf. Matt. 8:19-22)
- ➢ Even today we must be willing to leave all for Jesus, even if it comes at the cost of burning our bridges to a luxurious & promising future!

–***Tax collector***-Meaning: Jews who were hired by Rome to collect taxes for the state, mainly tariffs on goods (grain, wine, fruit, animals, etc.) Or transit dues for the use of roads, bridges, and harbors. Jewish Tax Collectors were regarded as traitors and collaborators by their own countrymen for their willingness in helping support a pagan Roman government. They were also considered sinners because of both their dishonesty in extorting more taxes than what was owed, as well as the fact that their work brought them into contact with unclean Gentiles.

-***Followed him***-Matthew's response is attributed to either:

- The powerful impact Jesus made on Matthew's heart & soul.
- Having already been familiar with Jesus' popularity as a Rabbi, understood the grace in which Christ was bestowing upon him.

⊶ Today the Church needs to take the same initiative in accepting people as they are, providing an environment where less-than-perfect people can find love, acceptance, and the encouragement to grow.

9:10 While Jesus was having dinner at Matthew's house, many tax collectors (i.e. Matthew's former associates.) **and "sinners"** (Syn.-thieves, scam artists, con artists, frauds, swindlers-L.B.V.) **came and ate with him and his disciples.**
11 When the Pharisees saw this, they asked his disciples, "Why does your teacher eat (Metph.-associate, defile himself.) **with tax collectors and sinners'?"** (Expresses: Not a sincere inquiry, but an accusation of religious impiety, having ceremonially defiled Himself by eating with those considered unclean. That if Jesus was a pious teacher as He claimed, how could He associate Himself with sinners? Suggests: Possibly a ploy to draw the disciples away from Jesus by causing them to revolt over such scandalous behavior.)

The Pharisees accuse Jesus of defiling Himself by keeping company with outcasts and sinners.

Message & Application 💻=🌎

❖ Shows believers who have experienced the Lord's grace & forgiveness will want to introduce their family, friends, and neighbors to Jesus.
❖ Displays how believers will want to invite former partners in crime to the One who pulled them out of their life of crime, booze, and drugs.
❖ Calls believers in using whatever employments, resources, and networking we have in bringing others into an encounter with Jesus.
❖ Warns against allowing the criticism & disapproval of others to keep us from reaching out to those who need the Lord's healing touch.
❖ Calls for never drawing the line when it comes to witnessing. (Know that every person is worth more than their worst act!). (V. 11)
❖ Warns how judgmental and critical attitudes can become obstacles in Saving others. (Rather than be faultfinders, be well-wishers!) (V. 11)
❖ Demonstrates how those who are disingenuous in their own Salvation are rarely supportive in the Salvation of others. (V. 11)
⊶ Even today, believers are not to allow the opinions of others to keep us from inviting certain people to Church. Or from spending time with those who are drug addicts, or with those who are in hospitals, clinics, and prisons. (Are you willing to rub shoulders with unsavory people?).
☞ Though believers are to isolate ourselves from sin, we're not to isolate ourselves from sinners. (Hate the sin, love the sinner). (cf.1-Corn. 5:9-11)
➢ Matthew's purpose in holding a feast for Jesus is attributed to either:
- To honor Christ for the grace He showed to him.
- As an opportunity to witness and have his friends and associates meet and hear Jesus.
- Was a farewell banquet celebrating the end of his career as a tax collector, and the beginning of a new career as a disciple.

9:12 On hearing this, (i.e. The Pharisees finding fault with Jesus for keeping company with sinners.-{V. 11}) **Jesus said, "It is not the healthy** (whole-K.J.V., Metph-Self-righteous, perfect, know-it-all's. Suggests: In context the Pharisees-{V. 11}) **who need a doctor,** (Metph-Savior) **but the sick.** (i.e. Murderers, rapists, child abusers, homosexuals, prostitutes, drunkards, drug addicts, etc.) **13 But go and learn what this means: 'I** (God) **desire mercy,** (1656-*Undeserved kindness or good will towards the afflicted.* Syn.-compassion, pity, sympathy.) **not sacrifice.'** (Metph.-religious rituals, Sunday worship, Churchgoing.) **For I have not come to call** (Metph.-Save, invite) **the righteous,** (Syn.-pious, blameless, self-righteous.) **but sinners.** (To repentance.-K.J.V.) {Hos. 6:6}

Shows how God wants not religious performance, but a heart of compassion and mercy for sinners.

Message & Application

- ❖ Shows how God comes not for those who think their perfect but those who know they're a hopeless sinner who needs His forgiveness.
- ❖ Reminds believers rather than fall on others with judgment and criticism, fall on them with the love and compassion of Jesus.
- ❖ Calls believers in reaching out to sinners, letting them know that we're not there to judge them, but to help them and encourage them.
- ❖ Teaches how God would rather we come with merciful hearts, knowing that nobody's perfect, that we all sin and fall short.
- ❖ Teaches rather than having a self-righteous attitude that is avoiding & shunning sinners, we should be reaching out with God's love for them!
- ⊶ Even today Christians/Church's should be places where sinners can come to get help and not feel judged and condemned.
- ☞ In a wider context teaches how Christ came not for the righteous but for those who know their lost sinners who need God's forgiveness. That the Gospel's invitation is open to everyone who is willing to throw themselves completely on God's Saving mercy & grace.

Ways to grow in Mercy & Compassion:

- Be willing to see potential & worth in others, rather than just their bad qualities.
- Be willing to seek God's help for those you discriminate against, or those who you are prejudiced against and find hard to love.
- Be willing to reach out and connect with those that you would normally avoid and shun.

From this verse here (V. 14) to verse (V. 17) Jesus teaches how religion must be practiced for the right reasons.

Jesus questioned About Fasting-(N.I.V.)

9:14 Then John's disciples came and asked him, "How is it that we and the Pharisees fast (Required only one day a year, Day of Atonement.-{Lev.23:27} But Jews observed it twice a week.)-{Luke 18:12} **but your disciples do not fast"?**

Jesus' disciples are criticized for not being as religiously pious and devout as John the Baptist and the Pharisees.

Message & Application

- ❖ Shows believers the dangers of focusing only on the external and outward motions of religion while neglecting the inner heart devotion.
- ❖ Displays how some only put on a religious show as a way of making themselves look pious and spiritual before God. (cf. Matt. 6:16-18)
- ❖ Teaches how some will call our devotion into question just because it doesn't fit with what a pious and religious person should look like.
- ⊶ Even today we can get in the habit of making our praying, tithing, and churchgoing as some sort of fast-track for scoring points with God.

9:15 Jesus answered, "How can the guests (5207-*Servants of the bridal hall who provided provisions for the wedding festivities.* Metph-disciples.) **of the bridegroom** (Metph.-Jesus) **mourn** (fast) **while he is with them? The time will come when the bridegroom will be taken from them;**(Expresses Jesus' violent arrest and crucifixion.) **then they will fast.** (i.e. Only until Jesus' resurrection.)

Christ's coming was a time for celebration, only after His crucifixion would the disciples fast.

Message & Application

- ❖ Shows how believers are to see that we're always making it about a personal and intimate relationship with Jesus and not about religion.
- ❖ Teaches how God wants us to fast for the appropriate reasons & right time, and not as some form of spiritual discipline or religious duty.
- ❖ Displays how in light of who Jesus is and all that He has done, can we be just as joyous when bad news comes as when good news comes.
- ❖ Teaches the more time we spend with Jesus, the less time will we feel miserable and down when going through hard times.
- ⊶ Even today if you have no joy or peace, maybe you need to get off the religious hamster wheel to resting in the grace/finished work of Christ.

9:16 "No-one sews a patch of unshrunk cloth-◙ (i.e. unwashed cloth. Metph-Jesus' teachings, Gospel of grace, New Covenant/dispensation.) **on an old garment,** (Metph-Jewish Law of works, Old Covenant, dispensation.) **for the patch will pull away from the garment,** (Suggests: Do to shrinkage when washed.) **making the tear worse.** (Expresses: Jesus is not just giving a sewing lesson but a common sense principle against mixing old things with new things)
17 Neither do men pour new wine (i.e. Unfermented wine. Metph-Gospel message, Grace, New Covenant.) **into old wineskins.-◙** (Suggests: The practice of pouring squeezed grapes into animal skins that had the legs and neck sewn up. Metph-Jewish Law of works, Old covenant.) **If they do, the skins will burst, the wine will run out and the wineskins will be ruined.** (Suggests: Because of the buildup of gasses during the fermentation process would stretch & tear the bag.) **No, they pour new wine into new wineskins,** (Suggests: New wineskins would be flexible enough to withstand the expanding gasses.) **and both are preserved."** (And no one after drinking the old wine wants the new, for he says the old is better.-{Luke 5:39} Expresses the reluctance of some to accept change, that their content with the status quo, and happy the way they are.)

God's New Covenant of mercy & grace is incompatible with the Old Jewish religious system of Law & works.

Message & Application 💻=🌎

- ❖ Shows how Jesus didn't come just to reform & patch up our life with more religion but to change and transform us with a whole new life!
- ❖ Teaches how being a Christian is not simply about making little life changes here and there, but rather about a radical change of life!
- ❖ Teaches how being a Christian is not some new novelty or religious brand to be added on, but a whole new way of life.
- ❖ Teaches how Jesus didn't come to make us a little better, or to help us over the humps in life, but to change us and transform us forever.
- ❖ Displays how Jesus doesn't settle for occupying just a little corner of our lives, but rather He wants all of our lives!
- ❖ Warns how traditionalism and inflexibility in religion can stifle God from doing a work on our hearts in growing and moving us forward.
- ❖ Warns how will only end up frustrated and ruined when we try to hold onto the old life while trying to live out the Gospel message.

🗝 Even today, believers can make the same mistake in wanting Jesus to fix-up one part of their lives while still holding onto their old life. Or they only show up to Church, hoping God will patch up their finances, marriages, and health issues with no real desire in allowing God to change them at their core level. Or they want Jesus in one part of their lives and not in other areas they consider private and off limits.

From this verse here (V. 18) to verse (V. 26) Jesus demonstrates His power & authority over death.

A dead Girl and a Sick Woman-(N.I.V.)

9:18 While he was saying this, (i.e. Parable of the old cloth & new wine.-{Vs. 16-17} behold-K.J.V.-Expresses the unusual occurrence) **a ruler** (i.e. A synagogue official named Jairus-{Mark 5:22}) **came and knelt before him-◙** (worshiped him-K.J.V.-4352-*To prostrate and bow down, to extend reverence to, welcome respectively.* Expresses an act of deep humility in throwing himself on the mercy of Jesus.) **and said,** (pleaded earnestly-{Mark 5:23}) **"My daughter** (little daughter-{Mark 5:23}, only daughter a girl about twelve.-{Luke 8:42}) **has just died. But come and put your hand on her, and she will live."** (Expresses the ruler's unwavering faith in the power and goodness of Christ. Possibly having witnessed other miracles which Jesus performed in the same manner.)
19 Jesus got up (i.e. Having been reclining at the dinner table at Matthew's house. That the Lord takes time for those in need, or love makes time for others.) **and went with him, and so did his disciples.** (The crowds followed and pressed around him.-{Mark 5:24} The crowds almost crushed him.-{Luke 8:42b})

Jairus a synagogue ruler humbly places his faith in Jesus divine power & authority to revive his daughter.

Message & Application 

- ❖ Shows how we can bring our desperate & hopeless situations to Jesus for help. (Know you can go to Jesus for hope when there is no hope!)
- ❖ Calls for coming broken and humble, that we're not allowing pride or reputation to keep us from Jesus as the only One who can Save us.
- ❖ Displays how God often uses the trouble and mess we're in to bring us to falling on our knees and crying out to Him for help.
- ❖ Calls for a living faith that is believing Jesus can step into our situation and change it regardless of what the circumstances may say. (Heb. 11:6)
- ❖ Teaches where bold faith puts forth the effort the Lord will do the rest!
- ❖ Displays how Jesus always takes time to minister to the hurting.(V. 19)
- ❖ Displays how the tragedies and sorrows of life come to all people regardless of who they are. (Both the rich & poor will find themselves in desperate need for a healing touch from God!)
- ⊶ Even today when life throws an unexpected curveball, or when the bottom falls out in losing your job, health, retirement, marriage, child, etc. know you can always cry out to Jesus for help. (Never think that Jesus is too big or too busy to help you!).

9:20 Just then a woman who had been subject to bleeding (i.e. Possible a menstrual/period discharge making her ceremonially unclean.-{Lev. 15:19-33}) **for twelve years** (She had sought cures from many doctors, spending all she had.-{Mark 5:26}) **came up behind him** (Fearing Jesus would not risk touching her and becoming unclean.) **and touched the edge**(hem/tassels) **of his cloak.**-◙
21 She said to herself, "If I only touch his cloak, (i.e. Robe) **I will be healed."**

A woman who had been hemorrhaging for twelve years places her faith in Jesus' divine power to heal her.

Message & Application 💻=🌎

❖ Shows believers how Jesus is accessible & touchable for all who are in need of a divine breakthrough and healing in their lives.
❖ Displays how we can bring our lifelong struggles with addiction, drugs, alcohol, pornography, etc. to Jesus for healing and deliverance.
❖ Encourages the hurting when you find yourself rejected & shunned by family, friends, and society you can always reach out to Jesus for help.
❖ Calls for the same perseverance and steadfast faith in never allowing shame, guilt, or embarrassment to keep us from our healing.
⊶ Even today we need to keep pressing through to our breakthroughs, never allowing obstacles to keep us away from Jesus' healing touch.

9:22 Jesus turned (Realizing power had gone out from him.-{Mark 5:30}) **and saw her. "Take heart,** (Syn.-don't despair, fear not, take courage.) **daughter** (Expresses tender kindness, affection, acceptance.) **he said", "your faith** (Syn.-transparency, honesty, openness, candor.) **has healed you."** (Suggests: How it was her faith in Jesus, not her actions in touching His clothing that healed her.) **And the woman was healed** (i.e. physically & spiritually.) **from that moment.**

As a result of the woman's faith in Jesus' power & authority, she is immediately healed of her affliction.

Message & Application 💻=🌎

❖ Shows believers where true honesty & transparency is reaching out to Jesus comes healing and Salvation. (cf. Heb. 4:15-16, 11:1-6)
❖ Teaches only when we realize our true condition and confess it openly to Jesus, can the Lord begin to work on healing us and changing us.
❖ Displays Jesus' ability to meet not only physical needs but the deeper needs of the soul in bringing spiritual healing and forgiveness as well.
❖ Teaches it's not the amount of faith, but Christ the object that matters.
⊶ Even today if we're to be healed we need to bare our souls to Jesus telling Him about everything, no matter how sinful/shameful it may be.

9:23 When Jesus entered the ruler's house (i.e. Jairus's house-{Mark 9:35, Luke 8:41}) **and saw the flute players and the noisy crowd,** (Suggests: Professional wailers & mourners who were hired to help carry out the funeral reception.)
24 he said, "Go away. The girl (twelve years old-{Mark 5:42 b}) **is not dead but asleep."**(Only of the body, not of the soul, that the girl was only physically dead, yet her soul continued to exist in another realm.) **But they laughed at him.** (scorn-K.J.V. scoffed & sneered-L.B.V. Syn.-derided, ridiculed, mocked. Suggests: They were poking fun at Jesus for miss diagnosing her condition.)
25 After the crowd had been put outside, (Suggests: In order not to sensationalize the miracle. Or as an act of grief over the crowd's scornful attitude. Except Peter, James, and John, and the child's parents.-{Luke 8:51} The former being Jesus' inner circle of disciples in order to witness the miracle and encourage their faith.) **he went in and took the girl by the hand,** (Expresses compassion, or a deliberate act in overthrowing ceremonial taboos against touching a dead body.-{Lev. 21:11}) **and she got up.** (Suggest: The miracle was instantaneous, that she was completely restored to both life and strength.)
26 News of this spread through all that region. (i.e. Capernaum/Galilee.)

Jesus proves His divine power & authority over death, by raising the girl back to life.

Message & Application 💻=🌎

- ❖ Shows no matter how hopeless & terminal the situation is Jesus can make a difference when it seems too late for anyone else to help!
- ❖ Teaches how the eyes of faith will look beyond the natural to the supernatural, that its God who has the last word, not our circumstances.
- ❖ Reminds believers even though by outward appearances nothing makes sense, know that God is still in control of the situation!
- ❖ Warns rather than doubting, trust that when Jesus says He's going to do something He is able to perform what He promised! (V. 24)
- ❖ Calls for dismissing skeptics & doubters from around us. (Naysayers can undermine our faith and take our eyes off of Jesus!). (V. 25)
- ❖ Calls for ministering to people in genuine and real ways, that it's never about publicity or popularity, but about God's glory! (V. 25)
- 🗝 Even today, believers can take courage that with the Lord nothing is final. That Jesus can bring revival to any situation, whether it's a dead marriage, lifeless career, rebellious child, bad drug habit, backslidden walk, failed ministry, etc.
- ➢ Miracles metaphorical implications suggest:
  - Reveals Christ as the Resurrection and the Life.
  - Christ's ability to Save us out of the dead life we were in.
  - Gives hope in our own resurrection, that death is not the end.

From this verse here (V. 27) to verse (V. 34) Jesus demonstrates His power & authority over spiritual blindness and unbelief.

Jesus Heals the Blind and Mute-(N.I.V.)

9:27 As Jesus went on from there, (i.e. Leaving Jairus's house.) **two blind men followed him,** (Suggests: Being blind they were probably guided by their hearts & ears.-{cf. Rom. 10:17}) **calling out,** (Syn.-imploring, pleading, begging.) **"Have mercy** (Syn.-sympathy, compassion, pity) **on us,** (i.e. Cure our blindness.) **Son of David!"** (Expresses a Messianic title signifying the Messiah's royal descent.-{cf. 2-Sam.7:12-16} That they understood Jesus to be the fulfillment of the Messianic promises as foretold by the prophet Isaiah centuries earlier.-{cf. Is. 35.5-6})
28 When he had gone indoors, (i.e. Possibly Peter's house in Capernaum. Suggests: Not to remain aloof, but to encourage them further.) **the blind men came to him,** (Expresses their earnest and persistent faith.) **and he asked them, "Do you believe that I am able to do this?"** (i.e. Heal their blindness. Suggests: Not that Jesus couldn't heal them, but was meant to test the sincerity of their faith, or to encourage them towards the right object of faith.) **Yes, Lord** (2962-*Master, one having divine power & authority.*) **they replied.**

Jesus by questioning the blind men, tests the sincerity & earnestness of their faith.

Message & Application =

- ❖ Shows believers the need for a faith that recognizes Jesus as the only One who can meet our needs and all that we ask of Him! (cf. Eph. 3:20)
- ❖ Teaches what we would have Jesus do for us we must be fully assured He is able to do. (Do you expect Jesus to do a divine work in your life).
- ❖ Displays how cries to God must be for mercy and compassion, and not about merit, hardship, injustice, unfairness, fate, or what's due us.
- ❖ Teaches the importance of being earnest and persistent in faith. (Don't allow anyone or anything stop you from reaching out to Jesus).
- ❖ Calls for not allowing the world's view or life's circumstances to defeat us, that all things are possible with Jesus!
- ❖ Displays how God wants us to come by our own confession of faith, and not according to what our friends, parents, or feelings may say.
- ❖ Displays how sometimes God postpones or delays our prayer requests in order to test our faith and see where our hearts are at. (cf. James 1:3)

⊶ Even today, believers need the same kind of faith that is trusting that Jesus has an answer and solution for any need. That Jesus can heal our marriages, finances, guilt, sickness, addiction, wayward child, unsaved spouse, and any other issues we may be facing.

9:29 Then he touched their eyes and said, "According to your faith (4102-*assurance, belief, fidelity, conviction.* Syn.-trust, action, obedience, commitment.) **will it be done to you";** (Suggests: Not in proportion to their faith, but rather in response to their faith or Jesus as the object of their faith.)
30 and their sight was restored. Jesus warned them sternly, (straitly charged-K.J.V.-1690-*Snort with anger.* Syn.-firmly, strictly, authoritatively, no uncertain terms.) **"See that no-one knows about this."**(i.e. Not that they can now see, an impossible fact to hide, but that the miracle was performed by Jesus. That Jesus didn't want to be known simply as a faith healer and miracle worker.)
31 But they went out and spread the news about him all over that region.

Jesus restores the blind men's sight in response to their faith in His Divine power & authority to heal them.

Message & Application 💻=🌎

- ❖ Shows believers how faith opens the door that allows God's power and favor to flow into our lives. (cf. Heb. 11:6, James 1:6-7)
- ❖ Teaches the degree in which we exalt and lift Christ up as Lord determines the extent to which Jesus can move and work in our lives.
- ❖ Teaches how God honors the type of faith that doesn't put limits on what He can do & achieve in our lives and those around us. (Eph. 3:20)
- ❖ Displays how the greatest opposition to our faith is not people, critics, or even the devil, but rather it's our own skepticism and unbelief!
- ❖ Encourages believers how God responds to our faith and not according to our reputation, character, popularity, income, church attendance, abilities, or anything else.
- ❖ Warns how our misguided zeal can cause others in coming to Jesus for the wrong reasons. (Vs. 30-31)
- ❖ Warns believers against thinking we have a better way of helping to honor the Lord than what the Lord commands. (Vs. 30-31)
- ❖ Calls for a faith that will obey & submit to Jesus even after we get our miracle.(Will you still obey Jesus after your needs are met?) (Vs. 30-31)
- 🗝 Even today if we're to grow in our walk we need to do our part in devoting ourselves daily to reading, following, and acting on God's word, and before we know it our faith will start to grow in leaps and bounds as never before!
- ☞ The faith that Jesus is talking about here is not a blind leap in the dark, having all the answers, believing certain things, or assenting to church doctrines. But rather a faith that is trusting and taking God at His word and then acting upon it. One who is willing to obey and follow God even in the face of doubt and uncertainty. (cf. Rom. 4:18-22, Heb. 11:1-13)

9:32 While they were going out (i.e. The healed blind men. Or Jesus & His disciples.) **a man who was demon-possessed and could not talk was brought to Jesus.** (i.e. Either by the healed blind men or by his friends.)
33 And when the demon was driven out, the man who had been mute spoke. The crowd was amazed and said, "Nothing like this has ever been seen in Israel." (Not that Israel never saw miracles, for Moses & Elijah worked miracles. But there was never as many miracles brought in a single day by One person.)

Jesus' healing miracle of the mute man is taken as evidence of His Divine credentials & Messiahship.

Message & Application 💻=🌎

- ❖ Shows Jesus' power & authority in delivering us from the evil forces and influences that have taken hold of our lives. (cf. 1-Pet. 5:8-9)
- ❖ Teaches the importance of intercession in bringing those who are dumb and deaf to the grace and mercies of God.
- ❖ Gives assurance in Christ's power in delivering us from whatever kind of sinful vices and addictions we've opened ourselves up too.
- 🗝 Even today we can count on Jesus giving us the victory over the sinful voices behind drinking, gambling, pornography, and anything else!

9:34 But the Pharisees said, "It is by the prince of demons (i.e. Satan, devil) **that he drives out demons."**(Suggests: Because they could not deny the evidence of the miracle, they ascribed it the work and power of the Satan.)

Unable to deny Jesus' miracles, the Pharisees attribute it to the cooperation & power of Satan.

Message & Application 💻=🌎

- ❖ Shows believers how skepticism & hardness of heart can cause us to miss Jesus' divine presence and work in our own lives.
- ❖ Teaches how we respond when God does something great determines the condition of our hearts. (Are you happy to see people blessed, healed, and set free by God, or do you become envious and resentful?)
- ❖ Displays no matter how much proof you offer, you will never be able to convince those who are proud and hard at heart!
- ❖ Prepares believers in not becoming discouraged or defeated by those who will try to attribute false and ulterior motives to the good we do.
- 🗝 Even today many will try to discount what Jesus has done in our lives in having us believe that it was simply the product of our imaginations, power of suggestion, or some crutch or emotional crises, and not the intervention and supernatural work of God.

From this verse here (V. 35) to the end of the chapter, Jesus calls for Ministers in sharing the Gospel with the lost.

The Workers Are Few-(N.I.V.)

9:35 Jesus went through all the towns and villages (A circuit covering 200 cities) **teaching in their synagogues, preaching the good news of the kingdom** (i.e. Gospel, His arrival as Messiah.) **and healing every disease and sickness.**

Jesus confirms His Messiahship with a threefold ministry of teaching, preaching, and healing.

Message & Application

- ❖ Shows how believers are to have a heart like Jesus that's willing to go to where the lost/hurting are rather than waiting for them to come to us.
- ❖ Calls for sharing the good news of the Gospel with others, that they don't have to remain trapped in a life of sin and hopelessness.
- ❖ Reminds believers how being a Christian is more than just sitting in Church and listening to good sermons, but rather about going out and making a difference in the lives of others!
- ⊶ Even today if were to reach the lost for Christ we have to get out of our comfort zones and go to where they are. Even if it's in a drug infested area, seedy part of town, bad neighborhood, homeless shelter, etc.

9:36 When he saw the crowds, he had compassion on them (4697-*To have the bowels moved with love & pity for the ills of others.*) **because they were harassed** (fainted-K.J.V. Syn.-burdened, defeated, beaten down.) **and helpless like sheep** (lost, drifting, wandering) **without a shepherd.** (Metph. Teacher, spiritual leader. One who would follow any fad or guru that came along.)

Jesus takes compassion on the people because of their lack of spiritual care and guidance.

Message & Application

- ❖ Shows how believers are to have love & compassion for people who are lost & drifting, who have nowhere else to turn to for help & truth.
- ❖ Calls for helping those who've been disheartened, disillusioned and let down by religion, inviting them into a personal relationship with Jesus.
- ❖ Teaches how we're to be people that others can turn to for guidance and compassion when they feel lost, broken and isolated.
- ⊶ Even today we need less annoyance and disgust and more compassicn for the alcoholic, drug addict, unwed-mother, welfare case, and ex-con.

9:37 Then he said to his disciples, "The harvest is plentiful (Expresses people abundant/ripe for Salvation, souls/sinners ready to be Saved.) **but the workers** (Metph-Missionaries, ministers, preachers, evangelists.) **are few.**
38 Ask the Lord of the harvest, (i.e. Jesus-{Matt. 10:5}, God-{John 15:1}, Holy Spirit-{Acts 13:2}. That believers can go to God in prayer for the talents, wisdom, and gifts needed for ministry and outreach.) **therefore, to send out** (send forth-K.J.V.-649-*An Apostle, To send on a service or with a commission.*) **workers into his harvest field.-◙** (Metph.-world. Suggests: In the immediate context the land of Israel but in a wider context the whole world.-{Matt. 13:36-38, 28:18-20})

Because the Salvation of souls is so great Jesus calls for ministers to be sent out into the world with the Gospel.

Message & Application 💻=🌎

❖ Shows how it's every believer's responsibility in taking up the call in sharing the Gospel with those who are lost and headed for hell.
❖ Calls for being willing instruments in God's hands, that if we will put forth the effort and do our part, the Lord will do the rest!
❖ Teaches how we're insufficient in carrying out any work of ministry by our own strength, without going to the Lord in prayer first!
❖ Calls for rolling up our sleeves and getting our hands dirty, that ministering the Gospel will take a great deal of time, effort, and work.
❖ Teaches how witnessing the Gospel does not depend on how qualified or skilled we are, but rather on an open and willing heart.
🗝 Even today we should be praying for greater opportunities to be used by God in sharing the Gospel with our family and friends or inviting our neighbors and co-workers to church.
☞ Because there are many people who are ready to give their life's to Jesus, all they need is someone to show them how! (Are you willing to allow God to use you in bringing others to Jesus?).

Effective Ways for Witness:

- Always see people the way Jesus saw them.
- Always have a stack of gospel tracts, pamphlets, and pocket bibles with you.
- Always be prepared in season and out of season.
- Always be studied up and equipped with bible verses and apologetic answers.
- Always bear witness through personal testimony and right living.

Chapter Ten

Missionary Instructions to the Twelve

- **Missionaries**-Are to focus their ministry to one area.-(Vs. 5-6)
- **Missionaries**-Are to preach and minister the Gospel freely, and all without pay.-(Vs. 7-8)
- **Missionaries-**Are to rely on God' support and provision in ministry.-(Vs. 9-10)
- **Missionaries**-Are to lodge only with those who are open and receptive to the Gospel-(Vs. 11-13)
- **Missionaries-**Are free to absolve themselves from all those who reject the Gospel.- (Vs. 14-16)
- **Missionaries**-Are to be prepared for opposition in ministry-(Vs. 17-31)
- **Missionaries**-Are to stay loyal and committed in discipleship, preferring Christ above family.-(Vs. 32-39)
- **Missionaries**-Are promised no act of kindness will go unnoticed or unrewarded by God.-(Vs. 40-42)

Jesus Sends Out the Twelve-(N.I.V.)

10:1 He called (Syn.-summoned, authorized) **his twelve disciples** (3101-*students, learners, pupils.* Jesus chose Twelve as symbolic of the twelve tribes of Israel.) **to him and gave them authority** (Syn.-power, strength, ability, gifts) **to drive out** (i.e. Exorcism) **evil spirits and to heal every disease and sickness.**

Jesus commissions the Twelve disciples, empowering them for ministry.

Message & Application 💻=🌎

❖ Shows how believers are summoned to go out and spread the Gospel message with those who are lost and hurting.

❖ Teaches how the Lord will see to it that we're qualified and gifted in carrying out whatever ministry He's called us to.

❖ Teaches how the success of our service and work for the Lord is found not in ourselves but only in Jesus.

❖ Teaches whatever ministry we're called to, God will see to it that we're divinely empowered with the resources to accomplish the task.

❖ Teaches how believers can take comfort in the fact that wherever the Lord summons us to go do, He also supports us in it!

❖ Calls for witnessing the Gospel message with works of mercy and compassion. (Witness God's Saving grace through works of love!).

❖ Calls for seeing that divine gifts and talents we're given by God are always used for the blessing of others.

☞ Jesus is not saying that all believers will be able to work spectacular miracles like the Apostles. But rather is promising the Holy Spirits presence and God's empowerment for whatever field of ministry we're called to.

10:2 These are the names of the twelve apostles: (652-*"Sent-ones"*-{V. 5} Syn.- messengers, ambassadors, heralds) **first, Simon (who is called Peter) and his brother Andrew; James son of Zebedee, and his brother John;**
3 Philip and Bartholomew; Thomas and Matthew the tax collector; (publican-K.J.V.) **James son of Alphaeus, and Thaddaeus;**
4 Simon the Zealot (Ca-na-an-ite-K.J.V. i.e. Member of a subversive political party-L.B.V.) **and Judas Iscariot, who betrayed him.** (Suggests: Judas listed last as the least respected disciple, having handed Jesus over to be arrested).

Here the disciples are listed in pairs according to the order of their commission and prominence.

Message & Application 💻=🌎

❖ Shows believers no matter how inadequate we feel we are, God is able to use us in mighty ways. (It's not our ability but our availability).
❖ Teaches how God can use common and ordinary people from all walks of life, whether rich or poor, educated or uneducated.
❖ Teaches how God can take people with different character flaws, be it impulsive-(Peter), pessimistic-(Thomas), despised-(Matthew), or greedy-(Judas) and turning them into courageous witnesses for Christ.
☞ The arrangement of the names suggests their importance within the apostolic circle. The arrangement in pairs suggests the order in which they were sent out-(Mark 6:7), or their natural relations and friendships.
☞ Even today God can take men who are uneducated, weak, timid, faint-hearted, etc. and empower them to do His work. (cf. 1-Corn. 1:26-29)

The Twelve Disciples

Name & Surname	Occupation
Peter/Simon/Cephas-(Rock /Stone)	Fisherman
Andrew/Brother of Peter	Fisherman
James/Boanerges-(Sons of Thunder)	Fisherman
John/Boanerges-(Sons of Thunder)	Fisherman
Philip	Unknown
Bartholomew	Unknown
Thomas/doubting /Didymus-(Twin)	Unknown
Matthew/Levi/Thomas	Tax collector
James/James the Younger	Unknown
Thaddaeus/Judas	Unknown
Simon/The Cananean/Zealot	Revolutionist
Judas Iscariot/The Betrayer	Unknown

(See also the biography of the Twelve disciples Pgs. 11-14)

10:5 These twelve Jesus sent out (649-*"Apostle", to send on a service or a commission.*) **with the following instructions: "Do not go among** (i.e. Journey, travel, tour, minister) **the Gentiles** (1484-*"Non-Jew".*) **or enter any town of the Samaritans.** (Suggests: Only applied to that time and place.{cf. Matt. 28:19})
6 Go rather to the lost sheep of Israel (Metph-God's chosen people, Jews.)

Jesus confines the disciple's ministry field to Israel, since Salvation (Messiah) is to be offered first to the Jews.

Message & Application =

- Shows believers how the focus of Evangelism should be for those who really need it, who are truly hurting and lost in sin.
- Teaches the importance of recognizing the lost and dangerous condition of those around us who need Jesus' love and healing touch.
- Teaches how Evangelism can begin in one's own backyard, influencing our own family, friends, neighbors, and communities first.
- Teaches how believers can better effectively spread the Gospel by taking advantage of customs and cultures we're already familiar with.

-Not among the Gentiles-Meaning: Variously attributed to either:

- The disciples having not yet been empowered with the Holy Spirit, would not have been spiritually strong enough to undertake such a hostile mission. (Acts 1:8)
- The Gentiles having no understanding of the Jewish religion would not have been open to the idea of a Jewish Messiah.

–Or enter any towns of the Samaritans-Meaning: Attributed to either:

- Because the Samaritans were a mixed race (The Israelite having intermarried with the Gentiles during the Assyrians captivity-(Deut. 7:3, 1-Kings 11:2, 2-Kings 17:24-41) they were often at times hostile to the Jews. (Luke 9:51-53)
- Having different Jewish religious views & observances they would not have likely accepted the testimony of a Jewish Messiah unless Christ came to them personally. (John 4:9)

-Go to the Lost Sheep of Israel-Meaning: Variously attributed to either:

- Jews being the chosen Covenant people of God, Salvation was to be offered to them first. (Matt. Rom. 1:16, 2:9-10, 9:4-5)
- The Jews were allowed to stumble first, thereby opening the way of Salvation to the Gentiles.-(Rom. 9:32-33)
- The Jewish covenant was still in effect, only after Jesus' death would the way be opened for the Gentiles. (Matt. 26:28, Rom. 11:11-24, Gal. 4:24-31, Heb. 7:22, 8:6-13, 9:15)

"Two-part" Perspective of Commission:

The first part of the commission deals with the immediate situation, that is within the context of the disciple's ministry to Israel.-(Vs. 5-16) The second part of the commission envisages a later period when the Apostles will be engaged in a wider mission to the world after Jesus' resurrection.-(Vs. 17-23)

Why the Jews have Priority in Salvation

- The Jews are God's chosen people. (Gen.12:1-3, Deut. 14:2, Amos 3:2, Rom. 11:28-29)
- The Jews are guardians and custodians of God's special revelations, the Old Testament scriptures. (Rom. 3:1-2, 9:4)
- The Jews have the legal lineage of the Messiah Himself. Jesus Christ came to the Jews as a Jew. (Matt. 1:1-16, Rom. 1:3, 9:5)
- The Jews have the covenant promise of Abraham, Salvation is from the Jews. (John 4:22, Acts 3:25, Rom. 11:17-24, Gal. 3:7)

Principles for Evangelism:

- Know your targeted audience, minister in areas where the Gospel is not known.-(Vs. 5-6)
- Preach & minister the Gospel to everyone without thought of reward.-(Vs. 7-8)
- Trust God to supply the support and provisions in ministry.-(Vs. 9-10)
- Minister the Gospel in love without getting angry or resentful.-(Vs. 11-14)
- Be wise in preaching the Gospel without needlessly offending or provoking.-(V. 16)
- Expect opposition from the world and family.-(Vs. 17-23)
- Be encouraged by God's care and protection.-(Vs. 26-31)

10:7 As you go, preach this message: 'The kingdom of heaven is near.' (Expresses God's Saving reign, Salvation, Messiah's arrival.)
8 Heal the sick, raise the dead, cleanse those who have leprosy,-◙ drive out demons. Freely you have received, freely give. (Expresses how believers are to use Jesus' generous gifts, anointing, and powers to be a blessing to others.)

Disciples/Missionaries are to preach & minister the Gospel freely to others and all without pay.

Message & Application 💻=🌎

- ❖ Shows how believers are to spread the Good News of the Gospel to all people, sharing with them God's love, mercy, and forgiveness.
- ❖ Teaches how ministry should always come from the right place, out of gratitude for all that Christ has done for us, not for making money!
- 🗝 Even today, believers are to go out in Jesus' name, doing acts of kindness without thought of reward or what we can get out of it.

9 Do not take along any gold or silver or copper (i.e. Money) **in your belts;** (purses-K.J.V. i.e. money-belt, wallets, etc. They were to go depending on God.)
10 take no bag (scrip-K.J.V. Handbag, duffle bag-L.B.V., begging-bag-Possibly used for fundraising.) **for the journey, or extra tunic,-◙** (i.e. Coat) **or sandals** (extra) **or a staff-◙** (i.e. Walking stick) **for the worker** (Metph.-disciple) **is worth his keep.**(meat-K.J.V. i.e. Food, lodging, etc. That missionaries will be supported with room and board due to the valuable blessings they bring.)

Disciples/Missionaries can depend on God and the hospitalities of others for their daily provisions.

Message & Application 💻=🌎

- ❖ Shows how believers are to throw off all hindrances to the Gospel, always preaching out of care for people's souls and not their money.
- ❖ Gives assurance in all things necessary in ministry. (Know the "Will" of God will never lead you where the "Grace" of God can't keep you).
- ❖ Teaches how we can better display the sincerity of the Gospel when we carry it forth without excessive wealth, money, and worldliness.
- 🗝 Even today, believers are to see that we're not giving out the wrong impression in ministry, that it's all about money, wealth, jet airplanes, limousines, fancy suits, television shows, etc.

-***Take no money, bag, sandal, staff***-Attributed to either:

- The urgency of the mission and its temporary nature.
- To prevent the disciples from being hindered in their travels.
- To send a clear signal there would be no financial gain in ministry.

10:11 "Whatever town or village you enter, search (inquire-K.J.V. i.e. ask-about, seek-out.) **for some worthy person** (i.e. Pious, reputable, God-fearing, upright, charitable, open person.) **there and stay at his house until you leave.**
12 As you enter the home, give it your greeting. (salute it-K.J.V. Suggests: To extend friendship, be cordial, polite. Expresses not a mere formality, but to discern the host's warmth and receptiveness.)
13 If the home (i.e. Family) **is deserving,** (worthy-K.J.V. i.e. Open, receptive, hospitable, accommodating, godly home-L.B.V.) **let your peace** (i.e. Blessings, prayers, witness.) **rest on it;** (Expresses that the family be blessed by witnessing and sharing the Gospel with them.) **if it is not, let your peace return to you.** (Expresses: Don't stay, move on, offer the Gospel to someone else.)

Disciples/Missionaries are to find accommodations with those who are open & receptive to the Gospel.

Message & Application

- ❖ Shows how believers are to seek out & stay with those who are open and receptive to Christ and the Gospel message.
- ❖ Calls for being content with God's provisions. (Be willing to serve without the best of accommodations, comforts, perks, or ease). (V. 11)
- ❖ Calls for being courteous and polite while sharing the Gospel. (The appeal of love & kindness opens the door for further witness)
- ⊶ Even today, believers are to go into ministry with the peace of Christ, knowing that some will meet us with joy and others with resistance.

10:14 If anyone will not welcome you or listen to your words, (i.e. Preaching, Gospel-witness) **shake the dust off your feet** (Expresses a sign of protest, rejection, and renunciation.) **when you leave that home or town.**

Disciples/Missionaries are free to absolve themselves of all responsibility for those who reject the Gospel.

Message & Application

- ❖ Shows believers rather than get angry & resentful with those who reject our witness, we're to shrug it off and prayerfully move on.
- ❖ Teaches rather than get bitter or discouraged we're to move forward with God's peace in our hearts that we did our best. (cf. Acts 13:46)
- ❖ Calls believers in staying true to our witness without compromising the Gospel message just to accommodate or appease others.
- ⊶ Even today rather than haggle & argue with those who are not ready to receive Christ. We're better off handing them over to God in prayer, trusting Him to grow the seed in His own time and own way.

10:15 I tell you the truth, it will be more bearable for Sodom and Gomorrah {Gen. Chps. 18-19} **on the day of judgment** {cf. Rev. 20:11-15} **than for that town.**

Those who reject Christ will be held more guilty because they had greater opportunity to receive the Gospel than Sodom & Gomorrah.

Message & Application 💻=🌎

- ❖ Shows how believers are to share the Gospel with earnest compassion, letting others know of the eternal consequences of rejecting Christ.
- ❖ Calls for warning sinners of the ultimate destruction they will face in Hell if they are unwilling to repent and receive Christ as Savior.
- ❖ Warns how living sinfully is culpable, but to spurn the grace that forgives the sin is even more grievous!
- ☞ While preaching the harsh consequences for rejecting Christ may not be a popular message today, it's still the truth and must be shared.
- ☞ Some teach from this verse different degrees of punishment in Hell as measured by the amount of light a person receives. (cf. Heb. 10:26-29)
- ☞ Today some try to justify their homosexual lifestyle by claiming that the sin of Sodom & Gomorrah here is not referring to homosexuality, but to that of inhospitality. (A vast majority reject this interpretation!).

10:16 I am sending you out like sheep-◙ (Metph-defenseless, vulnerable, easy-pray) **among wolves.-◙** (Expresses: Work will be dangerous and hazardous.) **Therefore be as shrewd as snakes** (5429-*wise prudent, sensible.* Expresses: Not in the sense as being sneaky or deceptive. But of being tactful, savvy, and street-smart.) **and as innocent as doves.-◙** (185-*unmixed, simple, pure.* Expresses: To be innocent, blameless, un-provoking, and inoffensive.)

Disciples/Missionaries are to be wise in avoiding conflict while remaining unflinching in their commitment to God.

Message & Application 💻=🌎

- ❖ Shows how believers are to be wise in avoiding conflicts & attacks while remaining unwavering in our integrity and devotion to God.
- ❖ Teaches rather than being naive in ministry, we're to be wise in the ways of the world. (Be generous in stewardship, but not gullible!).
- ❖ Calls for finding a balance between wisdom and vulnerability, that we're not compromising our character and walk. (Don't allow bad company to corrupt good character!).
- 🗝 Even today, believers need to exercise caution and care, knowing how to preach the Gospel without needlessly offending, provoking, or antagonizing others. (Always preach out of love, not out of malice).

From this verse here (V. 17) to verse (V. 31) Jesus teaches on the costs & dangers in ministry.

The Costs in Ministry-(Authors Insert)

10:17 "Be on your guard (beware-K.J.V. i.e. Vigilant, alert, don't be naïve-M.B.V.) **against men; they will hand you over** (deliver up-K.J.V.-1325-*"to surrender", yield up, betray.*) **to the local councils** (i.e. Local courts) **and flog you** (scourge-K.J.V., whipped-L.B.V.) **in their synagogues.-◙** (Lit. Fulfilled in the life of the Apostles and Paul.-{cf. Acts 5:40, 2-Corn. 11:23-24})

18 On my account (i.e. Fidelity and loyalty to Christ, Christian profession.) **you will be brought before governors** (Lit.-Fulfilled as with Paul before Gallio-{Acts 18:12-14}, Felix-{Acts 24:1-2}, and Festus.-{Acts 25:1-5}) **and kings** (Lit.-Fulfilled as with James & Peter before Herod-{Acts 12:1-6}, and Paul before Agrippa and Caesar.-{Acts 25:12}) **as witnesses to them** (Suggests: Not for the purpose of denunciation, but rather as a platform and opportunity to preach the Gospel to them.) **and to the Gentiles.** (Suggests: Taken together there will be opposition from all areas, both from the world as well as from the halls of the religious.)

Disciples/Missionaries are to expect opposition from all areas of society.

Message & Application 💻=🌎

❖ Shows believers how sharing the Gospel & our faith is not going to be easy or well received by everyone. (Many will oppose our message!).

❖ Teaches that if ministry is going to be effective in reaching out to others with Christ's love, we have to chance that some are going to let us down, even hurting and betraying us.

❖ Teaches rather than trying to fit-in and accommodating every bodies opinion, we are to stand true to our convictions no matter the costs.

❖ Teaches how our Christian service is not about ease, comfort, or popularity, but rather about confronting difficult & controversial issues. (Be prepared to take on social, political, and religious issues).

❖ Calls for seeing troubles and opposition as confirmation of our faith. (Know that living for God will bring some form of persecution).

❖ Displays how God may be using our hardships and trials as an opportunity to witness the Gospel and our faith to others.

⊶ Even today, believers need to be on guard against the social pressures of society & religion, that we're not compromising and bending our convictions just in order to fit in. (cf. Matt. 16:6, Heb. 2:1, 2-Pet. 3:17, 1-John 4:15-16, 1-Tim. 4:16, 6:20)

10:19 But when they arrest you, do not worry about what to say or how to say it. At that time you will be given (i.e. Inspired, moved) **what to say,**
20 for it will not be you speaking, but the Spirit of your Father speaking through you. (For securing an acquittal, or for fearless witness and testimony.)

Disciples/Missionaries are promised wisdom and inspiration from the Holy Spirit in times of persecution.

Message & Application 💻=🌎

❖ Shows how believers can count on God giving us the sufficient grace & strength to speak the truth when our faith is challenged.
❖ Teaches how God will not leave us to our own resources but will provide the wisdom, means, and boldness when we really need it!
❖ Teaches how God expects not perfection, but our willingness and availability to be used by Him when the time comes.
⊶ Even today instead of getting discouraged about the jams we find ourselves in, trust God for the wisdom in finding our way out of them!
☞ Jesus is not condoning laziness, that believers don't need to study, but rather assures the Holy Spirit's help in providing the inspiration.

10:21"Brother (i.e. Unbeliever) **will betray** (deliver up-K.J.V. i.e. Inform on, rat-out.) **brother** (i.e. A true believer) **to death, and a father his child; children will rebel against** (i.e. Turn against) **their parents and have them put to death.**
22 All men will hate you because of me, (my names sake-K.J.V. Suggests-Attachment/loyalty to Jesus. Because our Christian witness exposes the sinful living of others.) **but he who stands firm** (i.e. To remain faithful & loyal to Jesus) **to the end** (i.e. Believers life, tribulation period, or Jesus' return.) **will be saved.**

Disciples/Missionaries who persevere in the faith without renouncing Christ will be rewarded with eternal life.

Message & Application 💻=🌎

❖ Shows believers how our faithfulness & commitment to Christ will be severely tested/challenged by family, friends, and the world around us.
❖ Warns against allowing peer pressure or popularity to compromise our witness, convictions, and what we know is right.
❖ Prepares believers how following Jesus will be difficult due to the fact that it's in complete opposition to the world's values and culture.
⊶ Even today, believers need to stay true to our convictions even if it means being shunned by family and friends because we're no longer fun to be around or to party with.

10:23 When you are persecuted (1377-*"To pursue in a hostile manner", follow after, harass, trouble, mistreat.* Suggests: Harassed for religious beliefs.) **in one place,** (City) **flee** (5343-*run away, shun, avoid, escape.)* **to another. I tell you the truth,** (verily-K.J.V. Expresses: A strong confirmation/reliability) **you will not finish going through the cities of Israel before the Son of Man** (Jesus. Expresses a Messianic title signifying the Messiah's human origins.) **comes.**

Disciples/Missionaries are allowed to flee from danger, but not from witness or service.

Message & Application =

- ❖ Shows how believers are allowed to flee from danger not from service. (Escape conflicts where you can, but never succumb or yield to it!).
- ❖ Calls for not allowing difficulties or trials to discourage us in our faith, or keep us from carrying on, that Jesus will bring about change.
- ❖ Teaches instead of getting spiritually defeated keep sharing your faith, trusting God to open up doors for greater witness and opportunity!
- ❖ Calls for not allowing persecution to deter or dampen down our faith, or take our focus off of Jesus and all that He has called us to do.
- ❖ Calls for being wise in knowing how to avoid trouble and confrontations while staying true to our faith and witness.
- ❖ Calls for perseverance, knowing there will always be other opportunities to witness and share our faith in other places.
- Even today, believers are to keep sharing our faith in living the Gospel message, giving ourselves fully to the work of Christ until He returns.

–Before the Son of Man comes-Variously interpreted as either:

- Jesus' return will not come until the evangelizing of Israel or the whole world is completed. (Widely accepted by most) (Matt. 24:15-30, 26:64)
- Jesus' coming in judgment against the Jews in the destruction of Jerusalem by Rome (Fulfilled in A.D. 70). (Generally accepted by some) (Matt. 23:37-39, 24:1-2)
- Jesus' appearance to the disciples following His resurrection from the dead. (Matt. 28:16-20, Luke 21:40)
- Jesus' presence in the outpouring of the Holy Spirit on the day of Pentecost. (Acts 2:1-4, John 14:17-18)
- Jesus would catch up later with the disciples before they finished their own ministry. (Luke 10:1)
- Jesus' arrival at His triumphal entry into Jerusalem. (Matt. 21:1-11).

Areas of Persecution Believers may face:

- **Religious persecution**-By way of cults, religious ideologies, false doctrines. (V. 17)
- **Political persecution-**By way of religious rights/freedoms, imprisonment.-(Vs. 18-20)
- **Family persecution-**By way of isolation, estrangements, disownment.-(V. 21)
- **Social persecution-**By way of Character assassination, discrimination, bullying, out-casted.-(Vs. 22-25)

How to Endure Persecution:

- Maintain a deep-rooted commitment and faith to Christ. (Acts 14:22, Col. 2:7)
- See persecutions as a way to bring glory to God, manifesting His grace by praying and blessing our persecutors. (Matt. 5:43-45, 1-Corn. 4:11-13, Rom. 12:14-21, 1-Pet. 3:9)
- See persecution and trials as God's way of building character and strengthening our faith. (Rom. 5:3-4, 2-Corn. 12:10, 4: 17, 2-Thess. 1:5, Heb. 12:5, 1-Pet. 1:6-7, James 1:2-4)
- Expect persecution as an inevitable part of being a Christian. (John 15:18-19, 1-Thess. 3:3-4, 2-Tim. 3:12, 1-Pet. 2:21, 4:12, 1-John 3:13)
- Rejoice in persecutions that you're found worthy in suffering for Christ. (Matt. 5:11-12, Rom. 8:17, Philip. 1:29, 1-Pet. 4:13-16)
- See Persecutions as insignificant compared to our eternal glory that awaits us. (Matt. 5:11-12, Acts 20:24, 2-Corn. 4:17-18, Heb. 11:35, Col. 3:4, 2-Thess. 1:7-10, 1-Pet. 1:13)
- See Persecutions as an opportunity to preach and bear witness to Jesus and the Gospel to others. (Acts. 26:1-23, Gal. 4:14)

10:24 "A student (Metph.-disciples) **is not above** (5228-*superior to, chiefest.* Syn. better, higher-up, out rank, better qualified, greater) **his teacher,** (Metph.-Jesus) **nor a servant** (Metph-believer) **above his master.** (Metph-Jesus)
25 It is enough (Syn.-sufficient) **for the student to be like** (as-K.J.V. Syn.-identified with, relate, same-shoes, share the fate of-L.B.V. content-N.E.B., M.B.V.) **his teacher, and the servant like his master. If the head of the house** (Metph-Jesus) **has been called Beelzebub,-◙** (954-*lord of dung, lord of flies, a term derived from the O.T. designation of the Philistine god worshiped at Ekron.*-{2-Kings 1:2-3} Suggests: The agent through whom the Pharisees attributed Jesus' miracle powers to.-{cf. Matt. 12:24}) **how much more the members** (i.e. believers) **of his household!** (Metph.-Christ's family, Church.)

Disciples/Missionaries should not expect to be treated any better than Jesus was treated.

Message & Application

- Shows how believers should expect to be mistreated & persecuted since Jesus was treated much in the same way. (cf. John 15:18-27)
- Prepares believers in expecting to be shunned, ridiculed, and misunderstood by others.
- Teaches how it's not about being liked, popular, or getting along with everybody, but rather about staying true to our convictions & beliefs.
- Gives believers comfort and peace in the midst's of suffering, knowing that we're walking in the highest good for Christ's cause and glory.
- Calls believers in seeing trouble and persecution as a sign of Christ-likeness. (See it as a badge of honor to suffer for Jesus!).
- Reminds believers no matter how much we're misunderstood by others, we're always to model Christ's compassion, patience, and forgiveness.
- Exhorts believers rather than trying to fit in or craving acceptance in not being disliked, patiently suffer for Christ. (As Jesus had love to suffer for me, that I might have faith to suffer for Him!). (1-Pet. 4:1-7)
- Moves believers away from pride and self-importance, to putting ourselves under Christ's authority and direction.
- Calls for fearless witness in staying true to Christ's principles & values no matter how much we're misunderstood, ridiculed, or mistreated.
- Teaches how our hardships and difficulties do not invalidate Christ's presence or call on our lives, but rather confirms it!

⊶ Even today, believers should expect to be shunned, excluded, and ridiculed. Some will even call us names like Jesus freaks, bible thumpers, fanatics, bigots, etc.

10:26 "So do not be afraid of them. There is nothing concealed that will not be disclosed or hidden that will not be made known. (Expresses a proverbial saying vindicating the disciple's innocence and integrity at Christ's return.)
27 What I tell you in the dark, (privately, secretly. i.e. Jesus' teachings, Gospel) **speak in the daylight;** (publicly, openly) **what is whispered in your ear,** (privately, secretly) **proclaim from the roofs.** (boldly, fearlessly, courageously.)

Disciples/Missionaries are encouraged no matter the opposition the truths of the Gospel will be known.

Message & Application

- ❖ Shows how believers are to be bold & open in our witness for Christ, knowing God will vindicate our testimony and integrity in the end.
- ❖ Warns against the temptation of covering up, or compromising the Gospel message out of fear of being ridiculed, rejected, or slammed.
- ❖ Teaches how we can have a greater impact by living transparently, without worrying what someone might find out about us.
- 🗝 Even today, believers can live bold & courageous lives, knowing that God's truth will win out in the end.

–*Nothing concealed will not be disclosed*-Interpreted as either:

- The disciple's innocence, integrity, and character will be vindicated by God on the day of judgment.(cf. 1-Corn. 4:5)
- The Gospel will be made known despite the plots of evil men who will try to oppose it. (cf. Luke 12:1-3)

10:28 Do not be afraid of those who kill the body but cannot kill the soul. Rather be afraid (Expresses: Not of terror or fear, but of utmost reverence.) **of the One** (i.e. God) **who can destroy both soul and body in hell.**

Disciples are to put their faith & commitment to God above that of what man can do to them.

Message & Application

- ❖ Shows how believers are to fear more of disappointing & letting God down in our witness, than the fear of what people might think of us.
- ❖ Reassures believers, though men may shake our confidence and hope momentarily, they will never steal our faith in God away from us.
- ❖ Teaches how holding a healthy fear of God can keep us from trouble, disaster, and making poor decisions in life. (cf. Prov. 3:7-8, 14:16)
- 🗝 Even today the greatest detriment to Evangelism among Christians is the fear of losing friends or a neighbor slamming the door in our face!

10:29 Are not two sparrows-◙ (4765-*any little brown birds)* **sold for a penny?** (farthing-K.J.V.-787-*Roman copper coin called an "Assarion", worth about 1/2 a cent.* Suggests: That they were the cheapest source of food or sacrificial offering sold in the marketplace to the poor. Are not five sparrows sold for two pennies.-{Luke 12:6}-Suggests: They were even cheaper when bought in bulk.) **Yet not one of them will fall to the ground** (i.e. Natural death or hunted.) **apart from the will** (Syn.-consent, permission, knowledge, concern.) **of your Father.**
30 And even the very hairs of your head are all numbered. (Expresses God's providential care, down to even the smallest details in a believer's life.)
31 So don't be afraid; you are worth more than many sparrows.

Disciples/Missionaries never have to fear harm or threats since they are under God's providential care.

Message & Application 💻=🌎

- ❖ Shows believers how God cares about every part of our lives, even down to the smallest details. (Know God's in every detail of your life).
- ❖ Assures of having God's complete control over our circumstance, that nothing can happen to us apart from the loving plan of God.
- ❖ Encourages believers that no matter how forsaken, abandoned, or worthless we feel we are, God has a purpose and plan for our life!
- ❖ Gives believers hope in facing the future, that nothing happens just by chance apart from God's sovereign providence and permission.
- ❖ Encourages believers how God is not just a spectator or bystander but takes a great interest and active role in our lives. (Know that God is never too big or too busy to care about each and every believer!).
- 🔑 Even today, believers can trust that everything is going according to God's plan, that even the trials and hardships we face are serving a greater purpose and good! (cf. Rom. 8:28-39, 2-Corn. 4:17)
- ☞ Jesus is not promising here that God is going to keep us from sickness or protect us from all of the troubles & trials of life. But rather nothing will ever separate us from God's love, purpose, and plan for our lives.

Disciples Incentives in Ministry:

- God's daily provision & support.-(Vs. 7-10)
- God's wisdom & strength.-(Vs. 19-20)
- God's vindication & defense.-(Vs. 26-27)
- God's providence & protection.-(Vs. 29-31)
- God's value & importance He sets on us.-(Vs. 40-42)

From this verse here (V. 32) to verse (V. 39) Jesus teaches on the need for loyalty and commitment in discipleship.

10:32 Whoever acknowledges me (confess-K.J.V.-3670-*To declare openly one's solidarity/worship*) **before men** (Publicly) **I will also acknowledge him** (Syn.-endorse.) **before my Father in heaven** (i.e. As truly Saved, faithful believer.)
33 But whoever disowns me (Syn.-renounce, apostatize, turn one's back on, ashamed of me.-{Mark 8:38}) **before men, I will disown him** (Syn.-reject, be ashamed.) **before my Father in heaven.** (i.e. Jesus' denial of them on the day of judgment, that they never had a personal relationship with Him.)

Believers must be bold & unwavering in their loyalty and commitment to Christ.

Message & Application 💻=🌎

- ❖ Shows believers how a true confession in Jesus as Lord & Savior will display itself by the way we live, worship, and first place we give Him.
- ❖ Warns how it's a great dishonor and disservice when we choose the world over our faith and duty to Jesus.
- ❖ Teaches how the true test of discipleship is seen in how one responds under pressure. (Are you Christ seekers or crowd pleasers?).
- ❖ Teaches how being a Christian isn't about trying to fit in or pleasing everyone, but about standing for Christ regardless of the peer pressure!
- ❖ Calls for boldness, that witnessing may at times seem awkward, embarrassing, and uncomfortable, but stay committed!
- 🗝 Even today, believers are to live in such a way that's always giving praise & credit to the Lord. That it was Jesus who got us that new job, or that it was Jesus who restored our health, or that it was Jesus who had given us the strength to overcome our addiction, etc. (1-Corn. 10:31)
- ☞ Jesus is not calling for bullhorns or passing out tracts every day but for a witness that comes by the way we live, worship, and priorities we set.
- ☞ Jesus is not saying that one moment of denial a person can lose their Salvation.-(Peter, Matt. 26:69-75) But rather is talking about the type of denial that is habitual, final, and lifelong with no repentance. (Judas)

Ways we can deny Christ:

- By our words & actions (or inactions).
- By our failure to love & forgive.
- By our false & hypocritical lives.
- By our poor devotion and walk.

10:34 "Do not suppose that I have come to bring peace to the earth. (Suggests: Jesus' goal was not to be a social reformer, or to bring world peace by ending wars. But rather of bringing peace with God through His redemptive work on the cross.) **I did not come to bring peace, but a sword.** (Metph.- division, decision. Suggests: Not the design or purpose of Jesus' coming, but rather the natural effect due to the hardness of men's hearts.)

Believers loyalty & commitment to Christ will bring unavoidable conflict and division.

Message & Application

- ❖ Shows believers how our faith & loyalty to Jesus will naturally cause conflict and division, even splitting family and friendships apart.
- ❖ Prepares believers in not expecting everyone to see eye to eye with our Christian beliefs, values, or priorities we set.
- ❖ Warns how witness will cause conflict, for no one likes being told they're a sinner and going to Hell unless they repent and accept Jesus.
- ❖ Teaches how following Jesus is not about comfort, ease, or popularity. (Expect family and friends to pull away from you).
- ❖ Calls for staying true to God, always doing what is right even if it costs us popularity, friendships, and conflict.
- ❖ Calls for staying true to our Christian principles and values without compromise, no matter how offending or unpopular it may be.
- ❖ Calls for seeing that we're always doing what Christ wants us to do, no matter how uncomfortable or disagreeable it may be to others.
- ☞ Jesus is not encouraging conflict or violence with others, but rather is preparing believers to expect our beliefs to be at odds with the world.
- ☞ In a wider context can also be applied to the inner battles & struggles of the sinful nature, calling us to be at odds even with ourselves!

Common Areas of Division:

The Church	The World
Jesus the only way to heaven.	Man can get to heaven by good works.
Jesus is God.	Jesus was just a good man and teacher.
Christianity the true religion.	All religions are the same.
Sinners are going to Hell.	A loving God does not send men to hell.
The Bible is the word of God.	Men wrote the Bible.
God is sovereign/Omnipotent.	Evil precludes God's power & existence.
Creation.	Evolution.

10:35 For I have come to turn (set at variance-K.J.V. Syn.-estrange, clash, put at odds) **a man against his father, a daughter against her mother, a daughter-in-law against her mother-in-law**(Suggests: Division due to one's faith in Christ)
36 a man's enemies (foes-K.J.V. Syn.-adversary, persecutors.) **will be the members of his own household.'** (Syn.-family. Suggests: That division will be unavoidable because some will respond to Jesus while others will not. {Mic.7:6})

Believers loyalty & commitment to Christ will result in opposition from their own family members.

Message & Application

- ❖ Shows how believers can expect hostility & opposition from family and relatives because of our love and devotion to Christ.
- ❖ Emphasizes how opposition will arise from conflicting family values, morals, lifestyles, commitments, and duties.
- ❖ Calls for staying true to Christ even if it means risking ostracism, alienation, and banishment from families and friends.
- ⊶ Even today, believers must be willing to risk tension, strife, and estrangement from family in our love and loyalty to Jesus.

10:37 "Anyone who loves (Syn.-favors, esteems, desires, prioritizes, devoted, cherishes, cares more for-N.E.B., prefers-M.B.V.) **his father or mother more than me is not worthy of me** (514-*Befitting, deserving.* Expresses to be valued as one of His own, or to bear the Christian name.) **anyone who loves his son or daughter mother more than me is not worthy of me;**

Believers must give their loyalty & commitment to Christ above that of family and natural affections.

Message & Application

- ❖ Shows believers how all other affections, including family, friends, and careers, should pale in comparison to our love for Jesus.
- ❖ Teaches even when we're forced to make a choice between family and Jesus, preference and loyalty must always go to the Lord!
- ❖ Warns against being drawn away from Christ out of fear of losing families validation, identity, affections, or securities.
- ❖ Warns how our service to God can get hindered when we allow family loyalties & parents aspirations (school, careers, marriage) to come first.
- ☞ Jesus is not calling for abandoning one's love and care for their family. But rather all love must be regulated in assigning the highest priority to Jesus first. (When forced to make a choice, side with Christ!).

10:38 and anyone who does not take his cross-◙ (Lit. The Roman custom of forcing convicted criminals to carry the cross to the place of execution. Metph- To die to sin, self, and worldly desires. Or to suffer hardships, burdens, persecution, even death in one's commitment to Jesus. Suggests: In context willingness to break with family ties.-{V. 37} daily-{Luke 9:23}) **and follow me** (Expresses to follow and obey Jesus's teachings, example, and pattern of living.) **is not worthy** (Syn.-befitting, deserving, honorable) **of me.** (Expresses to be regarded as a follower and disciple of Christ.)

Believers must be willing to put Christ as first priority in life even before self.

Message & Application 💻=🌎

❖ Shows how believers are to die daily to self, that it's no longer about us and what we want, but what God wants! (cf. Gal. 2:20, 6:14)
❖ Calls for setting aside our own self-centered interest and pursuits, to walking in the path that God has marked out for us. (cf. Matt. 7:13-14)
❖ Calls for patience in learning how to endure and bear up under any hardship, trial, and difficulty as we follow Christ. (cf. 1-Pet. 2:23)
❖ Calls for accepting God's path & will regardless of the costs or risks. (Know God's ways may not be the easiest way, but its the best way!).
🗝 Even today cross bearing can be anything from losing family, friends, job, career, reputation, even one's life. Or the inconvenience of having to help someone at the cost of our own time, money, and pleasures. Or even the day-to-day battles against the cravings of the flesh and temptations that the world throws at us, beckoning us to a life of sex, drugs, alcohol, and self-indulgence. (cf. Col. 3:5-10, Titus 2:12)
☞ This is not saying that we must patiently suffer from some irritation or inconvenient burden as a nagging wife, thankless job, poverty, chronic illness, etc. Or as the saying goes *"This is my cross I have to bear"*. But rather is talking about a complete life commitment to Jesus.

Types of Crosses believers are to Bear:

- Willingness to follow Jesus even if it means losing a job, promotion, and career.
- Willingness to follow Jesus even if it means being alienated from family and friends.
- Willingness to follow Jesus even it means enduring hostility, rejection, and shame.

10:39 Whoever finds (Syn.-acquires, procures, esteems, saves-{Matt. 16:25}, keeps-{cf. Luke 17:33}, loves-{John 12:25}) **his life** (5590-*soul, self, feelings, will, desires, affections, comforts, securities.* Suggests: Either to find satisfaction and comfort in life apart from Christ. Or one who attempts to preserve themselves from hardship & persecution at the cost of renouncing Christ.) **will lose it,** (Suggests: True Spiritual life or eternal life.) **and whoever loses his life** (Metph.-self-interests, comforts, securities, pleasures, physical life, etc.) **for my sake** (i.e. claims, interests, cause, loyalty, commitment. Suggests: In submitting to Christ's claims on their lives to His service, promotion of the Gospel.-{Mark 8:35}) **will find it.** (Suggests: Both spiritually and eternally.-{cf. John 12:25 b})

Believers must be willing to give up their own pursuits & desires in favor of the better life Christ can give them.

Message & Application 💻=🌎

❖ Shows how believers are to give up control in trying to run our own lives to allowing God to run it. (Will you let God in the driver seat?).
❖ Calls for accepting the fact that we can't fix our life or our problems on our own, that we need God to step in and take control over it!
❖ Calls for surrendering ownership over to God, that we no longer reserve the right to live as we want and do as we want. (1-Corn. 6:20)
❖ Warns believers against thinking that we know what's best for us, that we can run our lives a whole lot better than God can.
❖ Calls for getting to the point that we hate who we used to be, that we're not going to be that same old person who we were in the past!
❖ Warns against being the type of person who refuses to give up their rights, or give anyone authority in dictating how they are to use their time, money, or what pleasures they can enjoy in life.

⊶ Even today we try to save our lives in so many ways by pursuing careers, sports, relationships, etc. ahead of a relationship with God. Or we revolve ourselves around activities we enjoy, things that fit our schedule with no thought to church or spiritual things. (cf. Luke 10:38-42, 1-John 2:15-17)

☞ Today the world tells us to look out for number one, that we need to take control of our future, make our own destiny, etc. Not realizing that we're not that good at knowing what's best and right for us.

☞ This is not calling for radical renunciation or asceticism, that we must live miserably and poorly, that we must forgo earthly possession and avoid certain things. But rather is warning against one who is focused on themselves, fulfilling all their desires, dreams, and ambitions with no real interest in following or living for Christ.

From this verse here (V. 40) to the end of the chapter, Jesus teaches on God's care for Missionaries.

Hospitality Encouraged-(Authors Insert)

10:40 "He who receives you (Expresses: By way of welcoming with hospitality. Or who is open & receptive to the Gospel.) **receives me,** (A Saving conversion to Jesus.) **and he who receives me receives the one** (i.e. God) **who sent me.**

Whatever is done for Jesus' disciples is viewed by God as done in the service of Christ.

Message & Application

- Shows how believers can take comfort & encouragement in ministry, knowing that we're going out in Christ's name, authority, and presence.
- Calls for welcoming and supporting of others in ministry no matter who they are, because it is really the Lord we're serving.
- Emphasizes the importance that Christ sets on ministers of the Gospel, seeing to their honor, support, and welfare.
- Teaches whatever reception we receive from others (positive or negative) is no reflection on ourselves, but rather falls upon Christ.

10:41 Anyone who receives (Syn.-welcomes, shows hospitality, supports.) **a prophet** (i.e. Pastor, Missionary, Preacher.) **because he is a prophet will receive a prophet's reward, and anyone who receives a righteous man** (i.e. Devout, faithful, godly person.) **because he is a righteous man will receive a righteous man's reward.** (Suggests Spiritual rewards from their teachings or eternal rewards credited to their account due to their service to the Lord.)

Those who welcome and show kindness to Jesus' disciples are assured of being rewarded with them.

Message & Application

- Shows believers how even the smallest act of support & aid offered to others in ministry carries the same reward and importance with God.
- Reminds believers how we're all together in the spread of the Gospel.
- Teaches believers as we welcome and support ministers, we also share in the blessings of their testimony, witness, and teachings.

⊷ Even today, believers can take comfort, though we may be less important compared to others in ministry, yet we are no less valuable in God's eyes.

10:42 And if anyone gives even a cup (drink) **of cold water** (Expresses-The smallest act of kindness, favor, or service.) **to one of these little ones** (3398-*Used in regards to station, age, rank, or influence.* Syn.-new covert, young Christian, humble believer) **because he is my disciple,** (3101-*Leaner, pupil.* Suggests: Out of regard for being one of Christ's own, or in recognition of their Apostleship.) **I tell you the truth,** (Expresses a strong confirmation and reliability.) **he will certainly not lose his reward."** (Expresses to be eternally rewarded by God, divinely appreciated. Is meant to encourage charitableness towards all of Jesus' disciples, not just the most important ones.)

Even the smallest act of kindness shown to one of Jesus' disciples will not go unnoticed or unappreciated by God.

Message & Application

- ❖ Shows believers how even the smallest acts of love & kindness done for one of Jesus' disciples never escapes God's notice.
- ❖ Teaches how even the simplest acts of kindness can have such a huge impact on others, letting them know that they're loved by God.
- ❖ Teaches how our lives are not simply defined by great deeds done for the Lord, but by the tiny acts of love and compassion for others.
- ❖ Teaches only by reflecting God's love in our daily lives and actions can we hope to attract others into a Saving relationship with Jesus.
- ❖ Calls for a love that always finds acceptance of others despite their appearances, failures, or shortcomings.
- Even today the tiniest acts of love & kindness can have a transforming effect on others, whether it's a friendly hello, a listening ear, a ride to the doctor, or lending a helping hand.

Ways to Support Missionaries:

- Send them donations and care packages.
- Pray for them and their work in spreading the Gospel.
- Encourage them with letters & Emails.
- Provide them support & aid by the way of shelter, clothing, meals, etc.
- Send Christian literature, Bible studies, etc.
- Volunteer in Church missions and donate money to their outreach programs.

Chapter Eleven

Warnings against Rejection & Doubt

- **Jesus and John the Baptist-** Warnings against doubting & wavering in one's decision for Christ.-(Vs. 1-6)
- **God's Measure of Greatness-** Teaches the need for a consistent and uncompromising faith in Christ.- (Vs. 7-19)
- **Jesus' warnings to unrepentant cities-**Warnings on the dangers of un-repentance and unbelief.- (Vs. 20-24)
- **Rest for the weary-**Jesus' open invitation to sinners in humbly trusting in Him for Salvation.- (Vs. 25-30)

Jesus and John the Baptist-(N.I.V.)

11:1 After Jesus had finished instructing his twelve disciples, (i.e. Having advised on missionary observances.) **he went on from there** (Expresses: Jesus' unwavering commitment to His own ministry. Or because of the disciple's unwillingness to leave their Master.) **to teach and preach in the towns of Galilee.** (i.e. The cities where the disciples had previously evangelized, thereby confirming their ministry & testimony concerning Him. Or going ahead and preparing these cities for the disciple's arrival, thereby making ready their evangelizing prospects. Where they were scheduled to go.-L.B.V.)

Having sent the twelve on their Missionary journey, Jesus continues His own ministry in Galilee.

Message & Application 💻=🌎

❖ Shows how believers are to practice what we preach, that what we've instructed others to do we must be willing to do ourselves.

❖ Displays how Jesus' teachings & instructions are more than enough to prepare and equip us for the fields that He sends us into.

❖ Comforts believers in knowing that the Lord will always be there to follow up our ministry, witness, and prayer requests.

❖ Assures believers that where Christ started a work in us He will also see that it's finished! (Trust that Jesus will complete His work in you!)

❖ Calls for moving forward in ministry, that our labor and witness for the Lord is never finished. (No excuses for idleness or laziness!).

❖ Teaches how even in Christ's absence we need to be constantly engaged in the work He has given us to do. (cf. 1-Corn. 15:58)

⊶ Even today it's not our duty to see that we're converting everyone we meet, but rather that we're doing our part in planting the seed and trusting the Lord for the harvest in doing all the rest.

☞ This verse marks the end of the "second" five-set division discourses that began at 10:1, suggesting another turning point in Jesus' ministry.

11:2 When John heard in prison-◙ (i.e. John the Baptist having been imprisoned by King Herod in the fortress dungeon of Machaerus for reproving his marriage as adulterous for taking his brother's wife.-{14:3-12}) **what Christ was doing,** (i.e. Jesus' miracle healings.) **he sent his disciples**
3 to ask him, "Are you the one who was to come, (Expresses a common expectation of the future arrival of a conquering military Messiah.{Mic.5:2, Mal. 3:1} **or should we expect someone else?"** (Suggests: Not a lack of faith, since John already had confirmation of Jesus' Messiahship.{John 1:29-34} But rather a lack of understanding of the type of ministry the Messiah would bring.)

Jesus' humble ministry was not portraying the type of conquering Messiah that John expected, one who would overthrow Rome and usher in the Millennial Kingdom.

Message & Application

- ❖ Shows believers how even the greatest Saints can have moments of discouragement and doubt. (Take comfort that your in good company)
- ❖ Teaches how no one is immune, that if John the Baptist can have doubts so can we, that we're all prone to stumbling now and again.
- ❖ Warns how our spiritual eyes can fail us during hard & difficult times. (Don't think that God has abandoned you in your time of need!).
- ❖ Teaches how Jesus is the best source to go to when questions and doubts start to set in. (God sees "doubt" not as a weakness, but the growing pains of an eager and seeking heart!).
- ❖ Warns against allowing discouragement and disappointment to grow that it starts to become a stumbling block in our walk with the Lord.
- ❖ Warns against falling into doubt just because an expectation we had of Jesus went unfulfilled, or somehow the Lord had let us down.

⊶ Even today we can experience the same kind of discouragement. That even after we're doing everything we're supposed to be doing in serving God. We still find ourselves struggling with our health, finances, and legal issues. That if God is love and all-powerful why doesn't He answer me or deliver me from what I'm going through?

How to handle Discouragement & Doubt:

- Always remember God's love & goodness regardless of what you're going through.
- Always trust in God's wisdom & ways, that God has something better waiting for us.
- Always remember that God's power & strength is greater than our circumstances.

11:4 Jesus replied, "Go back and report to John what you hear (i.e. Jesus' teachings, preaching.) **and see:** (i.e. Jesus' miraculous healings.)
5 The blind receive sight, the lame walk, those who have leprosy-◙ are cured, the deaf hear, the dead are raised and the good news (Gospel) **is preached to the poor.**(Not those in poverty, but burdened by the weight of sin){Is. 35:5, 61:1}

Jesus reassures John that He is the Messiah, by showing how He's doing exactly what Isaiah had prophesied.

Message & Application 💻=🌎

- ❖ Shows believers how in times of discouragement & doubt always remember God's faithfulness and goodness in the past. (cf. Heb. 13:5)
- ❖ Displays Jesus' tenderness, that He doesn't knock us for our doubts, but allows unbelievers and skeptics the time to come to the truth.
- ❖ Teaches how Scripture is the best medicine for getting our focus off our problems and struggles, and setting it on the things of God.
- ❖ Displays how the fulfillment of God's word and promises should be sufficient to warrant our continued faith & belief without further proof.
- ⊶ Even today when we find ourselves doubting, all we have to do is reflect back on God's word and the countless life's, including our own, that God has Saved, healed, and changed since coming to Christ.

11:6 Blessed is the man (i.e. believer) **who does not fall away** (offended-K.J.V. Syn.-stumble, trip-up, dismayed.) **on account of me."** (Expresses a call against feeling scandalized by Jesus' humble appearance, sufferings, crucifixion, death.)

A word of approval for those who do not miss out on Jesus' true identity and work because of His crucifixion & death.

Message & Application 💻=🌎

- ❖ Shows how believers are not to allow current struggles & trials to cause us to second guess Jesus' love, care, and concern for us.
- ❖ Warns against jettisoning our faith or turning our backs on Jesus just because some want, desire, expectation, or prayer goes unfulfilled.
- ❖ Calls for staying faithful to Jesus despite the unexpected bumps in the road. (Don't blame God when life becomes hard or unfair!).
- ❖ Prepares believers just because things aren't going like you thought, don't allow it to start to question your faith, whether it was all worth it.
- ⊶ Even today rather than jump ship just because Jesus didn't answer our prayers in saving our marriage, getting us that new job, or keeping our child from dying. We need to stay trusting in the Lord, that it's not going to become a sticking point in our faith and walk with Jesus!

11:7 As John's disciples were leaving, Jesus began to speak to the crowd about John: What did you go out into the desert to see, A reed swayed by the wind?-◙ (Metph-fickle, wavering, compromising, flip-flopping, wishy-washy.)
8 If not, what did you go out to see a man dressed in fine clothes?- ◙ (Metph-Life of luxury, comfort, pleasure, ease.) **No, those who wear fine clothes are in kings' palaces.** (Suggests: John's ascetic lifestyle was the complete opposite.)
9 Then what did you go out to see? A prophet? Yes, I tell you, and more than a prophet. (Suggests: Because John inaugurated the Messiah's arrival.-{V. 10} Or it was the O.T. Prophets that prophesied his own coming.-{cf. Mal. 3:1, 4:5-6})

Jesus defends John the Baptist as a true prophet, one who was unwavering in His conviction & witness.

Message & Application 💻=🌎

❖ Shows how believers are to stand firm in our faith & convictions, always holding to the truth of God's word and not popular opinion.
❖ Calls for being people of conviction, that we're staying true to God and what is right even if it costs us comfort and popularity.
❖ Teaches ones miss-step and moment of doubt does not make up one's whole character. (Don't define a person on one moment of weakness).
❖ Teaches two essential facts, that truth is more important than life, and that greatness is found in humbly serving God! (cf. Matt. 18:4)
⊶ Even today we need to be people of character & conviction, that we're not telling people what they want to hear but what they need to hear, that abortion is wrong, adultery is a sin, and homosexuality is a choice.

11:10 This is the one about whom it is written: "'I will send my messenger ahead of you, who will prepare the way before you. (Expresses John's prophetic role in announcing the Messiah's arrival and call to repent.-{Mal. 3:1})

Jesus confirms John the Baptist prophetic role in announcing the Messiah's arrival.

Message & Application 💻=🌎

❖ Shows how believers are to go about sharing the good news of the Gospel, that a person's sins can be forgiven through Christ Jesus.
❖ Teaches how we don't need great faith, or have to be perfect and know everything in order to point and lead others to Christ. (1-Corn. 1:26-29)
❖ Displays how we can clear a path for others to come to the Lord when they see Jesus through our godly character and conduct. (cf. 1-Pet. 2:12)
⊶ Even today, believers can prepare people's hearts in coming to Jesus by showing them their sin, misery, and need for a Savior.

11:11 I tell you the truth: Among those born of women (i.e. Unequal in human history.) **there has not risen anyone greater than John the Baptist;** (John's commission in announcing Christ's arrival.) **yet he** (i.e. believer) **who is least in the kingdom of heaven is greater than he.** (Not in calling, but privilege in being under the new covenant of grace through Jesus' finished work on the Cross.)

Believers are greater than John the Baptist because John only announced the Kingdom, whereas believers possess it!

Message & Application

- ❖ Shows the believers privileged position in living on this side of Jesus' finished work on the Cross, bringing in our healing and Salvation.
- ❖ Teaches how will always be objects of God's love, joy, grace, and mercy no matter our failures and mistakes. (cf. Rom. 8:31-39)
- ❖ Gives believers all the confidence in the world in being overcomers with Jesus, having the Holy Spirit living on the inside of us.
- Even today for believers no matter our struggles & trials, we can take comfort in what we've received from God, that it will give us hope and encouragement in staying the course and pressing on. (cf. V. 12)

11:12 From the days of John the Baptist until now, the kingdom of heaven (Gospel Preaching) **has been forcefully advancing** (suffereth violence-K.J.V.-971-*To force, crowd into, press.*) **and forceful men lay hold of it.** (Violent take it by force-K.J.V.-726-*Earnest, eager, determined.* Expresses: Not physical violence, but a spiritual battle of the soul in pressing forward in one's Salvation)

Despite opposition (within & without) believers are to be earnest & determined in their Salvation.

Message & Application

- ❖ Shows how believers are to be bold & determined in our faith, allowing nothing to steal our Salvation or keep us out of heaven.
- ❖ Warns how half-hearted & middle-of-the-road Christianity won't cut it, that we can't just slide, skate, or coast our way into the Kingdom!
- Even today we must continually wrestle & fight in throwing off sin, Satan, doubt, and anything else that's trying to pull us away from God.

-Forcefully advancing/forceful lay hold-Variously interpreted as either:

- If in the passive tense-(K.J.V.) the Gospel is violently attacked and opposed by Jewish activists who did everything to destroy it. (11:2)
- If in the middle tense-(N.I.V.) the Gospel is advancing in making great strides against the powers of darkness. As displayed by the vast crowds of sinners who were laying claim to it. (cf. Luke 16:16)

11:13 For (Conclusion draw as to why the "Kingdom of Heaven is advancing".) **all the Prophets and the Law** (Entire O.T.) **prophesied until John.** (Expresses the end of the Old Covenant/Dispensation of Law, and the beginning of the New Covenant/dispensation of grace.)
14 And if you are willing to accept it he is the Elijah who was to come.(Not of reincarnation, but John having ministered in the spirit/power of Elijah) {Mal.4:5}
15 He who has ears, let him hear. (Expresses how spiritual truths demand close attention and an open heart. Suggests: In context, that if John the Baptist is the Messiah's forerunner than Jesus must be the Christ!)

Calls believers in accepting John the Baptist's prophetic role, having ministered in the spirit & power of Elijah.

Message & Application 💻=🌍

- ❖ Shows the need for keeping hearts open to God's word & truth even if it goes against common expectations and everything we believed.
- ❖ Warns how a closed heart can have serious consequences in removing ourselves from God's grace and only means of Salvation.
- ❖ Calls believers in not expecting everything to be just perfect and to our liking, that all the lines have to be dotted in order for us to believe.
- ❖ Warns how men will have no excuses for remaining unresponsive and indifferent to God's Saving work now fulfilled in Jesus. (V. 13)
- ❖ Calls for keeping our eyes and hearts open to the work of God even if we don't understand it all. (Better to error on the side of caution!)
- ❖ Calls for remaining humble enough to follow God even if it may not be what we wanted or expected.
- 🗝 Even today if we're going to hear from God we need to get the focus off our own ideas & notions. As well as away from the attitude that assumes that God has to cater to what is comfortable, agreeable, and acceptable to us before we're willing to believe & follow. (cf. Vs. 16-19)
- ☞ This is not saying the Law is completely done away with, but only the ceremonial types, shadows, and prophecy's that pointed to Christ

Ways that John Exemplified Greatness:

- John was honest about his doubts & weaknesses. (Vs. 2-6)
- John stood firm in his faith & convictions. (Vs. 7-9)
- John stayed consistent in his character & witness. (Vs. 7-8)
- John remained responsive to God's purpose & calling. (V. 10)

11:16 "To what can I compare this generation? (i.e. Religious leaders) **They are like children** (Metph.-critical, discontent, fickle, unsatisfied.) **sitting in the market-places-◙** (i.e. Town-squares that served as places for selling, buying, and socializing.) **and calling out to others:**(i.e. To their playmates or passersby)
17 "'We played the flute-◙ (Reed flute) **for you,** (i.e. Wedding song. Metph.-Gospel message of mercy, grace, hope, joy, eternal life.) **and you did not dance; we sang a dirge**(i.e. Funeral song. Metph.-John's warning of punishment & judgment.) **and you did not mourn.'**(Metph-repent, grieve, remorse over sin. Suggests: Taken together a children's game known as "Weddings & Funerals".)
18 For John came neither eating nor drinking, (Metph.-Ultra-conservative, stern, strict, ascetic, etc. Modern cliché-"Fire & brimstone preacher".) **and they say, 'He has a demon.'** (Metph.-deranged, fanatic, radical, crazy-L.B.V.)
19 The Son of Man (Jesus) **came eating and drinking,** (Metph.-Socializing, accepting) **and they say, 'Here is a glutton and a drunkard, a friend of tax collectors** (e.g. Matthew) **and "sinners".' But wisdom is proved right by her actions."** (children-K.J.V. Expresses how the changed life's of sinners who were flocking to Jesus & John the Baptist in repentance was proof enough that their ministries were correct. Modern cliché "The proof is in the pudding".)

No matter how appealing Jesus or John the Baptist made their ministries, the religious leaders were never satisfied.

Message & Application 💻=🌎

- ❖ Shows rather than criticize & make excuses for not believing, have the heart to admit your a sinner who needs to repent and be Saved.
- ❖ Displays how some are unwilling to face the truth about themselves because that would require them to confront God & change their ways.
- ❖ Teaches no matter how hard you try, those who are in denial will never be satisfied regardless of what you say or do. (cf. Luke 16:19-31)
- ❖ Warns against thinking that God dances to our tune in what we deem as comfortable & acceptable before we're willing to believe & follow.
- ❖ Displays the patience of God's mercy & grace in trying all ways to appeal to men in getting them to deal with their sin and turn to Him!
- ❖ Teaches if God's going to help change us and grow us, we need to be a little less critical and fickle, and more open and receptive!
- ❖ Warns against the tendency of judging a person on their idiosyncrasies or how unconventional and eccentric they may be. (V. 19)
- ⊶ Even today those who want to justify their rejection and not face the truth will do so by using any excuse; *"There's too many hypocrites in the Church"*, or *"It's all about prosperity & wealth"*. Or they'll go so far as to blame Christians for being too judgmental, intolerant, and narrow-minded, that Jesus is the only way to heaven.

From this verse here (V. 20) to verse (V. 24) Jesus warns on the dangers of Unrepentance & unbelief.

Jesus' Warnings to Unrepentant Cities-(Authors Insert)

11:20 Then Jesus began to denounce (unbraid-K.J.V. Syn.-rebuke, reprove) **the cities in which most of his miracles had been performed, because they did not repent.**(3340-*Turning from sin & turning to God, a change of heart & mind*". Jesus' Messianic works should have caused people to turn to Him for Salvation)
21 "Woe to you, (Expresses a mixture of judgment, sorrow, pity, doom.) **Korazin! Woe to you Bethsaida** (i.e. Jewish towns near the Sea of Galilee. Was also the home of Andrew, Peter, and Philip. Expresses: Their guilt & culpability, having been ministered to directly by Jesus.) **If the miracles that were performed in you had been performed in Tyre and Sidon,-◙** (i.e. Phoenician cities on the Mediterranean coast. Expresses: Euphemism for all that is Idolatrous, corrupt, and pagan.) **they would have repented long ago** (i.e. In Ezekiel's day.) **in sackcloth-◙** (4526-*Woven goats hair.*) **and ashes.** (Rubbed on the head as a symbolic display of sincere sorrow, remorse, and grief over sin.)
22 But I tell you, it will be more bearable for Tyre and Sidon on the day of judgment than for you. (Suggests: The former only had the voice of the prophets, whereas the latter rejected the testimony of the Messiah Himself!)

Jesus holds these Jewish cities more accountable on the day of judgment because far worser cities would have responded & repented on lesser evidence.

<u>Message & Application</u> 💻=🌍

- ❖ Shows the dangers of remaining unresponsive & indifferent to God's Saving work. (How has your life changed after coming to Jesus?)
- ❖ Teaches how Jesus' Saving work should effect some sort of change and response. (Does your life bear evidence you belong to Christ?).
- ❖ Calls for making good on God's kindness & mercy in all that He has done by giving up our sinful and rebellious ways!
- ❖ Warns how complacency and indifference is more serious and scandalous to the Lord than even the most grievous sins!
- ❖ Warns against thinking that we can just live and do what we want, that there's no day of judgment or accountability coming. (cf. Heb. 9:27)
- ❖ Warns the dangers of knowing Jesus and do nothing about it. (It's one thing to hear the Word, and another not to do anything with it!)

🗝 Even today many only want the benefits & blessings of being forgiven by Jesus and going to heaven. While still wanting to do their own thing in living as they please and doing as they please.

11:23 And you, Capernaum,-◙ (A village on the northern shore of the sea of Galilee.) **will you be lifted up to the skies?** (exalted unto heaven-K.J.V. Expresses: The city expected to be eternally privileged by God as a result of its being Christ's hometown & headquarters for His ministry. Or they had a high view of themselves, convinced that they were the chosen people of God who were heading for heaven.) **No, you will go down to the depths.** (Hell-K.J.V. Expresses their punishment in hell for rejecting Christ. Or denoting destruction of their city as fulfilled by Rome in 70 A.D. {cf. Is. 14:13-15}) **If the miracles** (i.e. Jesus' display of divine power & authority as in the healing of the Centurion's servant, Peter's mother-in-law.-{8:5-15}) **that were performed in you had been performed in Sodom,** (Expresses: Euphemism for all that's immoral & wicked.) **it would have remained to this day.** (Would not have been destroyed by God.-{Gen.19:1-29} Would have served as a monument of God's mercy & grace.)
24 But I tell you that it will be more bearable (Syn.-tolerable) **for Sodom on the day of judgment than for you."** (Suggests: Because Capernaum received greater light having the Messiah/Christ personally minister among them.)

Capernaum will be held more accountable on the day of judgment than Sodom because they had far greater privilege & opportunity to receive Jesus as the Messiah.

Message & Application 💻=🌎

❖ Shows believers the severe consequences of remaining unrepentant & unchanged after all the advantages & opportunities God has given us.
❖ Warns against hardening our hearts to the kindness of God in giving us chance after chance to turn our life's around. (cf. Rom. 2:4-5)
❖ Warns of the dangers of allowing the privileges & opportunities to get right with God to go unanswered and unappreciated. (cf. Heb. 2:3)
❖ Warns against having a smug and high opinion of ourselves that won't accept the idea that we're a sinner who needs to repent.
❖ Warns against allowing pride and complacency get the better of us, thinking that our sins aren't that bad, that nobodies perfect.

⊶ Even today, believers who have been privileged in knowing the truth of God's word and what the bible says are expected to act upon it with a life of repentance, service, and righteous living. (cf. Heb. 10:29-39)

☞ Many teach from these verses that there will be varying degrees of punishment in Hell as determined by the amount of revelation & light a person receives. That it's better not to have known Jesus than to know Him and reject Him. (cf. Rom. 1:18-23, Heb. 10:26-29, Matt. 26:24)

☞ Jesus is not here being overly critical or harsh on believers. But rather is giving us a wake-up call, that He loves us too much in allowing us to go down the wrong path. (cf. Gal. 6:9)

From this verse here (V. 25) to the end of the chapter, Jesus reveals Himself as the means of Salvation & rest.

Rest for the Weary-(N.I.V.)

11:25 At that time (i.e. Disciples return from missionary work.-{Luke 10:17,21}) **Jesus said, "I praise you Father, Lord of heaven and earth,** (Expresses a prayer that recognizes God's sovereign rule over all things.) **because you have hidden these things** (i.e. Gospel message) **from the wise and learned** (Perfect, proud, know-it-alls.) **and revealed them to little children.** (Metph.-Humble, teachable) **26 Yes, Father, for this was your good pleasure.**(Not that God hides Salvation, but gives people over to their hardness of heart in choosing their own way.)

Jesus praises God for concealing the Gospel from the self-righteous and revealing it to the humble.

Message & Application 💻=🌎

- ❖ Shows believers the need in recognizing our miserable & helpless condition, that we're sinners who need God's forgiveness. (Ps. 51:1-17)
- ❖ Warns how being wise and self-sufficient in our own eyes can become a barrier to crying out to God for help. (cf. Matt. 5:3, 1-Corn. 1:18-31)
- ❖ Teaches when it comes to the biggest questions in life you can't think, reason, or work your way out of it, you have to hand it over to God!
- 🗝 Even today are you willing to kneel down and admit your need of God's help, that you can't fix your life or problems on your own?
- ☞ Jesus is not against wisdom or intellect, but a heart that is so prideful, arrogant, and self-righteous, it won't acknowledge their need for help.

11:27 All things (i.e. Grace, Salvation, truth, forgiveness.{Jn. 1:14,17}) **have been committed to me by my Father.** (i.e. God) **No-one knows the son except the Father, and no-one knows the Father** (i.e. God's love, mercy, grace, goodness, holiness.) **except the Son and those to whom the Son chooses to reveal him.**

The whole administration of the Gospel and God's Saving grace is committed and revealed by Jesus.

Message & Application

- ❖ Shows how there is only One hope for healing & Salvation, and it's found in the name of Jesus! (cf. John 3:35-36, 6:44, 14:6-7, 17:23, Acts 4:12)
- ❖ Teaches the sooner we see Jesus as our only hope, the easier we can release our sin, guilt, and burdens over to Him. (cf. Vs. 28-30)
- ❖ Teaches how we have in Jesus the full revelation of God's love, grace, and forgiveness. (That to know God we have to look too Jesus!)

11:28 "Come to me, (Expresses an invitation to follow, trust, believe on Jesus.) **all you who are weary** (labour-K.J.V. Syn.-Dismayed, worn out, beaten down, end of one's rope, burned out.) **and burdened,** (heavy laden-K.J.V. Expresses: To be overburdened with religious traditions and rules of the Pharisees. In a wider context to be weighed down by the difficulties of life, or the burdens of sin, guilt, shame, sickness, addiction, etc.) **and I will give you rest.** (Expresses Spiritual rest of the soul in finding peace, hope, rest, and forgiveness in Jesus.)
29 Take my yoke-◙ upon you (Lit. A wooden beam placed over the neck of two animals so they can work together in sharing heavy loads in pulling carts and plowing fields. Metph-To live under the grace and forgiveness of Jesus.) **and learn from me, for I am gentle** (Syn.-loving, kind, patient, considerate, long-suffering.) **and humble in heart** (Metph.-merciful, compassionate) **and you will find rest for your souls** (Expresses: Assurance of Salvation, release from shame, guilt, despair. As well as the freedom from legalism and work righteousness, no longer having to prove oneself, or from trying to earn God's favor/acceptance.)
30 For my yoke (Metph-teachings, commands.) **is easy** (Syn.-good, kind, well-suited, easy-fitting, tailor-made, accommodating, etc.) **and my burden** (Metph-religion, way of life.) **is light."** (Syn.-easy. Expresses the importance of walking in the love, grace, mercy, and forgiveness of Jesus and the Holy Spirit.)

Jesus invites all those who are burdened under the weight of sin & legalistic religion to come to Him for grace & Salvation.

Message & Application 💻=🌎

- ❖ Shows how those who are overwhelmed by the burdens of sin & guilt can come to Jesus for forgiveness and Salvation.
- ❖ Invites those who are tired and fed up of living life their way and always failing, to surrendering it over to Jesus' way of living.
- ❖ Encourages the hurting, when nothing is working in your life and your at the end of your rope, you can reach out and turn it over to Jesus.
- ❖ Allows those who are struggling to find purpose and meaning in life, to finding satisfaction and fulfillment in Jesus. (cf. John 14:27, 16:33)
- ❖ Invites all who are worn-out from a system of religious performance, achievements, and rule keeping to one of grace and acceptance.
- ⊶ Even today if your exhausted with searching for God through religious rituals, works, rules, books, fasts, diets, yoga, meditation, self-help groups, 12-step programs, etc. then you need to come and rest in Jesus.
- ☞ Jesus is not promising physical rest from all the trials, struggles, and difficulties of life. But rather is talking about a spiritual rest of the soul that's allowing Jesus to carry it. Or a religious rest from trying to win God's favor through works, to resting in Jesus' finished work on the Cross.

How to find Rest in the Lord:

- Repent & confess to the Lord your sins, guilt, shame, weaknesses, and failures.
- Come to the Lord in faith, repentance, submission, and humility.
- Rest in Christ's grace & forgiveness, and not in your own works or efforts.
- Surrender all your burdens, struggles, doubts, and fears over to the Lord.
- Submit to the Lord's guidance, direction, and control over your life.
- Find all your hope, needs, wants, and desires fulfilled and met in Jesus.

Types of Rest Jesus Brings:

- Freedom from sin and guilt of the past.
- Deliverance from fear and despair.
- Deliverance from pride, arrogance, self-centeredness, self-importance.
- Assurance of God's love & forgiveness.
- Release from religious pursuits, legalism, and work-righteousness.
- Freedom from getting caught up the lust of the flesh and the things of the world.

The Sinners Prayer:

Father I know I am a lost and hopeless sinner who needs Your forgiveness. I believe that Your Son died on the cross for my sins and rose three days later from the dead. I ask you right now Jesus to come into my life and be my Lord and Savior. I repent of my sins and surrender my life over to you from this moment on.
(Note: This prayer must be sincere and heartfelt!)

Chapter Twelve

Pharisees Opposition to Jesus

- **Lord of the Sabbath**-Warns against legalistic religion- (Vs. 1-16)
- **God's chosen Servant**-Teaches on Jesus' humble/compassionate nature in ministry-(Vs. 17-21)
- **Jesus and Beelzebub**-Warns against unbelief & hardness of heart.-(Vs. 22-30)
- **Blasphemy of the Holy Spirit**-Warns of the unpardonable sin in rejecting the Holy Spirit.-(Vs. 31-32)
- **Character & Profession**-Teaches on character of the heart-(Vs. 33-37)
- **Sign of Jonah**-Teaches on positive volitions in faith & walk.-(Vs. 38-42)
- **Parable of the Empty House**-Warns against reform without commitment.-(Vs. 43-45)
- **Jesus' mother and brothers** – Teachings how spiritual bonds and relationships are stronger than physical relationships.-(Vs. 46-50)

12:1 At that time (Jesus' Galilean ministry) **Jesus went through the cornfields on the Sabbath. His disciples were hungry and began to pick some ears of corn** (Wheat or barley.) **and eat them.** (Allowable under Law.-{Deut. 23:24-25})
2 When the Pharisees saw this, they said to him, "Look! Your disciples are doing what is unlawful on the Sabbath. (Violation seen as; Plucking the corn constituted "reaping". Rubbing the corn in the hands constituted "threshing".)

Pharisees accuse Jesus' disciples of violating the prohibition against working on the Sabbath.

Message & Application 💻=🌎

❖ Shows how those who are legalistic at heart will see religion about rules and regulations as to what you can and cannot do.
❖ Warns believers how will always have people watching our every step, just waiting to jump on us for breaking some petty rule.
❖ Teaches how as Christians we will always have critics in our lives just waiting to catch us in saying or doing something wrong.
❖ Calls for not allowing the legalistic & superstitious beliefs of others to undermine our faith, that if we fail to follow some rule or observe some commandment God will be angry with us and punish us.

-Sabbath-Meaning: The seventh day of the week (Saturday) which was to be set apart as a day of rest. A time to remember and reflect on God's goodness in all that He had done in His work of creation.-(Gen. 2:1-3) But the Pharisees took the day, which was meant for rest & worship, and made it a burden with their rules as to what constituted work.

🗝 Even today Church's that are legalists will have their own set of rules as to how you can dress, what length your hair can be, what foods you can eat, what music you can listen to, what movies you can watch, etc. (cf. Col. 2:16-23)

12:3 He answered, "Haven't you read (snub) **what David did when he and his companions were hungry?** (i.e. David and his fighting men while fleeing Saul.)
4 He entered the house of God, he and his companions ate the consecrated bread-◙ (i.e. 12 loaves of Holy Bread that was set before God in the Tabernacle) **which was not lawful for them to do, but only for the priests.**-{1-Sam. 21:1-7}
5 Or haven't you read in the Law that on the Sabbath the priests in the temple desecrate the day (i.e. By their cultic duties.) **and yet are innocent**
6 I tell you that one (Jesus) **greater than the temple is here.** (Expresses Jesus' work in our atonement and redemption should be the focus of our worship.)

If scripture did not condemn David's unlawful act, or the Priest's for working on the Sabbath how much less the disciples who serve Christ.

Message & Application 💻=🌎

- ❖ Shows believers how mercy & human need trumps religious rules and rituals. (Put acts of love and necessity over religious legalism!)
- ❖ Calls for looking beyond religious rules to the heart of God and what He would want you to do. (Know that it's never a sin to do good).
- ❖ Teaches when law & morality come into conflict, doing the moral and loving thing always wins out! (Put the law of love over rules!).
- ⊶ Even today meeting the pressing needs of others should always win out over religious rules and orthodoxy no matter what!
- ☞ This is not saying its alright to sin under some circumstances, but rather is teaching a lesson on being less dogmatic and more flexible.

12:7 If you had known what these words mean, 'I desire mercy, (1656-*To have compassion for the afflictions of others.*) **not sacrifice,** ({Hos. 6:6} Syn.-religious rules.) **you would not have condemned the innocent.** (i.e. Jesus' disciples.)

If the Pharisees realized how God desires mercy & compassion above rituals, they would not have criticized Jesus' disciples.

Message & Application 💻=🌎

- ❖ Shows believers how God desires not religious rules, but a heart that is loving, kind, and compassionate of others. (cf. Luke 10:29-37)
- ❖ Calls for having less of a critical & intolerant spirit, and more love for others, knowing how much God forgave us when we didn't deserve it.
- ❖ Calls for always putting our love and concern for the lost and hurting above some petty rule or religious formality.
- ⊶ Even today, believers are not to be so zealous & critical about our religious devotions and walk with God that it gets in the way of seeing others healed, Saved, and set free.

12:8 For the Son of Man (Expresses a Messianic title signifying the Messiah's human & divine nature.) **is Lord of the Sabbath."**(Expresses Jesus' divine sovereignty and authority on how the Sabbath should be observed.)

Since Jesus created the Sabbath & Fulfilled it He has authority over how the Sabbath is to be observed.

Message & Application 💻=🌎

- ❖ Shows how believers can rest in the finished work of Jesus, that we no longer have to work our way into heaven or try to win God's favor.
- ❖ Calls for always making it about Jesus, that we're allowing Christ to determine as to what is right and good. (cf. Col. 2:16-17, 2-Corn. 3:17)
- ❖ Invites believers in finding in Jesus a place of genuine renewal & rest from a bunch of silly rules and regulations. (cf. Matt. 11:28-30, Is. 30:15)
- 🗝 Even today the only requirement is that whatever we observe that it's all done with a reverent heart and an eye on glorifying the Lord.
- ☞ Jesus is not here commanding that the "Sabbath" still be observed, but that He is the ultimate fulfillment of our "Sabbath rest"! (cf. Heb. 4:1-16)

12:9 Going on from that place (Grain fields) **he went into their synagogue,-◙ 10 and a man with a shriveled hand** (Suggests: Some form of Paralysis due to injury or disease.) **was there.** (Suggests: Possibly deliberately planted there by the Pharisees as a pawn to trap Jesus.) **Looking for a reason to accuse Jesus, they asked him, "Is it lawful to heal on the Sabbath?"**(Suggests: Since Rabbinic law only allowed Sabbath healings that were a matter of life & death, they were really trying to trap Jesus, since the man did not meet that criteria.)

The Pharisees try to trap Jesus into working a miracle, whereby they could charge Him with breaking the Sabbath.

Message & Application 💻=🌎

- ❖ Shows how Christ meets us at the point of our greatest need, putting Himself in the place where healing and wholeness are needed most.
- ❖ Calls for not allowing our handicaps to keep us from seeking the Lord' help. (Where faith puts forth the effort, the Lord will do the rest!).
- ❖ Warns how being religious & legalistic can make you unloving and uncaring of others, that you stop seeing people to seeing only rules.
- ❖ Displays the dark side of legalism, that you care more about proving yourself right or defending some religious rule than about people.
- 🗝 Even today, believers are not to get so caught up in our religious convictions and personal beliefs that it keeps us from loving and helping certain people.

12:11 He said to them, "If any of you has a sheep and it falls into a pit-◙ (i.e. Well, ditch.) **on the Sabbath,** (i.e.-Saturday, or the Lord's Day.) **will you not take hold of it and lift it out?** (Suggests: Do to its monetary value.)
12 How much more valuable is a man than a sheep!-◙ (Suggests: Because man is made in the image of God.) **Therefore it is lawful** (Syn.-morally right, ethical) **to do good** (Syn.-show kindness, compassion, mercy.) **on the Sabbath."**

Jesus exposes the Pharisee's inconsistency, that if they could rescue a sheep on the Sabbath, how much more people who need healing.

Message & Application 💻=🌍

- ❖ Shows how we're to keep our values & priorities straight, always putting compassion and human need above religious traditions.
- ❖ Teaches how acts of kindness/compassion are always proper & right!
- ❖ Teaches how as Christians every day is a day for reaching out with the love and grace of Jesus in doing good to those around us.
- ❖ Teaches no matter how fallen and wrecked our lives become, God still loves us, wanting to lift us out of the pit of misery and despair.
- ❖ Warns how we can come off as hypocritical and uncaring when we put more value on religious obligations than on doing good for others.
- 🗝 Even today we're to put the needs of others first, even if it means missing Church because we're giving someone a ride to the doctor.

12:13 Then he said to the man, "Stretch out your hand". (i.e. Any paralysis) **So he stretched it out and it was completely restored, just as sound as the other.**

By healing the man Jesus puts compassion for the hurting & suffering over legalistic rules.

Message & Application 💻=🌍

- ❖ Shows how believers are to always put the welfare & concern of people first, despite what the religious rules and traditions may say.
- ❖ Calls for obeying God's commands without pausing to examine our abilities. (Know that God never commands without enabling!).
- ❖ Promises those who reach out in faith to Jesus can be fully restored & made whole again. (There's no sin that Jesus can't break and deliver!).
- ❖ Teaches how true faith acts obediently regardless of apparent obstacles or disabilities. (Excuses can hinder God's work in your life!).
- ➢ Miracles metaphorical implications suggest:
  - Christ's ability to free us from what is paralyzing our lives.
  - Christ's ability to bring hope & revival back into our withered lives.
  - Christ's ability to Save all who reach out to Him in faith.

12:14 But the Pharisees went out (i.e. From the Synagogue.) **and plotted** (held council-K.J.V. Syn.-conspired, schemed.) **how they might kill Jesus.** (Suggests: Attributed Jesus' healing the man as a direct violation of the Sabbath, punishable by death-{Ex. 31:14} or felt publicly humiliated by Him.)

Convinced Jesus had violated the Sabbath & undermined their authority the Pharisees wanted Him dead.

Message & Application 💻=🌎

❖ Shows believers when the word of God exposes our faults & legalistic hearts, rather than rebel were to humble ourselves & accept correction.
❖ Warns rather than respond with anger & hurt when God reveals an area that's not right in our lives, we're to fall down to Him in repentance.
❖ Warns how a hardened heart only plunges us deeper & deeper into sin.
🗝 Even today some would rather salvage and preserve their religious beliefs at all costs, rather than admit that they may be flawed.
☞ Note the Pharisee's hypocrisy, though they opposed Sabbath healings, yet felt no qualms in plotting the murder of a man on the Sabbath.

12:15 Aware of this (Expresses Jesus' divine omniscient in knowing their plan to kill Him.-{V.14}) **Jesus withdrew** (i.e. Not out of fear, but a tactical retreat, that His hour had not yet come.) **from that place.** (Synagogue) **Many followed him, and he healed all their sick,** (That Jesus heals all, turning none away.)
16 warning (charged-K.J.V., cautioned-L.B.V.) **them not to tell who he was.**

Knowing their plot to take His life, rather than provoke them Jesus humbly retreats.

Message & Application 💻=🌎

❖ Shows how believers are not to allow the hate & negativity of others to dampen our spirits, or keep us from serving and doing God's will.
❖ Teaches how even in the midst of opposition, criticism, and unfairness, continue the work of sharing the Gospel and God's love.
❖ Displays the need for avoiding useless confrontations and debates that will only distract us from God's work. (cf. Ne. 6:1-4, 2-Tim. 2:4)

–***Warning not to tell who he was***-Variously attributed to either:

- Jesus knew that His time to die had not yet come.
- Jesus did not want to provoke the religious leaders further.
- Jesus did not want to be known as a national liberator.
- Was in character with the humble ministry of the messiah.(Vs. 17-18)

🗝 Even today, believers are not to allow the threats & objections of bullies to keep us from pressing forward in ministering to others.

From this verse here (V. 17) to verse (V. 21) teaches on Jesus' humble & compassionate nature in ministry.

God's Chosen Servant-(N.I.V.)

12:17 This (i.e. Jesus' meek withdrawal and call for silence.-{V. 16}) **was to fulfill what was spoken through the prophet Isaiah:** (Prophesized 700 years earlier.)
18 "Here is my servant (Son/Jesus) **whom I** (God) **have chosen,** (i.e. In the work of Salvation.) **the one I love,** (Expresses: God's beloved Son. Declaration fulfilled at Jesus' baptism.-{Matt. 3:17}) **in whom I delight** (Expresses God's approval in Jesus' obedience in bearing the sins of the world. Declaration fulfilled at Jesus' baptism.) **I will put my Spirit** (Holy Spirit) **on him,** (Suggests: For fitting and anointing Jesus' human nature for His earthly ministry. Fulfilled at Jesus' baptism.) **and he will proclaim justice** (judgment-K.J.V.-2920-*Opinion or decision, to take a wrong and make it right.* Expresses: Not restitution or fairness, but more of acquittal and pardon.) **to the nations.** (Gentiles-K.J.V.-Any person who was not a Jew. i.e. The world. Expresses Jesus' work in satisfying God's justice in the punishment of sin by dying on the Cross.) {Is. 42:1 LXX}

Jesus' meekness was in character with the type of Messiah that Isaiah predicted who would carry out God's work of Salvation.

Message & Application

- ❖ Shows Jesus' work in setting things right between us & God by suffering and dying on the Cross for our sins. (cf. John 3:16, Rom. 5:6-11)
- ❖ Displays Jesus' love and concern for all people, that there's nothing He won't do for us and in us. (cf. Philp. 2:4-8)
- ❖ Comforts believers in knowing that no matter the evil, violence, and injustices we experience, Jesus will come back to set things right!
- ❖ Teaches how God will see that we're fully empowered and qualified in carrying out the service and work He has called us to do.
- ❖ Calls for coming with a servant's heart that's humbly submitting to God's will and purposes in all that He asks of us.
- ⊶ Even today we're to have a servant's heart in bringing the Gospel to a lost and hurting world. (Is there someone today you can take the Gospel to who needs Jesus' deliverance and healing touch?)

–***Proclaim justice to the nations***-Variously interpreted as either:

- Jesus' work in satisfying God's demands for justice in the punishment of sin.
- Jesus work in bringing about on earth the righteous requirements that God desires.

12:19 He will not quarrel (Syn.-argue, dispute.) **or cry out;** (Protest, threaten) **no-one will hear his voice in the streets** (i.e. Jesus would not seek publicity or popularity, that ministry would be conducted in a gentle manner.) {Is. 42:2 LXX}

Jesus' ministry would be conducted in a gentle and gracious manner.

Message & Application 💻=🌎

❖ Shows believers Jesus' meekness & gentleness in never becoming harsh, critical, judgmental, or threatening with us. (cf. Zech. 9:9)
❖ Calls for ministering the Gospel with gentleness and sensitivity. (Better to be a listener than quarrelsome or argumentative!).
❖ Teaches how the Gospel is better witnessed when people see the gracious/loving character of God through our peaceful & gentle lives.
⊶ Even today we're to carry out the ministry of the Gospel without the need for recognition, fanfare, celebrity, gimmicks, or pressure tactics.
☞ In context fulfilled by Jesus' withdraw from the controversies with the Pharisees and peoples false view of Him as a political Messiah.

12:20 A bruised reed-◙ (A cracked or worn flute made of bamboo. Metph.-One who is crushed in spirit, broken/beat up by sin.) **he will not break,** (Syn.-reject, turn away) **and a smouldering wick-◙** (A poorly trimmed lamp. Metph-One who is wavering, doubting, burned out, backslidden, end of one's rope.) **he will not snuff out,** (Expresses Jesus' patience and compassion in never leaving, abandoning, or giving up on us.) **till he leads justice** (judgment-K.J.V. Syn.-Gospel, Salvation, redemption) **to victory.** (Expresses Jesus' mission, that the work He began in us He will see it to the end.–{cf. Philp. 1:6}) { Is. 42:3 LXX}

Jesus is patient & tender in bearing with sinners, not wanting anyone to lose out on Salvation.

Message & Application 💻=🌎

❖ Shows Jesus' patience & compassion for those who are lost & broken by a life of sin, despair, and hopelessness. (cf. Matt. 11:28-30)
❖ Comforts the broken, that no matter how useless, worthless, or waste of time you feel you are, Jesus has a great plan for your life!
❖ Encourages believers that no matter our sins, failures, and weaknesses the Lord will never give up on us. (cf. Eph. 3:16-21, Heb. 7:25, Jude 1:24)
⊶ Even today instead of writing off the drunk, the drug addict, the homosexual, that their getting what they deserve, that their misery is a result of they're own sinful behavior. We're to be reaching out to them with the love, mercy, and compassion of Christ. (cf. Philp. 2:3-4)

12:21 In his name (Expresses Jesus' work in forgiveness, Salvation, and redemption as Lord & Savior) **the nations** (Gentiles-K.J.V.-1484-*Any nationality not a Jew.*) **will put their hope."** (Syn.-faith, trust, dependence, confidence security, refuge. Expresses the conversion of many people from around the world who will place their faith in Jesus for forgiveness & Salvation.){Is. 42:4 LXX}

Many people from all around the world will come to place their faith in Jesus as Lord & Savior.

Message & Application 💻=🌎

- ❖ Shows how believers can go to Jesus in having our sins forgiven, our burdens lifted, and our lives set free. (cf. Rom. 15:12-13, Eph. 1:12-13)
- ❖ Calls for trusting that no matter the weight and guilt of our sin we can run to Jesus for mercy and forgiveness! (cf. Rom. 5:20-21)
- ❖ Calls for putting our lives in Jesus' hands that He is our only hope for Salvation, change, and eternal life.
- ❖ Calls for trusting that Jesus has an answer and solution to any problem, difficulty, or dilemma we may be struggling with.
- ❖ Teaches no matter how much we've been rejected by family, friends, and the world, we can look forward to one day reigning with Christ.
- ❖ Teaches rather than finding our hope and security in our family, friends, government, technology, bank accounts, achievements, success, education, wits, etc. find it in Jesus who never disappoints!
- ❖ Gives believers the strength & courage in facing the future, undaunted by life's challenges and trials, knowing that the Lord is with us!

🗝 Even today, believers can go to Jesus for help in seeing us through whatever difficulties we're facing, whether its a health issue, marriage problem, drug habit, financial crises, job loss, rebellious child, future retirement, unemployment, etc.

☞ This verse is not saying that God is going to solve all our problems or take the pains of life away. But rather is promising that God will be there beside us through our struggles, giving us hope for the future.

Areas that Jesus provides hope:

- When we need comfort & forgiveness.
- When we need guidance & direction.
- When we need freedom & deliverance.
- When we need purpose & meaning.
- When we need healing & wholeness.

From this verse here (V. 22) to verse (V. 33) Jesus warns against unbelief and hardness of heart.

Jesus and Beelzebub-(N.I.V.)

12:22 Then they (i.e. Possibly friends or family members.) **brought him a demon-possessed man who was blind and mute** (2974-*Deaf, mute, dull in speech or hearing.* Metph.-The spiritual condition of mankind who are lost and blind to sin and God.) **and Jesus healed him so that he could both talk and see.**
23 All the people were astonished (Syn.-amazement, wonder) **and said, Could this be** (Perhaps, possibly) **the Son of David?** (Suggests: Jesus' healing work did not fit the expectations of a political Messiah that many expected. Or feared any open confession would invite a hostile response from the religious leaders.)

Displays the power & grace of Jesus in freeing men from the sin and bondage that is plaguing their lives.

Message & Application 💻=🌎

- ❖ Shows Jesus' power & authority in freeing those who are under the bondage & control of Satan and demonic forces.
- ❖ Displays Jesus' ability in opening the eyes of those who are blind and dumb to the things of God, that they may see the light of the Gospel.
- ❖ Displays Jesus' ability to liberate us from whatever sin and affliction that is controlling our lives.
- ❖ Teaches how with Jesus we no longer have to buy into Satan's lies that he's been feeding and speaking into our lives.
- ❖ Calls for always approaching Jesus with the same awe & expectation of faith that He is who He says He is! (V. 23)
- ❖ Warns how sitting on the fence about Jesus can give the enemy the opportunity to plant the seeds of doubt. (cf. V. 24)
- ❖ Teaches those who stay humble and simple in their faith will always find Jesus in any and every situation! (V. 23)

⊶ Even today will be able to look back and see how Jesus had broken the spell that cursing & foul language had over our lives. Or how He had replaced our anger & hate with love & forgiveness. Or how He freed us from a life of sin and addiction to one of hope and a new future.

➢ Miracles metaphorical implications suggest:
  - Jesus' power to deliver men from the bondage and blinding effects of sin.
  - Jesus' power in opening the eyes of those who are blind to the grace & mercies of God.

12:24 But when the Pharisees heard this, they said, "It is only by Beelzebub,-◙ (954-*Lord of flies or dung. Philistine god of Ekron. Was used as a euphemism for Satan.)* **the prince of demons, that this fellow** (pest) **drives out demons.**

Unable to deny Jesus' miracles, the Pharisees attribute it to sorcery & being in league with Satan.

Message & Application 💻=🌎

- ❖ Shows those who's hearts are obstinately opposed to the Gospel will find some excuse not to believe no matter how absurd it may sound.
- ❖ Displays the stubborn hearts of some people who will reject the truth no matter how clear the light or overwhelming the evidence.
- ❖ Teaches those who can't argue with our wisdom will try to undermine our credibility by calling into question our character & motives instead.
- 🗝 Even today many will look for any excuse not to accept Jesus rather than have to admit that everything they believed and built upon was wrong all along and will come crashing down.

12:25 Jesus knew their thoughts (i.e. Malicious hearts/attitudes.) **and said to them, "Every kingdom** (Metph-person) **divided against itself will be ruined, and every city or household divided against itself will not stand.** (Expresses a truism, that inward division naturally leads to strife and self-destruction.)
26 If Satan drives out Satan, (i.e. Demons, evil spirits) **he is divided** (fighting-L.B.V.) **against himself. How then can his kingdom** (Syn.-rule, sphere) **stand?**

If Satan was allowing Jesus to cast out demons he would be fighting against himself and undoing his own work.

Message & Application 💻=🌎

- ❖ Shows how believers can't be following & serving the Lord while holding onto a voice of pride and self-sufficiency. (cf. 2-Corn. 3:5, 12:9)
- ❖ Displays how we can't hide from the Lord, that He knows our every thought, that even the motives of the heart are open to Him! (Heb. 4:12)
- ❖ Warns how a faith that is not firmly grounded will eventually end in destruction. (Either determine your own beliefs or someone else will!)
- ❖ Teaches the importance of knowing the bible, that we're not just blindly following the false teachings of others. (cf. Acts 17:11, 1-Pet. 3:15)
- ❖ Warns if not fully assured in our own hearts we can be led astray from the truth. (If you're not standing for something you'll fall for anything)
- 🗝 Even today we need to be sure of what we believe and why we believe it. That if we're not standing firm in the faith we can start to bend and compromise our belief's for whatever teaching comes along.

12:27 And if I drive out demons by Beelzebub, {See V. 24} **by whom do your People** (Followers, disciples.) **drive them out?** (Expresses: What they attributed to the power of God to their own disciples, they would also have to attribute to Jesus as well.) **So then, they will be your judges.** (Syn.-Accusers, witnesses, condemners. Suggests: Their own followers will condemn them on the day of judgment for suggesting they to exercised their power through Satan.)

If they're going to accuse Jesus of using Satanic powers then their going to have to condemn their own disciples for doing so as well.

<u>Message & Application</u> 💻=🌎

- ❖ Shows believers the hypocrisy of holding a double standard, that we can condemn in others what we allow in ourselves. (cf. Rom. 2:1-5)
- ❖ Calls believers in having the heart and courage in admitting our inconsistencies when there exposed by Christ.
- ❖ Teaches if we're to have Jesus' help, we need to be honest and up front with Him about those areas of our lives that are slanted.
- ❖ Warns of the deceptive strategies and tactics of Satan in making sin, dishonesty, and half-truths seem less terrible than it really is.
- 🗝 Even today we need to hold ourselves accountable for the areas of our lives that are inconsistent and at odds with God's word and truth.

12:28 But if (Since, seeing that) **I drive out demons by the Spirit of God** (i.e. Power of God, finger-{Luke 11:20}) **then the kingdom of God** (Metph.-Messiah's arrival, God's reign, power, rule.) **has come upon you.** (Suggests: Jesus' healing miracles was evidence that God's power was present and at work.)

Jesus by casting out demons proved that the Messiah's rule & Kingdom had arrived.

<u>Message & Application</u> 💻=🌎

- ❖ Shows believers how Jesus' power is stronger & bigger than Satan's grip. (Know that Jesus is stronger than your weaknesses & habits!).
- ❖ Teaches where Christ's rule is sought and submitted to, the controlling influences of Satan and sin will be pushed back and ultimately fall.
- ❖ Reminds believers how the victory over sin & evil has already been won by Christ, we just need to walk in our healing! (cf. Eph. 6:11-12)
- ❖ Assures believers as we stay filled with God's word and the Holy Spirit's presence, sins rule and control will start to slowly fall away.
- 🗝 Even today believers can take comfort & encouragement that the reign of Satan and sin is over, that Satan's grip and control has been pulled down by Jesus as never before!

12:29 "Or again, how can anyone enter a strong man's house (Metph-Satan's dominion/realm.) **and carry off his possessions** (spoil his goods-K.J.V. Metph.-People who are bound by fear, drugs, alcohol, licentiousness.) **unless he first ties up the strong man? Then he can rob his house.** (Expresses Jesus' work in having disarmed Satan's power through His death and victory on the Cross!-{cf. Heb. 2:14-15})

Far from being in league with Satan, Jesus came to conquer and spoil his kingdom.

Message & Application =

- ❖ Shows believers Jesus' power & authority in overthrowing the hold that the enemy has over our lives. (cf. Col. 1:14-15, 2:15, 1-John 3:8)
- ❖ Teaches the importance of spiritual warfare and planning in binding Satan's weapons and avenues of attack. (cf. Eph. 6:11-18, 1-Pet. 5:8-9)
- ❖ Reminds believers rather than try to endure trials & temptations by our own strength, look to Christ's strength! (cf. Philp. 4:13,1-Corn. 10:13)
- ❖ Displays how we can't work our way out of our sin or addiction by our own efforts, but only through Christ's power. (cf. John 8:34)
- ⊶ Even today if we're to have any hope of escaping the power that drugs, alcoholism, and pornography has over us. We have to do it through Jesus' word and strength and not by our own efforts!

12:30 "He who is not with me is against me, (Suggests: The Pharisees, by accusing Jesus of using Satanic powers to cast out demons were in effect siding with Satan.-{V. 24}) **and he who does not gather with me scatters.** (Lit-The work of harvesting & sowing grain. Or of a shepherd's work in guarding their flock against attack. Metph.-To drive or hinder men from coming to Christ.)

The Pharisee's opposition to Jesus' ministry, was in effect, taking sides with Satan.

Message & Application =

- ❖ Shows believers how there can be no neutrality or middle ground when following Jesus. ("Middle of the road" Christianity won't cut it).
- ❖ Warns how being indifferent, uncommitted, and lukewarm in the faith is really the same as opposing Jesus and siding with Satan.
- ❖ Calls for standing faithfully on the side of Christ without compromise. (Allow no shades of gray, see issues as black & white, right & wrong).
- ⊶ Even today, believers need to realize that if we're not actively engaged in serving and laboring for the Lord in some way, we're only allowing sin & evil to grow and run rampant without any opposition!

From this verse here (V. 31) to verse (V. 32) Jesus warns of the unpardonable sin in rejecting the Holy Spirit's witness.

Blasphemy of the Holy Spirit-(Authors Insert)

12:31 And so I tell you, every sin and blasphemy (987-*To speak irreverently or profanely of God or of sacred things.)* **will be forgiven men, but the blasphemy against the Spirit** (i.e. Holy Spirit) **will not be forgiven.**
32 Anyone who speaks a word against the Son of Man (Suggests: In context The Pharisees attributing Jesus' miracles to the work of Satan.-{V. 24}) **will be forgiven, but anyone who speaks against the Holy Spirit** (Suggests: Denying the Holy Spirit' witness of the Gospel and offer of Salvation.) **will not be forgiven, either in this age** (i.e. Lifespan, Gospel dispensation.) **or in the age to come.** (i.e. Resurrected life or eternal life. Expresses irreversible condition.)

Men can reject Jesus' miracles & teachings, but those who reject the Holy Spirit's offer of Salvation will never be forgiven.

Message & Application

- ❖ Shows how there's no sin that can't be forgiven except the sin that persistently rejects Jesus as Lord & Savior. (cf. 1-John 2:22-24, 4:15)
- ❖ Warns against closing our ears and hardening our hearts to the Holy Spirit's voice to the point we no longer recognize the need to repent.
- ❖ Warns the only sin that can't be forgiven is the sin of not wanting Jesus in your life or the sin which says forgiveness is not wanted or needed.
- ❖ Warns believers against spurning the pleading and promptings of the Holy Spirit to repent and turn back to God. (Heb.10:26-29, 2-Pet. 2:20-21)

–***Blasphemy against the Spirit***-Meaning: This is not talking about taking the Lord's name in vain, being angry with God, or committing some heinous sin. But rather it is one who persistently and willfully rejects the Holy Spirit's witness of the Gospel and God's offer of forgiveness & Salvation. Or one who willfully falls away from God, reverting back to their old life of sin.(cf. Heb. 6:4-6, 2-Pet 2:20-22, 1-John 5:16-17) Some reject this based on the belief that *"Once Saved always Saved"*.-(John 10:27-28). Others contend that they were never Saved in the first place.

☞ The differences between the two blasphemy's, suggests the former is committed by a non-believer and therefore forgivable upon repentance. Whereas the latter is committed by believers, therefore more grievous.

☞ These verses have caused a great anxiety for many sincere Christians who fear they may have committed this unpardonable sin. Those who worry about it is really a good indication that they have not, for they would not have been grieved over such a sin in the first place!

From this verse here (V. 33) to verse (V. 37) Jesus teaches on the inner character and condition of the heart.

12:33 Make (assume, consider) **a tree** (heart) **good** (regenerate, born-again) **and its fruit** (conduct, speech) **will be good,** (honest, forthcoming) **or make a tree bad and its fruit will be bad, for a tree is recognized by its fruit.** (Expresses how a persons character will reveal itself by their actions & words.)

Pharisee's accusations that Jesus was working by the power of Satan was inconsistent with the good works He was doing.

Message & Application 💻=🌎

- ❖ Shows believers who are truly Saved & Born again will reflect it in a change of life, character, and speech. (cf. Gal.5:22-25, Col. 3:5-10)
- ❖ Teaches if we're to be known as followers of Christ then we need to act and talk as followers of Christ. (cf. 1-Corn. 11:1, 1-John 2:6)
- 🗝 Even today we need to ask ourselves is our action & speech consistent with a life that's been Saved by God. Or does it reflect someone who's always hurtful & cruel, or who's always grumbling & complaining?
- ☞ Jesus is not expecting sinless perfection in never doing wrong when in truth will often mess up and blow it at times. But rather that we're honest and upfront with God about those areas that need changing.

12:34 You brood (offspring) **of vipers,-◙** (i.e. Small poisonous snakes) **how can you** (Pharisees) **who are evil** (i.e. Malicious & prideful at heart.) **say anything good? For out of the overflow of the heart the mouth speaks.** (Expresses what one truly is in heart will naturally show up in one's character & speech.)

The Pharisee's malicious words towards Jesus revealed the true color & character of their hearts.

Message & Application 💻=🌎

- ❖ Shows how believers are to guard our hearts against any negative words that can become a poor reflection on God and hurtful to others.
- ❖ Warns against the kind of fault-finding heart that is always critical and negative of others. (Can't say anything nice, don't say anything at all!).
- ❖ Teaches how its easy to be a good person when your not under a lot of pressure, but what about the times of stress, how do you respond then?
- ☞ Even today when life squeezes you, or when someone hurts you or offends you. Do you allow anger, hatred, and bitterness to flow out of your mouth or how God would want us to respond? (cf. Luke 23:34)

12:35 The good man (Born again believer.) **brings good things** (good treasure-K.J.V. i.e. godly-graces, affections.) **out of the good stored up in him** (Hearts treasures or core values.) **and the evil man** (Metph.-Unbeliever) **brings evil things** (i.e. Lust, pride, envy, bitterness, etc.) **out of the evil stored up in him.**

Men can only promote what they truly are in heart & character.

Message & Application 💻=🌎

- ❖ Shows where a heart is treasuring God's grace & forgiveness, will have a life of love, kindness, and generosity overflow to others.
- ❖ Teaches how we speak and conduct ourselves says a lot about our love and allegiance to Christ or lack thereof.
- ❖ Teaches those who's hearts are filled with love for Jesus and all that He has done can't help but talk about Him to others.
- ❖ Teaches how our praises & references to the Lord will naturally show up in our daily conversations, speaking of all that Jesus has done.
- 🗝 Even today the same principle applies as in *"garbage in garbage out"*, that what we're filling our minds with, God's word or trashy movies, books, and magazines will eventually come out. (Philp. 4:8. Ps.119:11-16)

12:36 But I tell you that men (Believers) **will have to give account on the day of judgment for every careless word** (idle-word-K.J.V.-692-*Barren, useless, unfruitful.* Syn.-ungracious words, injurious epithets, etc.) **they have spoken.**
37 For by your words you will be acquitted and by your words you will be condemned." (Words good or bad, will be used in estimating overall character.)

Because words are a true indicator of a person's heart & character it will be used to pass judgment upon them.

Message & Application 💻=🌎

- ❖ Shows believers how our daily character & speech reveals the inward condition of our hearts, whether we were truly Saved or not.
- ❖ Teaches how words that are hurtful, injurious, and uncaring of the feelings of others displays a heart that is far from God. (cf. Eph. 4:29)
- 🗝 Even today we need to be careful of the kind of humor we're using. That we can't say things that are hurtful one minute and then the next minute say *"I was just kidding"* or *"Can't you take a joke"*. (Eph. 5:4)
- ☞ Jesus is not saying here that by slips of the tongue or words spoken in anger and frustration one can lose their Salvation. But rather the overall character of one's conduct & speech will be used as evidence of whether or not a heart has been spiritually regenerated by God.

From this verse here (V. 38) to verse (V. 45) teaches on the need for positive volitions & decisions in faith.

The Sign of Jonah-(N.I.V.)

12:38 Then some of the Pharisees and teachers of the law said to him, "Teacher, we want to see a miraculous sign (i.e. Thunder, lighting, darkness) **from you".** (Suggests: Not a sincere request, but excuse to discredit Jesus.)

The Pharisees try to discredit Jesus, by asking for a Divine sign as absolute proof of His Messiahship.

Message & Application 💻=🌎

❖ Shows how seeking signs displays a lack of faith in what God has already done. (Seeking signs is evidence of unbelief rather than faith).
❖ Calls for a faith that is thanking Jesus for what He has already done, rather than looking for more and more truth to convince us.
🗝 Even today we're not to make demands of God to prove He's worthy of our devotion, or set standards for what we will believe and accept.

12:39 He answered, A wicked (Metph.-hardhearted) **and adulterous** (Metph.-unfaithful, unbelieving) **generation** (Religious leaders) **asks for a miraculous sign! But none will be given it except the sign of the prophet Jonah.**
40 For as Jonah was three days and three nights in the belly of a huge fish, (whale-K.J.V.) **so the Son of Man will be three days and three nights in the heart** (tomb/grave) **of the earth.** (Jesus' death, burial, resurrection. That Jesus dying for our sins and resurrecting is proof enough of God's love & forgiveness.)

Because of the Pharisee's unbelief & hardness of heart, the only sign they will get will be Jesus' resurrection from the dead.

Message & Application

❖ Shows how Jesus dying for our sins & resurrecting should be enough proof without the need for further signs. (cf. Luke 16:31, Rom. 10:6-10)
❖ Teaches where genuine faith is resting in all that Jesus has done for us on the Cross, no further proof or evidence should be needed.
-***Three days and three nights***-The majority interpret these *"Three days & nights"* as an "idiom" for any part of a day rather than a literal 72 hours. That Jesus was crucified late Friday and rose early Sunday.
🗝 Even today if God never works another miracle in our lives, just being forgiven and Saved by Jesus should be sufficient enough!
☞ Confirms for believers how Jonah was a historical figure and not just a myth, that scripture is true and historically accurate!

12:41 The men of Nineveh-◙ (i.e. Capital of Assyria in northern Iraq.) **will stand up at the judgment with this generation and condemn it;** (Suggests: Not as judges, but by witness & example.) **for they repented** (3341-*A turning from sin & turning to God.*) **at the preaching of Jonah** (Mere man, reluctant prophet.-{Jon.3:1-10})**and now one greater than Jonah** (i.e. Jesus in both nature & grace.) **is here.** (Expresses: Pharisee's culpability, that pagans & heathens responded to a mere man, while they failed to receive their own Messiah, God's very Son!)

The men of Nineveh will condemn Israel because they repented on less evidence, whereas they rejected Christ Himself, God's own Son!

Message & Application

- ❖ Shows how men will have no excuse for not repenting & turning to Jesus having mercy and forgiveness in His name. (cf. Philp. 2:9-11)
- ❖ Warns how there are no excuses for complacency or fence-sitting, having been given a second chance/opportunity to get right with God.
- ⊶ Even today we have no excuses having greater opportunities to hear God's word through great preachers, teachers, family, and friends.
- ☞ Jesus is not saying the Nivenvites of Jonah's day are eternally Saved but will provide a norm of comparison for the judgment of the Jews.

12:42 The Queen of the South-◙ (i.e. Queen of Sheba.-{1-Kings 10:1-13} A city in Saudi Arabia, either "Yemen" or "Ethiopia".) **will rise at the judgment with this generation and condemn it; for she came from the ends of the earth** (Metph.-Great distance/pains.) **to listen to Solomon's wisdom, and now one greater than Solomon** (i.e. Jesus. In both wisdom, work, and message.) **is here.**

The Queen of Sheba will condemn Israel because she traveled great distances to hear the wisdom of a mere man, whereas they refused to listen to the Messiah who was in their own midsts.

Message & Application

- ❖ Shows how believers will have no excuses for not responding and resting on the divine wisdom and Saving work of Jesus.
- ❖ Calls for making the most of every opportunity, that no sacrifices, obstacles, or hardships are too much in seeking after Christ.
- ❖ Teaches how a heart that is truly following after Jesus will long to be taught and ministered by Him, that we may know His wisdom & truth.
- ❖ Reminds believers if we're not living a victorious life that is empowered by God, the problem is not with the Lord, but with us!
- ⊶ Even today we can go to Jesus for the wisdom & grace in dealing with any problem, burden, and crises we may be struggling with.

Parable of the Empty House-(Authors Insert)

12:43 "When an evil spirit comes out of a man, (i.e. Christ's work in delivering men from evil demons.) **it goes through arid places** (Expresses: Dwelling places of demons.) **seeking rest** (i.e. Mischief, evil doings) **and does not find it.**
44 Then it says, 'I will return to the house (Metph.-person) **I left.' When it arrives, it finds the house** (Metph.-heart/mind) **unoccupied** (Spiritual vacuum) **swept clean and put in order.** (garnished-K.J.V. Lit.-In his right mind. Metph.-reformed, rehabilitated, drug-free, clean, sober. Suggests: The same way Jesus healed people of demons. But in a wider context, persons who's life's were reformed by the Gospel, yet devoid of Christ and the Holy Spirit's presence.)
45 Then it goes and takes with it seven other spirits (Metph.-lusts, pride, vices, insecurities.) **more wicked than itself, and they go in and live there. And the final condition of that man is worse than the first. That is how it will be with this wicked generation.** (i.e. Israel. Suggests: Because of Israel's unbelief, they were in danger of spiritual apostasy. In a wider context a heart not fully committed to Christ will find itself given over to greater sin and bondages.)

Jesus having cleansed the nation of Israel of evil spirits, yet because of their rejection & unbelief of Him as the Messiah, they were in danger of a worse spiritual state.

Message & Application =

- ❖ Shows believers how it's not enough to reform & clean up our life, we have to invite Jesus into our hearts and be filled with His word/truth!
- ❖ Warns believers against simply cleaning up our act and turning over a new leaf, without giving Jesus control and authority over our lives.
- ❖ Warns how being indifferent and callous in our walk with the Lord can leave us vulnerable to temptation and relapse. (cf. 2-Pet. 2:20-22)
- ❖ Warns without Christ ruling and dwelling in our hearts we can slowly fall back into sin. (An ounce of prevention is worth a pound of cure).
- ❖ Warns how we can make ourselves easy targets for Satan to exploit when we start to compromise our walk with Jesus for other things.
- ❖ Warns how a heart that is void of Christ will only leave a vacuum, yearning to be filled with other things, usually unhealthy things!

¬***Seven other spirits***-Meaning: Since *"Seven"* in scripture is usually symbolic of perfection & completeness. It is seen here as representing the number of evil spirits needed to bring about the man's complete depravity. Or as the number of vices that Satan could use against him.

⊶ Even today, believers need to see that we're filling our lives with the things of Christ, Church, bible study, and prayer. Or we can slowly slip back to our old sinful lifestyle and habits of drinking, partying, and hanging around the wrong people. (cf. Eph. 4:22-29)

Jesus' Mother and Brothers-(N.I.V.)

12:46 While Jesus was still talking to the crowd, his mother and brothers (i.e. James, Joses, Simone, and Judas.-{Matt. 13:55} Born either by Mary after Jesus, or were Jesus' step-brothers born to Joseph by a previous marriage.) **stood outside, wanting to speak to Him.** (Suggests: They were concerned that the strain of Jesus' ministry was affecting His mental health.{cf. Mark 3:21})
47 Someone told him, "Your mother and brothers are standing outside, (Suggests: We're never supporters of Jesus' ministry at this time.-{John 7:5} Or was simply due to the overcrowded house.{Luke 8:19} **wanting to speak to you.**
48 He replied to him, "Who is my mother, and who are my brothers?"
49 Pointing to his disciples, he said, "Here are my mother and my brothers. (Not literally but in the spiritual sense as in obedience, devoutness, and loyalty)
50 For whoever does the will of my Father in heaven, (i.e. To trust & believe on Jesus.-{John 6:28-29} Followed by a faithful/obedient relationship. Hear God's word and put it into practice.-{Luke 8:21}) **is my brother and sister and mother."**

Believers are to put spiritual ties & relationships above physical ties.

Message & Application 💻=🌎

- ❖ Shows how the mark of a true follower of Jesus will have a life that is faithfully devoted to obeying and serving Him. (cf. Matt. 7:20-23)
- ❖ Calls for seeing that our lives reflect that we belong to Jesus. (Can other people tell that you've given your life over to Jesus?).
- ❖ Displays how true followers of Christ will be hungry for His word and truth. (Do you see Jesus' words as the words of life?). (John 6:68)
- ❖ Gives comfort in having a greater spiritual family of love, support, and belonging than we could ever get from our relatives and friends.
- ❖ Teaches how God's love and Saving grace is equally open to all people regardless of age, race, gender, or social standing. (Vs. 49-50.)
- ❖ Warns how the good intentions of family & friends can sometimes be a believer's greatest hindrance in obeying God's will. (Family members will not always have the same interests, goals, or concerns in mind).
- ⊶ Even today a distinguishing mark of a true follower of Jesus will have a life that is becoming more and more loving, caring, kind, patient, generous, honest, truthful, holy, and forgiving of others. (Gal. 5:22-23)
- ☞ Jesus is not saying that He expects us to live a perfect sinless life, when will often blow it. But rather it is one who will continue to serve and follow after the Lord even when they stumble and fall into sin.
- ☞ Jesus is not being cold or indifferent to His mother, nor was He downplaying the importance of family. For He would later while hanging on the cross provide for His mother's security.(John 19:25-27) But rather was teaching the importance of prioritizing God's will and interests first.

Chapter Thirteen

Jesus' Teachings in Parables

- **"The Sower"-**Teaches on the extent people apply their hearts to the Gospel and Salvation.-(Vs. 1-9)
- **The Purpose of Parables-**Teaches on having open & receptive heart towards the Gospels(Vs. 10-17)
- **"The Weeds & Wheat"-**Teaches on the mixture of true and false believers.-(Vs. 24-30, 37-43)
- **"The Mustard seed & Yeast"-** Teaches on the inner growth and development of the Gospel.(Vs. 31-43)
- **"The Hidden treasure & Pearl"-** Teaches on the uncalculated value of the Gospel & Salvation-(Vs. 44-46)
- **"The Net"-**Teaches on the separation between genuine & false believers on the day of judgment-(Vs. 47-50)

The Parable of the Sower-(N.I.V.)

13:1 That same day Jesus went out of the house (Peter's)**and sat by the lake.**
2 Such large crowds gathered around him that he got into a boat and sat in it,
(Suggests: As a makeshift pulpit.) **while all the people stood on the shore.**
3 Then he told them many things in parables,(3850-*Denotes a placing beside, to throw or lay beside.)* **saying: "A farmer went out to sow his seed.**
4 As he was scattering the seed, some fell along the path (wayside-K.J.V. A.V. i.e. Foot pathways, common roads.) **and the birds came and ate it up.**
5 Some fell on rocky places, where it did not have much soil. It sprang up quickly, because the soil was shallow. (i.e. Having only a thin top soil.)
6 But when the sun came up, the plants were scorched, and they withered (Syn.-dried up) **because they had no root.** (i.e. Lacked moisture for growth.)
7 Other seed fell among thorns, which grew up and choked the plants.
8 Still other seed fell on good soil (i.e. fertile, rich) **where it produced a crop —a hundred, sixty or thirty times what was sown.**
9 He who has ears, let him hear." (Expresses: Calls for spiritual attention.)

(For the interpretation & application of this parable see exposition at verses-18-23)

Message & Application 💻=🌎

–***Path***-Meaning: A trail or footpath that was hard-pact by foot traffic and where a seed could not take root, making it easy pickings for birds.

–***Rocky places***-Meaning: Bedrock covered with just a thin layer of soil, preventing the plant's roots from finding sufficient moisture.

–***Thorns***-Meaning: Weeds or thorn bushes that were not pulled out after the field had been plowed. Such thorns would deprive the seed sprouts of nourishment, water, light, and space to grow.

–***Good soil***-Meaning: Well plowed, cultivated, and rich in nutrients.

From this verse here (V. 10) to verse (V. 17) Jesus teaches on the purpose behind His parables.

The Purpose of Parables-(Authors Insert)

13:10 The disciples came to him (Jesus) **and asked, "Why do you speak to the people** (crowds-V.2) **in parables?**(3850-*Placing of one thing beside another for comparison.* A simple story used to illustrate a moral lesson and spiritual truth.)
11 He replied, "The knowledge of the secrets of the kingdom of heaven" (Expresses: Not some secret mystery, formula, rite, or puzzle to be solved. But rather God's plan of Salvation now revealed in the Gospel.) **has been given** (i.e. Through divine illumination, God's revealing grace.) **to you,** (Jesus' twelve inner disciples.) **but not to them.** (i.e. crowds-V.2 Suggests: Because the disciples had open hearts, whereas the people had stubborn and unbelieving hearts.)

Jesus speaks in parables because only the disciples have open & receptive hearts to hear the Gospel and God's plan of Salvation.

Message & Application

❖ Shows how God gives spiritual understanding to those whose hearts are open & receptive and conceals it from those who are hard at heart.
❖ Displays those who come with open & teachable hearts will inquire further into Jesus' parables, while the careless and indifferent will not.
❖ Teaches how Saving faith and spiritual insight is not a result of one's wisdom, intellect, or diligent study but a gift of God's sovereign grace.
❖ Displays how those who are working out their faith & Salvation will come to Jesus in wanting to know more. (Philp. 2:12, 3:13-14, 2-Pet. 1:5-10)

Even today those who know the truth will see in Jesus' parables and teachings a spiritual lesson and important truth to be learned. While others will only see them as empty stories without much meaning.

Purpose of Jesus' Parables:

- To reveal spiritual truths to the earnest, and to conceal it from the disinterested at heart.
- To separate truth-seekers from curiosity-seekers.
- To teach a spiritual truth and moral lesson.
- To disarm opposition & bypass defensive instincts.
- To capture and hold a person's interest & curiosity.
- To show mercy by giving people time to grow.
- To fulfill prophecy of the coming Messiah.

Types of Parables used by Jesus:

Similitude: A figure of speech that draws the comparisons between two different things by using phrases that contain the words "As" or "like". ("The Kingdom of Heaven is "like" a mustard seed or "like" yeast".)

Metaphor: A figure of speech that makes comparisons between two objects by carrying over an earthly truth to teach a moral or spiritual lesson. Then allowing the listener to draw the comparison for themselves. ("You are the salt of the earth you are the light of the world".)

Allegorical: An extended metaphor that takes on the form of a story, usually with a beginning, middle, and end. ("Workers in the Vineyard", "Prodigal Son".)

Interpreting Parables:

- **Parable Lesson:** Parables usually have only one main point & message.
- **Parable Symbols:** Identify the allegorical types and symbols within the story.
- **Parable Interpretation**: Do not over-allegorize the parable, do not push every word in the parable to symbolize something else.
- **Parable Message:** Understand the moral lesson behind the parable (Do not try to find a spiritual truth in every detail of the story, only its main message).

Classification of Parables

Era of grace: Parables that deal with present duties, responsibilities, and obligations of the believer here and now, between Jesus' first and second Advents.

Eschatological: Parables that deal with events to take place at Jesus' second coming.

13:12 Whoever has (Saving faith, receptive heart) **will be given more,** (i.e. spiritual truth, discernment, insight) **and he will have an abundance.** (i.e. A life rooted in the ways of heaven, godliness, and holiness.) **Whoever does not have even what he has,** (i.e. Understanding of God's word.) **will be taken from him.**

Believers who have earnest & receptive hearts for God's word will be given more understanding.

Message & Application 💻=🌎

❖ Shows how those who's hearts are honestly responding to the light & truth that God has given them will receive more truth to lead them on.
❖ Teaches how those who have a ready heart for learning God's word and truth will grow more and more in their walk and understanding.
❖ Warns those who don't want to grow closer to God will get exactly what they ask for! (God does not go where He's not wanted!).
🗝 Even today the same principal applies as to the law of life. That if you don't practice a skill or exercise a muscle it will eventually grow weak and die. So too with our spiritual life's, that how much we're willing to learn & study God's word will determine whether we grow or regress. (How do you respond when you hear the word preached, or when someone says let's read the bible, are you excited or indifferent?)

13:13 This is why I speak to them in parables: "Though seeing, (Jesus' miracles) **they do not see;** (spiritually) **though hearing,** (Jesus' teachings, preaching) **they do not hear** (spiritually) **or understand.** (Suggests: Taken together, attributes their unbelief to spiritual dullness and hardness of heart.)

Jesus speaks in parables because of the people's spiritual dullness and hardness of heart.

Message & Application 💻=🌎

❖ Shows how Jesus speaks in parables for those who have closed their hearts to the truth, that they have a sin problem that needs fixing.
❖ Calls for always seeing things from God's point of view. (Never be blind or deaf to your own faults, failures, and shortcomings!).
❖ Calls believers in always taking God's word to heart, accepting the truth about ourselves even if it's not what we like or expected.
❖ Displays how people don't like to be told they need to repent because that would require them to admit there's something wrong with them.
🗝 Even today God has a remedy & diagnosis, but many just can't bring themselves to see that they're a sinner who needs to be healed. Or they'll remain in self-denial that there's anything wrong with them.

13:14 In them is fulfilled the prophecy of Isaiah: "'You will be ever hearing but never understanding; you will be ever seeing but never perceiving.
15 For this people's heart has become calloused; (waxed gross-K.J.V.-3975-*To render dull, stupid, and callous.* Metph.-insensitive, indifferent, close-minded, hardhearted.) **they hardly hear with their ears, and they have closed their eyes.** (Expresses obstinate and willful unbelief.) **Otherwise** (Expresses either: A "judicial" hardening on God's part in giving them up to their willful rejection. Or as in "bitter irony" having willfully given themselves over to their own hardness of heart.) **they might see with their eyes, hear with their ears, understand with their hearts and turn,** (be converted-K.J.V. Syn.-repent, surrender, yield) **and I would heal them.** (i.e. Pardon, Save, forgive.) {Is. 6:9-10}

The people's spiritual insensitivity fulfilled Isaiah's prophecy of those who hardened their hearts & closed their eyes to the Gospel.

Message & Application 💻=🌎

- ❖ Shows how believers are to come with open & prepared hearts in seeing ourselves as sinners who need God's mercy and forgiveness.
- ❖ Calls for keeping our hearts open to any sin, rebellion, or callousness that God is revealing in our lives.
- ❖ Warns against tuning God out, that you've already decided what you will believe and accept even before you give God's word a chance.
- 🗝 Even today many often turn a deaf ear to God's voice, that they are either too prideful to bow to the truth, that they're a sinner who needs to repent. Or they block God out, too afraid of what God's claims may entail in having to give up their sin and turn their life's over to Him.

13:16 But blessed are your eyes because they see, and your ears because they hear. (Expresses Spiritual perception and open hearts to hear the Gospel.)
17 For I tell you the truth, many prophets and righteous men (i.e. O.T. Saints, Patriarchs.) **longed to see what you see but did not see it, and to hear what you hear but did not hear it.** (Suggests: Jesus' ministry and work in Salvation.)

The Disciples were privileged in seeing the Gospel and God's plan of Salvation now fulfilled in Christ.

Message & Application 💻=🌎

- ❖ Shows believers how blessed & privileged we are in having God bring us to a place in seeing our sins and our need for a Savior!(1-Pet. 1:10-12)
- ❖ Warns of squandering the gracious opportunity to get right with God.
- 🗝 Even today, believers should be grateful for having the voice and word of God to direct our path and correct us when we go astray.

13:18 "Listen then to what the parable of the sower means:
19 When anyone hears the message about the kingdom (i.e. Gospel, the word of God.) **and does not understand it, the evil one** (Satan) **comes and snatches away what was sown in his heart. This is the seed sown along the path.**
20 The one who received the seed that fell on rocky places is the man who hears the word (Metph.-Gospel, Salvation) **and at once receives it with joy.**
21 But since he has no root, (Syn.-conviction, conversion, Saving faith) **he lasts only a short time. When trouble** (hardships) **or persecution comes because of the word** (Gospel) **he quickly falls away.** (i.e. loses faith, backslides, apostasies)
22 The one who received the seed that fell among the thorns is the man who hears the word, but the worries (Syn.-anxieties, worldly cares) **of this life and the deceitfulness of wealth** (Metph.-riches) **choke it, making it unfruitful.**
23 But the one who received the seed that fell on good soil (Metph.-receptive heart) **is the man who hears the word and understands it He produces a crop, yielding a hundred, sixty or thirty times what was sown.**

To what extent people respond & apply their hearts to the Gospel determines their Salvation and spiritual growth.

Message & Application =

– ***Path***-Meaning: A person who does not respond to the Gospel at all. One who hears the Word but does not allow it to take root in the heart. One who's heart is hard that the Gospel makes no impression on them.

–***Rocky places***-Meaning: A person who responds to the Gospel but who's faith is superficial and falls away at the first sign of hardships and persecution. Portrays a believer whose faith is shallow. One who allows the trials/adversities of this life to draw them away from Christ.

–***Thorns***-Meaning: A person who responds to the Gospel but is pulled away by the deceitfulness of riches. Portrays a believer who allows the Gospel to be crowded out by the cares of this life, the lure of money, wealth, fame. One who is preoccupied with wealth & life's pleasures.

–***Good soil***-Meaning: A person who sincerely responds to the Gospel. Portrays a believer who is growing in the word and bearing fruit in their lives.

Allegorical types

Path... = A believer whose heart is hard and unaffected by the Gospel.

Rocky places... = A believer whose heart falls away because of troubles & hardships.

Thorns.. = A believer whose heart falls away because of worldly lusts & pleasures.

Good soil..= A believer whose heart is growing in the word.

The Parable of the Weeds -(N.I.V.)

13:24 Jesus told them another parable: "The kingdom of heaven (Metph-Gospel dispensation) **is like a man who sowed good seed in his field.**
25 But while everyone was sleeping, (Expresses enemy's subtlety, craftiness) **his enemy came and sowed weeds among the wheat, and went away.**
26 When the wheat sprouted and formed ears (Heads of grain)**then the weeds also appeared.** (Thought by many to be a poisonous weed known as "darnel".)
27 "The owner's servants came to him and said, 'Sir, didn't you sow good seed in your field? Where then did the weeds (tares-K.J.V.) **come from?'**
28 "'An enemy did this,' he replied. "The servants asked him, 'Do you want us to go and pull them up?.
29 "'No,' he answered, 'because while you are pulling the weeds, you may root up the wheat with them. (Suggests: Darnels & Wheat looked exactly alike, only after the heads of grains developed could they be distinguished.)
30 Let both grow together until the harvest. At that time I will tell the harvesters: First, collect the weeds and tie them in bundles to be burned; (i.e. As a source of fuel for ovens) **then gather the wheat and bring it into my barn**

(For the interpretation & application of this parable see exposition at verses-36-43)

Message & Application

-Everyone was sleeping-Meaning: Not that the servants were neglectful, but rather signifies the stealthy and malicious character of the enemy. In a wider sense portrays believer's who become neglectful in their duties. Typifies spiritual slumber, laziness, indifference, moral decay.

–Enemy- Meaning: A common practice during warfare or personal feuds for an enemy to destroy the other nation's ability to feed and support its army. Or as an act of revenge for destroying someone's livelihood. Metaphorically portrays Satan's goal to harm and destroy the Church.

–Sowed weeds-Meaning: To fling seeds from a bag with a fan like motion. If it was a "darnel" type of seed it would cause nausea, dizziness, and even death for people who eat it. In a wider sense portrays the hatred, malice, and duplicity of Satan in trying to destroy our walk with God.

–Let them grow until the harvest-Meaning: The reason for forbidding the pulling up of weeds-(Vs. 28-29) was due to the fact that by this time the roots of the weeds had already entangled themselves around the roots of the wheat, making it impossible to uproot one without the other as well. In a wider sense reasons for forbidding the separation is due to either: Questioning a believer's faith could damage the Saved, thinking they were unjustly excommunicated and judged. Or that these people under God's grace & patience may later repent and become believers.

The parable of the Mustard Seed-(N.I.V.)

13:31 He told them another parable: "The kingdom of heaven (Metph.-Church, Gospel, God's grace.) **is like** (Expresses a Simile-parable.) **a mustard seed,-◙** (Metph.-small, insignificant) **which a man took and planted in his field. 32 Though it is the smallest of all your seeds,** (Lit. 1-ml. in size. Suggests: The Church starting off with only a handful of disciples.) **yet when it grows, it is the largest of garden plants and becomes a tree,-◙ so that the birds of the air come and perch in its branches.** (Metph-sanctuary, refuge, security, peace.)

Though the Church/Gospel starts out small it will eventually spread throughout the world.

Message & Application 💻=🌎

❖ Shows the growth of the Gospel starting out small & insignificant at first, with only 12 disciples, yet spreading throughout the world.
❖ Calls believers in not allowing the fact that we're not the biggest or most gifted keep us from being used by God in mighty/powerful ways.
❖ Teaches we may not know why God has planted us in a certain place, but we can be sure He will see that we bloom in doing great things.
❖ Encourages believers in never quitting or giving up. (Don't measure your success/efforts, or Christ's power on what you can see right now)
❖ Reminds believers no matter how small or insignificant we feel we are, God has a great plan for our life's. (Press on despite small beginnings).

-***Mustard seed***-Meaning: A seed that produces a tree known as the "Black mustard plant", which can grow 6' to 12' feet tall. Some have tried to disprove the bible, that Jesus got it wrong, that the smallest seed was not the "Mustard" but the "Orchid" or "Poppy". (Many counter this by pointing out that Jesus was only referring to the agricultural manner of planting seeds. That it was the smallest seed commonly planted in one's crop as opposed to something that grows wild).

🗝 Even today, believers can expect that wherever in life God has placed us or called us to do, He will use it in having a transforming impact on the people, world, and society around us.

☞ Because some interpret *"birds"* as a symbol of Satan & his evil forces. They see the parable as both a prediction & warning on the corruption of the Church by false teachers. (Not accepted by all scholars).

Allegorical types

Mustard seed… = Church/Gospel growth.
Man… = Jesus, God.
Field... = World, Israel.
Birds… = Sinners, lost souls.

Parable of the Yeast-(N.I.V.)

13:33 He told them still another parable: The kingdom of heaven (Metph-Gospel, God's rule) **is like yeast-◙** (leaven-K.J.V.-2219-*Acting agent used to make dough rise. Something that pervades a thing.*) **that a woman took and mixed into a large amount of flour** (three measures of meal.-K.J.V.-A common amount [50 lbs.] that a woman could knead at one time, feeding 100 people.) **until it worked all through the dough.** (Expresses the spreading influence of the Gospel in the world. Or the inner transforming power of God's word.)

Though the Gospel starts out small it will eventually permeate and spread throughout the world.

Message & Application 💻=🌎

- ❖ Shows the invisible rule & reign of God in the hearts of believers, slowly changing and transforming us from the inside out.
- ❖ Displays the inner transforming work of God's word, turning our hearts from the power and love of sin to the love of God.
- ❖ Teaches even though we can't see what God is doing, we can trust that He's working/moving in our life's whether we feel it or not.
- ❖ Calls for patience, though growth/change is slow at first, it will come! (Know you're a work in progress, that God isn't done with you yet!).

-Yeast- Meaning: Since *"yeast"* in scripture is nearly always used to symbolize evil & wickedness. Some view the depiction of yeast here in a bad sense, as in the influence of false teachers & doctrines within the Church. (Most reject this interpretation based on the fact that "yeast" can be a mixed metaphor denoting both a negative & positive force, as "Lion" can be used both for Satan & Christ. (1-Pet. 5:8, Rev. 5:5)

🔑 Even today believers can count on God's continuing work in gradually changing our hearts bit by bit. Helping us to say "No" more & more to sin, and saying "Yes" to righteousness and His ways.

☞ While the previous parable of the "Mustard seed" spoke of the visible outward growth of the Church and our faith upon the world. (Vs. 31-32) The parable of the "Yeast" here speaks of the inward spiritual growth of God's Word/Gospel upon the heart and life of a believer.

Allegorical types

Yeast… = Gospel's influence, God's rule/grace.
False believers/doctrines -(Not universally accepted)
Flour/dough… = World, heart, soul.
Woman… = Christ, God, Church, Ministers of the Gospel.
Apostate Church-(Not universally accepted)

13:34 Jesus spoke all these things to the crowd in parables; (i.e. Forgoing parables of the "Sower", "Wheat & Weeds", "Mustard Seed & Yeast".-{Vs. 3-33}) **he did not say anything to them without using a parable.** (3850-*A placing of one thing beside another for comparison.* Suggests: A story that was intended to teach a moral lesson and a spiritual truth.)
35 So was fulfilled what was spoken through the prophet: "I will open my mouth in parables, I will utter (Syn.-discourse, teach, discuss, explain-L.B.V.) **things hidden** (Suggests: Not enigmatical sayings, but rather Gospel truths of God's plan of redemption & Salvation.) **since the creation of the world."** {"Asaph's"-Ps. 78:2-LXX} Expresses how Jesus was making known through His life, teachings, and miracles for the first time in history the nature of God's righteous acts in mankind's Redemption and Salvation.)

Jesus used parables to excite men's attention and curiosity, as He revealed God's plan of redemption & Salvation.

Message & Application 💻=🌎

- ❖ Shows believers the need to keep our hearts open & teachable if we're going to have a deeper understanding of God's word. (cf. V. 36)
- ❖ Encourages believers how we have in Jesus' parables hidden truths that have the power to help us grow, enriching our life's.
- ❖ Teaches if we're going to get to know God better we must be willing to spend time reading, studying, and meditating on His Word. (Do you faithfully attend bible study on a regular basis?).
- ❖ Teaches how there's a moral lesson and spiritual principle to be learned from God's word. (How has a story in the bible changed you?)
- ❖ Calls for putting ourselves in Jesus' parables, that there's always a truth to be learned and applied. (Much as you are doing right now!).

***-He did not say anything without using a parable*-**Does not mean that Jesus spoke nothing but parables (e.g. Sermon on the Mount). But rather He taught nothing without incorporating some sort of metaphor or analogy. That parables were an essential part of Jesus' teaching ministry used to illustrate spiritual truths and stimulate thinking.

🗝 Even today, believers must always view Jesus' teachings as containing some spiritual truth or important lesson to be learned and lived out in our daily lives.

☞ In context, the quoted Psalm was a historical overview of God's redemptive acts with His people Israel. From the time of their Slavery in Egypt to David's reign. That despite their sin and unfaithfulness God was still willing to redeem His people.

Jesus' other Parables:

- **The Growing seed-**Teaches on the transforming power of the Gospel and the believer's spiritual growth.-(Mark 4:26-29)
- **The Watchful & Faithful Servant-**Teaches on the importance of constant vigilance and stewardship, always being prepared for Christ's return by faithfully carrying out one's duties.-(Luke 12:35-48)
- **The Moneylender-**Teaches on how all are sinners and debtors to God. That the true appreciation of God's mercy & forgiveness expresses itself in deeds of love and gratitude. -(Luke 7:41-43)
- **The Good Samaritan**-Teaches on the importance of compassion and mercy towards others, that love will display itself by action. -(Luke 10:30-37)
- **The Rich Fool-**Teaches on the dangers of greed and self-centeredness. That the true meaning of life is found in following and serving God. -(Luke 12:16-21)
- **The Lowest Seat at the Feats-**Teaches the importance of humility and the need to extend mercy & hospitality to all without distinction. (Luke 14:7-14)
- **The Great Banquet-**Teaches on the dangers of making up excuses in putting Christ off. That God provides sufficient provisions of Salvation for all.-(Luke 14:16-24)
- **The Lost Sheep/Lost Coin-**Teaches how God actively seeks out lost sinners. That each individual soul is precious in God's sight. -(Luke 15:3-10)
- **The Lost/Prodigal Son-**Teaches on God's love, patience, and compassion for the repentant sinner, and the dangers of remaining self-righteous. -(Luke 15:11-32)
- **The Shrewd Manager-**Teaches on the importance of prudence and foresight, and the proper use of wealth and talents for the benefit of others. -(Luke 16:1-13)
- **The Rich Man and Lazarus-**Teaches on the dangers of self-centeredness, self-gratification, uncharitableness, and the finality of judgment and eternal destinies.-(Luke 16:19-31)

The Parable of the Weeds Explained-(N.I.V.)

13:36 Then he left the crowd and went into the house. His disciples came to him and said, "Explain to us the parable of the weeds in the field."
37 He answered "The one who sowed the good seed is the Son of Man.{12:8}
38 The field is the world, (i.e. mankind) **and the good seed stands for the sons of the kingdom.** (Metph.-Believers, Saints, the Saved.) **The weeds** (Metph-false believers, hypocrites, the unsaved.) **are the sons of the evil one,** (i.e. Satan)
39 and the enemy who sows them is the devil. The harvest is the end of the age, (i.e. Day of Judgment.) **and the harvesters are angels.**
40 As the weeds are pulled up and burned in the fire, so it will be at the end of the age. (i.e. Christ's return, final day of judgment.-{cf. Rev. 14:14-15})
41 The Son of Man (Jesus) **will send out his angels, and they will weed out of his kingdom** (Church, Christendom) **everything that causes sin and all who do evil.**(Expresses one who's a stumbling block or undermines the faith of others.)
42 They will throw them into the fiery furnace, (Metph.-Hell, Lake of fire) **where there will be weeping and gnashing of teeth.** (Expresses sorrow and remorse mixed with pain and suffering in hell.)
43 Then the righteous (i.e. Not sinless, but who are sincere & upright, who are clothed with Christ's righteousness.) **will shine like the sun in the kingdom of their Father.** (Expresses believers glorious state in heaven.) **He who has ears let him hear.** (Calls for the greatest care and attention in having a teachable spirit, that there's a spiritual truth/principle and lesson to be learned.)

Describes the mixture of true & false believers within the world/church and their separation at the final judgment.

Message & Application =

- ❖ Shows believers the need in uprooting the sin & false areas of our lives that's out of place and not in line with God's word. (2-Corn. 13:5)
- ❖ Calls for staying alert, that Satan is doing all he can to undermine our faith, destroy our walk, and steal our Salvation. (cf. 1-Pet. 5:8)
- ❖ Prepares believers in not being surprised when we find false and hypocritical Christians in the Church and the world around us.
- ❖ Displays God's patience & grace in giving people every opportunity to grow and bear fruit from being weeds to being wheat. (cf. 2-Pet. 3:9)
- ❖ Reminds believers how it's not our place to judge & condemn, but to warn & help others in choosing to be wheat, not weeds! (James 5:19-20)

⊶ Even today Satan will try to undermine our faith by planting false Christians into our lives who will try to lead us away from the truth, that you need Jesus plus works to be Saved. Or they'll try to get us to compromise our faith, that a little sin is no big deal, that you can sow your wild oats and still be right with God. (cf. 1-Corn. 5:1-11, Gal. 1:6-9)

Parable of the Hidden Treasure and Pearl-(N.I.V.)

13:44 "The kingdom of heaven (Metph.-Gospel, Salvation, eternal life, Jesus) **is like treasure hidden in a field.** (Suggests: Since there were no banks people buried their valuables in the ground for safekeeping.) **When a man** (i.e. Renter, hired laborer, trespasser. Metph.-Sinner, believer) **found it** (i.e. Possibly during plowing or sowing.) **he hid it again,** (i.e. Least the landowner claim it for himself.) **and then in his joy went and sold all he had and bought that field.**
45 "Again, the kingdom of heaven is like a merchant (i.e. Wholesale dealer) **looking for fine pearls-◙** (goodly pearls-K.J.V. Syn.-High-quality/grade, rare. Suggests: Not by diving for pearls, but by shopping the open market.)
46 When he found one of great value, (i.e. Flawless character, perfectly spherical, or rare in color.) **he went away and sold everything he had and bought it.** (Expresses no sacrifice too great, or the need for total investment.)

Salvation is of such great value that one should be willing to give up all they have to gain it.

Message & Application 💻=🌎

- ❖ Shows how believers will joyfully give up anything out of gratitude for all that Jesus has done in Saving us from our sins. (cf. Gal. 4:15)
- ❖ Displays the incalculable value of our Salvation, and the need for our total investment and commitment.
- ❖ Teaches how a relationship with Christ must stand supreme over everything and everyone else in our life's. (cf. Philp. 3:7-14)
- ❖ Teaches how nothing can compare to the new life that God can give us. (Are you aware of your sin sickness in light of God's mercy?).
- ⊶ Even today a believers Salvation and walk with Jesus should be so valuable that there's no sin, job, possession, relationship, habit, entitlement, etc. that we wouldn't gladly and joyfully walk away from.
- ☞ Jesus is not implying that one can purchase their Salvation with money or self-effort. Nor was Jesus teaching a lesson on the ethical or legality of the man's tactics. But is simply commending the man's correct value of things in capitalizing on the opportunities presented to him.
- ☞ Some view the parable as depicting the "Treasure/Pearl" as that of the Church. And the "Finder/Merchant" as Jesus who loved and valued us so much that He willingly gave up His life to purchase us for Himself.
- ☞ Some make distinctions between the two men. How some find Salvation by "happenstance" (finder) and the other (Merchant), only after a lifetime of diligent searching. The self-righteous & religious after years of struggle, whereas the humble and contrite immediately.

The Parable of the Net-(N.I.V.)

13:47 Once again, the kingdom of heaven (Metph.-Gospel age, age of grace.) **is like a net that was let down**-◙ (Suggests: A "dragnet" towed behind two boats and then drawn to shore. Metph.-The preaching of the Gospel message.) **into the lake** (Metph.-World, lost souls/humanity.) **and caught all kinds of fish.** (Metph-Mixed nationalities, races, characters, backgrounds, etc.)

48 When it was full, the fishermen pulled it up on the shore.-◙ (Metph.-Day of judgment, no reprieve or second chances.) **Then they sat down** (Expresses: Care, evaluation, estimation. That God's judgments are never rash or hasty, that He has all the details and facts of our lives before passing sentence.) **and collected the good fish** (Lit.-Ceremonially clean, marketable. Metph.-True-believer, born again, redeemed, converted.) **in baskets,**-◙ **but threw the bad** (Unclean/unmarketable. Metph.-unbeliever, unrepented, unconverted.) **away.**

49 This is how it will be at the end of the age. (i.e. Day of judgment.) **The angels will come and separate the wicked** (Metph.-hypocrite, unbeliever, false Christians.) **from the righteous** (Suggests: Not those who are sinless and perfect,-{cf. Rom. 3:10} but those who have been Saved by the blood of Christ.)

50 and throw them into the fiery furnace, (Metph-Hell, lake of fire.-{Rev.20:11-15} **where there will be weeping and gnashing of teeth.**-(Expresses sorrow and remorse mixed with pain and suffering in hell.)

On the day of judgment, God will separate truly born again believers from unbelievers.

<u>Message & Application</u>

❖ Shows how believers are to see that we're born again, that we've truly trusted and believed on Jesus for Salvation. (cf. Col. 1:23, 2-Pet. 1:10-12)

❖ Calls for seeing that we're Christians not just in name and profession only, but also in practice. (Are you the real deal or merely pretending).

❖ Displays the universal nature of God's grace, how it's open to all people, good or bad. (God doesn't discriminate, neither should we!).

❖ Teaches those who've been swept up in the Lord's Saving grace will reflect it in a change of life that is loving, caring, and pleasing to God.

❖ Warns how you may think that you have your Church, Pastor, and family fooled, but you cannot fool God who sees the real you!

❖ Displays the difference between those who are allowing God to have His way in their lives and those who are not.

⊶ Even today, believers need to know exactly where we stand in our relationship with the Lord. That its not about how loving, generous, or good we were. Or how much we attended church, tithed, or obeyed the commandments. But rather about whether we've truly repented and put our faith in Jesus for Salvation! (cf. Matt. 3:9, 2-Corn. 13:5, Heb. 4:1)

The Parable of the House Holder-(Authors Insert)

13:51 "Have you understood all these things?" (i.e. The seven previous parables and their spiritual truths.) **Jesus asked. "Yes," they replied.** (Expresses: Possibly presumptuous enthusiasm with only intrinsic knowledge.) **52 He said to them, "Therefore every teacher of the law** (scribe-K.J.V. i.e. Preacher, minister.) **who has been instructed** (Syn.-taught, trained, commissioned.) **about the kingdom of heaven** (Metph.-Gospel, eternal life, Salvation.) **is like the owner of a house** (Head of household. Metph.-Great authority, responsibility, steward.) **who brings out of his storeroom-◙** (cellar, pantry. Metph-wealth, values, experiences, knowledge.) **new treasures as well as old."**(Lit.-Last year's crops, this year's harvest. What is necessary for the welfare of the family. Metph.-Gospel teachings/applications, spiritual truths.)

Shows believers how we have in God's word a rich storehouse of spiritual truths & graces to which we can draw from.

Message & Application

- ❖ Shows how believers have been richly blessed with all the resources in God's word to draw from in living productive and transformed lives.
- ❖ Assures believers of having in Jesus' teachings all the practical guidelines for moving forward in our Christian faith and walk.
- ❖ Teaches how believers have a responsibility and duty to study God's word, that we may share it with others.
- ❖ Teaches the more we read God's word the more will get out of it, always discovering new things/truths we didn't see before.
- ❖ Teaches the importance of investing time in God's Word, that we may have a word of comfort, hope, and encouragement.
- ❖ Displays how we have in God's Word a wealth of resources to draw from in meeting any challenge, temptation, or trial facing us!

-***New treasures as well as old***- Variously seen as either:

- Adapting new & fresh insights to Jesus' teachings and parables to daily life.
- Interpreting Old Testament prophecies and promises in light of New Testament fulfillments.
- Utilizing the whole council of God's word, both O.T. & N.T.

⊶ Even today as we continue to grow in God's Word, will learn how to handle/cope with everyday problems and situations God's way. That we can become an inspiration and encouragement to others by sharing a teaching or a verse of scripture from God's word, and how it had helped us with our own struggles, doubts, and failures.

From this verse here (V. 53) To the end of the chapter, Jesus teaches on expecting rejection in discipleship.

A Prophet without Honor-(N.I.V.)

13:53 When Jesus had finished these parables, (i.e. The previous eight parable-{Vs. 3-49, 51-52}) **he moved on from there.** (i.e. Left the house in Capernaum-{V. 36}. That the disciples were well equipped to teach the people.)
54 Coming to his home town,-◙ (i.e. Nazareth, a village of about 1500 people.) **he began teaching the people in their synagogue,-◙** (Jewish places of worship) **and they were amazed.** (Syn.-astonished, blown away) **"Where did this man get this wisdom** (Expresses: Meant to criticize Jesus' lack of formal education, having never gone to Rabbinic school.) **and these miraculous powers?" they asked.** (Suggests: Taken together was meant to diminish Jesus' credentials.)
55 Isn't this the carpenter's son (i.e. Adopted son of Joseph. Possibly Jesus was brought up in the family trade.) **Isn't his mother's name Mary, and aren't his brothers** (i.e. Half-brothers) **James, Joseph, Simon, and Judas?**- {See 12:46-47}
56 Aren't all his sisters (i.e. Half-sisters) **with us?** (Suggests: Possibly that the sisters had remarried and remained in Nazareth.) **Where then did this man get all these things?"** (Expresses: Taken together because of Jesus' common and ordinary upbringing He didn't fit the Messiah's credentials.)

Because of Jesus' ordinary upbringing and lowly status, the people were unwilling to accept Him as the Messiah.

<u>Message & Application</u> 

- ❖ Shows how people can miss the message & work of Jesus when they only see Him from a worldly/human perspective. (cf. 2-Corn. 5:16)
- ❖ Warns how we can limit Jesus' healing power in our lives when we marginalize and box Him in.
- ❖ Calls for trusting that no matter our education or upbringing, God will equip us with the talents and ability do what He's called us to do!
- ❖ Warns how an unbelieving and resistant heart will always make up excuses and deny the obvious, rather than have to admit accountability.
- ❖ Warns the danger of familiarity, thinking we know everything about God's Word that it becomes an obstacle to spiritual growth and change. (When you get to the point that you've heard it all and there's nothing more to learn, that's when you begin to slip backwards!). (cf. Matt. 7:7-8)
- ⊶ Even today our preconceived views & criteria's about Jesus can become a barrier to what Christ can do in our lives, preventing Him from changing and transforming us.

13:57 And they took offense at him. (4624-*To stumble or trip up as in a snare, scandalize.* Syn.-contempt, prejudiced, refused to believe-N.L.T. Modern cliché *"Familiarity breeds contempt"*. Having been put off by Jesus' humble upbringing, they were unwilling to acknowledge Him as the Messiah.) **But Jesus said to them, "Only in his home town and in his own house** (Syn.-family, kinfolk) **is a prophet without honor."** (Expresses a common proverb that prophets are more accepted by others than their own countrymen or family. That because of pride and envy many will not accept being taught and preached to by one of their own peers.)
58 And he did not (could not-{Mark 6:5}) **do many miracles there because of their lack of faith.** (Suggests: Jesus could not perform miracles there because of their unbelief. Or chose not to do any more miracles in an atmosphere of unbelief "No point in working miracles for those who don't believe")

Because of the people's envy & hardness of heart they couldn't come to believe in Jesus as the Message.

Message & Application 💻=🌎

❖ Shows believers how pride & unbelief can rob us of our anointing, and keep us from experiencing God's highest and best for us.
❖ Calls for staying true to our faith and walk with Jesus no matter how many family and friends we lose along the way. (V. 57)
❖ Teaches how some of the toughest people to witness to are those in our own family. (Many will only see you for your past, and who you used to be, and not for who you are today!).
❖ Because family/friends are less likely to take our faith seriously due to our past history, all the more to witness not by words but by behavior!
❖ Teaches rather than taking offenses personally, respond with love and kindness, understanding people's fears, misconception, and errors.
❖ Calls for taking to heart that when our witness falls on deaf ears we're in good company, for Jesus was rejected by His own people.
❖ Warns against putting Jesus off just because He doesn't fit into the mold of our agendas, or conform to our wants and expectations.
❖ Warns how unbelief can hinder and shut us off from God's work in doing great and extraordinary things in our life's.
🗝 Even today, believers can't expect breakthroughs in our lives in an atmosphere of skepticism, doubt, and unbelief.
☞ Today many are only willing to follow Jesus as long as it doesn't cost them too much, come too uncomfortable, or force them to give up their pet sins.

Chapter Fourteen

Jesus' withdrawal & Unwavering Compassion

- **John the Baptist beheaded-** Teaches on staying true to our convictions regardless of the consequences.-(Vs. 1-14)
- **Jesus feeds the five thousand-** Jesus reveals Himself as the Messiah and the source of eternal life.-(Vs. 15-24)
- **Jesus walks on water-**A miracle attesting to Jesus' presence and protection in the storms of life.-(Vs. 25-36)

John the Baptist beheaded-(N.I.V.)

14:1 At that time (i.e. During Jesus' preaching ministry in Galilee.) **Herod** (i.e. Herod Antipas ruler of Galilee.) **the tetrarch** (5076-*A governor who rules over a fourth part of a country.)* **heard the reports about Jesus** (i.e. Jesus' miracles.)
2 and he said to his attendants This is John the Baptist; he has risen from the dead! That is why miraculous powers are at work in him. (Expresses: Herod having felt guilty for executing John, or saw in Jesus' miracles as evidence that John the Baptist had come back to life to haunt and exact revenge against him. Or that he was only repeating rumors held by others.-{cf. Luke 9:7})

Herod feeling guilty for killing John the Baptist thinks he has returned through Jesus to avenge his death.

Message & Application 💻=🌎

❖ Shows how guilt if not confessed & dealt with will only fester and grow. (Rather than try to silence or cover up sin, confess it to God!).
❖ Warns how unconfessed sin, if not repented of, will only haunt us with guilt. (Will you allow Jesus to clean the skeletons out of your closet?).
❖ Warns how holding onto sin can affect our lives, leading to all sorts of worries, fears, and misconceptions, not to mention guilt and self-pity.
❖ Calls for helping those who misunderstand Jesus to know Him better, that He's not out to punish or condemn, but to heal and Save!
❖ Teaches how only by coming clean and confessing our sins to God can real healing, freedom, and peace be found. (cf. 1-John 1:9)
❖ Calls for seeing that we're standing on God's word of forgiveness, that were not allowing Satan to bring up some sin over and over again.

🗝 Even today, believers can proclaim God's mercy & grace. But will not allow themselves to move on, thinking that some sin they committed in the past is too great for God to forgive. Not realizing that all their sins past, present, and future have already been forgiven and taken care of by Jesus once and for all on the Cross. (cf. Rom. 8:1-4, Eph. 1:7-9)

14:3 Now (Expresses: Used to explain the reasons for Herod's guilty conscience for having killed John.-{V. 2}) **Herod had arrested john and bound him and put him in prison-◙** (i.e. The prison at Machaerus in Perea, four miles east of the dead sea.) **because of Herodias, his brother Philip's wife,** (i.e. Herod had arrested John to please his wife's wishes.)
4 for John had been saying to him: (Expresses: Not a mild rebuke, but to repeatedly reprove over and over again, either privately or publicly.) **"It is not lawful for you to have her."** (Expresses either the marriage was adulterous because it was his brother Philip's wife. Or the marriage was incestuous, due to the fact that it was legally his niece, daughter of his half-brother Aristobulus.)
5 Herod wanted to kill John, but he was afraid of the people because they considered him a prophet. (Expresses how Herod feared for his own safety, or of his position as governor, that the people would revolt and start a riot.)

Herod arrested John for denouncing his marriage as adulterous for marrying his brother's wife.

Message & Application 💻=🌎

- ❖ Shows how believers are to have the courage in speaking the truth regardless of the consequences. (Be reformers, not compromisers!).
- ❖ Calls for doing what is right even if it's unpopular. (Will you remain uncompromising in your convictions or go along with the crowd?).
- ❖ Calls for being people of conviction & courage, confronting lifestyles that are contrary to the word of God, even if it offends others.
- ❖ Calls believers in always stepping up and doing the right thing even if it means paying the price for it later on if it doesn't go over well.
- ❖ Warns against becoming bitter and angry towards those who reprove us of our sin. (Know it's for your own spiritual welfare!). (V. 5)
- ❖ Teaches the importance of mildness/modesty, that we're not reproving others out of anger or indignation, but out of love and concern!
- ❖ Teaches the importance of not budging on issues that we know is wrong, even if it means rejection and fallout with others.

⊶ Even today rather than just sugarcoat or look past a person's immoral behavior. We need to confront them with the hard truths about their sinful lifestyle even if it results in confrontation, resentment, and backlash.

–***Herodias***-Granddaughter of "Herod the Great" daughter of Aristobulus half-brother of Antipas. She was first married to "Herod Philip" whom she left to marry his brother Antipas. John's denunciation of the marriage was based on the grounds that Mosaic law had forbidden the marriage to a brother's wife while he was still alive.-(cf. Lev. 18:16).

14:6 On Herod's birthday the daughter of Herodias (i.e. Salome, 12-17 years old.) **danced for them-◙** (Suggests: The custom of dancing seductively, provocatively, and erotically.) **and pleased** (Syn.-aroused) **Herod so much**
7 that he promised with an oath to give her whatever she asked.
8 Prompted (Syn.-coached, urged, instigated) **by her mother, she said, "Give me here on a platter-◙** (charger-K.J.V. Syn.-plate, dish) **the head of John the Baptist."** (Suggests: She was manipulated by her mother in exacting revenge against John for condemning her marriage as adulterous.-{cf. Mark 6:19})
9 The king was distressed, but because of his oaths and his dinner guests (i.e. Political officials, military commanders. That he feared he would lose face, appearing not a man of his word.) **he ordered that her request be granted**
10 and had John beheaded (i.e. By sword) **in the prison.** (i.e. Machaerus.)
11 His head was brought in on a platter and given to the girl, who carried it to her mother. (As confirmation that her mother's wishes were carried out.)

Herod fearing he might lose face and appear that he was not a man of his word has John beheaded.

Message & Application 💻=🌎

- ❖ Shows how believers are to have the moral courage in doing what is right regardless of the social pressures.
- ❖ Calls believers in staying true to our Christian morals even if it means appearing weak, humiliated, and embarrassed in front of others.
- ❖ Warns rather than allow fear to choose our course or sway our decisions in life, stay true to who you are in Christ!
- ❖ Warns against giving into peer pressure. (Don't compromise your walk and Christian principles out of fear or disapproval).
- 🗝 Even today if not careful we can cave under peer pressure, that we put more fear of looking bad at a party than doing what is right.

14:12 John's disciples came and took his body (i.e. Minus the head-{V. 11}) **and buried it. Then they went and told Jesus.** (i.e. Of John's execution.)

After giving John's body a proper burial his disciples warn Jesus of Herod's murderous act.

Message & Application 💻=🌎

- ❖ Shows believers how in times of tragedies & sorrows of life we can always come to Jesus for comfort and consultation. (Acquaint Jesus with your miseries and losses so He can help you move on!).
- ❖ Teaches how believers can go straight to Jesus in times of grief and distress. (Better to come to Christ in times of sorrow than not at all!).

14:13 When Jesus heard what had happened (i.e. John the Baptists execution-{V. 12}) **he withdrew** (departed-K.J.V.-402-*To retire, give place, turned aside.* Syn.-retreated, escaped. Expresses: Not of fear, but a tactical withdrawal in order to avoid Herod's violence, because His time to suffer had not yet come.) **by boat privately to a solitary place.** (Syn.-unpopulated, isolated. Suggests: Northeast shore of the Sea of Galilee.-{cf. John 6:1}) **Hearing of this, the crowds followed him on foot** (i.e. By land.) **from the towns.** (Suggests: The crowds ran by foot along the shoreline, while keeping the course of Jesus' boat in sight, even getting there ahead of Him.-{cf. Mark 6:33})

In order not to escalate the danger to His own life, Jesus finds safety across the lake outside of Herod's jurisdiction.

Message & Application 💻=🌎

- ❖ Shows how we can seek encouragement & comfort from God in times of tragedies. (Seek alone time with God to grieve and recover).
- ❖ Teaches believers how in times of grief and peril its good to get away that we may seek safety, rest, and time to pray.
- ❖ Teaches the importance of eagerly seeking and following after Christ regardless of the journey, hurdles, and obstacles. (V. 13b)
- ⊶ Even today when faced with the death of a loved one, a sick child, a hard day at work, etc. you can seek alone time with God to recover.

14:14 When Jesus landed and saw a large crowd, he had compassion on them (4697-*To have the bowels moved with compassion, pity, and sympathy.*) **and healed their sick.**

Jesus takes compassion on the people in seeing to their physical & spiritual needs.

Message & Application 💻=🌎

- ❖ Shows Jesus' love & compassion in always putting the lost & hurting first! (God always meets us at the point of our greatest need!)
- ❖ Calls believers in always seeing to the needs and concerns of others first before our own needs, wants, and comforts.
- ❖ Reminds believers regardless of our own personal crises, turmoil's, and grief's, always prioritize the welfare and needs of others first.
- ❖ Teaches how even in the midst of our own grief and heartbreak, we need to remember others and not wallow in our own self-pity.
- ⊶ Even today, believers are not to be so focused & self-absorbed with our own problems and issues, that we can't take time out to minister to the needs of those around us.

Jesus Feeds the Five Thousand (Jews)-(N.I.V.)

14:15 As evening approached, the disciples came to him and said, "This is a remote place, (i.e. Out of the way, isolated, unpopulated.) **and its already getting late. Send the crowds away, so that they can go to the villages and buy themselves some food."** (victuals-K.J.V.-Meat, foodstuff, etc.)
16 Jesus said, They do not need to go away. You give them something to eat.
17 "We have here only five loaves of bread-◙ and two fish," (Here is a boy with five small barley loaves and two small fish.-{John 6:9a}) **they answered.**
18 "Bring them here to me," he said.
19 And he directed the people to sit down on the grass. (Suggests: Early Spring.) **Taking the five loaves and the two fish and looking up to heaven, he gave thanks** (i.e. Gave the blessing) **and broke the loaves. Then he gave them to the disciples, and the disciples gave them to the people.**
20 They all ate and were satisfied, and the disciples picked up twelve basketfuls-◙ (2894-S*mall hand basket.* Symbolic of the Twelve tribes of Israel, or the Apostles, one for each disciple.) **of broken pieces that were left over.**
21 The number of those who ate was about five thousand men, besides women and children.(Estimates put the total number between 10,000-20,000.)

By miraculously feeding the multitudes, Jesus reveals Himself as the source and bread of life.

Message & Application

- Shows the sufficiency of Christ in satisfying the spiritual needs and deepest longings of the soul and even more! (cf. John 6:32-35)
- Teaches as we bring our limited resources, gifts, time, and talents to God, He will bless them and multiply them. (cf. Philp. 4:19)
- Displays God's abundant provision in providing the resources and solution for any problem, challenge, and obstacle we might face!
- Even today rather than focusing on our inadequacies; *"I don't have enough talent, abilities, training, etc. how can God use me*"? Believers are to trust that nothing is too big or too impossible for God to do!

Additional Lessons from Feeding the 5000

- God makes up for those areas where we're lacking.
- God wants us to take part in sharing in His work of blessing and meeting the needs of others.
- Believers are always to give thanks to God for everything, no matter how little we have.
- God wants us to be good stewards with what He gives us, not allowing anything to go to waste.

14:22 Immediately Jesus made (constrained-K.J.V.-315-*To compel by threat, force, or persuasion.*) **the disciples get into the boat and go on ahead of him to the other side,** (i.e. The west shore of the Sea of Galilee, Bethsaida-{Mark 6:45}) **while he dismissed the crowd.** (i.e. With a parting blessing.)

Fearing the disciples would fall in with the crowd's misguided zeal to make Him king by force, Jesus compels them to leave.

Message & Application 💻=🌎

❖ Shows the intervening work of Christ in keeping us from falling into spiritual pride and going down the wrong path. (cf. Prov. 16:9)
❖ Warns the dangers of falling in with the crowd. (Don't allow yourself to be influenced by the misguided zeal of others).
❖ Displays how Christ takes the time to protect us from our own misguided plans & desires when they start to run afoul of God's plans.
❖ Calls for trusting that whatever actions the Lord has directed us to take, that it's for our own good, even if it means rough sailing ahead!
⊶ Even today we can trust that Jesus has our best interests at heart, that sometimes what we want and what we need are two different things.

14:23 After he had dismissed them, (i.e. Sent them home.) **he went up on a mountainside by himself to pray.** (i.e. Either for Himself, the crowd, or the disciple's misguided plans.) **When evening came, he was there alone,**
24 but the boat was already a considerable distance from land, (i.e. About three miles from shore,-{John 6:19}, middle of the lake.) **buffeted** (tossed) **by the waves because the wind was against it.** (i.e. Were in grave danger of sinking.)

Jesus prays for the disciple's safety & protection in the trials and struggles that lie ahead.

Message & Application 💻=🌎

❖ Shows believers the importance of spending alone time with God in prayer over the temptations, distractions, and diversions of life.
❖ Encourages believers that if Christ is leading us in storms, He will also be there to see us through them! (cf. Rom. 8:34-35, Philp. 1:6)
❖ Teaches how Jesus knows the storms we're facing and is praying for us. (When you're in the place of peril, Jesus is in the place of prayer!).
❖ Teaches no matter how distant or far away the Lord seems to be, know that He is right there interceding for us. (cf. Heb. 8:1-2, 1-Tim. 2:5)
⊶ Even today just because we suffer & struggle when we're obeying the Lord and doing right, does not mean that the Lord isn't watching over us, or that Jesus doesn't care or doesn't love us!

Jesus Walks on the Water-(N.I.V.)

14:25 During the fourth watch of the night (3:00-6:00 A.M. Jewish practice of dividing the night into 4 parts.) **Jesus went out to them, walking on the lake.**
26 When the disciples saw him walking on the lake,-◙ they were terrified. (Syn.-Terror-stricken, freaking out) **It's a ghost, they said, and cried out in fear.**
27 But Jesus immediately said to them Take courage! It is I. Don't be afraid.
28 "Lord, if it's you "Peter replied, "tell me to come to you on the water."
29 "Come," he said. Then Peter got down out of the boat, walked on the water and came towards Jesus.
30 But when he saw the wind, (the wind boisterous-K.J.V. Suggests: Squall like conditions) **he was afraid and, beginning to sink, cried out, "Lord, save me !"** (Syn.-Rescue, deliver, etc. Expresses a cry to keep him from drowning.)
31 Immediately Jesus reached out his hand and caught him. "You of little faith," (Syn.-skeptical, doubting, distrusting) **he said, "why did you doubt?"**
32 And when they climbed into the boat, the wind died down.

Jesus gives the disciples a glimpse of His divine power and sufficiency in Saving all who come to Him by faith.

Message & Application 💻=🌎

- ❖ Shows how believers can call out to Jesus in the storms of life. (Trust Jesus to come to you in your darkest hours and trials of life!).
- ❖ Teaches how there's no storm of life that Christ cannot subdue. (Know there's nothing outside Christ's ability to quell or control).
- ❖ Teaches how sometimes Christ may not always come in the fashion we expect, but He will come in the form we need Him most. (Trust Jesus to come to you in your storm in whatever means He provides).
- ❖ Calls for stepping out of our comfort zones, be willing to give up whatever lifestyle, job, relationship, etc. that is holding you back.
- ❖ Warns believers of what can happen when we begin to take our focus off of Jesus and start to look at our circumstances instead. (V. 30)
- ❖ Displays how quickly our trials & situation will start to change and get better as soon as we invite Jesus into our lives. (V. 32)

🗝 Even today for believers no matter how gloomy things may look, or how much we're in over our heads when it comes to our mortgage, credit cards, car payment, hospital bills, school tuition, etc. we can always count on the Lord's help in keeping our heads above water.

➢ Miracles metaphorical implications suggests:
- Willingness to step out in faith in following Jesus.
- Jesus reaches out & rescues all who call out to Him for Salvation.
- Jesus' ability to rescue believers in times of trouble.

14:33 Then those who were in the boat (i.e. The twelve disciples and or possibly mariners as well.) **worshiped him,** (4352-*To give homage or reverence to, an act of bowing down or prostrating oneself.)* **saying, "Truly you are the Son of God."** (Expresses of being divine, Messiah, Christ.-{cf. Matt. 26:63})

Convinced of Jesus' divine nature the disciples confess their faith in Him as God.

Message & Application =

- ❖ Shows how those who have been rescued & delivered by Jesus will owe all glory, praise, worship to Him. (Our deliverance is His praise!).
- ❖ Reminds believers how it's only because of Jesus' presence and divine power that has brought us this far, and made us who we are today!
- ❖ Demonstrates how faith after crises and conflict is often strengthened. (Our victories bring greater praise and glory to Christ)
- ⊶ Even today God may be using our trials & difficulties, and how He gets us out of them as an opportunity to grow our faith. (1-Pet. 1:6-7)

14:34 When they had crossed over,(Sea of Galilee) **they landed at Gennesaret.** (A three and half mile wide tract of land just south of Capernaum, being a lush garden area with fertile vegetation and abundant fruits.-{Josephus, War 3. 10. 8}) **35 And when the men of that place recognized Jesus,** (i.e. Only as a miracle worker who healed many in nearby Capernaum.) **they sent word to all the surrounding country. People brought all their sick to him**(For physical healing) **36 and begged him** (besought-K.J.V. Syn.-pleaded, requested, implored) **to let the sick just touch the edge** (hem-K.J.V. tassels, fringe, border.) **of his cloak,** (Robe. Suggests having heard reports of the hemorrhaging woman who had been healed in the same way.-{9:20}) **and all who touched him were healed.**

The people were only seeking Jesus out for their physical needs rather than their spiritual needs.

Message & Application =

- ❖ Shows believers how Jesus is open & available for all who need a miracle and healing touch in their life's no matter who they are.
- ❖ Displays how Jesus graciously & lovingly rewards any expression of faith that is placed in Him, no matter how small or imperfect it may be.
- ❖ Warns how many can come with the wrong motives in only seeking to have their physical bodies healed and not their souls. (cf. 1-Corn. 15:9)
- ⊶ Even today if not careful we can bring people to Jesus for the wrong reasons in only having their health issues and financial problems fixed, rather than having their sins forgiven and their lives changed by Jesus.

Chapter Fifteen

Teachings on Rituals & Traditions

- **Clean & unclean-**Teaches how religion is a matter of the heart, and not external rules.-(Vs. 1-20)
- **Canaanite woman-**Teaches the importance of earnest & persistent faith.-(Vs. 21-28)
- **Jesus feeds the four thousand-** A miracle attesting to Jesus' authority & mission in extending Salvations to the Gentiles and all of humanity.-(Vs. 29-39)

Clean and unclean-(N.I.V.)

15:1 Then some Pharisees and teachers of the law came to Jesus from Jerusalem (Suggests: Official delegation sent to investigate Jesus.) **and asked**
2 "Why do your disciples break the tradition of the elders? (A meticulous set of Oral-Traditions meant to bring a Jew in compliance with the Law of Moses.) **They don't wash their hands before they eat!"** (Issue was not about hygiene, but of ceremonial defilement. Was only meant for the Priesthood.{Ex. 40:12-15})

The religious leaders accuse Jesus' disciples of breaking with their oral traditions on ritual purity.

Message & Application 💻=🌎

- ❖ Shows believers how holiness should always be an inward matter of the heart, and not just an outward matter of external rules.(cf. Rom. 2:29)
- ❖ Warns against seeing sin as something external, or something that we can easily remedy and avoid through religious disciplines.
- ❖ Warns against making our walk with God a religious checklist of "do's'" & "don'ts", rather than a heart relationship. (cf. Col. 2:20-23)
- ❖ Teaches how those who are legalistic will find fault with the practices of others, that if we're not doing what they're doing we're sinning.
- 🗝 Even today many have created their own rules of holiness, that if they just abstain from certain forms of entertainment, movies, music, books, foods, drinks, etc. that it will make them more favorable to God.
- ☞ Church Traditions are not inherently a bad thing, some can be very helpful in providing comfort & stability. But it's when those traditions start to conflict with the spirit and truth of God's word, or when they become rigid to God's heart and leading can they become harmful!

The Dangers of Traditions:

- They can undermine the authority of God's word.
- They can lead to superficial & shallow worship.
- They can trick one into feeling smug and Saved.
- They can exalt man above God.

15:3 Jesus replied, "And why do you break the command of God for the sake (Syn.-benefit, interest) **of your tradition** (i.e. Religious rules, observances, etc.)
4 For God said, 'Honour (Syn.-love, respect, support, care for) **your father and mother'**{Ex. 20:12} **and 'Anyone who curses** (Syn.-neglects, abandons) **his father or mother must be put to death.'** {cf. Ex. 21:17}
5 But you say that if a man says to his father or mother, 'Whatever help (i.e.-support) **you might otherwise have received from me** (In the way of assisting and caring for aged parents.) **is a gift devoted to God,'** (Corban.-{Mark 7:11b})
6 he is not to 'honour his father' with it. Thus, you nullify (Syn.-undercut, sidestep, override, circumvent) **the word of God for the sake of your tradition.**

Shows the hypocrisy of the Pharisees religion that circumvented the authority of God's word for their own rules and traditions.

Message & Application 💻=🌎

- ❖ Shows believers if not careful manmade rules & traditions can start to get elevated over time, becoming more important than God's word!
- ❖ Warns how religious causes can be made to sound very spiritual and godly when in reality it's only done for serving self. (cf. 2-Tim. 3:2-7)
- ❖ Warns against justifying some extravagant purchase and selfish want, and then say it was all done for serving the Lord.
- ❖ Displays how many will twist God's word around in order to serve their own selfish desires, while still making it seem their pursuing God.

-gift devoted to God-(Corban-Mark 7:11) By reciting the word "Carbon" became a formula that allowed a son to vow to God his inheritance, which released his obligations of supporting his parents. Some suggest that the vow was grossly misused by a Jew, who out of greed or anger against his parents used it as a legal loophole in keeping all his wealth.

🔑 Even today many will often hold tightly to their religious customs and traditions, that following religious rules is simpler than heart devotion. That it's easier to embrace external rules & rituals than to do the harder things in having to love the unlovely, help the needy, and care for the poor at the cost of their own time, money, and pleasures.

Other Traditions that Circumvent God's word

- The word of God describes baptism by immersion, human traditions says pouring or sprinkling is just as good. (Acts 8:39)
- The word of God proclaims all foods clean, human traditions says you can't consume pork, alcohol, or caffeine. (Mark 7:19)
- The word of God proclaims the Lord's day as the day of worship, human tradition says it's the Sabbath. (Acts 20:7)

15:7 You hypocrites! (5273-*Play actor who wore a mask.*) **Isaiah was right when he prophesied about you**(Not Pharisees outright, but of having the same type of spirit that Isaiah experienced by his own contemporaries. {cf. Is. 29:13})
8 "'These people honour me (draweth nigh-K.J.V. Syn.-worship, praise) **with their lips, but their hearts** (Syn.-love, affection, devotion) **are far from me.**
9 They worship me in vain; (Syn.-hollow, shallow, empty, self-serving, no purpose, pointless, farce-N.L.T.) **their teachings are but rules taught by men.'"**

The Pharisees professed their devotion to God, but in reality, their religion was hollow & empty.

Message & Application 💻=🌎

- ❖ Shows how God wants heart devotion and not religious lip service!
- ❖ Teaches how some can have all the outward forms of being religious, but not the inner realities that go with it! (cf. Rom. 2:19-24, 2-Tim. 3:5)
- ❖ Warns against proclaiming that we live by the bible and uphold God's word, and then do what we want and live like we want! (cf. Tit. 1:16)
- ⊶ Even today we can make the same mistakes of simply going through the motions of showing up to Church, mouthing the songs, say all the hallelujahs, etc. all the while our hearts and minds are elsewhere.

15:10 Jesus called the crowd to him and said, "Listen and understand. (Calls for the highest attention, that there's a spiritual principle to be learned.)
11 What goes into a man's mouth does not make (Syn.-render, constitute) **him 'unclean',** (defiled-K.J.V. Syn.-unrighteous, unholy, profane, sinful) **but what comes out of his mouth,** (Metph-inner-self/heart. e.g. dishonesty, lies, gossip, slander, curse joking, anger, bitterness, rudeness, filthy language, etc.) **that is what makes him 'unclean'."**(Syn.-sinful, immoral, unholy, ungodly, etc.)

What renders a person sinful to God is not outward things, but the inner condition of their heart.

Message & Application 💻=🌎

- ❖ Shows how sin is not a physical problem, but a moral & internal problem of the heart. (We're not what we eat, but what we speak!).
- ❖ Teaches how God is more concerned with who we are on the inside than about our outward appearance and performance! (cf. 1-Sam. 16:7)
- ❖ Warns against putting more value on looking right than on being right. (God doesn't want good religious habits, but a good heart!)
- ⊶ Even today God is not concerned with our worship appearance, church attendance, charity, or anything else that we think of as being good Christians. But rather about what's going on in our hearts instead.

15:12 Then the disciples came to him and asked, "Do you know that the Pharisees were offended (i.e. Infuriated, irate, called-out on) **when they heard this** (i.e. Having their hypocritical practices and empty rituals exposed.{Vs. 7-9} That truth always makes people uneasy when it exposes who they are at heart) **13 He replied, Every plant** (Pharisees false traditions.) **that my heavenly Father has not planted** (God's grace/faith in the heart) **will be pulled up by the roots. 14 Leave them;** (Expresses not to give into their religious ritualism and legalism.) **they are blind guides.** (Metph.-False spiritual leaders.) **If a blind man leads a blind man, both will fall into a pit".** (Suggests: Those who teach false doctrines will lead both them and their followers into spiritual ruin & disaster!)

Since God did not appoint or authorize the Pharisees oral traditions they will be rejected as Israel's spiritual leaders.

<u>Message & Application</u> 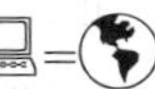

- ❖ Shows believers the need to see that we're coming by God's plan of Salvation through grace and not by religious works. (cf. Gal. 3:3)
- ❖ Calls for seeing that we're not falling into the trappings of external religion, but following God from the heart. (cf. Col. 2:8, Heb. 13:9)
- ❖ Teaches rather than get offended when our false and hypocritical lives are exposed, have the heart to face the truth and change! (V. 12)
- ❖ Warns how just being active in religion without being rooted in God's word/grace won't last, but only lead to failure, ruin, and doom!
- ❖ Calls for rejecting any religion that promotes formalism, ritualism, and externalism at the expense of heart purity and inner change.
- ❖ Warns how being wrapped up in old traditions can keep us in the dark to the truth and inner change that God is trying to work in us.
- ❖ Warns against following those who have strayed from God's word, or who fail to teach biblical principals correctly! (V. 14, cf. Acts 17:11)

⊶ Even today no matter how spiritual or religious something sounds, or how popular it appears, or how holy it makes you feel. If it's not based on God's word don't buy into it, be sold out to God, not religion!

☞ Jesus is not saying that every false teaching & doctrine is going to be uprooted. But is contrasting those who are internalizing God's word & grace upon their hearts, from those who are only religious outwardly.

<u>How to be Trees of God's Planting:</u>

- See that you're truly born again, that you've put your faith in Jesus and not in your own good works?
- See that your rooted & growing in God's word, and not in a religion of external rules and traditions.

15:15 Peter said Explain the parable to us. (i.e. Metaphor made at Vs. 10-11.)
16 "Are you still so dull?" (Viz. Spiritually sluggish/slow.) **Jesus asked them.**
17"Don't you see that whatever enters the mouth goes into the stomach and then out of the body? (cast out in the drought?-K.J.V. A.V. i.e. Toilet, latrine.)
18 But the things that come out of the mouth (i.e. Filthy talk, profane speech) **come from the heart** (True self) **and these make a man 'unclean'.** (i.e. Unholy)

What renders a person unholy is the corrupt character of their own hearts.

Message & Application 💻=🌎

- ❖ Shows believers how God is more concerned with the inner spiritual state of the heart than about outward appearances. (cf. 1-Sam. 16:7)
- ❖ Teaches how defilement is of a spiritual nature than physical, that our biggest problem is not outward appearances, but who we are at heart!
- ☞ Jesus is not saying that we can't be affected by the sinful things we put into our bodies/minds, that it's O.K. to do drugs & watch pornography. But rather is simply teaching that the source of sin lies in our hearts.

15:19 For out of the heart (2588-*Inner-self, true being.*) **come evil thoughts,** (malicious, spiteful, hurtful) **murder,** (homicide) **adultery,** (infidelity) **sexual immorality** (fornications-K.J.V., pornography, homosexuality) **theft,** (robbery, fraud, embezzlement) **false testimony,** (deceit, lying) **slander** (insult, vilify, slur)
20 These are what make a man 'unclean'; (Syn.-unholy, profane, corrupt, sinful, etc.) **but eating with unwashed hands does not make him 'unclean'."**

It's from a corrupt & sinful heart that gives rise to wrong actions & behavior.

Message & Application 💻=🌎

- ❖ Shows since sin & immorality begins in the wrong desires of the heart, its the heart that needs to be renewed the most and changed!
- ❖ Displays how all the religious rituals and hand washings in the world won't purify an ugly and corrupt heart! (You can't legislate morality!)
- ❖ Teaches how the root problem of sin lies not in a poor environment, lack of education, bad genetics, or a rough upbringing, but in our self!
- ❖ Warns against thinking we can simply control sin by regulating and filtering out the bad influences without dealing with the heart first.
- ⊶ Even today, believers should be less concerned about our religious fasts, diets, and hand washings and more concerned about the spiritual state of our hearts. That we don't need more religion, but more of our hearts being washed, sprinkled, and scrubbed by the blood of Jesus!

From this verse here (V. 21) to verse (V. 28) teaches on the need for earnest and persistent faith.

The Faith of the Canaanite Woman-(N.I.V.)

15:21 Leaving that place, (i.e. Gennesaret-{14:34} or Galilee in general.) **Jesus withdrew** (Expresses a tactical withdrawal, either for rest.-{Mark 7:24} Or for safety away from the Pharisees opposition.) **to the region of Tyre and Sidon.-** (i.e. Two seaport cities on the Mediterranean coast, modern day Lebanon and Syria. The territory being prominently Pagan and Gentile in nature.) {Map Pg. 6}
22 A Canaanite woman (Expresses an outdated term meant to draw out the tenuous meeting, being that they were Israel's old enemies.-{Deut.7:1-4}. Greek born in Syrian Phoenicia.-{Mark 7:26}. That she was a Gentile from the land of Canaan who worshipped many false god's & goddesses.) **from that vicinity came to him, crying out,** (Syn.-imploring, pleading, begged.-{Mark 7:26} Expresses: Her dire desperation/need.) **"Lord,** (Syn.-Sir, Master) **Son of David,** (Expresses a Messianic title signifying the Messiah's royal descent.-{2-Sam. 7:12} That she had heard rumors about Him.) **have mercy on me!** (Expresses: She was making her child's misery her own, identifying with her daughter's plight.) **My daughter is suffering terribly from demon-possession."**(Suggests: Demonic influences, causing her to be physically or mentally ill.)

Jesus departs for the Mediterranean coast of Tyre & Sidon, extending His mission to the Gentiles.

Message & Application =

- ❖ Shows how believers can take our dire needs & desperate situations to the Lord for help. (cf. Matt. 7:7, Ps. 4:1, 6:2, Prov. 3:5-6)
- ❖ Teaches how when those who want to quarrel and argue over religion, its best to move on. (Christ is patient, but to a point). (V. 21)
- ❖ Teaches how true faith recognizes there's only "One" who can resolve our problems. (Do you run to Jesus or to other things for solutions?).
- ❖ Encourages believers that when we have nowhere else to turn, we can always take our problems, burdens, and troubles to the Lord!
- ❖ Calls for a faith that presses forward regardless of cultural boundaries, social taboos, or religious hurdles we have to jump. (V. 22)
- ❖ Calls for seeing that we're coming to Jesus for mercy, and not by way of rights, entitlements, demands, pledges, or what is owed us. (V. 22)
- ❖ Encourages mothers & fathers that no matter how bound and enslaved our children are to sin we can bring them to the Lord in prayer. (V. 22)
- ❖ Teaches how sometimes God allows trials & crises to come in order to bring us to see our desperate need for His help. (cf. Matt. 11:28-30)

15:23 Jesus did not answer a word. (Expresses not that Jesus was being cold or indifferent, but rather His silence was meant to encourage her faith.) **So his disciples came to him and urged him, "Send her away, for she keeps crying out after us.** (Suggests: They saw her as an annoyance and nuisance.)
24 He answered, "I was sent only to the lost sheep of Israel." (Metph.-Jews)

By refusing to answer the woman, Jesus tests & encourages her faith.

Message & Application 💻=🌎

- ❖ Shows believers rather than be discouraged by God's silence, stay persistent in prayer! (Stay determined when God stands silent!).
- ❖ Calls for not allowing the disapproval & brush-off of others to keep us from seeking the Lord. (Don't let naysayers discourage you!).
- ❖ Warns against getting so caught up in our own spiritual needs and comforts that we neglect the lost and hurting souls around us.
- ❖ Teaches when prayers go unanswered, rather than give up trust that the Lord hears your cries and will respond in His own time and own way.
- ⊶ Even today if not careful we can become just like the disciples in our lack of compassion. That we would rather not deal with difficult people, wishing they'd take their problems and issues elsewhere.

15:25 The woman came and knelt before him.-◙ "Lord, help me!" she said.
26 He replied It is not right to take the children's (Jews) **bread** (Metph-Gospel) **and toss it to their dogs.-◙** (292-*Pet, puppy.* Metph-Gentiles. By using "Family Pets" and not "Wild Dogs", Jesus leaves the woman an open door of hope!)
27 Yes Lord, she said (Expresses as in "Fair enough", "Be that as it may".) **but even the dogs eat the crumbs that fall from their masters table.-◙** (Expresses her faith that Jesus' mission was for all people, not just the Jews. Or that just a fraction of Jesus' power was all that was necessary to heal her daughter.)

As God's chosen people it was wrong to take the Messiah's ministry/Gospel from the Jews and give it to the Gentiles.

Message & Application 💻=🌎

- ❖ Shows how we're to come to the Lord in meekness & humility, that we're all sinners undeserving of God's mercy & grace. (cf. James 4:6)
- ❖ Calls in forgoing pride, self-reliance, and self-sufficiency. (Know that you stand before God as unworthy and undeserving!).
- ⊶ Even today, believers are to come in humility, accepting whatever mercies & graces God supplies, that God does not owe us anything!

15:28 Then Jesus answered "Woman, you have great faith! (3173-*Mega, large.* Syn.-strong, persistent, persevering, enduring, steadfast, unwavering.) **Your request** (Syn.-prayer, petition) **is granted." And her daughter was healed** (Syn.-cured, made well. Suggests: The demon was exorcised from her daughter.) **from that very hour.** (i.e. Instantly, immediately, completely.)

Because of the woman's earnest & persistent faith, Jesus grants her requests and heals her daughter.

Message & Application 💻=🌎

- ❖ Shows believers how God honors the type of earnest & persistent faith that overcomes barriers and obstacles to come to Him.
- ❖ Calls for a faith that trusts that the Lord can heal & Save us no matter our history, background, our what we've done. (cf. Rom. 8:1, Heb. 7:25)
- ❖ Calls believers for the kind of faith that doesn't quit, shrink, collapse, or give up under any circumstances.
- ❖ Calls for a faith that stays obedient to God, accepting His decisions in whatever He chooses and decides, whether we like it or not.
- ❖ Calls for the sort of faith that does not waver or bail just because our prayers go unanswered by God. (cf. 2-Corn. 12:7-10)
- ❖ Calls for the kind of faith that endures, wrestles, and perseveres in God's goodness, even though there's so much we don't understand.
- ❖ Teaches how when faith stands firm in God, great/powerful changes and breakthroughs will start to take place in our lives!
- ❖ Displays the intercessory power of faith & prayer for the healing and Salvation of our children, family, friends, and those around us.

-***Great faith***-meaning: Her faith is praised for overcoming obstacles as:

- **Her little means**-That having never seen Jesus' miracles, yet trusting in His power to heal her daughter.
- **Her race-**That being Gentile exempted her as part of Israel's elect.
- **Her gender**-That Rabbis normally did not acknowledge women.
- **Her pagan religion**-That she was willing to abandon her own heathen practices & beliefs, to putting her faith in Israel's Messiah.

☞ Other virtues of the woman's great faith can be seen in her wit, wisdom, love, patience, humility, perseverance, and determination.

➢ Miracles metaphorical implications suggests:

- The importance of humility and persistent faith.
- Christ's power and authority over sin, death, and Satan.
- God's grace & mercy extends to all people & nationalities.
- Ministry transcends all racial and ethnic boundaries.

15:29 Jesus left there (i.e. Tire & Sidon, having ministered to the Canaanite woman.-{Vs.21-28}) **and went along the Sea of Galilee.** (i.e. Northern top of the Sea of Galilee, arriving in a prominently Gentile region know as the Decapolis Grk. "Ten Cities".-{Mark 7:31}) **Then he went up on a mountainside and sat down** (Suggests: For better ease of access to Him for healings and blessings.)
30 Great crowds came to him, bringing the lame (disabled/handicapped) **the blind, the crippled, the mute and many others, and laid them at his feet;** (Expresses a gesture of humility, compassion, and pity.) **and he healed them.**
31 The people were amazed when they saw the mute speaking, the crippled made well, the lame walking and the blind seeing. And they praised (Syn.-Glorified, exalted) **the God of Israel.** (Suggests: Confirms Gentile nationality.)

Jesus extends His mission & ministry in bringing hope & Salvation to the Gentiles.

Message & Application 💻=🌎

- ❖ Shows Jesus' love & compassion for the broken and hurting. (Know Jesus is here for you in whatever area you need fixing!).
- ❖ Displays how Jesus is approachable and accessible to all, no matter what sin or disability you may have. (Jesus is handicap friendly!)
- ❖ Displays how there's nothing that Jesus can't fix or solve, that Jesus has a remedy and solution for any condition we find our self's in.
- ❖ Teaches how we don't have to clean up our act first, that we can come to Jesus with all our garbage & issues and find healing & forgiveness.
- ❖ Teaches how we can lay all our burdens and worries at Jesus' feet. (Know you can bring all your pains & struggles to Jesus for healing!).
- ❖ Calls for a love & compassion for others that it draws people to praise and glorify God. (What are you doing to bring others to Jesus?) (V. 13)

🗝 Even today Jesus deals with each sinner according to their specific needs. That Jesus can rehabilitate those who's lives have been crippled by sin, drugs, alcohol, pornography, etc. bringing recovery & sobriety. Or those who have been handicapped spiritually or emotionally by the things of doubt and unbelief, bringing peace & hope back to their life.

☞ According to Mark's Gospel, describes the healing miracle of a deaf & mute man, and the unusual method Jesus used to cure him, putting His fingers in the man's ears, spitting and touching the man's tongue, then praying in Aramaic "Ephphatha" meaning *"be opened"*.-(Mark 7:31-35)

➢ Miracles metaphorical implications suggests:
  - Served as proof of Christ's Messiahship foretold by Isaiah.
  - God's grace and compassion for all sinners.
  - Extends the Messiah's mission to the Gentiles.

Jesus Feeds the Four Thousand-(Gentiles)-(N.I.V.)

15:32 Jesus called his disciples to him and said, "I have compassion for these people; they have already been with me three days and have nothing to eat. I do not want to send them away hungry, or they may collapse on the way".
33 His disciples answered, "Where could we get enough bread in this remote place (wilderness-K.J.V. i.e. Unpopulated, rural) **to feed such a crowd?"**
34 "How many loaves do you have?" Jesus asked. "Seven," they replied, "and a few small fish." (Suggest: Possibly a small number of Sardines.)
35 He told the crowd to sit down on the ground. (Organize/accurate count.)
36 Then he took the seven loaves and fish, and when he had given thanks, he broke them and gave them to the disciples, they in turn to the people.
37 They all ate and were satisfied. (Metph.-Spiritual sufficiency of Christ.) **Afterwards, the disciples picked up seven** (Expresses: Symbolic of Divine completeness and fullness.) **basketfuls** (4711-*hamper-size basket.*-{cf. Acts 9:25} Symbolic of God's superabundant grace.) **of broken pieces that were left over.**
38 The number of those who ate was four thousand, besides women and children. (Suggests: Estimates put the total number between 9,000-12,000.)

By miraculously feeding the multitude, Jesus reveals Himself as the bread of life and the source of Salvation for all people.

<u>Message & Application</u> 💻=🌎

- ❖ Shows Christ's sufficiency in satisfying the spiritual needs and deepest longings of the soul. (cf. John 6:32-35, Matt. 4:4)
- ❖ Calls for always having a heart of compassion in meeting the needs and welfare of those who are around us. (V. 32, Rom. 9:2-3)
- ❖ Warns how sometimes we can experience all the amazing things God has done for us in the past, yet still distrust Him for the present.
- ❖ Assures believers how Christ is more than enough in fulfilling all that we could ever need or ask for! (V. 37, cf. Eph. 3:20)
- 🔑 Even today Jesus will provide all we need, that we no longer have to find satisfaction and significance in money, relationships, or things, but in Christ alone.
- ➢ The disciple's question arises, not as a result of having forgotten the earlier feeding of the 5000-(14:15-21), but rather due to either:
  - A) Assumed that as Israel's Messiah, Jesus would not perform the same miracle on a Gentile crowd as He did for the Jews. (14:13-21)
  - B) That Jesus would not perform the same miracle as a result of the first crowds attempt to make Him king by force. (cf. John 6:15)

15:39 After Jesus had sent the crowd away, (Suggests: Dismissing the people with a parting blessing, or exhorting them towards thankfulness and sanctity of life.) **he got into the boat and went to the vicinity of Magadan.-◙** (Magdala-K.J.V. Suggests: Leaving the Decapolis Jesus crossed back over to the Western side of the lake of Galilee, arriving in the Jewish village of Magdala, just south of Capernaum. Dalmanutha.-{Mark 8:10 b}-Suggests: Either a variation of the same name or separate village in close proximity. *"Magadan"* was also the home of Mary Magdalene, whom Jesus had exorcised seven evil spirits from.)

Having ministered to the Gentiles, Jesus returns to Galilee continuing His ministry to the Jews.

Message & Application 💻=🌍

- ❖ Shows the power & sufficiency of Christ, that no one is ever left wanting or unsatisfied who come to Jesus!
- ❖ Assures believers that what Christ supplies is enough to live the abundant life He promised! (cf. John 10:10)
- ❖ Displays how God's word is more than enough to continue to instruct our souls and heal our bodies.
- ❖ Teaches how Christ never sends those who have hung in there away empty handed, without blessing them.
- ❖ Teaches how God always blesses us that we may move on to the next big thing He wants to accomplish in our life's. (cf. 1-Corn. 15:58)
- ❖ Teaches how God would rather we move forward in daily witness and ministry than be detained in the duty of worship & praise.
- ❖ Teaches believers how ministry and witness begins first at home.

–***Magadan-***A region that derives its name from a city found in that area called "Magdala". Though it's exact location is unknown, best estimates have placed it on the Westside of the Sea of Galilee about five miles south of Capernaum and three miles north of Tiberius. It is also the place from which Mary Magdalene received her name.

⊶ Even today, believers can move forward in our healing, that God's provisions are more than sufficient in meeting any need we may have later on down the road.

☞ Interesting to note that this crowd did not think of making Jesus king by force as did the other multitude of 5000 Jews that Jesus fed earlier. (cf.14:22, John 6:14-15) (Which has been explained in part as either: A result of their Gentile nationality, they were unfamiliar with the O.T. concept of "Manna" and its Messianic overtones. Or that Jesus did not preach to this crowd His sermon on the "Bread of life" as He did after the feeding of the 5000 Jews) (cf. John 6:25-40)

Chapter Sixteen

Warnings against the Religious Leaders

- **The Demand for a Sign.-** Warnings against spiritual blindness & unbelief.-(Vs. 1-12)
- **Peters Confession of Christ-** Teaches on finding our identity Jesus as Lord & Savior.-(Vs. 13-20)
- **Jesus Predicts His death-** Jesus prepares the disciples for His suffering & death.- (Vs. 21-23)
- **Costs in Discipleship-**Teaches on the costs and sacrifices in discipleship.-(Vs. 24-28)

The Demand for a Sign-(N.I.V.)

16:1 The Pharisees and Sadducees came to Jesus (Expresses an unusual alliance of two common enemies coming together in their hatred of Jesus.) **and tested him** (tempting-K.J.V.-3985-*To pressure, try, trap, and ensnare.* Syn.-trip-up, stump, discredit, test.) **by asking him to show them a sign from heaven.** (4592-*"Mighty act as a token of divine authority/power".* e.g. Thunder, lightning, hail. Suggests: Unsatisfied and unconvinced by Jesus' earthly miracles-{Matt. 12:24} they sought a divine act to prove that God was with Him.)

The religious leaders attempt to discredit Jesus' authority & claims by showing His inability to perform a divine miracle.

Message & Application 💻=🌎

❖ Shows how we're not to set terms & conditions on God for what we will believe. (Only those who are blind with unbelief seek after signs).

❖ Warns against expecting God to prove everything to our satisfaction before we're willing to commit and follow. (Take God at His word!).

❖ Teaches how those who ask for miraculous signs do so to justify their unbelief. (Demands for proof are usually smoke screens for unbelief!).

❖ Warns against thinking that God operates on our terms and conditions, or by what we will believe & accept. (God is not a puppet on strings!)

❖ Displays how many can come with their minds already made up about Jesus, that their only looking to pick a fight/argument and not for truth.

❖ Warns against thinking that we need certain issues answered, or some deep mystery resolved before we're willing to believe and follow God.

⊶ Even today, believers need to see that we're seeking God for wisdom, truth, and understanding, and not just for testing God's faithfulness or looking to disbelieve.

☞ Today many set arbitrary terms on God before they're willing to believe, such as: *"Lord, give me a sign so that I may know your real"*. Or they will try to bargain with God by setting specific requests such as: *"Lord heal my daughter"*, *"Fix my relationship"*, *"Pay my bills"*, etc. and I'll serve you forever, or I'll never miss Church again!

16:2 He replied, "When evening comes, you say, 'It will be fair weather, for the sky is red,' (Suggests: A sign of calm and clear weather ahead.)
3 and in the morning, 'Today it will be stormy, for the sky is red and overcast.- ◙ (Suggests: A phenomenon in which the sky appears redder as the rising & setting of the sun shines through dust particles in the atmosphere indicating stormy weather ahead. Expresses a mariners rhyme; "Red sky at night sailors delight, Red sky in the morning sailors take warning".) **You know how to interpret the appearance of the sky,** (i.e. Forecast the weather) **but you cannot interpret** (discern) **the signs of the times.** (i.e. They failed to see in Jesus' miracles that the Messiah was among them. Or prophecy being fulfilled.)
4 A wicked and adulterous generation (Metph.-Skeptical, unbelieving, hard-hearted. Expresses the religious leader's unfaithfulness to God in their rejection of Jesus as the Messiah.) **looks for a miraculous sign, but none will be given it except the sign of Jonah".** (i.e. As Jonah was three days in a belly of a great fish.-{Jon. 1:17} Jesus will be buried and resurrected three days later. That Jesus dying for our sins and resurrecting is enough evidence, that no other proof is needed.) **Jesus then left them and went away.** (Expresses judgment, that Christ does not tarry long with those who have hardened their hearts.)

If the religious leaders could discern the weather, they should have seen from Jesus' miracles that He was the promised Messiah.

Message & Application

- ❖ Shows believers how pride & hardness of heart can blind us to the sin in our lives and our need to repent and confess it to God. (Eph. 4:17-18)
- ❖ Calls for recognizing the plight of sin and what it's done to our lives if we're going to understand our desperate need of God's forgiveness.
- ❖ Teaches how disbelief is not an intellectual issue or a lack of evidence, but rather a problem of the heart that is unwilling to acknowledge sin!
- ❖ Teaches how the biggest barrier is not more proof or some religious experience, but a heart issue that is unwilling to see oneself as a sinner.
- ❖ Teaches the importance of staying spiritually minded on the things of God if we're to avoid the evil and moral decay around us.
- ❖ Teaches where genuine faith is resting in all that Christ has done in dying for our sins and resurrecting no further proof should be needed.
- ❖ Calls for paying less time on the earthly & temporal, and more time on the spiritual needs and welfare of the soul. (cf. Matt. 16:26, Col. 3:2)
- ⊶ Even today, believers can care more about the things of politics, sports, work, school, careers, stock-market, facebook, etc. than about the spiritual state of their souls when it comes to sin, death, and eternal judgment. (Men can draw from the evidence of God's world, but will not examine the evidence of their own life's!).

The Yeast of the Pharisees & Sadducees-(N.I.V.)

16:5 When they went across the lake the disciples forgot to take bread.
6 "Be careful," Jesus said to them. Be on your guard against the yeast (leaven-K.J.V. Metph-False teachings, attitudes, influence, hypocrisy, unbelief, etc.) **of the Pharisees and Sadducees."** (Expresses: Taken together their skepticism, legalism, liberalism, exclusivism, rationalism, religiosity, narrow-mindedness.)
7 They discussed this among themselves and said, "It is because we didn't bring any bread." (Suggests: They missed the spiritual implication and took it only as a precaution against buying bread from the Pharisees & Sadducees.)
8 Aware of their discussion, Jesus asked, "You of little faith (Syn.-forgetful, distrusting.) **why are you talking among yourselves about having no bread?**
9 Do you still not understand? Don't you remember the five loaves for the five thousand, and how many basketfuls you gathered. {14:15-21}
10 Or the seven loaves for the four thousand, and how many basketfuls you gathered? (Suggests: Taken together was ample proof of Jesus' Messahiaship.)
11 How is it you don't understand that I was not talking to you about bread? But be on your guard against the yeast of the Pharisees and Sadducees."
12 Then they understood that he was not telling them to guard against the yeast used in bread, but against the teaching of the Pharisees and Sadducees. (i.e. Their being sign-seekers, or their spirit of skepticism and unbelief.-{V.1})

Jesus having already proved to the disciples that He was the Messiah, warns them against being influenced by the skepticism and unbelief of the religious leaders.

Message & Application 💻=🌎

- ❖ Shows how believers are not to allow the false doctrines & beliefs of others to derail our faith or draw us away from Jesus!
- ❖ Warns how the preoccupation with the cares & anxiety of this life can cause us to fail in grasping spiritual lessons God is trying to teach us.
- ❖ Assures believers in the sufficiency of Christ, that He is more than capable in providing all we need! (Vs. 9-10)
- ❖ Warns against allowing the doubt and limitations of others to poison our capacity of what we believe God can do in our own lives.
- ❖ Warns believers if not careful a little doubt and unbelief can slowly creep in and start to deteriorate into open rebellion against God!
- ❖ Warns against allowing others to poison our walk with God in thinking that a little sin or a little wrong can't possibly affect us.
- 🗝 Even today, believers need to be careful of the corrupting influences that are slowly slipping into the Church. Coming in the form of anything from a prosperity Gospel of health & wealth to a new age movement of spiritualism, liberalism, and moralism/legalism.

From this verse here (V. 13) to verse (V. 20) teaches on the need of finding our identity and Salvation in Christ.

Peter's Confession of Christ-(N.I.V.)

16:13 When Jesus came to the region of Caesarea Philippi,-◙ (A Roman city located at the foot of Mtn. Hermon, who's worship was dedicated to the pagan god "Pan"-◙ Suggests: Used as a backdrop for all that is idolatrous, secular, worldly.) **he asked his disciples, Who do people** (family, friends, Hollywood) **say the Son of Man is?**(Christ/Messiah. That Jesus was speaking of the prevailing opinion as what the word on the street was concerning Himself.)
14 They replied, "Some say John the Baptist; (A popular belief that Jesus was John the Baptist raised from the dead.-{Matt.14:1-2}) **others say Elijah;** (Similarities being that Elijah performed the same type of miracles. Or since Elijah never saw death, he would return, ushering in the Messiah's arrival.-{2-Kings 2:1-12, Mal. 4:5}) **and still others, Jeremiah** (Similarities being that both ministered with the same zeal, sorrow, and judgment.) **or one of the prophets.** (Suggests: The prophet Moses predicted would come.-{cf. Deut. 18:15-18})

The popular consensus of the day was that Jesus was categorized as just another prophet among many prophets.

Message & Application 💻=🌎

- ❖ Shows how Saving faith in Jesus is not based on a popularity poll or public opinion, but rather on one's own personal decision.
- ❖ Teaches how God wants us to come by our own spiritual journey and declaration of faith than rely on the beliefs and opinions of others.
- ❖ Teaches rather than depending on the world's view of Jesus, we need to go straight to the source, God's own word and find out for our self's.
- ❖ Teaches how we can better witness in leading people to the truth by knowing what their opinions, beliefs, and views are concerning Jesus.
- ❖ Displays how it's up to us to make a personal decision for Jesus, that our church, pastor, and family can't make that choice for us!
- ⊶ Even today we're reminded that when all is said and done, what matters most is not what our parents, spouses, friends, co-workers, or neighbors think about Jesus, but what we believe in our own hearts.
- ☞ Today believers need to stand against a godless and pluralistic culture where everything goes. That it doesn't matter who or what you believe in, as long as you believe in something, that all roads lead to God.
- ☞ Today many share the same sentiments, who can have good thoughts & opinions about Jesus that *"Jesus was a great teacher & good man"*, *"A caring humanitarian"*, etc. but stop short of declaring Him God!

16:15 "But what about you?" he asked. "Who do you say I am?"(Expresses a self-declaration of Jesus' own divinity, being that the term "I Am" was a title used only by God.-{cf. Ex. 3:14} That faith and Salvation is a personal decision.)
16 Simon Peter answered, "You are the Christ, (5547-*Grk-"Anointed One", "Messiah".)* **the Son of the living God"** (Expresses how unlike the dead pagan idols made of wood & stone, Jesus is the divine and immortal God!)

Peter confesses Jesus as Lord & God!

<u>Message & Application</u> 💻=🌎

- ❖ Shows believers the need for a confession of faith that is willing to give divine ownership over to Jesus as Lord & Savior! (cf. Rom. 10:9)
- ❖ Calls for a personal decision that owes Jesus as our only answer, hope, joy, peace, refuge, and Salvation!
- ❖ Calls for a faith declaration that there's no detail of our life's that Jesus can't fix, cure, and rescue us from.
- ❖ Calls for a faith confession that bears evidence in the way we live and the choices we make. (Don't profess with lips, then deny by life).
- ❖ Calls for a faith confession in Christ as the One who reigns supreme over everyone and everything in our lives, who alone sustains us.
- 🗝 Even today our faith declaration in Jesus is not just a onetime act done in front of the Church. But rather a confession that is spoken and lived out daily throughout our lives by the decisions and choices we make.
- ☞ Other proof texts that testify and bears witness to Jesus' Divinity: John 1:1, 8:58, 10:30, 17:11, 20:28, Rom. 9:5, 14:11, 2-Corn. 4:4, 1-Corn. 8:2, Philp. 2:6-8, Col. 1:15, 19, Titus 2:13, 3:4, Heb. 1:2-3, 8-9, 1-John 2:22.
- ☞ Today this question here is the most important one you will ever have to answer when coming to Jesus. Because the decision you make will determine the road you will walk and the eternal destiny of your soul! (If you haven't already, repent & receive Jesus as Lord & Savior now!) (See the "Sinners Prayer" on Pg. 188)

<u>Reasons in Confessing Jesus as Divine:</u>

- Allows one to die-to-self and surrender their life's over to Jesus' divine rule, authority, and control.
- Allows one to go to Jesus in confession, repentance, and forgiveness of sins, casting ourselves on His mercy.
- Allows one to go to Jesus for divine healing & wholeness, trusting in His power to reverse the sin in our lives.
- Allows one to know that Jesus is actively involved in our lives, that His presence is always with us.

16:17 Jesus replied "Blessed (Spiritually favored) **are you Simon son of Jonah,** (Bar-jona-K.J.V.-*Heb.-Son of John.* Expresses Peter's earthly nature according to the flesh, or Peter's vacillating character.) **for this was not revealed to you by man** (i.e. Books, tapes, human reasoning, intellect, etc.) **but by my Father in heaven.** (Expresses how spiritual insights are always a work of God not of self.)

Peter's ability to confess Jesus as Lord & Savior came not by human effort but by divine revelation.

Message & Application 💻=🌎

- ❖ Shows how believing in Jesus as Lord & Savior is not a result of our own insights, but a work of God's grace. (John 14:6, Eph. 2:5-8, 2-Tim.1:9)
- ❖ Calls for realizing that our Salvation was not a result of how smart, holy, or special we are, but completely a work of God's grace!
- ⊶ Even today we must give all praise & glory to God for opening our eyes to the sin and bondage we were in and our need for Jesus!

16:18 And I tell you that you are Peter, and on this rock (4073-*Peter himself by the Grk. form of "Petros"-small stone, fragment. Or as Christ Himself by the Grk. form of "Petra" bedrock, foundation.* Suggests: In context Peter's faith confession in Christ as Lord & Savior.-{V.16}) **I will build my church** (1577-*Greek-"Ekklesia", assembly or body of believers, the called-out ones of God.* {cf. 1:Pet. 2:9}) **and the gates** (Metph.-power/forces/principalities) **of Hades** (Hell-K.J.V. Grk.-Abode of the dead) **will not overcome it.** (Expresses either the Church's success in fending off Satan's attacks in trying to ruin and destroy it. Or the Church's assault against the dominions of darkness and evil, freeing people from the power of Satan, sin, and death through the Gospel/Cross.)

The Church is to be built upon the truth of Peter's confession that Jesus is Lord & Savior.

Message & Application

- ❖ Shows believers how professing Jesus as "Lord & Savior" is to be the foundation and confession of our faith. (cf. Rom. 10:9-10, Philp. 2:11)
- ❖ Teaches how with Christ as our foundation and rock, there's nothing that can ever sink, defeat, or overwhelm us. (cf. Matt. 7:24-27)
- ❖ Assures the eternal security of the believer, that there are no forces in hell or earth that can remove us from Christ's Saving hand. (Jn. 10:28)
- ❖ Teaches how the Church is not a building, business, or social club, but a place for witness, outreach, ministry, and evangelism.

-one this rock-Historically understood by the Church as referring to:
1) Peter himself 2) Christ Himself 3) Only of Peter's confession

16:19 I will give you (i.e. Peter/believers) **the keys-◙** (Metph-power, authority, grace, faith, Gospel-truth, knowledge.-{Luke 11:52}) **of the kingdom of heaven;** (Metph.-Gospel message of Salvation/forgiveness.) **whatever** (i.e. Decisions, beliefs, sins, etc.) **you bind** (Forbid, prohibit) **on earth will be bound** (ratified, endorsed) **in heaven,** (Expresses a perfect tense as in "have been". That is to say Heaven doesn't follow our decisions, but rather we act according to what has already been determined by God.) **and whatever you loose** (Permit, allow) **on earth will be loosed in heaven.** (Expresses a legal term used by Rabbis when interpreting the Laws applications in the area of rules & practices. In context, Christ's sanctioning Peter's authority in opening the door of Salvation to the Gentiles. In a wider sense gives the Church the authority to explain and declare God's word & will as based on scripture.-{cf. Matt. 18:18-20, 2-Tim. 3:16})

Peter is given divine authority in opening the door of the Gospel and Salvation to all people.

Message & Application 💻=🌎

❖ Shows how believers have in the Gospel the authority to proclaim the promises of God that our sins are forgiven. (cf. 1-John 1:8-10)
❖ Teaches how we have in the Gospel the authority to declare that those who receive Jesus into their lives are Saved from their sins!
❖ Assures believers that whatever service & work the Lord has called us to, He also equips and empowers us with the ability to fulfill it.
❖ Teaches how we have in the Gospel everything necessary to bind sin, Satan, shame, guilt, doubt, unbelief, and anything else. (cf. Eph. 6:10-18)
❖ Displays how believers have in the Gospel the power to set people free from the guilt, bondage, and power of sin.

🗝 Even today, believers can proclaim the promises of the Gospel. That if we or someone else feels worried or ashamed on whether or not a certain sin has been forgiven by God. We have the ability and duty to loose them from it, reminding them how they no longer have to keep punishing themselves with guilt since God has already forgiven them for it. (cf. Philp. 3:13-14)

☞ The book of Acts recounts how Peter exercised that authority when he opened the door of faith first to the Jews on the day of Pentecost, then later to the Gentiles in the home of Cornelius. (cf. Acts 2:14-41,10:34-48)

☞ The Catholic Church uses this verse to teach the primacy of Peter and the Papal supremacy over the Church. Even giving legend to Peter standing at the "Pearly Gates" as to who can enter and who cannot.

☞ This verse is not saying that the Church has the power to say who's Saved and who's not Saved. But rather when judgments and decisions are in accordance with God' Word we have God's endorsement.

16:20 Then he warned his disciples (Suggests: The plural implies that all the disciples shared Peter's conviction.-{V. 16}) **not to tell anyone that he was the Christ.** (5547-*Grk. "Anointed one", Heb.-Messiah"*. Suggests: Peter's revelation was to remain a secret until after the Lord's suffering, death, and resurrection.)

Because people did not yet understand the Cross or a suffering Messiah, the disciples were to wait until after Jesus' resurrection.

Message & Application

- ❖ Shows believers how Jesus' passion, death, and resurrection is to be the defining mark and essential work of Salvation. (cf. 1-Corn. 2:1-2)
- ❖ Teaches how apart from the Cross & Resurrection people won't have a right understanding of Jesus and His mission in dying for sinners.
- ❖ Teaches the importance of getting the identity and mission of Christ right, or people will be coming to Jesus for all the wrong reasons.
- ❖ Calls for seeing that we're bearing proper witness or we can lead others in having unrealistic & unbiblical expectations about Jesus.
- ❖ Displays how divine truths must be shared in a timely manner. (Men must be ready to come to Christ for the right reasons!).
- ❖ Warns if not properly preached the Gospel can get distorted by well-meaning but ill-informed people. (Prosperity Gospel a good example).
- ❖ Teaches how Jesus wants to deliver us from the deeper pains/bondages of our sins, and not one who is only there to meet our needs & wants.

⊶ Even today we need to see that were always making it about the Cross, and not about health, wealth, or prosperity. Or how Jesus is there to pamper to their every need in getting them that new job, house, car, spouse, etc. and not for the greater things in having their sins forgiven.

☞ Jesus' call for silence was only temporary, where we are now free to proclaim the Gospel in telling others the "Good News" of the death and resurrection of Jesus to all who will listen and believe. (28:19-20)

–***Not to tell anyone***-Meaning: Silence is attributed to either:

- The disciples did not yet understand the aspect of a suffering Messiah or fully understand the cross/resurrection. (Vs. 21-23)
- Jesus wanted people to come to Him for Saving faith, and not just as a miracle worker or faith healer. (Vs. 15-18)
- The out-pouring of the Holy Spirit had not yet come upon the disciples to empower them for witness. (Luke 24:29, Acts 1:8, 2:1-4)
- The announcement would have only aroused a Jewish political movement to make Jesus a victorious king. (John 6:15)
- The announcement of Jesus as the Messiah King would have been seen as a threat to Rome, resulting in Jesus' premature death.

From this verse here (V. 21) to verse (V. 23) Jesus prepares the disciples for His suffering and death.

Jesus Predicts His Death-(N.I.V.)

16:21 From that time on (i.e. From the time of Peter's faith confession in Jesus as Christ.-{V. 16}) **Jesus began to explain to his disciples that he must** (Expresses the necessity of the Cross and God's plan of Salvation in connection to the suffering Servant of Isaiah.-{cf. Is. 50:4-11, 53:1-12}) **go to Jerusalem** (Being divinely ordained in fulfillment of O.T. Prophecies, as the city of sacrifices, He was to be the Passover lamb.) **and suffer many things** (i.e. An array of assaults, beatings, and mocking's while on His way to the Cross.) **at the hands** (Syn. agency, influence, instigation.) **of the elders, chief priests and teachers of the law,** (i.e. Jewish religious leaders who would be the initial instigators in Jesus' suffering & death.) **and that he must be killed** (i.e. Crucified in obedience to the divine plan in the redemption of mankind.) **and on the third day be raised to life.** (i.e. Resurrected. Suggests: As predicted by the Prophet Hosea.-{6:1-2})

Jesus prepares the disciples for His crucifixion & death, detailing how it will be at the hands of the Jewish religious leaders.

Message & Application 

- ❖ Shows Jesus' willingness in fulfilling God's plan of Salvation by suffering & dying on behalf of sinners. (cf. John 3:16-18, Rom. 3:25-28)
- ❖ Calls for a redemptive love that puts the eternal stakes and welfare of others first before our own interests. (cf. Rom. 15:1-3, Philp. 2:1-8, 4:14-19)
- ❖ Teaches how the impact and success we have is dependent on making use of the glorious opportunities and resources God places before us.
- ❖ Calls for trusting when our prayers and plans don't get answered in the way we like, that God has a greater purpose than what we can now see.
- ❖ Comforts believers how even the trials, suffering, and seeming defeats of life are not meaningless, but often serves a greater purpose!
- ❖ Teaches how triumph and glory are only achieved through hardship and self-sacrifice. (cf. Rom. 2:6-7, Philp. 3:10-12, Col. 3:23-24, Heb. 4:1-11)
- ❖ Displays how Jesus always prepares us ahead of time for the sorrows, turmoil's, and pains of life in order that our faith will not be shaken.
- ❖ Teaches how life isn't about ease or comfort, but about putting the will of God foremost before us, that His work is fully accomplished.
- 🗝 Even today, believers can take comfort that even in the trials and tragedies of life God has a greater purpose in all that happens. That even our hardships, struggles, and sufferings are often God's triumphs!

16:22 Peter took him aside (i.e. Privately or pulled Jesus away by the arm.) **and began to rebuke him.** (Syn.-protest, discourage, dissuade, talk-out-of, set straight) **Never, Lord! he said. "This shall never happen to you!"** (Expresses a form of protest as in "Heaven forbid", "Parish the thought", "God be gracious") **23 Jesus turned** (Away from Peter, or looked sternly upon him. At his disciples.-{Mark-8:33) **and said to Peter, "Get behind me"** (i.e. Get packing, beat it, or refocus, support.) **Satan!** (Not Peter literally but in sentiment & disposition.) **You are a stumbling-block to me;** (offence-K.J.V.-4625-*Snare or obstacle.* Syn.-diversion, hindrance.) **you do not have in mind** (savourest-K.J.V. Syn.-relish, interests, desire.) **the things of God,** (i.e. God' plan of Salvation & redemption.) **but the things of men."**(i.e. Worldly advantages, power, pomp, glory, etc.)

Peter unwittingly shares Satan's plan in tempting to divert Jesus away from the Cross to establishing an earthly kingdom.

Message & Application 💻=🌎

- ❖ Shows believers the need in sticking with the plans & purposes of God, even when it conflicts with our own interests, desires, and wants.
- ❖ Warns how when we start to argue with God's word and plans we begin to open the door to Satan's lies and deceptions.
- ❖ Displays how in times of trials and stress will often offer God an alternative plan, quick fix, or an easy way out.
- ❖ Warns against looking to do things our way rather than God's way. (Don't think you're wiser or understand things better than God!).
- ❖ Warns how when we allow our fleshy interests to jump in we can start to look at things from a worldly point of view rather than God's view.
- ❖ Teaches even when we're at our strongest spiritually we can still fall into Satanic traps if not careful. (Don't allow spiritual victories fool you into thinking your safe from Satan's attacks!).
- ❖ Teaches how the ultimate good from God does not always mean ease, success, and glory. (Be willing to get out of your comfort zone, know that God's way home doesn't always follow the safe path!).
- ❖ Warns believers against allowing the sentiments of loved ones to deflect us from the path of obedience to God.

🗝 Even today Satan often tempts us through the unsuspecting hands of our closest friends, using such appeals as; *"Surely God doesn't want you to go through this"*, or *"Spare yourself all the trouble & pain"*.

☞ Many resolve the contradiction of Peter's "Rock like faith" in V.18 to being a "Stumbling stone" here-(V. 23). By pointing out that Peter was only a stumbling stone during Jesus' earthly ministry, but would later become a "Foundation stone" after Jesus' resurrection.

From this verse here (V. 24) to end of chapter, Jesus teaches on commitment in discipleship.

16:24 Then Jesus said to his disciples, "If anyone would come after me (i.e. To be a disciple of Christ.) **he must deny himself** (533-*disown any connection with self.* Expresses a willingness to die to self-rule, self-centeredness, self-reliance, self-importance, carnal-nature.) **and take up** (Syn.-assume, bear, submit, daily.-{Luke 9:23}) **his cross** (Lit. The Roman practice to which a criminal was forced to carry their cross to the place of execution. Metph.-One who will follow Christ no matter the hardships, trials, or risks.) **and follow me.** (One who is willing to follow Christ's leading, direction, service, and example.)

Believers must be willing to die to self & anything else that keeps us from following God's will for our life's.

Message & Application 💻=🌎

❖ Shows how believers are to die daily to self, that it's no longer about us and what we want, but what God wants. (cf. Rom. 12:1-3, Gal. 2:20)
❖ Calls for recognizing that we no longer reserve the right to live as we want, that God is now in charge and control of our lives, not self!
❖ Calls for getting self out of the way to handing the reigns over to God, that we're no longer the boss of our lives God is!
❖ Portrays one who is patiently willing to suffer shame, ridicule, and rejection, even persecution as we follow Jesus. (cf. 1-Pet. 2:21-24)

–***Deny himself***-Does not mean some sort of act of self-denial or to take a vow of poverty, or to withdraw from the world. Nor is it simply giving up some guilty pleasure, like saying no to chocolate, junk food, and reality T.V. shows, etc. But rather it's one who is willing to give up personal ambitions, goals, and desires as they serve and follow Christ.

-***Take up his cross***- Is not meant in simply bearing with some tragedy, hardship, or inconvenient burden as in a nagging wife, thankless job, bad health, difficult neighbor, etc. Or as the saying go's *"We all have our crosses to bear"*. Nor is it a work of self-discipline in enduring some sort of affliction as an act of penance, or a religious fashion statement we wear. But rather it's one who is willing to pay the price no matter the costs, risks, or hardships as we follow after Christ.

⊶ Even today cross bearing can be anything from losing family, friends, job, reputation, career, or even one's life as we follow Christ.
Or even the day-to-day battles against the cravings of the flesh, or the daily temptations that the world throws at us. (cf. Eph. 4:17-24)

16:25 For whoever wants to save (run, preserve, hang-onto, retain ownership, play-it-safe, love.-{Jn.12:25}) **his life** (self, comforts, ease, security.) **will lose it,** (Eternal life or transformed life/character.) **but whoever loses** (Surrenders, renounces, puts-off, hates.-{Jn.12:25}) **his life for me** (Love for Jesus, and the Gospel.-{Mark 8:35}) **will find it.** (Life eternal, life of purpose, worth, fulfillment.)

Believers who want to retain ownership & control over their lives above Christ's claims & interests will lose out on eternal life.

Message & Application 💻=🌎

❖ Shows how believers are to give up control in trying to run our own lives to allowing God to run it. (Will you let God in the driver's seat?)
❖ Warns against thinking that we know what's best, that we can manage our lives a whole lot better than God can.
❖ Calls for coming to an end in ourselves, that we can't fix our lives on our own without God's help. (Will you stop fighting and let God in?).
⊶ Even today we try to save our lives in so many ways. We try to save our lives by pursuing careers, sports, relationships, etc. with no time for God. Or we revolve ourselves around activities we enjoy, things that fit our schedule with no thought to church or to spiritual things.
☞ Today the world tells us to look out for number one, that we need to take control of our future, make our own destiny, etc. Not realizing that we're not that good at knowing what's right and best for us.

16:26 What good will it be for a man if he gains (Syn.-profits, hoards, reaps, procures.) **the whole world,** (Metph-money, riches, honors, pleasures, fame, etc.) **yet forfeits** (Syn.-loses, squanders) **his soul?** (Metph.-Salvation, eternal life, very self.-{Luke 9:25}) **Or what can a man give in exchange** (Syn.-ransom, atone, redeem.) **for his soul?** (Expresses a negative reply as in "Nothing"!)

Salvation & eternal life with God should be more important than anything else in the whole world.

Message & Application 💻=🌎

❖ Shows how believers are to make the pursuit of God & Eternal life more important than a life of sin and temporary pleasures. (Col. 3:1-5)
❖ Teaches how there's nothing that this world has to offer that is worth going to hell for or losing our Salvation and soul over.
❖ Warns the folly of trading in a short time of fun and pleasure in this life now for a life of eternity in hell later! (cf. Philp. 3:7-9)
⊶ Even today are you willing to trade in a life of money, wealth, power, fame, popularity, success, etc. at the cost of losing your Salvation?

16:27 For the Son of Man (Expresses a messianic title signifying Messiah's human origins and headship over humanity.) **is going to come in his Father's glory** (i.e. Divine splendor and authority.) **with his angels,** (Expresses Christ's second coming on the day of judgment, with His Saint's/angels serving as His instruments of judgment.-{19:27-28, 25:31-33}) **and then he will reward each person** (i.e. Believer) **according to what he has done.** (Works-K.J.V.-4234-*Practiced, doing, a mode of being and acting.* Syn.-suffered, sacrificed, lived-out, put-off, dedicated, etc. Expresses: Not of isolated acts of good deeds, but more of the general course of one's life and conduct. In what one has practiced, risked, borne, and endured. Suggests: In context believers who have denied themselves and taken up their cross.-{Vs. 24-26} *If anyone is ashamed of me and my words, the Son of Man will be ashamed of him when we comes in his glory.*-{Luke 9:26} Expresses a warning against shrinking back to the point that we stop talking to others about Jesus, or we stop reading our bibles in public out of fear of what others may think. Or we stop inviting our friends and acquaintances over to study the bible with us out of fear of being labeled odd.)

Whatever sacrifices believers suffer for Christ's sake will be eternally rewarded by Him in the next life.

Message & Application 

❖ Shows believers how we serve & live for Christ today matters for eternity, and will one day follow us into heaven. (cf. Rom. 14:12)
❖ Prepares believers how we will have to give an account for our time here on earth, how we invested our life's for Christ's service.
❖ Comforts believers in knowing that every hour & every day we spend in Christian service will not go unnoticed by the Lord. (cf. John 6:27)
❖ Invites believers in giving our all for Christ and His cause, that our labor for the Lord will not be lost or in vain.(cf. 1-Corn. 15:58, Rev. 14:13)
❖ Calls believers in holding nothing back, that we're making the most out of our lives for Christ's cause and glory.
❖ Teaches how keeping eternal perspectives will enable us to cultivate godly values and priorities throughout our lives. (cf. Rom. 8:18)
❖ Teaches how those who keep their eyes focused on Jesus and the joys of heaven, nothing will be too hard to endure, bear, or give up for Him.

⊶ Even today, believers need to stay the course in never giving up, that whatever sacrifices and hardships we have to endure in our service and walk with the Lord can't even compare to what God has waiting for us in heaven. (cf. 2-Tim . 1:7-12, 4:1-8)

☞ Jesus is not here talking about earning or securing our Salvation by good works. But rather, our works will be the natural evidence and outworking of our faith, service, and obedience to God. (Matt. 25:31-46)

16:28 I tell you the truth, (Expresses a strong confirmation & reliability.) **some who are standing here** (i.e. Peter, James, and John.) **will not taste** (Syn.-experience, see) **death** (i.e. Physical.) **before they see the Son of Man** (Jesus) **coming in his kingdom.**(932-*power/splendor/glory.* Suggests: In the immediate context Jesus' transfiguration a week later.-{17:1-2} But in a wider context the spiritual rule of Christ in the believer's life. come with power.-{cf. Mark 9:1b})

Peter, James, and John will get an advance preview of Jesus' divine glory when He transfigures Himself before them.

<u>Message & Application</u>

- ❖ Shows believers the regenerating power & work of Christ upon our lives as we stay following, serving, and living for Him.
- ❖ Teaches those who open their hearts up to Jesus will see more and more of His power bearing fruit in their lives!
- ❖ Displays the life changing and transforming work of Jesus throughout our lives as we continue to serve and follow after Him.
- ❖ Reassures believer's that the good work that Jesus has begun in us, He will see it through to the end. (cf. Philp. 1:6, Eph. 4:15)
- ❖ Teaches how growing in virtues does not come by way of our own special efforts, but rather are a work of God's grace.
- ❖ Teaches how obedience and perseverance opens our lives up to seeing glorious experiences with God.
- ❖ Assures believers that when we set our life's according to Christ's values and principles, we will always come out winning!
- ⊶ Even today as we continue to live for Jesus, will see more and more of His transforming power & presence unfolding in our lives, slowly freeing us from the sinful habits, patterns, and addictions that have been plaguing our lives.

-***Son of man coming in his kingdom-***Variously interpreted as either:

- Jesus' transfiguration that Peter, James, and John would witness a week later. (Favored do to the context in which all three synoptic Gospels follow this statement). (Matt. 17:1-2, Mark 9:2-4, Luke 9:28-29)
- Outpouring of the Holy Spirit on the day of Pentecost. (Acts 2:1-4)
- Jesus' resurrection & ascension that many of the disciples would witness. (cf. Matt. 28:16-17, Luke 24:36-43, John 20:19-29, Acts 1:3-11)
- The internal development of Christ's power and spiritual rule on the believer's heart and life.
- The generation of believers who will be living during Jesus' return.
- The destruction of Jerusalem by Rome 40 years later in 70 A.D.

Chapter Seventeen

Jesus' Transfiguration

- **The transfiguration-**Jesus reveals His divine glory to Peter, James, and John.-(Vs. 1-12)
- **Elijah's return-**Jesus confirms John the Baptist fulfillment of Elijah's role, by coming in the spirit & power of Elijah.-(Vs. 10-13)
- **Healing of a boy with a demon-**Jesus teaches on appropriating the right kind of faith-(Vs. 14-21)
- **Son of man betrayed-**Jesus prepares disciples for His betrayal & death-(Vs. 22-23)
- **The Temple tax-**Jesus' provision in atonement & redemption.-(Vs. 24-2)

The Transfiguration-(N.I.V.)

17:1 After six days Jesus took with him Peter, James and John (Jesus' inner circle) **the brother of James, and led them up a high mountain** (Unknown. Possibly Mtn. "Tabor"-[1,886 ft.] or Mtn. "Hermon"-[9,200 ft.]-◙) **by themselves.**
2 There he was transfigured (3339-*Greek-metamorphosis, to change, transform.)* **before them. His face shone like the sun, and his clothes became as white as the light.** (Expresses: Jesus' divine radiance and heavenly glory.-{Heb. 1:3})
3 Just then there appeared before them Moses (Repr. Law) **and Elijah,** (Repr. Prophecy) **talking with Jesus** (i.e. Jesus' approaching death.-{Luke 9:31-32})
4 Peter said to Jesus, "Lord, it is good for us to be here. If you wish, I will put up three shelters-◙ (Suggests: As makeshift Shrines)**—one for you, one for Moses and one for Elijah."** (Suggests: Peter's attempt to make Jesus equal with Moses & Elijah. He did not know what he was saying.-{Mark 9:6, Luke 9:33})
5 While he was still speaking, a bright cloud enveloped them and a voice from the cloud said, "This is my Son", whom I love; with him, I am well pleased. Listen to him. (Expresses God's approval of Jesus' qualifications, obedience, and complete fulfillment of the Law & Prophets.{cf. Deut. 18:15})

Jesus transfigures Himself, giving the disciples a revelation of His divine glory & ultimate reign.

Message & Application 💻=🌎

- ❖ Shows believers the assurance of our ultimate transformation & future share in Christ's glorious Kingdom.(cf. 2-Corn. 3:18, Col. 3:4, 2-Pet. 1:16-19)
- ❖ Teaches how life is not lived on mountain tops (spiritual highs) but in serving the suffering & hurting in the valley's below.(V. 4, cf. Vs. 14-16)
- ❖ Gives hope in times of trials & struggles, that there's a glorious future in store for us. (Always see the glory on the other side of suffering!).
- 🗝 Even today rather than allow the pressures of a bad day, a breakup, a job loss, etc. to bring us down, we need to keep our gaze on Jesus and the glorious life that awaits us! (cf. Rom. 8:18, 1-Corn. 9:24-27, Heb. 12:1)

17:6 When the disciples heard this, (i.e. God's voice-{V.5}) **they fell face down to the ground, terrified.** (Expresses a mixture of both reverent fear and awe.)
7 But Jesus came and touched them. (Suggests: For strength & comfort, or to assure them He was not an apparition.) **"Get up," he said. "Don't be afraid."**
8 When they looked up, they saw no-one except Jesus. (Suggests: The absence of both the luminous cloud and the prophets Moses & Elijah.)

Believers only have to look to Jesus as Savior

Message & Application 💻=🌎

❖ Shows believers how Christ always meets us where we're at, reaching out with God's love, mercy, and forgiveness.
❖ Displays the healing touch of Jesus, bringing comfort, security, and peace. (Know Jesus will always be there when others desert you!).
❖ Teaches believers how we don't need a lot of money, or a lot of friends, but only Jesus.
🗝 Even today, believers are not equal or sufficient to any task without the Lord's personal touch, support, and direction.

17:9 As they were coming down the mountain, Jesus instructed them, "Don't tell anyone what you have seen, (i.e. Jesus' transfiguration.) **until the Son of Man has been raised from the dead."**

The Cross and Christ's resurrection are to be the supreme Saving event in our life's.

Message & Application 💻=🌎

❖ Shows believers how Jesus' work on Calvary is to be the Saving event in our life's, and not our spiritual experiences. (Col. 2:18, 2-Corn. 12:1-9)
❖ Teaches the importance of seeing that we're leading people to Christ for the right reason, for healing & Salvation, not for signs and wonders.
🗝 Even today divine visions & spiritual experiences are sometimes meant to be just between us and God, and not to be paraded around.

*–Don't tell anyone-*Prohibition is variously attributed to either:

- The resurrection was to be the supreme witness of Jesus' authority & Messiahship. (Matt. 12:39-40, 28:13, John 2:18-21)
- The resurrection would give the disciples a better testimony to declare to the people. (John 20:25-28, Acts 2:14-36)
- Jesus' suffering would have shaken the disciples' faith and quickly disillusioned those who were following Him.
- Others would infer that Peter, James, and John were entitled to special rights and privileges above the other disciples.

From this verse here (V. 10) to verse (V. 13) Jesus confirms John the Baptist's role by coming in the spirit & power of Elijah.

17:10 The disciples (i.e. Peter, James, and John) **asked him, "Why then do the teachers of the law say that Elijah must come first?"**(Suggests: Having just seen Elijah during Jesus' transfiguration, assumed he should have preceded the Messiah before the "Great Day of the Lord".-{cf. Mal. 3:1-5, 4:5-6})
11 Jesus replied, "To be sure, (Viz.-No doubt, they're correct.) **Elijah comes and will restore all things.** (Suggests: By calling for repentance and reform in preparation for the Messiah's arrival.-{cf. Mal. 3:1, 4:1-6})
12 But I tell you, Elijah has already come, (Suggests: Not in the appearance on the mount,-{V. 3} or as in reincarnation. But in the spirit, power, and character of John the Baptist.-{Luke 1:17}) **and they did not recognise him, but have done to him everything they wished.** (listed-K.J.V. A.V.-Syn.-desired, intended, hoped for. Suggests: The religious leader's rejection of John's message and consenting in part, to His arrest & death by king Herod.-{cf. Matt. 14:6-11}) **In the same way, the son of man** (i.e. Messiah/Jesus) **is going to suffer at their hands.** (Syn.-instigation, provocation. That they will accuse Jesus of being a blasphemer/pretender resulting in His arrest and death.)
13 Then the disciples understood that he was talking to them about John the Baptist. (For more examples of John's fulfilling Elijah's role see Pg. 182.)

John the Baptist fulfilled Elijah's role by coming in the spirit and power of Elijah.

Message & Application

- ❖ Shows how believers can become blind to what God wants to do in our lives when we already decided how things should turn out.
- ❖ Teaches how God's word is often fulfilled in ways that most people are not prepared to recognize. (We often reject that which does not match up with our popular expectations!). (cf. 2-Tim. 4:2-5)
- ❖ Teaches how when confused over scripture difficulties we can go to the Lord in prayer for understanding & enlightenment.(V. 10, Philp. 3:15)
- ❖ Prepares believers in expecting to be treated with rejection & contempt by the world and people in general as we serve Christ. (2-Tim.1:8-9, 4:5)
- ❖ Calls for boldly confronting sin and speaking the truth of God's word, even if it means being treated harshly and unfairly. (V. 12)
- ⊶ Even today we need to be prepared for the unexpected ways that God may be working in our life's in whatever He is leading us to do. (Will you give up your own agendas and accept God's plan without knowing all the facts, risks, and challenges that lay ahead?).

From this verse here (V. 14) to verse (V. 23) Jesus teaches the importance of appropriating the right kind of faith.

The Healing of a Boy With a Demon-(N.I.V.)

17:14 When they (Jesus, Peter, James, and John) **came to the crowd** (Among whom the scribes were debating with the disciples, trying to discredit Jesus' power & authority due to their failure to heal a boy.-{Mark 9:14-18}) **a man approached Jesus and knelt before him.** (Expresses to bow down in humility.)
15 "Lord, have mercy (Syn.-compassion, pity) **on my son,"** (my only child.-{Luke 9:38}) **he said. "He has seizures** (he is a lunatic-K.J.V.-4583-*Moon-struck, crazy, epileptic.* Suggests: The boy was suffering from some form of Epilepsy.) **and is suffering greatly.** (i.e. Epilepsy was causing the boy tremendous affliction.) **He often falls into the fire or into the water.** (Expresses how the child's life was in constant danger as a result of his epileptic seizures, causing him to tumble into fireplaces, resulting in severe burns, or into lakes resulting in near drowning's.)
16 I brought him to your disciples, (i.e. The nine) **but they could not heal him."**

A father humbly places his faith in Jesus' power & compassion to heal his epileptic son.

Message & Application =

- ❖ Shows how believers can take our desperate needs and hopeless situations to Jesus for mercy, compassion, and deliverance.
- ❖ Gives believers hope that even in the midst of our limitations and powerlessness we can always go to Jesus for help.
- ❖ Teaches how we can have mountaintop experiences one moment and the next moment back into the valley of failures, struggles, and defeats.
- ❖ Warns how opening ourselves up to Satan and demonic influences will often plunge us into greater evil, misery, and destruction. (V. 15b)
- ❖ Teaches how as Christians and followers of Jesus we're expected to pray and minister to those whom God puts in our path. (V. 16)
- ❖ Displays how faith and virtue can quickly wane when Jesus is taken out of the picture or is no longer a central part of our lives. (V. 16)
- ❖ Teaches how we can be fully empowered and qualified with all the resources needed to defeat the enemy but not the faith. (10:1, Luke 10:17)
- ❖ Warns how failure brings disgrace not only upon ourselves, but also robs the Lord of His glory and gives the enemy a chance to criticize.

⊶ Even today it's a great shame and disservice to Christ when the lost and hurting come looking for answers in their time of need only to find nothing that believers can offer, eventually causing them to look elsewhere, that maybe Jesus isn't as powerful as we claimed He was.

17:17 "O (Expresses dismay/disappointment.) **unbelieving** (Syn.-skeptical, doubtful) **and perverse** (1294-*Denotes to turn aside from the right path, crooked, twisted, distorted.* Not a moral perversion, but rather a spiritual perversion in having a lack of faith and wrong view of God.) **generation,"** (1074-*By implication an age, people, or nation living in the same time period, those who share the same interests & attitudes.* Taken together Jesus' disappointment in either the disciples, the father, or the crowd & scribes in general-{Mark 9:14-25} for their spiritual dullness, having failed in appropriating the power and authority already granted them.) **Jesus replied, "how long shall I stay with you? How long shall I put up with you?** (suffer-K.J.V. Syn.-bear, endure, tolerate. Expresses: Jesus' self–awareness of His origin, destiny, and approaching death. Is not meant to criticize or slam the disciples, but rather to encourage them towards greater exercise of faith.) **Bring the boy here to me."**
18 Jesus rebuked the demon, and it came out of the boy, and he was healed from that moment.(very hour-K.J.V. i.e. Immediately, instantaneously.)

Jesus rebukes the disciples for failing to appropriate the right kind of faith & power already granted them.

Message & Application 💻=🌎

- ❖ Shows how believers can be a great disappointment to Jesus when we profess our faith in Him, yet distrust in His power/authority to deliver.
- ❖ Displays how it grieves the Lord when we fail to abide in His word, promises, and anointing He so graciously grants us.
- ❖ Warns against acknowledging Jesus as Lord & Savior one day, then the next day distrusting that He can do anything for us.
- ❖ Displays how some can know all that the Lord has done, yet remain slow to believe and slow to put their trust in Him.
- ❖ Teaches how God expects more, that our lives should be marked with a greater exercise of faith, joy, and hope than the world around us!
- ❖ Displays Jesus' patience & compassion, that no matter how imperfect our faith, we can still bring our problems & struggles to Him for help. (Where faith fails, Christ still provides, rescues, and delivers!).
- ❖ Calls parents in never giving up, that we can bring our children to God in prayer, that they may be rescued & delivered from the powers of sin that are enslaving them.
- 🗝 Even today the same type of inconsistent faith is often displayed by some believers, who can one day make grand claims about Jesus and the next day be found complaining and expressing doubt in Him.

17:19 Then the disciples came to Jesus in private (Suggests: They were embarrassed for their failure.) **and asked, "Why couldn't we drive It out?"** (Suggests: They were only focusing on their own strength rather than on God.)
20 He replied, "Because you have so little faith. (unbelief-K.J.V. Syn.-inactive, distrusting, ineffectual, skeptical, misplaced. Not that the disciples lacked faith, for they would not have tried to cast the demon out in the first place. But rather the misplacement of their faith, focusing on their own efforts rather than God's power.) **I tell you the truth, if you have faith as small as a mustard seed,** (Suggests: Not in quantity, but in quality.) **you can say to this mountain,** (Mtn. of Transfiguration.) **'Move from here to there' and it will move. Nothing will be impossible for you."** (Expresses in overcoming great obstacles, trials, struggles, and difficulties. Not that will get whatever we pray for, but only that which is in accordance with the Gospel and in harmony with God's will.)
21"However, this kind does not go out except by prayer and fasting." –(K.J.V.- Not found in the most authentic Greek MSS. Suggests: Victory over sin & evil is dependent on a disciplined life of prayer, communion, and devotion to God.)

Believers with just a mustard seed of faith rightly placed in God can accomplish the impossible.

Message & Application 💻=🌎

- ❖ Shows believers the need to see that we're placing our faith in the power and authority of God and not in our own strength and abilities.
- ❖ Teaches how it's not the amount of faith that one has, but rather it's about the person (God) in whom our faith is placed in that matters!
- ❖ Teaches how even the smallest amount of faith rightly focused on God can overcome even the greatest obstacles and difficulties.
- ❖ Teaches if we're to grow and mature in our faith we need to take ownership of our failures as to where we went wrong. (V. 19)
- ❖ Calls for a faith that is leaning more and more on God's power, and less on our own resources and self-sufficiency. (cf. Philp. 4:12-13)
- ❖ Displays how it's not a lack of God's love or willingness, but rather about our doubts and misgivings.
- 🗝 Even today when we feel weak & powerless we need to examine our faith. That we're making God the object and confidence of our faith and not our own strength and abilities. (Know that it's not about the size of your faith, but about the size of your God!).
- ☞ Jesus is not saying that we can literally move mountains, or promising that if we pray hard enough will get whatever we want. But rather is promising believers in having the power to accomplish all that God has commissioned and called us to do in the work of serving Him and sharing the Gospel with others.

From this verse here (V. 22) to verse (V. 23) Jesus for the second time prepares the disciples for His death.

17:22 When they came together in Galilee, he said to them, "The Son of Man (i.e. Jesus. Expresses: A Messianic title signifying the Messiah's human origins & headship over humanity)**is going to be betrayed** (3860-*To deliver treacherously over to an enemy by way of betrayal.*) **into the hands of men.** (Suggests: By Implication Judas Iscariot who would betray Jesus by turning Him over to the Jewish and Roman authorities.-{cf. 26:21-25, 47-50})
23 They will kill (i.e. Crucify) **him, and on the third day he will be raised to life."** (i.e. Resurrected) **And the disciples were filled with grief.** (exceedingly sorry-K.J.V. Syn.-grief-stricken, heartbroken. Expresses the disciple's love and affection for Jesus. That the disciples were only focusing on Jesus' death, completely missing the point of the Transfiguration and Resurrection.)

Jesus again for the second time prepares the disciples for His death, this time adding the element of betrayal.

Message & Application 💻=🌎

- ❖ Shows Jesus' willingness in staying obedient to God's plan and purpose in suffering and dying on the Cross for our sins. (Philp. 2:1-8)
- ❖ Gives hope and encouragement in the plans and purposes of God, even in the face of loss and defeat. (cf. Rom. 8:28)
- ❖ Teaches how Christ prepares us beforehand for the severe trials that lie ahead. (The Lord will see to it that our faith is not shaken!).
- ❖ Teaches the importance of giving spiritual comfort when bearing painful announcements. (Always speak of Christ's won victories and glories when delivering bad news!).
- ❖ Displays how obedience and commitment to God brings new life, power, and transformation. (V. 23)
- ❖ Calls for trusting that despite the terrible & unjust things that happen to us, God is working it all for His purpose and glory. (V. 23)
- ⊶ Even today, believers can be so focused on the loss and pain of a situation, that we fail to hear God's promises of hope, comfort, and relief. (Always trust that God will bring good out of a bad situation!).
- ☞ According to Luke's Gospel the disciples: *"Did not understand what this meant. It was hidden from them, and were afraid to ask him about it"*-(Luke 9:45).(Suggests they were still holding on to the traditional view of a conquering Messiah and earthly pomp. Or they feared Jesus would reproach them for their spiritual dullness.-(Mark 8:17-18)

From this verse here (V. 24) to the end of the chapter, Jesus assures His work in our atonement & redemption.

The Temple Tax-(N.I.V.)

17:24 After Jesus and his disciples arrived in Capernaum, the collectors (i.e. Not Roman, but Jewish officials.) **of the two-drachma-tax-◙** (i.e. A Greek silver coin worth about two days wages.) **came to Peter** (Suggests: Observing Peter as standing out as the official spokesperson among the 12. Or because it was Peter's house that Jesus was staying at.-{V. 25}) **and asked, "Doesn't your teacher pay the temple tax?-◙ "**(tribute money-K.J.V. Suggests: A Jewish Atonement tax voluntarily paid annually by every male 20 years and older.-{cf. Ex.30:11-16} That they were testing Jesus' patriotism or religious devoutness.)
25 "Yes, he does," he replied. (Suggests: That Jesus had done so before. Or Peter was simply covering up for His boss.) **When Peter came into the house,-◙ Jesus was the first to speak.** (prevented-K.J.V.-Expresses an old English word meaning to "Speak before" or "To anticipate". Suggests: Jesus' divine omniscience, knowing Peter's guilt for failing to consult with Him first, or Peter's anxiety over the lack of funds.) **"What do you think, Simon?" he asked. "From whom do the kings of the earth collect duty and taxes- from their own sons** (Families) **or from others?"**(i.e. Commoners, foreigners-L.B.V.)
26 "From others, "Peter answered." Then the sons (Metph.-Jesus and the disciples.) **are exempt,"** (Syn.-free, tax-exempt) **Jesus said to him.**

Since Jesus is the Son of God and owner of the temple, He was exempt from having to pay taxes.

Message & Application

- ❖ Shows believers Jesus' work in our atonement & redemption, having made full payment for our sin debts owed to God. (cf. 1-John 2:2, 4:10)
- ❖ Teaches the responsibility of every believer in freely bearing witness of Christ, always exalting His integrity, truth, and honor. (V. 24)
- ❖ Displays how Christ already knows our needs, struggles, and moral conflicts even before we ask. (V. 25)
- ❖ Warns how those who know the true identity of Jesus should always speak better claims of Him and His work.
- ⊶ Even today, believers must keep our focus on the divine providence, provisions, and work of Christ. That Jesus must stand supreme over everything and everyone else in our lives. (cf. Eph. 1:15-20, Gal. 4:4-10)
- ☞ Jesus is not just giving a lesson on paying taxes. But rather is drilling home the importance of remembering His sovereign jurisdiction over all things, having made full payment for our sin debts owed to God.

17:27 "But so that we may not offend them (4624-"*To put a snare or stumbling block in the way*". Syn.-insult, scandalize, turn-off, create a crisis.) **go to the lake**(Sea of Galilee) **and throw out your line.-◙** (Fishing line) **Take the first fish you catch;** (i.e. Possibly a catfish who were know to swallow shiny objects.) **open its mouth and you will find a four-drachma coin.-◙** (i.e. A Greek silver coin equal to an average days wage. Not that Jesus created the coin in the fish's mouth, but rather arranged a fish that had swallowed a coin to be caught by Peter.) **Take it and give it to them for my tax and yours.** (Most assume that Peter obeyed and succeeded in what Jesus had commanded.)

Jesus submits to paying the tax for the sake of witness and out of respect for the religious establishment.

Message & Application 💻=🌍

- ❖ Shows believers Christ's humility in emptying Himself in making full redemption for our sin debts owed to God. (cf. 2-Corn. 8:9, Eph. 1:6-8)
- ❖ Teaches how it's better to keep the peace than to stand on our own personal rights. (Don't allow your freedom to hurt your witness and testimony with others!). (cf. Rom. 14:13-21, 1-Corn. 8:13, 2-Corn. 6:3)
- ❖ Teaches how it's better to give in and waive rights for the sake of unity and peace. (Avoid unnecessary offenses that can ruin God's work!).
- ❖ Teaches though our citizenship is in heaven, we're still obligated in obeying the laws & customs of the land in which we live. (Rom. 13:1-8)
- ❖ Reminds believers, though ultimately all that we have comes from God, but we still need to be active and engaged in the process.
- ❖ Teaches believers how God often meets our needs by putting our natural abilities and skills to work in what we already enjoy doing.
- ❖ Calls for trusting in divine providence, that God can meet our needs in a variety of ways. (Expect money and provisions from unexpected sources).

–***Not offend them-*** Jesus submits in order not to offend Jewish religious customs. But in a wider context suggests that believers, for the sake of witness and out of respect for the religious scruples of others, are called to sacrifice our liberties so as not to offend. (cf. Rom. 14:1-23)

⊶ Even today God's provisions often comes from unexpected sources as we're going about our daily routine. (Trust that the Lord is working behind the scenes as you go about your daily business!).

☞ This is not teaching that God will always work a miracle in getting us out of the jams we're in. But rather, God will provide whatever is necessary when we're pursuing a path of love, peace, and goodwill towards others.

Chapter Eighteen

Teachings on Relationships among Believers

- **Greatest in the Kingdom-**Teaches greatness measured not by rank, but by humility & service.-(Vs. 1-9)
- **"Lost Sheep"-**Parable on seeking out those who go astray.-(Vs. 10-14)
- **Brother who sins against you-** Teachings on 4 steps in reconciling a sinning believer.- (Vs. 15-20)
- **"Unmerciful Servant"-**Parable teaching on the principles of unlimited forgiveness.-(Vs. 21-35)

The Greatest in the Kingdom of Heaven-(N.I.V.)

18:1 At that time (i.e. Temple-tax incident.-{17:24-27} Or Jesus' Transfiguration.-{17:1-5}) **the disciples came to Jesus** (Suggest: For the purpose of resolving an argument between them.-{Mark 9:33}) **and asked, "Who is the greatest** (3187-*Comparative in degree, rank*. Syn.-chief, top-dog, head-honcho, #1, etc.) **in the kingdom of heaven?"**(Expresses Christ's Millennial Kingdom and Earthly reign.)

The disciples want to know which of them will hold the highest honor & status in Jesus' Kingdom.

Message & Application 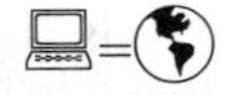

- ❖ Shows how believers can sometimes get our priorities mixed up in wanting to be served rather than serving.
- ❖ Warns against coming with the wrong attitude in thinking we can be great with God just because of what we do. (cf. Philp. 2:3-8)
- ❖ Warns against thinking what we've achieved, suffered, and sacrificed gives us some special honor and standing with God. (Never think that somehow God owes you for all the things you've done for Him).
- ❖ Warns against seeking places of honor and recognition for having done some generous, benevolent, or pious act.
- ❖ Warns how pride and competitive spirit can turn to sin because it looks to exalts self above others, that what we do for God makes us better!

Examples of a Competitive Spirit:

- Do you feel that you have to tell everyone how successful your ministry is doing?
- Do you find yourself having to brag about someone that you brought to Christ?
- Do you feel the need to tell someone how mightily God had used you in some situation?
- Do you find yourself trying to impress others with your bible knowledge when they're around?

18:2 He called a little child (i.e. Between two & six years old.) **and had him stand among them.** (Suggests: To be used as an object lesson and visual aid.)
3 And he said "I tell you the truth unless you change (be converted-K.J.V. Syn.-about-face, complete U-turn. Expresses: Not a faith Saving conversion to Jesus. But rather a radical change of mentality and thinking, from one of pride to one of humility.) **and become like little children**, (Metph-humble, lowly, trusting, teachable, flexible.) **you will never enter the kingdom of heaven.** (i.e. To assume the characteristics and qualities that are in line with heaven.)
4 Therefore, whoever humbles (5012-*Lowliness of mind, meek, modest, Unassuming.*) **himself like this child is the greatest in the kingdom of heaven.**

Greatness in Christ's kingdom is measured not by rank, but by humility and service to others.

Message & Application 💻=🌎

- ❖ Shows how true greatness is adopting a humble & submissive attitude, that it's not about being served but about serving others!
- ❖ Teaches how just like children we're to have no achievements or accomplishments to offer or commend ourselves on before God.
- ❖ Teaches how just like children we're to have no concerns for degrees of honor, status, or rank. (It's not about celebrity, but service!).
- ❖ Teaches the more we're willing to humbly agree with what God says about us is true, the more He can begin to lift us up and change us.
- ❖ Teaches believers only when we get "Self" out of the way can God then begin to work on reshaping and remolding us.
- 🗝 Even today we need to see ourselves as weak, broken, and helpless, that we bring nothing to the table, but are solely and completely dependent on God's mercy & grace! (cf. Matt. 5:3)
- ☞ Jesus is not calling for childish behavior. But rather a whole radical change of thinking and being. From an attitude of self-importance and self-sufficiency to one of inadequacy and dependence.

Other Humble Qualities of Children:

- They respond without reservation, trustingly.
- They are free of pride, selfish ambition, envy.
- They have no regard for worldly values/status.
- They possess a willingness to learn, grow, and be instructed (i.e. teachable, receptive).
- They are dependent on the help & care of others.
- They do not boast about their talents & abilities.

From this verse here (V. 5) to verse (V. 10) Jesus teaches on the responsibility of looking after weaker believers.

18:5 "And whoever welcomes (receives-K.J.V.-1209-*hospitality, takes in.* Syn.-loves, accepts, treats-kindly, befriends, esteems.) **a little child** (Metph.-New-convert, babe in Christ, new-born believer. Not limited to, but also including shut-ins, inmates, the elderly, etc.) **like this in my name** (i.e. As one who is a believer and follower of Christ, on my behalf-N.L.T.) **welcomes me.** (i.e. Acceptance that Jesus too was of little worldly importance and status, or will be divinely evaluated as though done for Christ personally.)

Whatever is done for the least of Christ's disciples is reckoned as done for the Lord.

Message & Application 💻=🌎

- ❖ Shows believers how true greatness is about serving others who have nothing to give, or whether they can repay us or not.
- ❖ Calls for always ministering to others without expecting anything in return, or how we can benefit from it. (cf. Philp. 2:3-4)
- ❖ Calls for ministering to everybody that God puts in our path, whether we get noticed or recognition for it or not. (cf. Matt. 25:34-40)
- ❖ Warns against failing to do something just because we think it's beneath us, or not according to our liking.
- ❖ Calls believers in coming with the same love and compassion of Jesus for those who are overlooked, forgotten, and left out.
- ❖ Teaches how true servants will minister to the weak, despised, and marginalized just as Jesus did. (cf. Philp. 2:5-7)
- ❖ Teaches how we're no longer defined by how we measure up to others, but where we stand in our relationship to Jesus!(Rom. 12:3, 2-Corn. 10:12)
- ❖ Teaches its not about seeking that job or position that the world thinks important, but about heeding God's call in what He would have us do.
- ❖ Gives encouragement to those who's call & walk is less than perfect, that they don't have to measure or compare themselves to some great preacher or saint, that Jesus accepts them just the way they are.

🗝 Even today rather than think that we have to be somebody great, that we need the best-paying job, the highest position in the company, or the top leadership role in the church. We should be putting our focus and ambition on serving Jesus in whatever area He has called us to. Whether it's sweeping the church parking lot, working in the soup kitchen, visiting the shut-ins, ministering to the homeless, etc.

18:6 But if anyone causes one of these little ones (i.e. New-convert, weak-believer, young believer in the faith, humble-Christian, etc.) **who believe in me to sin,** (shall offend-K.J.V.-4624-"*To trip up as in a snare, stumbling block in the way, scandalize.* Expresses to cause another to sin, stray, or lose faith, either by our actions or inactions.) **it would be better for him to have a large millstone-◙** (Suggests: A large circular stone weighing several hundred pounds that was pulled around in a circle by a donkey in grinding grain into flour.) **hung around his neck and to be drowned in the depths** (i.e. bottom/middle) **of the sea.** (Suggests: The ancient practice of the Greeks & Romans in punishing criminals by tying a stone around the condemns neck, and then tossing them into a lake, assuring their death by drowning.)

Warns those who cause new born believers to sin or go astray, drowning will seem mild compared to the severe punishment God will inflict on them.

Message & Application 💻=🌎

❖ Shows how believers are to take great care & attention in not allowing what we're doing to cause weaker Christians to stumble or go astray.
❖ Warns believers against persisting in any kind of behavior that can ruin or scandalize another's faith and walk.
❖ Teaches the importance of always making choices for the sake of weaker believers. (cf. Rom. 14:13-15, 19-21, 1-Tim. 4:3)
❖ Reminds believers since our children, friends, and fellow church members are watching us, we have a greater responsibility and obligation to be examples and role models for them to follow!
❖ Calls for being sensitive to the vulnerabilities & weaknesses of others. (Abstain from any liberty that would pressure, embolden, or encourage another believer to sin by going against their own conscience).
❖ Calls for being responsible for our behavior & conduct around others. (Are you watchful over your language, jokes, and humor, or do you say things that are insensitive, hurtful, and offensive to others.)
⊶ Even today if you truly loved your Christian brother you wouldn't seek a drinking buddy who's an alcoholic, or invite a vegan over for Thanksgiving dinner, or a recovering gambler to bingo night, or dress seductively around a brother who is easily tempted. (cf. Rom. 14:17-23)
☞ Jesus is not just talking about the obvious sins like causing someone to steal or lie. But rather about the little gray areas that are not spelled out in scripture like smoking, drinking, dancing, going to the movies, playing cards, playing the lottery, etc. that can violate the conscience and convictions of a weaker believer.

18:7 "Woe (Expresses judgment/doom.) **to the world because of the things that cause people to sin!** (Offences-K.J.V. Syn.-Tempt, ensnare, entice, and trip-up) **Such things must come,** (i.e. Because we're living in a fallen world and the sinful nature/flesh. Or that God has a greater purpose in them to mature & grow us spiritually.) **but woe to the man** (Believer) **through whom they come!**

Things are bound to cause believers to sin, but they are not to be the agency through which they come.

Message & Application 💻=🌎

❖ Shows how believers are to see that we're not leading others down a wrong path by our poor example, negative attitudes, and bad advice.
❖ Warns how the sovereign purpose and plan of God does not absolve or excuse us from the guilt of our sinful actions and decisions.
❖ Warns if not careful we can cause someone to stop believing in God and stop going to church by something we inadvertently said or did.
🗝 Even today we can lead others indirectly into sin by our lack of love and concern, triggering a resentful and angry reaction in them. Or by flaunting our blessings & success, causing them to envy and covet. Or even by our tolerance, causing them to feel comfortable in their sins.

18:8 If your hand or your foot (Metph-sinful activities.) **causes you to sin,** (offend-K.J.V.-4624-*Trip up, entice, stumble.*) **cut it off and throw it away. It is better for you to enter life** (Eternal life/Heaven) **maimed or crippled than to have two hands or two feet and be thrown into eternal fire.** (Metph-Hell)
9 And if your eye (Metph-sinful desires.) **causes you to sin,** (offend-K.J.V. Syn.-stumble) **gouge it out and throw it away. It is better for you to enter life with one eye than to have two eyes and be thrown into the fire of hell.**

Believers are to take radical & decisive measures in removing any sin that may cause others to stumble.

Message & Application 💻=🌎

❖ Shows how believers are to take decisive measures in removing any sin or offense that may cause others to stumble or go astray.
❖ Teaches how we're responsible not only for our own spiritual welfare but also the spiritual welfare of fellow believers as well.
🗝 Even today we need to take drastic action in removing any behavior, habit, attitude, and relationship that can cause others to fall into sin.
☞ Jesus is not literally teaching self-mutilation or physical surgery. But rather the spiritual surgery of the heart in dealing with any practice, activity, or poor behavior that can lead others to stumble.

18:10 "See that you do not look down on (despise-K.J.V.-2706-*To think slightly of or down upon.* Syn.-demean, spurn, belittle, write-off, ridicule, neglect, indifferent.) **one of these little ones.** (i.e. Weak-believer, young-convert, babes in Christ, wayward Christian.) **For I tell you that their angels in heaven always see the face of my Father in heaven.** (Expresses: Continual free access to God's presence, having Divine protection, care, and concern.)
11 For the Son of man (i.e. Jesus) **is come to save that which was lost**-(K.J.V. i.e. sinners.-[Note: This verse is not found in the earliest or most authentic Greek MSS]. Expresses: Christ's special care for believers, having given His life for their redemption and Salvation.)

Warns against demeaning & belittling weak believers because God places special importance on them.

Message & Application

- Shows how believers are not to spurn or belittle weaker Christians because they are dearly loved and cherished by God.
- Warns against slighting the failure and weaknesses of others. (Rather than writing others off, give them hope and encouragement).
- Teaches instead of judging, shunning, and looking down on wayward believers, always hold out love and concern for them.
- Teaches the importance of never giving up on wayward believers. (Have less of a critical spirit and more of a compassionate heart!).
- Warns how our negative words can make a person feel inadequate, discouraged, and shamed to the point of giving up.
- Warns against faulting, criticizing, or condemning others just because they don't measure up. (Know that nobodies perfect, that we all sin and fall short!). (cf. James 3:2)
- Calls for using whatever means (spiritual or scriptural) we have in always helping weaker believers in living out the Christian life.
- Even today a believers criticism & skepticism; *"I don't believe His repentance is genuine"* or *"He's bound to fall again"* can have a negative effect in discouraging wayward Christians into giving up.
- The reason weak believers are not to be belittled or ignored is because it can undermine their faith and walk with God.
- From this verse, many put forward the doctrine that all believers have guardian angels looking over them. (cf. Acts. 12:15, Heb. 1:14, Ps. 91:11). Others suggest that the "angels" here are not guardian angels, but rather the spirits of humble believers after death. And therefore they are not to be despised because they will have constant personal access to report to God how they were treated by the Church.

From this verse here (V. 12) to verse (V. 14) Jesus teaches on the importance of seeking out others who go astray.

The Parable of the Lost Sheep-(N.I.V.)

18:12 "What do you think? (Expresses Spiritual contemplation.) **If a man** (Metph.-God) **owns a hundred sheep,-◙** (Metph.-Believers) **and one of them wanders away,** (i.e. Strays, backslides, falls into sins.) **will he not leave the ninety-nine on the hills and go to look for the one that wandered off?** (Expresses God's love and concern for believers who have strayed.)
13 And if he finds it, I tell you the truth, he is happier about that one sheep than about the ninety-nine (Metph.-faithful) **that did not wander off.**
14 In the same way your Father in heaven is not willing that any of these little ones(weak-believer, young-convert, wayward Christian)**should be lost.**(parish-K.J.V. Metph-Given up on or given over to sin, spiritual ruin, and eternal doom.)

Believers are to have the same Godly compassion and concern in helping to restore others who go astray.

Message & Application =

- ❖ Shows how believers are responsible in reaching out and helping others who have backslidden and strayed away from Jesus.
- ❖ Calls for putting the value and security of lost souls above our own interests and comforts. (Spare no expense, effort, or cost in seeking out the lost, take the initiative, be diligent!).
- ❖ Teaches how there should be no chiding or upbraiding the lost, but a steering them back to God with acts of love and encouragement.
- ❖ Calls for always having a pastoral concern for each other.
- ❖ Warns of the misery that comes when we drift away from Christ, the isolation, loneliness, and aimless wondering as a result of sin.
- 🗝 Even today, believers must take the initiative in coming to the rescue of wayward believers, getting them back on track by helping them with their struggles and sins.

Additional Lessons drawn from Parable:

- The importance & great value that God places on sinners.
- God's love & concern in seeing sinners Saved and restored back to Him.
- The need for follow-up ministries.
- The believer's eternal security.

From this verse here (V. 15) to verse (V. 20) Jesus teaches on 4 steps in reconciling a sinning brother.

A Brother Who Sins Against You-(N.I.V.)

18:15 "If your brother (i.e. Fellow believer) **sins against you,** (trespass-K.J.V. Syn.-Offends, injures, leads astray. Suggests: Issues involving personal injuries, not differences of opinions; e.g. Church policies, goals, worship.) **go** (Suggests: When possible face to face rather than social media, email, or texting.) **and show him his fault,** (Not in a judgmental or a self-righteous way, but in a loving and humble way, not to slam but to help them.) **just between the two of you.** (i.e. Privately) **If he listens to you,** (apologizes, confesses the sin) **you have won your brother over.** (i.e. Restored back into fellowship with oneself, or showed him the error of his ways, bringing him back into a right relationship with God.)

The first step in reconciling a sinning brother is to reprove them privately.

Message & Application

❖ Shows believers how seeking out reconciliation privately give's the offender the opportunity to repent and correct the sin themselves.
❖ Teaches believers who are wronged are not to wait but are obligated to initiate the process of reconciliation. (Don't wait for an apology, be willing to forgive and forget, end the rift, mend fences, etc.).
❖ Believers by confronting the offender personally can keep us from harboring feelings of bitterness, anger, and resentment towards them.
❖ Believers by confronting the offender personally can keep us from further negatively gossiping and slandering them for their wrong.
❖ By confronting the offender privately demonstrates our humility and love in wanting to be back in a right relationship with them. (Shows the concern you place on their soul and spiritual well-being).
⊶ Even today we must confront others for their own spiritual welfare, helping to bring them to their senses in seeing and escaping the sin.

–***Just between the two of you***-Privately confronting serves to either:

- Protects the offender's reputation, saves from embarrassment.
- Enables the guilty to be more readily to acknowledge their sin.
- Allows the offender the opportunity to correct the sin privately, without bringing reproach or dishonor upon Christ or the Church.
- Saves the dignity of the accuser in case their accusations were wrong (Know that you're not infallible!).
- Preserves the peace, keeps factions from developing.

18:16 But if he will not listen, (i.e. Remains unrepentant, unreformed, unapologetic, un-convicted. Denies by way of justifying, excusing, or defending it.) **take one or two others along,** (Suggests: Persons of influence or authority, good reputations, spiritual.) **so that 'every matter may be established** (Syn.- validated, corroborated, verified, proved, confirmed-N.L.T.) **by the testimony of two or three witnesses.'** (Suggests: Based on the Law of Moses that required two or three witnesses to bear evidence to the charge. -{Deut. 19:15})

The second step in reconciling a sinning brother is to reprove them with the help of other believers.

Message & Application

❖ Shows how seeking out reconciliation with the help of others can convict the offender of his or her sin by their wise and godly counsel.
❖ Teaches rather than write others off, take every step necessary, seek additional help and whatever means available to convict them!
❖ By seeking the help of others can witness to the sin, bringing greater appeal, can act as mediators in bridging the communication gap.
❖ Believers by seeking the help of others can receive the proper counsel, alleviates the burden by sharing it with them. (Can also help in assisting them in taking the right approach).
❖ Believers by seeking the help of others shows that it's not a personal vendetta, but something that affects everyone and all involved.

-***One or two others***-Taking other witnesses along serve's to either:

- Supports the accusation and convicts the person by bringing additional testimony.
- Their presence may induce the guilty to listen, being influenced by their authority, reputations, and character.
- By being present they can listen to both sides and give their own unbiased opinion.
- They can certify that a sincere effort was made, or that the guilty did acknowledge the wrong and promised to correct it.
- They can protect the accused in the event that the offended brother was unjustly critical or too judgmental.

Four Steps in Reconciling a Sinning Brother:

Step 1 Reprove the offender privately.-(V. 15)
Step 2 Reprove the offender with two witnesses.-(V. 16)
Step 3 Reprove the offender with Church support.-(V. 17)
Step 4 Reprove the offender by breaking off fellowship.-(V. 17)

18:17 If he refuses to listen to them, (i.e. Confess, apologize, reform) **tell it to the church;** (i.e. Church leaders, Pastor, elders, local congregation-N.E.B.) **and if he refuses to listen even to the church,** (i.e. Church's reproof, remedial advice.) **treat him as you would a pagan or a tax collector.** (ostracize, shun, expel, excommunicate-L.B.V. Expresses have no fellowship with them, yet still holding out hope in their Salvation/restoration. Start from scratch, confront him with the need of repentance, and offer again God's forgiving love.-M.B.V.)

The third and fourth steps in reconciling a sinning brother is to reprove them with the Church's help and if that fails to break off fellowship with them.

Message & Application 💻=🌎

❖ Shows how seeking out reconciliation with the Church's help can convict the offender of his sin and need of God's forgiveness.
❖ Calls for the Church in getting involved in the reconciliation of believers. (Only in the atmosphere of Christian love, prayer, and fellowship can personal relationships be righted and corrected).
❖ Warns against fellowshipping with obstinate sinners until they're willing to repent. (Break off fellowship, but not hope or love!).
❖ Teaches the importance of not allowing the sinful behavior of others to influence the Church. (The unity, purity, and peace of the Church must always come first!). (cf. 1-Corn. 5:6-7)
❖ Teaches those who remain obstinate and unrepentant forfeit the right of the support, fellowship, and blessing of the Church.

–***Tell it to the Church***-By bringing the matter before Church serves to:

- Allows for the highest level of persuasion and Pastoral appeal.
- Renders a final verdict on the matter.
- Administers disciplinary action.

-***Treat him as a pagan or tax collector***-Variously interpreted as either:

- **Excommunicate them**-With the purpose of shaming them into repentance, that they may know the seriousness of their sin. (Traditionally supported by most.) (1-Corn. 5:1-13, Matt. 18:18, 1-Tim. 1:20, Titus 3:10-11, 3-John 1:9-10)
- **Withhold fellowship, but not love**-With the purpose that your kindness will lead them to repentance, feeling guilt and shame for how they have treated you. (2-Corn. 2:5-8,)
- **Regard them as an Evangelistic prospect**-With the purpose of restoring them back to God, explaining again God's love, grace, and forgiveness to them. (1-Corn. 5:5, Heb. 6:6)

18:18 "I tell you the truth, (verily-K.J.V.-Expresses: a strong confirmation, reliability. Modern cliché "You can take it to the bank".) **whatever you** (i.e. offended believer/Church.) **bind** (Metph.-forbid, prohibit, disallow) **on earth** (i.e. Church) **will be bound in heaven,** (Viz. By God/Christ) **and whatever you loose** (Metph.-permit, grant, allow) **on earth will be loosed** (Syn.-honored, supported, endorsed) **in heaven.** (i.e. By God. Expresses the cultural practice of Rabbis in determining decisions in regard to conduct based on scriptural applications. In a wider context gives the Church permission to act with divine authority based on God's word.)

The Church is to be under the authority of God's word when making disciplinary decisions and judgments.

Message & Application 💻=🌎

- ❖ Shows how believers have the full authority to tell an unrepentant brother when they have fallen out of line with God's word.
- ❖ Teaches how all Church rulings & decisions must be scriptural and biblical. (Decisions must reflect Godly principles, not own opinion!).
- ❖ Teaches the importance of using biblical principles in resolving conflicts and disputes. (Always handle problems God's way!).
- ❖ Assures the Church that when decisions and judgments are based on the principles of the Gospel they will have God's support.
- ❖ Teaches how all Church disciplinary actions must be biblically and scripturally supported. (Don't take any disciplinary action if you can't in good conscience find it supported in God's Word).
- ❖ Gives the Church the power & authority to declare in God's name all disciplinary actions and judgments.
- ❖ Teaches how the Church is responsible for guiding believers in the kind of behavior that is pleasing to God.
- ❖ Calls for concurring and supporting Church decisions that are only based on the word of God.
- ❖ Exhorts the Church to be at its best spiritually and scripturally when taking disciplinary actions.

–***Bind & loose-*** In the immediate context, the Church's allowance in taking disciplinary actions in regards to a sinning brother. But in a wider context can also be applied to the Church's authority in regulating other practices and affairs as well.

☞ Some misapply this verse as teaching on spiritual warfare, giving believers authority in binding Satan & demonic spirits/forces operating against them. (Though this may be biblically correct when one is living according to God's word, but it's not found in this context).

18:19 "Again, I tell you that if two of you on earth agree (4856-*To sound together, to be in accord, to be harmonious, a symphony.* Syn.-approving, concurring, same heart, mind, feelings, and opinion.) **about anything you ask for,** (as touching.-K.J.V. Syn.-concerning, relating, pertaining. In context of reconciling differences between believers.)**it will be done for you by my Father in heaven.** (Suggests: Only in matters that are in agreement with God's will.)
20 For where two or three come together (Suggests: In context the injured party & offender. Or the three witnesses who were called to help to reprove the sinning brother.) **in my name,** (Syn.-authority, honor, cause, sake.) **there am I with them".** (i.e. Spiritually, omnipresence. Suggests: In context Jesus' presence in assisting, guiding, campaigning in the reconciliation of believers.)

Believers are to join together in prayer when seeking divine guidance in making important decisions.

Message & Application 💻=🌎

- ❖ Shows how believers are to always go to God in prayer when seeking His guidance and intervention in resolving conflicts.
- ❖ Teaches how all church disciplines and decisions must be humbly and earnestly prayed upon. (Pass no sentence that you cannot in good faith ask God to confirm and support).
- ❖ Teaches how when we're pursuing our brother in disciplinary love and prayer we will find divine encouragement and guidance.
- ❖ Teaches how God answers prayers where strength, wisdom, insight, and courage are being sought.
- ❖ Displays how will not have to go through making difficult decisions alone, that we can go to God for guidance and direction.

☞ This is not giving a blanket promise, that if two or three Christians come together in prayer that Jesus is going to automatically answer their requests. But rather in context, this is only promising of having the assurance of divine assistance when it comes to resolving conflicts or for making important Church decisions when it comes to sin, fellowship, and discipline.

Three Principles in Intercessory Prayer:

- Prayer must be something specific which all are agreeable to. (V. 19)
- Prayer must be according to God's will. (V. 19 b)
- Prayer must be made in Jesus' authority and for His glory. (V. 20)

From this verse here (V. 21) to the end of the chapter, Jesus teaches on the principles of unlimited forgiveness.

The Parable of the Unmerciful Servant-(N.I.V.)

18:21 Then Peter came to Jesus and asked, "Lord, how many times shall I forgive (863-*"To send forth, send away".)* **my brother** (Fellow believer, Church member, anyone.) **when he sins against me?** (Expresses any form of wrong or offense.) **Up to seven times?"** (Suggests: Peter was being very generous, due to the fact that Rabbis taught that "Three times" was sufficient. {cf. Amos 2:1-6})
22 Jesus answered, I tell you, not seven times, but seventy-seven times. (Expresses endlessly, indefinitely, unconditionally, often as needed, etc.)

A believer's forgiveness is to be unlimited.

Message & Application 💻=🌎

- ❖ Shows how we're never to stop forgiving, that mercy & forgiveness should know no bounds, that we should forgive as much as we have to.
- ❖ Warns against attempting to regulate mercy on our terms and conditions. (Men are prone to fix bounds to their charity).
- ❖ Teaches the importance of taking into account that no one is perfect, that we all stumble and therefore will always need to be forgiven.
- ❖ Calls for always laying aside thoughts of malice, revenge, and grudges toward others. (Harbor not a critical spirit, but a forgiving spirit).
- ❖ Warns how holding onto unforgiveness can harm our spiritual life, often leading to depression, addictions, and substance abuse.

☞ Jesus is not here teaching that we're are to diminish, excuse, or close our eyes to the offense. Nor is it about trusting them again, shaming them, or done only out of duty and obligation. But rather it's about us letting go of our anger, resentment, and revenge, to always do them good and leaving them in God's hands.

Benefits of being Forgiving:

- Allows the victim to let go of the feelings of anger, resentment, bitterness, revenge, grudges, etc.
- Allows the victim to find healing, peace, joy, happiness, and spiritual well-being.
- Allows the victim to give it over to God, no longer having to carry it around with them.
- Allows the offender to see the errors of their ways, leading to remorse, repentance, and reconciliation.

18:23 "Therefore, the kingdom of heaven (Metph.-God's mercy, forgiveness) **is like a king** (Metph.-God) **who wanted to settle accounts with his servants.**
24 As he began the settlement, a man who owed him ten thousand talents (Suggests: A unit of weight of money [silver or gold]. 1 talent equals 75-95 pounds, equaling close to a million pounds. In today's currency equals about 10 million dollars. Metph.-Great Sin debts owed to God) **was brought to him.**
25 Since he was not able to pay, the master ordered that he and his wife and his children and all that he had be sold to repay the debt.
26 "The servant fell on his knees (Expresses: Desperation, earnest plea.) **before him. 'Be patient with me,' he begged, 'and I will pay back everything.'**
27 The servant's master took pity on him, canceled the debt and let him go.
28 "But when that servant went out, he found one of his fellow-servants who owed him a hundred denari.-◙ (Hundred pence-K.J.V. i.e. A Roman silver coin, equaling about 50 dollars. Metph.-Small and insignificant sins committed against us.) **He grabbed him and began to choke him.** (Suggests: Not literally, but to throttle, wring, and censor)**'Pay back what you owe me!' he demanded.**
29 "His fellow-servant fell to his knees and begged him, 'Be patient with me, and I will pay you back.'(Expresses: Same appeal made by his creditor.-{V. 26})
30 "But he refused. Instead, he went off and had the man thrown into prison until he could pay the debt. (i.e. A debtor's prison until restitution is made.)
31 When the other servants saw what had happened, they were greatly distressed and went and told their master everything that had happened.
32 "Then the master called the servant in. 'You wicked servant,' he said, 'I canceled all that debt (Metph.-sins) **of yours because you begged me to.**
33 Shouldn't you have had mercy on your fellow-servant as I had on you?'
34 In anger, his master turned him over to the jailers to be tortured until he should pay back all he owed.
35 "This is how my heavenly Father will treat each of you unless you forgive your brother (i.e. Fellow Christian) **from your heart."**(Syn.-sincerely, truly.)

Believers must be willing to always forgive others since God has forgiven all their sins.

Message & Application 💻=🌎

- ❖ Shows how there's no amount of wrongs that can't be forgiven towards others in light of the amount of mercy & grace that God has shown us.
- ❖ Teaches that when we compare all the sins we committed against God, a fellow brother's offense will seem quite small and insignificant.
- ❖ Teaches how forgiveness must be genuine and sincere, letting go the feelings of resentment, rage, wrath, revenge, retaliation, etc.
- ☞ Jesus is not saying that God will revoke our Salvation. But rather that God will withhold His daily mercies to us if were unmerciful to others.

Chapter Nineteen

Jesus' Final Journey to Jerusalem

- **Divorce-**Teaches on the importance of fidelity and commitment in marriage.-(Vs. 3-12)
- **Little Children and Jesus-** Teaches on the need for humble & trusting faith .- (Vs. 13-15)
- **The Rich young ruler-**Teaches on the importance of forsaking all to follow Christ.-(Vs. 16-26)
- **Rewards in discipleship-**Teaches on the costs and rewards in discipleship-(Vs. 27-30)

Jesus begins Judean Ministry-(Authors Insert)

19:1 When Jesus had finished saying these things, (i.e. Jesus' teachings on relationships among believers.-{18:1-35}) **he left Galilee** (departed-K.J.V.-Expresses: Jesus' purposeful determination to complete His mission by dying on the cross in Jerusalem.-{cf. Luke 9:51}) **and went into the region of Judea to the other side of the Jordan.-◙** (Suggests: Jesus skirted around Samaria-[possibly to avoid their hostility towards Him]-{Luke 9:51-56}] crossing over to the east side of the Jordan river in a region known as Perea.{See Map pg. 6})
2 Large crowds followed him, (Suggests: Only for healing of their bodies and not the healing of their souls.) **and he healed** (taught-{Mark 10:1} **them there.**

Jesus sets out resolutely towards the Cross as He makes His final journey towards Jerusalem.

Message & Application 💻=🌎

- ❖ Shows how believers are to remain true to God's calling & ministry regardless of the hardships and challenges that lie ahead.
- ❖ Teaches even though the transitions of life can sometimes be hard and difficult, we need to stay active in the work God has given us!
- ❖ Reminds believers despite the crises that may lie ahead, keep having love and compassion for the hurting and needy around you.
- ❖ Displays how Christ always meets us where we're at, having a cure and remedy for any pain, hurt, sickness, or issue we may have.
- ❖ Teaches how when Christ departs its best that we follow Him if we're going to have His help in other areas elsewhere as well.
- 🗝 Even today rather than run and hide when stress & pressures start to rise, we need to remain true to who we are and not compromise the love and compassion that God has conferred upon us to help others.
- ☞ This verse here marks the end of the "fourth" five-set division discourse that began in 18:1, suggesting another turning point in Jesus' ministry. (See Gospel Introduction; "Structure of Gospel")
- ☞ This would be Jesus' final departure from Galilee until His resurrection.

From this verse here (V. 3) to verse (V. 12) Jesus teaches on the importance of fidelity & commitment in marriage.

Divorce-(N.I.V.)

19:3 Some Pharisees came to him to test him. (tempting-K.J.V.-3985-*Ensnare, trip-up, entangle, prove wrong.* Syn.-bait, discredit, bring down.) **They asked, "Is it lawful for a man to divorce his wife for any and every reason?"** (Assumes one can divorce his wife on any grounds no matter how frivolous or trivial the reason, spoiling his supper, burning his bread. That it was a loaded question guaranteeing that any answer Jesus gave would offend someone and stir up controversy, similar to today's debates over birth control and gun control.)

The Pharisees attempt to discredit Jesus by getting Him to contradict the Law of Moses that gave concession for divorce.

Message & Application 💻=🌎

❖ Shows how believers must never justify some sin or wrong action based on the ambiguity of scripture. (Hold to the Spirit's leading and convictions where scripture is silent). (Rom. 14:14-23, 1-Corn. 6:12, 8:4-13)

❖ Warns against playing it fast & loose with scripture, looking for loopholes in God's word to wiggle out of the things we don't like.

❖ Warns how many will split hairs over scriptures in order to avoid obeying the clear teaching of God's word.

❖ Calls for accepting the teachings of scripture without adapting it to legitimize our choices, or to make us feel more smug in our Salvation.

🗝 Even today those who are not interested in the truth will always find clever ways to excuse their accountability or to justify some sin.

–***Test him-***The trap is variously seen as either:

- To trap Jesus into contradicting the Law of Moses, thereby losing His popularity and favor with the people. (Deut. 24:1-4)
- To trap Jesus into an ongoing controversy between the two rabbinic schools of Shammai & Hillel (see below).
- To involve Jesus in the Herod & Herodias's affair, that He too might be arrested and taken away like John the Baptist. (14:3-11)

☞ Most conclude the question stems from a hotly debated issue within Judaism between the schools of "Hillel" & "Shammai" based on the ambiguity of the word *"Indecent"* as found in Deut. 24:1. The former (Hillel) taking a more liberal approach, allowing divorce for any trivial dislikes. Whereas the latter (Shammai) taking a more conservative approach, allowing divorce only on the grounds of adultery.

19:4 "Haven't you read" he replied, "that at the beginning the Creator (God) **made them male and female"**(Adam & Eve. Suggests: Purpose for procreation)
5 and said, 'For this reason, a man will leave his father and mother and be united to his wife, and the two will become one flesh' (Expresses permanent union, commitment, soul mates, monogamy, fidelity, equality, procreation.)
6 So they are no longer two, but one. Therefore what God has joined together, let man not separate." (i.e. divorce-L.B.V.)

God's original purpose in creation was for marriage to be a permanent union between a man & woman.

Message & Application 💻=🌎

❖ Shows how we're to follow God's ideal of marriage as a lifelong commitment. (Stop looking for a way out and live by God's design).
❖ Teaches the importance of always basing life's decisions on God's word, and not what we think is best, or what the world has to say.
❖ Calls for always living life as God intended, that it doesn't matter what anybody else thinks, but it's what God says that counts!
❖ Calls for always sticking with the divine pattern, that God's way is the best way! (Abide in the natural order that God has created!).
❖ Teaches how couples can find victory and success in marriage through their spiritual values, principals, and shared core beliefs.
❖ Teaches those who view marriage as a lifelong commitment will be more readily to forgive, reconcile, and work through their differences.
❖ Couples who grow in their spiritual devotion to the Lord and each other can find stability, security, and strength in difficult times.
🗝 Even today couples who have God at the center of their lives are better able to weather any illness, storm, or marital issue facing them.

-What God has joined together-God's plan in marriage seen in 3 facts:

A) God created only one couple male & female.-(V. 4)
(Suggests if God expected Adam to have more than one wife, He would have created more than one female)
B) God ordained a stronger bond between a husband & wife than that of a relationship between parents and children -(V. 5)
C) God's providence in bringing together soul mates.-(V. 6)

Only Scriptural Grounds for Divorce:

1) The death of a spouse-(Rom. 7:1-3)
2) The act of infidelity by a spouse- (Matt. 5:32)
3) The desertion of an unbelieving spouse- (1-Corn. 7:10-15)

19:7 "Why then," they asked, "did Moses command that a man give his wife a certificate of divorce and send her away?"-{cf. Duet. 24:1-4}
8 Jesus replied, "Moses permitted you (suffered-K.J.V. Expresses: Not a command, but a concession.) **to divorce your wives because your hearts were hard.** (Metph.-stubborn, unforgiving, unbending) **But it was not this way from the beginning.** (i.e. Before Adam & Eve's fall in the garden of Eden.-{Gen. 3:1-7})

God only gave concession for divorce because of the sinful and hardhearted nature of man.

Message & Application 💻=🌎

❖ Shows believers how there would be no need for divorce if we simply had hearts that were less hard and more loving, yielding, and forgiving.
❖ Warns how our own selfish plans and self-centeredness is the number one causes that brings ruin upon our homes and marriages.
❖ Displays God doesn't intend for one to stay in a marriage where there's abuse, or where the spouse's life, health, and children are in danger.
❖ Teaches God's mercy provides concessions where the heart falls short.
❖ Warns believers if not careful our rebellious nature can start to creep back in, slowly turning our hearts away from the things of God.
⊶ Even today couples who are in a troubled marriage should be heading to God in prayer and counseling instead of running for the exit door.
☞ God only allowed divorce in order to prevent greater evils, which the wicked passion of men would otherwise commit; such as spousal abuse, slander, murder, etc. *"Better to divorce than to do worse"*.

19:9 I tell you that anyone who divorces his wife, except for marital unfaithfulness, (Syn.-adultery, infidelity, extramarital affairs, fornication-K.J.V.-4202-*Any illicit immorality including; adultery, homosexuality, bestiality, incest, prostitution, sodomy*) **and marries another woman commits adultery."**

Jesus sets marriage as indissoluble on any grounds except where adultery is committed.

Message & Application 💻=🌎

❖ Shows the binding nature & sacredness that God sets on marriage, allowing divorce only where adultery is committed. (cf. Mal. 2:16)
❖ Displays how marriage is not to be entered into lightly or carelessly, but thoughtfully and prayerfully, that marriage is for life!
⊶ Even today no matter how much you try to whitewash divorce by claiming; *"Irreconcilable differences"*, *"We've grown apart"*, *"We're not in love anymore"*, etc. does not hold water in God's eyes.

19:10 The disciples said to him, "If (Syn.-since) **this is the situation between a husband and a wife,** (i.e. That marriage is a permanent union, couples bound for life.-{V. 9}) **it is better** (expedient-R.S.V. Syn.-advantageous, advisable, practical) **not to marry."** (i.e. To remain single, celibate, unattached. Expresses: A common Jewish proverb; *"Better no marriage than an unhappy marriage"*, that it would be unbearable to be stuck in a bad marriage with no way out!)
11 Jesus replied, "Not everyone can accept (receive-K.J.V. Syn.-find room for, cope with.) **this word,** (i.e. Either Jesus' teaching on the indissoluble nature of marriage.-{V.9} Or the disciple conclusion it is better to remain celibate/single.-{-V.10}) **but only those to whom it has been given.** (Suggests: Those who feel God has put it on their hearts to be single should stay single, or vise versa.)

Celibacy or Singleness is not for every believer, but only for those who have been called to it by God.

Message & Application 💻=🌎

❖ Shows believers how celibacy or singleness should be a personal decision that one feels God has put on their heart and called them to.
❖ Teaches how those who are not "Spiritually empowered" in living a single life would be happier in a loving, supportive, and committed relationship. (cf. 1-Corn. 7:6-7)
❖ Calls for taking into consideration the sexual urges, passions, and lusts that come with celibacy. (Better to marry than burn with lust!).
❖ Warns how we can miss God's calling when we rush into marriage for the wrong reasons, looking only for financial security, children, completeness, freedom from sinful habits, etc.
❖ Teaches celibacy is not to be used for personal space and ease of never having to be tied down or having to check in, but for serving the Lord.
❖ Calls for prayerfully seeking God's help before taking on religious vocations in which we are unqualified or unprepared to perform.
❖ Assures believers that where there's a calling, there's a corresponding grace. (Know that where God calls, God also supplies!) (V. 11)
❖ Teaches how self-control and even self-denial is not something we can master ourselves without divine intervention. (V. 11)
❖ Teaches how Christian character is not achieved within ourselves but must be prayerfully sought with God's help and assistance. (V. 11)
🗝 Even today those who've been called to a life of celibacy/singleness is usually a work of the Holy Spirit in putting on their heart a consuming passion and desire for a life of ministry. (cf. Acts13:2, 1-Cor. 12:11)
☞ Jesus is not saying believers who are celibate/single are more spiritual than those married, for some of the greatest Evangelists were married! e.g. Billy Graham, D.L. Moody, John Wesley, George Whitefield, etc.

19:12 For some are eunuchs (2135-*Castrated male, (c) chamberlain, royal attendant.)* **because they were born that way;** (Suggests: As a result of physical birth defects, impotent or malformed testicles.) **others were made that way by men;** (Suggests: Were surgically castrated in order to serve in a kings Harem.{cf. Es. 2:3 Acts. 8:27, 32-39} Or as a result of imprisonment.) **and others have renounced marriage** (made themselves eunuchs-K.J.V. Suggests: Not literally, but rather the voluntary practice of remaining celibate for religious purposes.) **because of the kingdom of heaven.** (i.e. To better serve the Lord, Church/Gospel.) **The one who can accept** (Syn.-embrace, receive, adopt) **this should accept it."** (Expresses should welcome it, not fight it, embrace it, receive it joyfully. See it as divinely ordained as God's best for us.)

Believers who remain single are able to give themselves more fully to the work of Christ without distractions.

Message & Application 💻=🌎

- ❖ Shows believers who are single are better able to give their devotion and service to the Lord without worldly cares and distractions.
- ❖ Teaches those who are single are freed from all the cares that come with marriage, making them more disposed to the duties of God.
- ❖ Calls believers in finding contentment and fulfillment in whatever graces and duties the Lord has called us to.
- ❖ Teaches how God has a specific purpose and plan for our lives that should be fully embraced if we are going to find fulfillment in life.
- ❖ Calls believers in having such a devotion to the Lord that there's no part of ourselves we wouldn't voluntarily give up.
- ☞ Jesus is not teaching that believers should literally castrate themselves. But rather is simply emphasizing that celibacy is something that must be voluntarily embraced solely for serving God.
- ☞ Some twist this verse around to justify homosexuality, that Jesus is saying some are born gay with same-sex attractions and should accept it.

Determining Factors for Celibacy:

- Was a believer already single when they were Saved? (1-Corn. 7:17-28)
- Does a believer have control over their sexual passions and desires? (1-Corn. 7:8-9)
- Vocation & calling-(e.g. Missionary work)
- Does marriage or relationships distract from one's devotion to the Lord? (1-Corn. 7:34)

From this verse here (V. 13) to verse (V.15) Jesus teaches on the need for humble & trusting faith.

The Little Children and Jesus-(N.I.V.)

19:13 Then little children (infants-K.J.V., babies-{Luke 18:15}, young children.-{Mark 10:13}) **were brought to Jesus for him to place his hands on them and pray for them** (i.e. blessings & praying over them.) **But the disciples rebuked** (Syn.-Chased-away, ran-off) **those** (Parents.) **who brought them.** (Suggests: Disciples thought the children were unworthy to occupy their Master's attention or saw them as little importance.)
14 Jesus said, Let (suffer-K.J.V. Syn.-allow, permit) **the little children come to me, and do not hinder them,** (By word/example.) **for the kingdom of heaven** (God's Saving grace) **belongs** (Syn.-pertains, extends, relates) **to such as these."** (Not literally children, but childlike qualities of faith, humility, simplicity.)
15 When he had placed his hands on them, he went on from there. (i.e. Departed for "Perea".-{V. 1} That Jesus' blessings are enough to sustain us!)

God's Saving grace extends to those who exhibit humble and childlike faith in Jesus.

Message & Application

- Shows believers the type of humble & child-like faith needed when coming to Jesus for Salvation. (cf. Eph. 2:8-9, 1-Pet. 5:5)
- Displays how some believers can be close to the Lord in proximity, yet far from Him in priority, heart, and mission!
- Teaches how the Lord's grace has ample room for everyone, that no one is outside God's love, care, and concern no matter who they are!
- Warns how we can steer others away from coming to Jesus by our poor example, selfishness, and neglect. (cf. Rom. 2:24, 14:10-21)

Even today we can become a barrier to our children coming to Jesus when we neglect to bring them up in the ways of the Lord or take them to Church. Or when we fail to share the Lord's love for them, or how God has a purpose and plan for their lives.

How we hinder children from coming to Jesus:

- By our lack of humility, hypocrisy, and prideful attitude.
- By our lack of patience, kindness, and forgiveness.
- By our lack of faith & confidence in the Lord.
- By our lack of witness & example.
- By our lack of love, commitment, and devotion.

From this verse here (V. 16) to verse (V. 26) teaches how Salvation & eternal life comes by surrendering all to Jesus.

The Rich Young Man-(N.I.V.)

19:16 Now (and behold-K.J.V.-Expresses an exclamation of shock & surprise due to the man's religious and devout background, prominence, and wealth.) **a man** (certain ruler.-{Luke 18:18} -A member of an official council or Synagogue. Possibly introduced to contrast the difficult hang-ups that adults have in exhibiting the humble faith of children.-{Vs. 13-15}) **came up to Jesus** (ran up and fell on his knees.-{Mark 10:17}-Expresses youthfulness and eagerness.) **and asked, 'Teacher** (Suggests: The man only saw Jesus as a religious teacher/guru, and not as God incarnate!-{V.17}) **what good thing** (i.e. Good works, religious deeds, charitable acts, etc.) **must I do to get** (Syn.-earn, merit, secure) **eternal life?**(222-*"Zoe" absolute fullness & fulfillment of life which belongs to God.* i.e. To enjoy the fullness of God's presence & peace here now and in eternity.)

The man wrongly assumes that Salvation and eternal life could be earned by good works.

Message & Application 💻=🌎

❖ Shows believers how Salvation comes not by our own good deeds and efforts, but by trusting in Jesus alone. (cf. Rom. 3:10-12)
❖ Teaches how Christ is the right place to go to in getting our needs met, that Jesus can fill the deepest longings of the soul. (cf. John 6:35)
❖ Teaches that no matter how moral or religious a person is there will always be a void and emptiness that only Jesus can fill!
❖ Displays how some can have it all, money, wealth, power, fame, success, etc. yet still feel there's something missing in their life's.
❖ Warns how it's not about earning points with God or keeping a checklist of "do's" & "don'ts", but it's about a surrendered heart!
❖ Calls for resting in God's mercy & grace, that there's nothing more we need to do to earn God's forgiveness or make God love us more. (Know that it's not "you" + "rules" that Saves, but God alone!).
❖ Warns how some can come with the wrong motives, looking only for a magic pill, quick fix, or easier path than having to fully surrender.
⊶ Even today many think that if they just do some religious work or follow some religious rule they can make it into heaven. Or if they just be a good person and live a decent life they'll be accepted by God. All the while they unwittingly miss out, just as this young man did in never reaching that place of SURRENDER!

19:17 "Why do you ask me about what is good?" Jesus replied. "There is only One who is good. (18-*Pre-eminetly of God.* Suggests: That Jesus was really challenging the man if he was willing to own Him as God. That it's not about what he does, but what he believes Jesus can do for him. When you call me good you are calling me God-L.B.V.) **If you want to enter life,** (i.e. Eternal life) **obey the commandments."**(i.e. Ten Commandments. Expresses: Not that eternal life can be earned by good works.-{Eph. 2:8} But rather to impress upon the man his failure in living up to God's standards and his need for God's grace)
18 Which ones the man enquired. Jesus replied Do not murder, (6th) **do not commit adultery,** (7th) **do not steal,** (8th) **do not give false testimony,** (9th)
19 honor your father and mother,'(5th) **and 'love your neighbor as yourself.'"**(Lev. 19:18) Since Jesus quotes commandments that all deal with relationships with others suggests the man's self-centered wealth & greed was keeping him from obeying God's command in loving his neighbor as himself.)

Since no one can live up to God's perfect standards, eternal life cannot come by good works but by faith in Christ alone.

Message & Application

- Shows believers how Salvation & eternal life is not dependent on what we can do, but what Jesus can do for us and through us!
- Calls for an honest evaluation, that we will always fail in measuring up to God's righteousness. (Know that no matter how moral, religious, or good you are you'll always fall short!). (cf. Rom. 7:7-7-9. 7:14-25)
- Teaches the importance of recognizing our spiritual poverty and bankruptcy before God. (Know that you stand condemned as a lost and helpless sinner before a Holy God). (cf. Matt. 5:3, Rom. 7:18, Rev. 3:17)

–***Only one who is good-*** Jesus is not denying His own deity or sinless character, (cf. John 1:1, Philp. 2:6-8) but rather was meant as either:

- To test the man's faith to see if he was willing to own Him as God.
- To show the man all but God are sinners and the futility in seeking eternal life by good deeds in the presence of absolute holiness.
- To focus the man off himself to what Jesus could do for him.

-Obey the commandments-Jesus is not giving a road map to Salvation by way of following the commandments, but was meant as either:

- To impress upon the man the high standards required by God and the futility of trying to seek Salvation by his own merits.
- To convict the man of sin by showing him he had not kept them and therefore needed to be Saved by God's grace.
- To direct the man's attention away from the external Law to the moral & spiritual intent of the law. (cf. Matt. 5:21-28)

19:20 "All these I have kept," (Only of the letter, not the spirit. From my youth up.-K.J.V.) **the young man said. "What do I still lack?"** (Suggests: Religious and morally upright, but having no inner peace and fulfillment. That no amount of religious observances or works can ever fill the empty void of the soul.)
21 Jesus answered, (looked at him and loved him.-{Mark 10:21}-Expresses that Jesus was pleased with the man's earnestness and sincerity.) **"If you want to be perfect,**(5049-*Complete, finished, mature.* Expresses: Not sinless perfection, but undivided loyalty, commitment, sold out, etc.) **go, sell your possessions and give to the poor,** (Suggests: His possessions were an idol hindering him from fully surrendering to God.) **and you will have treasure in heaven.** (i.e. Joy, peace, forgiveness in Christ, etc.) **Then come, follow me."**(Expresses a call to fill the void with a life of service and discipleship in ministering for the Lord.)

Jesus exposes the man's one failure of idolizing his wealth before God.

Message & Application 💻=🌎

- ❖ Shows believers the need of laying down that thing that's blocking us from surrendering our lives fully over to Jesus.
- ❖ Warns how obeying the commandments is no assurance of Salvation because we will never know if we've ever done enough! (V. 20)
- ❖ Displays how Jesus wants to get to the deeper issues of the heart in what's holding us back from truly following Him.
- ❖ Displays how every person will have some sort of sin, vice, habit, etc. that they must be willing to leave at the alter if they're to follow Jesus.
- ❖ Calls believers in stepping away from that "One thing" that's keeping us from being sold out to God? (cf. Philp. 3:8-9)
- ❖ Calls for walking away from things that are coming between us and God. (Will you make God first in your life or other things?)
- ❖ Teaches when Jesus touches a nerve or puts His finger on a certain area or thing that needs to be surrendered over to Him. Know that it's for our best interest and welfare no matter how much it hurts.
- 🗝 Even today the same truth exists, that there's usually "One thing" that keeps a person from being sold out to God. Be it money, drugs, pride, status, wealth, fame, possessions, popularity, relationships, careers, etc.
- ☞ Jesus is not saying here that every person must sell everything they have and take a vow of poverty in order to follow Him. Or one can buy their way into heaven and God's good graces by some charitable act. But only of those things that are keeping us from following Him.
- ☞ The author can't answer what that something is that's standing between you and God. The reader must search his or her own heart for that thing they're still holding onto and confess it openly to God.

19:22 When the young man heard this, (Sell all his possessions.-{V. 21}) **he went away sad,** (sorrowful-K.J.V.-3076-*Distressed, grieved, gloomy, storm clouds gathering"*. Syn.-mournful, disheartened, dismayed, regretful) **because he had great wealth.** (possessions-K.J.V., very rich-L.B.V. Suggests: Assumes the man was unwilling to leave all for Christ, that the sacrifice was just too great!).

The man's love of his wealth kept him from surrendering his life to Christ.

Message & Application 💻=🌎

❖ Shows how believers are not to allow the love of stuff to come before our love for Jesus, no matter how valuable or dear it may be to us.
❖ Warns how allowing money, wealth, and possessions to define us can cause us to miss out on our healing and best that God has for us.
❖ Warns against finding our identity, value, worth, security, etc. in stuff and possessions rather than in a relationship with Jesus.
❖ Rather than give into defeat, thinking some habit is too difficult to give up or break, trust Jesus to give you the strength to walk away from it!
❖ Warns against ignoring and walking away from an opportunity to get right with God, that it may not come again! (cf. Heb. 10:18-27)
⊶ Even today for believers there's usually some sin, lust, habit, attitude, lifestyle, bitterness, relationship, entitlement- *"What's in it for me"*, etc. that stands in the way from fully following Jesus.
☞ Today many want Salvation on their own terms so long as it doesn't cost them too much. Or they give into discouragement, thinking the sacrifices are too great, e.g. *"Ask me anything, but don't take this"*!
☞ Whereas for each believer the sacrifice may be different, but no less difficult. We may not have much, but even giving up little things as food, friends, clothes, etc. can have just as powerful hold on us as well.
☞ Some praise the man's honesty in not being a hypocrite in pretending to live up to the standards he knew he could not attain. Others assume the man went back to his religious ways or kept searching for something to fill the void in his life only to die and face eternity in hell.

Obstacles to Surrendering all to Christ:

- Fear the cost too great in losing life's luxuries/pleasures.
- Fear of losing your reputation, comforts, and freedom.
- Fear of how friends, family, and peers will judge you.
- Fear of giving up control, admitting defeat, weakness.
- Fear of failing, not measuring up, being inadequate.
- Fear of the self-sacrifices, struggles, and hardships.

<u>How to Identify the False Idols in your Life:</u>

- **What do you complain about the most:**
  Are you always worried about financial status, the car you drive, the clothes you wear, the house you live in, your self-appearance, etc.
- **What do you sacrifice most of your time for:**
  Are you investing most of your time into making money, work, career, school, the stock market, retirement fund, house payment, children, etc.
- **What do you turn to find comfort & security in:**
  Are you seeking comfort & security in personal achievements, relationships, friends, possessions, bank accounts, technology, computers, video games, music, alcohol, drugs, sports, sex, food, etc.

<u>How to get Rid of the Idols in Your Life:</u>

- Repent & turn from the things that are trying to rule, control, and pull you away from God.
- Go to God in prayer for the grace & strength to break its control over you.
- Get rid and separate yourself from any people, objects, images, material, literature, pictures, videos, etc. that supports your idol.
- Fill the vacuum & emptiness with the things of God. Find your needs & desires as being met and fulfilled by God. Make God your drive, purpose, and satisfaction in life!
- Know when something is God-pleasing & honoring. Ask yourself are these things bringing glory and praise to God or to self?
- Remember that we're only stewards of the things God has blessed us with, that it is really all His anyway.

19:23 Then Jesus said to his disciples, "I tell you the truth, it is hard (Not impossible) **for a rich man to enter the kingdom of heaven.** (i.e. To be Saved.)
24 Again, I tell you it is easier for a camel to go through the eye of a needle-◙ (Lit.-Knitting tool. Expresses a hyperbole emphasizing that which is extremely difficult and impossible.) **than for a rich man to enter the kingdom of God."** (Suggests: Because they trust more in their wealth rather than in God.)

Warns of the extreme difficulties for those who trust in wealth to put their faith in Christ for Salvation.

Message & Application

❖ Shows believers how wealth, success, and fame can have such a powerful hold that we no longer see a need for God.
❖ Warns how the riches and cares of this world can be a distraction, diverting our priorities away from the Lord. (cf. 1-Tim. 6:9-10, 6:17-19)
❖ Warns how money and wealth can distort one's perspective, producing a sense of false security, self-satisfaction, and self-sufficiency.

–***Camel-*** Some suggest that because of the similarities to both spelling and sound, the word for "camel" (Kamelos-2574) was mistranslated from the Greek word for "cable" or "rope" (Kamilos-4979) and that Jesus is really making reference to a large "Rope" measuring up to 2 inch's in diameter used aboard ships rather than an actual camel.

-Eye of a needle- Some understand this not as a literal sewing needle. But rather that it's in reference to small doors in large wooden gates of a walled city called "The Needles Eye" to which a camel, only by unloading its cargo and kneeling down could just barely crawl through.

☞ Jesus is not here teaching that the rich can't be Saved. But rather is merely pointing out the insurmountable barriers rich people face in allowing their wealth to take the place of God in their life's.

☞ The dangers of wealth are not its possessions, for many righteous men such as Abraham, Job, Solomon, David, Joseph of Arimathea, etc. were wealthy, but rather about its rule and control over our lives.

Types of Barriers the Rich Face:

- They are more prone to rely on money to solve their problems rather than turning to God.
- Gives them a false sense of independence, security, self-reliance, and no need of God.
- Their attention/energy is drawn away from God.
- They have greater temptations to resist.

19:25 When the disciples heard this, they were greatly astonished (Suggests: Their shock was attributed to the fact that the Jews saw wealth as a sign of God's favor & blessing for being good.-{cf. Deut. 28:1-14}) **and asked, "Who then can be saved?"**(Assumes if those who have been prosperously blessed by God can't make it to heaven, what hope is there for the rest of us!)
26 Jesus looked at them (beheld them-K.J.V.-1689-*Earnest looking.* Expresses Jesus' loving concern, and reassurance.) **and said, "With man this is impossible,** (Suggests: Failure due to human weakness, fallen sinful nature, power of sin, etc. Or the failure of philosophy, religion, and good works.) **but with God all things** (i.e. Salvation, Saving faith, eternal life, healing, transformation, new heart, etc.) **are possible."**(141-*strength, power, and ability to do. To excel and grow.* Suggests: God's powerful effect on the heart in bringing a person to see their sin and need of His mercy and grace.)

Salvation comes only by the intervention & supernatural work of God's mercy and grace upon the human heart.

Message & Application 💻=🌎

- ❖ Shows how we can't Save ourselves through our works & efforts, but only through God's power and strength. (cf. 2-Corn. 3:4-5, Philp. 4:13)
- ❖ Displays the need of God's grace, that no matter how good we are or how hard we try we're incapable of obeying God perfectly.
- ❖ Promises in having God's help in stripping away the barriers of sin, pride, greed, lust, and any other issues that are gripping our hearts!
- ❖ Teaches how there is no sin, vice, habit, or addiction that is too big or too insurmountable that God can't deliver us from! (cf. Eph. 3:20)
- ❖ Gives believers hope in never giving up on ourselves or others, that God can reach and penetrate the most hardened hearts.
- ❖ Assures God's continual work on our hearts in tearing down those barriers that are keeping us from truly following Him!
- ❖ Warns how we can put limits and boundaries on God when we think there's something in our lives that God can't forgive or deliver us from. (Never assume that your too far lost for God to do anything about!)
- 🗝 Even today, believers no longer have to give into failure or defeat, that God is bigger than our struggles. That God will give us the strength to walk away from that relationship, addiction, habit, and anything else that's holding us captive/back!
- ☞ Today believer's don't have to give into discouragement or lose hope in seeing a friend or family member Saved. That we can go to God in prayer that He may touch and open their hearts as well, no matter how remote or impossible it may seem. (cf. Luke 16:31, 1-Corn. 1:20-25)

From this verse here (V. 27) to end of the chapter, Jesus teaches on the costs & rewards in discipleship.

Rewards in discipleship-(Authors Insert)

19:27 Peter answered him, "We have left everything (i.e. Business, homes, occupations, livelihoods.-{Matt. 4:18-22}) **to follow you!** (Expresses Peter wasn't just blowing smoke, that the disciples really had left everything to follow Jesus, unlike the rich man who chose his possessions over Christ.-{19:22}) **What then will there be for us?** (Expresses not a self-promoting or presumptuous attitude on Peter's part, but rather for reassurance and encouragement.)
28 Jesus said to them, "I tell you the truth, at the renewal of all things, (Regeneration-K.J.V.-3824-*New heaven, earth, birth, Messianic age, restoration.* Christ's Second coming & Millennial Age.-{Rev. 20:4-6, 21:1-7}) **when the Son of Man** (Expresses a Messianic title signifying the Messiah's human origins and divine headship over humanity.) **sits on his glorious throne, you who have followed me** (The twelve disciples, excluding Judas, who would be replaced by Mathias.) **will also sit on twelve thrones, judging** (Syn.-presiding, ruling) **the twelve tribes of Israel.** (We cant be entirely sure of what this means at this time. Some view it as the disciples judging Israel for their rejection of Christ, or their ruling over the Church during Christ's Millennial reign.)

Because of the disciple's sacrificial service, they will be rewarded with a glorious future of ruling with Christ in the Millennial age.

Message & Application 💻=🌎

- ❖ Shows believers whatever we have to give up now for Christ pales in comparison with the eternal riches of being with Jesus in heaven!
- ❖ Calls for being heavenly minded, that whatever sacrifices we endure now will be well worth the future glory that awaits us in heaven!
- ❖ Calls for living like pilgrims here on earth, knowing that our true citizenship is in heaven. (cf. Philp. 3:19-21, Heb. 11:13-16, 1-Pet. 2:11)
- ❖ Teaches how our service to the Lord will find its own reward in heaven. (Know you will never regret what you give up for Christ!).
- ⊶ Even today if our lives were nothing but hardships, struggles, and difficulties, just being Saved and reigning one day with Jesus makes it all worth it and we would happily do it all over again if we had too!
- ☞ God's purpose in postponing rewards later in eternity may be for our own good. That if God gave material rewards for every good deed we did, we would get prideful of our achievements or act out of wrong motives.

19:29 And everyone who has left (forsaken-K.J.V. i.e. Renounced, shunned, put-off.) **houses** (Possessions) **or brothers or sisters or father or mother or children** (Relationships, wife-K.J.V.) **or fields** (Occupations, jobs) **for my sake** (Suggests: In service to Christ, and the Gospel.-{Mark 10:29}) **will receive a hundred times as much** (Expresses not in the sense of a 100 to 1 payoff, for who can have 100 mothers. But of untold riches in the form of spiritual growth, joy, peace, and comfort in the Holy spirit, good conscience, Church family, etc. And with them persecutions.-{cf. Mark 10:30} Expresses a natural part of God's growing and refining process.) **and will inherit eternal life.**
19:30 But many who are first (Metph.-Spiritually proud) **will be last, and many who are last** (Metph.-Humble, lowly) **will be first.** (Expresses how in God's economy worldly values are turned upside-down. That it's not about merit, importance or time served, but about God's grace.)

Believers who sacrifice all for Christ & the Gospel will be abundantly rewarded now and in eternity.

Message & Application 💻=🌎

- ❖ Shows whatever we forsake for the Lord will be compensated hundredfold by God, though not necessarily in the same form.
- ❖ Assures believers in having God's loving care & provision in life. (Trust God to compensate for any losses you have to endure!).
- ❖ Teaches how we can't "Out-give" God, that God will bless us far more than what we're giving up. (cf. Luke 6:38, 2-Corn. 2:9)
- ❖ Teaches how we couldn't make a better investment, that the dividends we gain in following Jesus far outweigh any losses! (cf. Philp. 3:7-8)
- ❖ Teaches how no one will be the loser for having made a decision for Christ. (No one will say "I was better off in my sins than with Jesus").
- ❖ Teaches when God asks us to give up something that's dear to us, know that it's for our best interest, that will be the better person for it!
- ❖ Teaches whatever empty holes, lostness, or missing out feelings we experience in giving up so much, will eventually go away with Christ!
- ❖ Encourages believers whatever we lose for Christ we gain in a richer fellowship of love, support, and security than our family can offer.
- 🗝 Even today, believers will look back over our lives being thankful that we put off a certain promotion, job, relationship, career, hobby, etc. in order to know the Lord better, even wishing we had done more!
- ☞ Jesus is not saying that believers can abandon their responsibilities to family. But rather that our love & devotion to Him must transcend all other relationships. Nor is Jesus saying that by sowing money into a Church or ministry that God will bless us financially a hundred times over.

Chapter Twenty

Teachings on Greatness among Believers

- **"Workers in the Vineyard"-** Parable teaching on how God rewards Salvation to all, regardless of merit-(Vs. 1-16)
- **Jesus again predicts His death-** Jesus for the third time prepares disciples for His death-(Vs. 17-19)
- **A Mothers Request-**Teaches how greatness is measured not by rank, but by humility & service. -(Vs. 20-28)
- **Two Blind Men-**A miracle attesting to Jesus' ability to remove spiritual blindness.-(Vs. 29-34)

Workers in the Vineyard-(N.I.V.)

20:1 For the kingdom of heaven (i.e. God's Saving grace) **is like a landowner who went out early in the morning to hire men to work in his vineyard.-◙**

2 He agreed to pay them a denarius-◙ for the day and sent them into his vineyard. (Lit.-To harvest grapes. Metph.-Church, body of believers.)

3 "About the third hour (9:00 A.M.) **he went out and saw others standing in the market-place doing nothing.** (Expresses Spiritual idleness, slothfulness.)

4 He told them, 'You also go and work in my vineyard, and I will pay you whatever is right.' (Expresses: God's grace, mercy, justice, sovereignty.)

5 So they went. "He went out again about the sixth hour (12:00 P.M.) **and the ninth hour** (3:00 P.M.) **and did the same thing.**

6 About the eleventh hour (5:00 P.M.) **he went out and found still others standing around. He asked them, 'Why have you been standing here all day long doing nothing?'** {See V. 3}

7 "Because no-one has hired us they answered. "He said to them, 'You also go and work in my vineyard".(Metph.-Church, body of believers, Christian dome.)

8 "When evening came, (6:00 P.M.) **the owner of the vineyard said to his foreman, 'Call the workers and pay them their wages, beginning with the last ones hired and going on to the first.'**

9 "The workers who were hired about the eleventh hour (5:00 P.M. Metph.-Latest possible moment, last minute.) **came and each received a denarius.**

10 So when those came who were hired first, they expected to receive more. But each one of them also received a denarius.(Rom. Coin=Days wage)

11 When they received it, they began to grumble against the landowner.

12 'These men who were hired last worked only one hour,' they said, 'and you have made them equal to us who have borne the burden of the work and the heat of the day.' (Expresses Spiritually superior, Self-righteous, legalistic.)

13 But he answered one of them, Friend, (Expresses: Reproof as in "Pal".) **I am not being unfair to you. Didn't you agree to work for a denarius?**

14 Take your pay and go. I want to give the last man the same as I gave you.

15 Don't I have the right to do what I want with my own money? Or are you envious (jealous/spiteful) **because I am generous?**(Syn.-gracious, forgiving.)

16 So the last will be first, and the first will be last. (i.e. The humble & proud.)

God rewards Grace & Salvation equally to all believers, regardless of their labor or sacrifices.

Message & Application 💻=🌎

❖ Shows believers how Salvation is a gift from God and not a result of our own merits or how much we sacrificed.
❖ Calls for seeing that we're always serving God freely without the expectation of receiving something in return.
❖ Cautions against making our importance to God based on how much we gave, achieved, or put off as compared to others.
❖ Warns believers against envy and ulterior motives in serving God. (Labor for God out of love and devotion, not out of rewards!).
❖ Assures God's love & forgiveness, that no matter where we are in our walk, or how far we drifted, we're just as Saved as the next guy!

–***The last will be first/first will be last-*** In the immediate context, those who serve God out of pride and selfish ambition, looking only for a reward will be humbled, whereas those who serve out of love without thought of reward will be exalted.

🗝 Even today those who have been Christians for a long time can sometimes struggle, thinking it's unfair that someone who has lived a wild life, never gone to church, never prayed, etc. yet still be Saved & forgiven. Or they struggle in believing God can look past the horrible things they've done and still be loved and accepted by Him.

☞ Today many often serve God with a commercial or mercenary spirit, *"I should get more because I gave more"* or *"What's in it for me"*.

➢ The laborers have been variously identified as either:
- The morally upright & flagrant sinners.
- Those who respond early & late in life.
- The participation of the Jews & Gentiles in Salvation.

➢ Additional lessons drawn from Parable:
- God has grace on whom He chooses.
- God rewards eternal life equally to all believers.
- God treats all believers with justice and fairness.

Allegorical Types

Landowner…... = God/Christ.
Vineyard………= Church/world.
Hired workers… = Believers of various; ages, service, office, vocation.
Denarius……… = Salvation, grace, mercy.

From this verse here (V. 17) to verse (V. 19) Jesus for the third time prepares the disciples for His approaching death.

Jesus Again Predicts His Death-(N.I.V.)

20:17 Now, as Jesus was going up to Jerusalem, (i.e. To celebrate the Passover. Expresses Jesus' resolute determination in facing all that was going to happen to Him.) **he took the twelve disciples aside and said to them,**
18 "We are going up to Jerusalem, and the Son of Man (Expresses a Messianic title signifying the Messiah's human origins.-{cf. Dan 7:13-14}). **will be betrayed** (Syn.-double crossed, stab in the back, sell out, turncoat. i.e. By Judas Iscariot-{26:21-25, 47-50}) **to the chief priests and the teachers of the law.** (i.e. Jewish religious leaders.) **They will condemn him to death**
19 and will turn him over to the Gentiles (i.e. Pontius Pilate. Suggests: Because Israel was under Roman rule, capital punishment cases had to be carried out by Rome.-{John 18:31}) **to be mocked** (i.e. Ridiculed by Roman soldiers.-{Matt. 26:67-68) **and flogged-◙** (scourged-K.J.V. Syn.-whipped, beaten, lashed) **and crucified.** (4717-*Execution by nailing to a cross.)* **On the third day he will be raised to life!"** (Suggests: Jesus' resurrection from the dead three days later.)

For the third time, Jesus predicts His death, adding the details of His suffering, crucifixion, and resurrection.

Message & Application 💻=🌎

- ❖ Shows believers the amount of suffering & abuse Jesus was willing to endure in satisfying God's wrath against sin that we may have life.
- ❖ Calls for having the same resolve, putting ourselves in the center of God's will no matter the hardships or sacrifices we have to endure.
- ❖ Assures believers that no matter how discouraging, bleak, or hopeless things may look, know that Jesus is in control.
- ❖ Teaches how Christ prepares us beforehand for the severe trials that lie ahead so that when they do come our faith may not be shaken!
- ❖ Teaches the importance of giving spiritual comfort when bearing painful announcements. (Always speak of Christ's won victories and glories when delivering bad news!).

☞ According to Luke's Gospel *"The disciples did not understand any of this. Its meaning was hidden from them, and they did not know what he was talking about"*.-(Luke 18:34) (Suggests they were still thinking of a conquering Messiah who would set up a literal worldly Kingdom. Or they took the announcement only as a parable of which they were unable to understand, or was a result of divine providence.-(Luke 24:25)

From this verse here (V. 20) to verse (V. 28) Jesus teaches on the need for humility in leadership & service.

A Mother's Request-(N.I.V.)

20:20 Then (i.e. After Jesus just announced His suffering & death.-{Vs. 18-19}) **the mother** (i.e. Salome) **of Zebedee's sons** (i.e. James & John) **came to Jesus with her sons and, kneeling down, asked a favor of him.**
21 "What is it you want?" he asked. She said, "Grant that one of these two sons of mine may sit at your right and the other at your left in your kingdom." (Expresses thrones closest to Jesus having positions of honor & power. The request was possibly made in response to the twelve thrones already promised to the disciples, leaving only the question of precedence.-{cf. 19:28} That the disciples were still thinking of an earthly kingdom with worldly pomp and power. Or they were using their close relationship with Jesus, being part of His inner circle.)

The Mother of James & John is seeking that her Sons be granted positions of honor and authority in Jesus' kingdom.

Message & Application 💻=🌎

- ❖ Shows how believers can get their priorities mixed up in wanting the honor, fame, and glory without the labor or sacrifices.
- ❖ Warns against serving Christ out of selfish ambitions or what we can gain. (Serve out of love and not out of personal advancement!).
- ❖ Displays how many can do the right things, but for the wrong reasons and motives in doing it for self and what they can gain. (cf. James 4:3)
- ❖ Teaches how we must bring our children to Jesus for what He thinks is best and not what we think is best. (You may think you know what's right, but Jesus knows better!)
- ❖ Warns rather than seeking our path in what will benefit and bless us, we should be seeking God's path in what He would have for us.
- ❖ Displays the insensitivity of some people, that they can start to ask for favors from God during the trials and crises of others.-(V. 20)
- ❖ Calls for always striving and excelling in grace, service, and holiness, rather than in honor or self-importance.

🗝 Even today, believers can make the same mistake in thinking only of rights and privileges. That following Jesus entitles us to some reward or big payoff. Or we will use our relationship with Jesus for personal gain and advancement. (What motivates you for joining a church, is it to worship and serve God or to ask for favors?)

20:22 "You don't know what you are asking," Jesus said to them. (i.e. James & John, that it was they that put their mother up to the request.-{V. 20}) **"Can you drink the cup** (4221-*Afflictions, sufferings, one's lot or appointment, God's judgment against sin.* Metph.-sufferings, trials, hardships.) **I am going to drink?"**(Expresses Jesus' suffering in bearing the cup of God's wrath against sin. Modern cliché *"Are you willing to walk in my shoes"*. And be baptized with the baptism that I am baptized with?-K.J.V.-{Not found in earliest or most authentic Grk. MSS}) **"We can," they answered.** (Expresses bravado or pride rather than real knowledge. Their later desertion of Jesus at His arrest in Gethsemane would reveal just how unready they really were.-{cf. Matt. 26:56})
23 Jesus said to them, "You will indeed drink from my cup, but to sit at my right or left (Metph.-To share power & glory) **is not for me to grant. These places belong to those for whom they have been prepared by my Father."**

Jesus is asking James & John if they are willing to suffer for Him and the Gospel.

Message & Application 💻=🌎

- ❖ Shows how believers can be eager for duties without understanding the costs & sacrifices involved. (Many want the glory without the Cross).
- ❖ Warns how we can be overly presumptuous, thinking we're strong enough to handle any difficulty, trial, or hardship that comes our way.
- ❖ Calls believers in knowing what we're signing up for, that living for Jesus will involve great hardships, struggles, and sacrifices.
- ❖ Warns against overestimating our abilities, assuming we can do anything for God's glory by our own strength and efforts.

🗝 Even today we may not have to lay our life's down by way of physical sufferings or martyrdom. But it may entail laying it down in the little daily sacrifices by way of temptations, losses, trials, and setbacks.

–***You will indeed drink from my cup***-Expresses a prediction of the brothers own suffering & death. As fulfilled in James being the first disciple to be martyred/beheaded with a sword by Herod Agrippa.-(Acts 12:2) And John the last disciple to die as an exile on the island of Patmos.-(Rev. 1:9) Others see it only in reference to the Last Supper and the brothers participating with Jesus in the Eucharist.-(cf. Matt. 26:27-28)

-***Prepared by my Father***-Variously interpreted as either:

- God determines places of honor on the basis of those who suffered & sacrificed most for Christ.
- God determines places of honor according to humility and selfless service.

20:24 When the ten (Disciples) **heard about this** (James & John's power grab- {V.21) **they were indignant** (upset/resentful) **with the two brothers.** (Because the brothers beat them to the punch in asking for those lofty positions.)

The other disciples were jealous of James & John due to their own desires for those lofty positions.

Message & Application 💻=🌎

- ❖ Shows how believers can become jealous & resentful at others when our own selfish ambitions and interests are affected.
- ❖ Displays how we can get angry & disgusted at the prideful hearts of others, and gloss over it when it pops up in our own life.
- ⊶ Even today we often get offended by those who think they're closer to God than we are, or that they're a better Christian than we are.

20:25 Jesus called them together and said, "You know that the rulers (i.e. Governors) **of the Gentiles**(Non-Jews) **lord it over them, and their high officials** (i.e. Kings/Caesars) **exercise authority over them".** (Expresses one who plays the boss, one who is on a power trip, or who lets power go to their heads.)
26 Not so with you. Instead, whoever wants to become great among you must be your servant (140-*Slave, table waiter, an under-rower in galley ship.*)
27 and whoever wants to be first (chief-K.J.V. Syn.- #1) **must be your slave—**
28 just as the Son of Man (Jesus) **did not come to be served, but to serve, and to give his life as a ransom** (3083-*Price paid to set a slave free.)* **for** (behalf-of) **many.** (Expresses Jesus' substitutionary Atonement in paying the price for sin.)

Greatness in Christ's kingdom is measured not by worldly power or authority, but by humble service.

Message & Application 💻=🌎

- ❖ Shows believers how greatness is not determined by positions of power or authority, but by humbly serving the needs of others.
- ❖ Reminds believers how no job or service should be too low, too menial, or too beneath us to perform. (cf. John 13:5)
- ❖ Displays how true leadership lives and leads by example, that it's never about us and what we can get, but about what we can give!
- ⊶ Even today many only go to church for getting their needs met with no real heart desire to serve. That yes they like to hear good preaching, teaching, and music. But they don't want to get involved in counseling anyone, volunteering anywhere, or having to do outreach ministry.
- ☞ Today Jesus is the supreme example of humility and selfless service, having laid His own life down in dying for our sins! (cf. Philp. 2:3-8)

From this verse here (V. 29) to the end of the chapter, Jesus displays His ability to remove spiritual blindness.

Two Blind Men Receive Sight-(N.I.V.)

20:29 As Jesus and his disciples were leaving Jericho a large crowd followed him. (i.e. Pilgrims heading with Jesus to attend the Passover feast in Jerusalem)
30 Two blind men were sitting by the roadside, (A common practice for seeking alms from passerby's.) **and when they heard that Jesus was going by, they shouted, Lord, Son of David** (Messiah's royal descent) **have mercy on us!**
31 The crowd rebuked them and told them to be quiet, (Suggests: Thought it beneath the Messiah to associate with sinners & beggars.) **but they shouted all the louder** (Expresses: Boldness) **"Lord, Son of David, have mercy on us!"**
32 Jesus stopped and called them. "What do you want me to do for you?" he asked. (Suggests: Not that Jesus was ignorant of their wants, but meant to inspire their faith, to see if they were willing to ascribe divine power to Him.)
33 "Lord," they answered, "we want our sight." (i.e. To cure their blindness.)
34 Jesus had compassion on them and touched their eyes. Immediately they received their sight and followed him. (i.e. To Jerusalem or discipleship.)

Jesus takes compassion on two blind men and heals their sight.

<u>Message & Application</u> 💻=🌎

❖ Shows how the Lord is never too busy or too preoccupied for those who cry out to Him for mercy & compassion. (Ps. 4:1, 18:6, James 4:10)
❖ Prepares believers in not allowing others to deter us in accepting that our case is hopeless for Christ to do anything about. (V. 31)
❖ Calls for an earnest & persistent faith that doesn't quit or give up no matter how much we're discouraged, ridiculed, or laughed at! (V. 31)
❖ Warns against allowing opportunities to get right with God pass us by. (Know the day of Salvation is now, that there may not be a tomorrow).
❖ Teaches the importance of being persistent and specific in our requests to God. (No room for doubt, reservations, or half-heartedness).(Vs. 32)
❖ Teaches those who are grateful for Christ's mercies and all that He has done will give all devotion, worship, and service to Him. (V. 34)

🗝 Even today we need to see our lost & broken condition, that we're poor, blind, and wretched with no hope in sight without Jesus!

➢ Miracles metaphorical implications suggests:
- The need for persistence in prayer & faith.
- Jesus' ability to remove spiritual blindness.
- Jesus Saves all who cry out to Him for Salvation.

Chapter Twenty One

Jesus' Triumphal Entry

- **Triumphal entry-**Jesus humbly presents Himself as Israel's long-awaited king-(Vs. 1-11)
- **Jesus at the Temple-**Jesus cleanses the temple of fraud & corruption.-(Vs. 12-17)
- **Withering fig tree-**A miracle judgment of Israel's spiritual bareness & unbelief- (Vs. 18-22)
- **Authority of Jesus questioned-** Teaches on surrendering one's life over to Jesus' authority- (Vs. 23-27)
- **"Two Sons"-**Parable contrasting Israel's failure to respond to the Gospel & Sinners who did-(V. 28-32)
- **"The Tenants"-**Parable teaching on God' rejection of Israel & extending Salvation to the Gentiles-(Vs. 33-46)

The Triumphal Entry-(N.I.V.)

21:1 As they approached Jerusalem and came to Bethphage on the Mount of Olives,-◙ (i.e. A village on a hilltop ridge of olive groves.) **Jesus sent two disciples,** (Unknown, possibly Peter & John being two of Jesus' inner circle.)
2 saying to them, "Go to the village ahead of you, and at once, you will find a donkey-◙ tied there, with her colt by her. Untie them and bring them to me.
3 If anyone (Owner.-{Luke 19:33} Citizens of the city.-{Mark 11:5}) **says anything to you, tell him that the Lord needs them, and he will send them right away."** (Expresses Jesus' Omniscience, knowing exactly where the donkey would be.)

Jesus prepares His humble ride into Jerusalem as Israel's long-awaited Messiah and King.

Message & Application =

- ❖ Shows believers where the Lord leads & instructs, He also supplies the provisions and resources to carry it out! (cf. 2-Corn. 9:8-11, Philp. 1:6)
- ❖ Teaches how Christ makes our gracious service to Him possible in always preparing the way before us. (cf. Deut. 31:8, 1-Corn. 2:9)
- ❖ Teaches how those who love the Lord will never draw the line when it comes to their possession but will give all that Jesus asks for!
- ❖ Teaches that no matter how stubborn and mule-headed we are, God can still use us, that He has a purpose and plan for our lives.
- ❖ Displays how we can expect divine intervention to show up at the right time and the right place when we need it most!
- ❖ Calls for the willingness in relinquishing our possessions over to the Lord when He has need of it since it all belongs to Him anyway.

⊶ Even today, believers can take comfort that whatever the Lord has called us to do, whether it's confronting a difficult situation, taking on a new job, ministry, or moving to a new city. Jesus is in complete control of the situation and will help us deal with the load.

21:4 This took place to fulfill what was spoken through the prophet {Zech. 9:9} **5 "Say to the Daughter of Zion,** (Expresses: A personification of Jerusalem.) **'See, your king** (Lord/Savior) **comes to** (for) **you, gentle** (Syn.-humble, meek) **and riding on a donkey,-◙ on a colt,-◙** (calf) **the foal** (young) **of a donkey."**

Jesus fulfills Zechariah's prophecy by arriving in Jerusalem not as conquering ruler, but as a humble Prince of peace.

Message & Application 💻=🌎

- ❖ Shows believers the humble & gentle arrival of Christ into our lives, that He came not to slay and condemn, but to Save and forgive!
- ❖ Displays how Christ is not a tyrant who's cruel & oppressive, but loving & gentle. (Later Jesus will come on a Warriors horse-Rev. 19:11)
- ❖ Teaches that for the word and promises of God to be fulfilled it takes some cooperation and obedience on our part. (V. 4)
- ❖ Teaches how God often fulfills His promises in ways we don't expect. (Will you accept God's plan & will no matter how it shows up?)
- 🗝 Even today God often works quietly just under the surface where we need healing and victory the most, and not where we want it the most.

21:6 The disciples went and did as Jesus had instructed them. (Expresses how true devotion always obeys without question, protest, or debate.) **7 They brought the donkey and the colt,** (Suggests: The mother mare to nurse the cult, or to keep it calm. Which no one has ever ridden-{Mark 11:2}-i.e. Unbroken) **placed their cloaks-◙** (robes) **on them,** (i.e. The cloaks as a makeshift saddle for Jesus to sit on. Or the donkeys themselves, not knowing which one Jesus would ride.) **and Jesus sat on them.** (i.e. The disciple's cloaks.)

The disciples construct a makeshift saddle out of their coats as a token of Jesus' royalty.

Message & Application 💻=🌎

- ❖ Shows how true faith obeys without objection or protest, that doing things Jesus' way is the best way, even if we don't understand it!
- ❖ Calls for serving Jesus by whatever accommodations we have. (Nothing should be so dear to part with in our service to Christ).
- ❖ Teaches how true and authentic worship will do all things to exalt Christ's honor and glory before others.
- 🗝 Even today it's every believer's duty in using whatever time, talents, resources, and gifts we have in carrying Jesus' message of love and forgiveness further down the road.

Palm Sunday - (Cont.)

21:8 A very large crowd (Pilgrims on their way to celebrate the Passover feast.) **spread their cloaks-◙** (coats, robes) **on the road, while others cut branches** (palm branches.-{John 12:13}) **from the trees and spread them on the road.-◙** (Expresses an act of homage and honor paid to a king, similar to the modern-day proverbial "Rolling out the red carpet" for VIP's. Lit.-The purpose being to keep the dust from rising and getting Jesus' feet dirty.)
9 The crowds that went ahead of him and those that followed shouted, "Hosanna (5614-*Heb.-"Save now or Save we pray". A hymn taken from Psalm 118:25-26.* Syn.-Hallelujah, Praise God.) **to the Son of David!"** (Expresses a Messianic title signifying the Messiah's royal descent.) **"Blessed is he who comes in the name of the Lord!" "Hosanna in the highest!"** (Expresses Glory to God forever. That they were only celebrating Jesus' arrival as political king, someone who would liberate them from Roman rule.)

The crowds only pay political homage to Jesus as their long awaited Messiah King.

<u>Message & Application</u> 💻=🌎

❖ Shows how we're to receive Jesus for who He is, and not for who we want Him to be, or who's only there to meet our needs and demands.
❖ Warns against only looking to Jesus for fixing our problems and jams we're in and not our greater need in having our sins forgiven!
❖ Calls for seeing that we're truly seeking Jesus and not just jumping on the bandwagon and following the crowd because it's popular.
❖ Teaches how we should be worshipping and praising Jesus for who He is and not just lip-service for getting what we want.
❖ Warns believers against reducing Jesus to some sort of "Genie in a bottle" who's only there for getting our wishes met.
❖ Calls for laying our all under Christ's feet. (Give not only your best but all the rest! Make Christ the rightful King over your life!).
❖ Teaches how we should be seeking Jesus in rescuing us out of our sin, and not about how prosperous or blessed we can become.
❖ Teaches rather than trying to fit Jesus into our expectations, it is we who are to tailor our lives around Him and what He determines.
🗝 Even today many only rally around Jesus when things are going good, or when it suits their interests in getting them that new house, car, job, promotion, healing, etc. only to fall away when it doesn't pan out.
☞ The crowd's superficial cries of acclamations are made even clearer by the fact that only a week later, this same crowd who were cheering Jesus as king, would later be calling for His crucifixion. (Mat.27:22-23)

Palm Sunday - (Cont.)

21:10 When Jesus entered Jerusalem,-◙ (Tradition locates the entrance as the eastern gate, known today as the "Sheep Gate".) **the whole city was stirred** (4579-*To rock to and fro, as a city shaken by an earthquake, To agitate the mind with fear or emotion.* Syn.-commotion, turmoil, flurry, hubbub. Suggests: Because of the crowds Messianic overtones.-{V. 9}) **and asked, "Who is this?"** (Suggests: Since Jesus' ministry was mostly in Galilee, He was virtually unknown to them. Or they were asking not of His identity, but only of His purpose.)
11 The crowds (i.e. Galilean pilgrims who were celebrating Jesus' arrival as Messiah.) **answered, "This is Jesus, the prophet** (Expresses the Messiah as the One promised by Moses.-{Duet. 18:15-18}) **from Nazareth in Galilee."** (Expresses a correct, but incomplete answer. That Jesus' arrival should have had a greater witness and impact on them.-{cf. John 1:45-46})

The crowds miss Jesus' true identity and only see His arrival as a prophet and not as Savior.

Message & Application 💻=🌎

- ❖ Shows believers the need for a larger view & understanding of Jesus or we can come up short in our Christian witness and walk.
- ❖ Warns how not pressing far enough can cause us to miss Christ's rightful Lordship over our lives and all that He can do for us.
- ❖ Calls for a heart that is stirred up in wanting to know Jesus better and all that He is doing. (Are you excited about the things of Christ?).
- ❖ Displays the life changing effect that Christ will have in shaking us out of the sin and rut we're in, never leaving us the same again!
- ❖ Warns how an inadequate confession of Christ can cause us to fall short in both our devotion and how we live our life's!
- ❖ Displays how failure to grow is no fault of God, but often our own lack of interests in getting to know and understand Jesus better!
- ❖ Calls for a declaration of Jesus that goes beyond the general and generic, to one that speaks to who He is and all that He's done! (Is Jesus just your role-model & teacher, or is He your everything!)
- ❖ Warns how an emotional & mental agreement with Jesus without true conviction and faith will have little impact on changing our lives.
- ❖ Calls for seeing that our Christian profession and the words we speak reflect an expectancy that matches the promises of God.

🗝 Even today if we're to have any hope of seeing victories in our lives, we must take great pains in having a proper understanding of Jesus and all that we ask of Him or we can come up short in our growth and walk with Him.

Chronology of Jesus' Passion Week:

Sunday-Jesus' triumphal arrival in Jerusalem-
(Matt. 21:1 11, Mark 11:1-11, Luke 19:28-44)

Monday-Jesus' cleansing of the Temple.
(Matt. 21:12-17 Mark 11:15-18, Luke 19:45-48)
Jesus curses Fig tree-(Matt 21:18-22, Mark. 11:12)

Tuesday-Jesus' controversy with the religious leaders-
(Matt. 21:18-46, 22:1-46, Mark 11:12-14, Luke 20:20-44)
Jesus' denunciations of the religious leaders-
(Matt. 23:1-39, Mark 12:38-39, Luke 20:45-46)
Jesus' Olivet discourse on Tribulation & return.
(Matt. 24:1-51, 25:1-46)

Wednesday- Jesus anointed by a sinful woman.-(Mark 14:1-11)
Judas bargains to betray Jesus-(Luke 22:3-6)

Thursday-Preparations for the Passover.
Jesus shares last supper with disciples.-
(Matt. 26:1-30, Mark 14:12 26, Luke 22:7-23)

Friday-Jesus' betrayal, arrest, crucifixion, and burial-
(Matt. 26:47-74, 27:11-61, Mark 14:43-72, 15:1-47,
Luke 22:47-62, 23:1-56, John 18:28-19:37)

Saturday-Jesus in the tomb/Jewish Sabbath-(Matt. 27:62- 66)

Sunday-Jesus' Resurrection-(Matt. 28:1-13, Mark 16:1-20,
Luke 24:1-49, John 20:1-31)

From this verse here (V. 12) to verse (V. 17) Jesus demonstrates His power & authority in cleansing the sin & corruption from our lives.

Jesus at the Temple-(N.I.V.)

21:12 Jesus entered the temple area-◙ (i.e. Court of the Gentiles) **and drove out all who were buying and selling there. He overturned the tables of the money-changers-◙** (Suggests: Those who exchanged Roman currency for the Temple shekel at inflated rates.) **and the benches of those selling doves.** (Those who sold birds for sacrificial offerings to the poor at excessive prices.)
13 "It is written," he said to them, "'My house-◙ (i.e. Temple) **will be called a house of prayer,'** (Syn.-Worship, supplication, intercession. {Is. 56:7, Jer. 7:11}) **but you are making it a 'den of robbers'.** (Expresses a criminal environment, favorable for committing extortion, fraud, bribery, and racketeering.)

By cleansing the Temple of corruption & extortion Jesus restores God's house to its proper use of prayer & worship.

Message & Application 💻=🌎

❖ Shows believers Jesus' cleansing effect upon our hearts & souls, purging the sinful corruptions and idols out of our lives! (Eph. 5:25-27)
❖ Calls for welcoming the Lord's work in overturning and driving out the false and hypocritical areas of our lives. (cf. 1-Corn. 6:19-20)
❖ Calls for self-examination, that we're not accommodating any sin, attitude, or practice that's out of line with God's word.
❖ Calls for having the same zeal and love for God that wants to speak up when we know something is out of place and not right.
❖ Reminds believers how our bodies are a temple to the Lord, and not a playground for sin, immorality, or abuse! (cf. 1-Corn. 6:19-20)

🗝 Even today, believers are responsible for our own housecleaning, that we're not compromising on some sin, or allowing certain things in our lives that we wouldn't have had when we first came to Jesus.

☞ Jesus is not forbidding Church fundraising, bingo-nights, swap-meets, or pot-lucks. But rather against religion that is commercialized and mechanical, to one that is spirit-filled and flows from the heart.

☞ Today the same parallels can be seen by those who take advantage of others for financial profit and doing it all in the name of religion.

☞ Some try using Jesus' display of anger & violence here as running contrary to His sinless character. (Many counter this by arguing that Jesus was only responding from a place of righteous indignation and not of anger or hate).

21:14 The blind and the lame (i.e. Crippled, disabled, maimed) **came to him at the temple,** (Expresses how Jesus reestablishes the Temple back to its proper use as a place for healing and prayer.-{cf. 2-Sam 5:8}) **and he healed them.**
15 But when the chief priests and the teachers of the law (i.e. Religious leaders.) **saw the wonderful things he did** (i.e. Jesus' Miracles, teachings-.{Mark 11:18b}) **and the children shouting in the temple area, "Hosanna** (5614-*Heb.-"Save now" or "Save we pray", exclamation of praise & adoration.* Syn.-Hallelujah, God bless-L.B.V.) **to the Son of David,"** (Expresses the Messiah's royal descent from King David. That the children were reenacting the Messianic praises that the crowds were shouting earlier.-{V. 9}) **they were indignant.** (23-*"Stirred up with righteous anger".* sore displeased-K.J.V. Syn.-resentful, disapproving, annoyed. Suggests: Their disapproval of Jesus in allowing Himself to be praised as the Messiah, or by the presence of the lame & blind in the Temple area. Or even possibly their fear of Roman reprisal.)

Jesus returns the Temple to its proper use for people to be healed and ministered to.

Message & Application

- ❖ Shows Jesus' tender love & compassion for the lost, least, and left-out, who need His healing and forgiveness.
- ❖ Displays Jesus' acceptance of outcasts and sinners no matter how flawed, broken, or imperfect they are! (God's mercy is for everyone!)
- ❖ Portrays Jesus' concern for the poor, powerless, and excluded who need His help in fixing and straightening out their lives.
- ❖ Warns how it's usually a sign of pride and a wrong heart when we see God doing wonderful things and still get bent out of shape over it.
- ❖ Warns how when we harden our hearts in defending our positions and entitlements we often in the process miss God's work in our lives.
- ❖ Teaches believers rather than respond with a critical spirit, always have a heart in seeing sinners healed and addicts set free. (V. 15)
- ⊶ Even today Church's should be a place where less-than-perfect people can go for healing and wholeness over any sin, vice, or addiction, without the fear of shame, criticism, or judgment.
- ➢ Miracles metaphorical implications suggests:
  - Christ's willingness & readiness to Save all who seek Him.
  - Christ's loving concern for the lost, broken, and hurting.
  - Christ's power and goodness in removing spiritual blindness.

21:16 "Do you hear what these children are saying?" (i.e. The Messianic accolades being made of Jesus.) **they asked him. "Yes, replied Jesus "have you never read, 'From the lips** (Syn.-mouths) **of children and infants you have ordained** (perfected-K.J.V.) **praise?** (Syn.-glory, worship, devotion.{cf. Ps. 8:2})
17 And he left them (Expresses an act of abandonment/judgment, that Jesus doesn't tarry long with those who have hardened their hearts.) **and went out of the city** (Jerusalem) **to Bethany** (A village that laid on the southeast side of the Mt. of Olives.) **where he spent the night.** (Suggests: Due to the overcrowding of Jerusalem at Passover there were no vacant lodges. Or to avoid further confrontations with the religious leaders. Jesus probably sought out the hospitality of Marry, Martha, and Lazarus who resided in Bethany.)

By citing Psalm 8:2 Jesus supports the children's praises and devotion to Him as Lord & God.

Message & Application 💻=🌎

❖ Shows believers how true worship will give all praise & glory to Jesus for who He is and all that He has done in our life's.
❖ Teaches how those who have experienced Christ's amazing grace will find all their joy, hope, and needs met in Him.
❖ Prepares believers in not allowing the enemy to discourage us in our praise and worship, or take away our trust and confidence in God.
❖ Displays the sustaining power of worship and praise in getting us through any crises and difficult challenges we may be facing.
❖ Reminds believers how celebrating God's love and goodness can keep the enemy from stealing our hope and joy away.
❖ Displays how by speaking praises of God we're allowing the Lord to have the last word and not Satan or the circumstances surrounding us.
❖ Warns believers how dissatisfaction and discontent with Jesus will often drive Him far from us. (V. 17)

🗝 Even today, believers can speak victories into our lives, that God's breakthroughs are coming. That it is God who holds and defines who we are and not our circumstances, situations, or problems!

Benefits of Praising Jesus as Lord:

- Gives believers hope when suffering loss, loneliness, and despair.
- Strengthens a believer's faith, allowing God to move and work on our behalf.
- Reminds believers of God's power, goodness, and presence in our lives.

From this verse here (V. 18) to verse (V. 22) Jesus warns of the dangers of living barren & fruitless lives.

The fig Tree Withers-(N.I.V.)

21:18 Early in the morning, (i.e. Monday) **as he** (i.e. Jesus) **was on his way back to the city** (i.e. Jerusalem) **he was hungry.** (Expresses: Christ's humanity.)
19 Seeing a fig-tree by the road, he went up to it but found nothing on it except leaves.-◙ (Since early figs-buds usually sprouted first, a tree that was in full-leaf should have had figs. Metph.-To appear outwardly religious but spiritually barren. That Israel professed their worship of God but lacked faith in Jesus as the Messiah.) **Then he said to it, "May you never bear fruit again!" Immediately the tree withered.** (i.e. Dried and shriveled up, or rotted away.)
20 When the disciples saw this, they were amazed. How did the fig-tree wither so quickly? They asked. (i.e. Only how it was done, not what it meant.)
21 Jesus replied, "I tell you the truth, if you have faith and do not doubt, not only can you do what was done to the fig-tree, but also you can say to this mountain (i.e. Mtn. Olives. Metph.-Great-obstacles) **Go throw yourself into the sea,**(Dead Sea.) **and it will be done.** (Expresses: Nothing will be impossible.)
22 If you believe, you will receive whatever you ask for in prayer." (Suggests: In context not of material things, but life's that are fruitful and pleasing to God.)

Jesus curses the fig tree as an act of judgment upon fruitless Israel, who professed their faith in God but rejected Him as the Messiah.

Message & Application 💻=🌎

- ❖ Shows believers how God expects us to live differently, that our Christian profession is marked by fruitful and productive lives.
- ❖ Teaches how God doesn't want those who are merely looking and sounding religious, but Christians who are the real deal.
- ❖ Calls for seeing that we're producing Spiritual fruit in our lives, and not simply maintaining outward appearances. (cf. Gal. 5:22-25)
- ❖ Displays the power of prayer in removing whatever obstacles that are standing in the way of bearing fruit in our Christian life. (V. 21-22)
- ❖ Promises that where prayers are seeking more of Christ's rule and ways perfected in them will be heard and answered by God!
- 🗝 Even today we can go to God in prayer for strength in dealing with whatever mountainous barriers of legalism, religionism, externalism, doubt, unbelief, and anything else that's rising up and holding us back.
- ☞ Today the same hypocrisy is seen by some who can look & sound like Christians, who can go through all the motions of attending Church, praying, fasting, etc. but bear no evidence of a relationship with God.

From this verse here (V. 23) to the end of the chapter, teaches on the importance of submitting to Jesus' rule & authority.

The Authority of Jesus Questioned-(N.I.V.)

21:23 Jesus entered the temple courts,-◙ (i.e. Court of the Gentiles.) **and, while he was teaching, the chief priests and the elders of the people came to him.** (Suggests: Used as an opportunity to humiliate and discredit Jesus.) **"By what authority** (Syn.-Divine right, prerogative, manner) **are you doing these things?"**(i.e. Jesus' Triumphal entry and cleansing of the Temple.) **they asked. "And who gave you this authority?** (Suggests a call for divine credentials. Was not a sincere inquiry in wanting to know the truth, but rather a smokescreen to undermine and discredit Jesus before the people as being unqualified.)

The religious leaders try to trap Jesus into acknowledging His Messiahship so they could accuse Him of blasphemy.

Message & Application 💻=🌎

- ❖ Shows believers how it's not Jesus who must validate & prove Himself to us, but it is we who must adjust and conform to Him!
- ❖ Teaches how God doesn't owe us an explanation or have to prove everything to our satisfaction before we're willing to believe & follow.
- ❖ Warns how when we start to question Christ's authority in one area of life, will begin to question His authority in other areas as well.
- ❖ Warns against thinking we know better than God in how to run our own lives & choose our path, only to end up paying the price later on.
- ❖ Teaches how we don't need a doctorate to do what God has laid on our hearts to do, or prove to anyone we're qualified to preach the Gospel.
- ❖ Prepares believers who are trying to do good will find their efforts constantly challenged and called into question.
- ❖ Displays how men will call into question another's credentials when their own hypocritical practices are being challenged and threatened.

-***Who gave you this authority***-Was meant to trap Jesus by putting Him on the horns of a dilemma. That if Jesus answered that His authority came from God, they could accuse Him of blasphemy. Or if Jesus answered that His authority was His own, they would make him look like a fanatic and heretic, losing His influence with the people.

🗝 Even today, believers need to take a hard look at how we respond to those that God brings into our lives for reproof and correction. Do we respond favorably when a brother or sister confronts us about a certain sin or an area of weakness, or do we respond negatively?

21:24 Jesus replied, "I will also ask you one question. If you answer me, I will tell you by what authority I am doing these things.
25 John's baptism—(Ministry) **where did it come from? Was it from heaven,** (God) **or from men?"**(i.e. Human origins, man-made. Expresses Jesus' wisdom in turning the tables on them, putting them in a similar predicament.) **They discussed it among themselves and said, "If we say, 'From heaven',** (God) **he will ask, 'Then why didn't you believe him?'** (Suggests: John's message and testimony about Jesus being the Messiah.)
26 But if we say, 'From men'—we are afraid of the people, (i.e. Fear of a riot, they will stone us.-{Luke 20:6}) **for they all hold that John was a prophet."**
27 So they answered Jesus, "We don't know." (Expresses not of ignorance, but a cop-out, that any answer they gave they would be condemning themselves.) **Then he said, "Neither will I tell you by what authority I am doing these things.** (Suggests: If they're not going to be honest, why should Jesus tell them what they already knew, but were unwilling to admit!)

The Religious leaders saw their dilemma, if they accepted John's work as Divine they would have to accept Jesus as the Messiah.

Message & Application

- ❖ Shows how believers can't expect the Lord's help in changing us if we're unwilling to face the hard questions and truth about ourselves.
- ❖ Warns instead of skirting around the difficult and hard parts of God's word, have the guts in admitting the areas where you fall short.
- ❖ Displays how our actions and words communicate a great deal as to who's going to have ultimate authority over our lives, God or others!
- ❖ Warns believers against putting status and popularity above staying faithful and true to God and His ways.
- ❖ Demonstrates how some people are more concerned about saving face at any cost than about truth.
- ❖ Displays how some people would rather go against the evidence of their own consciences than to admit defeat or their own accountability.
- ⊶ Even today rather than cave into the social pressures around us, we need to stand up for God and our convictions regardless of the fallout.
- ☞ Teaches a common principle, that we cannot learn new truth if we are unwilling to obey what God has already told us. (If you want answers, deal rightly with the truth that the Lord has already revealed!).
- ☞ In effect, Jesus turned the tables on the religious leaders putting them on the horns of a dilemma. That if they said John's ministry was from heaven (God) they would incriminate themselves for not repenting at John's preaching of Jesus. But if they said it was from men they feared the people would riot and stone them, holding John to be a prophet.

The Parable of the Two Sons-(N.I.V.)

21:28 "What do you think? There was a man who had two sons. He went to the first (older boy) **and said, 'Son,** (Metph-sinners) **go and work today in the vineyard.'**(Metph-Believe on Christ, Gospel dispensation, Church.)
29 "I will not,' he answered, (Expresses: Rebellious, disrespectful.) **but later he changed his mind** (Syn.-repented, remorseful, contrite, regretful) **and went.**
30 "Then the father (Metph-God) **went to the other son** (Metph-religious leaders) **and said the same thing. He answered, 'I will, sir,' but he did not go.**
31 "Which of the two did what his father wanted?" "The first," they answered. Jesus said to them "I tell you the truth, the tax collectors and the prostitutes (Metph.-Sinners, outcasts, low-life's, lowest of the low, etc.) **are entering the kingdom of God ahead of you.** (i.e. Receiving Christ/Salvation.)
32 For John came to you to show you the way of righteousness, (i.e. John's work in calling for repentance, reform, and faith in Jesus.) **and you did not believe him but the tax collectors and the prostitutes did. And even after you saw this,** (Sinners repenting and transformed life's.) **you did not repent** (3340-*A changed mind or purpose, a turning from sin to God.*) **and believe him.**

Contrasts the difference between the self-righteous religious leaders who did not repent and believe on Christ whereas Sinners who did.

Message & Application

- ❖ Shows believers how God expects profession to be followed by a life of repentance and obedient living. (cf. James 1:22, 2:22)
- ❖ Warns against giving lip-service to God with no real heart to follow through or obey Him. (God wants obedience, not Lip service!)
- ❖ Calls for a repentance that goes beyond just words to a change of life and behavior. (God wants possession, not just profession!).
- ❖ Teaches how it's one thing to say you live to serve Christ, but another thing altogether to actually obey and follow through with it!
- ❖ Teaches no matter what we've done or how far we've strayed we can turn back to God and be forgiven. (V. 29, 1-John 1:9, Luke 15:11-32)

⊶ Even today, believers can say the same things, promising God they're going to go to church more often, or they're going to spend less time on Facebook and more time in God's book, or their going to add more time to their prayer life, with no real heart to follow through with it.

☞ The parable teaching is not that one son was better than the other, but rather it exposes the hypocrisy between profession and practice.

➢ Additional lessons drawn from Parable:
- God's graciousness despite our former sins, mistakes, and errors.
- God's goodness & patience for all sinners.

***Parable of the Tenants*-(N.I.V.)**

21:33 Listen to another parable: There was a landowner (God) **who planted a vineyard.**-◙ (Israel) **He put a wall around it, dug a winepress-**◙ **in it and built a watchtower.**-◙(Expresses: God's protection, care, provision.) **Then he rented the vineyard to some farmers** (Religious leaders) **and went away on a journey.**
34 When the harvest time approached, he sent his servants (O.T. prophets) **to the tenants** (i.e. Israel) **to collect his fruit.** (Metph-Repentance, faith)
35"The tenants (i.e. Israel's religious leaders.) **seized his servants;** (O.T. Prophets, Saints.) **they beat one, killed another, and stoned a third.**
36 Then he sent other servants (i.e. John the Baptist.) **to them, more than the first time, and the tenants treated them in the same way.**
37 Last of all he sent his son (Jesus) **to them. They will respect my son he said.**
38 "But when the tenants (Israel's rulers) **saw the son,** (i.e. Jesus) **they said to each other, 'This is the heir. Come, let's kill him and take his inheritance.'**
39 So they took him and threw him out of the vineyard and killed him. (Lit. Fulfilled by the religious leaders in having Jesus crucified outside Jerusalem.)
40 "Therefore, when the owner (i.e. God) **of the vineyard comes, what will he do to those tenants?"** (Metph. Unrepentant Israel)
41 "He will bring those wretches (rotten men) **to a wretched** (bloody) **end," they replied,** (Lit. Fulfilled in the destruction of Jerusalem by Rome in 70 A.D.) **and he will rent the vineyard to other tenants,** (Gentiles) **who will give him his share of the crop at harvest time.**(i.e. Repentance, faithfulness, righteousness.)

Because of Israel's unbelief & rejection of Jesus, God now extends the Gospel & Salvation to the Gentiles.

Message & Application 💻=🌎

- ❖ Shows how believers are expected to make good on God' Saving grace with a life of fruitful labor and obedient living. (cf. John 15:1-5, 2-Pet. 3:9)
- ❖ Warns against making light of God's endless patience and kindness by remaining unrepentant and unchanged. (cf. Rom. 2:4-5)
- ❖ Displays the intervening work of God in providing every opportunity and means necessary to turn back to Him before it's too late.
- ❖ Displays God's rightful claim upon our lives in expecting us to live a more committed and devoted life after all He has provided.
- 🗝 Even today, believers can get in the habit of serving self in doing our own thing with no thought of giving back to God our time, tithes, prayers, witness, or service after all He has done for us.
- ➢ Additional lessons drawn from Parable:
  - God's loving kindness, mercy, and grace.
  - God's long-suffering, patience, justice, and forbearance.
  - God expects faithful stewardship in all areas of life.

21:42 Jesus said to them, "Have you never read in the Scriptures: "'The stone (Metph-Jesus) **the builders** (Religious leaders) **rejected** (Expresses: The practice of masons throwing aside stones that were unusable. Metph-Israel's unbelief of Jesus) **has become the capstone-◙** (Syn.-cornerstone. Fulfilled in Jesus' finished work on the Cross in dying & resurrecting.) **the Lord has done this, and it is marvellous in our eyes'?**(Expresses: How God' work in our Salvation is always to be seen as an object of joy, thankfulness, and praise! {Ps.118:22-23, Is. 28:16})

Israel having rejected Jesus, God now exalts Christ as the principle means of Salvation.

Message & Application 💻=🌎

- ❖ Shows how believers are to see that we're making Christ' Saving work the bases & foundation stone of our lives. (cf. Rom. 9:30-33, 1-Pet. 2:4-10)
- ❖ Calls for making Jesus the foundation stone and strength of our lives. (Know you can lean on Jesus for stability and support!)
- ❖ Warns how without Jesus as the cornerstone of our lives, everything else would just crumble and fall apart.
- ❖ Warns how carelessness and miss opportunities can cause us to miss out on God's leading and what's best for our lives.

–***Capstone-***A architectural term denoting the principle stone that formed the foundation of a building, or a support stone used in an arch, or the top stone of a pyramid. Metaphorically the culmination and crowning achievement of Christ's work on the Cross in securing our Salvation.

🗝 Even today many can get their values & priorities mixed up in what's really important in life. Or they will see life going along well and have no need for Jesus, that He doesn't fit their plans and goals.

21:43 "Therefore I tell you that the kingdom of God (Metph.-Gospel, Salvation.) **will be taken away from you** (i.e. Jewish religious rulers. Or the nation in general.) **and given to a people** (Gentiles.) **who will produce its fruit.** (Metph-faith in Christ, repentance, righteousness, holiness, obedience, etc.)

Because of Israel's rejection of Christ, the Gospel will be taken from them and given to the Gentiles who will believe.

Message & Application 💻=🌎

- ❖ Shows believers how God expects the fruit of a repentant & believing heart that is trusting in Jesus for Salvation.
- ❖ Warns against remaining neutral & indifferent to God's Saving grace.

🗝 Even today, believers who are professing their faith in Christ should be bearing fruit in their lives, bringing glory and honor to His name.

21:44 He (i.e. Sinner) **who falls** (Metph-Surrenders, brokenness, repents.) **on this stone** (Metph-Jesus) **will be broken to pieces** (Lit.-As a lower cornerstone protrudes too far out from a foundation causing one to trip over it, injuring themselves. Metph.-One who is crushed and broken in spirit having been affected by their own sinfulness in light of Jesus' mercy & forgiveness.{cf. Ps. 51:17} Or one who stumbles in disbelief over Jesus to their own ruin and loss.) **but he** (i.e. unrepentant) **on whom it falls will be crushed."** (Lit.-As an upper capstone is dislodged, sending it crashing on top of a person's head killing them. Metph.-Christ's second coming in judgment upon the unrepentant. {Dan.2:34-35} Grind him to powder-K.J.V.-[Not omitted by all Bible translations])

Israel's stumbling in disbelief over Jesus now will be to their own ruin & loss. But those who persistently reject Christ will be to their own eternal doom & destruction.

Message & Application 💻=🌎

- ❖ Shows how we have two choices, we can come broken, falling on Jesus for mercy & grace now, or we can resist Him and be lost forever.
- ❖ Warns rather than seeing our self's as so wise and sufficient in our own eyes, we need to come broken and defeated. (cf. Ps. 51:17)
- ❖ Instead of coming by our own efforts and goodness we need to come weak and broken. (Will you come proud or on your hands & knees?)
- ❖ Calls for getting right with the Lord, that any way we look at it there's things in our life we just can't fix or change. (cf. Is. 6:5, Rom. 7:21-24)
- ❖ Warns when we rebel & resist the things the Lord is trying to break us of, it's only us who suffer. (Do you fight God every step of the way?)
- ❖ Teaches only by coming broken and defeated can the Lord begin to reform us and put us back together as the person we were created to be.
- ❖ Calls for allowing God to break us as long as necessary and as often as necessary, that He may keep us humble and teachable. (cf. 2-Corn. 11:30, 12:5-10)
- ❖ Teaches how we cannot expect to come out of our encounter with Jesus as we were when we went in, without leaving a changed person!

–***Falls on this stone broken to pieces***-Variously interpreted as either:

- Those who come broken over their sin, humbly falling on Jesus for mercy and forgiveness.
- Those who stumble in unbelief over Jesus to their own eternal ruin and destruction.

🗝 Even today many stumble in the same way, thinking they have it all figured out and don't need God's help, that they can fix themselves. Or they'll come prideful & self-righteous, refusing to be broken down, that who's to tell them there's anything wrong with them.

21:45 When the chief priests and the Pharisees heard Jesus' parables, (Suggests: Previous parables of "The stone"-{Vs. 42-44} "The Two Sons"-{Vs. 28-31} and "The Tenants".-{Vs. 33-41}) **they knew he was talking about them.**
46 They looked for a way to arrest him, but they were afraid of the crowd (i.e. Passover pilgrims.) **because the people held that he was a prophet.** (Suggests: They feared the people would riot, holding that Jesus was the prophet foretold by Moses.-{Deut. 18:18} So they left him and went away.-{Mark 12:12 c}-Suggests: They consulted together for a better opportunity to trap or seize Jesus.)

Knowing Jesus' parables were condemning them, the religious leaders wanted Jesus dead but feared a riot if they arrested Him.

Message & Application 💻=🌎

- ❖ Shows rather than get offended & hurt when God's word exposes our sins, see it as helping us to recognize our need to repent and change.
- ❖ Warns how we can't be seeking God and His truth, and then reject it when it gets too personal, too uncomfortable, or too convicting.
- ❖ Calls for staying more in tune with God's will, and less governed and controlled by peoples opinions and views.
- ❖ Calls for being less concerned about our own comfort and more obedient to God's will regardless of what it might cost us personally.
- ❖ Displays how Godly counsel often passes unheeded by those who have already hardened their hearts against the truth.
- ❖ Teaches how men often try to stifle their consciences by removing the burden of their guilt and accountability. (A guilty conscience needs no accusers!).
- ❖ Teaches how men can be more in fear of the social and political repercussions of their sins than the eternal consequences.
- ❖ Displays how God has many ways of restraining the wicked plans of others for our own protection. (V. 46)
- ❖ Teaches how the best way to come to Christ's defense is to live life's of honor and obedience to Him. (V. 46)
- ❖ Teaches how only by being open & public in our support of ministers, can we protect their characters and reputations. (V. 46b)

🗝 Even today when God confronts us with a truth about ourselves or exposes something in our lives that's out of character with His word. Do we get angry and ignore it, or explain it away as not applying to us, or do we confess it and get rid of it?

☞ Today as so often happens many Christians passively tolerate flagrant sins and blatant untruths out of fear of being too controversial or too political, that the confrontations and fallouts are just not worth it.

Chapter Twenty Two

Religious Leaders Controversies with Jesus

- **"Wedding Banquet"-**Parable teaching on Israel's rejection of the Gospel, Salvation now goes to the Gentiles.-(Vs. 1-14)
- **Paying Taxes to Caesar**.-Religious leaders attempt to trap Jesus into appearing seditious towards Rome.-(Vs. 15-22)
- **Marriage at the Resurrection-** The Sadducees attempt to discredit Jesus concerning the resurrection-(Vs. 23-33)
- **Greatest Commandment-** Religious leaders attempt to discredit Jesus by drawing Him into unsolvable debate- (Vs. 34-39)
- **Whose Son is the Christ-**Jesus confronts the religious as to the Messiah's origins.- (Vs. 40-46)

The Parable of the Wedding Banquet

22:1 Jesus spoke to them again in parables, saying:
2 "The kingdom of heaven (Metph-Gospel dispensation) **is like a king who prepared a wedding banquet for his son.** (Metph.-Jesus)
3 He sent his servants to those who had been invited to the banquet to tell them to come, but they refused to come. (Expresses: Insolence, ingratitude)
4 "Then he sent some more servants and said, 'Tell those who have been invited that I have prepared my dinner: My oxen and fattened cattle have been slaughtered, and everything is ready. Come to the wedding banquet."
5 "But they paid no attention (Expresses indifference) **and went off—one to his field, another to his business.** (Expresses-Put worldly concerns/values first)
6 The rest seized his servants, ill-treated them (e.g. Peter & the Apostles-{Acts 5:17-41}) **and killed them.** (e.g. Stephen-{Acts 7:54-60}, James-{Acts 12:1-2})
7 The king was enraged. He sent his army and destroyed those murderers and burned their city. (Fulfilled by Rome in destroying of Jerusalem in A.D. 70.)
8 "Then he said to his servants, 'The wedding banquet is ready, but those I invited did not deserve to come. (Suggests: Unmoved by faith & repentance.)
9 Go to the street corners and invite to the banquet anyone you find.'
10 So the servants went out into the streets and gathered all the people they could find, both good and bad, and the wedding hall was filled with guests.
11 But when the king came in to see the guests, he noticed a man there who was not wearing wedding clothes. (Metph.-Robe of faith and righteousness.)
12 'Friend,' he asked, 'how did you get in here without wedding clothes?' The man was speechless. (Suggests: Having no excuse or defense, convicted.)
13 "Then the king told the attendants, (Metph-Angels) **'Tie him hand and foot, and throw him outside, into the darkness,** (Metph-Hell) **where there will be weeping and gnashing of teeth.'**(Expresses sorrow, remorse, pain, anger.)
14 "For many are invited, (called-K.J.V.) **but few are chosen."**

(For Interpretation & Application see following Pg. 321)

Israel having neglected to respond to the Gospel's invitation, God now extends Salvation to the Gentiles.

Message & Application

- ❖ Shows how believers are expected to respond to God's Saving grace with a life of faithful and obedient living. (cf. Rom. 6:13, Rev. 19:7-8)
- ❖ Warns against dishonoring all that God has done and provided for us in thinking we have more important things to attend and pursue.
- ❖ Teaches how God's provision of Salvation is tailored-fit for everyone, covering up any sin, shame, guilt, or wound.
- ❖ Warns against treating the things of God lightly or with indifference by choosing our own ways. (cf. Rom. 2:4-29, Rev. 3:15-16)
- ❖ Warns against thinking we can accept God's offer of Salvation and yet go on living according to our own terms and conditions.
- ❖ Teaches how Salvation is not a free ticket to live as you please but must prove itself genuine through holy living. (cf. Eph. 5:25-27)

–***Many invited, but few are chosen***-Expresses the "General call" of sinners to Salvation through the Gospel, but who fail to heed the call by way of faith, repentance, and righteous living.

⊶ Even today many people can display the same attitude when they hear the Gospel, but ignore it by putting more concern in pursuing everyday activities of work, school, and careers. Or they put off Church, bible study, and prayer by making up excuses for being too busy or too tired.

➢ Additional lessons drawn from parable:
- God's impartiality, extending Salvation to all people regardless of race, gender, social status, or character.
- God's love, patience, and provision in not wanting any to be lost, but for all to come to repentance & Salvation.
- God expects Salvation to be evidenced by a life of repentance and obedient living.

Allegorical Types

King....................= God.
Wedding banquet... .= Gospel invitation, eternal life, Messianic banquet.
Son......................= Jesus.
First guests............. = Jewish religious leaders.
Second guests.......... = Gentiles, Sinners, You.
Wedding clothes......= Righteousness, holiness, faith, Salvation, repentance, good works.

From this verse here (V. 15) to verse (V. 22) the Religious leaders attempt to trap Jesus in making Him appear seditious towards Rome.

Paying Taxes to Caesar-(N.I.V.)

22:15 Then the Pharisees went out and laid plans to trap him in his words. (entangle-K.J.V.-3802-*To ensnare, entrap, provoke, to make an elicit remark.)*
16 They sent their disciples to him (Suggests: To look less like tempters and more like sincere learners.) **along with the Herodians.**–(Suggests: Supporters of Rome who would report any seditious remarks made by Jesus to the authorities.) **"Teacher," they said, "we know you are a man of integrity** (Expresses a false sense of flattery meant to butter Jesus up into answering their question.) **and that you teach the way of God in accordance with the truth. You aren't swayed by men because you pay no attention to who they are.** (Expresses one who is impartial, uninfluenced by threats of power, doesn't play favorites, calls it like it is. Modern cliché "To call a spade a spade".)
17 Tell us then, what is your opinion? Is it right to pay taxes to Caesar or not?" (i.e. An annual census-tax paid by Jews to Rome. Was not a legal question, but a moral one in paying tribute to a pagan god. Was meant to trap Jesus in a dilemma. That if Jesus acknowledged that it was "lawful", He would appear unpatriotic, losing His popularity with the people. Or if Jesus said it was "unlawful", He would appear seditious towards Rome, resulting in His arrest.)

The Pharisees attempt to trap Jesus in appearing either unpatriotic to Israel or seditious towards Rome.

Message & Application =

- ❖ Shows how believers should be seeking God for truth, and not trying to justify some sin, or see what we can get away with.
- ❖ Warns against praising Jesus' wisdom and greatness while having no real heart or interest in following His teachings and advice.
- ❖ Calls for being people of integrity, that we're standing on the truth of God's word no matter what others may think or say about us.
- ❖ Warns against allowing others to butter us up to the point that we start to compromise the Word of God just to make them feel good.
- ❖ Teaches those who pay excessive flattery usually have ulterior motives in mind. (Don't fall prey to false praise!). (V. 16. cf. Rom. 16:17-18)

⊶ Even today, believers need to see that we're staying true to scripture and not fudging on some sin. Thinking maybe we were too hard on ourselves, that God's word wasn't prohibiting this as I thought it once did. Or maybe I shouldn't allow this to violate my conscience as I did before.

22:18 But Jesus, knowing their evil intent, (maliciousness) **said You hypocrites** (See 15:7) **why are you trying to trap me?** (i.e. Ensnare, trip-up, corner, etc.)
19 Show me the coin used for paying the tax. They brought him a denarius-◙ (i.e. A Roman silver coin worth about a day's wage for a common laborer. By asking for the coin Jesus exposes their hypocrisy, that by having Cesar's coin on them it was they, not Him, who were collaborating with a pagan government.)
20 and he asked them, "Whose portrait is this? And whose inscription?"-◙ (Suggests: A portrait of "Tiberius Cesar" with the subscription: *"Tiberius Caesar Son of the Divine Augustus"*. Reverse side: *"Pontifex Maximus High Priest".)*
21 "Caesar's" they replied. Then he said to them give to Caesar what is Caesar's, (Taxes, civil-obedience, honor, respect) **and to God what is God's.** (Heart, worship, love, praise, devotion, submission, obedience, soul, self, etc.)
22 When they heard this, they were amazed. So they left him and went away. (Expresses defeat, humiliation, shame, disappointment.)

Jesus avoids the trap by showing how they were obligated to obey both God and Government.

<u>Message & Application</u> 💻=🌎

- ❖ Shows how we bear duel citizenships, having both a civil obligation to the state, but more importantly a spiritual & moral obligation to God.
- ❖ Teaches though we live in the world our ultimate devotion is to God having been made in His image and likeness. (cf. Gen. 1:26-27)
- ❖ Teaches how its every believers duty to be good citizens and witnesses in all spheres of life that God ordains. (cf. Rom. 13:1-8, 1-Pet. 2:12-17)
- ❖ Calls for getting our priorities straight that we march to a different drummer and answer to a higher authority and calling.
- ❖ Teaches those who find their ultimate value and hope in God nothing will be an issue or too hard to submit, surrender, or get along with.
- ⊶ Even today, believers can have both earthly responsibilities when it comes to work & paying the bills. And spiritual responsibilities when it comes to matters of faith and practice. That yes, we may have to support and feed ourselves, but were not going to bend to what culture dictates, or sell out our integrity and Christian morals/values just in order to fit in and go along with the crowd. (cf. Eph. 6:12, Col. 3:2-5)
- ☞ Jesus is not just calling believers to be good citizens in paying our taxes or the need for separation of Church & State. But rather it's about knowing where the world's claims end and where God's begins!
- ☞ For the most part, there is usually no conflict between the believer's duty to "Government" and duty to "God". Only when those loyalties conflict are believers to obey God! (Acts 4:19-20, Ex. 1:15-21, Dan 3:1-18)

From this verse here (V. 23) to verse (V. 33) the Sadducee's attempt to discredit Jesus concerning the resurrection.

Marriage at the Resurrection-(N.I.V.)

22:23 That same day the Sadducees, who say there is no resurrection, (i.e. No life after death. Suggests: A theology embraced due to its absence from the "Torah", first five books of Moses. {Gen-Deut.}) **came to him with a question.**
24 "Teacher," they said, "Moses told us that if a man dies without having children, his brother must marry the widow and have children for him. (Suggests: The Jewish marriage custom stipulating that it was the brother's responsibility in carrying on the family name and inheritance. {cf. Deut. 25:5-6})
25 Now there were seven brothers among us. The first one married and died, and since he had no children, he left his wife to his brother.
26 The same thing happened to the second and third brother, right on down to the seventh. (Suggests: Not literally, but hypothetically.)
27 Finally, the woman died.
28 Now then, at the resurrection, whose wife will she be of the seven, since all of them were married to her?" (Expresses not a sincere inquiry, but rather meant to discount the resurrection based on the absurdity and immoral dilemma it presented in a wife having seven husbands in the next life.)

Sadducees try to discredit Jesus on the resurrection by questioning the morality of a wife having seven husbands in the next life.

Message & Application 💻=🌎

❖ Shows how believers are to stand on the truth of God's word rather than try to find angles to reason it away or claim it doesn't apply to us.
❖ Warns against seeking inconsistencies in God's word as smokescreens in order to avoid our accountability and go on living as we please.
❖ Calls believers, rather than manipulate our way around the hard parts of God's word, seek to find out what it means and how to apply it!
❖ Teaches instead of sitting in judgment over God's word, have the humility to accept God's infinite wisdom and not your own logic!
⊶ Even today we must always stand on the truth of scripture, that God's word always supersedes logic and reason. (Will you keep following God even if it doesn't always fit your rationale or pattern of thinking?).
☞ Today many try to justify their unbelief by raising bible discrepancies. Today it's: *"How could all the animals fit on Noah's Ark"* or "*Where did Adam's son Cain find a wife*", or *"How could a loving God destroy Canaan"*, or *"If God gives free will, what about Pharaoh"*?

22:29 Jesus replied, "You are in error because you do not know the Scriptures (i.e. The O.T.) **or the power of God.** (i.e. God's Omnipotence.)
30 At the resurrection people will neither marry nor be given in marriage; (i.e. Brides) **they will be like the angels in heaven.** (i.e. Immortal, spiritual.)
31 But about the resurrection of the dead—have you not read what God said to you, (i.e. God speaking to Moses via the burning bush.-{Ex. 3:4})
32 I am (Present tense) **the God of Abraham, the God of Isaac, and the God of Jacob He is not the God of the dead, but of the living.** (Suggests: When God spoke this to Moses, though the patriarchs had passed on, Abraham 300 years earlier, they were still alive and eternally present with God in heaven.)
33 When the crowds heard this, they were astonished at his teaching. (Suggests: At Jesus' wisdom, exegetical skills, and insight into the Torah.)

Jesus proves the resurrection on two accounts: God's omnipotent power and how its clearly taught in scripture.

Message & Application 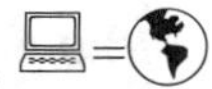

- ❖ Shows believers who are faithfully standing on God's word & power, nothing will seem too impossible or too difficult for God to do.
- ❖ Calls for seeing that we're appealing to scriptures when correcting the false views and doctrines of others, and not by our own arguments.
- ❖ Teaches the power and authority we give to God determines what we believe He can do, achieve, and accomplish in our lives. (V. 29)
- ➢ Even today no matter how hopeless & terminal things may look, know that God can take a dead marriage, relationship, job, career, child, and anything else and turn it around into something great. (Prov. 3:5-6)

-Like the angels in heaven-Variously interpreted as either:

- Believers will have no need for procreation.-(Gen. 1:28)
- Believers will no longer be lonely or need companionship, having a deeper relationship with God and others in heaven.-(Gen. 2:18)
- Believers will no longer have carnal & fleshy interests/desires, having been raised a spiritual body.-(Rom. 14:17, 1-Corn. 15:35-50)

☞ Jesus is not saying family relations will not exist, or that we will have no distinct memories or personalities. But is simply teaching how we must not think of heaven as merely an extension of this life here.

Questions & Areas of conflict:

1) Paying Taxes- (Vs. 15-22)	Political
2) The Resurrection (Vs. 23-33)	Theological
3) #1 Commandment (Vs. 34-40)	Moral
4) Messiah's origins (Vs. 41-45)	Doctrinal

From this verse here (V. 34) to verse (V. 40) the Pharisees & Sadducees attempt to trap Jesus into an unsolvable religious debate.

The Greatest Commandment-(N.I.V.)

22:34 Hearing that Jesus had silenced, (i.e. muzzled, routed, checkmated.) **the Saddducees, the Pharisees got together.** (i.e. Having seen the Sadducees defeated by Jesus, they began plotting their own strategies for ensnaring Him.)
35 One of them, an expert in the law, (One who was learned & skilled in the Law of Moses.) **tested him** (3985-*To ensnare, trap, trip up)* **with this question:**
36 "Teacher, which is the greatest (Syn.-weightier, important) **commandment in the Law?"**(first five books of Moses. Not a sincere inquiry, but was meant to make Jesus appear incompetent in solving a debate that had perplexed other Rabbis. Or to catch Jesus in elevating one commandment over another.)

The Pharisees try to trap Jesus into an unsolvable debate over which commandments were the most important in the law.

Message & Application 💻=🌎

- ❖ Shows how we're to be seeking to better follow & obey God, and not just trying to win an argument that we were right and they were wrong.
- ❖ Warns how spiritual victories and breakthroughs are usually followed by demonic forces who will try to take us down. (V. 34, cf. 1-Pet. 5:8-9)
- ❖ Teaches how truth often gets lost when we're only trying to show someone up. (See that your real motive is about truth, not pride!).
- ❖ Reminds believers rather than worrying about what we should not do, we should be thinking about how to better display God's love.

–***Which is the greatest commandment***-Rabbis had listed some 613 commandments into two categories, the weightier (248) and lighter (365). The debate was whether the important ones were ceremonial (Sacrifices, circumcision, ritual purity, Sabbath keeping) or Moral (stealing, coveting, adultery). Others suggest the debate was between the Oral Tradition & written Law of Moses. Or between the first half of the Ten Commandments & second half of the Ten commandments.

⊶ Even today when it comes to religion many want everything to be boiled down to one simple formula/rule they can easily follow without having to give their hearts fully over to God and all that He requires.

☞ Today Church's can get into the same habit of splitting hairs over the technicalities of religious observances. Today it's: *"Should baptism be by immersion or sprinkling"*? Or *"Should Worship be contemporary or traditional"*? Or *"Should women or just men be Pastors"*? Or *"Should modern bible translations be used or just the K.J.V."*? etc.

22:37 Jesus replied: Love (Syn.-worship, cherish, embrace) **the Lord your God with all your heart** (Syn.-affections, emotions, desires) **and with all your soul** (Syn.-will, purpose, drive, inner-being.) **and with all your mind.**-{Deut.6:4-5} Syn.-thoughts, choices, determination, resolve. With all of your Strength.-{Mark 12:30}-Syn.-money, power, wealth, talents, gifts, resources, time, abilities, etc. Expresses: Taken together to love God with every fiber & core of one's being.)
38 This is the first and greatest commandment.
39 And the second is like it: 'Love (25-*Grk-"Agape", active-love, self-giving, unconditional-love.*) **your neighbor** (Syn.-fellow being, sphere of influence) **as yourself.'**-{Lev. 19:18} (Expresses a redemptive love that treats others with the same affection, kindness, and consideration as you would like to be treated.)
40 All the Law and the Prophets (Expresses: Taken together the entire O.T. As to the Law; The spirit in which it was given. And the Prophets, by their call for maintaining justice, mercy, and charity.–{Jer. 7:5) **hang on** (Syn.-Hinges, springs, rooted, based on.) **these two commandments."** (Suggests: All underlining principles of God's commandments can be traced to this one rule of "Love"!)

Jesus displays how loving God & others is the greatest commandment because it embodies all other commandments.

Message & Application 💻=🌎

❖ Shows how loving God with all of our being & everything we do is to be the first and foremost priority in life. (cf. Rom. 12:1-2, 2-Corn. 5:14-15)
❖ Calls for seeing that every aspect of our lives, choices, and decisions are a reflection of God's honor and glory in mind. (cf. 1-Corn.10:31)
❖ Teaches how our relationship with God is both vertical and horizontal, that our love for God will flow out in our love for others. (1-John 4:20)
❖ Teaches those who put the love of God and others as a first principle, all other obedience's, charities, and mercies will naturally follow.
❖ Teaches only when we put our energy into loving God first, they'll be no room in our lives for idols, hatred, envy, or bitterness.
❖ Calls for a love that always puts the interests and welfare of others first. (If you truly loved your neighbor as yourself you wouldn't sleep with his wife, steal from him, lie to him, or hurt him!).(cf. Rom. 13:8-10)

⊶ Even today, believers who love God with all their heart, mind, and soul, will be less consumed with the worldly things of T.V., Internet, video games, Facebook, sports, etc. and more filled with the things of God, bible study, church, witnessing, and ministering to others. (cf. Rom. 8:4-6, Col. 3:1-2, Eph. 4:17-24, 1-John 2:15-16)

☞ The love Jesus is asking for here is never within one's own strength. But comes with the Holy Spirit's help in reshaping and transforming us, gradually chiseling away the rough and hard areas of our hearts.

Whose Son Is the Christ?-(N.I.V.)

22:41 While the Pharisees were gathered together Jesus asked them,
42 "What do you think about the Christ?{16:16} **Whose son is he?" "The son of**
David," they replied. (Expresses a Messianic title signifying the Messiah's royal
descent and Kingly status.-{2-Sam.7:12-14} A correct but incomplete answer.)
43 He said to them, "How is it then that David, speaking by the Spirit,
(i.e. Inspiration of the Holy Spirit) **calls him 'Lord'? For he says,**
44 The LORD (03068-*"Jehova/Yahweh"* i.e. God) **said to my Lord:** (2962-*"Adonai", God, Master.* i.e. Jesus) **"Sit at my right hand** (Expresses-Divine honor/authority. Fulfilled in Jesus' resurrection & ascension into heaven.) **until I put your enemies under your feet.**-{Ps. 110:1} (Metph.-Victory/Rulership. To be fulfilled at Jesus' second coming and ultimate victory over sin & death.)
45 If then David calls him 'Lord', (i.e. God/Divine) **how can he be his son?"**
(Suggests: If David attributes deity to Him, He must be more than human!)

By quoting David's Psalm Jesus proves His Divine Sonship as Lord & God!

Message & Application

- ❖ Shows believers the need to take Jesus' divine authority & nature to its logical conclusion or we can come up short in our walk & devotion
- ❖ Calls for keeping a right perspective of Jesus as the only One who can rescue us from our sins, solve our problems, and meet our every need.
- ❖ Teaches rather than force our point of view, sometimes it's better to reason with others, allowing them to see the failure in their own logic.
- ❖ Calls for seeing scripture as nothing less than the divinely inspired and authoritative word of God for our lives. (cf. 2-Pet. 1:19-21)

⊶ Even today we can make the same mistake in only looking at Jesus in one dimension, as a loving and forgiving person who died on the Cross for our sins. Without also understanding Jesus' divine Lordship as the One who is interceding for us, who answers our prayers, and is involved in our lives!

☞ This question here is of great importance, for what you think of Jesus will determine how you live your life. Take a "Low" view of Jesus and you'll always struggle, questioning Jesus' faithfulness & goodness. Or take a "High" view of Jesus and you'll give yourself freely, joyfully, and fully to Him!

➢ The quoting of Psalm 110:1 draws out several implications:
  - Confirms the Holy Spirit's role in the divine inspiration of scripture.
  - Confirms the Messianic fulfillment of Jesus' Divinity & Lordship.
  - Confirms the Trinity, God the Father, the Son, and the Holy Spirit.

22:46 No-one (i.e. Religious leaders) **could say a word in reply, and from that day on** (Expresses: Having failed to catch Jesus at His words, they would from this point on secretly plot His death.) **no-one dared** (durst-K.J.V.-5111-*To be bold, courageous.* Syn.-Challenge, test, confront.) **to ask him any more questions.** (Suggests: Fearing Jesus' wisdom, they dare not enter into further debates with Him, least He become more convincing and they more indictable. The crowd listened to him with delight-{Mark 12:37b} and the common people heard him gladly.-K.J.V.-Expresses unlike the religious elite who were too proud, the humble were willing to place their faith in Christ.)

The Pharisees saw their dilemma, either acknowledge the deity of Jesus or confess their own ignorance.

<u>**Message & Application**</u> 💻=🌎

❖ Shows believers how pride & stubbornness of heart can cause us to miss out on the truth of Jesus and all that He is.
❖ Teaches rather than become defensive to the truth that God is revealing to us, be willing to submit and accept correction!
❖ Calls for standing in agreement with what the Lord says about us, even if it's not what we expected.
❖ Warns against going to God for questions and advice, and then not listen to the answer He gives us just because it's not to our liking.
❖ Teaches instead of walking away we must be willing to confront the hard truths about ourselves if we're going to be changed by Jesus.
❖ Warns against allowing tough questions and unanswerable issues to sidetrack us from moving forward in our faith and walk with God.
❖ Teaches how we don't have to have all the answers and understand everything, we just have to believe and follow through.

–***No one could say a word in reply***-Not that they were unable to answer, or were completely confounded by such a deep question. But rather were afraid to take Jesus' reasoning to the logical conclusion, that Jesus must also be Divine!

🗝 Even today, believers have only two choices. Either we can become "Prideful & Defensive" and miss the truth of what God is trying to tell us. Or we can come "Honest & Humble", accepting the truth and be changed by it! (Know the decision is all yours and no one else's!).

☞ Sadly today many respond in the same way to their own loss. That they can be awestruck but not converted, silenced but not convicted, humiliated but not humbled, reluctantly impressed yet unbelieving.

☞ This would be Jesus' last debate with the religious leaders, now going over their heads directly to the people. (e.g. Chap. 23)

Chapter Twenty Three

Denunciations against the Religious Leaders

- **Warning** -Against religion that does not practice what it preaches**.** Or makes a show of piety.-(Vs. 1-12)
- **Woe # 1-**Denunciation against religion that hinders others from following God**.**-(Vs.13-14)
- **Woe # 2-**Denunciation against religion that converts people only to corrupt them later.-(V 15)
- **Woe # 3-**Denunciation of religion that makes distinctions in God's word when its handy.- (Vs. 16-22)
- **Woe # 4-**Denunciation against religion that puts more emphasis on rituals than moral virtues.(Vs. 23-24)
- **Woe # 5-**Denunciation against religion that appears righteously outwardly, but lacks inward reality. -(Vs. 25-26)
- **Woe # 6-**Denunciation against religion that appears pious but is superficial in character-(Vs. 27-28)
- **Woe # 7-**Denunciation against religion that holds a double standard-(Vs. 29-32)

23:1 Then Jesus said to the crowds and to his disciples:
2 The teachers of the law and the Pharisees sit in Moses' seat.-◙(Stone seat in a Synagogue. Official successors who taught and interpreted the Law of Moses.)
3 So you must obey them and do everything they tell you. But do not do what they do, for they do not practice what they preach. (Suggests: They talked the talk but did not walk the walk, that they never lived it out in practice.)
4 They tie up (obligate, force) **heavy loads**(legalistic rules) **and put them on men's shoulders, but they themselves are not willing to lift a finger to move them.** (Expresses their insensitivity in even making the slightest effort to help others. They pressed rules that they were unwilling to observe themselves.)

The religious leaders proclaimed to teach the way of God's word & truth but lacked the character and integrity that go's with it.

<u>Message & Application</u> 

- ❖ Shows believers the need for a life that goes beyond just talk & show, to one that is lived out in life and practice.
- ❖ Teaches how believers can still follow good teaching even if it's being poorly carried out by hypocrites and bad ministers. (V. 3)
- ❖ Warns against religion that piles on the sin of failure and inadequacy while offering no remedy or cure. (It's easy to make a person feel guilty, but can you make them feel loved and forgiven by God?)
- ❖ Warns how we can set others up for failure when we load them down with guilt and condemnation, with no offer of hope or forgiveness.

⊶ Even today believers can preach God's grace and then give very little of it to others. Or they can talk about God's mercy & love and then live a life that is marked by unforgiveness, criticism, and insensitivity!

23:5 "Everything they do (i.e. Religious observance, prayers, alms, fasting, etc.) **is done for men to see:** (Syn.-flaunt, for show-L.B.V.) **They make their phylacteries wide-◙** (5440-*An outpost, fortification, preservative, prayer boxes.* Suggests: The Pharisees made their prayer boxes larger than normal to make them appear more pious. Today its extra large bibles or crosses.) **and the tassels on their garments long;-◙** (Suggests: They made the tassels on their robes longer to show that they were more pious and religious than others.)
6 they love the place of honor at banquets and the most important seats in the synagogues;(Jewish house of worship. Suggests: Seats nearest the platform for the reading of the Law were usually reserved for distinguished guests.)
7 they love to be greeted (Syn.-honored, recognized) **in the market-places** (i.e. Publicly, openly) **and to have men call them 'Rabbi'.** (Syn.-professor, scholar, master-L.B.V., doctor and reverend-M.B.V. Expresses: Taken together they loved spiritual grandstanding and having a holier than thou status.)

The religious leaders are denounced for making a show of their piety in order to be praised and admired by others.

Message & Application 💻=🌎

- ❖ Shows believers how true religion is about worshipping & serving God, and not about gaining praise and recognition for ourselves.
- ❖ Teaches rather than seeking our own glory, see that you're doing things for God and His glory. (Draw men to God, not to self!).
- ❖ Warns against taking advantage of ones status in order to enjoy certain perks/honors. (Serve God out of love not out of preferential treatment).
- ❖ Calls believers in always serving in a way that puts all the focus and attention on God and not on ourselves.

–***Phylacteries-***A small wooden box or leather pouch (1 ½' x 4') in which verses of O.T. Scriptures were kept. These boxes were usually worn on the forehead or left arm. The custom was instituted based on the literal reading of such passages as Ex. 13:9 and Deut. 6:8, 11:18.

-***Tassels on their garments long-***Loose threads (blue & white woven together) that hung down diagonally from the four corners of one's outer robe, serving as memory prods to remind the Jew of God's law. The custom was instituted in compliance to passages as Numb. 15:37-41.

🗝 Even today, believers need to be careful against thinking we're more spiritual than others just because we carry bigger bibles, lead a prayer group, head a bible study, or serve on the church board.

☞ Jesus is not here condemning all religious ceremonies or ornaments e.g. Crosses, fish symbols, bumper stickers, angel pins, etc. But only the ostentatious display of such ornaments in order to impress others.

23:8 "But you are not to be called 'Rabbi', (4461-*My master, great one.* Syn.-guru, spiritual guide) **for you have only one Master** (i.e. Christ Jesus Himself.) **and you are all brothers.** (Expresses spiritual equality & standing before God.)
9 And do not call anyone on earth 'father', (Expresses in the spiritual sense, e.g. Spiritual leader.) **for you have one Father,** (i.e. God) **and he is in heaven.**
10 Nor are you to be called 'teacher', for you have one Teacher, the Christ.

Believers are not to get caught up in the importance of titles & positions or allow others to put us on a pedestal.

Message & Application 💻=🌎

❖ Shows how believers are not to accept exalted titles & honors or allow ourselves to be worshiped and praised by those we lead.
❖ Reminds believers how God is the Author and Sustainer of our faith, not some preacher, teacher, or evangelist! (cf. 1-Corn. 3:4-23, Heb. 12:2)
❖ Teaches how true leaders will always point to Jesus as the source of all wisdom, authority, and truth, and not themselves! (cf. 1-Corn. 11:1)
❖ Warns against giving undue spiritual authority to any Church leader as if they were the sole source of all truth rather than God.
⊶ Even today, believers are to make God our sole authority and spiritual source of all strength and truth, and not that of men!
☞ Jesus is not saying here that believers cannot call a parent or priest father (Roman Catholics). But rather we are not to give the same spiritual distinction and honor that belongs only to God!
☞ Jesus is not speaking out against Church titles as Pastor, Bishop, Deacon, etc. But only the spiritual pride that accompanies such titles.

23:11 The greatest among you will be your servant. (Syn.-minister, deacon)
12 For whoever exalts himself (Syn.-praises, prides) **will be humbled, and whoever humbles himself will be exalted.** (Expresses a spiritual principle that the way to glory and true life is humbling serving and helping others.)

True greatness in discipleship is measured not by titles & status, but by humility and service.

Message & Application 💻=🌎

❖ Shows believers how greatness in God's Kingdom is not measured by power & status, but about humility and service to others.
❖ Calls for putting the service of others before our own honor and reputation. (Be willing to serve whether anyone notices it or not).
⊶ Even today a heart that is given over to the service and needs of others will keep us from a life of pridefulness in only focusing on ourselves.

From this verse here (V. 13) to verse (V. 33) Jesus gives Seven Warnings against false and hypocritical religion.

Seven Woes-(N.I.V.)

23:13 "Woe to you (Expresses a mixture of sorrow, grief, pity, doom.) **teachers of the law and Pharisees, you hypocrites!** (5273-*Play actor who wore a mask to portray a character in a play.*) **You shut the kingdom of heaven** (Metph-Gospel of Christ. Taken away the key to knowledge.-{cf. Luke 11:52}) **in men's faces.** (Suggests: By their false doctrines, legalistic rules, and hypocritical practices. Or kept people from receiving Jesus as the Messiah/Divine.-{9:33-34}) **You yourselves do not enter, nor will you let those enter who are trying to.**
14 Woe unto you, scribes & Pharisees, hypocrites! For ye devour widow's houses (Expresses how they would trick widows into signing over the title deed to their houses.) **and for a pretence** (show) **make long prayer:** (Suggests: For the purpose of appearing extremely sincere and devout, that they would never cheat anyone.) **therefore ye shall receive greater damnation** (K.J.V.-Not not found in the earliest or most authentic Grk. MSS. Expresses Jesus' denunciation of those who use religion for personal gain or to defraud people.)

The religious leaders are denounced for their hypocritical & legalistic religion that hindered others from coming to Jesus.

Message & Application

- Shows how legalistic religion can make it seem God's impossible to please, His commands difficult to obey, heaven an unattainable goal.
- Warns how we can turn people off from coming to the faith when we present God as a severe judge who leaves no room for mercy or grace.
- Warns how legalism can make it seem God is harsh and overbearing, or that God is simply a taskmaster who requires perfection.
- Calls for preaching a Gospel that is easy for sinners to accept without putting up a lot of roadblocks and hoops for them to jump through.
- Calls for always making it about a God who loves and forgives people and not One who is there to give them rules that they can't keep.
- Warns how we can drive people away from coming to Jesus when we come across as self-righteous, judgmental, and unforgiving.
- Even today, believers need to be aware of Church's that preach on everything else, but never on sin, grace, repentance, or how to be Saved. Or who preach a Gospel that says unless you worship on a certain day, dress a certain way, eat a certain way, be baptized a certain way, read a certain bible, tithe a certain amount, or speak in tongues you can't be Saved! (cf. Gal. 4:9-10)

23:15 "Woe to you, teachers of the law and Pharisees, you hypocrites! {V.13} **You travel over land and sea** (Metph.-Spared no pains, energy, or effort, went to the ends of the earth, etc.) **to win** (i.e. Gain) **a single convert,** (proselyte-K.J.V.-4339-*Gentile convert to Judaism.* Suggests: They were only looking for people to convert to their religion/party.) **and when he becomes one, you make him twice as much a son of hell** (Expresses a candidate worthy of going to hell.) **as you are.** (Suggests: Because their converts hung on to their old Pagan practices while adopting the Pharisees hypocritical & legalistic practices. Or that their converts were better than the Pharisees at legalism.)

The religious leaders are denounced for converting a person only to corrupt them later by their own hypocritical and legalistic practices.

Message & Application 💻=🌍

- ❖ Shows how believers are to see that we're winning souls over to Jesus, and not over to a religion of rule keeping and work-righteousness.
- ❖ Teaches rather than being more concerned about trying to get people to our Church, bring them into a Saving relationship with Jesus.
- ❖ Warns the dangers of misdirected zeal. (Win sinners over to Jesus, and not over to some denomination, program, church, or preacher).
- ❖ Teaches how it's about bringing people into a relationship with Jesus, not about getting them to be just like us or doing Church our way.
- ⊶ Even today, believers need to see that we're bringing people into a Saving relationship with Jesus, and not just about adding numbers to our Church, notches to our belts, or filling the pews to pay the bills.
- ☞ Jesus is not criticizing the religious leaders for their evangelistic zeal, but rather of perverting their converts by their legalistic practices.

Signs that you may be a Legalistic Pharisee:

- You are overly critical of other Christians who don't worship, dress, or act as you do.
- You base your Salvation on works rather than on Jesus.
- You think that showing up to Church every Sunday and tithing makes you right with God.
- You only read the bible to confirm & support your position, rather than allowing it to reshape you.
- You get angry & offended when someone tries to correct you in an area where you're wrong.
- You only see your church, denomination, and bible as the only right one and everybody else's as wrong.

23:16 "Woe (See V. 13) **to you, blind guides!** (Metph-false spiritual leaders) **You say, 'If anyone swears by the temple,-◙ it means nothing; but if anyone swears by the gold of the temple, he is bound by his oath.'**
17 You blind fools! (3474-*"Moros", Spiritually slow of heart.* Syn.-Morons) **Which is greater: the gold, or the temple that makes the gold sacred?**
18 You also say, 'If anyone swears by the altar,-◙ it means nothing; but if anyone swears by the gift on it, he is bound by his oath.' (he is guilty-K.J.V.)
19 Blind men Which is greater: the gift or the altar that makes the gift sacred
20 Therefore, he who swears by the altar, swears by it and everything on it.
21 And he who swears by the temple, swears by the one who dwells in it.
22 And he who swears by heaven, swears by God's throne and by the one who sits on it. (i.e. All oaths ultimately relate to God in one way or another.)

The religious leaders are denounced for making fine distinctions in God's word in order to get around from having to fully obey it.

Message & Application 💻=🌎

- ❖ Shows believers rather than live a life that is full of concession and compromise, have a heart that wants to stay true to God and His word!
- ❖ Teaches rather than look for angles & loopholes in getting away with as much as possible, have a heart that is staying accountable to God.
- ❖ Warns believers rather than trivialize and downplay God's word, we need to take it at face-value and live by it without excuse!
- ❖ Warns rather than rationalizing and excusing what we know is right, have the integrity in staying authentic and real with God.

🗝 Even today we play the same games with the commands of God. That what God has said in the past doesn't really apply today. Or we shade bible truths in order to cling to some sin. Or we make excuses in order to give ourselves a pass, saying things like *"I know I should give more to the Church, but I'm on a tight budget"*. Or *"We like to do more in ministry but were not that gifted or our work schedule won't allow it"*.

☞ Jesus is not simply calling for keeping oaths. But is warning against what's called "Casuistry". Which uses clever reasoning techniques to trick oneself in justifying some wrong action and feel good about it.

Other excuses believers often use:

- "I know I should be nice at work, but I'm just under a lot of pressure lately".
- "I know I should pray and read God's word more, but there's just not enough time in the day".
- "I know I should share my faith more, but I'm just too shy".

23:23 "**Woe-**{V. 13} **to you, teachers of the law and Pharisees, you hypocrites! You give a tenth** (i.e. To tithe 10% of one's income to God.) **of your spices—mint,-◙ dill,-◙ and cummin.-◙** (Tiny garden herbs. Expresses their meticulous observances in the smallest of details and minute matters.) **But you have neglected the more important matters of the law—justice,** (Syn.-fairness, quality, impartial) **mercy** (Syn.-Love, kindness, compassion.) **and faithfulness.** (i.e. Love for God or fidelity to one's promises.) **You should have practiced the latter, without neglecting the former.** (i.e. Both should have been practiced.)
24 You blind guides! (Metph-false spiritual leaders.) **You strain out a gnat-◙** (i.e. Any species of tiny flying insects.) **but swallow a camel** (Expresses the practice of filtering wine through a cloth or clinched teeth in order to sift out the smallest of unclean insects.-(Lev. 11:23) Metph.-One who can be so focused on avoiding the smallest of sins, they unwittingly commit even greater sins.)

The religious leaders are denounced for being more scrupulous in their religious practices & observance than on moral virtues.

Message & Application =

- ❖ Shows how believers can get so focused on the meticulous details of religion that they miss the heart behind it all. (cf. Matt. 5:20 Mic. 6:8)
- ❖ Displays how some can get wrapped up in the trivial and minor points of religion that they begin to lose sight of what really matters.
- ❖ Warns how getting sidetracked in the details & minutia can cause us to miss the great realities of the faith, that it's about Jesus, not religion!
- ❖ Teaches how people should remember us for our love, compassion, and generosity, and not for our religious zeal or Church attendance.
- ❖ Warns how religion is worthless if it's not making us more loving, kind, and compassionate people on the inside! (cf. 1-Corn. 13:1-8)
- ❖ Displays how many can wear they're Jesus crosses and hats without it being matched in a life of love for people or the way they treat others!
- ❖ Warns against fooling ourselves in thinking that obedience in one area excuses or justifies disobedience in another area.
- ❖ Calls for asking what's driving our lives, is it our religious observances, or is it wanting to look more and more like Jesus?
- ❖ Teaches how the devil doesn't have a problem with all the religious external stuff we do, so long as we don't have that vibrant relationship that is truly following and living for the Lord. (cf. 2-Corn. 11:3)

⊶ Even today, believers can take great care and attention in doing all the religious things, go to Church weekly, pay their tithes, attend prayer meetings, listen to Christian music, etc. While the rest of the time their gossiping about others, or their abusive to their wives, harsh to their children, cold to their neighbor, and horrible to their employees.

23:25 "Woe-{V. 13} **to you, teachers of the law and Pharisees, you hypocrites! You clean the outside of the cup and dish,** (Metph-outward conduct, behavior) **but inside they are full of greed** (extortion-K.J.V.-724-*Plunder, rob, rape.* Syn.-cheat, fleece, defraud, swindle.) **and self-indulgence.** (excess-K.J.V.-192-*lack of restraint, self-control.* The unrestrained pleasure and pursuits of pleasing self.)
26 Blind Pharisee! (Metph-false spiritual leaders.) **First clean the inside of the cup and dish,-◙** (Metph-heart, character.) **and then the outside** (i.e. Conduct and behavior.) **also will be clean.**
27 "Woe to you, teachers of the law and Pharisees, you hypocrites! You are like whitewashed tombs,-◙ (Expresses the practice of bleaching the outside of tombs in an effort to warn passerby's from becoming ceremonially unclean.) **which look beautiful on the outside** (i.e. Saintly, pious, righteous.) **but on the inside are full of dead men's bones and everything unclean.** (Expresses: Despite their religious display they were filled with corruption and hypocrisy.)
28 In the same way, on the outside (visibly, publicly) **you appear to people as righteous** (Holy/saintly) **but on the inside** (Privately) **you are full of hypocrisy** (Syn.-pretense, play acting) **and wickedness.** (Syn.-sin, corruption, immorality.)

The religious leaders are denounced for appearing righteous & pious outwardly while remaining wicked & sinful at heart.

Message & Application 💻=🌎

- ❖ Shows how God is more concerned with the inner character of the heart than with outward appearances & religious show. (1-Sam. 16:7)
- ❖ Warns, we might be able to fool people by putting on a good religious act, but we cannot fool God who sees the heart and real you!
- ❖ Teaches how God looks past our clothes, tithes, offerings, charity, and church attendance, to what's really going on in our hearts.
- ❖ Warns against thinking we can just polish up the outside with fancy clothes and fancy religion without ever really changing on the inside!
- ❖ Teaches if our hearts are right with God the rest will follow and take care of itself. (Know that image making begins from the inside out!).
- ❖ Teaches only by getting honest with God in cleaning up the inside first the outside won't come off as a sham!
- ❖ Warns rather than masking sin issues with good works, we need to get real with God about the dirt and filth that's going on the inside.

⊶ Even today, believers can go through the motions of looking and sounding holy. Go to Church regularly, wear the right clothes, say the right words, etc. All the while their cheating and defrauding other people. Or their drinking, partying and indulging in luxuries and lavish living. (cf. 1-Corn. 6:9-11, 2-Tim. 3:2-5, 1-Pet 2:11)

23:29 "Woe {V. 13} **to you, teachers of the law and Pharisees, you hypocrites! You build** (Syn.-rebuild, renovate, beautify) **tombs-◙** (5028-*Sepulcher, graves.* Syn.-memorials, monuments, shrines) **for the prophets** (Suggests: Martyred O.T. Prophets; e.g. Uriah-{Jeremiah-26: 20-24}, Zechariah-{2-Chron. 24:20-22}) **and decorate** (garnish-K.J.V. Syn.-beautify, maintain, repair, lay flowers on-L.B.V.) **the graves of the righteous.** (Suggests: Set up Memorials to honor O.T. Saints.)
30 And you say, (Suggests: As part of a commemoration speech.) **'If we had lived in the days of our forefathers,** (i.e. Ancestors) **we would not have taken part with them in shedding the blood** (Metph.-killing) **of the prophets.'** (Expresses a form of pride, self-righteousness, that they were above reproach.)
31 So you testify against yourselves that you are the descendants of those who murdered the prophets. (Suggests: Not literally, but rather as in spirit, attitude, and disposition. Modern cliché "Chips off the old block". That by decorating the tombs of the prophets they were unknowingly approving and condoning the crime of their forefathers! {cf. Luke 11:47-48})
32 Fill up, then, (i.e. Carry through, accomplish) **the measure of the sin** (Syn.-guilt) **of your forefathers!** (Expresses a prediction of their living up to their forefather's evil character and reputations by plotting to kill Jesus as well.)

The religious leaders professed themselves righteous yet were plotting to take Jesus' life.

Message & Application 💻=🌍

- ❖ Shows believers the dangers of overestimating our own goodness and righteousness, that we would never sin like other people.
- ❖ Displays the deceptive nature of the flesh in thinking we can keep God's Commandments when we really can't! (cf. Rom. 7:6-25)
- ❖ Teaches no matter how good a job we do in keeping all the rules, even on our best days we will always fall short. (cf. Rom. 3:23)
- ❖ Warns believers against trying to make ourselves feel better by minimizing our own sins by magnifying the sins of others.
- ❖ Warns against trying to build ourselves up by tearing others down. (Don't throw others under the bus just to make yourself look better)
- ❖ Teaches how it's not for us to find fault with others, but to understand our own failures, that we're no better than anyone else.
- ❖ Warns against thinking so smug & good of ourselves, that we have finally arrived and made it and don't need any more improvement.
- 🗝 Even today many can point out the sins & failures of others and say *"They would never do things like that"*. That they would never dress like that, talk like that, gossip like that, act like that, etc. All the while their taking in ungodly entertainment, movies, music, books, etc. that glorifies and celebrates the same kind of sin.

23:33 "You snakes! You brood of vipers!-◙ (Metph-deceptive, crafty, and malicious.) **How will you escape being condemned to hell?** (Suggests: As a result of their self-righteous views of themselves and rejection of Jesus. In a wider context all of mankind due to Adams & Eves fall in the garden of Eden.)
34 Therefore I am sending you prophets and wise men and teachers. Some of them you will kill (Fulfilled in Stephen being stoned.-{Acts 7:54-60} James being beheaded.{Acts 12:1-2})**and crucify;-◙**(Fulfilled in Peter being hung upside down on a cross.-{John 21:18}) **others you will flog-◙ in your synagogues and pursue from town to town.** (Fulfilled in Paul & Barnabas.-{Acts 8:3-4, 9:23-25, 13:52})
35 And so upon you will come all the righteous blood (Expresses: Judgments, due, accountability, guilt.) **that has been shed on earth, from the blood of righteous Abel** (i.e. Adams first son killed by Cain.-{Gen. 4:1-10}) **to the blood of Zechariah son of Barakiah,**-(Jehoiada-{2-Chron. 24:20} i.e. Last martyr.-{2-Chron. 24:20-22} Taken together the whole Hebrew Bible. From Genesis to 2-Chronicles, not Malachi.) **whom you murdered** (Stoned to death-{2-Chron.24:21}) **between the temple and the altar.-◙** (i.e. Outer courtyard of the priests that ran between the Temple and alter. Expresses not personally, but rather collectively, having the same heritage, disposition, attitude, and temperament.)
36 I tell you the truth, all this (i.e. Divine judgments.) **will come upon this generation.** (i.e. Jewish religious leaders, having culminated & exceeded them in guilt by shedding the most precious blood of all the Messiah, God's own Son!. Fulfilled 40 years later in the destruction of Jerusalem by Rome in 70 A.D.)

Because of Israel's rejection & killing of Christ, they will incur all the accumulation of Divine wrath since the beginning of the world.

Message & Applications

- Shows believers the love & patience of God in trying all ways to get us to repent of our sin & hypocrisy before it takes us straight to hell.
- Warns rather than ignore our hypocritical ways, or pretend sin doesn't exist, we need to acknowledge it openly and honestly to God.
- Teaches rather than get offended and hurt by those whom God sends to reprove us, have the courage to reform and accept correction.
- Teaches how sometimes the religious veneers need to be pulled away in order to keep us from going down a path of self-deception.
- Teaches how when the Lord exposes something that's not right in our lives, rather than become defensive have the heart to change!
- Reminds believers only when we face the real truth about ourselves can God's grace, mercy, and forgiveness begin to heal and change us.
- Even today, believers need to see that we're responding by taking action towards those false and hypocritical areas of our lives that God exposes, that we may confront and denounce it before it's too late!

23:37 "O Jerusalem, Jerusalem, (Expresses: The intense emotion and deep love of Jesus' heart for all people.) **you who kill the prophets** (i.e. O.T. Prophets, Uriah-{Jer. 26:23}) **and stone those sent to you,** (i.e. Zechariah.-{2-Chron. 24:21-22} Later Jesus' apostles, as in Stephen-{Acts. 7:54-60}, Paul-{Acts. 14:19} Expresses their habitual rejection of God's grace and numerous appeals to turn back to Him.) **how often I have longed to gather your children together,** (i.e. Israel/sinners.) **as a hen gathers her chicks under her wings,** (Expresses the custom of hens to shelter and protect their chicks in times of danger. Metph.-Jesus' tender love, care, and protection.) **but you were not willing.** (Expresses Israel's/sinners indifference and reluctance to come to Jesus for Salvation.)
38 Look, your house (Metph.-Temple, city, nation, life, soul.) **is left to you desolate.** (Expresses the danger of losing out on God's Saving grace by remaining in our unbelieving and self-righteous ways. In a wider context the Temples abandonment by God to the destruction of Rome fulfilled in 70 A.D.)
39 For I tell you, you will not see me again (i.e. Either the end of Jesus' public ministry or His departure by His death.) **until you say, 'Blessed is he who comes in the name of the Lord.'"** ({Ps. 118:26} Expresses Jesus' second coming, or until their ready to see Jesus for who He really is as Lord & Savior at their conversion. That this will be Jesus' last public appeal and warning to both Israel and us, that now is the day to cry out to Jesus for forgiveness and Salvation!)

Because of Israel's rejection of Jesus as Savior their Temple & Nation will be abandoned by God to the destruction of Rome.

Message & Application 

- ❖ Shows believers Jesus' willingness & readiness to forgive our rebellious and sinful ways if we will only turn to Him. (cf. 2-Pet. 3:9)
- ❖ Displays the gracious heart and love of God, that even in light of our hypocrisy and sin, He still wants to forgive us and Save us.
- ❖ Teaches how it breaks Jesus' heart when we fail to turn to Him, only to run headlong in our rebellious & sinful ways to our own destruction.
- ❖ Displays the patience and grace of God in wanting to turn us from our hypocritical ways before it's too late. (cf. Rom. 2:4-5)
- ❖ Warns how those who fail to turn to Jesus for Salvation do so at their own peril and choice! (Know the blame is not with God, but with us).
- ❖ Warns if not careful we can easily become callous & indifferent to our own sin/hypocrisy to the point that we no longer see a need to repent.
- ⊶ Even today when we feel there's a hypocritical & sinful area that's not right in our lives. Or we feel a disconnect between our motives and actions, or between our life and profession. Rather than continue to pretend it doesn't exist, we need to flee to the Lord for help in dealing and correcting those issues before we have to stand before Him.

Chapter Twenty Four

Jesus' Olivet Discourse

First 3 ½ years of the Tribulation

- The increase of false Messiah's claiming to be Christ.-(Vs. 4-5) (Church age)
- The increase in political upheavals/revolutions /world wars.-(Vs. 6-7 a) (Church age)
- The increase of natural disasters.-(V. 7 b) (Church age)
- World hatred against Christianity / Believers persecuted. -(V. 9)
- Apostasy within the Church / Many will turn from the faith.-(Vs. 10-13)
- Worldwide Evangelism of the Gospel.-(V. 14)

Second 3 ½ years of Great Tribulation

- Antichrist invades Jerusalem and desecrates the Temple.-(V. 15)
- Antichrist begins worldwide persecution of the Church-(Vs. 16-20)
- God pours out His wrath and judgments upon the earth-(Vs. 21-22)
- False reports of Christ's Second Coming-(Vs. 23-26)
- Christ's return will be sudden, self-evident, and universal.-(Vs. 27-31)
- **"Parable of the Fig Tree"** Teaches the certainty & nearness of Christ's return.-(Vs. 32-35)
- **"Day & Hour Unknown"-**Teaches the importance of vigilance and watchfulness.-(Vs. 36-51)

T u e s d a y - (Cont.)

Signs of the End of the Age-(N.I.V.)

24:1 Jesus left the temple (Expresses Jesus' final departure, having denounced the religious leaders hypocritical practices.-{23:13-39}) **and was walking away when his disciples came up to him to call his attention to its buildings.-◙** (The disciples were admiring the Temple's magnificent and beautiful structure, being made of white marble and gold. A real wonder of the ancient world.)
2 "Do you see all these things?" he asked. "I tell you the truth, (Expresses a strong confirmation and reliability.) **not one stone here will be left on another; every one will be thrown down."**(Lit. Fulfilled by Rome 40 years later in the complete destruction of Jerusalem and the Temple.)

Jesus predicts the complete destruction of the Temple.

Message & Application 💻=🌎

- ❖ Shows how believers are to see that our hearts are not captivated and preoccupied with the outward pomp & grandeur of organized religion.
- ❖ Warns how failure to receive Christ will drive Him far from us.
- ❖ Calls for seeing through the temporal prosperity of worldly things, keeping our attention on spiritual and eternal matters.
- ❖ Teaches how Christ is not interested in simply remodeling us but rather wants to completely rebuild and transform us.

24:3 As Jesus was sitting on the Mount of Olives,-◙ (A hilltop ridge of olive groves, across the Kidron valley, overlooking the Temple.) **the disciples** (Peter, James, John, and Andrew.-{Mark 13:3} **came to him privately. "Tell us," they said, When will this happen,**(Destruction of the Temple/Jerusalem.-{V. 2}) **and what will be the sign** (4592-*Mark, signal, event)* **of your coming** (i.e. Jesus' second coming.) **and the end of the age.** (World-K.J.V.-165-*An end of an era, period of time.* Not the literal end of the world, but end of the age, ushering in Christ's millennial reign. Most view this as "One single event". Others see it in three parts. The first being fulfilled by Rome in the destruction of the Temple in 70 A.D. The second of Christ's future return. And the third the end of the age.)

The disciples want to know what events will signal the destruction of the Temple & Jesus' second coming.

Message & Application 💻=🌎

- ❖ Shows how believers are always to be living with the readiness and expectedness for Christ's return, and not just idle curiosity.
- ❖ Teaches how believers can take to heart all that Christ teaches and instructs, never doubting its truth or the accomplishment of it.
- ❖ Displays how believers are to take all events of life as having meaning and relevance in our walk and relationship with Christ.
- ❖ Teaches how when confused we can go to Jesus for instruction, that He may give us what is best and the right way to proceed.

Scholarly view of Tribulation & Christ's Return:

1) A world dictator/antichrist will rise to power, making a seven-year peace treaty with Israel, which after 3 ½ years he will break it.-(Dan. 9:26-27)
2) Antichrist will invade Jerusalem and set an image of himself in the rebuilt Temple.-(Matt. 24:15, 2-Thess. 2:2-4)
3) Antichrist begins worldwide persecution of the Church, forcing all to worship him.-(Matt. 24:16-22, Rev. 13:1-18)
4) Jesus returns to reign on earth for a 1000 years.-(Rev. 20:1-6)
5) Antichrist will gather at Armageddon for a final war against Christ, at which he will be defeated. (Rev. 20:1-10)
6) Rapture of the Church.-(1-Corn. 15:51-58, 1-Thess. 4:13-18) (Some view as before the Tribulation)
7) Resurrection & final judgment.-(Rev. 20:11-14)
8) New Heavens & New Earth where believers will reign with Christ forever.-(Rev. 21:1-27)

24:4 Jesus answered: "Watch out (take heed-K.J.V. Expresses a call for prudence, patience, discretion, and evaluation.) **that no-one deceives you.** (4105-*Lead astray, seduce, wander.* Syn.-delude, charm, taken-in. Suggests: Either by signs, miracles, doctrines, or prophecies.)
5 For many will come (i.e. During Church interim or end of days.) **in my name,** (i.e. Title, rank, authority, office) **claiming, 'I am the Christ,' and will deceive many.** (Suggests: Into believing that Christ's second coming had arrived.)

A warning to believers to be alert for false messiah's who will try to deceive them into believing they are Christ.

Message & Application 💻=🌎

❖ Shows how believers are to stay faithful to Christ despite tumultuous times. (Trust in Jesus as the only source of hope for the future).
❖ Warns how false Christ's will press upon believers as their deliverer, promising happiness, abundance, and prosperity. (Those who are spiritually lost will cling to that which makes them feel good).
❖ Displays the importance of abiding in Jesus' teachings. (Don't allow others to deceive you by false doctrines and theologies, always compare their teachings with God's word).
❖ Teaches that when Christ returns, He will not need to try to convince or persuade believers, they'll know it in their spirit and hearts.
❖ Warns how false messiahs will portray themselves as Christ-like deliverers, offering themselves as solutions to the world's problems.
☞ Because of the difficult trials believers will endure leading up to the Tribulation period, some will be more vulnerable and receptive to false messiah's who will promise deliverance and safety.
☞ Though the Church has already seen a number of false Christ's, e.g. Jim Jones, David Koresh, Sung Myung Moon, Sergey Anatolyevitch, Torop, Wayne Bent, etc. But in context to the Tribulation period, there will be either an increase and surge of false Messiah's. Or of their growing persuasiveness in their ability to deceive people will be greater than in any other generation. (See Mark 13:22)
☞ Most view this as a general characteristic developing during the Church age only to increase more rapidly during the Tribulation.
☞ According to the book of Revelations a majority view this here as corresponding to the opening of the "First Seal" depicting the Antichrist or a "false spirit of conquest & delusion".-(See Rev. 6:1-2) (Most reject this due to their interpretation of the rider on the white horse in Revelation as being that of Christ Jesus Himself.-Rev. 19:11)

Dispensationalists Views of the Tribulation:

Pre-Tribers: (A growing popularity among Evangelicals)	Hold that Christ can return at anytime and rapture the Church before the Tribulation takes place. (See John 14:1-3,1-Thess. 4:14, Rev. 3:10, 4:1) (Dates back only to the 1800 & later)
Mid-Tribers: (Not universally accepted among most Christian denominations)	Hold that Christ will return and rapture the Church in the middle or before the second half of the Great Tribulation. (See Matt. 24:13-15) (Dates back only to the 1900 & later)
Post-Tribers: (Widely accepted among majority of Christian denominations)	Hold that Christ will return and rapture the Church near the end of the Great Tribulation. (See Matt. 13:37-43, 24:13, 24:29-31, Acts 2:19-21,1-Corn. 1:7-8, Philp. 1:10 1-Thess. 4:15-17, James 5:1-11, 2-Pet. 3:10, Rev. 7:13-15, 20:4-6) (Dates back to the Apostles and early Church fathers)

Millenarians Views of the Tribulation:

Pre-Millenarians: (Widely accepted among Evangelicals)	View a literal thousand year reign by Christ before the tribulation. Which will bring in a reign of peace and righteousness on earth.
A(no)-Millenarians: (Widely accepted by Jehovah's Witness, Mormons, Seventh-Day Adventist)	View a figurative thousand year reign by Christ after the tribulation. A time in which Jesus will reign in the hearts of believers, (or the souls of deceased believers) will also, see reestablishment of Israel.
Post-Millenaries: (Widely accepted by most Christian denominations)	View also a literal thousand year reign by Christ but after the tribulation period. A time in which the world will be Christianized, resulting in a long period of peace and prosperity.

24:6 You will hear of wars and rumors of wars, (i.e. World wars, future conflicts, threats of war, riots, saber-rattling, revolutions.-{Luke 21:9}) **but see to it that you are not alarmed.** (troubled-K.J.V. Syn.-anxious, panic, apprehensive, worry) **Such things must happen,** (Suggest: Brought about by man's own wickedness and fallen nature. Or God's judgments because of the sin and evil in the world.) **but the end** (i.e. Apocalypse) **is still to come.**
7 Nation will rise against nation (i.e. Civil wars, revolutions, conflicts.) **and kingdom against kingdom.** (Expresses internal conflicts, ethnic uprising, strife, economic collapse, religious ideologies.) **There will be famines** (Syn.-droughts, floods, hurricanes, starvation, diseases, epidemics. Brought on by mankind due to wars or by way of natural disasters.) **and earthquakes in various places.**
8 All these are the beginning of birth-pains. (Sorrows-K. J. V. Expresses: Things will get noticeably worse, greater calamities to come, or the distress of those days will soon be followed by new life and blissful times.) {cf. Is. 11:6-8}

A warning to believers not to mistake cataclysmic events such as wars & natural disasters as signs that the Apocalypse has begun.

Message & Application =

- ❖ Shows how believers are not to allow worldly calamities of wars and natural disasters to divert our attention from Christ and the Gospel.
- ❖ Warns believers against setting dates and times based on wars and natural catastrophes, that the immediate end is near.
- ❖ Calls believers in staying faithful in troubling times, that all things are working together towards our redemption. (See disasters as the ever-closer return of Christ!). (cf. Rom. 8:28)
- ❖ Teaches even when the world seems to be falling into chaos, trust in the sovereignty of God, that He is in ultimate control.
- ❖ Reassures believers despite the growing hatred and violence in the world, we can trust that God is able to bring good out of evil.
- ❖ Calls for travailing in trials and hardships, that not all is lost or hopeless, that God's deliverance is on the way.

–***Famines***-Possible theories have attributed it to being either a result of severe worldwide droughts, shortages caused by wars, or a crisis brought on by the increase of the world's population. (cf. Acts 11:28)

☞ Though the Church age has seen a number of wars (i.e. In our own era world wars 1 & 2) and natural disasters. But in context to the first half of the Tribulation period, these wars will increase significantly.

☞ According to the book of Revelations a majority view this as corresponding to the opening of the "Second, Third, and Fourth Seal judgments" depicting wars and famines.-(cf. Rev. 6:3-8)

24:9 "Then (i.e. During the birth pains and escalation of worldwide conflicts.-{V. 8}) **you will be handed over** (Syn.-betrayed, arrested, surrendered. Either by Jew, Gentile, or apostatized believers.-{V. 10}) **to be persecuted** (1377-*To put to flight, to pursue.* Syn.-despised, oppressed, tortured-L.B.V.) **and put to death, and you will be hated by all nations** (Expresses Worldwide animosity) **because of me.** (i.e. Because of Christians profession, loyalty, and allegiance to Christ.)

A warning to believers of worldwide hatred & persecution during the Tribulation period because of our Christian faith.

Message & Application

❖ Shows how Christians will be blamed & persecuted because of our witness and testimony of Christ. (Expect opposition from the world).
❖ Teaches believers how our faithfulness to Jesus will be severely challenged and tested during the Tribulation period.
❖ Prepare believers against allowing bullies and threats to deter our witness and testimony of Jesus.
❖ Reminds believers no matter the cost or dangers to our own lives, we are to stay true to Christ and the Gospel. (Don't be sidetracked by worldliness, or the fear of offending another's sensibilities).
❖ Displays how believers will be unjustly blamed for all the evils, calamities, and troubles throughout the world.
❖ Calls for patience & endurance in not giving into fear or threats.

–***Handed over-***Majority view that it will be of a political nature, whereby the official policy of governments will be to arrest Christians as enemies and threats to the new world order or to mankind in general. Others suggest in context to the following verse (V. 10) that such arrests will come as a result of the betrayal of relatives and apostatized believers. (cf. V.10, Mark 13:12-13)

☞ Though the Church age has seen many Christians persecuted for their faith, e.g. Polycarp, Wycliffe, Martin Luther, Jim Elliot, etc.
But in context to the Tribulation period, these persecutions will be accelerated and on an unprecedented worldwide scale.

☞ The book of Acts gives abundant proof in the fulfillment of these words as the early Apostles Peter, James, John, and Paul were met with such treatment. (See Acts 4:3, 5:17-21, 7:59, 12:1-5, 16:23-24, 21:26-33,

☞ According to the book of Revelations, a majority view this here as corresponding to the opening of the "Fifth Seal judgment" as depicting the souls of those believers who had been martyred during this Tribulation period for proclaiming the Gospel. (See Rev. 6:9)

24:10 At that time (i.e. During worldwide persecution of believers.-{V. 9}) **many will turn away from the faith** (be offended-K.J.V.-4624-*Scandalized, caused to stumble, trip up.* Suggests: Many believers will lose their faith and apostatize.) **and will betray** (i.e. Sell out, inform on, rat-out. Either by parents, relatives, or friends in revealing names, addresses, places of hiding.) **and hate each other,**
11 and many false prophets (Syn.-false preachers, teachers, cults) **will appear** (arise-K.J.V. Suggests: From within the Church, Christendom.) **and deceive many people.** (Suggests: By heretical doctrines and licentious practices.-{V. 12})

A warning to believers against Apostatizing from the faith because of persecution.

Message & Application 💻=🌎

- ❖ Shows how believers are not to allow persecution & mistreatment of others to cause us to fall away from the faith or our trust in God.
- ❖ Calls for not allowing anger or bitterness to turn us away from God.
- ❖ Teaches since its inevitable that people will hurt and injure us, all the more that we respond with patience, compassion, and forgiveness.
- ❖ Warns against allowing the disappointments, faults, and offenses of others to deter us in our faith and walk with God.
- ❖ Calls for enduring in the faith no matter how much people are unjustly judging, slandering, criticizing, or condemning us.
- ❖ Calls for not getting dismayed and angry with God just because bad things happen, or because our prayers and expectations go unfulfilled.
- ❖ Calls for seeing that our faith is deeply rooted in the goodness and faithfulness of God, and not in what others say and do!
- 🗝 Even today many false prophets have infiltrated our Church's, misleading people with promises of health, wealth, and prosperity.
- ☞ Though the Church age has seen a number of false prophets and cults e.g. "Jehovah Witnesses, Mormons, Seventh Day Advantest", etc., but in context to the tribulation period, these cults will greatly increase.

Why some Believers fall Away:

- They lack true conversion & commitment.
- They were never rooted in the word.
- They fail to grow and mature spiritually.
- They are led astray by false teachings.
- They grow weary and discouraged.
- They fall into pride and self-centeredness.

24:12 Because of the increase of wickedness, (iniquity-K.J.V.-458-*lawlessness, unrighteousness, no principals.* Syn.-immorality, depravity. Expresses the general profaneness of worldly morals and values.) **the love** (25-*Affection, charity, good will*) **of most** (i.e. Believers or people in general) **will grow cold** (Syn.-uncaring, unloving, indifferent, unsympathetic, etc. {cf. Rev. 2:4})
13 but he who stands firm (endures-K.J.V.-5278-*To persevere under trials, suffering, hardships.*) **to the end** (i.e. Not physical death, or earthly trials, but of remaining faithful to Christ and our Christian values.) **will be saved.** (Expresses one who does not allow themselves to fall into apostasy/depravity. Or allow the wickedness around them to steal their faith and devotion to God.)

Believers are not to allow the immorality & wickedness around us to tone down our love for Christ and others.

Message & Application 💻=🌎

- ❖ Shows how believers are not to allow worldly influences keep us from following God's standards in doing what is right. (cf. 2-Tim. 3:1-9)
- ❖ Calls for holding onto our moral integrity and Christian zeal. (Don't start tolerating sin just because everybody else is doing it!).
- ❖ Calls for staying true to the Lord, that we're not compromising our faith by giving into the sinful culture & wickedness that surrounds us.
- ❖ Warns against harboring hate and a critical spirit towards those who have hurt us or who have let us down. (Don't draw away from God because a Church or Pastor has hurt or wronged you).
- ❖ Calls for not allowing the moral failures and insincerities of other Christians to discourage us in God's power and work in our own lives.

–***the love of most will grow cold***-Variously attributed to either:

- Because of the world's sinful behavior, a believer's Christians standards & morals will slowly diminish.
- Because of the severe persecution of the Church will cause some to lose courage in their witness & profession.
- Because of the betrayal & apostasy of other Christians will cause some to grow shy and suspicious of fellow believers.

⊶ Even today one way we can tell if our love for God is waning is when our prayer meetings and bible studies become a drudgery, and our friends and movie night become a delight.

☞Though the Church's witness has declined at various times throughout history, e.g. the Inquisitions of the middle ages, moral lapses of priests, the acceptance of gay marriages, homosexual clergy, etc. But during the Tribulation, these evil acts will drastically increase.

24:14 And this gospel (2098-*Glad tidings, good news*) **of the kingdom** (Metph.-God's Saving grace, Jesus' redeeming work in Salvation.) **will be preached in the whole world as a testimony** (witness-K.J.V.) **to all nations,** (i.e. cultures, nationalities. Suggests: As warning for those who reject the Gospel, or as an extension of God's blessing of Salvation to all people.) **and then the end will come.** (i.e. Christ' return, day of judgment, destruction of Temple/Jewish state.)

Despite the apostasy & persecution of the Church, the Gospel will triumph in the end.

Message & Application 💻=🌎

- ❖ Shows believers that no matter how dark or gloomy things may look, the Gospel and our faith will prevail in the end.
- ❖ Teaches how God will give us the sufficient grace, strength, and wisdom in facing any trial or challenge to our faith.
- ❖ Moves believers in being fully invested in the work of spreading the Gospel message, knowing we have God's assurance of our success.
- ❖ Warns how we cannot plead inexperience or a lack of means or funds in spreading the Gospel since God promises us the ultimate victory.
- ❖ Displays how the Gospel is not confined to cultural or social borders, but reaches out with God's love and forgiveness to all people.
- ☞ Jesus is not saying every person will believe the Gospel. Nor was He proposing we can speed up His return by converting the whole world.
- ☞ Some use this verse to teach the nearness of Christ' return by pointing out how the explosion of technological advancements radio, television, satellite, internet has brought the Gospel to people around the world.
- ☞ According to the book of Revelations many view this as culminating in either the "144,00 Sealed" (Jewish evangelists -Rev. 7:1-8) or the preaching of the first of "The three angels"-(Rev. 14:6-7) or through the efforts of the "Two Witnesses" (Possibly Enoch & Elijah)-(Rev. 11:3-12)

Signs that Precede the Tribulation:

- Israel in their own land (fulfilled in 1948)
- Global economy.
- Increased technology.
- One world government.
- A restored Jewish Temple.
- Worldwide persecution against the church.
- Widespread apostasy within the church.

Beginning of 3 ½ years Great Tribulation

24:15 "So when you see standing in the holy place-◙ (Lit.-Temple sanctuary, Holy of Holies.) **the abomination** (946-*Idolatrous practice that's an affront to God's holiness and worship* [e.g. Antiochus's using the Temple altar to sacrifice pigs to the pagan god Zeus]-{1-Macc. 1:47}) **that causes desolation',-◙** (2049-*To lay waste, bring to ruin.* Lit. A future fulfillment by the Antichrist in setting himself up or a statue in the Temple, declaring himself God.) **spoken of through the prophet Daniel**-{Dan. 9:27} **let the reader understand**-(Calls for seeing Daniel's prophecy fulfilled and beginning of the Great tribulation period.)

Warns that when believers see Daniel's prophecy fulfilled of a world dictator/Antichrist setting himself up in the Temple to be worshiped as God, then they know that the Great Tribulation has begun.

Message & Application 💻=🌎

- ❖ Shows how many will try to destroy & corrupt our faith in turning our hearts from God to worshipping man-made idols and images.
- ❖ Calls believers in expecting assaults on our faith, beliefs, and practices, even the desecration of our Church's and places of worship.
- ❖ Warns against allowing idols to take the place of God in our lives. (Remove from your heart anything that competes with God!).
- ❖ Calls for standing firm with God without compromising to false religious cults, no matter how attractive or popular they may be.

–***Abomination that causes desolation***-In the immediate context the term refers to Daniel's prophecy concerning the destruction of the Temple by Antiochus Epiphanes, king of Syria, in erecting a pagan altar to Zeus in the temple and sacrificing pigs on it.-(cf. 1-Macc. 1:47, 54)
But in a wider context it also looks forward to a future desecration of a fourth rebuilt Temple (Ezek. Chaps. 40-48) by the Antichrist, either setting himself or an image of himself in the Temple forcing all to worship him as God. (Dan. 3:1-11, 12:11, 2-Thess. 2:3-4, Rev. 11:1-2, 13:4-6, 12-15)

☞ According to Revelations a majority view this as corresponding to the "Dragon of the Sea" (Satan) who gives the "Beast" (Antichrist) power to subdue and conquer the world-(cf. Rev. 13:1-15)

➢ A majority accept the desecration of a literal fourth Temple by the Antichrist due to its recurring theme throughout Israel's history:

- Solomon's Temple.....Desecrated by Nebuchadnezzar-(2-Kings 25:1-15)
- Zerubbabel's Temple..Desecrated by Antiochus Epiphanes-(1-Macc 1:47)
- Herod's Temple...........Desecrated by Roman Gen. Titus.-(Joseph. 6, 6:1)
- Ezekiel's Temple........Desecrated by the future Antichrist-(Dan. 9:27)

24:16 then (i.e. When the Antichrist invades Jerusalem and the Temple-{V. 15}) **let those who are in Judea flee to the mountains.** (Suggests: As a place of refuge from perusing armies. Judean hills-L.B.V.)
17 Let no-one on the roof of his house (Lit. Used as places of prayer or places to cool off on hot summer nights. Suggests: Those who will be on their day off, retired, or laid off.) **go down to take anything out of the house.** (Suggests: Persecution will be so swift with no time to collect personal belongings.)
18 Let no-one in the field go back to get his cloak.-◙ (coat. Suggests: Those who are at work will have no time to go home to change or collect belongings.)
19 How dreadful it will be in those days (i.e. The Great Tribulation period.) **for pregnant women and nursing mothers!** (Suggests: The dangers to both will be that they will not be able to move fast enough, exposing their life and the life of their child. [The Elderly and handicap would also fall under these hardships]. Some suggest that the tragedy is seen in the fact that these mothers, who do not make it out, will either force them to kill their babies, sparing them from brutal treatment of the enemy.-{cf. 2-Kings 15:16, Hos. 13:16} Or force them, because of the famine, to cannibalize their own babies.-{cf. Deut. 28:53-56})
20 Pray that your flight (Syn.-escape) **will not take place in winter** (Suggests: That harsh winter and cold conditions will make an escape that much harder, especially on snowy & muddy roads. Or rain flooded streams would be difficult if not impossible to cross.) **or on the Sabbath.** (i.e. Saturday, the Jewish day of no work. Suggests: That because many Jews would be observing the Sabbath, procuring transportation, food, or travel necessities would be difficult.)

A warning to believers that because of the swift persecution by the Antichrist they are to immediately flee to safety.

Message & Application 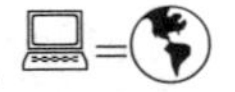

- ❖ Shows believers how much God loves us and does not want us lost or given over to evil and destruction.
- ❖ Calls for taking advantage of the doors the Lord opens for us in fleeing from sin, immorality, idolatry, and anything else God hates!
- ❖ Calls for placing our faith in God's grace and protection in difficult times and not in our assets or possessions.
- ❖ Teaches though we will always have pain and troubles in our lives, but we can count on Jesus' presence in helping us make the best of it.
- ❖ Displays how believers can always go to God in prayer, that He may secure our ease and safety in times of crises.
- ☞ According to the book of Revelations, a majority view this here as corresponding to the depiction of a "Woman fleeing from the Dragon" (Satan) where she is protected in the desert for 3 ½ years. (Rev. 12:1-17)

24:21 For then (From the time of the Antichrist's persecution.-{Vs. 16-20}) **there will be great distress,**(great tribulation-K.J.V.-2347-*Anguish, distress, calamity, suffering, troubles.* Syn.-persecutions, brutality, violence, horror.) **unequalled from the beginning of the world until now** (i.e. From the beginning of creation up to the Antichrist's persecution.) **and never to be equaled again.** (Expresses how all others atrocities will pale in comparison to the Antichrist' persecution.)

Warns believers that the persecution of the Antichrist will be on a scale that the world has never seen before.

Message & Application 💻=🌎

- ❖ Shows how believers are to be prepared & alert in not allowing times of severe trials and testing to turn our hearts away from the Lord!
- ❖ Exhorts believers in preparing ourselves for all manner of attacks and challenges to our faith that we may not fall away from Christ.
- ❖ Warns against allowing others to play on our fears. (Do not allow times of trouble to become times of temptation!).
- ❖ Calls for staying faithful to God, so that when the time of testing comes we will have the strength to stand our ground.
- ❖ Calls for always remaining faithful to God no matter trying times or difficult circumstance.

-***Great distress/Tribulation-***Many see this as a time of great persecution by the Antichrist when he breaks his treaty and turns against Israel in the middle of the seven year tribulation period,-(cf. Dan. 7:21-22, 11:40-45) eventually encompassing the entire world.-(cf. Rev. 12:9, 12-17, 13:7)

☞ Though the world has seen horrific persecutions throughout history, (6 million Jews killed in the holocaust, genocides in Rwanda, Bosnia, etc.) But the persecution under the Antichrist will pale in comparison.

☞ According to the Gospel of Luke expounds in more detail the nature of this Tribulation relating how: *"There will be great distress in the land and wrath against this people. They will fall by the sword and will be taken as prisoners to all the nations. Jerusalem will be trampled on by the Gentiles until the times of the gentiles are fulfilled.*-(Luke 21:23 b-24) (i.e. The Antichrist's and his armies invasion & siege of Israel & Jerusalem).

☞ Many compare this tribulation time to what Josephus recorded to what the Jews experienced under the Roman invasion of 70 A.D. Where 100,000 Jews were taken as prisoners, and another 1.1 million were either slaughtered or starved to death. (See Jos. Book V, chap. 12, 3.)

☞ Based on Revelations many view this as "The Beast" (Antichrist) who is given the power to make war against the "Saints"-(cf. Rev. 13:7-10)

24:22 If those days (i.e. The Tribulation period under the Antichrist.-{V. 21} **had not been cut short,** (2856-*To cut off, curtail, abridge.* Syn.-intervene, interrupt, suspend. Suggests: By the sudden return of Christ in destroying the Antichrist, or God's day of judgment against the wicked.) **no-one** (i.e. Believers or mankind in general, human race.-N.L.T.) **would survive,** (Suggests: If war would have continued unchecked man would have wiped himself completely out, either by famine or nuclear war.) **but for the sake** (Syn.-interest, benefit, well-being, welfare.) **of the elect** (Metph.-Believers, Saints, God's chosen people-L.B.V. Expresses: Christians or Saved believers during the Great Tribulation period.) **those days will be shortened.** (i.e. To only 3 ½ years.)

A word of encouragement how God will shorten the Antichrist's persecution in order to allow end time believers to survive.

Message & Application 💻=🌎

❖ Shows believers how God is ultimately in charge of history and will not allow evil to exceed the bounds He has set.
❖ Comforts believers in knowing that God is mindful of our times of affliction & distress. (Trust in God strength when facing severe trials).
❖ Displays how God's providence and grace always intervenes for the sake of believers in order to secure our safety and Salvation.
❖ Teaches instead of complaining about our afflictions, be thankful that they only last a short time. (When things look dreadful we should be thanking God that there not worse!).
❖ Teaches the importance of always remembering that when times of suffering and hardships come know that God is in control.
❖ Displays God's love & mercy towards His faithful. (Know that God's sovereignty will always see to your protection and welfare).
❖ Consoles believers that God will not allow His wrath to proceed without providing for our safety and deliverance.

*–days cut short-*Most understand as God's intervention by allowing the Tribulation period to last only 3 ½ years. Others understand as God literally shorting the daylight hours when most of the slaughter would occur.

*-for the sake of the elect-*Gives unmistakable & clear evidence in support of a post-rapture of believers near the end of the Great Tribulation.

☞ Jesus is not here promising that God will always protect believers from suffering and death, but rather will not allow trials to come to the point that they overtake our faith.

7-Year Tribulation Time Line

33 A.D.	70 A.D.	Church Age	Seven Year Tribulation Period: First 3 ½ Years	Seven Year Tribulation Period: Second 3 ½ Years	Christ's Second Coming and Millennial Reign	Judgment
Jesus' death (Dan. 9:26)	Destruction of Jerusalem and Temple (Matt. 24:2, Dan. 9:26)	Intermediate gap of unknown duration (33 A.D. to Present)	Increase of False Messiah's-(Vs. 4-5) Increase of political upheavals, revolutions, world wars-(Vs. 6-7) Increase in Natural disasters-(V. 8) Worldwide persecution against Church-(V. 9) Apostasy within the Church-(Vs. 10-13) Worldwide evangelism of the Gospel-(V. 14)	Antichrist invades Jerusalem, sets up image in Temple-(V.15) Dan. 9:27, Rev. 13:5-6) Antichrist' persecution of the church during the Great Tribulation-V. 21Dan 12:1,Rev.13:7-10) Raising up of false Christ's and false prophets-(Vs. 23-28, Rev. 13:11-18)	God's outpouring of wrath through cataclysmic events bringing the world/age to an end.-(V. 29, Is. 13:9-13, Rev. Chaps. 8-16) Jesus' second coming-V. 30, Rev. 19:11) Rapture of believers -(V. 31 1-Thess. 4:15-17, Rev. 14:16) Jesus' Millennial reign-(Rev. 20:1-6) Battle of Armageddon-(Rev. 19:19-21, 20:7-10)	Final day of judgment-Rev. 20:11-15) New heavens /New earth (Rev. 21:1-27)

(Note: The above 7 year Tribulation timeline is only a scholarly consensuses and not an exact view taken by every Church and Denomination.)

24:23 At that time (i.e. Great Tribulation period.) **if anyone says to you, 'Look, here is the Christ!'** (Expresses: Local reports, I witness accounts.) **or, 'There he is!'** (Expresses national, universal, widespread reports.) **do not believe it.**
24 For false Christ's (Syn.-Antichrist, Messianic pretenders.) **and false prophets** (Syn.-False religious leaders, supporters of the Antichrist.) **will appear and perform great signs** (e.g. Make fire come down from heaven.-{Rev. 13:13-14} **and miracles to deceive** (4105-*To lead away from the truth, seduce, go astray.* Suggests: To mislead others that they are Christ.) **even the elect—**(Metph.-Saved believers, Saints.) **if that were possible.** (Suggests: Those who are truly Saved and abiding in Christ and God's word will not be fooled or deceived.)
25 See, I have told you ahead of time. (Expresses: Believers have sufficient notice & warning not be caught off guard, stay spiritually prepared and alert.)

Warns believers how false Messiah's will attempt to deceive us into believing they are Christ.

Message & Application 💻=🌍

❖ Shows believers how Christ's arrival will not come in a heralded manner nor by supernatural feats. (Trust in God's word, not on signs).
❖ Warns against being mesmerized or hoodwinked by spectacular claims or achievements. (Test the spirits, not performances). (cf. 1-John 4:1)
❖ Calls for being spiritually prepared and alert, staying grounded in God's word, sound doctrines, and the Holy Spirit's guidance.
❖ Teaches those who are living Spirit-filled lives, truly following, obeying and treasuring God's word will never be deceived.
☞ Based on the book of Revelations, a majority view this as corresponding to the "Beast of the earth" (false prophet) who will be endowed by the "dragon" (Satan) with supernatural powers to perform miracles signs & wonders on his behalf.-(Rev. 13:11-18, 19:20, 2-Thess. 2:9)

How to Detect False Prophets:

- Their teachings are unbiblical. (Teachings & doctrines are not in line with the word of God).
- Their witness and walk does not agree with the inward witness of the Holy Spirit.
- Their prophecies fail to come true.
- They lead others to worship false gods. (They worship a different Jesus, one of wealth, health, and prosperity).
- They often exalt themselves rather than God.

24:26 "So if anyone tells you, 'There he is, out in the desert,' (Suggests: A monastic or apocalyptical community.) **do not go out; or, 'Here he is, in the inner rooms,'** (secret chambers-K.J.V. Suggests: Secrete conclaves, minority sects. Metph.-isolated, secluded, remote places, exclusivity.) **do not believe it.**
27 For as lightning that comes from the east is visible even in the west, (Expresses: Universal, public, unmistakable, clearly seen, obvious.) **so will be the coming of the Son of Man.** (i.e. Jesus/Messiah. Expresses: A Messianic title signifying the Messiah's human origins and headship over humanity.)
28 Wherever there is a carcass (Dead animal) **there the vultures will gather**.

A warning to believers that Jesus' second coming will not be in secret but will be obvious and visible to all.

Message & Application 💻=🌎

❖ Shows how Christ's return will be unmistakable, universal, and visible to all, that it will be impossible to miss!
❖ Teaches believers that if you have to be told that Christ has returned, you can bet for sure that He hasn't!
❖ Warns how believers can miss Christ's return when we stick to our own prophetic insights and imaginations.
❖ Teaches how Jesus' return will not only be evident to all, but also instant, sudden, and without warning. (c.f. 24:36-44)
❖ Prepares believers since Christ can come at anytime we need to make every moment of our life's count as we long for His return.
❖ Warns against being taken in by those who try to set times and dates for Jesus' return. (Know that Christ's return is not on our timetable).
❖ Teaches how we will not need any preacher, religious organization, or elaborate formulas to know that Jesus has returned.

-wherever there is a carcass vultures will gather-Interpreted as either:

- Just as the presence of vultures clearly indicates a carcass, so to will signs clearly indicate Jesus' arrival.
- Just as it is impossible for vultures to miss seeing a dead carcass, so to will it be impossible to miss Jesus' arrival.
- Where the lost and wicked are found, judgment will follow. (cf. Luke 17:26-37, Rev. 19:17-21)
- Apostate Israel being invaded by the powerful Roman army with their military eagle standards. (cf. Deut. 28:49)

🗝 Even today believers need to be aware of any Church that will try to mislead you into believing that Jesus' has already returned. (Know that Jesus hasn't forgotten you, that you have not missed the boat!).

24:29 "Immediately after the distress of those days (i.e. Great Tribulation, persecution of the Antichrist.) **"'the sun will be darkened,** (i.e. An eclipse of the sun, either by volcanic earthquake spewing up ash.-{Rev. 6:12} Nuclear winter, meteor impacts-{Rev.8:7-12}, or gravitational collapse.) **and the moon will not give its light;** (Due to the fact that the light of the moon is only a reflection of the sun.) **the stars will fall from the sky,** (Lit. meteors, comets, asteroids.-{Rev. 8:7-11}, or nuclear missiles.) **and the heavenly bodies** (i.e. The moon, sun, stars, planets.) **will be shaken.'** (Suggests: A shift in the natural forces of the universe or the orbital patterns of celestial bodies, thereby affecting weather & tides. Others take it figuratively of God's awful judgment on a fallen world.)

At the end of the Tribulation period, God will pour out His wrath through cataclysmic events bringing the world to an end.

Message & Application 💻=🌎

☞ According to Apocalyptical language many see these events as the outpouring of God's wrath & judgment upon unbelievers and the ungodly-(cf. Is. 13:9-13, 24:18-23, Jer. 4:27-28, Ezek. 32:7-8, Joel 1:15, 2:10-11)

☞ Scholars debate over the interpretation of these "signs", the majority take them as literal astral events. Others understand them as only symbolic signs signifying a violent political change. i.e. raising and falling of kings & nations, and the emergence of a new world order.

–***stars will fall from the sky***-According to the book of Revelations a majority view this as corresponding to the "Seven Trumpets" particularly the first, second, and third each depicting various meteor showers; "First Trumpet" showering down small meteors the size of hail stones, resulting in the third of the earth being burned up-(Rev. 8:7) "Second Trumpet" depicting a meteor the size of a mountain falling into the sea, resulting in the death of a third of all sea life as well as the destruction of a third of all ships.-(Rev. 8:8-9) "Third Trumpet" depicting a "Great star" which would be called *"Wormwood"* (bitter) falling on a third of rivers and fresh water springs turning them bitter. –(Rev. 8:10-11) Others apply it in the symbolic sense as in reference to the sounding of the "Fifth Trumpet" depicting a divine agent (angel)-(Rev. 20:1) who was given the keys to the abode to release evil forces upon the inhabitants of the earth to torture those who did not have the seal of God on their foreheads.-(Rev. 9:1-11)

☞ Based on Revelations some see this as corresponding to all three series of judgments "Seven Trumpets", "Seven Plagues", and "Seven bowls"-(Rev. Chp. 8-16) poured out by God upon sinners and unbelievers on earth.

Jesus' Second Coming-(Authors Insert)

24:30 "At that time (i.e. End of history/age/world-{V. 29} or fall of Jerusalem.) **the sign of the Son of Man** (i.e. Jesus) **will appear in the sky, and all the nations** (Syn.-peoples) **of the earth will mourn.** (2875-*Lament, wail.* Suggests: Because they will realize the day of judgment has come. Or Israel for having rejected Christ.-{Zech. 12:10}) **They will see the Son of Man coming** (3952-*Parousia, second advent, presence.* i.e. Jesus' second coming.) **on the clouds of the sky, with power** (i.e. divine authority, judgment.) **and great glory.** (Expresses: Taken together Christ's exaltation and enthronement.)
31 And he will send his angels (Suggests: Angels who will act as divine agents in carrying out Christ's will.) **with a loud trumpet-◙ call,** (Metph.-summons, command, assembly, judgment. Suggests: The sound of Christ's voice gathering and resurrecting believers.-{1-Thess. 4:16-17, 1-Corn. 15:52}) **and they will gather his elect** (Metph.-Saved believers, Christians.) **from the four winds,** (Expresses the entire globe, corresponds to the four points of a compass.) **from one end of the heavens to the other.**(Expresses: Every place under the sky, whole world.)

At the end of the world (history/age) Jesus will return from heaven to redeem(resurrect/rapture) believers from all over the earth.

Message & Application 💻=🌎

- ❖ Shows how Jesus will return in great glory & triumph, rescuing all those who have believed on Him, bringing them home to heaven.
- ❖ Teaches no matter what we're going through we can always rejoice that our ultimate Salvation and vindication is drawing near.
- ❖ Assures believers in the Lord' sovereign power to rescue and deliver those who believe and are looking for His coming.
- ❖ Teaches how God is in ultimate control of all things and is faithful to all His promises and prophecies in His word.

–***sign of the Son of Man***-Interpreted as either:

- The visible & bodily return of Christ Himself (Acts 1:10-11, Rev. 1:7)
- The appearance of a Cross or fish symbol in the sky.
- The "Shekinah" glory of Christ-(Ex. 13:21-22, 14:24, 40:34-35)
- The star of Bethlehem that marked Jesus' birth-(Matt. 2:7-10)

☞ Many use this verse here in support of the post-Tribers doctrine of the rapture of believers at the end of the tribulation period.

☞ Based on the book of Revelations a majority view these events as corresponding to the; "Sounding of the angel's seventh trumpet"-(Rev. 11:15-18) and the Rider on the White Horse.-(Rev. 19:11-16)

☞ According to Paul, the rapture takes place at this time.(1-Thess. 4:13-17)

From this verse here (V. 32) to verse (V. 35) Jesus teaches on the certainty & nearness of His return.

Parable of the Fig Tree-(Authors Insert)

24:32 "Now learn this lesson from the fig-tree:-◙ As soon as its twigs get tender (Suggests: Twigs beginning to sprout, germinate, branches full of sap.) **and its leaves come out,** (Syn.-bloom, bud. Suggests: Early Spring.) **you know that summer is near.**
33 Even so, when you (i.e. Believers in general.) **see all these things,** (i.e. Signs and events that signal the Tribulation period.-{Vs. 5-29}) **you know that it is near, right at the door.** (Expresses how Jesus' second coming is imminent and close at hand.)

Just as the budding of a fig tree indicates summer is approaching so to the Great Tribulation will indicate the nearness of Jesus' return.

Message & Application 💻=🌎

- ❖ Shows though we may not know the exact time or date of Christ's return, we will be able to know its general season and nearness.
- ❖ Calls for perseverance, watchfulness, and faithfulness. (Don't allow adversities and calamities to undermined your confidence).
- ❖ Calls believers to keep an eye on the prophetic unfolding of worldly events. (Stay apprised, but not engrossed!).
- ❖ Gives hope and encouragement in difficult times, knowing that it's almost over and that Jesus is coming soon to set things right.
- ❖ Displays the providence of God's work in our ultimate redemption, transformation, and perfection.
- ❖ Teaches how Jesus' coming should be a source of comfort and joy of renewed life and the promise of a new age of peace and blessings.
- ❖ Teaches believers though they be inflicted with troubles and turmoil's, we will emerge with more productive and fruitful lives.

-Lesson of the fig tree-Variously interpreted as implying either:

- Approaching events of the great tribulation/Jesus' return.
- Jesus is sure to return in early spring or summer.
- Was only pointing to the rebirth of the nation of Israel, fulfilled in 1948.

☞ Just as nature can indicate the arrival of the seasons, so to the events during the Tribulation period will indicate the arrival of Jesus' second coming.

24:34 I tell you the truth, this generation (1074-*Age, nation, race.* Metph.-believers, Christians. Suggests: Not the Apostles living at the time of Jesus, for they have all passed away. But rather the generation of believers living at the time of the Tribulation.) **will certainly not pass away** (3928-*To parish.* i.e. come to an end, come to its close.-L.B.V.) **until all these things have happened.** (i.e. Tribulation signs discoursed in verses 4-28, and Christ's final return.)
35 Heaven and earth (i.e. Universe, all of creation.) **will pass** (Syn.-melt) **away,** (Suggests: To be dissolved by fire.-{cf. 2-Peter 3:10, Rev. 21:1}) **but my words** (i.e. Jesus' warnings concerning the Tribulation period and His return.-{Vs. 4-28}) **will never pass away.** (Expresses the unfailing character of Jesus' predictions of the Tribulation are more certain and firmer than creation itself.)

The generation of believers who are alive during the Tribulation will see the end times & Christ's return.

Message & Application =

- ❖ Shows believers the truth & infallibility of God's word. (Know that there is nothing more sure and dependable in life than God's word!).
- ❖ Assures the absolute certainty of all of God's plans, purposes, and promises. (Know the firm foundation of your Salvation, eternal security, and future glory!).
- ❖ Warns against finding security in temporal things, but rather in the promises and assurances of God's word.
- ❖ Teaches how even in a world of ever-changing fashions, values, and lifestyles, we can trust in the unchanging certainty of God's word.
- ❖ Teaches that no matter how much man tries to destroy our faith or the bible, the word of God will endure to the end.

–***This generation***-Variously interpreted as either:

- Generation of believers living during the tribulation period will see the coming of Christ.
- God will preserve the Jewish people as a distinct race until the end of history and Christ's return.
- The present generation of Jews who will witness the destruction of Jerusalem and the Temple in their own lifetime. (Fulfilled 40 years later in 70 A.D.)
- The events of the Tribulation period will fall within one generation from start to finish.
- The present generation of Jewish unbelief will continue until the end and Christ's return.
- The present generation of wickedness and evil will continue until the end and Christ's return.

From this verse here (V. 36) to the end of the chapter, Jesus teaches on the importance of Vigilance and Watchfulness.

The Day and Hour Unknown-(N.I.V.)

24:36 "No-one knows about that day or hour, (i.e. Of Jesus' second coming/end of the world. Expresses: Precise moment, not the general signs-{cf. 24:32-33}) **not even the angels in heaven,** (Suggests: Because angles are finite creatures with limited knowledge.) **nor the Son,** (i.e. Jesus. Note: This omission is generally left out by some bible translation [e.g. K.J.V.] due to its absence in the earliest and most authentic Greek manuscripts.) **but only the Father.**

Since only God knows the exact time of Jesus' return believers need to be vigilant.

Message & Application 💻=🌎

❖ Shows how believers are not to attempt to predict precise dates and times for Jesus' return, or believing those that do.
❖ Calls for vigilance, preparation, and watchfulness. (Be less concerned about exact dates and more about being spiritually/morally prepared!).
❖ Warns against trying to use cleverly inventive formulas of scriptures, science, or astronomy to predict the exact day of Jesus' return. (Believers should always be about preparation, not calculation!)
❖ Calls for patience and attentiveness. (Our duty is to be faithfully carrying out the Lord's work, not speculating about unknowns).
⊶ Even today because Jesus' return will come suddenly & unexpectedly there will be no time for preparation. (Those who are living faithful and godly lives do not need precise dates and times for Jesus' return).
☞ Jesus is not here denying His divine nature, omnipotence, or deity. But rather by becoming human Jesus voluntarily gave up the unlimited use of His divine attributes (Omnisense) while here on earth.
☞ Such concealment is likely for our own good, that if we did know the exact time of Jesus' return we would naturally become lazy in our stewardship, or tempted to live in sin, only to repent at the last minute.
☞ This is one of the most disobeyed bible verses to which many cults and false prophets fail to heed, and as a result, always find themselves humiliated by their failed predictions.
☞ Though we can have a general idea of Jesus' return by calculating the length of the seven-year Tribulation period, specifically the last 3 ½ years after the desecration of the Temple-(V. 15) but we will never know the exact day or hour.

24:37 As it was in the days of Noah, so it will be at the coming of the Son of Man. (i.e. Just like in Noah's day, Jesus' return will sudden and unexpected.)
38 For in the days before the flood people were eating and drinking, (Expresses the pursuit of pleasures, self-gratifications, worldliness.) **marrying** (i.e. grooms) **and giving in marriage,** (Brides betrothed by parents.) **up to the day Noah entered the ark;-◙** (Expresses: Taken together of carrying on with the normal course of life and daily routines, oblivious to the warnings ahead.)
39 and they knew nothing about what would happen until the flood came and took (swept-K.J.V.) **them all away.** (Suggests: Not away in the rapture, but away in judgment.) **That is how it will be at the coming of the Son of Man.** (Expresses a Messianic title signifying the Messiah's human origins and headship over humanity.-{cf. Dan. 7:13-14} Suggests: Jesus' second coming will be similar to that of the flood, bringing immediate and sudden judgment.)

Jesus' return will bring an immediate and sudden judgment upon people when they least expect it.

Message & Application 💻=🌎

❖ Shows how believers must always be prepared, for judgment can come at any time when we least expect it.
❖ Warns against being so preoccupied with worldly affairs that we grow indifferent and unprepared for Christ's return.
❖ Teaches the dangers of refusing to heed the warnings and patience of God, living as if no judgment was coming.
❖ Teaches the importance of being found faithful and righteous as we wait for Christ's return.
❖ Cautions believers against allowing the distractions of everyday life to take our heart and focus away from Jesus.
❖ Calls believers in seeing that our lives are revolved around living for God and not for self!

-As in the days of Noah-The similarities that Jesus is stressing is not necessarily the "extreme wickedness" of Noah's days, though that may be true in the last days.-(cf. 24:12) But rather the people's indifference and unpreparedness. (After all, there is nothing sinful in eating, drinking, and marrying if practiced in moderation!).

⊶ Even today if not careful the preoccupations with the affairs of this life can slowly dull us to eternal and spiritual truths. (Don't allow the distractions of this life to take away from your spiritual life).

➢ Similarities and common features:
- People will be pursuing their own pleasures & delights-(V. 38 a).
- People will be going about their daily business and routines-(V. 38)
- People will be caught unexpectedly and without warning-(V. 39)

24:40 Two men (i.e. Father & son, brothers, coworkers, men-servants.) **will be in the field;-** (i.e. Plowing/sowing. Usual occupations, employments.) **one will be taken** (i.e. Sinner and unbeliever taken in judgment.) **and the other left.** (i.e. Believers who will share in Christ's Millennial reign on earth.)
41 Two women (i.e. Mother & daughter, sisters, house-maids.) **will be grinding with a hand mill;-◙** (Lit.-Small circular stones used to grind grain [wheat or barley] into flour in preparation for baking bread.) **one will be taken and the other left.** (Suggests: Destinations same as in verse 40.)

At Christ's return, the sinners will be taken into judgment and Saved believers will be left to reign with Jesus forever.

Message & Application

- ❖ Shows believers how Christ's return will be sudden and swift. (No time for last minute repenting or bargaining).
- ❖ Teaches the importance of living faithfully, that when Jesus returns they'll be no time for apologies or excuses.
- ❖ Teaches no matter how humble our stations in life or the places we may be, will never be overlooked or forgotten by Jesus. (Holds out hope for those who may be in prison or dispersed in various places).
- ❖ Calls for a heart that is faithful, consistent, and continually prepared for Christ's return.
- ❖ Teaches how Salvation will be based solely on one's faith-conversion to Christ, and not on religion, morals, or deeds.
- ❖ Teaches how we should be waiting for Christ's return, not on some mountain top, but by continually witnessing and laboring for the Lord.
- ❖ Warns how there will be no last-minute repenting or bargaining, that the choices we make in life will determine our eternal destinies.

–***Two men/two women***-Though people will outwardly appear the same but inwardly will have different convictions & beliefs. That no matter how close two people are in this life (marital, siblings) there will be no guarantee that they will share the same eternal destinies. May also stress the cleavage of the unbeliever to believers caused by Christ's arrival. May also serve as a word of encouragement for believers who, though intermixed or linked with others, either by society, habitations, or employments, will still be considered as true Christians.

–***One will be taken and the other left***-Variously interpret as either:

- The one taken is the unbeliever in judgment.
  (Widely supported by most, based on the parallel context of those taken in judgment by the flood -V. 39)
- The one taken is the rapture of the believer to heaven.

Parable of the Householder & Burglar-(Authors insert)

24:42 "Therefore (i.e. A conclusion.) **keep watch,** (Expresses: Not physical watching as in current events, but spiritual alertness and vigilance.) **because you do not know on what day your Lord will come.** (i.e. Jesus' second coming.)
43 But understand this: If the owner (Metph-believer) **of the house had known at what time of night the thief** (Metph-Jesus) **was coming, he would have kept watch and would not have let his house** (Metph.-soul, spiritual state/life/walk) **be broken into.** (Expresses the need for spiritual alertness in not be given over to sinful living, worldly pursuits, or Satan's temptations.)
44 So you also must be ready, because the Son of Man (i.e. Messiah/Jesus) **will come at an hour when you do not expect him.** (Expresses Christ's sudden return, or the believer's unexpected call home through sudden death.)

A warning to believers for constant vigilance against sin & temptation since Jesus can return at a time we least expect it.

Message & Application

- ❖ Shows believers the need to be living holy & sanctified lives since Jesus can return any day! (1-Thess.5:2-6, 2-Pet. 3:11, Titus.2:11-15, Rev. 16:15)
- ❖ Calls for living every day as if Jesus was going to return tomorrow. (Are you living as if the second coming could happen at any moment).
- ❖ Calls for taking inventory of our lives. (How would you want Jesus to find you living when He returns, faithful or disobedient?).
- ❖ Calls for knowing our weaknesses and the temptations we need to guard against, that we're not going to compromise with sin anymore!
- ❖ Calls for guarding our hearts, that we're not allowing the things of sin, Satan, doubt, unbelief, discontent, etc. to creep into our lives.
- ⊶ Even today, believers are responsible for being spiritually invested in our prayer life and walk with God if we're going to have the strength to resist the temptations and distractions around us. (cf. Eph. 6:10-13)
- ☞ Jesus is not saying that He expects us to be living perfect sinless lives when He returns, but that we're living repentant and consistent lives.

How to stay Prepared for the Lord's Return:

- Know that you're truly Saved, that you have responded to the Gospel and accepted Jesus as your Lord & Savior.
- Stay active in using your gifts & resources for serving and witnessing for the Lord.
- Stay living holy & sanctified lives that are pleasing to the Lord, becoming more & more like Him.

Parable of the Wise & Faithful Servant-(Authors Insert)

24:45 "Who then is the faithful (Syn.-dutiful, reliable, willing) **and wise** (Syn.-prudent, diligent) **servant,** (Metph-Pastor, minister, deacon) **whom the master** (Jesus) **has put in charge of the servants in his household** (Church) **to give them their food at the proper time?** (Expresses Spiritual and administrative duties including preaching, teaching, exhorting, instructing, and encouraging.)
46 It will be good (Syn.-profitable) **for that servant whose master** (i.e. Jesus) **finds him doing so when he returns.** (Expresses Jesus' second advent.)
47I tell you the truth he will put him in charge of all his possessions. (i.e. To be honored with a permanent position with Christ in His Millennial Kingdom.)
48 But suppose that servant is wicked (Syn.-slothful) **and says to himself, 'My master is staying away a long time,'** (Expresses a false sense of security, thinking he wont be held accountable since Christ isn't returning anytime soon.)
49 and he then begins to beat his fellow-servants (Expresses: To abuse one's position by being cruel, oppressive, and overbearing, throwing one's weight around.) **and to eat and drink with drunkards.** (Expresses to be lazy and self-indulgent, wasting their life's away on partying, drinking, and sinful living.)
50 The master of that servant will come on a day when he does not expect him and at an hour he is not aware of. (Expresses Jesus' unexpected Parousia.)
51 He will cut him to pieces (Expresses: Not literally to chop into pieces. But rather to severely punish, dissect, expose, and chastise.) **and assign him a place** (Syn.-portion) **with the hypocrites** (i.e. Unbelievers, pretenders.) **where there will be weeping and gnashing of teeth.** (Expresses: Taking together sorrow, regret, and remorse, mixed with physical suffering and torment in Hell.)

Displays how believers are to be found faithfully carrying out our responsibilities & duties when the Lord returns.

Message & Application 💻=🌎

- ❖ Shows how believers are to stay faithfully following & serving the Lord as we wait for His return!
- ❖ Calls for being diligent & dutiful in the things of the Lord and all He requires. (Are you discharging your duties faithfully to the Lord?)
- ❖ Teaches how one day will have to give an account of our stewardship in how we used our time, gifts, and resources that God has given us.
- ❖ Warns against allowing the Lord's delay to cause us to slack off, thinking we can put off Church and witnessing for another day.
- ❖ Warns of the dangers of becoming lazy, complacent, and self-serving in putting our own agendas above the Lord's work.
- 🗝 Even today, believers need to see that we're staying on-task, that we're not mishandling the privileges and resources that the Lord has given us for our own selfish ends, but for the Lord's honor and glory.

Chapter Twenty Five

Parables on Watchfulness & Readiness

- **"The Ten Virgins"**-Parable teaching on the importance of being prepared for Christ' return by living holy lives.-(Vs. 1-13)
- **"The Talents"**-Parable teaching on being productive & faithfully in serving Christ until He returns-(Vs. 14-30)
- **"The Sheep and the Goats"**-Parable teaching how the evidence of one's Salvation will display itself through acts of love and kindness to others.- (Vs. 31-46)

The Parable of the Ten Virgins-(N.I.V.)

25:1 "At that time the kingdom of heaven (i.e. State of the Church at Christ's return.) **will be like ten virgins** (3933-*Unmarried daughter, bridesmaids.)* **who took their lamps-◙ and went out to meet the bridegroom.** (i.e. Fiancé, husband to be. Expresses the rapture of believers at Jesus' second coming.)
2 Five of them were foolish (Metph.-Spiritually dull, lazy, and sluggish) **and five were wise.** (Metph.-Spiritually prudent, attentive, sensible, and practical.)
3 The foolish ones took their lamps but did not take any oil with them.
4 The wise, however, took oil (i.e. olive oil) **in jars-◙ along with their lamps.-◙**
5 The bridegroom was a long time in coming, (i.e. Interval between Jesus' first & second advents.) **and they all became drowsy and fell asleep.**(i.e. The former having fallen into spiritual slumber & complacency, the latter peace & security.)
6 "At midnight the cry rang out: (Expresses the call of believers at the Rapture or at death.-{1-Thess. 4:16}) **'Here's the bridegroom!** (Christ) **Come out to meet him!'**(i.e. Resurrection of believers in meeting the Lord in the air.-{1-Thess. 4:17})
7 Then all the virgins woke up and trimmed their lamps.-◙ (i.e. adjusted wicks)
8 The foolish ones said to the wise, 'Give us some of your oil; (1637-*Symbol of the Holy Spirit.* Expresses: Their need of grace, good works, righteous living. Or the indwelling presence of the Holy Spirit.) **our lamps are going out.'**
9 "'No,' they replied, 'there may not be enough for both us and you. Instead, go to those who sell oil and buy some for yourselves.' (Expresses how no believer has extra grace or righteous living they can share with another.)
10 "But while they were on their way to buy the oil, the bridegroom arrived. The virgins who were ready went in with him to the wedding banquet. (Expresses: Joy and blessing of spending eternity with Jesus in heaven.) **And the door was shut.** (Expresses the Irreversible condition of the lost in being barred from heaven, that there will be no bargains, excuses, or second chances!)
11 "Later the others also came. 'Sir! Sir!' they said. 'Open the door for us!'
12 "But he replied, 'I tell you the truth, I don't know you.' (Expresses: We're never true believers, lacked a personal relationship with Jesus as Lord & Savior)
13 "Therefore keep watch, because you do not know the day or the hour.

(For Interpretation and Application see next page 367)

A warning to believers in always being prepared for the Lord's return by living faithful & holy lives.

Message & Application 💻=🌎

- ❖ Shows how believers are to stay vigilant & alert for the Lord's return by living faithful and devoted lives. (cf. 1-Corn. 16:13, 1-Pet. 5:8-9)
- ❖ Teaches the importance of seeing that we're truly Saved & Born again, that we're not waiting until the last moment to put our faith in Jesus.
- ❖ Teaches how each person is responsible for his & hers own spiritual condition, that nobody can grow our faith for us without God's help!
- ❖ Warns how some are going to be sorry for neglecting their faith, even wishing they devoted more time to Church, bible study, and prayer.
- ❖ Warns against allowing Christ's delay to cause complacency/slackness thinking we have all the time in the world to clean up our lives.
- ❖ Warns against only waiting till the last minute to become the type of Christian we should have been a long time ago!
- ❖ Warns against waiting only until times of crises & trials to repent and get right with God, that there may not be a second chance! (Vs. 10-13)
- ❖ Calls for self-examination, are we committed and sold out to the Lord to the degree we should be, or is there something holding us back?
- ❖ Calls for seeing that we're growing in a personal relationship with Jesus, and not borrowing another's faith, convictions, or bible knowledge to get us through! (cf. Gal. 6:1-5)
- 🗝 Even today, believers need to see that we're not simply trying to ride into Christ's presence/heaven on the coattails of our grandparent's faith, or on some admired Preacher, Author, and Saint. But that we have truly trusted in Jesus as our personal Lord & Savior.
- ➢ Additional lessons drawn from parable:
  - Each believer is responsible for his or her own spiritual condition and personal choices.
  - That grace and truth comes directly from God, you can't borrow faith or Spirit-filled character.
  - Warning against attempting to convert or live righteously at the last moment before Christ returns

Allegorical Types:

Ten virgins……… = Believers, Christians, the Church.
Bridegroom…….. = Jesus.
Lamps………….. = God's word/truth, or profession, witness.
Oil……………… = Holy Spirits presence, true conversion, Salvation, or faith, grace, righteous living.

The Parable of the Talents-(N.I.V.)

25:14 "Again, it will be like a man going on a journey, (Expresses Jesus' ascension into heaven.) **who called his servants and entrusted his property**

15 To one he gave five talents of money,-◙ (5007-*Unit of weight in gold or silver. 1 talent equaling 20 years of work for a common laborer.* In today's market about 4 million dollars.) **to another two talents, and to another one talent,** (i.e. gifts.) **each according to his ability. Then he went on his journey.**

16 The man who had received the five talents went at once and put his money to work and gained five more. (Expresses: Diligence, faithfulness.)

17 Also, the one with the two talents gained two more.

18 But the man who had received the one talent went off, dug a hole in the ground and hid his master's money. (Expresses: Slothful, distrustful, fearful.)

19 "After a long time the master of those servants returned (Expresses Jesus' second advent.) **and settled accounts with them.** (i.e. Day of judgment.)

20 The man who received the five talents brought the other five. 'Master, he said, you entrusted me with five talents. See, I have gained five more.

21 "His master replied, 'Well done, good and faithful servant! You have been faithful with a few things; I will put you in charge of many things. (Suggests: higher position, greater opportunities for service.) **Come and share your master's happiness!** (Suggests: Blessings of eternal life with Christ.)

22 "The man with the two talents also came. 'Master,' he said, 'you entrusted me with two talents; see, I have gained two more.' (See V. 16)

23 "His master replied, 'Well done, good and faithful servant! You have been faithful with a few things; I will put you in charge of many things. Come and share your master's happiness!'

24 "Then the man who had received the one talent came. 'Master,' he said, 'I knew that you are a hard man, (Syn.-demanding, overbearing, severe.) **harvesting-◙ where you have not sown-◙ and gathering where you have not scattered seed.-◙** (Expresses one who expects a profit on his investment. Was not the character of Jesus, but the man's wrong impression of Him.)

25 So I was afraid and went out and hid your talent in the ground. See, here is what belongs to you.' (Suggests: Thought playing it safe better than risk.)

26 "His master replied, 'You wicked, lazy servant! So you knew that I harvest where I have not sown and gather where I have not scattered seed?

27 Well then, you should have put my money on deposit with the bankers,-◙ so that when I returned I would have received it back with interest.

28 "'Take the talent from him and give it to the one who has the ten talents.

29 For everyone who has will be given more, and he will have an abundance. Whoever does not have, even what he has will be taken from him.

30 And throw that worthless servant outside, into the darkness, (Metph-hell) **where there will be weeping and gnashing of teeth.'** (See 24:51)

(For Interpretation and Application see next page 369)

A warning to believers to be faithfully serving Christ with the gifts God has given them.

Message & Application 💻=🌎

❖ Shows how believers are to be faithful & productive in serving the Lord with whatever talents He gives as we wait for His return.
❖ Reminds believers whatever gifts God has given us, great or small, are expected to be used for God's service and glory.
❖ Displays how God knows each believers abilities & limitations, and will not give us more than what He knows we can handle.
❖ Teaches how all of God's gifts are precious and are not to be wasted. (Rather than play it safe, be faithful in what you have!).
❖ Warns against being neglectful & lazy, that our time here on earth should be used for doing something for the Lord. (Vs. 24-27)
❖ Displays how failure to understand God's love & mercy can lead to unnecessary fears, paralyzing our walk & service. (Those who think it is impossible to please God will not prosper!). (Vs. 24-25)
❖ Warns against allowing failure or embarrassment to stop you from succeeding in God's work. (Better to try and fail, than not try at all!). (Vs. 24-25)

-***Whoever has will be given more/or taken from him***-Teaches those who improve on God's gifts will have those gifts increased. But in a wider context may also apply to the amount one is willing to invest in their spiritual life will determine their spiritual growth.

🗝 Even today, believers are expected to make wise investments of this one life and the allotment of time that God has given us for His service and glory.

➢ Additional lessons drawn from parable:
- In God's eyes, all believers are equally important no matter their gifts or talents.
- Believers must be good stewards with all of God's gifts and resources.
- Even the smallest gifts and abilities can be capitalized on, if not by ourselves than by others.

Allegorical Types:

Master...........	=	Jesus/God.
Servants.........	=	Believers.
Talents..........	=	Spiritual gifts, skills, abilities, opportunities, resources.

The Sheep and the Goats-(N.I.V.)

25:31 "When the Son of Man {See 24:39b} **comes in his glory,** (i.e. Jesus' second advent) **and all the angels with him, he will sit on his throne in heavenly glory.**
32 All the nations (Suggests: Peoples, professed Christians.) **will be gathered before him, and he will separate the people one from another as a shepherd separates the sheep from the goats.**-◙ (Expresses the final day of judgment.)
33 He will put the sheep-◙ (Metph-True-believers, the righteous, gracious, compassionate, merciful, loving.) **on his right** (Metph.-honor, favor, exalted, blessed) **and the goats** (Metph-False-believers, unrighteous, slothful, wicked, graceless) **on his left.** (Metph.-dishonor, rejection, condemnation, disfavor.)
34 "Then the King (i.e. Jesus) **will say to those on his right, 'Come, you who are blessed by my Father;** (i.e. God) **take your inheritance, the kingdom prepared for you since the creation of the world.**
35 For I was hungry and you gave me something to eat, I was thirsty and you gave me something to drink, I was a stranger and you invited me in,
36 I needed clothes and you clothed me, I was sick and you looked after me, I was in prison and you came to visit me. (Suggests: The list includes anything from the homeless, refugee, the hospitalized, the infirmed, the persecuted.)
37 "Then the righteous (i.e. True believers) **will answer him, 'Lord, when did we see you hungry and feed you, or thirsty and give you something to drink?**
38 When did we see you a stranger and invite you in, or needing clothes and clothe you?
39 When did we see you sick or in prison and go to visit you?' (Displays how true faith & love responds naturally, spontaneously, and instinctively, without thought. Expresses their humility and unworthiness to be honored for what they unknowingly did.)
40 "The King will reply, 'I tell you the truth, whatever you did for one of the least of these brothers of mine, (i.e. Fellow believers who are poor and of little importance, and who cannot repay the favor in return.) **you did for me.'** (Suggests: As our love for Christ, that it is laid to His account, and He will repay.)
41 "Then he will say to those on his left, 'Depart from me, you who are cursed into the eternal fire (Metph.-hell) **prepared for the devil and his angels**
42 For I was hungry and you gave me nothing to eat, I was thirsty and you gave me nothing to drink,
43 I was a stranger and you did not invite me in, I needed clothes and you did not clothe me, I was sick and in prison and you did not look after me.'
44 "They also will answer, 'Lord, when did we see you hungry or thirsty or a stranger or needing clothes or sick or in prison, and did not help you?'
45 "He will reply, 'I tell you the truth, whatever you did not do for one of the least of these, you did not do for me.'
46 "Then they will go away to eternal punishment, (Metph.-Hell) **but the righteous to eternal life."** (Metph.-Heaven, paradise.)

(For Interpretation and Application see next page 371)

The evidence of one's Salvation & faith in Jesus will display itself through acts of love & kindness to others.

Message & Application 💻=🌎

- ❖ Shows believers how genuine faith & love for Jesus will display itself in doing good and helping others. (cf. John 13:35, 1-John 3:14-18)
- ❖ Calls believers for a commitment to Christ that is displayed not just in words, but through loving and generous lives. (cf. Matt. 7:21-23)
- ❖ Teaches those who have truly experienced God's grace & goodness will have that goodness flow out of them in doing good for others.
- ❖ Teaches how those who know all that Jesus has done in Saving and rescuing them cannot casually sit by and watch others suffer.
- ❖ Emphasizes how acts of love & service to Christ are done naturally and spontaneously, without thought of reward or recognition in return.
- ❖ Warns against allowing opportunities to share Jesus' love pass us by. (Better to do something than to live with guilt & regret of not trying!).
- ❖ Calls for not allowing a day to go by that we're not reaching out in witnessing to others in some loving and compassionate way!
- ❖ Teaches the true hallmark of a professed Christian is not his religious doctrines, dogmas, beliefs, or bible knowledge. But rather it is his love & compassion for those who are lost and hurting. (cf. James 2:14-24)
- ❖ Teaches even if we don't see results, or feel we're making a difference in what we're doing, know that it matters to God, that He sees it!
- 🗝 Even today, believers need to take an honest look at ourselves and ask is our faith authentic and real. Or are we just going through the motions of doing the bare minimum with no real heart for the poor, needy, and suffering around us? (If you were to stand right now before God what evidence would there be that you were a Christian?)
- ☞ Jesus is not saying that Salvation is only earned through good works. Or that if we've never taken a homeless person into our home and fed & clothed them we're going to hell. But rather is simply teaching how authentic faith always responds with acts of love & kindness to others.
- ☞ The list that Jesus presents here should not be limited to just the bare requirements. But rather describes the daily acts of mercy that people can do every day without thought of time, money, or effort.
- ➢ Additional lessons drawn from parable:
    - Love & charity for others will be the test of true faith.
    - No selfless act of service goes unnoticed by God.
    - Sins of omission are more serious than the sins of commission.

Chapter Twenty Six

Jesus' Betrayal & Arrest

- **Plot Against Jesus-**Religious leaders conspiracy in killing Jesus-(Vs. 1-5)
- **Jesus Anointed at Bethany-** Mary in an act of love anoints Jesus' body for burial-(Vs. 6-13)
- **Judas Agrees to betray Jesus-** Judas betrays Jesus to the religious leaders.-(Vs. 14-16)
- **The Lord's Supper-**Jesus institutes the Passover supper as a memorial to His suffering and death- (Vs. 17-30)
- **Jesus Predicts Peter's Denial-** Jesus predicts Peter's denial and desertion-(Vs. 31-35)
- **Gethsemane-**Jesus humbly submits to God's will in suffering for the sins of the world-(Vs. 36-46)
- **Jesus Arrested-**Judas betrays Jesus to religious authorities with a kiss.-(Vs. 47-56)
- **Jesus Before the Sanhedrin-**Jesus stands trial in a preliminary inquisition before the Sanhedrin.-(Vs. 57-68)
- **Peter disowns Jesus-**Peter denies knowing Jesus three times.-(Vs. 69-75)

Wednesday-

26:1 When Jesus had finished saying all these things, (i.e. The discourses given in the two preceding chapters.-{Chps. 24-25}) **he said to his disciples,**
2 "As you know, the Passover is two days away (i.e. Day after tomorrow indicating Friday.) **and the Son of Man** (i.e. Jesus) **will be handed over** (i.e. By the religious leaders to Rome.) **to be crucified."** (4516-*To impale on a cross.)*

For the fourth and final time, Jesus predicts His death, presenting Himself as the Passover lamb.

Message & Application

- ❖ Shows Jesus' willing sacrifice in our Salvation & redemption by voluntarily dying on the cross in our place.
- ❖ Teaches believers who have been fully instructed by Christ are better prepared for the trials and sufferings that lie ahead.
- ❖ Teaches the importance of knowing that even in life's unfairness and betrayals God is still in control.

–***Passover-***Commemorates Israel's deliverance from slavery in Egypt when God *"Passed-over"* Egypt, striking dead all the firstborn of the Egyptians. Typologically signifies Jesus' crucifixion, coinciding with the "Passover". Suggests Jesus offering His own life as the Passover sacrifice in the redemption of sin. (cf. John 1:29, 19:36)

☞ This verse here marks the end of the "fifth" five-set division of discourses that began at 24:1. (See Gospel Introduction)

From this verse here (V. 3) To verse (V. 5) the religious leaders hold council in plotting Jesus' arrest.

The Plot Against Jesus-(N.I.V.)

26:3 Then the chief priests and the elders of the people assembled in the palace (i.e. House) **of the high priest, whose name was Caiaphas,** (Suggests: An unlawful assembly of the Sanhedrin who normally met in the Temple court.)
4 and they plotted (Syn. Consulted, strategized, conspired) **to arrest Jesus in some sly way**(subtilty-K.J.V.-1388-*Cunning, crafty, guile, deceit)* **and kill him.**
5 "But not during the Feast," (Passover.) **they said,**(Expresses their fear was not out of respect for the sacred event, but rather because of the Messianic fervor that was generated during such an event, swelling the crowds to about 250,000.) **or there may be a riot among the people."** (Suggests: Because many people regarded Jesus as a prophet, or because many of Jesus' supporters from Galilee would be in Jerusalem celebrating the Passover at this time.)

The religious leaders conspire how they could arrest & kill Jesus without drawing public attention or starting a riot.

Message & Application

–***Caiaphas***-Full name "Joseph Caiaphas" served as high priest from A.D. 18-36. Was the son-in-law and successor of Annas (John 18:13). Was Appointed to the office of high priest by the Roman procurator "Valerius Gratus" in A.D. 18 was deposed by "Vitellius" in A.D. 36.

–***To arrests Jesus in some sly way***-Meaning a way to arrest Jesus without drawing public attention, eventually Judas Iscariots would solve their dilemma by providing them the opportunity they were looking for when he offered to betray Jesus by leading them to Him at night. (See Vs. 14-16, Luke 22:3-6)

Caiaphas's Position & Functions:

- Was heir and successor to the Aaronic priesthood.
- Belonged to the party of the Sadducees, served and officiated in the regular priestly tasks.
- Was the only priest who could enter the "Holy of Holies" once a year on the "Day of Atonement".
- Presided over important cases, was president of the Sanhedrin, was the chief representative of the people to the ruling officers of foreign powers (i.e. Rome).

From this verse here (V. 6) To verse (V. 13) Mary displays her act of love & devotion by anointing Jesus with oil.

Wednesday - (Cont.)

Jesus Anointed at Bethany-(N.I.V.)

26:6 While Jesus was in Bethany-(A village located on the eastern slope of the mount of Olives, approximately 2-miles east of Jerusalem.) **in the home of a man known as Simon the Leper,-◙** (Suggests: Nickname resulting from having been healed by Jesus, that he was hosting a dinner party in Jesus' honor.)
7 a woman (i.e. Mary, sister of Martha & Lazarus.) **came to him with an alabaster jar-◙** (i.e. A white or semi-transparent form of marble carved out of gypsum stone, used for storing various ointments & perfumes.) **of very expensive** (Syn.-rare, costly) **perfume,** (ointment-K.J.V., pint of pure nard.-{John 12:3} i.e. "Spikenard"-an aromatic oil extracted from the stem of plants imported from India to make perfumes and oils. That it was probably a family heirloom.) **which she poured on his head as he was reclining at the table.-◙** (Expresses the normal cultural custom of eating meals by reclining on a couch of pillows with the feet extended away from the table.)

Mary in an act of love & devotion anoints Jesus' body for burial.

Message & Application 💻=🌎

❖ Shows how believers must give their best to Jesus, that no price or sacrifice is too great or too good for all that Christ has done for us.
❖ Teaches how true love for Jesus will pour out all our gifts, talents, and possessions for Him, that nothing is too good for Jesus.
❖ Displays how our love and devotion to Jesus will sacrifice all regardless of the financial, social, or personal costs.
❖ Calls for the willingness in declaring openly and publicly our love for Jesus. (Are you ashamed to show your affections for Jesus?).
❖ Teaches how true love for Jesus does not count the cost. (There should be no limit or barrier to how much we're willing to give up for Jesus).
🗝 Even today, believers are to have the same unrestrained love and devotion to Jesus, that we will not allow finances, expenses, or costs to get in the way of serving and glorifying the Lord.

-Anointed Jesus with oil-Variously attributed to either:

- As an act of love and devotion to Jesus. (cf. Luke 7:37-47)
- As an act in recognition of Jesus' approaching suffering and death. (cf. 26:12, John 12:7, Mark 14:8)
- As an act of her faith in Jesus as Christ and Messiah.

26:8 When the disciples saw this, (i.e. Mary's extravagant expense in displaying her love to Jesus.-{V.7}) **they were indignant.** (23-*"Much displeased", grieved.* Syn.-resentful, angry, furious) **"Why this waste?"** (Syn.-loss, squander) **they asked.** (Privately within themselves,-{Mark 14:4} or directed towards the woman.-{Mark 14:5} Possibly having been led & instigated by Judas.-{John 12:5})
9 "This perfume could have been sold at a high price (three hundred pence/denari-K.J.V. Equivalent to about a year's salary of a common laborer.-{Mark 14:5} Translated into today's money about $20.000 to $30.000 dollars.) **and the money given to the poor."**

The disciples having missed the benevolent act of Mary's anointing of Jesus only saw the perfume as a waste of money.

Message & Application 💻=🌎

- ❖ Shows believers who put Christ first in their lives will often be misunderstood and criticized by others.
- ❖ Warns how greed often camouflages itself under the pretense of piety & pious concern for others. (Charity often serves as a cloak for greed).
- ❖ Prepares believers in expecting to be criticized by others when we give ourselves so openly and generously to the Lord. (Don't allow what you do for Jesus to be considered as time or money wasted!)
- ❖ Warns against allowing others to make us feel that our love and devotion to the Lord as being too fanatic or too over the top.
- ❖ Challenges believers in not allowing our form of worship & devotion to be dictated by others. (Many will call into question why we invest so much time to church, charities, ministry, and prayer).
- ❖ Displays how acts of devotion & mercy can often be misconstrued when not knowing the heart and motives of the believer.
- ❖ Though believers have a responsibility in how we invest our time and resources, in the end, it is only we who are answerable to God.
- ⊶ Even today, believers can expect that there will always be people in our lives who will question why we give so much time & money to the Church. (Don't allow the ridicule and criticism of others dampen your spirits or quench your fire in serving and glorifying the Lord!).
- ☞ According to the Gospel of John, it recounts that it was Judas who protested to the waste of perfume. Which leads here to believe that the rest of the disciples were instigated by him towards the protest. That his true motives were not that he cared for the poor but of his greed, having been appointed treasurer of Jesus' ministry he wanted the money to go towards the funds so he could embezzle it for himself. (See John 12:4-6)

26:10 Aware of this, Jesus said to them, "Why are you bothering (troubling-K.J.V. Syn.-censuring, condemning, criticizing-L.B.V.) **this woman? She has done a beautiful thing** (Syn.-admirable, befitting, loving, praiseworthy.) **to me.**
11 The poor you will always have with you, but you will not always have me. (Expresses Jesus' impending death. That caring for the poor will be a continuing concern for the Church, but not a primary purpose above serving Christ.)
12 When she poured this perfume on my body, she did it to prepare me for burial. (Jesus' arrest & crucifixion would not allow time for proper burial rites.)
13 I tell you the truth, wherever this gospel is preached throughout the world, what she has done will also be told, in memory of her." (Suggests: Mary's act would remain a model of devotion, and serve as an example to others. The truth of Jesus' words can be seen in the fact that all four Gospel's records the story. {c.f. Matt. 26:7, Mark 14:9, Luke 7:37-39, John 12:7})

Jesus praises Mary's anointing as an act of love in preparation for His suffering and death.

Message & Application 💻=🌎

❖ Shows believers how devotion & worship of Jesus should be the highest priority in life, even above that of charity and social services.
❖ Displays that no matter how scorned, demeaned, or ridiculed we are by others, will always be honored and approved by Christ. (Find your validation and approval in Jesus, not in others!).
❖ Teaches how those who know the infinite worth of Jesus' mercy and grace, will spare no expense in doing all we can to glorify Him.
❖ Teaches how selfless devotion to Christ will give their all, no matter how costly, foolish, and uncomfortable it may be.
❖ Displays how our daily expressions of love and devotion to Jesus can leave a lasting impression on others. (V. 13)
❖ Motivates believers in living generously for Christ, knowing that our works will never go unnoticed or unappreciated by God. (V. 13)
☞ Jesus is not here downplaying the importance of the poor or discouraging their relief. But rather is teaching the importance of putting spiritual needs first before religious services. That only when hearts are right with Him can we effectively carry out all other duties. (Some view this as a prophetic statement that the plight and conditions of the poor of the world will remain until Jesus' second coming).
☞ Some suggest Mary did not understand the full significance of what she had done but was only praised for the prophetic significance of the act, whether known to her or not. Others believe Mary purposely intended the act, having better understood Christ's predictions of His suffering and death than that of the disciples. (cf. Mark 14:8)

From this verse here (V. 14) To verse (V. 16) Judas agrees to betray Jesus to the religious authorities.

***Judas Agrees to Betray Jesus*-(N.I.V.)**

26:14 Then one of the Twelve—(Magnifies the betrayal, having been one of Jesus' closest disciples.) **the one called Judas Iscariot went to the chief priests**
15 and asked, "What are you willing to give me if I hand him over to you?" (deliver-K.J.V., betray-N.L.V.) **So they counted out for him thirty silver coins.**
16 From then on Judas watched for an opportunity to hand him over.

Judas out of his love & greed for money decides to betray Jesus to the religious leaders.

<u>Message & Application</u> 💻=🌎

- ❖ Shows those who hold Jesus of little value are the first to fall away. (Value Christ above money, wealth, prestige, and reputation).
- ❖ Warns against selling Jesus out in hopes of personal gain or worldly advantages. (You can either sell out to the world or sell out to God).
- ❖ Warns against abandoning Jesus when times get hard, or when our expectations of Jesus goes unfulfilled.
- ❖ Warns against following and serving Jesus only when it's to our profit.
- ❖ Warns no matter how close we are to Jesus we're all vulnerable to sin!
- ❖ Warns how a heart that is absent of love and devotion to Jesus can become easy targets for Satan and evil to exploit.

–***Thirty silver coins***-The amount may be based on the O.T. Law for the compensation of an injured slave.-(Ex. 21:32) Expresses their contempt for Jesus, placing no more value on Him than a slave. Or playing on Judas's greed, knowing he would sell out his master cheaply.

➢ Motives for Judas's betrayal has been variously attributed to either:
- Judas' greedy desire for money or Satan's influence in playing on Judas' lust for wealth. (John 12:4-6, 13:2, 27, Luke 2:3, 1-Tim. 6:10)
- Judas' disillusionment by the announcement of Jesus' death, saw his hopes of worldly power and prestige gone. (Matt. 20:18)
- Judas' attempt to force Jesus' hand in exercising His power in overthrowing Rome and establishing His Messianic kingdom.
- Judas' failure to understand Jesus' true identity as Savior, always addressing Jesus only as "Rabbi" and never as "Lord". (Matt. 27:22-25)
- Judas assumed Jesus would use His power and escape, that he would have his money and no harm done. (Matt. 27:3-5)
- Judas' being the only non-Galilean thought it his duty. (John 11:57)

Thursday - (2:00-6:00 P.M.)

The Lord's Supper-(N.I.V.)

26:17 On the first day (i.e. Thursday 14th of Abib-Nisan [March-April]) **of the Feast of Unleavened Bread,** (i.e. The day of Preparation for the Passover in which Jews would rid their houses of all yeast in commemoration of their haste in escaping their bondage in Egypt.-{Ex. 12:15-20}) **the disciples** (i.e. Peter and John.-{Luke 22:8}) **came to Jesus and asked, "Where do you want us to make preparations for you to eat the Passover?"** (Suggests: Consisting of buying and preparing the paschal lamb, as well as the unleavened bread, bitter herbs, wine, and other ceremonial dishes.)
18 He replied, "Go into the city to a certain man (A man carrying a jar of water.-{Mark 14:13}-Suggests: The man would easily be identified since it was customary for only women to carry water jars.) **and tell him, 'The Teacher says: My appointed time is near.** (i.e. Jesus' crucifixion & death.) **I am going to celebrate the Passover with my disciples at your house.'"**
19 The disciples did as Jesus had directed them and prepared the Passover.

Jesus arranges to eat the Passover meal with His disciples as His last supper before His crucifixion.

Message & Application

- Shows how the Lord's supper is always to be carried out with careful preparation, planning, and contemplation. (cf. 1-Corn. 11:17-22)
- Displays how when we have no idea of where we're going in our service to the Lord, Jesus will always give us a sign in the right course.
- Teaches how we're unqualified in undertaking any religious duties or ordinances without Christ's divine guidance and direction
- Calls for humbly serving the Lord without the need for recognition or approval. (V. 18)
- Assures believers that as we obey what Christ sets out for us to do, we will always find things just as He promised us! (V. 18)

–***Certain man***-The man's anonymity is variously attributed to either:

- To keep the man's identity hidden from Judas Iscariot, who was out to betray Jesus to the religious leaders. (V. 16)
- Was a private supporter of Jesus who wanted to keep his identity secret, out of fear of the religious leaders- (John 12:42)
- Was one of Jesus' lesser known disciple, not of the twelve. (Supported by some due to the expression: "The Teacher says My appointed time is near"-V. 18)
- To direct the disciples to the man by a miracle, thereby encouraging their faith that all things were under His control, including His crucifixion.

Following Elements of Jewish Passover meal:

a. **Passover lamb-**The taking of a one-year-old sheep without defect and having the priest slaughter it in the Temple then roasting it at home.(As a reminder of God having spared the firstborn of Israel by passing over their homes)-(See Ex. 12:21-23)
b. **Unleavened bread-**Bread that was baked in the home without yeast. (As a reminder of the swiftness of God's delivering the Israelites out of bondage in Egypt-(See Ex. 12:39) as well as their separation from all the sin in which Egypt stood).
c. **Bowl of sauce-**Called "Charoseth" made of stewed fruit, possibly dates, raisins, and vinegar used to dip bread in. (As a reminder of the clay in which Israelites used to make bricks while in captivity in Egypt).
d. **Dish of bitter herbs-**A kind of salad made up of a wild lettuce, chicory, pepperwort, chives, and dandelions. (As a reminder of Israel's bitter slavery in Egypt)-(See Ex. 12:8, Numb. 9:11)
e. **Cups of wine-**Called the cup of "Hallel" or cup of "Praise & Thanksgiving" in which each of the four cups of wine was followed by a benediction or hymn. (As a reminder of God's covenant blessings promised to Israel)-(See Ps. 113-118)

(Note: Jesus' fulfillment of these Passover rituals will be more fully explained in verses 26-30)

26:20 When evening came Jesus was reclining at the table-◙ with the Twelve.
21 And while they were eating, he said, "I tell you the truth, one of you (i.e. Judas.) **will betray me."**
22 They were very sad and began to say to him one after the other, "Surely not I, Lord?" (Expresses an acknowledgment only of their loyalty to Jesus, then an attempt to clear themselves from suspicion, or unsure of their own actions.)
23 Jesus replied, "The one who has dipped his hand into the bowl with me (Expresses: One who would be a close friend/trusted associate.) **will betray me**
24 The Son of Man will go (Expresses Jesus' crucifixion & death.) **just as it is written** (i.e. Prophesied) **about him.** (Expresses: Various O.T. passages such as Ps. 41:9, Is. 50:5-6, 53:1-12, Dan. 9:26, Zech. 12:10.) **But woe to that man who betrays the Son of Man! It would be better for him if he had not been born."** (Expresses: Compared to the eternal punishment that awaited the betrayer in hell. Though it was God's plan it does not relieve Judas's guilt or responsibility.)
25 Then Judas, the one who would betray him, said, "Surely not I, Rabbi?" (Suggests: Unlike the other disciples, Judas was unwilling to give Jesus the same honor of "Lord".-{V. 22}) **Jesus answered, "Yes, it is you."** (Suggests: A Private conversation, being that the disciples make no effort to stop Judas, or Judas being the closets reclining to Jesus, Viz.- *"You have said it yourself"*.)

Jesus identifies His betrayer as being a close friend who will act treacherously against Him.

Message & Application

- ❖ Shows the need to examine our own hearts & motives while serving Christ. (Stop pointing fingers and be honest and open with yourself).
- ❖ Teaches the importance of vigilance and humility. (Know that we all have the capacity to betray and fall away from Jesus).
- ❖ Displays the power of sin & temptation, that we should not be so confident in thinking we can overcome them by our own strength.
- ❖ Illustrates a divine truth, though an evil act is overruled for good, it does not lessen its guilt and penalty. (V. 24, cf. Rom. 6:1)

–***Dipped his hand into the bowl***-The cultural custom of taking a piece of bread or meat, and then dipping it into a bowl of sauce made up of stewed (pureed) fruit, possibly dates, raisins, and vinegar. In the social and cultural context, since the bowl was a common dish shared by all who were eating. Jesus' statement was meant not to identify the traitor, but rather to emphasize the treacherous act of the betrayer as being a friend, a trusted associate, and someone who was close.

☞ According to the Gospel of John, the disciples thought Jesus was telling Judas to buy something for the feast, or to give something to the poor, being that he was in charge of the money bag.-(John 13:23-29)

26:26 While they were eating, Jesus took bread, gave thanks {See V. 27} **and broke it, and gave it to his disciples, saying, "Take and eat; this is my body".** (Expresses a symbol of Christ's suffering and death, having His body broken & wounded on the cross for our sins.-{cf. Matt. 27:27-31, Is. 53:5, 1-Corn. 11:23-24})
27 Then he took the cup, (i.e. Third cup of Passover liturgy.) **gave thanks** (i.e. Gave the blessing) **and offered it to them, saying, "Drink from it, all of you.**
28 This is my blood of the covenant, which is poured out for many for the forgiveness of sins. (Expresses a symbol of Jesus' blood shed on the cross in ratifying a new covenant between man and God in the remission of sins.)
29 I tell you, I will not drink of this fruit of the vine (i.e. wine) **from now on until that day** (i.e. Jesus' second advent/coming.) **when I drink it anew with you in my Father's kingdom."** (Suggests: Christ's Millennial reign.)
30 When they had sung a hymn, they went out to the Mount of Olives.

Jesus institutes the Passover bread & wine as a symbolic memorial of His suffering & death in the Atonement of sins.

Message & Application 💻=🌎

❖ Shows how believers are to come to the Lord's Supper with open and prepared hearts, remembering all that Christ had suffered & sacrificed.
❖ Calls believers in keeping an eye on all that Christ has suffered for us.
❖ Displays the sufficiency of Christ's sacrifice, delivering believers from death and the bondage of sin.
❖ Calls for pledging our complete loyalty and commitment to Christ, having suffered in giving His life for us.
❖ Calls for finding in Jesus all the sustenance of life and the desires of the soul. (Look at Christ's work as food for the soul).
☞ These Eucharistic elements are not to be viewed as a means of grace, sacraments, or the physical means of Salvation. But rather are only a reminder of the believer's confession of faith and solidarity to Christ.
☞ Today Church's celebrate the Lord's supper in different ways. Some observe it every Sunday, others only three or four times a year. Some use unleavened bread and real wine, others unfermented fruit juice.

Elemental Aspects of Communion:

- The bread and wine become symbols representing the memorial of Christ's death and enduring sacrifice.
- The bread and wine become the actual body of Christ (Catholics doctrine of Consubstantiation).
- The bread & wine become the spiritual presence of Christ through the power of the Holy Spirit.

Following Passover Liturgy & Jesus' New institution:

1) The sharing of the first of four cups of wine, at which the head of the household gave a blessing before the meal. Also observed by Jesus-(See Luke 22:17) Followed by a ceremonial washing of hands and feet-Also observed by Jesus.-(See John 13:2-5).
2) The sharing of the second cup of wine at which time the meaning of the significance of the Passover feast is explained.-(Ex. 12:26-27) Followed by the singing of the first portion of the "Hallel" as found in Psalms 113-114.
3) The serving of the Paschal lamb-(Symbolizing God's redemptive act in sparing the firstborn of Israel by passing over their homes.-(Ex. 12:1-14) **Jesus' new institution of it as expressed by His sacrificial death for sin.**–(Vs. 26, 28, John 1:29, 36, Heb. 9:11-28)
4) The sharing of unleavened bread (Symbolizing Israel's deliverance from slavery in Egypt.-(Ex. 12:15-20) **Jesus' new institution of it as symbolizing His body given over on the cross as God's punishment for sin.**
5) The sharing of the third cup of wine at which time grace was said. (Symbolizing God's covenant blessings given to Israel) **Jesus' new institution of it as symbolizing His blood shed on the cross for the sealing of a New Covenant in the remission of sin.**
6) The sharing of the fourth cup of wine followed with the singing the second portion of the "Hallel" as found in Psalms 115-118. As also fulfilled by the disciples in the singing of a hymn after supper-(See Matthew 26:30, Mark 14:26)

Sacramental Elements of the Lord's Supper:

Bread.-Remembrance of Jesus' body given over to suffering and death in the redemption of sinners, as well as the source of eternal life.

Cup.-Remembrance of Jesus' blood shed on the cross for the remission of sin and the sealing of a New Covenant of grace.

Theological Elements of the Lords Supper;

- A proclamation of Christ's death on the cross as a substitutionary sacrifice in atoning for sin.
- A proclamation of the spiritual union & abiding presence of Christ with believers. (cf. John 6:56)
- A proclamation of the believer's continual dependence and future participation in Christ's eschatological kingdom. (Mark 14:25, Luke 22:18, 1-Corn. 11:26, Rev. 19:9)

Observing the Lord's Supper:

- **Participation:** Believers are to fellowship with each other and their Church on the first day of the week-(The Lord's day) (1-Corn. 11:18, 20) They are to share communion (bread & cup) with their congregation.-(1-Corn. 11:23-25)
- **Commemoration:** Believers are to remember the redemptive nature of Christ's substitutionary sacrifice. Believers are to identify with Christ's suffering in dying for our sins.-(1-Corn. 11:24) Believers are to remember Christ's blood shed on the Cross as God's provision in the Atonement of sin.-(1-Corn. 11:25)
- **Self-examination:** Believers are to guard their hearts and thoughts, confessing and repenting of known sins beforehand. Believers are to keep their attention and focus on the meaning and significance of the Lord's supper.-(1-Corn. 11:27-29)
- **Proclamation-**Believers by partaking in the Lord's supper are proclaiming Christ's sacrificial death on the Cross for our sins, their spiritual unity, and Jesus' second coming.-(Luke 22:16-18, 1-Corn. 11:26)

Good Friday - (10:00 P.M.-12:00 A.M.)

Jesus predicts Peter's Denial-(N.I.V.)

26:31 Then (i.e. While en-route to the Garden of Gethsemane.-{V. 30}) **Jesus told them, This very night you will all fall away** (646-*Apostatize, revolt, defect.* offended-K.J.V.-4624-*Scandalize, trip up.* Syn.-dismayed, distrust, forsake, ashamed, desert-L.B.V.) **on account of me,** (i.e. As a result of Jesus' arrests and crucifixion. Or because of Jesus' apparent defeat on the cross.) **for it is written:** (i.e. Prophesied in Zech. 13:7) **"'I** (i.e. God) **will strike the shepherd,** (Metph-Jesus. Expresses God's will in giving Jesus over to suffering and crucifixion at the hands of the Jews & Romans in bearing sins of the world. {cf. Is. 53:10, Acts 2:23, Rom. 8:32}) **and the sheep of the flock** (Metph-disciples) **will be scattered"** (Suggests: The disciples fleeing in fear for their own safety as a result of Jesus' arrest and crucifixion as a criminal.)
32 But after I have risen (i.e. Jesus' resurrection.) **I will go ahead of you into Galilee".** (Expresses Jesus' way of comforting and reassuring the disciples, that despite their own failure, He will not leave nor forsake them.)

As a result of Jesus' arrests and fear for their own lives, the disciples will desert Him, just as Zechariah prophesied.

<u>**Message & Application**</u> 

- Shows no matter how far we fall, Christ will never disown or forsake us. (Know Jesus' unfailing love no matter how far you backslide).
- Warns believers against falling away from Christ for fear of reproach, shame, or embarrassment.
- Displays how Christ is acquainted beforehand with our trials and weaknesses, knowing how to bear and deliver us in them. (Trust that Jesus who Saves, also knows how to keep us!).
- Reminds believers no matter how much it may seem that Satan or sin has the upper hand, know that God is always in control.
- Cautions believers against thinking we're stronger than we are, for it is Christ who keeps us. (Trust Jesus as the shepherd of your soul).
- Teaches the importance of acknowledging our weakness and continual need to depend on Jesus. (No matter how firm our faith, know that some temptations are too strong for us to bear alone).

–I will go ahead of you into Galilee-Variously interpret as either:

- Galilee being a principal field of Jesus' ministry, would be the natural place to commission the disciples to spread the Gospel.-(cf. Matt. 28:16-20)
- Galilee being the home of most of the disciples, making it the natural place they would flee too in taking refuge.-(cf. John 16:32)

26:33 Peter replied, "Even if all (Viz. Other 11-disciples.) **fall away** (be offended-K.J.V. {cf. V. 31}) **on account of you,** (i.e. In consequence of the stigma of shame and disgrace following Jesus' arrest and crucifixion.) **I never will."**
34 "I tell you the truth," (verily-K.J.V.-Expresses a strong confirmation and reliability.) **Jesus answered, "this very night, before the cock-◙** (i.e. Rooster) **crows,** (i.e. Sunrise, daybreak, within hours, at dawn-L.B.V., cock crows twice.-{Mark 14:30}-Expresses a reference to the Roman time periods of the second and third watch.) **you will disown me** (deny-K.J.V.-533-*To affirm that one has no connection or acquaintance with.* Syn.-renounce, disclaim.) **three times."**
35 But Peter declared, (Syn.-protested, emphatically.-{Mark 14:31}) **"Even if I have to die with you, I will never disown** (deny-K.J.V.) **you."** (Expresses: fidelity, loyalty.) **And all the other disciples said the same.**

Jesus predicts that before the night is over Peter will deny knowing Him three times.

Message & Application 💻=🌎

- ❖ Show how some can feel over confident & invincible in the times of safety, but not know their own weaknesses in times of trials & dangers.
- ❖ Warns against relying on our own strength rather than the Lords. (Know your vulnerability/weaknesses and total dependence on Jesus).
- ❖ Warns of the dangers of spiritual pride & presumption, thinking we would fare better in loyalty and faithfulness than other Christians.
- ❖ Warns against thinking that somehow we're better armed against sinning than anybody else. (Better to say "If others can fall so can I"!).
- ❖ Displays the vulnerability of pious men in being over-confident in their own strength and stability. (Sometimes we're nobler in our declarations than our living, better to learn to take heed then to fall!).
- ❖ Warns against thinking that we know ourselves better than God knows us. (Those who fail to listen to God are bound to stumble).
- ➢ Demonstrates the three greatest sins believers can fall into:
  - Failure to heed Jesus' words-(V. 31)
  - Contempt and superiority over others-(V. 33 a)
  - Spiritual pride and self-confidence-(V. 33 b)
- ☞ According to the Gospel of Luke, while predicting Peter's denial, Jesus also reassures Peter, that though his faith will falter it will not fail, and how he will be a source of encouragement to the other disciples. (See Luke 22:31-32)
- ☞ After the resurrection, these three denials will be recalled by Jesus during Peter's reinstatement, as a way of allowing Peter to reconfirm his love for Him three times.-(See John 21:15-17)

From this verse here (V. 36) To verse (V. 46) Jesus agonizes over His crucifixion & death while praying in Gethsemane.

Good Friday - (12:00 -1:00 A.M.)
Gethsemane-(N.I.V.)

26:36 Then Jesus went with his disciples (i.e. The Eleven.-{John 13:27-30}) **to a place called Gethsemane,-◙** (1068-*Heb.-Oil press.* i.e. An enclosed olive grove east of Jerusalem on the lower slopes of the mount of Olives.) **and he said to them, "Sit here** (i.e. At the entrance to the garden grove.) **while I go over there** (i.e. Further into the garden grove. For privacy in prayer.) **and pray."**
37 He took Peter and the two sons of Zebedee (James & John) **along with him** (i.e. Jesus' inner circle of disciples who were closest to Him.) **and he began to be sorrowful** (Syn.-grief stricken, mournful) **and troubled.** (85-*Distressed, great mental stress & anguish.* Deep distress, intense anguish, excruciating anxiety, Expresses a combination of mental stress compounded with fear and anxiety.)
38 Then he said to them, "My soul (i.e. Spirit) **is overwhelmed with sorrow** (deeply grieved-NASB, crushed with horror and sadness-L.B.V.) **to the point** (Syn.-degree) **of death.** (Expresses a sorrow so great that it almost kills, or that He could die from the sheer anguish.) **Stay here and keep watch** (Syn.-vigil) **with me."** (Expresses: To keep awake/vigilant, to sympathize or unite with another in prayer. Pray that you will not fall into temptation.-{Luke 22:40})

Jesus anguishes over the prospect of being made sin and separated from God as He bears the sins of the world.

Message & Application

- ❖ Shows believers the great amount of suffering & anguish Jesus was willing to undergo on our behalf. (Pray; "God help us to hate sin because of what it did to our Lord and Savior"!).
- ❖ Displays the importance of seeking the assistance of other Christians when we find ourselves in great trials and temptations. (V. 38)
- ❖ Teaches the importance of uniting with others in prayer, offering our support and comfort in their time of need. (V. 38)

–***Overwhelmed with sorrow***-Variously attributed to either:

- Jesus' fear of being forsaken & separated from God the Father, while bearing the sins of the world. (cf. Matt. 27:46, Mark 15:34)
- Jesus' anguish over the horrible prospect of taking upon Himself all the moral filth, perversity, and sins of the world.-(cf. 2-Corn. 5:21)
- Jesus' sense of loneliness having foreseen the disciple's desertion, Peters failure, Judas's betrayal, and the nation's rejection of Him.

26:39 Going a little farther, (i.e. Going deeper into the garden, to a more private spot, farther away from the three disciples, about a stone throw away.-{Luke22:41}) **he fell with his face to the ground and prayed,"**-◙ (Expresses a sign of anguish, earnest entreaty, submission. Church tradition has Jesus kneeling under an olive tree or upon a rock.) **My Father, if it is possible,** (Expresses: Not reluctance, but an alternative way that is still consistent with God's redemptive purposes.) **may this cup** (Metph.-God's judgment, wrath, sufferings, and trials. Expresses Jesus' approaching Passion & Crucifixion.) **be taken from me. Yet not as I will,** (Syn.-desire, wish, determine) **but as you will."** (Expresses Christ's voluntarily putting aside His own will and desires in favor of submitting to what God wants.)

Jesus humbly submits to God's will in suffering for the sins of the world.

Message & Application 💻=🌎

❖ Shows believers the great depth of Christ's love & mercy in His willing to suffer by standing in the place of sinners.
❖ Displays Jesus' tremendous love for us, having willingly taken upon Himself all of God's wrath for our sins.
❖ Calls for trusting our life's to God's wisdom, goodness, and mercy regardless of the trials and hardships we have to endure.
❖ Teaches where trials and hardships may be unavoidable, we can always pray to God for the grace & strength to bear up under them.
❖ Teaches how true faith always follows and trusts in the Divine will no matter the consequences or where it takes us.
❖ Characterizes the type of surrendered life God desires, one that is willing to trust in His providence even in times of our greatest peril.
☞ Jesus is not asking that God accomplishes His redemptive purposes by some other means other than Himself, nor was Jesus distrusting in the Father's will. But rather was concerned with being separated/forsaken (temporarily) from God the Father, while bearing our sins on the cross.
☞ According to the Gospel of Luke it records additional details, that as Jesus prayed; *"His sweat was like drops of blood falling to the ground"*.-(Suggests so intense was the emotional strain that Jesus was enduring that it caused what is known as "hematidrosis" a condition that occurs when a person who is under extreme anguish or emotional pain, will cause the capillaries in the sweat glands to dilate and burst, thereby producing a mixture of blood & sweat. Others interpret it only as describing "Profuse sweating", that sweat was pouring out like thick clots of blood on the ground.

26:40 Then he returned to his disciples (i.e. Peter, James, and John.) **and found them sleeping.** (Exhausted from sorrow.-{Luke 22:45 c}) **"Could you men not keep watch** (Syn.-vigil) **with me for one hour?"** (Expresses: Not bitterness, but rather disappointment and sadness.) **he asked Peter.** (Suggests: Peter singled out, having been the leader of the twelve. Or on account of Peter' prior bold assertion, having boasted in his fidelity in dying with Jesus.-{Vs. 31, 35})
41"Watch (1127-*Constant vigilant, spiritual alertness.* Metph-to be spiritually prepared and alert.) **and pray so that you will not fall** (Syn.-sub-come, yield) **into temptation.** (Syn.-sin, trials, apostasy. Suggests: The testing of their faith against deserting Jesus because of His arrest and death. Expresses: Not that believers be spared trials, but that they not be overcome by them.) **The spirit** (i.e. will, desires, best intentions) **is willing, but the body** (Fallen/sinful nature) **is weak."** (Expresses Jesus' sympathy, though the disciple's intentions were good, but human inadequacies would make it difficult for them to carry it out.)

Disciples are to pray that they remain faithful in not deserting Jesus when He is arrested and crucified.

Message & Application 💻=🌎

- Shows how sufferings & trials, if not prepared for, can become a temptation to our faith in deserting Jesus. (If we hope to reign with Christ, we must also be willing to pray and stand with Him!).
- Calls for the willingness in sharing in our brother's struggles, offering them our encouragement, support, and prayers.
- Calls for staying spiritually dependent on God's strength. (Know it's not within your own power to stand without God's help & assistance).
- Warns how if we can't keep our love and fidelity for Jesus in small temptations, how can we expect to stay committed to Him during greater trials. (If we can't endure words, how can we endure wounds).
- Warns the dangers of living in a state of false security. (Know that temptation, sin, and Satan's attacks are around every corner!).
- Displays how most temptations are a result of our own carelessness and negligence towards our spiritual lives.
- Teaches the importance of being spiritually prepared for Satan's attacks by devoting ourselves to prayer and bible meditation.
- Comforts believers in having the gracious provisions of Christ, always taking into considerations our shortcomings and failures.

-Found them sleeping-Does not mean the disciple were indifferent to our Lord's suffering. But rather was proof of their attachment to Him, being overwhelmed and exhausted from sorrow and grief over Jesus' announcement of His arrest and death. (cf. Luke 22:45)

26:42 He went away a second time and prayed, "My Father, if it is not possible for this cup (God's wrath/judgment against sin.) **to be taken away unless I drink it** (Expresses: Surrender/submission.) **may your will be done."**

Jesus voluntarily surrenders to God's will in suffering for the sins of the world.

Message and Application

- ❖ Shows Jesus' unceasing compassion & love for sinners in His willingness to suffer and die in our place.
- ❖ Calls for surrendering all to God no matter how trying or disagreeable it may seem at the time. (Know that obedience to God always gives way to victory and glory in the end!).
- ❖ Teaches how the true characteristics of a surrendered life is one that fully submits to the divine will in all things.
- ❖ Calls for always putting the purposes and plans of God before our own will and desires. (Trust that God knows what's best for us).

26:43 When he came back, (i.e. For support in His hour of agony.) **he again found them sleeping because their eyes were heavy.** (i.e. Though the disciples fought as much as they could from falling asleep, they eventually succumbed.)
44 So he left them (Expresses: Not rejection or disappointment, but Jesus' compassion in sympathizing with their weakness.) **and went away once more and prayed the third time, saying the same thing.** (Expresses: Not so much the same words, but rather of earnestness, determination, and purpose.)

Jesus obediently commits Himself to God's will in suffering for the sins of the world.

Message & Application

- ❖ Shows believers how the infirmities of the flesh, if not guarded against, can slowly rob us of our spiritual alertness.
- ❖ Displays Jesus' patience and compassions with human frailty, that Christ graciously pardons our weakness and infirmities.
- ❖ Teaches how sometimes Christ leaves us to our spiritual slumber in order to teach us a lesson against the false sense of security.

–***Prayed the third time-***The three petitions are interpreted as either:

- Was meant to convey the progression of Jesus' submission, surrender, and commitment-(Vs. 39, 42, 44)
- Was intended to contrast with Peter's three denials. (Vs. 31-35)
- Was an intercessory prayer needed for the disciples and for all believers-(cf. John 17:1-26, 18:1)

26:45 Then he returned to the disciples and said to them, "Are you still sleeping and resting? (Expresses a form of "irony" in light of the imminent danger unfolding before them, or in the sense of "lost opportunity", that the time for praying and preparation had passed.) **Look,** (behold-K.J.V. Expresses: Partly as a call to awaken the disciple's attention as well as to express the insolent and horrid actions of Judas.) **the hour is near,** (Syn.-imminent, at hand) **and the Son of Man** (i.e. Messiah/Jesus) **is betrayed into the hands of sinners.** (i.e. The arrival of Judas with Jewish authorities and Roman soldiers.)
46 Rise, (i.e.-Get up, make haste) **let us go!** (Suggests: Not in the sense of retreat, but rather to advance and to confront. Expresses Jesus' fortitude, willingness, and readiness to do God's will.) **Here comes my betrayer!"** (i.e. Judas. Suggests: Either Jesus' omniscience in what was unfolding, or having seen the gleam of torches descending the valley and coming towards them.)

The disciple's opportunity to prepare themselves for the crises ahead had now passed, for Jesus' arrest was close at hand.

Message & Application 💻=🌎

❖ Shows the need to stay spiritually prepared. (Don't give in to laziness when it comes to Church attendance, bible study, or prayer!).
❖ Teaches despite our spiritual slumber/neglect, Christ's love still goes out to us, strengthening and preparing us for the trials that lie ahead.
❖ Warns how the failure and neglect to pray now, can affect us in our preparation for the trials that lie ahead.
❖ Displays the powerful effect that prayer can have in disarming our fears, giving us the strength to meet the dangers that lie ahead. (Burdens that are not removed are overcome by perseverance).-(V. 46)
❖ Calls for embracing the divine paths God has called us to with obedience and faithfulness. (V. 46)

☞ According to the Gospel of Mark the call for attention is expressed as; *"Enough"*!- (Mark 14:41 b) Which has been variously interpreted as meaning either in the sense of "sufficient", that the disciples time for rest, watching, and praying was over. Or as of "compensation", that Judas had received the money for the betrayal. Or even in the sense of "settlement", that God's time for Jesus to go to the cross had come. Do to the context of *"The hour is near"*-(V. 45) most favor the latter interpretation.

Good Friday - (1:00-3:00 A.M.)

Jesus Arrested-(N.I.V.)

26:47 While he was still speaking, Judas, one of the Twelve, (Expresses: Magnifies Judas's treachery & betrayal, being one of Jesus' closest friends.) **arrived. With him was a large crowd armed with swords and clubs,** (Expresses a combination of Roman soldiers and Jewish Temple guards.) **sent from the chief priests and the elders of the people.**
48 Now the betrayer had arranged a signal with them: (i.e. Because Jesus was unknown to them.) **"The one I kiss is the man; arrest him."**(Expresses a common form of greeting by kissing the right and left side of the cheek. Used as a convenient way to identify Jesus without arresting the wrong man.)
49 Going at once to Jesus, Judas said, "Greetings, Rabbi!" (Expresses a false pretense of praise and respect, a form of mock respect.) **and kissed him.**
50 Jesus replied, "Friend, do what you came for."(Exposes Judas's hypocritical pretense of affection, or to convict him of his crime and treacherous act. That there will be no resistance from Jesus, all was going according to the divine plan.) **Then the men stepped forward, seized Jesus and arrested him.**

Under the false pretense of loyalty & affection, Judas identifies Jesus to the authorities with a kiss.

Message & Application

- ❖ Shows how believers must never allow the betrayal & treachery of our closest and dearest friends keep us from forgiving them.
- ❖ Displays how oftentimes the greatest of hypocrites are those who make the loudest of professions and attachments to Christ.
- ❖ Calls for not becoming bitter, discouraged, or resentful against those who have wounded or abandoned us in our time of crises.
- ❖ Teaches rather than rebel and revolt against Christ, speak honestly to Jesus about your hurts, wounds, and disappointments.
- ❖ Teaches how God's love never abandons even the most apostate.

-The one I kiss-Most interpret it simply as a way to identify Jesus to the soldiers without mistakenly arresting the wrong man. Others see it as emphasizing the insidious nature of Judas's crime, by using the pretense of his friendship and affection for Jesus to betray Him.

-Friend-Variously interpreted as either:

- A conciliatory appeal, expressing a spirit of forgiveness and grace extended to Judas.
- A scornful ironic rebuke, knowing Judas's treachery in betraying Him.
- To convict Judas of guilt and moving him to repentance.

26:51 With that, (i.e. Jesus having been seized and arrested.-{V. 50}) **one of Jesus' companions** (i.e. Simon Peter.-{John 18:10} Gospels probably conceal the name in order to protect Peter from future persecution.) **reached for his sword, drew it out and struck the servant of the high priest,** (Suggests: Was the closest in attempting to apprehend Jesus, or was the leader of the band. The Gospel of John identifies him as *"Malchus"*.-{John 18:10 b}) **cutting off his ear.** (i.e. Peter having missed a blow to the head, hits the man's ear instead.)
52 "Put your sword back in its place," Jesus said to him, "for all who draw the sword will die by the sword. (Expresses a proverbial maxim, that all who live violently will die violently, that violence only invites further violence. That Peter by drawing his sword he was needlessly endangering his own safety and the safety of the other disciples.)
53 Do you think I cannot call on my Father, (i.e. God) **and he will at once put at my disposal more than twelve legions of Angeles?** (i.e. A Roman army division of 6000 soldiers X 12 equaling 72,000 angels. A legion of angels for each disciple if needed. Expresses Heaven itself would come to Jesus' aid, that Jesus was in complete control, everything was happening with His permission.)
54 But how then would the Scriptures be fulfilled that say it must happen in this way?" (Suggests: In fulfillment with all the O.T. Prophesies concerning the suffering Servant and God's plan of Salvation.-{Is. 53:10-12, Ps. 22:11-16, 41:9})

Jesus offers no resistance because it was the prophetic plan of God that He suffer & die for the sins of the world.

Message & Application

- Shows believers how rash decisions & misdirected zeal can cause us to act out of the will of God and wrong motives.
- Warns believers against the temptation of putting our own ideas and plans ahead of God's will and plans.
- Teaches how God doesn't need our good intentions & sacrifices, but rather our uncompromising obedience. (None of us is indispensable).
- Comforts believers in knowing that when surrounded by enemies, we have divine protection on our side if needed.
- Calls for always approaching difficult situations, not by our own counsels or strengths, but by God's providence and grace.
- Warns how sometimes our good intentions, no matter how noble, can get in the way of God's plans and purposes for our lives.

☞ According to the Gospel of Luke after Peter cut off the servant's ear Jesus; *"touched the man's ear and healed him*"-(Luke 22:51) (Expresses Jesus' compassion even in our failures, that Jesus is willing and ready to clean up the messes we make!).

26:55 At that time Jesus said to the crowd, (i.e. The chief priests/temple guards.) **"Am I leading a rebellion,** (Syn.-revolution, insurrection, come against a thief-K.J.V., dangerous criminal-L.B.V.) **that you have come out with swords and clubs to capture me? Every day I sat in the temple courts-◙ teaching,** (i.e. Public places, chief priests own backyard.) **and you did not arrest me.**
56 But this has all taken place that the writings of the prophets {Is. 53:7-9, 12} **might be fulfilled. Then all the disciples deserted him and fled.**(forsook-K.J.V. cut and ran-M.B.V. i.e. They escaped for their own safety, fearing arrest.)

Jesus' humble restraint was all in fulfillment with scriptures.

Message & Application

❖ Shows Jesus' calmness & restraint in standing alone and abandoned as He awaits His fate in all that God had called Him to suffer.
❖ Teaches believers how our witness must stand on its own integrity and honor, and not by threat or intimidation of others.
❖ Teaches the importance of carrying out ministries peacefully. (Give enemies no excuse to justify their persecution of us).
❖ Displays the need for patience while under pressure, always reproving our enemies and persecutors calmly and intelligently.
❖ Warns how even the best of us can give in to fear, discouragement, and despair. (Know that no-one is perfect, we all fail!).
❖ Calls for constant vigilance and humility, for even the most faithful of us, can desert Christ in times of danger.

–***Then all the disciples deserted him***-Variously attributed to either:

- Having witnessed Jesus' arrest, feared for their own safety.
- Having lost faith, they fled in despair, seeing Jesus' arrest as an end to their hopes.
- Having feared that Peter's rash assault on the high priest's servant would be charged to them all.

☞ According to the Gospel of Mark, it adds that; *"A young man, wearing nothing but a linen garment* (i.e. undergarment, nightshirt, robe) *was following Jesus. When they seized him, he fled naked, leaving his garment behind".*-(Mark 14:51-52) (Scholarly consensus is that the young man was John Mark the author of his Gospel. That his house was near Gethsemane. That he been awakened by the commotion and in his haste, went out to investigate wearing only his nightgown. Expresses an ancient literary practice of inserting oneself into the epic, without divulging one's identity. That it was Mark's way of putting himself there as an eyewitness, saying that like the rest, he also deserted Jesus.

From this verse here (V. 57) To verse (V. 67) Jesus is taken to the high priest's house for a preliminary inquisition before the trial.

Before the Sanhedrin-(N.I.V.)

26:57 Those who had arrested Jesus took him to Caiaphas, the high priest, where the teachers of the law (Scribes-K.J.V.) **and the elders had assembled.** (Expresses: Taken together an informal trial before the Sanhedrin.)

58 But Peter followed him at a distance, (Expresses a mixture of curiosity, devotion, loyalty, and love for Jesus.) **right up to the courtyard of the high priest.-◙ He entered** (Suggests: With the help of another disciple, presumably John.-{John 18:15-16}) **and sat down with the guards to see the outcome.**

Because of their haste in putting Jesus to death before the Sabbath, the Sanhedrin hold a trial at the High Priest's house.

Message & Application 💻=🌎

- ❖ Shows the lengths that religion & sinful humans will go to in removing Jesus from their lives.
- ❖ Cautions believers against half-heartedness, don't allow fear, ridicule, or embarrassment keep you from proclaiming Christ.
- ❖ Warns the dangers of presumption and self-confidence by going headlong into temptation without God's protection.
- ❖ Warns the dangers of worldly associations, that when we choose to sit in the company of sinners trouble is bound to follow.
- ⊶ Even today is your walk with the Lord only at a distance. Are you ashamed of being seen carrying a bible, do you blend in with coworkers and friends so that no one can tell you're a Christian?

Those who oppose the legality of this trial do so by arguing:

A) Jewish law held that criminal trials could not be held at night. And that verdicts required two days to appeal capital cases.

B) Jewish law stipulated that trials of criminal cases could only be held at the Temple chamber of Hewn stone, and only in public.

C) Jewish law forbade the executions of criminals during major feasts days, except for the most heinous of crimes.

Those who support the legality of this trial do so by arguing:

A) Jewish laws stipulations were only theological formulations, never meant to be enforced by law.

B) Expedience was necessary due to the fact the leaders feared mob violence because of Jesus' arrest, therefore haste was required.

C) Since law allowed criminals to be crucified on feast days, they needed to move fast in putting Jesus to death on the Passover.

Chronology of Jesus' Trial:

An Inquisition Trial: (12 - 6 A.M.)

1) A preliminary hearing before Annas.-(John 18:12-14) (Deposed by Rome, Annas was still considered high priest. His preliminary findings would be used to advise Caiaphas).
2) An informal trial before Caiaphas & Sanhedrin.-(Matt. 26:57-68, Mark 14:53-65, Luke 22:54, John 19:24) (Where Jesus would be tried and condemned for blasphemy).
3) A second sentencing trial before the Sanhedrin just after daybreak.-(Matt. 27:1, Mark 15:1, Luke 22:66) (Unknown if there were two separate hearings before the Sanhedrin, one at night, then another in the morning, or a single trial extending to dawn).

A Criminal/Civil Trial: (7 – 11 A.M.)

1) A trial before Pontius Pilate.-(Matt. 27:2, 11-26, Mark 15:1-15, Luke 23:1-5, John 18:28-40, 19:1-16) (Where Jesus would be tried and condemned for sedition and insurrection)-(Luke 23:1-2).
2) A trial before Herod Antipas.-(Luke 23:6-12) (Jesus being a legal resident of Galilee, was under Herod's jurisdiction).
3) A retrial before Pontius Pilate.-(Luke 23:13-25) (Having been acquitted by Herod)-(Luke 23:13-15)

26:59 The chief priests and the whole Sanhedrin (i.e. Jewish Supreme court.) **were looking for false evidence** (false witnesses-K.J.V., witnesses who could lie.-L.B.V.) **against Jesus so that they could put him to death.**
60 But they did not find any, though many false witnesses came forward. (But their statements did not agree.-{Mark 14:56}) **Finally, two came forward** (Expresses the minimum number required under Mosaic Law.-{Deut. 17:6})
61 and declared, "This fellow (Expresses a contemptuous tone as in "chap" or "bloke".) **said, 'I am able to destroy the temple of God and rebuild it in three days.'"**(Suggests: A statement that Jesus said three years earlier in defending His authority in the cleansing of the Temple.-{cf. John 2:12-21} Expresses: Legality of the charge is seen as a blasphemous boast, a sacrilegious affront to God, or a Messianic claim.-{V. 63 b, Zech. 6:12-13, Luke 23:2})

Looking for a legal pretext to condemn Jesus, two witnesses come forward falsely accusing Jesus of blaspheming God.

Message & Application 💻=🌎

- ❖ Shows the need for standing true to Christ, having seen the false accusations that the Lord had unfairly endured for us.
- ❖ Teaches those who have already hardened their hearts will look for any evidence to reject Jesus than admit their own accountability.
- ❖ Displays how legalistic religion is more concerned about self-preservation than about truth.
- ❖ Warns how those who are unwilling to face the convictions of their own conscience will look for any means to prove it away.
- ❖ Calls for seeking God's guidance and intervention in not allowing bias or untruths to interfere with His will.
- ❖ Displays the malicious tactics of our adversaries, who, if they cannot find anything in our character, will use innuendos and hearsays.
- ❖ Warns how murder always begins with the mouth. (Gossip and tittle-tattle are a form of verbal bloodshed that begins in the heart).
- ❖ Teaches that no matter how many times we're misunderstood, take comfort that God knows the truth and knows your heart.
- ❖ Calls for exercising discernment in knowing how to sort out lies from the truth, and misunderstanding from facts.
- ❖ Warns against allowing the rumors and negative gossip to taint our view of others. (Get the facts straight before jumping to conclusions).

–***I am able to destroy the temple & rebuild it in three days***-Was a miss representation of what Jesus had actually said. Where Jesus was speaking metaphorically of His body and resurrection from the dead. But the Jews interpreted Jesus' words as a literal threat of destroying and replacing the Temple proper. (cf. John 2:18-22)

26:62 Then the high priest stood up (Expresses: Frustration, impatience.) **and said to Jesus, "Are you not going to answer? What is this testimony that these men are bringing against you?"**(i.e. The blasphemous Messianic claims.)
63 But Jesus remained silent. The high priest said to him, "I charge you under oath by the living God:(i.e. Unlike the dead idols made of wood/stone.) **Tell us if you are the Christ, the Son of God."**(Expresses not a sincere inquiry, but rather a way to get Jesus to implicate Himself of the blasphemous charges.)

Caiaphas attempts to get Jesus to acknowledge His Messiahship so he could condemn Him for blasphemy.

Message & Application 💻=🌎

- ❖ Shows Jesus' meekness & submission in staying true to the will and plan of God in suffering in the place of sinners.
- ❖ Calls believers in standing firm in our convictions. (Don't allow the opinions of others deter your faith in Christ).
- ❖ Displays how no amount of testimony or witness will convince those who have already hardened their hearts and are blind to the truth.

–***Jesus remained silent***-Not that Jesus lacked any words in His own defense, but rather was unwilling to interfere with the course of events. That His silence was in fulfillment of prophecy concerning the Suffering Servant as predicted by the prophet Isaiah. (cf. Is. 53:7)

26:64 "Yes, it is as you say, (Expresses an assent of Messiahship & divinity. Similar to the English idiom; *"You said it with your own lips"*. I am-{Mark 14:62} **"Jesus replied. "But I say to all of you: In the future** (i.e. Day of Judgment) **you will see the Son of Man** (i.e. Messiah/Jesus) **sitting at the right hand of the Mighty one** (i.e. God. Sharing in divine power and glory.) **and coming on the clouds of heaven."**(Expresses Jesus' second coming/advent in judgment. That the positions will be reversed, where Jesus on the day of judgment will be sitting in judgment upon His accusers!)

Jesus not only confesses His divine Messiahship but also warns of His returning one day in judgment against them.

Message & Application 💻=🌎

- ❖ Shows Jesus' humbleness & patience in wanting all to know the truth and come to repentance before the day of Judgment.
- ❖ Calls believers in staying true to Christ, always with an eye of faith that Jesus is who He claims to be, Lord and Savior!.
- 🗝 Even today we're to have the courage in acknowledging God's truth before men, regardless of the dangers & consequences that may follow.

26:65 Then the high priest tore his clothes (i.e. Robes Expresses horror, shock, grief. Was forbidden by law,-{Lev. 10:6} but was a common method of expressing grief.-{cf. 2-Kings 18:37, 19:}) **and said, "He has spoken blasphemy!** (987-*"Of those who speak contemptuously of God or sacred things".)* **Why do we need any more witnesses? Look, now you have heard the blasphemy.** (i.e. Jesus having asserted Messiahship and divine equality with God.-{V. 64 b})
66 What do you think? (Expresses: Is not calling for a formal verdict or judicial decision,–{27:1} but only of professional opinion since they had no power under Roman law to enforce capital punishment.) **"He is worthy** (guilty-K.J.V., deserving-R.S.V.) **of death, they answered.** (Suggests: As mandated by the Law of Moses.-{cf. Lev. 24:10-23, 1-Kings 21:10-13})

By claiming divinity & equality with God, Jesus is condemned for blasphemy.

Message & Application

- Shows the decision we make concerning Jesus' divine claims will either result in falling down & worshiping Him or rejecting Him.
- Warns against being influenced by the bigotry and prejudice of others. (Don't allow the authority of others to sway your judgments).
- Warns how failures in coming to Christ is not from the want of evidence, but the lack of will. (Don't reject Christ without thoroughly investigating and examining His claims!).
- Displays how many try to ease their consciences by finding others who are in agreement with their convictions. (Know that no amount of witnesses will clear a guilty conscience!).

-High priest tore his clothes-Some see a prophetic fulfillment in this action as the rendering and changing of the Aaronic priesthood and the abolition of the ceremonial law now more fully fulfilled by Jesus. Much in the same way, the veil in the Temple was torn in two from top to bottom at the moment of Jesus' death on the cross. (cf. Matt. 27:50-51)

Those Responsible for Jesus' Death:

- The whole human race because of our sin debt owed to God.(Acts 4:27, 1-Tim. 2:6)
- Satan/Judas. (Luke 22:3-4, John 13:27)
- Jewish religious leaders. (John 5:18, 7:1, 10:31)
- Roman political leaders. (Acts 4:27)
- Jewish population. (Matt. 27:22, Acts 2:36)
- God the Father's will. (Is. 53:10, Acts 2:23)

26:67 Then they (i.e. Members of the Sanhedrin council.) **spat in his face** (Expresses a form of extreme insult, disgrace, rejection, contempt, mocking.-{Luke 22:63}) **and struck him with their fists.** (i.e. Heavy and repeated blows to the head, face, and mouth.) **Others** (i.e. Jewish temple guards-{Mark 14:65, Luke 22:63-64}) **slapped him** (i.e. In the face as a form of shame, insult, contempt.)
68 and said, "Prophesy (4395-*"Of telling forth divine knowledge", predict, make known.)* **to us, Christ.** (5547-*"Anointed One", son of God,* Messiah!-L.B.V.) **Who hit you?"** (Expresses a form of taunting and ridicule. That Jesus was blindfolded.-{Mark 14:65} That it was a commonly held belief that the Messiah could judge without sight or hearing.-{cf. Is. 11:2-4, Ps. 17:37} A similar example is found in a children's game called "Blind Mans Bluff" in which one player is blindfolded and has to catch and identify other players by touch.)

The Sanhedrin expresses contempt for Jesus' Messianic claims by making a mockery of His Messiahship.

Message & Application 💻=🌎

- ❖ Shows Jesus' willingness in enduring mocking & humiliation as He suffers on behalf of sinners.
- ❖ Displays the wickedness of men to make sport of others in their misery. (There's nothing more malicious than to add insult to injury).
- ❖ Teaches the importance of maintaining peace and patience in the face of provocation. (Can you stay calm in the face of unfairness?)
- ❖ Calls for enduring all forms of insults and indignities that we might learn to suffer in silence like Christ without taking revenge.
- ❖ Characterizes the daily abuses done to Christ by those who partake of wickedness, thinking they can sin securely without Christ knowing.

–***Who hit you?***-Because Matthew does not mention Jesus being blindfolded as does Mark's Gospel.-(Mark 14: 65) Some interpret that what is being demanded is the names of those who were hitting Him, who being strangers to Jesus. Others interpret that the demand of their identities was a result of the vicious and disfiguring beating Jesus was enduring. (cf. Is. 52:14).

🗝 Even today there is no degree of insult, shame, or contempt that believers should complain about in bearing the name of Christ, having seen the amount of suffering that Jesus endured on our behalf.

☞ By enduring such treatment Jesus fulfilled the "Suffering Servant" predicted by the prophet Isaiah-(cf. Is. 50:6-7) as well as submitting to God's will in suffering for sin as part of the redemption of man-(cf. Is. 53:5-7, 1-Pet. 2:23, 4:1,Heb. 2:9, 12:3) Some see in it the exemplary example of Jesus putting into practice His own teachings. (cf. Matt. 5:39)

Good Friday - (5:00-6:00 A.M.)
Peter Disowns Jesus-(N.I.V.)

26:69 Now (i.e. During Jesus' trial proceedings.) **Peter was sitting out in the courtyard,**-◙ (i.e. Warming himself by the fire while waiting for the outcome of Jesus' trial.-{cf.-Mark 14:54, Luke 22:55}) **and a servant girl** (damsel-K.J.V.-3814-*"Denotes a young girl or female slave", bondmaid, maidservant.* Doorkeeper.-{cf. John 18:16}, of the high priest.-{cf. Mark 14:66}) **came to him. "You also were with Jesus of Galilee," she said.** (Expresses: By implication an accusation of being a follower, supporter, and disciple of Jesus.-{cf.-John 18:17})
70 But he denied it before them all. (i.e. Peter's denial was directed towards the girl, as well as to a group of bystanders.-{Luke 22:56, Mark 14:69}) **"I don't know**(understand-{Mark 14:68})**what you're talking about," he said.** (Expresses a form of denial, a pretense of ignorance, innocence, and indifference.)

Peter publicly denies Jesus by swearing ignorance and disassociation.

Message & Application 💻=🌎

❖ Shows how believers are not to allow embarrassment, ridicule, or persecution deter or intimidate our witness of Jesus.
❖ Warns believers against denying Jesus out of fear, or shifting our conversations so that we don't have to talk about Him.
❖ Warns those who are not strong in the Lord will easily fall by the slightest provocation. (If we are not spiritually sufficient in resisting small battles, how can we expect to stand during all out attack!).
❖ Warns how bad company corrupts good character. (Are you willing to praise Jesus just as much around friends as you are around enemies & strangers, or do you try to play off your faith to be part of the crowd?).
❖ Warns against allowing our disappointments or shattered dreams to change our perceptions of Jesus' power and love for us.

–***You also were with Jesus***-The servant girl had either seen Peter with Jesus in the temple days earlier, or she remembered admitting Peter in at the request of John, another of Jesus' disciples. (cf. John 18:16-17)

⊶ Even today, believers can sometimes fail Jesus when we refuse to speak up or come to His defense. (Do you disassociate yourself from Jesus in the presence of critics, employers, friends, neighbors, and strangers by remaining silent?).

☞ Some are apologetic towards Peter's response, that being in the enemy's camp he feared being identified and apprehended.
Others focus on the cowardliness of the act, by pointing out how Peter meekly recoils and falls away at the fear of a mere slave girl.

26:71 Then he went out to the gateway, (porch-K.J.V. Suggests: Peter's attempt to hide his identity in the darkened alcove, or to make his escape easier. May also express Peter's unwillingness to abandon Jesus completely.) **where another girl** (maid-K.J.V.) **saw him and said to the people there,** (i.e. Other servants/officers.) **"This fellow** (i.e. Possibly a euphemism of contempt.) **was with Jesus of Nazareth."**(Expresses: Disciple, supporter, compatriot. Possibly was meant in a derogatory manner, due to the contempt that many Judeans had for the poor reputations of those from Nazareth.-{cf. John 1:46})
72 He denied it again, with an oath: (3727-*"A fence, an enclosure, that which restrains a person", "formal or legal binding pledge, promise, vow"*. Expresses: Is meant to confirm the truthfulness of a statement by appealing to something sacred.) **"I don't know the man!"** (Expresses: Disclaimer, disassociation.)

For the second time, Peter denies Jesus, swearing on the truthfulness of his word.

Message & Application

- Shows believers the dangerous spiraling effects of sin. (Those who have fallen into sin always rush headlong from bad to worse!).
- Warns believers the more we're around the crowds of the world, the more temptation we have to sin and deny Jesus.
- Teaches that no matter how much we try to hide, our profession and character will always be under scrutiny.
- Warns believers that as long as we remain in a pattern of denial, we'll keep repeating the same mistakes over and over again.

Progression of Peter's Three Denials:

Defense:
1) A plea of ignorance or pretension.
2) A denial with an oath.
3) A denial with cursing and swearing.

Appeal:
1) Simple denial & evasion.
2) Personal assurance.
3) Violent affirmation/direct profanes.

Deposition:
1) Public declaration.
2) Legal/judicial affirmation.
3) Divine defense.

26:73 After a little while, (i.e. About an hour later.-{Luke 22:59}) **those standing there** (i.e. Servants & officers of the high priest.) **went up to Peter and said, "Surely you are one of them, for your accent gives you away".** (Suggests: Peter's Galilean dialect being different from that of Judeans, in which certain vowels were pronounced with a country drawl.)
74 Then he began to call down curses on himself (Expresses to validate the truthfulness of one's word by calling down misfortune on oneself, *"May God strike me dead if I'm lying"*) **and he swore to them,** (Expresses: Take a vow or an oath, "I swear to God" or "I swear on my life".) **"I don't know the man!" Immediately a cock** (i.e. Rooster, hen) **crowed.**
75 Then Peter remembered the word Jesus had spoken: "Before the cock crows, you will disown me three times." And he went outside (i.e. Out of fear of being suspected as a disciple, or as a result of his shame and guilt.) **and wept bitterly.** (Expresses Peter's guilt, regret, sorrow, remorsefulness, repentance.)

For the third time, Peter denies Jesus swearing on both his life and God as his witness.

Message & Application 💻=🌎

- ❖ Shows believers no matter how strong we are, we can all fail in our Christian faith and witness of the Lord.
- ❖ Teaches how we speak & talk reveals a great deal about our Christian character. (Fear of exposure often deteriorates into greater sins!).
- ❖ Impresses upon believers how nothing should grieve us more and call us to repentance than knowing that we have sinned against the Lord.
- ❖ Reminds believers of our own weakness in the face of danger and fear, that we're all prone to break our word and promises to the Lord.
- ☞ According to Luke's Gospel immediately following the rooster's crow; *"The Lord turned and looked straight at Peter"*(22:61) (Expresses: Not of wrath or resentment, but of compassion, mercy, and forgiveness).

Root causes of Peter's Downfall:

1) Peter's failure to listen to the word of God, having been warned by Jesus concerning his imminent fall.-(26:31)
2) Peter's pride and self-confidence, thinking he could fare better than others.-(26:33)
3) Peter's failure in staying spiritually alert by praying instead of sleeping.-(26:40-41)
4) Peter's overconfidence, placing himself in the dangerous situations of temptation and evil influences.-(26:58)
5) Peter's failure in giving into shame and discouragement, instead of focusing on Christ & His promises -(26:70-75)

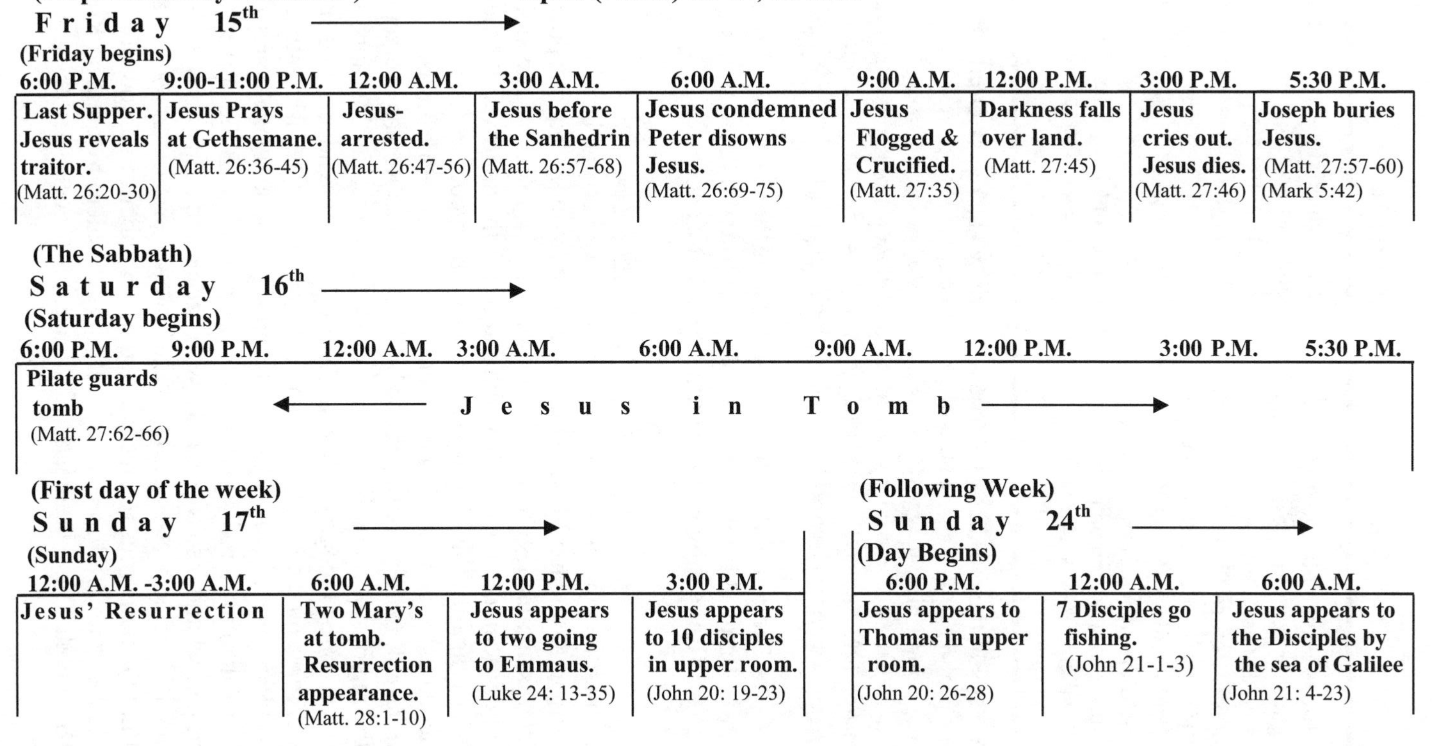

Time Line from Jesus' Last Supper to Resurrection

April (Nisan) 15-24, 30 A.D.

(Preparation Day / Passover)
Friday 15th →
(Friday begins)

6:00 P.M.	9:00-11:00 P.M.	12:00 A.M.	3:00 A.M.	6:00 A.M.	9:00 A.M.	12:00 P.M.	3:00 P.M.	5:30 P.M.
Last Supper. Jesus reveals traitor. (Matt. 26:20-30)	**Jesus Prays at Gethsemane.** (Matt. 26:36-45)	**Jesus- arrested.** (Matt. 26:47-56)	**Jesus before the Sanhedrin** (Matt. 26:57-68)	**Jesus condemned Peter disowns Jesus.** (Matt. 26:69-75)	**Jesus Flogged & Crucified.** (Matt. 27:35)	**Darkness falls over land.** (Matt. 27:45)	**Jesus cries out. Jesus dies.** (Matt. 27:46)	**Joseph buries Jesus.** (Matt. 27:57-60) (Mark 5:42)

(The Sabbath)
Saturday 16th →
(Saturday begins)

6:00 P.M.	9:00 P.M.	12:00 A.M.	3:00 A.M.	6:00 A.M.	9:00 A.M.	12:00 P.M.	3:00 P.M.	5:30 P.M.
Pilate guards tomb (Matt. 27:62-66)	← **Jesus in Tomb** →							

(First day of the week)
Sunday 17th →
(Sunday)

12:00 A.M. -3:00 A.M.	6:00 A.M.	12:00 P.M.	3:00 P.M.
Jesus' Resurrection	**Two Mary's at tomb. Resurrection appearance.** (Matt. 28:1-10)	**Jesus appears to two going to Emmaus.** (Luke 24: 13-35)	**Jesus appears to 10 disciples in upper room.** (John 20: 19-23)

(Following Week)
Sunday 24th →
(Day Begins)

6:00 P.M.	12:00 A.M.	6:00 A.M.
Jesus appears to Thomas in upper room. (John 20: 26-28)	**7 Disciples go fishing.** (John 21-1-3)	**Jesus appears to the Disciples by the sea of Galilee** (John 21: 4-23)

Chapter Twenty Seven

Jesus' Passion & Death

- **Judas Hangs himself-**Judas out guilt for betraying Jesus commits suicide-(Vs. 1-10)
- **Jesus Before Pilate-**Jesus stands trial before the Roman governor Pontius Pilate.-(Vs. 11-26)
- **Soldiers Mock Jesus-**Roman soldiers show contempt for Jesus' royal claims.-(Vs. 27-31)
- **The Crucifixion-**Jesus suffers God's wrath and punishment for the sins of the world-(Vs. 32-44)
- **The death of Jesus-**Jesus dies for the sins of the world.-(Vs. 45-56)
- **The Burial of Jesus-**Jesus is laid in the tomb.-(Vs. 57-61)
- **Guards at the Tomb**-Pilate posts Roman guards to secure the tomb-(Vs. 62-66)

27:1 Early in the morning, (i.e. 6:00 A.M. Friday.) **all the chief priests and the elders of the people came to the decision to put Jesus to death.**
2 They bound him, (Suggests: To make Jesus appear as a dangerous criminal and a threat to Rome.) **led him away and handed him over to Pilate, the governor.** (2232-*Roman procurator, Prefect.* Suggests: Being under Roman law, the Jews had no legal authority to execute capital punishment.)

The Sanhedrin having no legal authority to carry out capital punishment has Jesus handed over to the Roman governor Pontius Pilate for execution.

<u>Message & Application</u> 💻=🌎

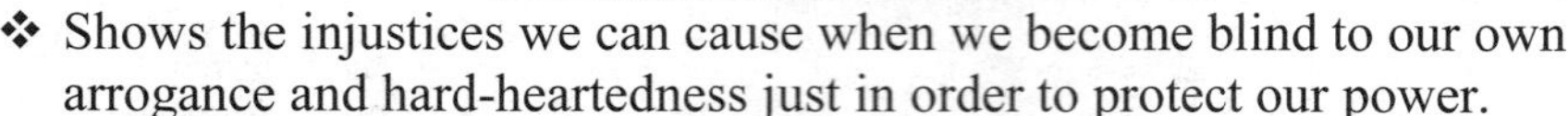

- ❖ Shows the injustices we can cause when we become blind to our own arrogance and hard-heartedness just in order to protect our power.
- ❖ Warns against legitimizing wrong decisions by seeking the aides of others. (Sin often gains its validity through the approval of others).
- ❖ Warns against thinking we can clear our own conscience and accountability by getting others to do our dirty work for us.

-Pilate-Full name "Pontius Pilate", who served as Roman prefect over the regions of Samaria & Judea from A.D. 26 to 36. Was appointed governor of Judea by Tiberius Caesar. Official residence was in Caesarea on the Mediterranean coast, but during Jewish festivals such as "Passover", in order to keep the peace he would take up residence in Jerusalem in Herod's palace. Sources outside the Bible portray Pilate as a cruel and insensitive ruler who had nothing but contempt for his Jewish subjects. (See Luke 13:1, Philo. "Embassy to Gaius" 299-305 p. 784). Pilate's murderous reign consisted of a number of provocations and clashes with the Jews such as defiling Jerusalem by erecting Roman banners that bore the image of Caesar.-(Josh. "Antiquities" Book 18, 3)

***Judas hangs Himself*-**(N.I.V.)

27:3 When Judas, who had betrayed him, saw that Jesus was condemned, he was seized (filled) **with remorse** (Syn.-regret, guilt, repented himself-K.J.V.) **and returned the thirty silver coins to the chief priests and the elders.**
4 "I have sinned," he said, (Expresses not a confession unto repentance that leads to Salvation, but only a contention of moral wrongdoing since the confession was made to the priests, not directly to God.) **"for I have betrayed innocent blood." "What is that to us?" they replied. "That's your responsibility.** (Expresses an attempt to shift their guilt & accountability.)
5 So Judas threw the money into the temple(i.e. To implicate the priests, or to clear his own conscience.) **and left. Then he went away and hanged himself.**

Judas thinking Jesus would be acquitted is now filled with remorse for betraying Him and commits suicide.

Message & Application

- ❖ Shows believers that without true repentance a man's humble confession and restitution can never cleanse his conscience.
- ❖ Warns against assuming that our sins are too great to be forgiven by God. (See your sin as bad, but not unpardonable, know that you're never beyond God's mercy & forgiveness!).
- ❖ Calls for always thinking about the grave and sinful consequences of our actions, before we do something that we will later regret.
- ❖ Warns how pleasures and vices may seem enjoyable at the time, but they will only become loathsome and repulsive later.
- ❖ Warns how a guilty conscience will not find comfort/sympathy from our old sinful companions. (Seek relief from God, not from friends!).

-Seized with remorse-Judas' remorse variously attributed to either:

- Assumed Jesus would be acquitted of all charges and set free, that he would have his money and therefore no harm done.
- Assumed Jesus would use His divine powers and miraculously escape His captors.

🗝 Today many people can have guilt and agony of conscience, but without true sorrow towards God, there can be no real repentance and no real change of heart and character.

☞ According to the book of Acts attributes Judas's death as a result of; *"Having fell headlong, his body burst open and all his intestines fell out"*.-(Acts 1:18) (Many resolve the discrepancies by suggesting that Judas after hanging himself, the rope or tree branch broke and his body, already in a state of decay and decomposition [bloated] fell hitting the ground below and bursting open.

27:6 The chief priests picked up the coins and said, "It is against the law to put this into the treasury, (2878-*Corban, a gift offered to God, alms chest.* Syn.-Donation box. Expresses the overall immorality of the act of bringing anything defiling into God's temple as based on Deut. 23:18) **since it is blood money."** (i.e. Money gained at the expense of another's life. In context money that had been used to bribe Judas, resulting in Jesus' death.)
7 So they decided to use the money to buy the potter's field as a burial place for foreigners. (i.e. A plot of ground on the southern slope of Mt. Zion that served as a place where potters had once dug for clay. It would later be used as a cemetery for strangers who should happen to die while in Jerusalem.)
8 That is why it has been called the Field of Blood to this day. (i.e. From the time Matthew wrote his Gospel. Suggests: Not by the chief priests, but by commoners as a memorial for their treacherous betrayal in killing Jesus.)

Since the money was used in a crime, it could not be used for sacred things, instead, it is given to charity.

Message & Application 💻=🌎

❖ Shows the depravity of some who can keep moral & ethical values while overlooking their own gross sins.
❖ Warns believers against thinking we can atone for our sins through charitable acts. (Many use honorable acts in an attempt to bury their crimes, know that your sins will eventually find you out!).
☞ Illustrates the hypocrisy of the chief priests, having no qualms about killing an innocent man, yet were concerned about sacred things.
☞ Some view the act as symbolically signifying the gracious favor of Christ's blood in purchasing the sinners Salvation and refuge.

27:9 Then what was spoken by Jeremiah the prophet (i.e. 500 years earlier.) **was fulfilled: "They took the thirty silver coins, the price set on him by the people** (i.e. Religious leaders.) **of Israel,** {See Zech. 11:12-13})
10 and used them to buy the potter's field, as the Lord commanded me.

The religious leaders by buying the field fulfilled Jeremiah & Zechariah's prophecy.

Message & Application 💻=🌎

☞ Because the prophecy is not found in Jeremiah but rather in Zechariah, many explain the discrepancy as either; Most O.T. Prophetic writings were naturally attributed to Jeremiah being the major prophet.
Or Matthew may have had both Jeremiah (32:6-9) & Zechariah (11:12-13) in mind, and therefore combined both passages into one.

Jesus Before Pilate-(N.I.V.)

27:11 Meanwhile (i.e. During Judas's remorse.-{Vs. 3-5}) **Jesus stood before the governor,** (i.e. Civil trial. Probably the judgment hall inside Pilate's temporary residence at Herod's palace.) **and the governor asked him, "Are you the king of the Jews?"** (i.e. Presupposes the formal charges of "Treason" brought by the Sanhedrin.- {cf. Luke 23:2}) **"Yes, it is as you say," Jesus replied.** (Expresses a confirmation with a qualification attached as in "Yes, I am the king of the Jews", but not in the political sense as Pilate understands it.)

Jesus only acknowledges His kingship, not as a political subversive, but as the promised Messiah king of the Jews.

Message & Application =

❖ Shows believers Jesus' Spiritual Kingship over us, having secured our redemption and Salvation by being made sin for us.
❖ Displays the importance of setting our enemies at ease, convincing them that they have nothing to fear in coming to Jesus.
☞ Christ holds His peace while accused that we may not be accused.

27:12 When he was accused by the chief priests and the elders, he gave no answer.(Expresses Jesus' unwillingness in defending Himself for our acquittal.)
13 Then Pilate asked him, "Don't you hear the testimony (charges-N.L.T.) **they are bringing against you?"** (Expresses the political nature of the charges of treason, carrying with it capital punishment.)
14 But Jesus made no reply, (i.e. Defense) **not even to a single charge—** (Expresses Jesus' unyielding determination in obeying the Fathers will in fulfillment of Isaiah 53:7.) **to the great amazement of the governor.** (i.e. Pilate's astonishment at Jesus' refusal to defend Himself, knowing of His innocence, or Jesus' determination and willingness to face the capital charges against him.)

Jesus' silence testifies to His willingness to suffer for the sins of the world.

Message & Application =

❖ Shows believers Jesus' willingness to stand condemned, taking the full penalty and punishment of our own sins upon Himself.
❖ Displays how Christ permitted Himself to stand accused and condemned that we may stand boldly before the throne of God.
❖ Teaches how we owe nothing to fear or threat, that everything is happening according to the Lord's will.
❖ Teaches the importance of following through with the will of God, regardless of personal cost, ridicule, or death.

27:15 Now it was the governor's custom at the Feast (Passover celebration.) **to release** (Syn.-pardon, clemency.) **a prisoner chosen by the crowd.**
16 At that time they had a notorious prisoner, (notable-K.J.V., A.V.-1978-*"In a bad sense as infamous"*. Syn.-legendary, disreputable.) **called Barabbas.**
17 So when the crowd had gathered, Pilate asked them, "Which one do you want me to release to you: Barabbas, (Heb. Yeshua Bar-Abba, "son of the father") **or Jesus who is called Christ?"**(5547-*"Anointed One: Messiah".)*
18 For he knew it was out of envy (Syn.-spite, resentment, malice.) **that they had handed Jesus over to him.** (Suggests: Pilate knowing that it was not out of loyalty to Rome, but out of spite because of Jesus' popularity with the people.)

Pilate attempts to escape responsibility for killing an innocent man by offering amnesty to a prisoner of their choosing.

Message & Application 💻=🌎

–***Governor's custom to release a prisoner-***Since there is no historical record, suggests it was a local practice instituted by Pilate to pacify his Jewish subjects. Some suggest a tractate from the Mishnah makes reference to this practice-("They may slaughter [i.e. Passover lamb] for one whom they have promised to bring out of prison".-(Pesahim 8:6)

–***Notorious prisoner-***Most identify him as a "Zealot or Insurrectionists", others as a "robber or thief". According to the Gospels of Mark, Luke, and John identifies Barabbas as being in prison for leading a rebellion against Rome, in which he, along with others, had committed murder in the uprising.-(cf. Mark 15:7, Luke 23:19).

27:19 While Pilate was sitting on the judge's seat, (i.e. Holding court) **his wife** (Claudia Procla) **sent him this message: "Don't have anything to do with that innocent man,** (Don't condemn Him.) **for I have suffered a great deal today in a dream because of him."** (Expresses: Not her defense of Jesus but rather her fear of divine reprisal on her husband/family if he condemns an innocent man.)

Pilate is warned not to condemn Jesus fearing divine retribution due to His innocence.

Message & Application 💻=🌎

- ❖ Shows how believers are to pursue friends & relatives, doing whatever we can to keep them from sinning against Christ.
- ❖ Assures believers of divine intervention and warning against sinful pursuits. (See divine warnings as God's great love & mercy for you).
- ❖ Displays the crowning qualities of a wife's wisdom. (Believers would do well if they would only listen more often to their wife's counsels).

27:20 But the chief priests and the elders persuaded the crowd (i.e. Not the same crowd pilgrims that celebrated Jesus' triumphal entry in Jerusalem earlier that week,-{21:8-10} but rather the people of the city. That they had either circulated stories of Jesus' threat to tear down the Temple.-{26:61} Or Jesus' blasphemous claims He made before the Sanhedrin.-{26:64-65}) **to ask for Barabbas and to have Jesus executed.**
21 "Which of the two do you want me to release (Syn.-pardon, amnesty, clemency) **to you?" asked the governor.** (Suggests: Pilate took to heart his wife's warning.-{V. 19}) **"Barabbas," they answered.**
22 What shall I do, then, with Jesus who is called Christ?" (5547-*"Anointed One", Messiah.)* **Pilate asked.** (Suggests: Pilate's assumes they would save one who was their Messiah and king.) **They all answered, "crucify him!"**(Suggests: The religious leaders influence prevailed in turning the crowd against Jesus.)
23 "Why? What crime has he committed?" asked Pilate. (I have found in him no grounds for the death penalty. Therefore I will have him punished and then release him.-{Luke 23:15-16}) **But they shouted all the louder, "Crucify him!"**

Despite Pilate's attempts to free Jesus the religious leaders persuade the crowd to call for Jesus' execution.

Message & Application

❖ Shows how we must never allow peer pressure or public opinion of others to influence us in choosing other things over Jesus.
❖ Warns believers if we're not watchful and careful, we can be hurried towards sin through the wicked and evil influences of others.
❖ Displays how some can have a profession and show of religion, but no real commitment or devotion to Christ when it really matters.
❖ Warns how we can crucify Jesus all over again when we choose other things over Him. (cf. Heb. 6:6)
❖ Teaches the importance of remaining faithful and committed to Christ even when all our hopes and dreams are shattered.
⊶ Even today many will praise Jesus when life is good and things are going their way, but blame Him when things go bad. (Praise God in good times and bad times).
☞ Every person will one day be confronted with their opinion of Jesus and forced to ask themselves the same question *"What do you do with Jesus, do you receive Him as Lord & Savior of your life"*? or *"Do you deny and reject His claims"*?
☞ According to John's Gospel, the crowd was able to pressure Pilate from releasing Jesus by calling into question his loyalty to Caesar and Rome. (cf. John 19:12)

27:24 When Pilate saw that he was getting nowhere, but that instead, an uproar (tumult-K.J.V., riot-L.B.V. Public disorder.) **was starting, he took water and washed his hands in front of the crowd.-◙** (Expresses a symbolic gesture of absolving oneself of any responsibility in the involvement of a crime.) **"I am innocent of this man's blood,"**(of this just person-K.J.V., A.V.) **he said. "It is your responsibility!"** (Syn.-liability, guilt, business, affair, etc.)
25 All the people answered, "Let his blood (i.e. death.) **be on us and on our children!"**(5043-*Jewish nation, citizens, posterity.* Expresses the people's attempt to persuade Pilate by accepting full responsibility for Jesus' death.)

Pilate attempts to absolve himself of guilt in Jesus' death, while the people assume full responsibility.

Message & Application 💻=🌎

- ❖ Shows believers rather than try to escape responsibility for our sins we need to confess them openly to Jesus, seeking His forgiveness.
- ❖ Warns how there can be no neutrality, passing the buck, or indifference when it comes to taking accountability for our sins.
- ❖ Warns how washing your hands of sinful affairs doesn't make the guilt go away, it just gives you a false sense of security. (Don't make excuses, take responsibility for the decisions and choices you make!).
- ❖ Teaches rather than cave into peer pressure stay uncompromising in your Christian principals and convictions.

*–Led his blood be on us and our children-*Some broaden the declaration as a prophetic curse bringing on themselves and nation divine wrath, as fulfilled in the destruction of Jerusalem by Rome in A.D. 70. Others see it as a prophetic prediction of divine mercy in the remission of sin to those Jews who would later come to put their faith in Jesus.

Pilates efforts to Escape Responsibility:

- Hoped to release Jesus through amnesty.-(27:15-18)
- Hoped to remove his responsibility by washing his hands of the matter.-(Matt. 27:24)
- Hoped to release Jesus having found no basis for a charge against Him.-(Luke 23:4, John 19:4)
- Hoped to escape responsibility by turning Jesus over to Herod Antipas' jurisdiction.-(Luke 23:6)
- Hoped to turn Jesus' case over to the Jewish rulers.-(John 19:6)
- Hoped to pacify the crowd by having Jesus scourged and then released.-(Luke 23:22)

27:26 Then he released Barabbas to them. But he had Jesus flogged,-◙ (scourged-K.J.V.-5417-*Lat.-flagellum, to whip or lash.* i.e. The Roman practice of flaying criminals with a whip.) **and handed him over** (i.e. To Roman soldiers) **to be crucified.-◙** (4716-*To be impaled on a stake or pole in the shape of a two beam cross, either in a form of a "T" or traditionally a "+".* i.e. The Roman practice of executing criminals by hanging the condemned on a cross.)

Pilate bound by his political duty, has Barabbas pardoned and Jesus publicly whipped and handed over for execution.

Message & Application

–***Flogged-***A form of corporal punishment practiced by Rome and other cultures. Flogging was administered by a type of whip (flagellum) made of leather cords, usually weighted on the end with pieces of metal or bones. The procedure would have the condemns upper body exposed with the hands tied to a post and would usually be whipped until the flesh was beaten to a bloody pulp or until bone appeared. Under Mosaic Law the number of lashes was determined by the crime and was limited to no more than 40 lashes.-(Deut. 25:1-3) Flogging was usually administered as punishment for certain crimes, or for obtaining confessions, or as a prelude to execution,-(Matt. 27:26), purpose being to weaken the prisoner in dying more quickly on the cross.

Purpose of Jesus' Passion & Suffering:

- In order to satisfy divine justice. It was God's punishment for sin. -(Is. 53:3-10, Ps. 40:6-8)
- Supreme test of Jesus' obedience/commitment in obeying God's will.-(Rom. 5:19, Philip. 2:6-8)
- To remind us of the great price that our sins cost Jesus, and the extent of God's profound love for us.-(Rom. 5:7-8, 1-John 3:1)
- Was prophesied in fulfillment with the role of the Suffering Servant.-(Is. 52:14-15, 53:5)
- Was in order that Jesus experience the full extent of human sufferings, helping us when we suffer.-(Heb. 2:10, 2:18, 5:8)
- Served as an example for believers to follow. (2-Corn. 1:5-6, 4:10-12, 11:23-25, Heb. 12:3, 13:13, 1-Pet. 2:21-23, 4:1, Philip. 2:5-8, 3:10, 1-John 3:16)

Good Friday - (9:00-12:00 P.M.)
The Soldiers Mock Jesus-(N.I.V.)

27:27 Then the governor's soldiers took Jesus into the Praetorium (4232-*Official residence of the governor, also the camp of the imperial Roman bodyguard".* armory-L.B.V.) **and gathered the whole company of soldiers** (4686-*Tenth part of a legion, consisting of 200 to 600 men.)* **round him.**
28 They stripped him and put a scarlet (i.e. red, crimson) **robe-◙ on him,** (Expresses a mock imitation symbolizing the robes worn by kings.)
29 and then twisted together a crown of thorns-◙ and set it on his head. (Expresses a mock imitation symbolizing the crowns worn by kings.) **They put a staff-◙ in his right hand** (Expresses mock imitation symbolizing the scepters held by kings.) **and knelt in front of him** (A mock imitation of offering homage to a king.) **and mocked him. "Hail, king of the Jews!" they said.** (Expresses: Taken together a mock imitation of salutations made to Emperors and kings.)
30 They spat on him, (i.e. Possibly in the face. Expresses deepest contempt, insult. Opposite of a kiss of homage normally reserved for kings.) **and took the staff and struck him on the head again and again.** (i.e. Possibly to drive the crown of thorns deeper into the flesh, or another form of torture.)
31 After they had mocked him, (1702-*"To deride, jeer at")* **they took off the robe and put his own clothes on him.** (Suggests: Partly to retrieve their own personal belongings, or not to offend Jewish sensibilities of a man's nakedness. Because no mention is made of removing the crown of thorns, many assume Jesus was crucified with it still on His head.) **Then they led him away to crucify him.** (i.e. To Golgotha located directly outside the city. Tradition has Jesus walking the route know as the "Via Dolorosa".)

The guards express contempt & ridicule towards Jesus by making a mockery of His royal claims.

Message & Application

- ❖ Shows believers the great amount of suffering & abuse Jesus was willing to endure in bringing about our healing and Salvation.
- ❖ Reminds believers how our light and momentary trials are nothing compared to all that Christ has suffered for us! (cf. 1-Pet. 2:21-24)
- ❖ Warns when we joke about our sins and continue to live the way we used to, we're just as guilty of mocking Jesus as the Roman soldiers.
- ❖ Warns how we can bring great dishonor and disgrace upon Jesus when we only pretend to worship Him. (Don't mock Christ by empty words of praise, profession, or devotion!).
- ⊶ Even today, believers can strip the royalty & majesty away from Jesus when we fail to give Him the supreme authority over our lives.

The Crucifixion-(N.I.V.)

27:32 As they were going out, (i.e. Leaving the city, possibly in observance against the Jewish law that prohibited criminals from being executed within the city.-{Lev. 24:14, Numb. 15:35-36}) **they met a man** (i.e. A chance passerby, by random, coming in from the fields.-{Luke 23:26} **from Cyrene,-◙** (i.e. A coastal city in north Africa, midway between Carthage and Alexandria, modern day Libya. That he was probably one of thousands of Jews on his pilgrimage into the city to celebrate the Passover.) **named Simon,** (Name suggests he was a Hellenistic Jew. The father of Alexander and Rufus.-{Mark 15:21}-Suggests: Due to the familiarity with his two sons suggests that Simon and his family later became Christians as a result of this incident.-{cf. Rom. 16:13}) **and they forced him** (compelled-K.J.V.-29-*"To impress into service", Roman authority to conscribe couriers for government service".* Syn.-recruited, drafted, pressed him into service.-N.E.B.) **to carry the cross.-◙** (i.e. Though it was a Roman custom that the condemned man carry his own crossbeam, weighing between 50 & 100 lbs. to the place of execution, purpose being for both pain and shame. But in Jesus' case, because the flogging had left Him severely weakened, they feared He would faint under it, so they forced Simon to carry it for Him.)

Jesus weakened by the severe flogging, Simon is randomly recruited by the Roman guards to carry the cross for Him.

<u>Message & Application</u> 💻=🌎

❖ Shows believers how true discipleship is about bearing crosses daily for Jesus as we follow Him. (cf. Matt. 10:38, 16:24)

❖ Teaches how sometimes God uses places & circumstances to draw us closer to Jesus. (Allow God to change the course of your life!).

❖ Moves believers towards humble service, always willing to serve and help carry the burdens and miseries of others.

❖ Calls believers in our willingness in enduring humiliation, shame, and disgrace as we identify ourselves with Jesus.

❖ Calls for the need of faithfully carrying out whatever tasks the Lord sets before us, no matter how unpleasant or unrewarding it may be.

–***Forced him to carry the cross***-Reluctance attributed to either:

- It was an unclean task, the cross being soaked in Jesus' blood, making him unfit from celebrating the Passover.
- It was a difficult task, the crossbeam weighing 50-100 lbs.
- It was an embarrassing task, fit for the worst of criminals.

⊶ Even today we shouldn't think it strange when crosses come upon us suddenly and unexpectedly. (Are you willing to accept hardships and burdens as you follow Jesus?).

27:33 They (i.e. The entourage of soldiers with Jesus.) **came to a place called Golgotha-◙ (which means The Place of the Skull).** (Latin- "Calvary")
34 There they offered Jesus wine to drink, mixed with gall; (vinegar-K.J.V.-5521-*A plant of bitter/poisonous fruit, opium poppy.* drugged wine-L.B.V., myrrh-{Mark 15:23} Used as a narcotic to reduce the pain of crucifixion. Expresses possibly their compassion, or a cruel act of torment, making the wine so bitter that it was undrinkable.) **but after tasting it, he refused to drink it.** (Suggests: Jesus having discovered the bitter narcotic. That He refused to alleviate any of His sufferings, wanted to be fully conscious until His death.)

Jesus is determined to keep His senses and endure the complete extent of suffering for our sins.

Message & Application =

–***Golgotha-***A name that owes its origins to either: The place where criminals were crucified and their skulls could be found lying around. Or the adjacent hill was in the shape of a skull. Today the Church of the Holy Sepulcher (Jesus' burial tomb) serves as near the traditional site which is located within the present walls of the old city (northern outer wall during Jesus' day). Others point to an area just outside the Damascus gate near a hill which is called *"Gordon's Calvary",* which even to this day the hill near the site still resembles a skull.
Some suggest the name is derived from the ancient tradition where the skull of Adam was said to be found. Because the site was outside the city and near a main road, executions held there served as examples to others and as a deterrent to criminals.

-***Wine mixed with gall-***A variety of plants that produced a bitter tasting fruit. Most scholars believe the one being referred to here is what is called the *"Papaver somniferum"* (i.e. "Opium poppy", today grown mostly in Afghanistan) to which the seed heads produces the narcotic opium, which is then used as a potent drug and pain reliever. Others who translate it as "Poison" suggests they were offering Jesus the opportunity to take His own life. According to ancient tradition, it holds that it was Jerusalem women who had offered the drink to Jesus as a customary practice in administering pain-killing narcotics to those who were about to be executed, as inspired from Proverbs 31:6-7.

–***Refused to drink it-***Reasons for Jesus keeping His senses intact:

- In order that His final seven statements could be heard.
- In order to minister Salvation to the dying thief.-(Luke 23:42)
- In order to help believers in their time of suffering.-(Heb. 4:15-16)
- In order to taste death for all sinners.-(Heb. 2:9)

27:35 When they had crucified him, they divided up his clothes (Suggests: The clothes were part of the executioner's fee. Or having heard of the cures of those who touched the hem of His garment, thought they possessed some magical virtue.) **by casting** (Syn.-throwing, tossing) **lots.-◙** (Expresses a form of gambling, similar to throwing dice or flipping a coin. They were probably some sort of marked stones or sticks. Because the inner garment was seamless it was gambled for separately.-{cf. John 19:23-24}) {cf. Ps. 22:18}
36 And sitting down, they kept watch over him there. (i.e. To ensure death. Or to hinder other people or the disciples from rescuing the condemned.)

By gambling for Jesus' clothes, the soldiers had unknowingly fulfilled Psalm 22:18.

Message & Application 💻=🌎

❖ Shows how believers can become reckless with their Salvation, knowing the sacrifice of Christ, yet continuing to live in sin. (Don't gamble that you will always have opportunities to repent later on!).
❖ Calls for joyfully suffering the confiscation of all our earthly goods and comforts, knowing that we have better treasures in heaven!
❖ Warns how those who reject Jesus today are gambling with their Salvation. (Don't place bets against the testimony of millions of people who have given their life's over to Jesus!).
❖ Warns against thinking we can forgo the path of holiness, service, and discipleship by placing all our bets on the grace of God.
❖ Displays how many can draw near to Christ, yet have their hearts far from Him. (Don't be blind to the mercies of Christ).

–***Crucified him***-The Roman method of execution in which a criminal was first laid on two crossed beams in the form of a "+" (traditional) then having his hands (wrists) extended and fastened to the crossbeam with nails, and then having the feet (ankles) crossed together and nailed in place on the upright beam (the purpose being to prevent the victim from using their legs to support themselves in order to breathe, was also why the legs would be broken.-(cf. John 19:32-33)
Then elevating the criminal while hanging on the cross in an upright position into a hole in the ground. The cause of death came either by asphyxiation (suffocation by restricting the diaphragm thereby making breathing impossible) or by exhaustion and dehydration. (For additional causes see notes on page 426)

🗝 Even today many only see personal opportunities in religion of how much they can get from Jesus without it costing them anything, that many want the blessings of Christianity but not the cross.

27:37 Above his head they (i.e. Roman soldiers.) **placed the written charge against him: THIS IS JESUS, THE KING OF THE JEWS.** (Suggests: Pilates' attempt to humiliate the Jews, or absolve himself before his Roman superiors by using the Jewish religious leader's accusations as the charge for Jesus' crucifixion.)
38 Two robbers (thieves-K.J.V., criminals-N.L.T.) **were crucified with him, one on his right and one on his left.-◙** (Suggests: By being positioned between the two thieves, Jesus was being portrayed as the worst of the three, or possibly the ringleader and chief malefactor. Some contend the two robbers were colleagues and co-conspirators of Barabbas. According to the Gospel of Nicodemus, they are named Dismas-[repentant thief] and Gestas.)
And the scriptures {Is. 53:12} **were fulfilled which saith, And he was numbered with the transgressors**-(Not found in the earliest or most authentic Greek MSS. - Suggests: Was added to complete and fill in the thought.)

Jesus by being crucified with common criminals voluntarily stands in the shame & disgrace of sinners.

Message & Application 💻=🌎

- ❖ Shows Jesus' willingness in bearing our humiliation, guilt, and sins so we won't have to. (There's no sin Jesus is unwilling to atone for!).
- ❖ Displays Jesus' willingness in identifying/standing with us in our sins. (Trust that Jesus will never leave you to suffer alone!).
- ❖ Portrays Jesus' love & acceptance, having shared in our disgrace and shame. (Whatever you've gone through, Jesus has been there!)
- ❖ Teaches how through divine providence God can use ordinary men to bear testimony to Christ. (V. 37)

–***The King Of The Jews***-Served as a warning to passerby's of the severe consequences for those who rebel against Imperial Rome. Was not meant to cause mockery towards Jesus, but rather to insult and mock the Jews who were at enmity towards Jesus. May have also served to vindicate Pilate of any involvement by putting the blame on the Jews who used this accusation when they accused Jesus before Pilate.

☞According to John's Gospel, the sign was written in Aramaic, (Hebrew) Latin (official Roman language) and Greek-(common language) (John 19:20) (Suggests: To ensure that all nationalities would not fail to read it). Also, according to John's Gospel the religious leaders had gone to Pilate protesting: *"Do not write, 'The King of the Jews', but that this man claimed to be the king of the Jews"*.(John 19:21) (That the religious leaders were protesting that the declaration should not have been written as a statement of fact, but rather as a mere claim, but Pilate would eventually overrule them.)-(cf. John 19:22)

27:39 Those who passed by (i.e. Jewish onlookers, that the place of crucifixion was near a main thoroughfare to warn people of the dire consequences for those who rebelled against Rome.) **hurled insults at him,** (reviled him-K.J.V.-987-*"To speak reproachfully or profanely", to vilify, defame.* Hurled abuse-L.B.V., derided him-R.S.V.) **shaking their heads,**(Expresses a token of contempt insult by moving one's head from side to side in a gesture of disgust.) {Ps. 22:7}
40 and saying, "You who are going to destroy the temple and build it in three days,(Suggests: They had witnessed the trial proceedings or heard secondhand reports of the charge in which Jesus was condemned before the Sanhedrin.-{26:61}) **save** (Syn.-rescue, deliver) **yourself! Come down from the cross, if you are the Son of God!"** (Suggests: Another rumor of the events that had taken place during Jesus' trial, having been found guilty of blasphemy before the Sanhedrin. Expresses: Possibly an echo of Satan's own temptation at Jesus' baptism.-{cf. 4:3})

The people taunt Jesus in using the same power that He boasted of in destroying the Temple to rescuing Himself from the cross.

Message & Application 💻=🌎

❖ Shows how many will go out of their way to kick us when we're down trying to shake our confidence in God's favor & blessing. (Many add insult to injury, using our misfortune as a sign of God's abandonment).
❖ Warns of those who will try to shake our faith by using our distresses as proof that our faith is hopeless, and God's promises have failed.
❖ Teaches how such skeptical language is often reminiscent of unbelief. (Many today often call for visible proof in order to believe).
❖ Warns how those who are consumed with success or material gain will miss the meaning of the cross.
❖ Warns against rejecting Christ just because He doesn't match the picture we expect of Him.
❖ Prepares believers how many will try to challenge our faith by having us put God's promises and power to the test.

–***Save yourself***-Does not mean that Jesus was not powerful enough to come down off the cross if He chose. But rather it is precisely why He did not save Himself in order that He may Save sinners. (Know that it was love, not nails that kept Jesus on the cross!).

🗝 Even today many will often use the injustices or failures of God in order to justify their unbelief, saying such things as; *"If God is almighty why doesn't He stop all the sin and evil in the world?"*

☞ By ridiculing and mocking Jesus the onlookers unknowingly fulfilled Psalm 22:7.

27:41 In the same way the chief priests, the teachers of the law and the elders (Expresses three major religious groups that made up the Sanhedrin.) **mocked him.** (i.e. poke fun at, ridicule, taunt. Not addressing Jesus directly, but rather speaking abusively about Him to the crowd or among themselves.)
42 "He saved others, "they said, (Expresses: Jesus having revived others from death through His miracle healings.) **"but he can't save** (Syn.-rescue, deliver) **himself!** (Expresses bitter irony, sarcasm, taunt, seeing how He was now nailed to the cross.) **He's the King of Israel!** (Suggests: A stinging innuendo to Pilate's inscription on the cross-{V. 37} or a reference to Jesus' own admission.-{V. 11.}) **Let him come down now from the cross, and we will believe in him.**
43 He trusts in God. Let God rescue him now if he wants him, (Expresses an ironic taunt, seeing how His crucifixion and misery was proof of God's abandonment, that He must be accursed by God.) {cf. Ps. 22:8a} **for he said, 'I am the Son of God.'"**(Suggests: A reference to Jesus' earlier admission before Caiaphas and the Sanhedrin.-{Matt. 26:63-64, John 10:36})

Despite the religious leaders attempt to make Jesus appear as a deceiver & imposter, Jesus remains on the cross to Save sinners.

Message & Application 💻=🌎

- ❖ Shows believers who have truly trusted in Christ shouldn't need spectacular miracles in order to prove our Salvation.
- ❖ Teaches a valuable lesson, that belief cannot be founded on outward signs of power, but instead must be taken on faith.
- ❖ Warns against making the wrong assumption, that belief is based on visible proof rather than on faith. (cf. Heb. 11:1)
- ❖ Warns against promising God our belief by prescribing the means & motives of our faith. (*"I'll believe you if you remove this cross"*)
- ❖ Teaches those who make arbitrary demands of Christ are usually blind at heart. (Many can have the fullest evidence yet remain unbelieving).
- ❖ Warns of those who will attempt to vilify Jesus as a fraud, or to drive us to despair in distrusting in God's power and love.
- 🗝 Even today many will promise to put their faith in Jesus if He will give them a sign or a supernatural feat. (Before demanding miracles, consider the abundant evidence you already have around you!).
- ➢ Three areas the religious leaders attempt to disprove Jesus' claims:
  - If Jesus could not save Himself, He, therefore, did not have the divine power as He claimed.
  - If Jesus could not save Himself, His pretense of Saving others was a fraud and delusion.
  - If Jesus was the Son of God, why would God abandon Him to the cross and so much misery?

27:44 In the same way the robbers (3027-*Thief, brigand, one who plunders openly and by violence.* malefactors-K.J.V.) **who were crucified with him** {cf. Is. 53:12} **also heaped** (Syn.-piled-up, laid-on) **insults on him.** (cast the same in his teeth-K.J.V.-Expresses: Remarks full of reproach and taunts, similar to the taunts made by the religious leaders.-{cf. Vs. 41-43} One who hung there hurled insults at him: *"Aren't you the Christ? Save yourself and us!"*.-{Luke 23:39})

The robbers ridiculed Jesus' for not using His power as the Messiah to rescue them all.

Message & Application 💻=🌎

- ❖ Shows how sinners can remain sarcastic & defiant till the very end.
- ❖ Warns against allowing our lowest points and darkest hours to keep us from Jesus. (Know Christ's love despite present sufferings!).
- ❖ Prepares believers in expecting suffering and persecutions as a result of our attachment to Christ.
- ❖ Cautions believers against hardening our hearts, know your guilt and condemnation before God.
- ❖ Calls for not allowing present sufferings to keep us from divine graces. (See crosses as God's way of moving you to repentance).

☞According to the Gospel of Luke, it records that one of these robbers would later repent confessing his sin and rebuking the other saying; *"We are punished justly, for we are getting what our deeds deserve. But this man has done nothing wrong"*. *"Jesus, remember me when you come into your kingdom"*. To which Jesus replies; *"I tell you the truth, today you will be with me in paradise"*.-(Luke 23:41-43) (Expresses: Those who cry out in mercy to Jesus will be Saved, that no one who comes to Jesus will ever be condemned. Emphasizes how it's never too late to repent and ask Jesus to Save you!)

Various types of People who Mock Jesus:

- **The Ignorant**-(Vs. 39-40)
  (Signifies those who are skeptical, indifferent, suspicious, uniformed.)
- **The Religious**-(Vs. 41-43)
  (Signifies those who are self-centered, prideful, envious, no place for Christ.)
- **The Condemned**-(V. 44)
  (Signifies those who are hard-hearted, bitter, resentful, rebellious, unrepentant.)

Good Friday - (12:00-3:00 P.M.)
The Death of Jesus-(N.I.V.)

27:45 From the sixth hour until the ninth hour (From 12:00-3:00 p.m. Friday.) **darkness came over all the land.** (i.e. Judea. Attributed to either, Supernatural act of God, a solar eclipse of the sun, [not universally accepted due to the fact that eclipses only last a few minutes] storm clouds, sand/dust storm. Metph.-A sign of God's displeasure and judgment against sin.-{cf. Amos 8:9-10, Joel 2:1-2})

For three hours of darkness, Jesus bears God's wrath & judgment for the sins of the world.

Message & Application 💻=🌎

❖ Shows how the full weight of God's judgment & punishment for sin has been poured out upon Jesus. (cf. 2-Corn. 5:21, Is. 50:3, 53:4, Amos 8:9)
❖ Displays Jesus' willingness in taking upon Himself all the darkness and blackness of sin and hell so that we won't have to. (cf. Col. 1:12-14)
❖ Warns how a soul void of God's presence and Saving grace leaves nothing but a life full of sorrow, misery, and gloom! (cf. Gen. 1:1-2)
❖ Displays the gravity of Jesus' death, that even the cosmos and nature itself was mourning the suffering of God's Son. (cf. Rom. 8:19)

–***Darkness came over the land***-Variously interpreted as signifying:

- Christ's being under God's judgment & wrath for sin.
- Christ's conflict with the powers of darkness and evil.
- Christ's lack of heavenly comfort as He bears the sins of the world.

4 Miracles accompanied by Jesus' death:

1. **Midday Darkness.** Signifies God's judgment and the outpouring of wrath upon Jesus for sin.
2. **Tearing of the Temple curtain in two.** Signifies the opening of Salvation to all people through the death of Jesus, and the permanent opening of God's presence to man.-(Heb. 9:3,8, 10:19-22)
3. **Earthquake.** Signifies Jesus having fulfilled the demands of the Law, the covenant inaugurated at Sinai is now ended. (Ex. 19:16, Heb. 12:18-24)
   Or God's power & judgment.-(Judg. 5:4, Joel 3:16)
4. **Opening of the Graves.** Signifies Christ's victory over sin & death. And assurance of our own resurrection.-(Eph. 4:8-9)

27:46 About the ninth hour (3:00 P.M.) **Jesus cried out in a loud voice, "Eloi, Eloi, lama sabachthani?"**(Expresses a mixture of both Hebrew & Aramaic.) **which means, "My God, my God, why have you forsaken me?** (Syn.- abandoned, deserted, forgotten, disowned. Expresses Jesus' anguish over being separated from God the Father as He bears the sins of the world.) {cf. Ps. 22:1a}

Jesus stands forsake & abandoned by God as He bears the sins of the world.

Message & Application 💻=🌎

- ❖ Shows the great amount of agony Jesus endured as He bore our sins so we won't have to. (Know that Salvation was anything but cheap!)
- ❖ Warns against taking for granted our Salvation, knowing the amount of suffering it cost Jesus in going through the hell that we deserved!
- ❖ Warns no greater sorrows than to go through life without God, hope, mercy, or love. (Spiritual sorrows are the worst of mental miseries!).
- ❖ Warns believers of the seriousness of sin, that it can leave us destitute, hopeless, and alienated from God the Father. (cf. Is. 59:2)

–***Why have you forsaken me***-Variously attributed to either:

- God had to judicially turn from Jesus as He bore our sin.
- God being holy could not look upon His Son being made sin.
- God's justice demanded that sin be punished.

🗝 Even today we can feel forsaken by God, wondering where God was in our time of pain, agony, and loneliness as when sickness strikes or the death of a loved one. Know that your not alone, that we can look up and cry out to God, that He hears our pain and suffering!

27:47 When some of those standing there heard this, they said, "He's calling Elijah."(Because Elijah never saw death, he would return to help the righteous.)

The bystanders misinterpret Jesus' words as calling on the prophet Elijah to rescue Him.

Message & Application 💻=🌎

–***He's calling for Elijah***-Variously attributed to either:

- If spoken by the soldiers was an ignorant mistake, misinterpreting the Aramaic pronunciation of "Eli" (Heb.-God) for "Elijah".
- If spoken by the Jews was a deliberate taunt meant to deride Jesus in misrepresenting Him as a false messiah who, being accursed by God, could only seek the help of a latter-day prophet to rescue Him. Or was meant to exonerate Jesus since it was thought that Elijah would return to rescue the righteous in times of trouble.-(2-Kings 2:11, Mal. 4:5)

7 Things Jesus said from the Cross:

1) ***"Father forgive them for they know not what they do"*** (Luke 23:34, Is. 53:12) Signifying: Jesus' forgiving His executioners. As well as His grace, mercy, and intercession for all sinners.
2) ***"Today you will be with me in paradise"-*** (Luke 23:42) Signifying: Jesus' promise to the penitent thief of his redemption as well assuring believers of their eternal security, Salvation, and happiness with Him in heaven.
3) ***"Here is your son, Here is your mother"-*** (John 19:26-27) Signifying: Jesus' committing His mother into John's care (or vice-versa). As well as the concern and welfare that Jesus places on all those who love Him.
4) ***"My God, My God, why have you forsaken me"*** (Matt. 27:46, Mark 15:34, Ps. 22:1) Signifying: Jesus' experiencing God's abandonment and wrath as He bears the sins of the world.
5) ***"I am thirsty"***-(John 19:28) Signifying: Jesus' physical suffering and spiritual thirst in desiring to see the fulfillment of God's plan of Salvation & redemption.
6) ***"Father, into your hands I commit my spirit"*** (Luke 23:46) Signifying: Jesus' firm confidence and trust in God, and voluntary act of yielding up His life in the place of sinners.
7) ***"It is finished"***-(John 19:30) Signifying: Jesus' victory over sin, man's sin debt is paid in full, God's wrath against sin is fully satisfied.

(Note: Though the exact chronology is unknown the above order represents the accepted consensuses)

27:48 Immediately one of them (one man.-{Mark-15:36}, soldiers.-{Luke 23:26}) **ran and got a sponge.-◙** (i.e. A sea-sponge used as a way of getting the liquid to Jesus' mouth without spilling it. Expresses: Possibly compassion, sympathy.) **He filled it** (i.e. Soaked it) **with wine vinegar,** (3691-*denotes sour wine, ordinary drink of laborers and soldiers.* Note: Not the same as the drug potion offered to Jesus earlier.-{V. 34} Was either a light wine turned sour and mixed with water. Or a wine turned bitter by the fermentation and aerobic bacteria.) **put it on a stick,** (i.e. So as to reach Jesus' lips, that the cross was high with Jesus several feet off the ground. A stalk of hyssop plant.-{John 19:29}) **and offered it to Jesus to drink.** (i.e. By sucking the liquid from it.)
49 The rest said, "Now leave him alone. (Expresses a mocking objection to the drink, that if any relief is to be given it should come from Elijah. Or was sufficient to revive Jesus long enough to see if Elijah would come.) **Let's see if Elijah comes to save him".** (Syn.-rescue, deliver. Suggests: Since Elijah never saw death, many believed he would return to rescue the righteous.)

A Roman soldier out of compassion offers wine-vinegar to Jesus to ease His suffering.

Message & Application 💻=🌎

- ❖ Shows how believers owe all love & devotion to Jesus out of all He suffered for us. (Refresh the Lord with your love!).
- ❖ Calls for showing compassion to others in their time of greatest need and suffering, regardless of who they are or what they've done.
- ❖ Warns against allowing others to dictate who deserves or does not deserve our help. (Don't allow others deter what you know is right).
- ❖ Warns against making a mockery of another's trials and sufferings.
- ❖ Demonstrates how many can fail to realize everything they already have in Christ, to always looking for more and more proof.
- ❖ Prepares believers in expecting our pious devotions to be ridiculed and abused by others.

*–Wine offered to Jesus to drink-*Variously attributed to either:

- A cruel act in an attempt to revive Jesus in prolonging His suffering (the vinegar acting as a stimulate) or hasten His death (the vinegar acting as a natural dehydrate). (See Ps. 69:19-21)
- A mocking reproach on the part of the soldiers to Jesus' royal claims since this type of wine was normally drunk by common people. (cf. Luke 23:36-37)
- An act of kindness and compassion.

27:50 And when (at the ninth hour.-{Mark 15:34}-i.e. 3:00 P.M. Suggests: The same time of the offering of the evening of sacrifice and the time when the paschal lamb was killed.) **Jesus had cried out again in a loud voice,** (Expresses a cry of triumph; *"It is finished"*-{John 19:30} or *"Father, into your hands I commit my spirit"*.-{Luke 23:46} Not of agony or exhaustion, but rather of Jesus dying in strength, self-will, and victory.) **he gave up** (Syn.-surrendered, yielded, dismissed.) **his spirit.** (i.e. Life, spirit. Yielded up the ghost.-K.J.V.-Expresses: Does not mean the Holy Spirit, but rather is a euphemism used for one who has died, expired, or breathed their last.-{Mark 15:37} Suggests: A deliberate and voluntary surrendering of Jesus' life. That Jesus' life did not ebb away slowly, but that He had voluntarily given up His life as a freewill offering in the remission and atonement of sin.)

Jesus voluntarily surrenders His life over for the sins of the world.

Message & Application 💻=🌎

❖ Shows believers Jesus' love for sinners in voluntarily dying in our place. (Jesus would rather die for us than live without us).
❖ Displays how Jesus freely lays down His life on His own accord in keeping with God's plan of Salvation and redemption of sinners.
❖ Assures believers of Jesus' triumph and victory over Satan and sin.
❖ Teaches the importance of yielding up our lives into God's hands in whatever He asks of us.
❖ Calls believers in sacrificing our time and efforts to God's service. (Will you gladly surrender your life to God's will and work?).
❖ Displays the kind of attitude we should all have of entrusting ourselves into God's hands at death or any other time. (1-Corn. 15:55)

–***Cried out in a loud voice***-Variously interpreted as indicating either:

- That Jesus' life was not taken from Him, that His death was voluntary. (cf. Luke 23:46) (Confirmed by the fact that those crucified normally suffered unconsciousness, eventually lapsing into a coma before dying).
- That Jesus' death was not a cry of weakness, but of strength & victory. (cf. John 19:30)

🗝 Even today we should be willing to yield up ourselves into God's hands in whatever area He has called us to, no matter how trying, difficult, or challenging it may be.

☞ According to John's Gospel, Jesus cried; *"It is finished"*-(John 19:30) Expresses how the work of atonement was complete, that the sin debt was paid for in full.

Purposes in Jesus' Crucifixion:

- Was a substitutionary sacrifice for the atonement of sin and redemption of man. (Mark 10:45, Acts 5:31, 13:38, 26:18, Rom. 3:24-25, 4:25, 6:10,1-Corn. 15:3, Eph. 1:7, Col. 1:14-22, 2:13, Heb. 9:12, 22-28, 1-Pet. 2:24)
- Provided reconciliation by making peace between man & God. (Matt. 27:51, Rom. 5:6-11, 11:15, 2-Corn. 5:18-19, Col. 1:19-22, Eph. 2:11-22, 1-Pet. 3:18, Heb. 10:19-22)
- Established a new covenant between God & man. (Matt. 26:28, Luke 22:20, Rom. 11:27, 1-Corn. 11:25, Heb. 7:22, 8:6-13, 9:11-20, 10:29, 12:24, 13:20)
- To meet the righteous requirements of the law on behalf of the believer. (Rom. 7:1-6, 8:3-4, 10:4, 1-Corn. 1:30, Eph. 2:15, Col. 2:14, Gal. 3:21-25, Titus 2:14)
- Serves as an example of the way of discipleship. (Matt. 10:38, 16:24-25, Rom. 6:5-8, Gal. 2:20, 5:20, 6:14, Col. 3:3-8, 1-Pet. 2:24, 4:1)

The Meaning of the Cross

- The Cross is Christ's work in dying for the sinner and bringing them back to God.
- The Cross is where the sinner finds God's forgiveness, mercy, grace, and love.
- The Cross is Grace unearned, Justice served, Wrath turned away, Ransomed delivered, and Sin conquered.
- The Cross is God's triumph and victory over sin, death, and Satan.
- The Cross is the promise of redemption and eternal life.
- The Cross is the wisdom and power of God.
- The Cross is the promise of redemption and resurrection.
- The Cross is the call to self-sacrifice, patience, and service.

The Medical Causes of Jesus' Death:

- **Asphyxia by suffocation**-With the fixed position of the body on the cross, having the arms outstretched prevented the chest (diaphragm) from expanding, causing Jesus to suffocate, being too weak from the scourging and beatings to lift Himself up on the cross to breathe.
  (Suggests: Why the legs of the other two criminals were broken in preventing them from leveraging themselves up to breathe.-(John 19:31-32) (Some reject this due to the fact that Jesus was able to give out a loud cry just before He died).
- **Hemorrhaging and excessive bleeding**-With the wounds suffered by both the flogging and the nails used to attach the body to the cross caused Jesus to bleed to death. (Some reject this due to the fact that loss of blood normally led to unconsciousness, whereas Jesus was fully awake right up until death).-(V. 50)
- **Pulmonary embolus/blood clot-** With the body in a fixed position on the cross and completely immobilized would cause blood to accumulate in the legs, causing Jesus to die of a cardiac rupture/heart attack). (Suggests: Why, when the Roman soldier pierced Jesus' side water & blood flowed, bearing evidence of a cardiac rupture.-(John 19:34) (Some reject this due to the fact even with the hands and ankles in a fixed position, the body and torso still had some freedom to move up and down and vertically by bending the knees).
- **Shock and exhaustion-**With the body severely beaten, flogged, and fixed to the cross, would have left Jesus dehydrated, weak, and critically ill, causing convulsions resulting in a heart attack or stroke. (Suggests: Why Jesus was too weak to carry the cross to the place of execution). (Some reject this due to Jesus' coherent statements from the cross which showed none of the hallmark signs of one dying from profound exhaustion or shock).

27:51 At that moment (i.e. At the time of Jesus' death, final cry.) **the curtain of the temple-◙** (veil-K.J.V. i.e. A curtain that served as a dividing wall between the Holy Place and the Holy of Holies, some 60 feet long and 40 feet high.) **was torn in two from top to bottom.** (i.e. From heaven to earth, The verification of this event must have been witnessed by the priests, who were at this time burning incense before the holy of holies.) **The earth shook** (Note: Unknown whether this earthquake was local [Temple mount] or widespread.) **and the rocks split.** (As a consequence of the earthquake. Expresses a symbol of God's judgment and overthrow/breaking in of Satan's kingdom.)

Jesus now gives believers permanent access to God's presence through His atoning & redemptive work on the cross.

Message & Application 💻=🌎

- ❖ Shows believers how through Christ's sacrifice we now have free access to the throne of God's mercy & grace. (Rom. 8:32, Heb. 10:19-20)
- ❖ Displays how nothing can hinder our way to heaven, that we can now have the confidence of entering into the presence of God.
- ❖ Teaches how we can now approach God with complete confidence and boldness, knowing all our sins are forever put out of His sight.
- ❖ Displays the incredible power of the Lord, having broken down the barrier of sin that's been separating us from God.
- ❖ Warns against staying in unbelief after all God has done. (V. 51b)

–***Curtain torn from top to bottom***-Variously signifying either:

- A symbol of the permanent opening of access to God's presence through the atoning death of Christ.
- A departure of God from the Temple, ending the old covenant with Israel.-(Ezek. Chaps. 10-11)
- A breaking down of the partition-wall between Jew & Gentile.
- A foreshadowing of the future destruction of the Temple. (Fulfilled by Rome in A.D. 70).

–***The earth shook/rocks split***-Variously interpreted as either:

- A symbol signifying the earthshaking event of Christ's death, affecting all of creation.
- An ending of God's covenant inaugurated at Sinai and the beginning of a new covenant of grace.-(Ex. 19:16-18)
- A manifestation of God's wrath and anger against those who wrongly crucified Jesus.
- A testimony of the earth's witness to Jesus' innocence.
- A means in which Christ's death would open the tombs of the deceased.-(V. 52)

27:52 The tombs (i.e. Graves) **broke open** (Suggests: As a consequence of the earthquake dislodging the stones.) **and the bodies of many holy people** (saints-K.J.V.) **who had died were raised to life.** (Not resurrected, but rather revived or resuscitated, raised to ordinary physical life.-{Matt. 9:23-25, Luke 7:11-15})
53 They came out of the tombs, and after Jesus' resurrection they went into the holy city (Uncertain whether they immediately went into Jerusalem at the time of Christ's death, or waited at their tombs until after Jesus' own resurrection.) **and appeared to many people.** (Suggests: They had been seen by their former relatives and friends, that they returned to their normal bodies and natural life.)

Jesus conquers the power over sin & death through His atoning and redemptive work on the Cross.

Message & Application 💻=🌎

- ❖ Shows believers the resurrecting power of Christ in raising us up to a glorious new life now and the hereafter! (cf. 2-Corn. 4:16)
- ❖ Displays the life-giving power of Christ, that no matter how dead we are in sin Jesus can lift us up and give us victory over it!
- ❖ Teaches the importance of living holy and faithful lives, that only the graves of Saints will be opened and raised to life. (cf. John 5:28-29)
- ❖ Calls for making our transformed lives visible to our family & friends as irrefutable proof of the resurrecting power and work of God.

–***Many holy people raised to life*** -Variously interpreted as either:

- Old Testament Saints and holy men who arose to bear witness to Christ's resurrection only to retire to their graves again. (Not widely supported due to the fact that the O.T. saints would not have been easily recognized.-cf. V. 53)
- Disciples/believers who had died before Christ's crucifixion and resurrection who were revived, returning to their natural life only to eventually die again.

🗝 Even today, believers can live more joyful & victorious lives, knowing God can rejuvenate and bring back to life a dead career, marriage, relationship, and anything else.

☞ Serves to confirm the general resurrection of the dead in the last day, that there is a glorious future in store for us in our own resurrection.

☞ Note: No biblical account of whether these risen Saints died again or had gone into heaven with Jesus. (Some hold that they arose receiving glorified bodies and after giving proof of the reality of the resurrection they ascended to heaven).

27:54 When the centurion-◙ (i.e. A Roman officer commanding a 100 men, sergeant-L.B.V.) **and those with him who were guarding Jesus** (i.e. The purpose being to prevent Jesus' rescue and to ensure that death was complete.) **saw the earthquake** (i.e. Physical signs) **and all that had happened,** (i.e. The darkness-{V. 45} natures convulsions/earthquake-{V. 51 b} opening of the graves-{Vs. 52-53}) **they were terrified,** (feared greatly-K.J.V., filled with awe-R.S.V. Syn.-awe stricken. Suggests: They saw the events as proof of divine judgment against them for having participated in the crucifixion, that such events had never been observed in previous crucifixions.) **and exclaimed, "Surely he was the Son of God!"** (i.e. Divine being, Messiah, holy, innocent. Suggests: Being well seasoned in carrying out all sorts of crucifixions, Jesus' death was unlike anything he had ever witnessed before. That Jesus never cursed, never retaliated against those who mocked, taunted, and ridiculed Him but rather forgave them. Praised God and said, *"Surely this was a righteous man"*.-{Luke 23:47}-Expresses Jesus' innocence as well as divine vindication.)

The supernatural events and signs that followed Jesus' crucifixion convinced the Roman Soldiers of Jesus' vindication and innocence.

Message & Application 💻=🌎

- ❖ Shows how Saving faith will confess Christ's Lordship and divine authority. (Will you acknowledge that Jesus is who He says He is?)
- ❖ Displays the glorious Saving work of God in taking callous and hardened sinners and turning them into worshippers of Christ.
- ❖ Teaches how true faith will see God's love and presence even in a world that seems harsh, brutal, and unfair.
- ❖ Calls for always speaking the sure truth and glory of Christ. (Will you praise Jesus as Lord no matter what all the others say?).
- ❖ Displays the extent of God's Saving grace even to those who seem the most unlikely to believe on Christ.
- ❖ Teaches how there's no person too cold-hearted, rebellious, or too proud that the power of Christ can't break and humble.
- ❖ Emphasizes the difference between those who see their life's as being judged and punished, and those who see God's mercy & forgiveness.
- ❖ Displays how God can take what seems to be a tragedy & total failure and turn it into an opportunity to bring praise and glory to His name.
- ⊶ Even today every person will have to at some point in their lives, make their own personal decision about Jesus. Either He was just another great teacher who was dealt a bad hand, and as a result was crucified on a cross. Or He will be known to them as their Lord & Savior who Saved them from their sins.

27:55 Many women were there, watching from a distance. (i.e. Not of their aloofness our detachment, but rather out of fear for their own safety, being that the cross was surrounded by soldiers. Or out of love, not bearing to watch Jesus' sufferings or modesty due to Jesus' nakedness. Expresses the woman's affectionate attachment to Jesus.) **They had followed Jesus from Galilee to care for his needs.**(i.e. They had cared and supported Jesus during His ministry out of their own means, possibly even financing Jesus' final trip to Jerusalem)
56 Among them were Mary Magdalene, (i.e. A woman whom Jesus had earlier expelled seven demons from.-{Luke 8:2} Last name identifies her place of origin or hometown of "Magdala", a village near Capernaum in Galilee.) **Mary the mother of James and Joses,** (i.e. Mary the wife of Clopas-{cf. John 19:25 b} or possibly Jesus' mother and step brothers.-{cf. Matt. 13:55}) **and the mother of Zebedee's sons.** (i.e. Salome-{Mark 15:40, 16:1} and her two sons, James & John.-{Matt. 20:20-21} Others identify her as possibly also the sister of Mary, mother of Jesus.-{cf. John 19:25})

Unlike most of the disciples, these women remained faithful to Jesus unto death.

Message & Application 💻=🌎

❖ Shows how true believers will stay loyal & committed to Jesus when everyone else bails.
❖ Calls for not allowing tragedies, sufferings, or grief to keep us from Christ. (Those who truly love Jesus will remain faithful, drawing near and standing with Him no matter what!).
❖ Calls for taking advantage of the opportunities given us in doing what we can in our service to Christ. (When restrained from doing what you would, do what you can!).
❖ Calls for making ourselves available to Christ. (Can Jesus count on your support and willingness to serve Him regardless of the difficulties or discouragements you may face?).
❖ Prepares believers against thinking it's strange that when we suffer, our best friends may shy away from us. (Remember it was out of love that many could not bear to look at Jesus when He suffered).
☞ This verse is often used in validating & approving a woman's right in entering into the ministry. (Male believers would do well to remember that it was a woman who anointed the Lord while the disciples murmured-(Matt. 26:7) That it was women who were at the cross while all the disciples [except John] had fled-(Mark 14:50) That it was a woman who came to the tomb and who was the first to announce the Lord's resurrection-{28:1-10} while the rest of the disciples were cowering in a house in fear of the Jewish authorities & Roman reprisal-(John 20:18-19).

Good Friday -(3:00-6:00 p.m.)

The Burial of Jesus-(N.I.V.)

27:57 As evening approached, (i.e. Between 3:00 & 6:00 p.m. Ending of Friday and beginning of Saturday [Sabbath], before sunset.) **there came a rich man from Arimathea,** (i.e. A town 20 miles northwest of Jerusalem. That he was a native of Arimathea arriving in Jerusalem to celebrate the Passover.) **named Joseph, who had himself become a disciple of Jesus.** (Suggests: Secretly because he feared the Jews.-{cf. John 19:38 b} Or that he feared being expelled from the Sanhedrin because of his association with Jesus.)
58 Going to Pilate, he asked (begged-K.J.V.-154-*To call for, require, demand.* The Greek verb suggests boldly, fearlessly, and courageously. No doubt needed due to the fact that not being a relative, he would have to explain his reasons.) **for Jesus' body, and Pilate** (having been reassured by the centurion that the death had already taken place.-{John 19:33-34}) **ordered that it be given to him.**

Joseph in observance of Jewish law & approaching Sabbath goes boldly before Pilate in asking to bury Jesus' body.

Message & Application 💻=🌎

- ❖ Shows where there's true love & devotion to Christ, no service will seem too low, or labor too hazardous in serving Him.
- ❖ Calls for using whatever advantages we have in our service for Christ. (Will you make use of every opportunity & resource to glorify God?).
- ❖ Displays the providence of God in providing the courage and strength to fearlessly do the work He's called us to do.
- ❖ Calls believers in expecting blessings and aid from unlikely sources and supporters.
- ❖ Inspires believers in knowing the kind of impact we can make when we're courageous and compassionate for the things of Christ.

–***Joseph of Arimathea***-According to the other Gospels accounts identify him as being a member of the "Sanhedrin"-(Mark 15:43, Luke 23:50 a) That he was a good and upright (honorable) man, that he had not consented to Jesus' execution-(Luke 23:50 -51)-(Suggests: Possibly he was not present during the sentencing trial or was outvoted by the majority vote) That he was waiting for the kingdom of God-(Luke 23:51) (Suggests he was not a Sadducee but a Pharisee and follower of Jesus)

☞ Joseph's exemplary character can be seen in the costly risk in identifying himself with Jesus. That he had used his influence to gain an appearance before Pilate. That Joseph was willing to use his financial wealth to bury Jesus.

27:59 Joseph took the body, (i.e. Down from the cross or from the hands of those who had been ordered by Pilate to deliver it to him.) **wrapped it in a clean linen cloth,-◙** (i.e. Burial clothing.)
60 and placed it in his own new tomb that he had cut out of the rock.-◙ (i.e. A burial chamber carved out of a stone cliff. Church tradition identifies the site in what is known today as the "Church of the Holy Sepulcher" located within the Christian quarter of the old city.) **He rolled a big stone in front of the entrance to the tomb-◙** (i.e. A disk-shaped stone, about three feet in diameter and weighing 1-2 tons. rolled into place in a groove cut into the rock to protect against wild animals and grave robbers. With the slot on an incline would make the stone easy to roll shut but difficult to open, taking possibly several men to roll the stone back up the incline in order to open it.) **and went away.** (Suggests: Being that the Sabbath, a day of rest and no work was fast approaching, there was nothing left to do but go home and rest.)
61 Mary Magdalene and the other Mary (i.e. Wife of Clopas-{V. 56, John 19:25}) **were sitting there opposite the tomb.** (i.e. No doubt their mourning for Jesus as they watched His burial. As well as taking note of the place where Jesus was buried in order to return after the Sabbath to finish anointing the body and completing the burial.-{Matt. 8:1, Mark 16:1, Luke 23:55-56, 24:1})

Joseph in accordance with Jewish customs wraps Jesus' body in grave clothes and lays Him in his own tomb.

Message & Application 💻=🌎

☞ According to the Gospel of John, Joseph was assisted by Nicodemus who was also another secret disciple of Jesus'. That the preparations of Jesus' burial consisted of a mixture of myrrh and aloes, weighing about seventy-five pounds-(John 19:39-40)

Jewish Burial Practices & Customs:

1) The body is first washed and then perfumed and preserved with myrrh [gum resin or sap produced from various trees and bushes] and aloes [extracts produced from various tree leaves].
2) The body is then wrapped in a fine linen cloth with the spices mixed in between the folds (Some believe the "Shroud of Turin" is what remains of that cloth.)
3) The body is then laid upon a rock-shelf cut out from the inside walls of the tomb.

Saturday -(6:00 p.m.)
The Guard at the Tomb-(N.I.V.)

27:62 The next day (i.e. 6:00 p.m. Saturday/Sabbath) **the one after Preparation Day** (i.e. Friday.) **the chief priests and the Pharisees went to Pilate.**
63 "Sir," they said, "we remember that while he was still alive that deceiver (i.e. Jesus. Syn.-liar, fraud. Expresses their contempt for Jesus, believing He was subverting the nation with His teachings.-{cf. Luke 23:2}) **said, 'After three days I will rise again.'** (A reference to what Jesus had spoken earlier to them concerning the sign of the prophet Jonah as a symbol of His own resurrection in three days.-{Matt. 12:38-40} Or was in reference to Jesus' saying; "Destroy this temple, and I will raise it again in three days".-{cf. John 2:19-22})
64 So give the order for the tomb to be made secure until the third day. Otherwise, his disciples may come and steal the body and tell the people that he has been raised from the dead. This last deception will be worse than the first." (Suggests: The deception of Jesus' resurrection would be greater than His deception of claiming to be the Messiah.)
65 "Take a guard," Pilate answered. "Go, make the tomb as secure as you know how." (i.e. Using either their own Temple-guards or the Governor's soldiers. Or meant as a cynical taunt of their cowardice in fearing a dead man.)
66 So they went and made the tomb secure by putting a seal on the stone-◙ (i.e. By fastening the stone cover with cords and uniting them together with an official wax or clay seal stamped with the Kings signet, thereby ensuring the security of the grave. Purpose being to deter fraudulent tampering, possibly in preventing the guards from being corrupted and bribed in permitting the theft.) **and posting the guard.** (i.e. Roman guards or Temple police.)

The religious leaders, fearing the disciples will proclaim Jesus' resurrection by stealing His body ask Pilate to guard the tomb.

Message & Application

- ❖ Shows how many try to do everything they can in denying God. (Men would rather bury their convictions than admit accountability).
- ❖ Warns how many will try to discourage our faith in Christ, keeping Jesus from releasing His power to heal and transform us.
- ❖ Warns against sealing Christ out of your life. (Many are willing to welcome Jesus, but block Him from changing the way they live).
- 🗝 Even today many people will do all they can to keep Jesus in the grave, today its science, liberalism, secularism, and cultism.
- ☞ Demonstrates the hypocrisy of the priests, who were scrupulous about keeping the Sabbath, but did not mind profaning the day by consulting with a foreign governor in securing and sealing up an unclean grave.

Chapter Twenty Eight

Jesus' Resurrection

- **The Resurrection-**Jesus raises from the dead and appears to the two women.-(Vs. 1-10)
- **The Guards Report-**Religious leaders bribe the guards into saying that the disciples stole Jesus' body.-(Vs. 11-15)
- **The Great Commission-**Jesus commissions the disciples in preaching the Gospel throughout the world, baptizing believers in the name of the father, Son, and Holy Spirit.-(Vs. 16-20)

S u n d a y -(6:00 a.m.)

The Resurrection-(N.I.V.)

28:1 After the Sabbath, at dawn on the first day of the week, (i.e. 5:00-6:00 A.M. Sunday.) **Mary Magdalene** (i.e. Whom Jesus cast out seven evil spirits) **and the other Mary** (i.e. Mary the wife of Clopas.-{John 19:25}) **went to look at the tomb.** (i.e. To anoint Jesus' body & finish the burial rights.-{Mark 16:1-3})
2 There was a violent earthquake, for an angel of the Lord came down from heaven and, going to the tomb, rolled back the stone and sat on it.
3 His appearance was like lightning, and his clothes were white as snow.
4 The guards were so afraid of him that they shook and became like dead men. (Expresses: They either fainted in terror or were paralyzed with fear.)
5 The angel said to the women, "Do not be afraid, (Syn.-agitated, troubled. Suggests: Not to be alarmed by the disappearance of Jesus' body.) **for I know that you are looking for Jesus, who was crucified.**
6 He is not here; he has risen, just as he said. (i.e. Predictions concerning His death & Resurrection-{16:21,17:23,20:19}**Come and see the place where he lay.**
7 Then Go quickly and tell his disciples: 'He has risen from the dead and is going ahead of you into Galilee. There you will see him. Now I have told you."

An angel confirms Jesus' resurrection to two women, calling them to share the good news with His disciples.

Message & Application 

- ❖ Shows those who aspire in their love & devotion to Jesus will not be disappointed. (Know your worship & devotion will not be in vain!).
- ❖ Assures believers of living a victorious life, having God' power to roll away the stones of sin, doubt, despair, and addictions out of our lives.
- ❖ Teaches believers who seek Christ as their Lord & Savior no longer need to fear sin, death, or Satan's attacks.
- ❖ Displays how God often uses different means and agencies in confirming and validating our faith.
- ⊶ Even today we're to share the good news with others, that Jesus is alive, willing to Save & rescue them from their sins and bondages.

Purposes for Jesus' Resurrection:

- Proves Jesus' victory over sin & death, that Jesus made full payment for our sin debt owed to God. (See Rom. 5:12-21, Heb. 2:14-15, 1-Corn. 15:17, 15:54-57)
- Proves that our sins have been forgiven, that the sacrifice was acceptable to God. (See Rom. 4:25, Heb. 10:5-18, 1-Pet. 3:18)
- Attests that Jesus is Lord & Christ, and confirms Jesus as the Son of God.-(See Acts 2:32-36, John 20:28, Rom. 1:4, Heb. 10:5-12, 1-Pet. 3:18)
- Encourages believers in our own resurrection, giving hope of eternal life with Jesus.-(See Rom. 8:23-25, Heb. 9:28, 1-Pet. 1:3, 21, 2-Corn. 1:9-10, Philip. 3:20-21, Titus 1:2, 1-John 3:2-3, 2-Tim. 1:10)
- Assures believers that Christ is alive, ruling and interceding on our behalf.-(See Rom. 8:34, 14:9, Heb. 4:14-15, 7:24-25, 1-John 2:1)
- Gives believers a living hope, someone we can live for.-(See 2-Corn. 5:15, 1-Peter 1:3-5)
- Serves as a source of power for victorious Christian living.-(See Acts 4:10, Rom. 6:4-14, 7:4, 1-Thess. 5:1-11)
- Proves that there is a future judgment.-(Matt. 25:31-32, Acts 10:40-43, 17:31, Rom. 14:9-12, 1-Corn. 4:5, 2-Corn. 5:10, 1-Thess. 1:10, Rev. 11:11-13)
- Allows believers to receive the indwelling presence of the Holy Spirit.-(See Acts 2:33, John 7:39, 14:15-19, 16:7, 20:21-22, Rom. 8:11, 2-Corn. 5:5)
- Fulfilled prophetic promises made in the O.T.- (See Acts 2:29-32, 13:30-32, 1-Corn. 15:3-4)

28:8 So the women hurried away from the tomb, afraid (with fear-K.J.V. A.V. Expresses: A mixture of wonder and awe produced from the angels appearance. awe-N.E.B., deep in wonder-M.B.V. Trembling and bewildered-{Mark 16:8}) **yet filled with joy,** (Suggests: By the angels glad tidings of Jesus' resurrection.) **and ran to tell his disciples.**
9 Suddenly Jesus met them. "Greetings," (All hail-K.J.V.-5463-*"To rejoice", used as a salutation upon meeting or parting,* Syn.-good wishes/health, God's speed, blessings) **he said. They came to him, clasped his feet** (Expresses: A token of humility, reverence, and veneration.) **and worshiped him.**
(Expresses: Knelt or prostrated themselves before Him as an act of divine adoration, owing Him as their Lord and God.)
10 Then Jesus said to them, "Do not be afraid. Go and tell my brothers (i.e. The Twelve Disciples) **to go to Galilee; there they will see me."** (Suggests: Reconfirms Jesus' earlier promise made to the disciples in the Garden-{cf. 26:32} or to reconfirm the angel's testimony.-{V. 7} Reasons for the rendezvous see analysis at 26:32. Expresses: A tender gesture of kindness & forgiveness, having deserted Him in His sufferings, yet He still lovingly keeps fellowship with them.)

Jesus appears before the women reassuring them of His presence and love for the disciples.

<u>Message & Application</u> 💻=🌎

- ❖ Shows how we're not to loiter or lose time in the errands God sends us on. (A ready heart makes quick work of the Lord's instructions).
- ❖ Assures believers that when we're in the path of duty we can be dependent on Christ's blessings, presence, and instructions.
- ❖ Displays how Jesus never breaks his promises, that He will always keep His word. (Do not waver or doubt, bank on Christ' promises).
- ❖ Teaches how by virtue of our faithfulness and commitment to Christ, do we find words of victory, assurance, and blessings.
- ❖ Assures believers that despite our failures Christ still loves us. (V. 10) (Know that Jesus will never desert or break fellowship with you).
- ❖ Teaches the importance sharing our comforts and encouragements we receive from God with others. (Encourage others by sharing the truths of the scriptures and spiritual insights). (V. 10)
- ❖ Calls for courageous witness in telling others of the victories and deliverances that Christ has brought in your life. (V. 10) (Share with others Jesus' Saving grace).
- ☞ This verse here is often used to support the right of women in ministry, having been used by Christ as the first messengers of the Gospel. (Some see it as a fitting duty since it was a woman (Eve) that led man to sin, it should be a woman that brings the good news of Salvation).

The Guards' Report-(N.I.V.)

28:11 While the women were on their way, (i.e. To share the good news with the disciples of Jesus' resurrection.) **some of the guards** (i.e. Roman soldiers) **went into the city** (Jerusalem) **and reported to the chief priests** (i.e. Annas & Caiaphas. Having been assigned to the Jewish authorities, or feared to report their negligence to their own Governor.-{V. 14}) **everything that had happened.** (i.e. Earthquake, angel's appearance, stone rolled away, empty tomb.-{28:2})
12 When the chief priests had met with the elders and devised a plan, they gave the soldiers a large sum of money, (i.e. To bribe and induce them to lie.)
13 telling them, "You are to say, 'His disciples came during the night and stole him away while we were asleep.'
14 If this report gets to the governor, we will satisfy him and keep you out of trouble."(i.e. They would persuade Pilate not to punish them for sleeping on duty, a capital offense which under Roman law was punishable by death.)
15 So the soldiers took the money and did as they were instructed. And this story has been widely circulated among the Jews to this very day. (i.e. The writing of Matthew's Gospel.)

In order to keep Jesus' resurrection quiet, the Roman guards are bribed in saying the disciples stole the body.

Message & Application

- Shows that when we give ourselves up to sin, we are often entangled in new crimes. (New lies are often used to cover up old lies!).
- Warns against guarding our reputations at the expense of leading others away from Christ. (Better to owe up to your mistakes.)
- Teaches that if we would only investigate the issues for ourselves, we will find false claims made about Christ will never hold water.
- The absurdity of the explanation fails in many ways:
  1) If it occurred while the soldiers were sleeping, how could the guards know who took the body.
  2) If the disciples were truly being accused why had not the religious leaders arrested and prosecuted them.
  3) If the soldiers confessed to such a story, it would mean a breach of negligence, punishable by death.
- Other erroneous theories skeptics use to deny the resurrection:
  - Jesus did not really die but was only unconscious.
  - Jesus' body was stolen.
  - The disciples had gone to the wrong tomb.
  - The disciples had hallucinated His appearance.
  - Jesus' followers had made it all up.

(For a counter rebuttal to all such theories see Pg. 438)

Evidence for the Resurrection:

The Stone & Seal:

- Because of the Roman guard's strict discipline and allegiance to the Emperor, any attempt to move the stone would have been prevented. Even if the soldiers were all asleep, no one would have been able to move the stone without waking at least one of them up.
- Because the "Seal" stood for Roman power & authority, no one would have removed it, exposing themselves to execution.

The Empty Tomb:

- Because the tomb was in close proximity to Jerusalem, claims of the resurrection could immediately and easily have been disproven by simply going to the tomb to check for oneself.
- Empty tomb is acknowledged by both Jesus' opponents & disciples. (Former would have certainly refuted this by producing the body!).
- Jesus' tomb was never venerated as a shrine.
- Because the testimony of women in 1st-century Jewish culture was considered worthless. If the empty tomb was simply legend the male disciples would have been made the first to discover the empty tomb.

The Grave Clothes:

- Because the linen grave clothes lay neatly aside along with the head covering-(John 20:1-10) proves that Jesus' body was not stolen, for thieves would not have taken the time to carefully remove and neatly fold the wrappings. Or if Jesus simply recovered from passing out He would not have left the tomb naked.

The Roman Guards:

- The Roman soldiers would not have allowed the body to be taken either by desertion or sleep, for such negligence of duty under Roman law was punishable by death.
- Because the soldiers had to be bribed by the religious leaders, proves the truth of their testimony of the miraculous event.

The Disciples:

- The transformed lives of the disciples, from one of fear & cowardice to bold witness and unflinching courage confirms the resurrection.
- The disciple's willingness to proclaim the resurrection despite the dangers to their own lives. (No one would propose to die or expose themselves to persecution if they knew their beliefs were a lie!).

Counter Theories & Rebuttals for the Resurrection:

The Theft Theory- ***"That the disciples stole Jesus' body"***
Rebuttal:

- The disciples had neither the opportunity nor the power to remove Jesus' body with Roman soldiers guarding the tomb.
- The disciple's grief and cowardice would have prevented the daring courage needed to face a detachment of Roman soldiers.
- Because the disciples did not yet fully understand the resurrection they had no motive to remove the body.
- The enemies of Jesus' would not have stolen His body, for that would have only confirmed belief in His resurrection.

The Swoon Theory-*"That Jesus did not die but merely fainted"*
Rebuttal:

- The amount of massive blood loss, torture, and stab wounds to Jesus' body and side argues against this.
- The Roman soldiers being proficient in crucifixions would not have failed in their duties, which by Roman law was punishable by death.
- The probability that Jesus having survived the crucifixion with the wounds to His side, feet, and hands, and still having the strength to move a two-ton stone away, then over power Roman soldiers, and then walk several miles are very unlikely.
- Jesus' ability to wrangle free from grave clothes tightly wrapped around Him and heavily soaked with gummy embalming spices, without leaving them disarranged is very improbable.

The Hallucination Theory-*"People hallucinated Jesus' appearance"*
Rebuttal:

- More than 500 people could not all have had the same hallucination.
- The Jewish or Roman authorities could have produced Jesus' body, putting an end to the illusion once and for all.
- The fact that Jesus allowed Thomas to touch His hands and side, and later ate with the disciples disproves the hallucination theory.

The Wrong Tomb Theory-*"Everyone went to the wrong tomb"*
Rebuttal:

- The women certainly would have known the right tomb having witnessed Joseph of Arimathea bury Jesus' body the previous day.
- The religious leaders could have gone to the right tomb & produced Jesus' body dispelling the claims of the resurrection once and for all.
- Joseph of Arimathea, owner of the tomb would have corrected them.

28:16 Then the eleven disciples (i.e. Excluding Judas, who had committed suicide.-{cf. 27:5}) **went to Galilee, to the mountain** (i.e. Possibly Mtn. Tabor or the Mtn. of the Beatitudes.) **where Jesus had told them to go.**
17 When they saw him, they worshiped him; (i.e. Owed divine honor, homage, and adoration to Jesus.) **but some doubted.** (1365-*"To stand in two ways", to waver.* Suggests: Not all the disciples, but rather like Thomas, some were hesitant at first, that it was really Jesus and not a ghost.-{V. 18, Mark 16:14, Luke 24:37-38, John 20:25} Or that there was a larger group present with the disciples who were not yet confirmed believers.-{cf. 1-Corn. 15:5-6})

While most of the disciples worshiped Jesus some were hesitant at first that it was really Him.

Message & Application 

- Shows believers only when we make Jesus the object of our faith & worship can we find purpose, assurance, and hope in uncertain times.
- Teaches those who would maintain a relationship with Jesus must attend to Him in the place He has appointed them.
- Teaches the importance of making work of the things of Christ no matter the journey or how far it takes us. (Don't hesitate in giving Christ control over your life, no matter where it may lead).
- Teaches only when we respond obediently to Jesus' Lordship can we triumph over our doubts, insecurities, and uncertainties.

Consensus of Resurrection Appearances:

Sunday Morning:
- Mary Magdalene- (First appearance) (Mark 16:9-11)
- Other two Mary's(Second appearance) (Matt. 28:8-10)
- Peter-(Third appearance) (1-Corn. 15:5)

Sunday Afternoon:
- Two on the road to Emmaus-(Fourth appearance)(Mark 16:12)
- Ten Apostles, Thomas absent-(Fifth appearance) (Luke 24:36)

Following Sunday:
- Ten Apostles, Thomas presents(Sixth appearance) (John 20:26)

Following 32 days:
- Seven by the Sea of Galilee-(Seventh appearance) (John 21:1)
- 500 believers in Galilee-(Eighth appearance) (1-Corn. 15:6)
- James half brother of Jesus-(Ninth appearance) (1-Corn. 15:7)
- 11 disciples on Mount Tabor-(Tenth appearance) (Matt. 28:16)

28:18 Then Jesus came to them (i.e. Twelve Disciples, while in Galilee.) **and said, All authority in heaven and on earth** (Christ' dominion over all creation.) **has been given to me.** (i.e. As a result of Jesus having died & conquered death.)
19 Therefore go (Expresses: Not a suggestion but a command.) **and make disciples** (Believers/Converts.) **of all nations,** (Expresses: A call to go and Evangelize the world with the Gospel.) **baptizing them** (907-*To dip/immerse in water.* i.e. Confirming them.) **in the name of the Father** (God) **and of the Son** (Jesus) **and of the Holy Spirit,**
20 and teaching them to obey everything I have commanded you. (i.e. Church doctrines, as in repentance, confession, baptism. But also Christian character as well, as in the way of Christlike love, charity, and forgiveness.) **And surely I am with you always, to the very end of the age."** (i.e. The World, Gospel age.)

Jesus Commissions the Twelve Disciples to preach and spread the Gospel to all people.

Message & Application 💻=🌎

❖ Shows how all believers have a responsibility to share the Gospel message of God's love & forgiveness to a lost and hurting world.
❖ Teaches how Jesus didn't just Save us so we could have a free train ticket to heaven, but rather that we may serve and witness for Him.
❖ Assures believers in having success in accomplishing whatever task the Lord has called and commissioned us to do.
❖ Teaches how Jesus is always to have an authoritative role in our life's.
❖ Encourages believers in having Christ's guidance, presence, and support as we go out to serve and minister for Him. (V. 20)
🗝 Even today the "Great Commission" is not just about Alter Calls, or getting people to say a prayer, sign a decision card, or take a dip in the baptismal pool. But rather it's also about teaching the Word of God and helping them in their spiritual walk as well.
☞ Jesus is not calling on every believer in becoming a missionary in some foreign country. But rather, He does expect us to use whatever opportunities we have to share the Gospel as we go about our daily routines of going to work, school, gym, or to a neighbors house, etc.

Ways to Fulfill Christ's Commission:
- Through our Words & Witness
- Through our Prayers & Invitations
- Through our Offerings & Donations
- Through our Love & Support

Cross References

The following "Cross reference" index is given here to guide the reader to other bible passages that will help aid in studying other verses on the same subject as well as give additional applications to the teaching.

The following list of Cross references is not exhausted in itself, but rather focuses only of those verses that are critical to the main subject matter.

It is encouraged that the reader and student use bible Concordances and Chain References works (e.g. "R.A. Torrey's Treasury of Scripture Knowledge") to do their own investigation as well.
(Bible chapter & verse are in **boldface type**, followed by their corresponding verses from other books of the bible).

(**1:1-**Gen. 12:3, 13:15, 22:18, 2-Sam. 7:12-13, 22:51, 2-Corn. 1:18-20, **1:2-**Gen. 38:1-29, 49:1-12, **1:21-**John 3:16, Acts 4:12, Col. 1:20-23, 1-John 2:1-2, 3:5, Ps. 130:7-8, Is. 12:1-2, 45:21-22, **1:22-23-**Matt. 28:20, Rev. 21:3, John 1:1-3, 14:19-21, Philp. 2:2-7, Heb. 4:15, Rom. 8:35-39, **2:5-6-**Matt. 10:6, John 7:42, 10:11-14, Heb. 13:20, 1-Pet. 2:25, 5:4, Ps. 78:71-72, Is. 9:6-7, 40:11, Jer. 23:4-6, Ezk. 34:23-24, **2:14-15-**Gen. 45:4-11, Ex. 4:22-23, 12:31-42, 1-Pet. 2:9, **3:1-2-**Matt. 21:28-32, Acts 2:38-39, 3:19, 19:19, Rom. 12:2, 2-Corn. 7:8-11, Is. 59:20, Ezk. 14:6, 18:30-32, Rev. 9:20-21, Luke 15:11-32, 2-Pet. 3:9, Rev. 2:21, **3:5-6-**Acts 8:18-23, 19:18, James 5:16, 1-Tim. 6:12, 1-John 1:8-10, **3:7-**Matt. 5:20, Luke 7:30, 7:36, 18:9-14, John 3:1-15, 4:1, 7:48, 9:16, 12:42, Rom. 2:4-5, **3:8-**Luke 3:10-14, Matt. 7:15-18, 21:28-32, Acts 11-27, 19:18-20, 26:20, Rom. 2:4-7, 2-Corn. 7:10-11, Gal. 5:22-24, Philp. 1:11, Eph. 4:21-24, Is. 55:7, **3:9-**John 8:33-40, Luke 16:24-31, Rom. 2:28-29, 4:1-17, 9:6-8, 11:16, Gal. 1:15, 3:6-9, 3:26-29, Eph. 2:8-10, 1-Thess. 2:12, Heb. 5:4, Ezk. 33:24, Is. 51:1-2, 55:6-7, **3:10-**Is. 5:2-7, 10:33-34, Mal. 4:1, John 15:1-8, Matt. 7:19, 13:1-9, 24-30, 21:18-19, Ps. 80:8-11, Ezk. 15:2-6, Rom. 2:4-11, 1-Corn. 6:9-10, Eph. 1:4, 5:5-6, Gal. 5:19-21, Heb. 10:26-27, 1-Pet. 4:17-18, 2-Tim. 3:5, **3:11-**Acts 1:4-5, 2:3-4, 1-Pet. 1:7, Titus 2:14, 3:3-7, Jer. 9:7, Zech. 13:9, Mal. 3:2-3, Rev. 3:18, **3:12-**Luke 3:17,12:51-53, 19:22, Matt. 7:13-14, 13:24-30, 37-43, 49-50, 25:31-33, 1-Corn. 3:11-15, 2-Corn. 10:3-5, Col. 3:5, 2-Thess. 1:7, Deut. 8:2, Is. 41:16, Jer. 15:7, Dan. 2:35-36, Mal. 4:1, Heb. 12:5-11, 1-Pet. 3:18, 4:17, 2-Pet. 3:7, Ps. 1:1-6, **3:15-**Luke 1:6, John 4:34, 2-Corn. 5:21, Heb. 10:5-7, Ps. 40:7-8, **3:16-**Is. 11:2, 42:1, 59:21, 61:1-3, Ps. 2:7, 8:4-8,89:26-29, Ezk. 1:1, 2:2, Matt. 12:18, 22:41-45, John 1:34, 5:31-37, 19:7, Acts 7:56, Heb. 1:5-8, **4:2-**John 10:10, Eph. 6:11-12, 1-Pet. 5:8, Gen. 4:7, James 1:13-14, 1-John 5:19, **4:3-**Gen. 3:1-6, Luke 22:31-32, Matt. 27:40, 1-Thess. 3:5, 1-John 2:15-17, Heb. 2:18, James 1:14, **4:4-**Luke 12:1, Eph. 6:16-17, John 4:32-34, 6:27, 30-35, 48-58, 63, Acts 6:1-4, 14:17, 17:28, 1-Corn. 8:8, 10:1-11, Heb. 5:12-14, Ps. 1:2, Josh. 1:8, **4:7-**Ps. 78:18,41, 95:9, Is. 7:10-12, Nub. 14:22, Matt. 16:1-4, Mark 8:11-1w, Acts 5:9, 1-Corn. 10:9, Heb. 3:7-9, **4:8-9-**Matt. 16:26, Ps. 49:16-17, 72:11, Heb. 11:24-26, 1-John 2:15-16, rev. 11:15, Ps. 72:11, John 13:3, **4:11-**Heb. 1:4-8, 1-Corn. 10:13, Matt. 26:53, 1-Tim 3:16, **4:13-16-**Matt. 4:23, John 1:4-5, 9, 3:19, 8:12, 12:46, 1-John 1:5-7, 2:8, 1-Pet. 2:9, 2-Corn. 4:6, 1-Thess. 1:4-5, 5:5-8, Eph. 5:8-14, Col. 1:12-13, Ps. 23:1-6, Job 33:28,**4:17-**Acts 2:38, 3:19,10:36-38, 11:18, 20:21, **4:20-** Matt.10:37, 19:27, Mark10:29-30, Ps.119:60, **5:3-** Luke-18:10-14, Rom. 7:18, 24, 1-Corn. 2:1-5, Philip. 2:5-8, 3:7-10, James 4:6-10, Ps. 34:6, 18, 51:17, Prov. 16:19, 29:23, Is. 66:2, Rev. 3:17-

18, **5:4**-Matt. 9:15, Luke 7:38-50, 16:25, John 14:1-4, 16:20-22, Rom. 5:3-5, 7:14-24, 8:23, 12:15, 2-Corn. 1:4-7, 5:4, 7:9-10, James 1:2-4, 12, Heb. 13:5-6, Is. 61:1-3, **5:5**-Matt. 11:28-29, 12:14-21, Rom. 12:12-19, Gal. 5:22-23, Eph. 4:2, 12, 32, 5:23, Philip. 2:3-11, Col. 3:12, 1-Pet. 2:18-23, 3:4, 14-15, 1-Tim. 6:11, Titus 3:12, Ps. 37:11, 29, **5:6**-Matt. 6:33, John 4:14, 6:26, 6:48-58, 7:37, Rom. 8:29, 7:18, 12:8, Philip. 1:11, 2:3-4, 1-Pet. 1:15-16, 2-Pet. 3:13, Heb. 2:10-1, 5:7- Matt. 6:12-15, 18:21-38, 23:23, 25:34-45, Luke 6:35-36, 10:30-37, Eph. 4:32, 5:1, Gal. 5:22, Col. 3:12, Heb. 4:15-16, 2:13, 1-Tim. 1:13-16, 2-Tim. 1:17-18, **5:7**-Matt. 18:28-35, Rom. 15:7, Gal. 6:9-10, Col. 3:13-15, 1-Thess. 5:14-15, James 2:13, 1-John 4:19, Prov. 3:27, 21:13, **5:8**- Matt. 6:22-24, 7:19-21, 23:25-28, Philip. 2:12-15, Col. 3:1-10, James 3:14-17, 4:7-8, 1-John 1:7-8, 3:1-3, 1-Pet. 1:16, Heb. 10:22, 12:14, Titus 1:15-, 2:14, 2-Tim. 2:22, Rev. 21:27, 4:8, Deut. 6:5, 1-Chron. 29:17-19, Ps. 24:3-6, 51:10,68:11, **5:9**- Luke 17:3-4, John 20:21, Rom. 12:18-21, 14:1, 17-19, 1-Corn. 7:15, Eph. 2:14-17, 4:3, Philip. 2:1-3, Col. 3:15, James 3:16-18, Heb. 12:14-15, 2-Tim. 2:22-24, 1-Pet. 3:10-11, 1-John 3:1, **5:10**-Matt. 10:23, John 3:20-21, 7:7, 15:19-21, Rom. 8:35-36, 2-Corn. 4:8-11, James 1:12, 5:10-11, 1-Pet. 3:13-14, 4:12-16, 2-Tim. 2:12, 3:10-15, 1-John 3:12-12, **5:11-12**-Matt 10:18,-25, 24:9, Luke 7:33-34, John 15:20, Acts. 5:40-41, Rom. 5:3-5, 8:36, 2-Corn. 1:3-11, 4:10-11, 1-Pet. 1:6-8, 4:14-16, James 1:2-4, **5:14-16**-John 12:35-36, Acts 26:18, Rom. 2:19-20,13:11-14, 1-Corn. 14:24-25, 2-Corn. 3:12-18, 4:1-15, Eph. 5:8-14, Philip 2:15, 1-Tim. 5:10, 6:18, Titus 2:7,1-Pet. 2:9,12, 3:1, **5:17**-Rom. 3:21-31, 7:1-4, 8:1-4,10:4, Gal. 3:23-25, Col. 2:12-13, Eph. 2:8-9, Heb. 8:7-13, Jer. 31:33, **5:19**-Matt. 8:1-4, Gal. 3;10-13, Heb. 8:8-10, James 2:10, 3:1, 1-Tim. 1:8-11, 6:3-4, Deut. 12:32, Mal. 2:8-9, Rev. 2:14-15, 20, **5:20**-Matt. 7:13-14, 7:21, 22:1-14, 23:2-5, 23-28, Luke 16:14-15, 18:9-14, Rom. 9:30-32, 10:2-4, Philip. 3:7-9, Gal. 5:19-23, Heb. 4:11, 12:14, Rev. 21:27, 1-Sam. 16:7, 1-Kings 1-Chron. 28:9, 3:6, Ps. 15:2, 32:11, 37:31, 40:8, **5:21-22**-Luke 9:35, Acts 3:22-23, Eph. 4:26-27, 31-32, Gal. 5:19-21, Col. 3:6-8, James 1:19-20, 3:5-10, 1-John 3:15, 1-Sam 20:30-34, Gen. 4:6-8, Ps. 4:4, 37:8-9, Prov. 29:8, 11, **5:23-24**-Matt. 5:9, 6:14-15, 9:13, Gen. 4:4-7, 1-Corn. 6:7-8, James 1:20, 3:14-18, 1-Tim. 2:8, **5:25-26**-Matt. 5:40, Rom. 13:1-8, 1-Corn. 6:6-7, Eph. 4:26, **5:27-28**- Matt. 5:40, Rom. 13:1-8, 1-Corn. 6:6-10, Eph. 4:26, **5:29-30**-Rom. 6:6, 12, 8:13, 1-Corn. 9:27, Gal. 5:24, Col. 3:5-17, 1-Thess. 4:3-7, 1-Pet. 4:1-3, Luke 9:24-25, **5:31-32**-Matt. 19:1-12, Mark 10:6-12, Heb. 13:4, Mal. 2:14-16, **5:33-36**-Matt. 23:16-22, Matt. 10:29-30, James 5:12, **5:37**-2-Corn. 1:17-20, Eph. 4:25, Col. 3:9, 4:6, James 5:12, John 8:43-44, **5:43-45**-Luke 6:28, Acts. 7:59-60, Rom. 12:17-18, 1-Corn. 4:13, Col. 4:6, Eph. 4:31-32, 5:1-2, **5:46-47**-1-Pet. 2:20-23, Matt. 9:10-11, 11:19, **5:48**-Luke 6:40, Eph. 5:1-2, 1-John 4:17-19, James 1:4, **6:1**-Matt. 25:40, Luke 6:15, John 5:44, 12:43, Philip. 2:18, 1-Pet. 2:12, 2-Cor. 9:9, Matt. 10:42, 16:27, 1-Corn. 9:17, 2-Corn. 5:10, Eph. 6:6, Gal. 1:10, 1-Thess. 2:4, Heb. 6:10, 2-John 1:8, Rev. 22:12, **6:2**-Matt. 23:13-29, John 5:41, 44, 7:8, 1-Thess. 2:3-6, 2-Corn. 9:13-15, **6:3-4**-Matt. 8:4, 9:30, 12:19, 25:37-39, Luke 14:13-14, John 7:4, **6:5**-Eph. 6:18, Col. 4:2, Luke 18:10-11, **6:6**-Matt. 14:23, Mark 1:35, Luke 5:16, 2-Kings 4:33, Is. 26:20, Dan. 6:10, Acts 9:40, 10:30, **6:7-8**- Matt. 15:8, 1-Kings 18:26-29, Acts 19:34, Ecc. 5:2-3, Rom. 8:26, Philip. 4:6, Luke 12:30, John 16:23, Is. 65:24, **6:9**-Luke 11:1-2, Matt. 23:9, Ezk. 36:23, Rom. 8:15, Gal. 4:6, 1-Pet. 1:17, Rev. 16:9, **6:10**-Is. 2:2, Dan. 2:44, 7:27, Rev. 11:15, 19:6, Rom. 12:2, Eph. 6:6, Heb. 10:36, 13:21, 1-Pet. 4:2, Ps. 103:20-21, **6:11**-Prov. 30:8, Luke 11:3, **6:12**-Matt. 26:41, Luke 22:31-40, Ex. 34:7, 1-John 1:7-9, Matt. 18:21-34, Col. 3:13, **6:13**-1-Corn. 10:13, 1-Pet. 5:8, 2-Pet. 2:9, **6:14-15**-Matt. 18:21-35, 2-Corn. 2:7, 10, Eph. 4:31-32, James 2:13, 1-John 3:10, **6:16**-1-Kings 21:7, Ps. 35:13, Dan. 9:2, Zach

7:5, Acts 13:2-3, 14:23, 1-Corn. 7:5-K.J.V., **6:17-18-**Luke 18:9-14, Rom. 2:6, 2-Corn. 10:18, Col. 3:22-24, 1-Pet. 1:7, **6:19-21-**Matt. 13:22-, 13:44-46, Mark- 10:17-30, Luke 12:13-21, 12:32-34, 14:12-14, 16:1-13, 19-25, John 6:27, Acts 2:42-45, 4:36, 5:1-6, Philip. 3:7-8, 4:10-19, 1-Tim. 6:6-10, 6:17-19, Heb. 10:34, 11:26, 1-Pet. 1:3-4, 1-John 2:15-16, Job. 31:24, Ps. 62:10, Prov. 11:4, 19:17, Ecc. 5:10-14, Is. 33:6, **6:22-23-** Mark 4:19, Eph. 6:5, Col. 3:22, Rom. 12:8, 2-Corn. 8:2, 9:11, 13, 11:3, James 1:8, 1-Tim. 6:9-11, 6:17, **6:24-**James 4:4, **6:25-**Matt. 6:11, 13:22, Luke 10:38-42, Rom. 8:32, 1-Corn. 7:32, Philip. 4:6, 11, 2-Tim. 2:4, Heb. 13:5-6, 1-Pet. 5:7, Ps. 55:22, **6:26-** Matt. 10:29-31, Luke 2:16-21, 2-Thess. 3:10-12, 1-Kings 17:5-6, Job 38:41, Ps. 145:15-16, 147:9, **6:30-**James 1:10-11, 1-Pet. 1:24, Prov. 90:5-6, Is. 40:6-8, Matt. 8:26, 14:31, 16:8, 17:17, John 20:27, Heb. 3:12, **6:31-32-**Matt. 4:4, 15:33, Ps. 78:18-31-**(V. 31,)** Eph. 4;17, 1-Thess 4:4-5, Luke 11:11-13, **6:33-**Mark 10:29-30, Luke 1:5-6, 12;32, Rom. 14:17, Eph. 1:3-4, Col. 3:1-10, 1-Tim. 4:8, 1-Pet. 5:7, 2-Pet. 1:10-11, Ps. 37:3-4, 25, 55:22, Prov. 2:1-9, 3:9-10, **6:34-**Acts 14:22, Philip. 4:19, James 4:13-15, Ex. 16:18-20, Prov. 27:1, John 14:27, Philp. 4:6, Heb. 13:6, 1-Pet. 5:6-7, **7:1-2-**Matt.5:7, Luke 18:11, Rom. 2:1-2, 14:3-4, 10-13, 1-Corn 4:3-5, 5:12-13, James 2:13, 3:1-2, 4:11-12, 5:9, Ps. 18:25-26, Ob. 1:15, 2-Thess. 1:6-7, **7:3-5-**Matt. 18:15-17, Luke 18:9, John 8:7-9, Rom. 2:21-23, 12:3 1-Corn. 11:31, 2-Corn. 1:306, Gal. 6:1, 2-Sam.12:4-7, **7:6-**Matt. 13:44-46, Luke 23:9, Acts 13:44-46, 1-Corn. 2:13-16, 2-Corn. 6:14-18, Philip. 3:2, 2-Pet. 2:22, **7:7-8-**Matt. 5:6, 21:22, Luke 18:1-8, John 14:13-14, Philip. 4:6, James 1:2-8, 4:2-3, 1-Pet. 3:12, 1-John 3:22, 5:14-15, **7:12-**Matt. 22:37-40, Mark 12:30-33, Rom. 13:8-10, Gal. 5:13-14, James. 2:8, **7:13-14-**Matt. 3:8, 22:14, Luke 13:23-27, Deut. 30:15-19, Ps. 1:1-6, 1-Corn. 6:9-12, 9:26-27, 2-Corn. 4:4, 6:17, Gal. 5:19-21, Eph. 2:2-3, Philip. 2:12-14, 3:17-20, 1-Pet. 4:17-18, **7:15-**Matt. 24:4-5, Acts 17:11, 20:28-30, 2-Cor. 11:11-15, Philip. 3:2, 1-Tim. 4:1-3, 2-Tim 2:14-19, 3:6, 4:3-4, 2-Pet. 2:1-3, 1-John 2:18-27, 4:1-6, Jude 1:3-19, Deut. 13:1-11, 18:20-22, Jer. 6:13-15, 23:21-32, Ezk. 13:1-12, **7:16-18-** Matt. 12:33-35, Rom. 16:17, 2-Thess. 3:6, 2-Pet. 2:10-18, Jude 1:10-19, James 3:12, 1-Tim. 1:3, 4:6, Eph. 5:9, Col. 1:10, James 3:17-18, Gal. 5:17, 2-Tim. 3:5, 13, 1-John 2:26, 3:9-10, 4:1, 2-John 1:9-10, **7:19-20-**John 15:1-10, 2-Corn. 10:4-6, Eph. 2:10, Philp. 1:9-11, 1-Pet. 2:5-9, 4:7-11, 1-John 2:4-6, 2-John 7-11, **7:21-22-**Matt. 12:50, 21:28-32, 23:25-28, 25:1-13 Luke 6:46, 10:20, John 7:17, Rom. 10:9, 12:2, 16:18, 1-Corn. 13:1-3, 2-Corn. 11:13-15, 13:5, 2-Tim. 3:5, James 1:22-27, 2:14-18, **7:23-**Matt. 10:32, 25:31-46, John 10:14, 27, Acts 19:13-17, Ps. 1:6, 6:8, 1-Corn. 9:25-27, 2-Tim 2:19, 1-John 2:4, 2-Pet. 2:20-22, Heb. 10:26-27, **7:24-27-**Matt. 13:21, 23, 16:18, John 14:15, 1-Corn. 3:13-15, 2-Corn. 13:5, 2-Tim. 3:1-7, James 1:21-27, 2:14-22, 1-Pet. 1:6-7, 1-John 1:6, 2:4, Titus 1:16, **7:28-29-** Matt. 28:17-18, Luke 4:22, 32, John 1:1, 5:27, 7:2, 15, 7:46, Jude 1:25, Prov. 15:2, 28, **8:10-12-**Matt. 15:28, 24:31, Rom. 9:1-33, 10:16-21, Eph. 2:11-20, Gen. 12:3, 22:18, Ps. 22:27, Is. 2:2-3, 11:10, Mic. 4:1-2, **8:19-20-**Matt. 10:24-25, Mark 10:29-30, Luke 2:7, Ps. 84:3, 104:17, Is. 53:2-3, **9:12-13-**James 1:27, 3:17, 1-Tim. 5:4, Matt. 23:23, 25:34-46, Luke 10:25-37, 18:10-14, Gal. 5:6, 6:9-10, 1-John 3:17-19, Job 29:12, Is. 1:17, Micah 6:8, **9:16-17-** Matt. 13:52, Jos. 9:4, 13, Ps. 119:83, Is. 58:6, Rom. 7:6, 2-Corn. 5:17, Gal. 3:24-25, 4:23-24, Eph. 2:8-9, 4:21-22, Heb. 8:7-13, **9:36-**Matt. 23:1-4, 13-14, Heb. 4:15, 5:2, Numb. 27:17, Is. 56:11, Jer. 50:6, Ezk. 34:3-6, Zech. 10:2, **9:37-38-**Matt. 28:19-20, Luke 10:2, John 4:35-38, 2-Thess. 3;1, Eph. 4:11, Ps. 68:11, Acts. 8:4, **10:16-** Rom. 16:19, 1-Corn. 16:13, 2-Corn. 11:3, 12:16, Eph. 5:15-16, Col. 4:5-6, James 3:13-17, 1-Pet. 3:15, Prov. 15:1, **10:17-18-**John 16:1-4, 16:12-13, Acts 9:4-5, 12:1-2, 22:25, 26:1-32, 2-Corn. 11:23-24, Philip. 1:12-13 Matt. 5:10-12**,** **10:23-**Matt.4:12, 7:6, 10:16,

12:14-15, John 7:1, 2-Corn. 11:23, Philip. 1:20-26**, 10:24-**25-1-Thess. 3:3-4, 2-Tim. 3:12, 1-Pet. 2:21, 4:12-13, **10:32-33-**Matt. 7:21-23, 16:15-16, Luke 8:13, John 3:36, 9:22, Rom. 1:16, 10:9-13, 1-Corn. 12:3, 16:13, 1-Tim. 6:12-14, 2-Tim. 1:8-10, 2:10-13, 19, Heb. 10:26-31, 13:15, 1-John 2:22-23, 4:2-3, Rev. 2:13, 3:5, 21: 8, Prov. 3:5-6, **10:38-**Matt. 5:11-12, John 16:33, Gal. 2:20, Philips. 1:20, 29, Rev. 2:10, **10:39**-Matt. 16:26, 1-Corn. 10:24, Gal. 2:24, 5:17, Philip. 3:7-8, 2-Tim. 4:6-8, 1-John 2:15-17, **10:40**-Matt. 25:34-40, 2-Corn. 5:20, Gal. 4:14, Heb. 6:10, 2-John 1:9, **11:4-5-**Luke 4:16-21, John 3:2, 5:36, 10:38, 14:11, Is. 35:4-6, 42:7, 61:1, **11:12-**Matt. 7:7, 7:13-14, 13:44-46, 21:23-32, 16:24-26, Mark 3:10, Eph. 6:11-13, Col. 3:5, Philip. 2:12, 3:12-16, **11:13-**Matt. 5:17-18, 16:16, Luke 24:27, 44, John 3:30, 5:39, 46, Acts 3:22-24, Rom. 3:23, 1-Pet. 1:10-12, Heb. 1:1-3, 8:7-13, **11:20-22-**Luke 12:48,19:37, John 10:25, 38, 14:11, 15:24, Acts 2:22, 21:1-7, 2-Corn. 2:22, Heb. 2:3-4, **11:23-24-**Luke 14:11, Rom. 2:4-6, 2-Pet. 2:4-9, Ezk. 16:48-50, Jude 1:7, Rev. 11:8, **11:25-26-**Rom. 10:3, 20, 1-Corn. 1:18-29, 2:6-8, 2:14, 10:11-12, 2-Corn. 4:3-6, Eph. 2:8, 2-Thess. 2:13-14, James 4:6, Eph. 1:9-11, **11:27-**John 1:17-18, 3:34-36, 6:44-48, 10:28-30, 14:6- 9, 24, 15:16, 17:2-8, 25-26, 1-Corn. 15:25-27, Eph. 1:4, 20-23, Philip. 2:10-11, Heb. 2:8-10, 1-Pet. 3:22, 1-John 5:20, **11:28-30-**Gal. 6:9, Heb. 12:3, Ps. 62:1, Is. 40:29-31, **12:19-**Matt. 26:51-52, Zech. 9:9, John 18:36-38, 2-Corn. 10:1, 2-Tim. 2:24-25, 1-Pet. 3:15, **12:21-**Luke 24:47, John 1:12, 20:31, Acts 9:15, Is. 11:10, Rom. 15:12, Eph. 1:12-13. Philp. 2:9-11, **12:22-23-** Matt. 9:32-33, Mark 9:17-26, John 7:31, Is. 29:18, 32:3-4, 35:5-6, **12:25-26-**John 17:21-22, Rom. 1:28-32, 8:13-14, 1-Corn. 1:10-31, 3:1-3, 2-Corn. 10:5, Gal. 5:15-26, Eph. 4:3-6, Gen. 3:1-6, Titus 3:3, 2-Tim. 3:2-5, James 3:13-17, 4:1-10, **12:28-**John 12:31-32, Acts 10:38, 26:18, Rom. 6:17-22, Eph. 2:3-10, Col. 1:13, Heb. 2:7-14, 12:28, 1-Pet. 2:9, 1-John 3:8, **12:29-**Is. 49:24-26, 53:12, John 8:36, 1-John 3:8, 4:4, 1-Tim. 1:15-16, 2-Tim. 2:26, Eph. 2:2, 4:8-9, 6:11-12, 6:16, James 4:7, Heb. 2:14-15, 1-Pet. 5:8, **12:31-32-**Luke 10:16, 12:8-10, John 15:22-26, 16:7-14, Rom. 1:22-28, 1-Thess. 4:8, Heb. 6:4-6, 10:26-31, 1-John 5:16-17, 1-Tim. 1:13, 2-Pet. 2:21, Ezk. 3:20, 18:24, **12:35-**Rom. 6:4, 12:1-2, 2-Corn. 10:5, Eph. 4:29, 5:2, 5:15, Gal. 2:20, Col. 1:10, 3:16, 3:20, 4:6, Philp. 1:11, 1:27, 4:8, 1-Thess. 2:12, 4:1, Heb. 10:22, James 1:19-20, 2-Pet. 1:3, 2-Tim. 1:9, Prov. 23:7, **12:36-37-**1-Corn. 12:3, Eph. 5:4, Col. 4:6, Prov. 15:4, 17:28, Rev. 16:9, Rom. 10:9, James 1:26, 2:20, **12:39-40-**Matt. 17:23, 27:63-64, 1-Corn. 1:22-24, 2-Corn. 5:7, Jon. 1:17, Hos. 6:2, James 4:4, **12:43-45-**1-Pet. 5:8, Eph. 2:2, 4:20-24, 6:12, 1-Thess. 2:15-16, Heb. 10:26-31, 2-Pet. 2:20-22, **12:46-50-**Matt., 7:21-22, 10:37, 19:29, Luke 6:46, John 6:28-29, 8:31, Rom. 2:13, 8:2-17, Eph. 1:3, 5:2-17, 6:6, Philip. 2:1-11, Col. 3:17, 1-Tim. 5:8, 1-John 2:15-17, 3:21-24, Heb. 2:12-13, 4:6, James 1:22, 2:20-26, 1-Pet. 2:15, 4:2, Titus- 1:16, Prov. 3:5-7, **13:10-11-**Matt. 11:25-26, 16:17, Rom. 1:28-32, 1-Corn. 2:7-10, 14, 4:1, Eph. 1:18, 3:9 James 1:16-18, 1-Tim. 3:16, Is. 1:4, **13:12-**Mark 4:24-25, Luke 8:18, 12:20-21, John 15:2-5, Rom. 10:17, **13:13-**John 12:47-50, Deut. 29:3-4, Is. 42:18-20, 44:18, Ezk. 12:1-2, Mark 8:17-18, John 9:39-41, 1-Corn. 2:14, 2-Corn. 4:3-4, **13:14-15-** John 8:43-44, 12:37-40, Acts 7:57, 28:26-27, 1-Corn. 2:14, 2-Corn. 4:3, Eph. 4:18-20, 5:15-17, Heb. 4:7 5:11, 2-Tim. 4:4, James 4:7-8, **13:16-17-**Rom. 16:25-26, Heb. 11:13, 25-26, 1-Pet. 1:10-12, 2-Pet. 1:19, Eph. 3:3-5, **13:31-32-**Matt. 5:13-16, Rom. 11:11-24, Ezk. 17:23, 31:6, Dan. 4:9-18, Ps. 72:17-19, 104:12, 1-Corn. 1:26-29, 2:1-5, 2-Corn. 4:7, Philp. 1:6, **13:33-**John 3:8, Matt. 5:13-16, 24:14, 26:13, Luke 16:16, 17:20-21, 24:47, Acts 8:4, Philp. 2:12-13, 3:8-15, Heb. 4:12-13, **13:36-43-**Zeph. 1:2-3, Mal. 4:1,Matt.5:45, 7:21-23, 24:31, Rom. 2:8-9, 16, 1-Pet. 5:8, 2-Pet. 2:1-3, 3:8-9, 1-Corn. 15:41-54, Eph. 5:8-12, 2-Thess. 1:6-10, Heb. 10:26-31, 2-Tim. 4:2-4, 1-John 3:7-9,

13:47-50-Zeph. 1:2-3, Mal. 4:1,Matt.5:45, 7:21-23, 24:31, Rom. 2:1-16, 1-Pet. 5:8, 2-Pet. 1:10-11, 2:1-3, 3:8-9, 1-Corn. 4:5, 15:41-54, 2-Corn. 13:5, Eph. 5:8-12, Philp. 2:12, 2-Thess. 1:6-10, 2-Pet. 1:10-11, Heb. 10:26-31, 2-Tim. 4:2-4, 1-John 3:7-9, 5:12, Rev. 21:7-8, **13:51-52-**Matt. 5:19, Acts. 7:1-53, 17:11, Rom. 15:4, 1-Corn. 3:2, 7:10-12, 25, 11:23, Eph. 3:2-9, Philip. 1:9, Col. 2:2-3, 3;16, Gal. 6:6, 2-Tim. 2:15, 3:15-17, Heb. 5:12-13, 6:1, 2-Pet. 3:17-18, James 1:21-24, 1-John 2:7-8, Titus 1:9, Lev. 26:9-10, Song. 7:13, Ezr. 7:10, **13:53-56-**Matt. 2:23, Luke 4:16, John 1:11, Ps. 22:22, 40:9-10, John 1:45-46, 7:15-16, 41-42, 9:29, Acts 4:13, John 6:42, 2-Corn. 5:16**, 13:57-58-**Matt. 11:6, John 4:44-45, 6:57-61, Jer. 12:5-6, Ps. 22:6, Is. 8:14, 49:7, 53:3, Luke 2:34-35, Rom. 11:7-11, 1-Corn. 1:23-28, 1-Pet. 2:8, James 1:19, **14:1-2-** Ps. 32:3-6, 35:2, Prov. 28:17, Rom. 2:15, 1-Corn. 4:4, Philp. 3:13, Heb. 9:14, 10:19-24, 1-John 1:9, **14:6-11-**Ester. 5:1-8, 7:1-10, Matt. 17:12, 21:35-36, 22:3-6, Mark 9:13, Luke 9:9, **14:25-32-**Philp. 4:7-8, Heb. 12:2, Ps. 23:4, 55:22, 69:1-2, **15:3-6-**Matt. 5:33, 12:7, 23:16-18, Ps. 76:11, Prov. 19:26, 20:25, 23:22, 28:24, Eph. 6:1-3, Col. 3:6-8, 1-Thess. 5:21, 1-Tim. 5:4, 8, 16, 2-Tim. 3:16, Jer. 8:8, Rom. 3:31, **15:7-9-** Ezk. 33:31, Jer. 12:2, Prov. 23:26, Is. 1:13-15, Deut. 12:32, Eph. 4:18-19, Col. 2:18-23, 1-Tim. 1:4, 4:1-7, Heb. 13:9, Rev. 3:16, **15:10-11-** Matt. 12:34-35, Luke 11:39-41, Rom. 3:13-14, 14:14-23, Philp. 4:8, James 3:1-12, 1-Tim. 4:3-5, Col. 3:8-9, 2-Pet. 2:18, **15:12-14-**Matt. 3:10-12, 8:11-12, 13:36-43, John 15:2, 6, Rom. 2:19, 1-Corn. 3:6-8, 12-15, Heb.-12:15, 2-Pet. 2:1-22, 1-Tim. 4:16, James 3:1, Is. 9:16, 42:18-20, Mal. 2:8, Ezk. 14:10, Rev. 19:20, **15:15-18-**Rom. 3:10-19, 7:21-23, Philp. 1:27-28, 1-Tim. 4:3-6, James 1:14, 3:6, Luke 6:45, 19:22, 1-Corn. 6:13, Col. 2:21-22, Gen. 6:5, 1-Sam.16:7, **15:19-20-**Gen. 3:4-7, Ex. 20:13-16, Is. 59:7, Jer. 17:9, Rom. 1:28-32, 3:10-19, 8:5, 12:2, 1-Corn. 6:9-18, 2-Corn. 7:1, 10:4-6, Eph. 2:1-3, 4:29-31, Philp. 4:8, Col. 3:1-3, 5-10, James 1:14-15, Titus 3:2-3,1-John 1:5-7, Prov. 4:23, 6:14, 6:16-19, Is. 59:7 Jer. 17:9, **15:28-**Matt. 7:7-11, 8:8-10, Luke 18:2- Rom. 4:19-20, Heb. 3:14, 10:35-36, 11:6, Gen. 32:26, Job 13:15, 23:10, Ps. 145:19, **16:2-4-**Eph. 5:15-17, 1-Pet. 5:8-9, **16:5-12-**Luke 18:9-14, Ex. 12:15-19, 1-Corn. 5:6-8, Gal. 3:1-3, 5:9, 6:1, Col. 2:8, Heb. 3:12, **16:16-17-**John 6:69, 20:31, 1-John 4:15, 5:5, 20 Matt. 11:25-27, John 6:45, 17:6-8, Rom. 10:9-10, 1-Corn. 2:12-14, 12:3, Eph. 1:17-18, Gal. 1:11-12, 16, **16:18-**Matt. 22:41-43, John 20:28, Acts 2:21, Rom. 8:31-39, 10:9-13,1-Corn. 3:9-12, 2-Corn. 10:4-5, Philip. 2:11, 1-Pet. 3:15, 2-Pet. 2:1, Jude 1:4, **16:19-**Luke 11:52, Acts. 11:1, 14:27, Is. 22:20-22, 2-Corn. 13:10, 1-Thess. 4:8, Rev. 1:18, 3:7-8, **16:22-23-**James 4:7, Is. 55:8-9, 1-Corn. 2:12-16, Col. 3:1-2, **16:24-**Matt. 10:24-25, 38-39, 19:12, 26:39, Mark 10:21, Luke 14:26 John 5:30, 13:15, Acts 14:22, Rom. 12:1-2, 14:7-9, 15:2-3, 26:39, 1-Corn. 1:11, 2-Corn. 4:10-11, 5:15, Gal. 2:20, 5:24, 6:14, Philip. 2:3-8, 3:7-10, Col. 3:5-15, 1-Thess. 3:3-4, Titus 2:12, Heb. 5:7-9, 11:24-26, James 5:10-11, 1-Pet. 2:13-23, 4:1-2, John 12:25-26, **16:25-**Matt. 6:24, Luke 12:16-21, John 12:25, 21:15, Deut. 30:11-20, Acts 20:23-24, Rom. 6:6 Eph. 4:17-24, Col. 3:3-10, 1-Tim. 6:17-10, 2-Tim. 4:10, **16:26-**Matt. 4:8-10, 6:19-24, 13:22, 13:44, 19:16-30, 1-Tim. 6:9, 17-18, James 1:10-11, Job 2:2-5, **16:27-**Rom. 2:6-7, 1-Corn. 15:58, 2-Corn. 5:9-10, Eph. 6:8, Gal. 6:7-9, 2-Thess. 1:7-10, 4:13-18, 5:1-11, Jude 1:14, Ps. 62:12, Philp.2:12-13, 2-Tim.4:7-8, Heb. 1:3-14, 12:1-3, 1-Pet. 1:17, 3:22, 2-John 1: 8, Rev. 2:23, 22:12, **17:1-5-**2-Pet. 1:16-18, Mark 9:1, John 1:14, 12:30, 17:24, Ex. 33:18-19, Ps. 63:2, Acts 22:6-11, Rom. 8:18, 2-Corn. 3:18, 4:6, 6:9-10, Philp. 3:21, Heb. 1:1-3, 12:2, Rev. 1:14-16, Prov. 4:25-27, **17:10-13-**Matt. 11:13-14, 14:3-10, John 1:11, Acts 2:23, 7:52, 13:24-28, Is. 53:3-12, **17:17-18-**Deut. 32:5, 20, Numb. 14:11, Mark 16:14, **17:19-20-**Matt. 14:30-31, 21:21, Luke 1:37, 1-Corn. 13:2, Philip. 4:13, **17:22-23-**Matt. 16:21, John 16:5-23, Acts 2:23-31,

17:24-26-Matt. 12:5-6, John 1:12, Col. 2:16-23, Gal. 5:1-10, Neh. 10:32, **17:27-**Rom. 12:18, 14:1-23, 1-Corn. 8:9-13, 9:19-23, 10:23- 33, Philp. 2:3-8, **18:2-4-**Matt. 5:3, 20:25-27, 23:11-12, Mark 9:35, 4:7-11, Luke 18:14, John 13:3-17, Rom. 12:2-8, 1-Corn. 14:20, 2-Corn. 10:1-18, Eph. 4:1-2, Col. 3:12, Philip. 2:3-8, Heb. 13:17, 1-Pet. 5:1-5, James 4:10, **18:5-**Matt. 10:40-42, 25:31-46, Luke 14:12-14, John 13:13-15, Rom. 12:16, 1-Corn. 12:12-31, James 2:1-5, 1-John 4:20-21, **18:6-**Rom. 14:13-21, 15:1-3, 1-Corn. 8:9-13, 10:32-33, Gal. 4:14, 5:15, 2-Thess. 1:6-9, Ps. 105:15, **18:7-**Matt. 13:41-42, 2-Thess. 3:8, 1-Tim. 4:1-3, 2-Pet. 2:22, **18:8-9-**Matt. 5:29-30, Rom. 13:12, 15:1, Philip. 3:8, Is. 2:20, 30:22, Ezk. 18:31, 2-Thess. 1:8-9, Rev. 21:27, **18:10-**Luke 18:9, 1-Corn. 12:12-25, Heb. 1:14, 13:2, 1-Tim. 4:12, Gen. 28:12, 1-Kings 19:5-8, Job. 1:6, 2:1, **18:12-14-**John 10:1-16, 21:16-17, Ezk. 34:1-31, James 5:19-20, Heb. 12:13-15, 1-Pet. 1:4-5, 2:25, 2-Pet. 3:9, 1-John 5:16, Jude 1:22-23, Ps. 78:52, 119:176, **18:15-**Luke 17:3, Rom. 12:21, Gal. 6:1-5, Lev. 19:17, 1-Corn. 6:1-8, James 5:19-20, Ps. 141:5, Prov. 11:30, 25:9-10, **18:16-**2-Corn. 13:1-2, Numb. 35:30, Deut. 17:6, John 8:17, 1-Tim. 5:19, **18:17-**Acts 6:1-3, 1-Corn. 5:1-13, 6:1-4, 2-Corn. 2:6-7, 3-John 1:9-10, 2-Corn. 6:14-17, 2-Thess. 3:6, 3:14-15, 1-Tim. 1:20, 5:20, Titus 3:10-11, 1-Pet. 5:7, Ps. 147:3, **18:21-22-**Matt. 6:12-14, Luke 17:3-4, Rom. 12:18-21, Eph. 4:26, 4:31-32, Col. 3:13,Heb. 12:14-15, Lev. 19:18, **19:4-6-**Mal. 2:14-16, 1-Corn. 6:16, 7:10-14, Eph. 5:31, **19:7-8-**Mal. 2:14-16, 1-Corn. 6:16, 7:10-14, Eph. 5:31, **19:9-**Matt. 5:32, Rom. 7:2-3, 1-Corn. 7:10-13, 39, **19:10-11-**1-Corn. 7:1-8, James 1:14, **19:13-15-** Matt. 11:25, 18:1-14, 1-Corn. 14:20, Eph. 6:4, 1-Pet. 2:1-2, Mark 10:15, Luke 18:17, 1-Tim. 4:12, Deut. 6:4-7, Prov. 22:6, **19:17-19-**Matt. 5:3, Rom. 7:18, James 1:17, 2:10, 1-Pet. 2:3, Lev. 18:5, Is. 64:6, Ezr. 20:11, Gal. 3:11-13, **19:20-21-**Matt. 6:19-21, 24, Luke 14:33, 16:9, Acts 2:45, 4:32-35, Rom. 3:19-20, 1-Corn. 13:3, Phil. 3:1-9, 1-Tim. 6:10, 17-19, Heb. 10:34, 1-John 1:8, **19:23-24-**Matt. 7:13-14, 13:22, 23:24, Luke 12:15-21, 16:13, 1-John 2:15, 1-Tim. 6:9-10, 17, James 5:1-4, Ps. 49:6-7, Prov. 11:28, **19:25-26-**Rom. 8:35-39, 2-Corn. 12:9-10, Eph. 2:3-9, 3:7, 6:11-13, Heb. 6:17-19, Ps. 3:8, Jer. 13:23, 32:27, Gen. 18:14, 1-Tim. 1:12-18, 2-Tim. 1:8-9, Titus 3:3-5, 1-John 4:4, 2-Pet. 1:3-4, **19:27-28-**Dan. 7:13-14, Rom. 5:3-5, 8:18, 1-Corn. 2:9, 6:2-3, 2-Corn. 4:17-18, 5:16-18, Col. 3:1-4, Heb. 2:5-8, 2-Tim. 2:12, 1-Pet. 1:6-9, 5:8-10, Rev. 2:26-27, 3:21, **20:17-19-**Matt.16:21, 17:22-23, Mark 10:32-34, John 18:28-38, Acts 3:13-16, Ps. 35:16, **20:20-21-**Matt. 4:21, John 15:7, Rom. 12:10, Mark 16:19, Col. 3:1, **20:22-23-**Matt. 26:39-42, 26:35, John 18:11, Rom. 8:17, Prov. 16:18, Col. 1:24, 2-Tim. 2:11-12, 1-Corn. 2:9, Philp. 1:29, Heb. 11:16, **20:25-28-**Matt. 8:8-9, 18:1-3, John 13:4-17, 1-Pet. 5:1-5, Philip. 2:4-8, 1-Tim. 2:6, Is. 53:4-12, Dan. 9:24-26, Rom. 3:24-26, Gal. 5:13, Eph. 1:7, 5:2, Heb. 9:28, **20:29-34-**Matt. 7:7-8, John. 9:1-12, Philip. 4:6, Ps. 146:8, Heb. 4:15-16, Is. 29:18-19, 35:5-6, 42:16, **21:1-3-**Mark 11:1-6, Luke 19:28-34, John 12:12-14, 1-Pet. 3:15, 2-Tim. 2:15, **21:4-5-**Is. 12:6, Gen. 49:10-11, Ps. 9:14, Zeph. 3:14-15, **21:10-11-**1-Sam. 16:4, Matt. 2:23, 13:44, Luke 19:41-44, John 1:45-46, 1-Pet. 3:15, **21:16-17-**Acts 16:23-26, Philp. 4:6-7, Heb. 13:15, Rev. 4:11, Ps. 34:1, 63:3-4, 2-Sam. 22:4, 2-Chron. 20:9, 20:17-22, Jonah 2:1-10, **21:18-22-**Matt. 7:17-18, 23:27-28, Luke 13:6-9, John 15:1-8, Rom. 11:15-24, Eph. 2:10, Gal. 5:22-23, Philp. 1:11, 2-Tim. 3:5, James 2:14-18, Jer. 8:4-13, Hos. 10:9-16, **21:28-32-**Matt. 7:21-22, John 15:14, Titus 1:15-16, James 1:23-24, 2:14-26, 1-John 3:18-19, Ps. 51:16-17, **21:42,** Matt. 7:25-27, Acts 4:8-12, 1-Corn. 3:10-11, Eph. 2:11-22, 1-Pet. 2:4-7, Is. 28:16, Zech. 3:8-9, **21:43-**Matt. 8:11-12, Acts 13:46, 1-Pet. 2:9, Is. 26:2, **21:44-**Is. 8:13-15, 60:12, Rom. 9:30-33, 1-Corn. 1:23, 1-Tim. 1:15, James 4:6, 1-Pet. 2:6-8, 1-John 1:8-10, Dan. 2:34-35, 44-45, Luke 2:34, Heb. 2:2-4, Rev. 6:15-17, Ps. 51:17, 34:18,

22:1-14-Matt. 7:21, 13:22, Luke 14:15-24, Acts. 13:44-47, Rom. 10:1-3, 1-Corn. 6:9-11, Eph. 4:21-24, Col 3:5-14, Rev. 19:7-9, **22:15-17-**Matt. 17:24-25, Deut. 17:14-15, Ezr. 7:24, Acts. 5:37, **22:18-22-**Matt. 17:24-27, Prov. 24:21, Luke 23:2, Rom. 13:7, 1- Pet. 2:13-17, **22:29-33-**1-Corn. 15:35-50, Ps. 8:5, Heb. 11:16, **22:37-40-**Matt. 7:12, Luke 10:25-37, Acts 17:28, Rom. 12:1-2, 13:8-10, 1-Corn. 10:31, 2-Corn. 10:3-5, Philp. 4:8, 1-John 3:10-18, 3:21-22, 4:7-21, 5:2-5, Deut. 10:12, 11:8-19, Gal. 5:14, James 2:8, Rom. 15:2, 1-Corn. 13:1-13, Ps. 119:33-35, **22:41-45-**Matt. 1:1, 1:23, Acts 2:34-36, Rom. 1:3-4, 10:9-10, 1-Corn. 15:23-26, 2-Corn. 4:4, Philp. 2:9-11, Col. 1:15, Heb. 1:3-6, 2:7-9, 10:11-14, Is. 9:6, **23:5-7-** Matt. 6:1-5, Luke 16:15, 14:7-14, John 5:44, Rom. 12:10, 12:43, Philip. 1:5, 2:3, 2-Thess. 2:4, James 2:1-4, **23:8-10-**2-Corn. 1:24, 4:5, 1-Pet. 5:3, John 13:13-14, Rom. 12:3-8, 14:9-10, 1-Corn. 1:12-13, 3:3-5, Rev. 19:10, Matt. 6:9, Rom. 8:14-15, James 2:1, **23:11-12-**Matt. 20:25-27, John 13:12-17, 1-Corn. 9:19, 2-Corn. 4:5, 11:23, Philip. 2:5-8, 1-Pet. 5:5-6, James 4:6, **23:13-**Rom. 2:17-21, **23:15-** Acts 13:43, 26:11, Rom. 10:2-3, 1-Corn. 2:4-5, Gal. 4:17, 6:12, Philip. 3:6, **23:16-22-** Matt. 5:33-34, 15:5-6, Deut. 23:23, James 5:12, **23:23-24-**Matt. 5:19-20, Luke 18:11-12, Hos. 6:6, Mic. 6:6-8, 1-Corn. 13:1-13, Eph. 5:1-2, Gal. 5:6, 5:22-23, James 1:27, 2:15-16, Mica 6:6-8, Jer. 9:24, **23:25-28-**Matt. 5:8, 12:33-35, Luke 6:45, 16:15, Rom. 2:28-29, 2-Corn. 7:1, James 4:8, Prov. 4:23, Ps. 51:6, Is. 55:7, Jer. 4:14, 17:9-10, Ezk. 18:31, Acts 23:3, 1-Sam. 16:7, **23:29-32-**Matt. 21:35-36, 2-Chron. 36:15-16, Luke 19:22, Acts 7:51-52, Job. 15:5-6, Ps. 64:8, 1-Thess. 2:14-16, Gen. 15:16, Numb. 32:14, Zech. 5:6-11, James 4:4, 8, **23:33-36-**Matt. 10:17, John 16:12, Gen. 4:10, 15:16, Deut. 21:1-9, 2-Chron. 24:22, 2-Kings 21:16, 24:3-4, Is. 26:21, 65:6-7, Jer. 26:15, 23, Lam. 4:13-14, **23:37-39-**Luke 19:41-44, 20:9-16, Acts 7:52, 1-Thess. 2:15, 2-Chron. 36:15-16, Ps. 17:8, 36:7, 57:1, 91:4, Is. 31:5, Jer. 4:14, 25:3-7, 35:15, 44:4, Neh. 9:26, Ps. 17:8, 36:7, 63:7, Is. 64:10-11, Jer. 12:7, Dan. 9:26, Matt. 24:2, 2-Chron. 7:20-21, Is. 40:9-11, Zech. 12:10-14, Hos. 3:4, Rom. 11:25, 2-Corn. 3:14-18, **24:4-5-**Jer. 29:8, 2-Corn. 11:13-15, Eph. 4:14, 5:6, 2-Thess. 2:3, 2-Pet. 2:1-3, 1-John 4:1-3, **24:6-8-**Dan. 9:26 b, Ezk. 7:26, 14:17-21, 2-Thess. 2:2, 1-Pet. 3:14-15, Ps. 27:1-3, 33:19, 37:19, 46:1-3, 112:7, John 14:1, 14:27, Job. 5:22, Rom. 8:20-22, **24:9-**Matt. 10:17-25, 22:34, John 15:18-21, 16:2, **24:10-11-**Matt. 13:20-21, 26:21-24, Acts 20:28:31, Rom. 16:18, 1-John 2:19, Mic. 7:5-6, Matt. 7:15, Eph. 4:14, Philip. 2:3, 2-Thess:2:1-3, 2-Pet. 2:1-3, 1-John 2:18, 26,1-Tim. 3:9, 4:1-16, 2-Tim. 4:3-4, **24:12-13-**Eph. 4:25-32, 1-Corn. 6:7-9, 1-Thess. 5:19, James 4:1-4, 5:1-6, Rev. 2:4-5, **24:14-**Matt. 28:19, Mark 16:15-16, Luke 24:47, Acts 1:2-8, Rom. 10:18, 15:18-21, **24:15-**2-Thess. 2:1-4, Hos. 9:10, **24:16-20-**Gen. 19:15-17, Prov. 22:3, Matt. 5:10-12, 10:23, Acts 22:4, Matt. 6:25, 16:25, Gen. 39:12-18, 2-Kings 4:29, Is. 3:6, 2-Sam. 4:4, 2-Kings 15:16, Luke 23:29-30, Ex. 16:29, **24:21-**Dan 9:26, 12:1, Joel 1:2, 2:2, Jer. 30:7, 1-Thess. 5:1-8, **24:22-**Is. 1:9, 6:13, 65:8-9, Zech. 13:8, Rom. 11:26, **24:23-24-**Matt. 7:21-23, 24:5, Luke 17:23, John 10:4-5, 2-Pet. 2:1-3, 3:17, John 6:39, 10:28-30, Rom. 8:38-39, Mal. 4:5, **24:26-28-**Acts 1:11, 21:38, 1-Thess. 5:1-4, James 5:8, 2-Pet. 3:3-4, Job. 39:27-30, **24:30-31-**Matt. 3:11-12, 13:24-30, 16:27, 26:64, 1-Thess. 4;16-18, 2-Thess. 1:7, Ps. 18:9-13, Dan. 7:13-14, Acts 1:9-11, Rev. 1:7, 14:14-20, **24:37-39-**Luke 14:16-24, Rom. 13:13-14, 14:17, 1-Corn. 7:29-31, 1-Thess. 5:1-9, 2-Pet. 2:5-9, 3:3-13, **24:42-44-**Luke 12:35-40, 21:36, Rom. 13:11, 1-Corn. 6:13, Eph. 5:15-17, 1-Thess. 5:1-10, 1-Pet. 4:7, 5:8, 2-Pet 3:10, Rev. 3:3, 16:15, Ex. 22:2-3, **24:45-51-** Matt. 13:52, Luke 12:47-48, 16:10-12, John 21:15-17, Acts 20:28, 1-Corn. 3;1-2, 1-Pet. 4:10-11, 5:2-3, James 4:17, 2-Tim. 4:5, Matt. 7:15, Prov. 28:3, Rom. 16:18, 2-Corn. 11:20, Philip. 3:19, Titus 1;11-12, 1-Pet. 5:3, 2-Pet. 2:13-14, 3-John 1:9-10, **25:1-13-** Matt

22:1-14, Luke 12:35, 1-Corn. 15:59, Gal. 5:22-23, 2-Thess. 3:11-13, 2-Pet. 3:14, Rev. 2:5, 3:2-3,-Heb. 10:36-38, 1-Thess. 5:6-8, **25:14-30-**Matt. 7:21, Luke 19:11-27, Rom. 12:6-8, 1-Corn. 3:5, 12:4-29, 15:10, 15:58, Eph. 4:11, 1-Pet. 4:9-11, 2-Tim 4:5-8, Heb. 6:12, John 15:2, **25:31-46-**Matt. 16:27, John 5:27-29, 2-Thess. 1:7-8, Acts 17:30-31, Dan. 7:9-14, Ezk. 34:23-31, Zech. 14:5, Joel 3:1-12, Rom. 14:10-12, 1-Corn. 4:5, 2-Corn. 5:10, Heb. 6:10, James 2:14-26, 1-John 4:20, **26:6-7-**John 12:2-3, Ex. 30:23-33, Ps. 133:2, **26:17-19-**Ex. 12:1-28, 13:6-10, Lev. 23:4-8, Numb. 9:1-14, Deut. 16:1-8, **26:26-30-**Ex. 24:7-8, Lev. 17:11, John 6:25-59, Acts. 20:7, 1-Corn. 5:7, 10:16-22, 11:24-29, Eph. 1:7, Col. 1:20, Heb. 9:14-22, 10:4-14, Is. 53:10-12, Jer. 31:31-34, **26:36-38-**Job. 6:2-5, Ps. 18:4-6, 43:5, 55:4-8, 61:1-3, 88:1-7, 14-16, 116:3-4, Is. 53:3,John 12:27, Rom. 8:32, 2-Corn. 5:21, Gal. 3:13, Heb. 5:7, **26:40-41-**Matt. 6:13, 13:20-21, 25:1-13, 1-Corn. 16:13, Eph. 6:18, 1-Pet. 4:7, 5:8, Ps. 51:12, Rom. 7:18-25, Gal. 5:16-17, 24, **26:51-**Matt. 4:6-7, 2-Corn. 10:4, Gen. 9:6, Matt. 5:39-41, Rom. 12:19, 1-Corn. 4:11-12, 1-Thess. 5:15, 1-Pet. 2:21-23, 3:9, Rev. 13:10, Jude 1:14, Dan. 7:10, Luke 24:26, 44-46, Acts 2:23, 4:27-28, **26:65-66-**Matt. 9:2-3, Luke 5:21, 22:70, John 10:33, 36, 19:7, Lev. 24:16, **26:73-75-**Jud 12:6, Ne 13:24, Gen. 42:21, Rom. 9:3, Rom. 7:18-20, 2-Corn. 7:10-11, **27:3-5-**2-Corn. 7:10, Gen. 42:21-22, 1-Sam. 15:24, Luke 23:41, John 19:10, Rom. 3:19, Ps. 55:23, Acts 1:18, Zech. 11:13, **27:24-25-**Matt. 21:43-44, 23:35-36, Acts 4:27, 5:28, 7:52, **27:27-31-** Ps. 22:6-7, Matt. 20:19, Ps. 35:15-16, 69:7, 19-20, Is. 49:7, 53:3, Jer. 20:7, Matt. 26:67, Job 30:8-10, Is. 50:6, 53:7, Mic. 5:1, Matt. 21:39, Heb. 13:12, 1-Pet. 2:19-23, **27:32-**Heb. 13:11-12, Acts 2:10, 6:9, 11:20, 13:1, **27:38-**Matt. 26:55, Mark 15:28, Luke 10:30, John 19:18, **27:39-40-** Matt. 16:4, Luke 16:31, John 2:19-22, Ps. 22:17, 31:11-13, 35:15-21, 69:7-12, 69:20, 89:51, 109:25, Lam. 2:15-17, **27:41-43-**Ps. 3:2, 35:15, 42:3, 10, 71:11, **27:45-**Amos. 8:9, Ex. 10:21-23, Joel 2:31, Is. 50:3, Rev. 8:12, Is. 53:11, **27:46-**Ps. 22:1, 71:11, Heb. 5:7, Gal. 3:13, **27:50-**Matt. 20:28, John 10:11, 15, 17-18, Gen. 3:15 b, **27:51-**Eph. 2:13-18, Heb. 6:19, 9:2-3, 8, 10:20-22, **27:52-53-**Rom. 6:22-23, 1-Corn. 15:19-23, Philip. 3:21, Col. 1:18, Is. 26:19, Dan. 12:2, Hos. 13:14, John 5:25-29, 1-Thess.4:14, Rev.1:5, **27:54-**Matt.8:11-12, Luke 23:40-41, John12:32, Rom.1:4)

If you have any questions or comments
feel free to contact me at:

ministercosta@yahoo.com (primary)
Or
costa.david4@gmail.com

Web Address is:
www.matthewlifeapplication.com